Effective Training

Systems, Strategies, and Practices

FOURTH EDITION

P. Nick Blanchard
Eastern Michigan University

James W. Thacker
University of Windsor

D1361356

Pearson Education
Boston   Columbus   Indianapolis   New York   San Francisco
Upper Saddle River   Amsterdam   Cape Town   Dubai   London   Madrid
Milan   Munich   Montreal   Paris   Toronto   Delhi   Hong Kong   Mexico City
Sao Paulo   Seoul   Singapore   Sydney   Taipei   Tokyo

Editorial Director: Sally Yagan
Editor in Chief: Eric Svendsen
Acquisitions Editor: Jennifer M. Collins
Editorial Project Manager: Claudia Fernandes
Director of Marketing: Patrice Lumumba Jones
Marketing Manager: Nikki Jones
Marketing Assistant: Ian Gold
Senior Managing Editor: Judy Leale
Project Manager: Holly Shufeldt

Senior Art Director: Jayne Conte
Manager, Rights and Permissions: Charles Morris
Cover Photo: Frank Pedrick/The Image Works
Full-Service Project Management:
  Ravi Bhatt/Aptara®, Inc.
Composition: Aptara®, Inc.
Printer/Binder: Hamilton Printing Co.
Cover Printer: Demand Production Center
Text Font: Palatino

Credits and acknowledgments borrowed from other sources and reproduced, with permission, in this textbook appear on appropriate page within the text.

If you purchased this book within the United States or Canada you should be aware that it has been wrongfully imported without the approval of the Publisher or the Author.

Prentice Hall
is an imprint of

10 9 8 7 6 5 4
ISBN 10:   0-13-510592-7
ISBN 13: 978-0-13-510592-4

Dedication

This edition is dedicated to sons, Mike and Brandon;
who knew they would make me so proud; and to my wife,
friend, and partner in all things, Claudia.
N. B.

This book is dedicated to Gabrielle, my wife of 45 years,
without whom none of this would have happened.
And to Larry; I miss you old friend.
J. T.

BRIEF CONTENTS

Contents

PREFACE

The idea for this book came while fishing on a beautiful lake in northern Manitoba. Both of us were teaching a course about training and were unsatisfied with the texts available at the time. Our main concern was that we really needed two texts for the course: one providing the theory and scholarship surrounding the learning-teaching experience, and the other providing the application and "how-to" part of the experience. This text is still the only one (in our minds at least) that accomplishes this. The fourth edition retains the integration of theory with effective and practical training applications and adds new material while enhancing the ease of reading and understanding.

GENERAL AND SPECIFIC CHANGES TO THE FOURTH EDITION

General Changes for Fourth Edition

- Updated information for research and applications in each chapter.
- Added new cases.
- Some minor changes to the Training Process Model (labeling feedback loop, adding the delivery of the training, etc.).

Specific Chapter Changes

Chapter 1 (Training in Organizations)

- Added a "careers in training" section.
- Expanded discussion legal issues related to training.
- Deleted "Opportunities and Challenges" section and added "Trends in Training" section.

Chapter 4 (Needs Analysis)

- Expanded discussion of how to create effective questionnaires.

Chapter 5 (Training Design)

- Expanded coverage of Gagne's 9 Events of Training.
- Made several changes to the "Learning Objectives" section.

Chapter 6 (Traditional Training Methods)

- Changed "visual aids" section to include photos, power point presentations, etc., and deleted older methods (overhead transparencies, photographic slides, etc.).
- Expanded and modified the "coaching" section.
- Updated listing and description of "business games".
- An additional table has been added showing the methods, their purpose, and when to use them.

Chapter 7 (Computer-Based Training Methods)

- Updated content for current technology and provided some additional examples.

Chapter 8 (Development and Implementation of Training)

- Modified the model and the related discussion to include actual delivery of training after the dry run.

Chapter 9 (Evaluation of Training)

- Expanded the discussion of how to measure Organizational Results in the Kirkpatrick model.

Chapter 10 (Key Areas of Organizational Training)

- Added Cross Cultural Training as a section (upgraded from a sub-topic).
- Deleted discussion of the Learning Organization.
- Connected the phases of the Training Process Model to each of the major topic areas.

Chapter 11 (Employee and Management Development)

- Major revision and updating of material based on the Winter, 2007, Personnel Psychology Review of the book.

We've added some new examples to show how theory, concepts, and principles can be translated into practical application by organizations around the world. Make sure to go through the Fabrics, Inc., case throughout the book. The case takes the reader through what actually occurs in the development of a training program, beginning with Chapter 4 on needs analysis and then, step-by-step through design, development, and evaluation. We have provided a lot of detail so that the reader can see what is actually done. We have added a section on careers in training to Chapter 1 and expanded the coverage of legal issues. Chapter 11, which used to be called Management Development, is now titled Employee and Management Development, with all the expanded coverage this implies. We continue to differ from other training books in that we place training activities in the context of organizational strategy. Whether you are a student or a practitioner, this book will be of both conceptual and practical value for developing training programs that meet strategic and tactical needs. At the same time, an overarching model of the training process will guide you step-by-step through the training procedures, from initial needs analysis through the evaluation of training's effectiveness. As human resource (HR) competencies become a significant competitive advantage, the pace and intensity of organizational training increases dramatically. Human resource development (HRD), or "performance improvement," departments must demonstrate that their programs enhance competencies that are of strategic value. As a company's strategies change, the types of management competencies and styles also need to change, and HRD is responsible for this alignment. We address these and related issues, because we believe that effective training practices are determined by the organizational context in which they occur.

UNIQUE CHARACTERISTICS OF THIS BOOK

This book differs from others on the same topic in a number of ways. For example, we

- demonstrate how HRD fits into the strategic planning process;
- show the important relationships between organizational development (OD) practitioners and trainers;
- provide an overarching model of the training process, with a more detailed model of each phase of the process, making it easy to see how each phase connects and contributes to achieving training objectives;
- include a small-business perspective to training and its implementation;
- provide a step-by-step process for developing learning objectives with many examples of good and bad objectives;
- integrate learning and design theory into the creation of training programs so the reader can see how these theories help in the design of effective training;
- incorporate both micro and macro theories of design perspectives into the design of training;

- provide the Fabrics, Inc., case, which runs throughout the text, demonstrating the step-by-step process of developing an actual training program from needs analysis through evaluation;
- provide numerous examples of actual training situations (called Training in Action) throughout each chapter to highlight important aspects of the training process;
- use a contingency approach for each training process, rather than a "one best way," identifying alternative approaches and their associated strengths and limitations; and
- provide a comprehensive case in Chapter 2 that is applicable throughout the text and is often referred to in the remaining chapters.

Other aspects of the text that we believe are important are as follows:

- Learning objectives at the beginning of each chapter
- Key terms are identified in each chapter, and a glossary providing their definitions is at the end of the book
- A case at the beginning of each chapter
- Questions, cases, and exercises at the end of each chapter
- An instructor's manual with sample syllabi, suggested answers to questions at the end of the chapters, and a "test bank" of questions
- PowerPoint slides of all tables and figures.

Learning objectives provide trainees with an understanding of what the training is trying to accomplish, and so they are an important part of the training process. Better learning is achieved if, at the beginning of training, people know where they should focus their attention. Therefore, at the beginning of each chapter, we identify its learning objectives, stating what the reader should be capable of doing after completing the chapter. (The value of learning objectives and the characteristics of good objectives are discussed in depth in Chapter 5).

Following the learning objectives is a case example to stimulate the reader to think about the issues that will be raised in the chapter. Throughout the chapter, we refer back to the case to make specific points, asking the reader relevant questions about the case. Some of the cases are presented in totality at the beginning of the chapter; others are split into two parts: the first part stopping at a critical point and the remainder presented at the end of the chapter. This allows the reader to apply the concepts and principles from the chapter in evaluating the actions taken and how the issues were handled. It also allows the reader to see the resulting consequences.

At the end of each chapter are discussion questions, cases, and exercises to enhance understanding. The instructor's manual provides more information about this material and offers additional ideas for teaching. It also includes sample course outlines and a test bank. PowerPoint slides for each chapter are available from the publisher.

Another important difference in this book is the overarching model of the training process and its subprocesses. This model provides an understanding of the logical sequencing of training activities, from needs analysis to implementation and evaluation. The model demonstrates training as a system and how its processes are interconnected. Thus each phase of the training process (i.e., needs assessment, design, development, implementation, and evaluation) is covered in its own chapter. These chapters begin with a description of the types of input needed to complete that phase and the types of output produced. The bulk of each chapter provides a step-by-step description of how the input is transformed into the output. The output from one phase then becomes the input for the next.

As with earlier editions, for ease of reading, we have not used the he/she convention when the context of the material requires a gender reference. Instead, we alternate the use of gender throughout the text. Reviewers were universally appreciative of this aspect of the text.

Most training books focus on large organizations that have access to many resources, ignoring the smaller companies with more limited resources. We address the training issues faced by smaller businesses in two ways. First, the contingency approach provides alternative activities and procedures—some of them compatible with limited resources. Throughout the book, we address the applicability of various approaches to the smaller business. Second, many of the chapters include sections directed specifically at the small business. These sections provide possible alternatives and describe what some small businesses are actually doing in these areas. Unfortunately, the literature on small-business training practices is relatively sparse. If you know of successful small-business practices, we would love to hear about them and include them in subsequent editions.

We are committed to continuously improving this book to enhance learning and make teaching from it a joy. To that end, we ask you to contact us with your thoughts, applications from the research, training techniques, exercises, and so on, so that we can share them with others. **You can reach us at Nick.Blanchard@emich.edu or jwt@uwindsor.ca.** Of course, you will be acknowledged for your contribution if it is included in future editions.

ORGANIZATION AND PLAN OF THE BOOK

We begin Chapter 1 with an overview of training, its roles, and its goals, using an open systems perspective. In this section, we discuss how training fits into the HR function, and how the training function fits into the structure of large and small companies. This section also presents the overarching training process model, which is used to outline the organization of the book and provide an overview of the content of the remaining chapters. This is followed by current trends in HRD. Included is a discussion of the legal issues that affect HRD activities such as equity, required training, and liability. We conclude this chapter by defining the key terms used throughout the text.

Chapter 2 discusses strategic planning and the roles HR and HRD play in this process. Here we show how input from the HR function in general and the HRD function in particular can influence strategic direction. We then proceed to discuss how these functions develop internal strategies to support the overall strategic plan. The case at the start of the chapter provides a discussion point for many of the topics in this and subsequent chapters, allowing the student to walk through a case from the beginning of the strategic plan to the development of training. Throughout the text, we often refer back to this chapter to demonstrate how strategic issues drive HRD decisions. We also provide an important link between OD practitioners and trainers, showing how the competencies of each of these disciplines complement and support the objectives of the other. In the remaining chapters, we use an OD philosophy to address ways in which the training process and outcomes can be integrated into other organizational systems. This integration of the training process into a systems perspective provides the reader with an understanding of where training fits in the organization and how it operates. This is followed by a discussion of how strategies for overcoming resistance to change are applicable to training activities.

Chapter 3 provides the theoretical and conceptual framework for understanding the training process. It begins with a short discussion of the value of theory in leading to new and practical applications. A model of the factors that determine human performance (motivation, knowledge, skills, abilities, and environment) is followed by a review of theories of motivation and learning. These theories are discussed in terms of their application to training. This is followed by a discussion of overcoming resistance to learning and designing training that motivates trainees to learn. The concepts and principles developed here are referred to throughout many of the following chapters, tying particular practices to the theoretical rationale for those practices.

Chapter 4 addresses needs analysis, the first phase of the training model presented in Chapter 1. An expanded graphic of this phase is presented and discussed at the outset so the reader will understand the organization of the chapter. The philosophy of needs analysis is discussed in terms of both its proactive use (as related to the strategic plan) and its reactive use (to deal with immediate concerns and changing conditions). The relationship between these two approaches is also explored. The steps involved in the needs analysis are discussed, along with the sources from which data can be gathered and to set training priorities. The chapter ends with a real example of a training process for Fabrics, Inc., walking the student through the needs analysis as it is actually done for the company.

Chapter 5 begins with the second phase of the training model: training design. The outcomes of the needs assessment phase are shown as inputs to this phase. The chapter then identifies the activities conducted in the design phase of training. First is the development of the training/learning objectives. Here a formula for development of learning objectives is provided along with numerous examples of effective objectives. We then provide a table that provides actual first tries at writing objectives and those same objectives after being refined.

The discussion then moves to the identification of organizational constraints on training and factors that will facilitate learning. The learning facilitation factors focus separately on the trainee and the training design. Next, factors that facilitate the transfer of learning back to the trainee's job are discussed. These factors are broken down into training design factors and organizational systems factors back on the job. We then discuss a macro theory of design and demonstrate how this design theory facilitates the overall design of training. This is followed by a micro theory of design. Here we demonstrate how the micro theory helps in the step-by-step design of a training program. We also integrate this micro theory of design with social learning theory to demonstrate the relationship between the two. At the end of the chapter, Fabrics, Inc., is revisited, and the process of design is examined step-by-step.

Chapter 6 provides information on traditional methods of training, including lectures, cases, games, simulations, and on-the-job training. Using learning theory as a framework, the various methods of training are described, along with their strengths and limitations. Included here are the effectiveness at developing knowledge, skills, or changing attitudes; the relative costs; trainer versus trainee control over what is learned and how; and issues related to training group characteristics. Included in the discussion of each method is the practical application, or how to actually use the method effectively.

Chapter 7 focuses on what we call computer-based training (CBT). However, this encompasses all training that is created and delivered electronically. Again, using learning theory as a framework, the various forms of this approach are described along with their respective strengths and weaknesses. In addition, the discussion covers the various methods of delivery (the Internet, intranet, CD, etc.) and learning management systems.

Chapter 8 is divided into two parts: development and implementation of training. It begins with a summary table showing the relative effectiveness of the various methods for enhancing knowledge, skill, and/or attitudes. The development of the training program is discussed in terms of our model of the process. The inputs from previous phases are discussed in terms of their influence on the characteristics of the training program being developed. Here actual forms that you might use, tables that provide step-by-step procedures for developing aspects of training, issues to consider in developing training using different methods, and so forth, are provided. At the end of this chapter, Fabrics, Inc., is revisited to show some developmental outputs.

The model for implementation is then provided, with the outputs from the development phase becoming the inputs for implementation. Here we describe the process of putting on the training and what needs to be done to ensure success. Again the focus is on practical applications, beginning with hints to assist trainers in effective use of the lecture method. Then we present a practical guide related to things to consider in the implementation of training, including a dry run and pilot program. Finally, we address some of the critical issues related to transfer of training.

Chapter 9 begins with the model for evaluation and addresses the issues and activities involved in the evaluation phase of the overarching training model. While various evaluation issues are discussed in each phase of the training model, we provide the bulk of the information at this point in the book (after development and implementation). However, we stress the importance of incorporating appropriate evaluation activities into each of the other phases of the model. We provide guidance and actual examples of the various types of evaluation that can be used. At the end of the chapter, we again revisit Fabrics, Inc., to provide the process that takes place at this stage of training. Here, we provide actual evaluation forms that are used to test employees from Fabrics, Inc., at the end of training. We also have an appendix to this chapter that provides a more advanced discussion of reliability and validity issues.

Chapter 10 contains two parts. First, the focus is on five special training topics: orientation, diversity, sexual harassment, team training, and cross-cultural training. For these first five topics, we provide information on what companies are currently doing and why it is important. Then, for each of the five, we discuss in detail how to develop that type of training, using the model provided in the previous chapters. For the orientation training (sometimes referred to as "onboarding"), we provide a hypothetical example for readers to follow. Of course, we also provide a detailed discussion on how to develop the training. Finally, several other special training topics are addressed in terms of what organizations are doing and why it is important.

Chapter 11 begins with a focus on employee development and how it can help in retaining employees and keeping them motivated while providing increased organizational flexibility. Different approaches to employee development are discussed, including development in the current job, job rotation, and special assignments. The responsibilities of the employee, the supervisor, the HR unit, and the organization in terms of employee development are also identified.

We then turn to management development with an explanation for why managers are singled out. Managerial competencies, in addition to personal traits or styles, are discussed in terms of effectiveness. We adopt a contingency approach to management development in the sense that we provide a model that allows the training professional to determine what competencies a manager in a particular organization needs. The model integrates the competitive strategy, organizational structure, and technology literature into a continuum that describes the organizational context in which managers must operate. This context then determines the relative value to the company that various managerial competencies and characteristics (such as style) are likely to provide. This chapter also discusses three important areas of managerial knowledge and competency: understanding of the organizational context, self-awareness and diagnostic skills, and adaptability. The chapter also includes a discussion of the special needs of technical managers, and a specific section is provided to highlight the special issues related to the training of top managers and executives.

ACKNOWLEDGMENTS

Ever since we conceived of the book on that sunny day on a boat in northern Manitoba while catching our share of walleye, there have been many who have contributed to its success. We are immensely grateful to all of them. Of course, any errors, omissions, or other mistakes can be attributed to us.

We hope you find this book useful and easy to understand. Many have contributed to this goal. The people at Prentice Hall, as always, were very helpful. Thanks to our editor, Jennifer Collins, and our project manager at PH, Claudia Fernandes, who carried us into final production. We are very appreciative of the hard work put in by our production editor, Holly Shufeldt, and the team at Aptara®, Inc., whose diligence and skill in copyediting and production created the final images, text, and layout for this edition. They have made the book better than it otherwise would have been. Thanks also to Charles Morris for securing those pesky permissions.

We would like to acknowledge the contributions of both the academics and practitioners who have shared their insights with us. Specifically, we would like to thank Mitchell Fields, University of Windsor, whose examples and suggestions have stood the test of time. Special thanks also go out to Greg Huszczo, Rick Camp, Mary Vielhaber, and Jane Stephenson, all of Eastern Michigan University. Each has made valuable contributions that are incorporated in this edition. Finally, but most importantly, a very big thank you to the reviewers of the Third Edition of this book, whose feedback helped us make improvements.

ABOUT THE AUTHORS

P. Nick Blanchard

Nick completed his undergraduate studies in psychology at UCLA, his master's degree in psychology at San Diego State University, and his doctorate in industrial/organizational and social psychology at Wayne State University. He is currently a professor in the College of Business at Eastern Michigan University, where he has also served as dean, associate dean and head of the management department. His writings appear in both scholarly and applied publications, including *International Journal of Training and Development, Human Resource Development Quarterly, Journal of Managerial Psychology,* and *Basic and Applied Social Psychology*. His earlier books in training are *Toward a More Organizationally Effective Training Strategy and Practice* and *Effective Training*. Dr. Blanchard has served as consultant and trainer to many organizations including Bethlehem Steel, Chrysler Corporation, Domtar Gypsum, Ford Motor Company, and Navistar in the private sector and the cities of Ann Arbor and Ypsilanti and the State of Michigan Department of Transportation in the public sector.

James Thacker

Jim received an undergraduate degree in psychology from the University of Winnipeg in Winnipeg, Manitoba, and his doctorate in industrial and organizational psychology from Wayne State University. He is currently professor emeritus at the University of Windsor's Odette School of Business following his retirement in 2007, after 25 years of teaching, publishing, and otherwise doing his part for the greater good. His research has been published in both academic journals (*Journal of Applied Psychology, Personnel Psychology,* and *Academy of Management Journal*) and practitioner journals (*Journal of Managerial Psychology* and *The Human Resource Consultation: An International Journal*). He coauthored the first Canadian edition of *Managing Human Resources* with Wayne Cascio, published in 1994, and, with Nick Blanchard coauthored *Effective Training: Systems, Strategies, and Practices,* published in 1999, 2004, and 2007.

Jim has been a consultant and trainer in the private sector (Ameritech, Ford, Hiram Walker's, Navistar, H.J. Heinz, and Honda Canada) and public sector (Revenue Canada, CanAm Friendship Center, and City of Windsor). Before obtaining his doctorate, Jim has worked for a gas utility as a tradesman and served as vice president of his local union (Oil, Chemical, and Atomic Workers) for a number of years. This firsthand experience as a tradesman and union official, combined with his consulting and academic credentials, provides Jim with a unique combination of perspectives and skills.

Chapter 1

Training in Organizations

Learning Objectives

After reading this chapter, you should be able to:

➤ Describe the components of a general open systems model.

➤ Describe how an open systems model applies to the training unit of an organization.

➤ List and describe the interrelationships among the five phases of the training process model.

➤ Explain how the training model can be applied to organizational improvement and problem solving.

➤ Describe the challenges/opportunities facing training.

➤ Define key terms used in the training literature.

➤ Describe the benefits of integrating organizational development and training principles.

➤ Describe the differences in how small and larger businesses might implement the training process model.

CASE: Taking Charge at Domtar: What It Takes for a Turnaround*

Domtar is the third largest producer of uncoated freesheet paper in North America. In the decade prior to 1996, Domtar had one of the worst financial records in the pulp and paper industry. At that time it was a bureaucratic and hierarchical organization with no clear goals. Half of its business

---

*Swift, A. "Royer's Domtar turnaround." *Financial Post* (October 6 2003), FP3. Allen, B. 2003. The Domtar difference. www.pimaweb.org/conferences/june2003/ BuddyAllen.pdf. Anonymous (January 2001) Partnership between Domtar and Cree First Nations brings results. www.diversityupdate.com. Richard Descarries, Manager, Corporate Communications and External Relations, Domtar, personal communication (2004).

(*continued*)

was in "trouble areas." Moreover, the company did not have the critical mass to compete with the larger names in the field. The balance sheet was in bad shape, and the company did not have investment-grade status on its long-term debt.

In July of 1996, Raymond Royer was named president and chief executive officer (CEO). This was quite a surprise because, although Royer had been successful at Bombardier, he had no knowledge of the pulp and paper industry. Many believed that to be successful at Domtar, you needed to know the industry.

Royer knew that to be effective in any competitive industry, an organization needed to have a strategic direction and specific goals. He decided to focus on two goals: return on investment and customer service. Royer told Domtar executives that to survive, they needed to participate in the consolidation of the industry and increase its critical mass. The goal was to become a preferred supplier. The competitive strategy had to focus on being innovative in product design, high in product quality, and unique in customer service. At the same time, however, it had to do everything to keep costs down.

When Royer took over at Domtar, he explained to the executive team that there were three pillars to the company: customers, shareholders, and ourselves. He noted that it is only "ourselves" who are able to have any impact on changing the company. He backed up his words with action by hiring the Kaizen guru from Bombardier. Kaizen, a process of getting employees involved by using their expertise in the development of new and more effective ways of doing things, had been very effective at Bombardier. Royer saw no reason why it would not be successful at Domtar. Royer also knew that for the new strategic direction and focus to be successful, everyone needed to both understand the changes being proposed and have the skills to achieve them. The success of any change process requires extensive training; therefore, training became a key part of Royer's strategy for Domtar.

This last point reflects the belief that it is the employees' competencies that make the difference. The Domtar Difference, as it is called, is reflected in the statement, "tapping the intelligence of the experts, our employees." Employees must be motivated to become involved in developing new ways of doing things. Thus, Domtar needed to provide employees with incentives for change, new skills, and a different attitude toward work. The introduction of Kaizen was one tactic used to achieve these goals.

Training at Domtar went beyond the traditional job training necessary to do the job effectively and included training in customer service and Kaizen. This is reflected in Domtar's mission, which is to

- meet the ever-changing needs of our customers,
- provide shareholders with attractive returns, and
- create an environment in which shared human values and personal commitment prevail.

In this regard, a performance management system was put in place to provide a mechanism for employees to receive feedback about their effectiveness. This process laid the groundwork for successfully attaining such objectives as improving employee performance, communicating the Domtar values, clarifying individual roles, and fostering better communication between employees and managers. Tied to this were performance incentives that rewarded employees with opportunities to share in the profits of the company.

(*continued*)

Has Royer been successful with his approach? First-quarter net earnings in 1998 were $17 million, compared with a net loss of $12 million for the same time period in 1997, his first year in office. In 2002, third-quarter earnings were $59 million and totaled $141 million for the year. That is not all. Recall his goal of return on equity for shareholders. Domtar has once again been included on the Dow Jones sustainability index. Domtar has been on this list since its inception in 1999 and is the only pulp and paper company in North America to be part of this index. To be on the list, a company must demonstrate an approach that "aims to create long-term shareholder value by embracing opportunities and managing risks that arise from economic, environmental, and social developments." On the basis of this, it could be said that Royer has been successful. In 2003, Paperloop, the pulp and paper industry's international research and information service, named Royer Global CEO of the year.

It was Royer's sound management policies and shrewd joint ventures and acquisitions that helped Domtar become more competitive and return their long-term debt rating to investment grade. However, joint ventures and acquisitions bring additional challenges of integrating the new companies into the "Domtar way." Again, this requires training.

For example, when Domtar purchased the Ashdown Mill in Arkansas, the management team met with employees to set the climate for change. The plan was that within 14 months, all mill employees would complete a two-day training program designed to help them understand the Domtar culture and how to service customers. A manager always started the *one-day customer focus* training, thus emphasizing the importance of the training. This manager returned again at lunch to answer any questions as the training proceeded. In addition, for supervisor training, each supervisor received skill training on how to effectively address employee issues. How successful has all this training been? Employee Randy Gerber says the training "allows us to realize that to be successful, we must share human values and integrate them into our daily activities." The training shows that "the company is committed to the program." Tammy Waters, a communications coordinator, said that the training impacted the mill in many ways and for Ashdown employees it has become a way of life.

The same process takes place in Domtar's joint ventures. In northern Ontario, Domtar owns a 45 percent interest in a mill, with the Cree of James Bay owning the remaining 55 percent. Although Domtar has minority interest in the joint venture, training is an important part of its involvement. Skills training still takes place on site, but all management and teamwork training is done at Domtar's headquarters in Montreal.

Royer's ability to get employees to buy into this new way of doing business was necessary for the organization to succeed. Paperloop's editorial director for news products, Will Mies, in describing why Royer was chosen for the award, indicated that they polled a large number of respected security analysts, investment officers, and portfolio managers as well as their own staff of editors, analysts, and economists to determine a worthy winner this year. Raymond Royer emerged a clear favorite, with voters citing, in particular, his talent for turnaround, outstanding financial management, and consistently excellent merger, acquisition, and consolidation moves as well as his ability to integrate acquired businesses through a management system that engages employees. Of course, that last part, "a management system that engages employees," could be said to be the key without which most of the rest would not work very well. That requires training.

Overview of Training

Everyone in an organization is affected by training. Everyone receives training at one time or another, usually multiple times. Managers and supervisors need to be sure that their direct reports have the competencies required to perform their jobs. Subject matter experts (managers and others) are asked to provide training. Significant budget dollars are allocated to training employees. The troubles with the U.S. economy have decreased the total amount of the corporate budget going toward training. In 2008, training budgets for U.S. companies with 100 or more employees totaled just over $56 billion, a decrease of about 4 percent from 2007.[1] However, this is still an increase of 9 percent over 2004. The economic recession of 2008–09 has resulted in a reduction of staffing in the training function, but it still exceeds the 2004 levels.

Why does this corporate emphasis on training exist? What difference does training make to the bottom line? Evidence continues to grow showing that companies investing more in training produce improved financial results in terms of higher net sales, gross profits per employee, stock growth, and ratio of market to book value.[2] For example, in a Mutual of Omaha study, it was determined that those with higher levels of training generated, on average, an additional $150,000 of new business premium each year. However, training doesn't always lead to an improved bottom line. Many companies report that they perceive little value from their training initiatives.[3] Obviously, companies that report very positive improvements are using more effective training practices than those that do not. Effective training differs from ineffective training in terms of the processes used to determine what employees need to learn and how training is designed and implemented. The first three chapters of this book provide you with an understanding of the context and theoretical foundation on which effective training is based. Chapters 4 through 8 provide you with an in-depth understanding of how to determine training needs and how to design, develop, and implement training to meet those needs. Even companies that have reported unsatisfactory results from their training efforts are doing at least one thing right—they are evaluating their training and can take corrective action. Companies that don't evaluate their training don't have a clue about its effectiveness. We believe that it is useful, first, to give an overview of what an effective training unit should accomplish in an organization. This chapter and the next cover a broad set of organizational issues that provide the context for developing and implementing effective training. As we discuss this context, we will be referring back to the Domtar case from time to time, to illustrate in concrete ways how training relates to organizational effectiveness.

Training System and Processes

Training provides employees with the knowledge and skills to perform more effectively. This allows them to meet current job requirements or prepares them to meet the inevitable changes that occur in their jobs. However, training is only an opportunity for learning. What is learned depends on many factors, such as the design and implementation of training, the motivation and learning style of the trainees, and the organization's learning climate.

Training is also part of an integrated system in which performance is measured against criteria (best practices benchmarks) that are tied to strategic objectives. Training is used extensively to help employees understand how they can assist in meeting corporate objectives. Clearly, Domtar knows that. Recall, when Domtar purchased the Ashdown Mill, training was an immediate focus. Within 14 months, all mill employees completed a two-day training program so they would understand Domtar's culture and know how to service customers in the appropriate manner. Always having a manager kick off the training and later return to answer questions shows the importance Domtar attached to training. But effective training requires more than just having key managers available. It requires that effective systems are in place to address the performance issues facing the organization. With that in mind, we turn to the design of an effective training system.

Training as an Open System

Figure 1-1 shows a general **open systems model**.[4] Open systems have a dynamic relationship with their environment; closed systems do not. Obviously, a business must interact with its environment, making it an open system.

As Figure 1-1 indicates, an open system depends on the environment for the input that supports the system. A business, for example, needs raw materials, capital, and employees in order to operate. The environmental inputs are transformed into outputs by the system's processes. For a business, these would include its products and services. The system's outputs flow into the environment and might or might not influence future inputs into the system. In effective systems, the system output influences the environment to supply new supportive input to the system.

A system, such as a business, must be responsive to the needs and demands of its environment because the environment provides the input needed for the system to replenish itself. For example, if a business is responsive to the needs of society by providing valued goods and services (output), it receives financial and goodwill credits (input). The business uses these inputs to continue operating. If the business does not provide sufficient value to its environment, it will fail because the environment will not provide the necessary input for the system to replenish itself.

Many open systems exist as part of another open system and, therefore, are called subsystems of that larger system. For example, a product assembly system is a subsystem of a manufacturing system, which itself is a subsystem of the company, which is a subsystem of the industry, and so on. Training can be seen as a subsystem within the larger human resources (HR) unit, which itself is a subsystem of the company. Figure 1-2 illustrates some of the exchanges that take place between the

Figure 1-1
General Open Systems Model

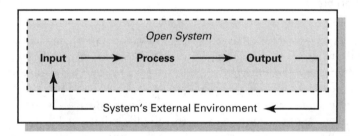

Figure 1-2
Training as a Subsystem Within the Organizational System

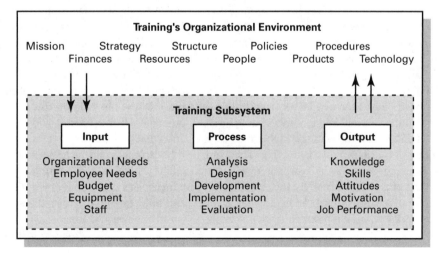

training system and the larger organizational system. The organization's mission, strategies, resources, and the like, all represent sources of input into the training subsystem. Of course, if the training department is part of a larger HR function, then these inputs would be filtered through that system. Organizational and employee needs, training budgets, staff, equipment, and so forth, are all inputs from the organization to the training subsystem. Training processes transform these inputs into usable output for the organization (improved knowledge, skills, and attitudes; job performance; and so on). Looking at the training unit from an open system perspective shows how interconnected training activities are with what is happening elsewhere in the organization. The point here is that the organization invests money in the training function, for which it expects a favorable return. Periodically, the organization will examine the returns from training and determine whether the training system is working properly and what further investment is appropriate. Training in Action 1-1 demonstrates the consequences of a poor match between the training system and the organizational environment.

The Training Process Model

This book will take you through the complete training process as it would be conducted under ideal conditions. Unfortunately, most organizations do not operate in ideal conditions. Insufficient financial resources, time, and training professionals represent just a few of the challenges faced by most companies. Recognizing these limitations, we also provide variations to training practices and systems that, although not ideal, do a reasonable job of accomplishing **training objectives.** Of course, these shortcuts exact a price, and we identify the major consequences associated with these shortcuts. Thus, we try to provide both "ideal" and more practical approaches to implementing the training processes. Nonetheless, even in less-than-ideal

TRAINING IN ACTION 1-1
Team Building Sizzles, Then Fizzles

The director of a city utilities department felt that creating employee problem-solving teams would improve the quality of operations and the efficiency of the department. All employees were provided the opportunity to participate in team-building and problem-solving training. About 60 percent of the employees, including the director and his management group, signed up for the training. Three-hour training sessions took place once a week for ten weeks. Working on a common process within their department, employees were grouped into teams for three weeks of team-building training and seven weeks of problem-solving training.

At the beginning of the problem-solving training, each team identified a problem in its area of operation. Each team then worked through the problem as they progressed though each step of the training. The team members were delighted to be learning new skills while working on a real problem. By the end of training, each group actually solved, or made significant progress toward solving, the problem it was working

on. Evaluations taken at the conclusion of training indicated that trainees enjoyed the training and understood the steps, tools, and techniques of team building and problem solving. The director was pleased with the results and submitted a report documenting the successes of the training to the city manager.

Follow-up evaluation conducted six months later showed only one team still in operation. The other teams fell apart for various reasons, such as excessive workloads, little recognition being given when problems were solved, nontrained employees resisting making changes in work processes, or teams being ridiculed by those who had not participated in training. Clearly, the training did not achieve the desired outcomes. If the director had understood the system and what was and was not rewarding, a more successful outcome could have been achieved. By using the analysis phase of the Training Process Model, the relevant aspects of the system would have been identified and adjustments to either the system or the training could have been made.

Figure 1-3 Training Processes Model

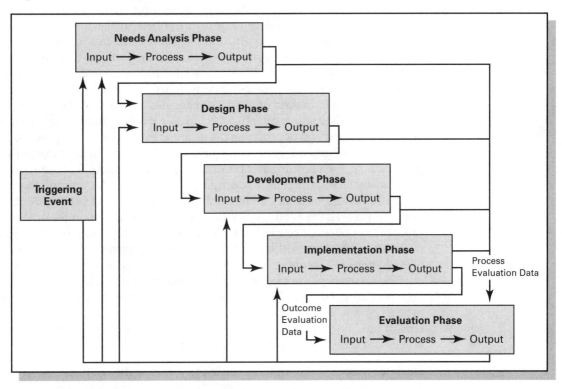

conditions, all of the training processes are critical to the success of training. Although less-than-ideal methods may be used to carry out the training processes, elimination of one or more of the processes places the entire effort at grave risk.

An effective training system is a set of processes designed to transform organizational inputs into output that meets organizational needs. Training is not just running training programs or putting a large percentage of employees through some training. Viewing training as simply a program or set of programs is too shortsighted. Training should be viewed as a set of integrated processes in which organizational and employee needs are analyzed and responded to in a rational, logical, and strategic manner. When training is conducted in this manner, the organization will improve, the value of the training unit will increase, and further investment in training is likely to occur. Our model of training processes, depicted in Figure 1-3, reflects this approach.

Figure 1-3 is merely an overview of the process. A more detailed figure for each phase is provided at the beginning of each relevant chapter, with the input and output of each process described in considerably more detail. For now, we will briefly describe the purpose of each of the phases and their relevant inputs and outputs.

The training process begins with some type of triggering event. A **triggering event** occurs when a person with authority to take action recognizes that **actual organizational performance (AOP)** is less than the **expected organizational performance (EOP).** For example, the quality standard (the EOP) at Company X is three rejects per thousand. An examination of the data for last month indicates that the actual quality level (AOP) was 17 rejects per thousand. If a person with authority to take action sees this gap as a concern, it would trigger an analysis of why the number of rejects is so high. This analysis is discussed below.

Analysis Phase   The **analysis phase** begins with the identification of the **organizational performance gap** (AOP is less than EOP). Things such as profitability shortfalls, low levels of customer satisfaction, or excessive scrap are all examples of a current performance gap. Another type of performance gap is future oriented. Here, the company is seen as likely to perform poorly in the future unless changes are made. For example, if an organization wanted to install robotic equipment in six months but employees were not able to program the robots, then there is an expected performance gap in the future. Once a performance gap exists, the cause must then be determined. Once the cause(s) is determined, and its elimination is believed to be important, the elimination of the cause becomes a "need" of the organization.

The analysis phase is often referred to as a **training needs analysis (TNA).** However, *both* training and nontraining needs are identified with this process. The cause of the performance gap might be inadequate knowledge, skills, or attitudes (KSAs) of employees. If so, then training is a possible solution. However, KSA deficiencies are only one of many reasons for performance gaps. Other reasons for performance gaps, such as motivation issues or faulty equipment, must be separated from KSA deficiencies, as these are nontraining needs and require a different solution. In the analysis phase, the cause of the performance gap is identified, separating KSA from non-KSA causes. Those performance gaps caused by KSA deficiencies are identified as "training needs" because training is a solution. All other causes are defined as nontraining needs.

The analysis phase also attaches priorities to the training needs that are identified. Not all needs will have the same level of importance for the company. This process of data gathering and causal analysis to determine which performance problems should be addressed by training is the analysis phase of the training process. It will be discussed in great detail in Chapter 4.

Design Phase   The training needs identified in the analysis phase, in addition to areas of constraint and support, are the inputs to the **design phase.** An important process in the design phase is the creation of training objectives. These provide specific direction for what will be trained and how. These objectives specify the employee and organizational outcomes that should be achieved as a result of training and become inputs to the remaining phases of the model.

Another part of the design process is identifying the factors needed in the training program to facilitate learning and its transfer back to the job. These include identifying alternative methods of instruction, amount of practice required, the organization of the training content, and much more. This phase is the topic of Chapter 5. Chapters 6 and 7 provide detailed descriptions of the various methods that can be used to deliver the content of the training.

Development Phase   **Development** is the process of formulating an instructional strategy to meet a set of training objectives as well as obtaining or creating all the things that are needed to implement the training program. The **instructional strategy** consists of the order, timing, and combination of methods and elements used in the training program. Inputs into this phase are provided by the design phase and include alternative instructional methods and the information relating to learning facilitation and transfer. Even though the training objectives are not direct inputs to this phase, they influence program development through their influence on the direct inputs. Outputs from this phase are all of the things needed to implement the training program. These include the specific content for of the training, instructional methods used to deliver the content, materials to be used, equipment and media, manuals, and so forth. These are integrated into a coherent, well-organized training plan focused on achieving the training objectives. These outputs of the development phase serve as inputs to the implementation phase. The development phase is the focus of Chapter 8.

Implementation Phase   All the aspects of the training program come together during the **implementation phase;** however, it is a mistake to assume that everything will happen as planned. Therefore, it is useful to conduct a dry run and even a pilot of the program.

Evaluation Phase   Although we discuss this phase of the model last, it actually begins during the development phase. Recall that evaluation objectives are an output of the design phase. These outputs become inputs to the **evaluation phase.** Another input is the organizational constraints. Time, money, and staff all affect how training is evaluated. Two types of evaluation are useful. First, **process evaluation** determines how well a particular process achieved its objectives (i.e., outputs). In other words, did the trainer follow the exact training process suggested? For example, if role-plays were in the design, were they used properly? Collecting and analyzing process data can provide early warning of potential problems in the training program.

Outcome evaluation is the evaluation conducted at the end of training to determine the effects of training on the trainee, the job, and the organization. This type of evaluation uses the training objectives as the standard. Outcome evaluation can also be used to improve training processes. Outcome evaluation data by themselves do not provide enough information for program improvement, but in combination with process evaluation data, they serve as a powerful tool for improving programs. For example, if one or more objectives are not achieved, the training process evaluation data can then be used to identify problems in the process and corrective action can be taken. Chapter 9 provides a detailed discussion of the evaluation process.

TRENDS IN TRAINING

The business environment in North America will continue to change rapidly. These changes bring both challenges and opportunities. Successful companies in most industries must constantly realign their activities to meet new conditions while remaining true to their mission and strategic direction. As companies adapt, their training function also needs to adapt. Multiple surveys over the last several years have asked HR executives and human resource development (HRD) managers to identify their organization's needs for the next several years. What are the trends in training for the near future?[5]

- Aligning training with business strategy
- Managing talent due to changing demographics
- Improving the training function
- Quality
- Legal issues

Each of the above issues is discussed below in terms of the opportunities and challenges it presents to the training function. The ways in which companies are addressing these issues are covered in more depth in Chapter 10, Key Areas of Organizational Training.

Aligning Training with Business Strategy

For the past five years, virtually all the surveys show that aligning training with business strategy is a top priority not only of training managers, but also of HR managers and other business executives. Why is it such a high priority? First, it is only in the last decade that reliable evidence of training's impact on the bottom line has surfaced. Second, and just as important, the business environment over the last decade has been changing rapidly, and all signs indicate that this will continue. Most companies will need to continuously realign their activities to meet new conditions. This requires people at all levels in the organization to be able to make day-to-day decisions that support the business strategy. Training initiatives will need to support the strategic direction of the company and the people who carry it out. Organizations now realize that effective training is a tool for getting better job performance, better bottom-line results, and creating organization-wide adaptability.

What actions did Domtar take to align its training with its business strategy? One component was the institution of Kaizen methods and the associated training. This aligns with the strategic goal of "tapping the intelligence of the experts, our employees." Was the money Domtar spent on this training worth it? It would seem so. Using the Kaizen approach, employees developed a new way of cutting trees into planks. The result was fewer wood chips to transport and more logs produced per tree. Since 1997, it is estimated that Kaizen has saved Domtar about $230 million in production costs. Two of their mills are among the lowest-cost mills in North America. Clearly, the training at Domtar was aligned with its strategic goals.

Companies are now realizing that worker knowledge is a competitive advantage and that training is a strategic tool. As Angela Hornsby, V.P. of learning and development at Carlson Restaurants Worldwide, says: "Things are changing so much more quickly these days, and companies have to adapt so much faster than before to remain competitive. The fact is that one of the most powerful tools we have at our disposal to change performance and help people to adapt more readily to that change is learning."[6] Even though aligning training with business strategy is an important goal, it isn't as easy to do. We will discuss this in more depth in Chapter 2, providing suggestions for how to meet this challenge and take advantage of the opportunities it affords.

Managing Talent Due to Changing Demographics

Major demographic shifts have occurred in North America that affect businesses now and will for the next 15 years. Principal among these demographic shifts are as follows:

- Increased gender, ethnic, and age diversity in the North American workforce
- Aging of the population (baby boomers)

Diversity

Hispanics will soon become the largest minority group in the U.S. workforce. All other minority groups are increasing in size while the percentage of Caucasians will decrease. The number of women will increase to about 50 percent of the workforce.[7] Increased diversity brings both the opportunity for new ways of approaching business issues and the challenge of finding ways to integrate these differing perspectives. We will discuss the legal side of diversity in the "Legal Issues" section. Along with more diversity in terms of gender, ethnicity, and so forth, the workforce is becoming more diverse with respect to age. Four distinct generations are currently in the workforce. Each generation has a different set of values relating to the role of work in their life. The average age of the population is increasing with about 14 percent of the labor market 55 or older. By 2015, over 20 percent are expected to be in this range. As these people retire from their jobs, many will return to the workforce on a part-time basis because of the demand for knowledgeable workers and the insecurity of retirement income. However, these people will not be looking for traditional full-time jobs. Rather, they will be looking for jobs that allow them to enjoy significant periods of time away from job responsibilities. Younger workers want a more balanced work and nonwork life and are more conversant with technologies that allow them to work from anywhere. We are seeing more training focused on building bridges between the older managers and the younger subordinates and programs for team skills that focus on cooperation and problem solving. In general, there are increasing demands for these programs to be aligned with business goals rather than focusing on diversity for its own sake.

Developing the Right Talent

Some have suggested that most companies, now or in the near future, will face a severe shortage of all types of labor. The worldwide economic recession that began in 2008 has certainly eliminated that concern, at least in the near term. Nonetheless, it is now and will continue to be important for most businesses to secure workers with the right skill sets.[8] Baby boomers with the highest knowledge and skill levels will be the ones most likely to leave the workforce, as they will have higher levels of retirement income. Because of changes in technology, job design, and the like, it is estimated that more than 75 percent of the workforce needs retraining just to keep up with the changes in their current jobs. It is projected that the forces identified above will combine by 2020 to create a shortage of 20 million workers, especially in jobs that require the most skill and provide the highest economic value.[9] A survey of senior executives in manufacturing firms indicates that replacing retiring skilled workers will cost their companies up to $20 million a year and will continue for at least five years.[10] Where will the needed talent come from in the next few years? The traditional source of talent coming out of the colleges and technical schools will be fought over fiercely, because there won't be enough to go around. To make up the shortage, many companies will create their own talent. For example, in 2005, Hewlett-Packard addressed this issue by increasing their training budget by 16 percent, bringing the total to $300 million. Raytheon Vision Systems realized that over 35 percent of their workforce would be eligible to retire by 2009. This not only would create a huge loss of people, but also would represent a critical loss of institutional knowledge. Many of those set to retire were the inventors of the knowledge. Raytheon set up a "Leave a Legacy" program, pairing vital-knowledge experts with high-potential subordinates in mentoring relationships. In addition to the shortage of new talent, existing employees will need training to keep up with the changes brought on by new technologies. Thus, in many organizations, you will find the training function focusing on the following types of initiatives:

- Programs that focus on the recruiting and selection process (such as recruiter training, behavioral based interviewing, etc.)
- Programs that improve retention of knowledge workers (e.g., orientation, performance review)
- Programs that assess and track job requirements and employee competencies (HRIS systems)
- Development of innovative knowledge delivery systems that increase the speed with which knowledge is obtained and provide an increased breadth of training opportunities is another way in which companies are creating more knowledgeable workers more quickly (computer-based and other electronic forms of training)

In addition to technological innovation, the competitive environment demands that organizations continuously upgrade the knowledge of their workforce. Consumer demands for higher-quality products and services and the fiercely competitive global economy require employees at every level who are more knowledgeable, more committed to quality, show better judgment, and demonstrate more competencies than ever before.

Tied to the increased level of knowledge expected of all workers is the speed with which knowledge is acquired. In today's competitive business environment, most companies have minimized the time it takes to move a product from the idea stage to the marketplace. This, however, puts great strains on the ability of the employees to be up to speed on the new products and production processes. The smart companies are now making "time to knowledge" as important as "time to market." By getting the training department involved early in the product development stage, companies are able to provide just-in-time training and increase the breadth of training opportunities.

Training in Action 1-2 describes how the United Farm Workers union was able to work with farm owners and managers to create more knowledgeable farm workers. This is especially interesting since many unions have resisted increased knowledge requirements of the jobs they represent.

Quality and Continuous Improvement

Training must be seen as an integral part of the organization's performance improvement system. If not, it will continue to be seen as a cost center, providing less valued contributions to the organization. Training was a critical part of Domtar's change process. It helped educate employees regarding the mission, strategy, and objectives of the organization and how these objectives translated to each employee's job behaviors. Experienced trainers know that effective training is structured as a continuous performance improvement process that is integrated with other systems and business strategies, just as at Domtar. While several models exist for continuous improvement, common to them all are the following:

- Identification of performance improvement opportunities and analysis of what caused the opportunity to exist (gap analysis)

TRAINING IN ACTION 1-2
FIELD Partners with Growers

A more knowledgeable workforce is a double-edged sword for unions. On the one hand, union leadership demands that employers provide training for the rank and file to keep them up to date with modern operating methods. On the other hand, union leadership also understands that more knowledgeable workers improve the efficiency of the company, resulting in reductions in the size of the bargaining unit. A major challenge for the future is finding a way for both the company and the union to prosper under intensely competitive conditions, where a knowledgeable workforce is a competitive advantage. Some progress in this area is evident from the development of partnerships between unions and employers to create education and training programs that develop less skilled employees and increase productivity. Even at the lowest levels of the agriculture industry, more knowledgeable workers can improve the bottom line.* The Farmworker Institute for Education and Leadership Development (FIELD) serves as an intermediary between management and community organizations and provides direct training to both current employees and potential employees. FIELD was founded by the United Farm Workers (UFW) union to foster the economic and social prosperity of the low-income and low-skill farm workers and their families. Working in partnership with agricultural owners and managers, FIELD provides classroom training, educational literacy programs, and cross training to prepare workers for jobs in agriculture. It also provides training for those already employed, on the basis of employer needs. These programs include upgrading job skills, communication, quality management, leadership development, and conflict resolution. For example, FIELD trained over 900 workers at seven companies in health and safety. FIELD also provides customized training, as it did for Monterey Mushrooms, a California-based distributor of fresh and processed mushrooms with a UFW workforce. The training developed by FIELD reinforced the company's "be the best" principles and encouraged collaboration and conflict resolution. The company has benefited from the training with higher productivity and fewer accidents.

*Source: "Grab your partner." *Training* (June 2004), pp. 32–38

- Identification of alternative solutions to the opportunity and selection of the most beneficial solution. A training program is one of many possible performance improvement solutions
- Design and implementation of the solution (training if it is one of the selected solutions)
- Evaluation of results to determine what, if any, further action should be taken

Each of the above steps matches well when placed against the Training Process Model. That is because effective training is a continuous performance improvement process. Training does not stop and start with each program. The training function in organizations continuously searches for performance improvement opportunities, develops and implements solutions, and evaluates the effectiveness of the solutions.

Quality improvement is a key component of most continuous improvement processes. High-quality products and services are necessary to stay in business in today's competitive markets and thus have high priority for most businesses. This is especially true for businesses that provide products or services directly to other businesses. Typically, these companies must demonstrate the quality of their products through quality systems developed by the purchasing company or by some globally accepted agency. For example, the major automobile manufacturers impose their quality systems on suppliers. The **International Organization for Standardization (ISO),** located in Geneva, Switzerland, developed a set of worldwide standards to ensure consistency in product quality by all companies that become certified. In general, there are five stages in the certification process:

1. Preaudit: assessing how you are doing now
2. Process mapping: documenting the way things are done
3. Change: developing processes to improve the way things are done to reach a desired level of quality
4. Training: training in the new processes
5. Postaudit: assessing how well you are doing after the changes and continuing the improvement process.

Once certified, there are continuing audits to ensure company compliance with the standards. Thus, training is an important part of attaining ISO certification and is required on a continuous basis to maintain certification. The certification process also helps improve training. A research study showed improvements in TNA, design, delivery methods, and evaluation following certification.[12] This study also found that these companies provided more hours and more types of training and had a larger training budget following certification.

In addition to improved training processes, companies with ISO certification also find the following advantages:[13]

- Improved efficiency
- Higher productivity
- Better internal communication
- Improved quality image and market competitiveness
- Increased customer preference
- Increased awareness of opportunities for process and quality improvements
- Reduced costs and improved ability to document quality control processes to their customers

Glen Black, president of the Process Quality Association in Canada, compared ISO-certified companies with those not certified. He found that certified companies are six times less likely to experience bankruptcy, average 76 percent lower warranty costs in customer-discovered defects, and allow 36 percent less bureaucracy within their company structure.[14] A cost comes with achieving these benefits, however. Once the company makes the decision to seek certification, it must be prepared to engage in a substantial amount of training that can be costly. Furthermore, training is only one part of the overall cost, so each business must determine whether the costs of ISO certification are justified by the benefits.

Legal Issues

Equal employment opportunity, affirmative action, sexual harassment, and related legislation have placed legal requirements on businesses regarding specific types of training. You will learn in detail the training issues related to sexual harassment and equity (specifically related to females in nontraditional jobs, the glass ceiling, and the disabled) in Chapter 10. In addition, trainers need to be aware of liability issues, copyright infringement, and other legal concerns. The discussion of these issues is not intended to provide technical legal information, but rather to provide a general (and understandable) description of the important legal issues related to training activities.

Equity

In North America, federal, state, or provincial law and associated court rulings provide the complex legal framework within which businesses must develop their HR policies and practices. Even though legislation initially focused on the selection of people into the organization, there are many areas related to training that also require attention. This is especially true as the legal battlegrounds have shifted from employment to career opportunities over the last decade. Since this is not a text on training liability issues, we will address the topic only in a general way. Those wishing a more in-depth coverage might want to read "Avoiding Legal Liability: For Adult Educators, Human Resource Developers, and Instructional Designers."[15]

United States federal law makes it illegal to exclude people from training on the basis of gender, race, age (employees aged 40 or older), and disabilities. Generally, the above categories are referred to as "protected," as they belong to a "protected group." Employers must make sure that criteria for selecting people into training programs are based on bona fide job requirements (not race, gender, age, etc.). Employees targeted for promotion generally receive training and developmental experiences to prepare them for the new position. The legal issue here is that those in protected classes may claim that they did not receive the training needed to be promoted. In general, the law says that those in protected groups must be given equal opportunity for promotions. If members of a protected group can demonstrate that they have been adversely affected (e.g., fewer promotions, lower pay) because they did not receive training that was provided to those who received those benefits (e.g., promotions), the burden of proof falls on the employer to demonstrate that its practices are job-related and consistent with business necessity. In the case of promotions, a company can avoid such claims by providing equal access to training for all employees in a job classification. Once it is determined that someone in the classification will be promoted, that person can receive additional training to prepare for the new position. The legal issue of equal opportunity then focuses on the selection process rather than the training opportunities.

For employees with disabilities (physical or mental), the employer must not only ensure equal opportunity for training, but also make reasonable accommodation. Reasonable accommodation means making training facilities and materials readily accessible and useable to those with a disability. Depending on the disability, this could include instructional media and/or providing readers. If the training is considered to be related to essential job functions and the disability prevents the person from participating in the training, then, unless undue hardship can be demonstrated, the employer is obligated to provide alternative training that develops the same set of competencies.

Not only do protected groups need equal access to training, they must receive equal treatment while participating in training. This means that the training must provide equal opportunities for learning, practice, and feedback.

Required Training

Some training is required by law. Failure to provide this training will subject the company to sanctions from the courts or federal and state regulators. For example, the Occupational Safety and Health Act requires employers to provide periodic training on the handling of hazardous materials and the use of safety equipment. Flight crews on passenger airlines must complete a set of mandated training courses. In other cases, courts have ordered companies to provide specific types of training to redress problems identified in court proceedings. Companies that have lost employment discrimination cases have been ordered to provide diversity training, and those losing sexual harassment cases have been ordered to provide sexual harassment training.

In other cases, even though training is not legally required, it makes good legal sense to provide the training. In a 1999 ruling, *Kolstad v. American Dental Association,* the Supreme Court recognized the good-faith effort of employers to implement and enforce measures to prevent discrimination and harassment in the workplace.[16] Essentially, the court found that even though an individual might behave in a manner that violated the federally protected rights of another employee, no damages would be awarded if the company was shown to have made a good-faith effort to prevent the activity. One component of such a good-faith effort is to provide training aimed at preventing the illegal behavior. Another component is the implementation of policy and procedure for addressing the behavior, should it occur, and finally, the application of sanctions to individuals found to have engaged in the behavior. We discuss how this is done and provide examples in Chapter 10. The number of sexual harassment claims has decreased over the last few years, but the number of discrimination claims of all types has remained steady.

In designing training programs to deal with discrimination and harassment, trainers need to avoid training that itself is discriminating or harassing. For example, in the early 1990s, it was documented that women aircraft controllers who had to walk down long aisles populated by their mostly male colleagues would find themselves subject to jeers and/or sexual comments, and, on occasion, would have their dresses pulled up. After repeated complaints about such behavior, the Federal Aviation Administration (FAA) arranged for training to be provided to its 8,000 employees. A part of the training involved men walking down a gauntlet of women coworkers, who now did the jeering, sexual commentary, and groping. It was intended that the men get a firsthand understanding of what the women had experienced. One of the male participants was outraged by the experience. He stated that he did not treat others in this manner and did not expect to be treated that way himself. In the program he was accused, as a white male, of being in sexist denial. He complained to his supervisors in the FAA but little was done. Shortly thereafter, he filed a $300,000 lawsuit for sexual harassment. He won, and the FAA's director of training was fired.[17]

Liability for Injury or Illness

Some types of training programs have the potential to cause physical or psychological injury or illness to participants. For example, some simulations that require trainees to use tools or equipment might cause injury if they are used incorrectly. Training in other instances might involve the use of chemicals that can cause illness if inhaled. In many states, the employer is responsible for financial damages resulting from injuries or illness caused by participation in training. This is true even if the training is provided by an outside vendor. Trainees need to be warned of any dangers associated with training, be trained in methods of preventing the dangers from occurring, and be provided with safety equipment. Employers are also liable for injuries to nonemployees resulting from a poorly or incorrectly trained employee.

Confidentiality

An employee's performance during and at the conclusion of training is confidential in the same manner as other employee information. Thus, if performance in training is to be used in promotion or salary decisions, the employee must be informed that it will be used in that way. Unless permission has been granted, or the trainee is informed prior to training that such discussions would occur, trainers must also avoid discussion of the trainee's performance with other employees.

Copyrighted Materials

The use of any copyrighted material without the permission of the owner is illegal. If your training vendors infringe on the copyrighted material of others while providing your company with services, your company could be liable for damages. Thus, as the training manager, you would want to make sure that your contract with the vendor required the legal use of any copyrighted materials.

CAREER OPPORTUNITIES IN TRAINING

To understand the types of career paths training offers, it is necessary to understand how the training unit fits in the organization. This can vary considerably across organizations. For example, large companies typically separate management training and development from the training of the nonmanagement employees. Each of these areas might be further divided into more specialized activities. For example, the employee development area might contain separate units focused on training in customer service, employee orientation, health and safety, and each of the organization's major operation areas (sales, manufacturing, etc.). If the company is very large, it might also have specialists working in evaluation and research, program design, materials development, and needs analysis. The person in charge of customer service training, for example, would work with specialists in these areas to do the following:

- Determine the customer service training needs in the organization.
- Develop training programs to meet those needs.
- Develop materials to support the instructional methods to be used in the programs.
- Evaluate the effectiveness of the programs.

Entry-level positions in a large company's HRD department are usually at the specialist level. Thus, a new hire with little experience but a good education in the training area could start out as a materials designer or a stand-up trainer, depending on her KSAs. In a large organization, a career path might look like the one shown in Figure 1-4. The early rotation through the various specialist positions provides the novice trainer with firsthand experience in all aspects of the training system. When a person has a solid grasp of the system (i.e., how it is "supposed" to work and how it "actually" works), she is able to supervise or coordinate one of the specialist areas. Some large companies also require their HRD personnel to spend time in a line position, to better understand the needs of line personnel. Thus, at some point in the career ladder pictured in Figure 1-4, the training practitioner could find himself supervising or working in a line operation for a period of 6 to 12 months, although this requirement is still fairly unusual. Supervisors will often also rotate across specialist areas before moving into a manager's role, such as manager of employee development. After sufficient experience and success as a manager, the trainer may

Figure 1-4
Possible Career
Path in Training

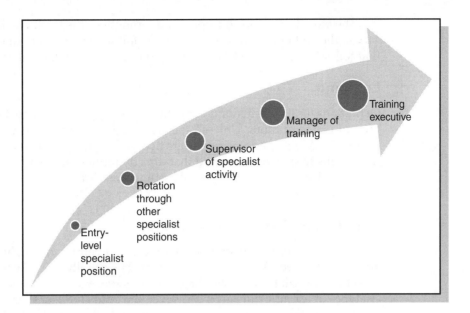

be asked to assume responsibility for all training and development activity in the organization—the training executive position.

The smaller the organization, the greater the breadth of responsibility each person in the training unit will have. In a medium-sized company, with around 1,000 employees, the HRD activities of employee and management training may not be separated into separate units, but carried out by the same small group of people under the guidance of an HRD manager. Each individual is expected to perform all (or most) aspects of each of the activities. Smaller companies (100–300 employees) may not have an HRD or training department at all. Instead, a single individual may be responsible for all training activities. In even smaller businesses, many of the HR responsibilities, including training, are decentralized out to the line managers. HR departments may consist of only one or two people who handle the core HR activities and act as consultants and facilitators for the line managers in carrying out their HR responsibilities, such as training.

Another career path for a training and development professional is as a member of a training or consulting firm. Requirements here vary greatly. There are a large number of one- or two-person consulting businesses that do training. These people market some core set of knowledge they have acquired through their work experience, education, or both. There are also some very large training or consulting firms that operate on a national or global basis. These firms hire specialists in certain areas such as instructional design, materials development, and evaluation. However, these firms also prefer employees to have several years of experience as well as advanced degrees. Generally, they are able to recruit a sufficient number of applicants who meet the experience and education requirements, because their compensation package is typically much better than that of the smaller firms, although compensation levels vary considerably from firm to firm.

IMPORTANT CONCEPTS AND MEANINGS

The literature in training and development, as in other professional disciplines, is continually evolving. As such, you will often find different meanings attached to the same terms. Thus, it is important for us to be clear about the terms and concepts we are using. It is also useful for you, the reader, to have a good understanding of how terms are commonly used in the field and how they will be used throughout the text.

The basic terms and concepts used throughout the book are defined in the glossary at the end of the book. However, the following terms are the foundation for all that follows, and we need to be clear about meanings at the outset.

Learning

Definitions for learning found in the literature vary according to the theoretical background of the authors. Unless otherwise indicated, the term **learning** in this text means a relatively permanent change in cognition (i.e., understanding and thinking) that results from experience and that directly influences behavior. This definition, of course, reflects our own theoretical assumptions. We will discuss this definition and others at length in Chapter 3.

Knowledge, Skills, and Attitudes

What is learned can be separated into different categories. Again, how these categories are defined differs according to the source. Historically, organizational psychologists used the acronym KSAs to stand for the terms *knowledge, skills, and abilities*—the different types of learning outcomes. However, the term *attitudes* is increasingly being substituted for the term *abilities*. As it turns out, the definitions given to *skills* and *knowledge*, taken together, are not that different from the definition of abilities. Thus, the term *abilities* is redundant with knowledge and skills. Abilities, for example, are defined as ". . . general capacities related to performing a set of tasks that are developed over time as a result of heredity and experience."[18] Skills are defined as ". . . general capacities to perform a set of tasks developed as a result of training and experience."[19] The only difference seems to be whether heredity is involved. The existing scientific evidence suggests that skills are influenced by heredity as well as by experience. Some authors make a distinction by categorizing skills as being psychomotor (behavioral) in nature, whereas abilities are categorized as cognitive. In this case, abilities do not differ from how knowledge is defined. The most commonly accepted definition of knowledge covers both the facts that people learn and the strategies that they learn for using those facts. These are cognitive in nature. Although some would argue that abilities are still distinguishable from knowledge and skills, we believe the distinction to be of minimal value. On the other hand, attitudes are relatively easy to distinguish from knowledge or skills. In addition, it is scientifically well established that attitudes influence behavior, and they are learned.[20] Thus, to our way of thinking, attitudes must be part of any holistic attempt to describe learning/training outcomes.

In this book, the acronym **KSAs** refers to the learning outcomes, **knowledge, skills,** and **attitudes.** These three outcomes of learning are depicted in Figure 1-5. The ways in which the three types of learning occur are interrelated but quite different. We will discuss these in depth in Chapter 3. The definitions for the three types of learning outcomes are as follows.

Knowledge
Knowledge is an organized body of facts, principles, procedures, and information acquired over time.[21] Thus, learning refers to:[22]

- the information we acquire and place into memory (declarative);
- how information is organized for use, into what we already know (procedural); and
- our understanding of how, when, and why information is used and is useful (strategic).

Declarative knowledge is a person's store of factual information about a subject. Facts are verifiable blocks of information such as the legal requirements for hiring,

Figure 1-5
Classification of
Learning Outcomes

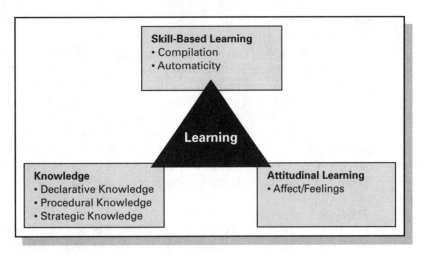

safety rules, and the like. Evidence of factual learning exists when the learner can recall or recognize specific blocks of information.

At a higher level is the person's understanding about how and when to apply the facts that have been learned. This is referred to as **procedural knowledge.** It assumes some degree of factual knowledge, because some information must be known about an object or activity before rules for its use can be developed. For example, one could not know when to apply the steps in an employment interviewing process (procedural knowledge) if one does not know the steps (declarative knowledge). Procedural knowledge allows trainees to understand the underlying rationale and relationships surrounding potential courses of action so they can apply their factual knowledge appropriately.

The highest level of knowledge is **strategic knowledge.** This is used for planning, monitoring, and revising goal-directed activity. It requires acquisition of the two lower levels of knowledge (facts and procedures). Strategic knowledge consists of a person's awareness of what he knows and the internal rules he has learned for accessing the relevant facts and procedures to be applied toward achieving some goal. When this type of knowledge is the focus of training or education, it is often called a "learning how to learn" program. For example, Bill has the task of ensuring that the hiring process for his company is both legal and effective at identifying the best candidate for the job. He would have to review and evaluate the various employment procedures to determine which, if applied correctly, would result in the selection of the best candidate *and* would fit within the law. He would have to have previously acquired procedural and declarative knowledge related to employment law and to effective hiring procedures. He would be using his strategic knowledge to access and evaluate the procedural and declarative knowledge to achieve his goal of a legal and effective hiring process.

Skills
Knowledge is a prerequisite for learning skills. A person must know "what" to do and "when" to do it. However, a gap separates knowing those things from actually being able to "do" them. A skill is a proficiency at being able to do something rather than just knowing how to do it. By skills, we mean the capacities needed to perform a set of tasks. These capacities are developed as a result of training and experience.[23] A person's skill level is demonstrated by how well she is able to carry out specific actions, such as operating a piece of equipment, communicating effectively, or implementing a business strategy.

There are two levels of skill acquisition: **compilation** (lower level) and **automaticity** (higher level). These reflect differences in the degree to which a skill has become routine or automatic. When a person is learning a particular skill or has only recently learned it, he is in the compilation stage. Here he needs to think about what he is doing while performing the skill. After a person has mastered the skill and used it often, she has reached the automaticity stage. Here the person is able to perform the skill without really thinking about what she is doing. In fact, thinking about it may actually slow her down. Learning how to play tennis is a good example of the different stages of skill development. When you are first learning to play, you must constantly think about each aspect of hitting the ball, such as where to stand on the court, and so on. Gradually, changes in how you grip the racket and your movement on the court become automatic, and thinking about them actually might reduce your effectiveness. One of the values of "practicing" as a learning technique is that through practice the behavior becomes more automatic.

Attitudes

Attitudes are employee beliefs and opinions that support or inhibit behavior.[24] In a training context, you are concerned about employees' attitudes in relation to their learning the training material and their job performance. The beliefs and opinions the person holds about objects or events (such as management, union, empowerment, and training) create positive or negative feelings about those objects and events. Thus, changing a person's beliefs or opinions can change the desirability of the object or event. For example, if an employee has positive feelings about a supervisor, those positive feelings are likely to become associated with the employee's job. If the employee learns from a coworker that the supervisor said negative things about her, job satisfaction is likely to be reduced, even though nothing about the job itself actually changed. What changed is the employee's belief about the supervisor's opinion of her.

Attitudes are important to training because they affect motivation. **Motivation** is reflected in the goals people choose to pursue and the effort they use in achieving those goals. Goals and effort are influenced by how a person feels about things related to the goal (i.e., attitudes). Because a person's attitude influences behavior, attitudes that motivate employees to perform or learn more effectively need to be addressed through training. Do you think Domtar employees immediately embraced the new way of doing business? Were they eager to get involved in making the company more profitable before the training and other changes were implemented? It's highly unlikely. That is why it is important to address attitudes as well as skills in a training program.

Consider the situation Lockheed Corporation faced about a decade ago. Concerned about the security of their products and product development processes, Lockheed realized that it needed either to significantly increase the current security force (which was costly) or include security in the job descriptions of all employees. Lockheed chose the latter approach, implementing security awareness training and annual security refresher training. The sessions were designed to change employees' attitudes about their jobs. Employees saw workplace security as part of their individual responsibility rather than only the responsibility of the security department. Five years after the program started, the number of reports of "suspicious incidents" increased by 700 percent.[25] Training in Action 1-3 illustrates the importance of examining not only knowledge and skills, but also attitudes when designing training programs.

Competencies

A **competency** is a set of KSAs that enables a person to be successful at a number of similar tasks. In the broadest sense, a job is broken down into a set of tasks, and the competencies required to perform the job are determined through an analysis of the tasks. A competency is more than just KSAs; it is the ability to integrate and use

The offices of the president and provost at a large university were receiving many complaints about the registration office being unresponsive to student problems during registration for classes. The director of registration felt that, because of the high turnover in customer service representatives (CSRs) who handled student problems, most CSRs did not know the proper procedure. The director wanted to initiate training in registration procedures immediately and called in a consultant to help develop and conduct the training.

After listening to the director's description of what was wanted, the consultant said, "You're probably right. Of course, we could conduct a training needs analysis to clarify the exact nature of the performance problem." The director was concerned about the time required for a needs analysis and wanted to get training started right away. However, in agreeing that the needs analysis would determine specific problem areas, the director said, "Okay, do the analysis, but let's get started on training right away. I want them to know exactly what they are supposed to do."

The needs analysis revealed the steps and procedures that an effective CSR was required to complete in dealing with an unhappy customer. For example, one of the first steps for the CSR was to identify and clarify the customer's problem and to acknowledge the feelings the customer was displaying (e.g., anger or frustration) in a friendly and empathetic manner. Once these feelings had been acknowledged, the CSR was to determine the exact nature of the customer's problem through nonevaluative questioning (i.e., determining the facts without placing blame for outcomes).

Interviews with the CSRs established that they all knew the correct procedure and most could quote it word for word. However, observation of the CSRs at work showed marked differences in how the procedure was carried out. Further analysis of each CSR's skills in performing these tasks revealed that the primary causes of unsatisfactory performance were low skill levels and inappropriate attitudes. Even though nearly everyone "knew" what to do, some were not good at doing it. Others did not believe that it was important to follow every step. One CSR said, "Hey, if they get their problem solved, what do they care if I acknowledged their feelings?"

Certainly training was required in this case, but not the "knowledge" training the registration director thought was necessary. For those CSRs who lacked the behavioral skill to carry out the procedures, demonstrations and practice sessions with immediate feedback were provided. For those CSRs who had the skill but did not understand the importance of all the procedures, training sessions were conducted in which the CSRs reevaluated their attitudes through various educational and experiential activities.

the KSAs to perform a task successfully. A carpenter, for example, has knowledge about different types of wood, tools and their uses, and types of finishes that can be applied to wood. This knowledge alone will not make that person a good carpenter. The carpenter also might possess a set of skills such as cutting, shaping, joining, and finishing. These skills alone will not make a good carpenter. The carpenter might love working with wood, place a high value on quality, and find great satisfaction working on the details of planning a project. These factors alone will not make a good carpenter. It is the combination of these KSAs and others such as hand-eye coordination, visual acuity, patience, and judgment that allow the carpenter to become proficient. To be successful at carpentry, or at any other occupation, a person must acquire multiple competencies. A trainer can identify the key KSAs that make a master performer successful at a given job and then group these KSAs into appropriate clusters. This provides a broad set of competencies required for the job. Linking these competencies to a set of behaviors that allow trainers to "know it when they see it" provides a valuable tool for hiring, training, and determining pay rates for the job. We spend a great deal of time discussing KSAs because they are the foundation of competencies. Competencies are useful for understanding how the KSAs combine to influence job performance. The KSAs determine what types of training will improve competencies and, thus, lead to improved job performance.

Training, Development, and Education

The terms *training, development,* and *education* are used in different ways by various authors. Here, the terms *training* and *development* refer to distinct, but related, aspects of learning. Training is a set of activities, whereas development is the desired outcome of those activities. **Training** is the systematic process of providing an opportunity to learn KSAs for current or future jobs; **development** refers to the learning of KSAs. In other words, training provides the opportunity for learning, and development is the result of learning. "Training departments" are now called Human Resource Development departments, and "management training" is called management development. These changes in terminology reflect the change from a focus on the process (training) to a focus on the outcome (development).

Education is typically differentiated from training and development by the types of KSAs developed, which are more general in nature. While training is typically focused on job-specific KSAs, education focuses on more general KSAs related, but not specifically tailored, to a person's career or job.

FOCUS ON SMALL BUSINESS

Most business texts, especially those covering human resource management (HRM), focus on medium- to large-sized businesses for a number of reasons, including the following:

- Research typically requires a larger sample size.
- Larger firms have the budgets to support research.
- Policies and procedures are more formalized, thus easier to track.
- Techniques described in HR texts usually require a formal HR function containing multiple areas of specialization, such as compensation, HRD, selection, and so on.

When small businesses are overlooked, a major component of the economic engine that runs North America is ignored. Small- to medium-sized business firms account for more than 60 percent of the private sector's contribution to the economy. Most of the workforce is employed at companies employing fewer than 100 people. Almost all businesses (98 percent) employ fewer than 100 employees, and 93 percent employ fewer than 20. No size criterion is universally accepted in the literature for categorizing a business as large or small. We generally use the term **small business** to refer to organizations with fewer than 100 employees, but on occasion, we use examples with about 150 employees. Larger companies that employ between 150 and 500 people are usually considered to be medium-sized.

The model of the training process that we present is applicable to both large and small businesses, but the ways in which it is implemented can differ dramatically with the size of the company. One difference is the number of employees that need to be trained. Because larger companies train greater numbers of employees, they must use a more systematic and controlled method of determining what training needs exist. In smaller companies, the owner or president can have a close working knowledge of each employee and his or her training needs. Another difference is in developing training programs. The smaller business can easily determine what types of training are more or less important to the company's objectives and can design training accordingly. In larger companies, again, a more systematic and formal approach is needed because the firm's strategies and objectives are more complex. In larger companies, economies of scale can be obtained if common training needs across the workforce are identified, thus reducing the per-person cost of training.

However, a more rigorous approach to identifying needs is required because more employees are involved.

Another difference between large and small companies is that small companies can use less costly and formalized methods for evaluating training because the results are more easily observed. Throughout the following chapters, where applicable, we will have a "Focus on Small Business" section. Here, we will identify strategies and practices that might be more appropriate for the smaller business. Where research results are applicable, we highlight their implications. When research is not available, we offer logic and applied examples.

SUMMARY

Training was described in terms of an open system in which it receives inputs from other parts of the organization and the external environment. That input is transformed by processes in effective training units into output that meets the organization's needs. Effective training occurs as a set of phases. In each phase, input is acquired, a set of processes are engaged, and output needed for subsequent phases is produced. The training process model provides a visual understanding of how the phases relate to each other. Although the model shows the phases occurring as sequential steps (needs analysis, design, development, implementation, and evaluation), in fact these phases occur in a dynamic fashion with feedback from one phase leading to the next phase and recycling through some aspects of the previous phase.

Training faces increasing demands to demonstrate results in terms of return on investment. With these demands come increased opportunities for the training function to influence the direction and operations of the company. In higher-performing organizations, training activities are aligned with the organization's strategies. The challenge for training units is to align its resources with activities that provide the best match with strategic objectives.

Changing demographics, steadily increasing market competitiveness, high demand for and short supply of knowledge workers, and customer demands for high-quality products and services all challenge companies and their training departments. Companies are becoming more concerned with creating their own talent, as significant losses to the workforce will occur from retirements over the next ten years. Successful companies build their training units to serve as a continuous improvement system and problem-solving tool. Evidence is accumulating that those companies that spend more on training are achieving better financial results. Improved operating methods (such as ISO and increased employee competencies are also resulting in declining union membership. This trend places the leadership of unions in the dilemma of demanding increased training for their membership to ensure job security, while at the same time recognizing that higher-skilled employees allow the company to do more with fewer people.

The legal environment places requirements on the training system in terms of providing mandatory training and ensuring equitable treatment of employees. Training units also have responsibilities for making sure that training is safe for trainees and that the training is consistent with protecting the safety of those with whom trainees come into contact after training. The increased use of outside training vendors requires due diligence to prevent copyright violations.

In large organizations, the training unit is divided into specializations. The most typical entry point into a training career is in a large company as a specialist in one part of the training process (e.g., needs assessment, instructional design). From there, the progression is much like any other functional area with rotation through the different specializations before moving into a managerial position. In smaller organizations, a few people will handle all training responsibilities, while in very small businesses, all HR functions are usually divided among the few people in management-level positions.

Important concepts and terms in the field of training were defined and discussed, including *competencies, learning, knowledge, skills*, and *attitudes*. The rationale for substituting attitudes for the "abilities" concept was provided. Though differing opinions exist in the field of training about what constitutes training versus development and education, training in this text will be considered to be the experiences provided to people that enable them to learn job-related KSAs. Education will be considered to be the experiences that enable people to learn more general KSAs that are related to, but not specifically tailored to, a person's job. Development will be considered to be the learning that occurs as a result of training or education.

KEY TERMS

- Actual organizational performance (AOP)
- Attitudes
- Automaticity
- Competency
- Compilation
- Declarative knowledge
- Design phase
- Development
- Development phase
- Education
- Evaluation phase

- Expected organizational performance (EOP)
- Implementation phase
- International Organization for Standardization (ISO)
- Knowledge
- Knowledge, skills, and attitudes (KSAs)
- Learning
- Motivation
- Analysis phase
- Open systems model

- Organizational performance gap (OPD)
- Outcome evaluation
- Procedural knowledge
- Process evaluation
- Skills
- Small business
- Strategic knowledge
- Training
- Training needs analysis (TNA)
- Training objectives
- Triggering event

CASE QUESTIONS

1. How did Domtar's strategies align with its mission? Explain your answer.
2. Given the difficulty of organizational change, what factors contributed to the success at Domtar? How did Domtar's management at all levels contribute to reducing resistance to change? What else might they have done?
3. What were the major HRD challenges associated with Domtar's acquisitions and joint partnerships? How were these challenges addressed, and what were the risks associated with these approaches?
4. Take the critical facts in the Domtar case and place them into the appropriate phases of the training model presented in the chapter. Begin with the triggering event and provide a rationale for why each fact belongs in the phase in which you have placed it.

EXERCISES

1. Review the material in Training in Action 1-3. Assume that you were hired to develop a training program for these CSRs. Write down what you believe are the four most important KSAs your training must address and your reasoning for selecting these. If done as a group exercise, allow each member of the group to share the KSAs she identified and her reasoning. Then reach a group consensus as to the four most important KSAs and your rationale for including each KSA. Each group will then report to the rest of the class.

2. In small groups, discuss the training responsibilities of supervisors and managers who are not part of the HRD department. Prepare a list of what those responsibilities might be and a rationale for your choices.
3. Identify two organizations with different environments and core technologies. Describe what these differences are. Indicate how the HRD strategies of these companies might be similar or different. Provide a rationale for your conclusions based on concepts in the chapter.
4. Conduct an interview with a small business owner or manager. Get a good understanding of how the company approaches training. What differences do you see between how this company approaches training and what was described in this chapter? What are the reasons for this difference?

QUESTIONS FOR REVIEW

1. Describe the relationship between the HR and the HRD functions in a large organization. How might a small organization handle the responsibilities of these two areas?
2. Consider the following problem-solving model. On the basis of the discussion in this chapter, describe how the training process model is or is not consistent with this model.

Problem-Solving Process
- Define and understand the problem.
- Determine the cause of the problem.
- Identify potential solutions to the problem.
- Select the solution that provides the most benefits for the least cost.
- Develop an action plan for putting the solution in place.
- Implement the solution.
- Evaluate and, if necessary, modify the solution.

3. What are the significant legal issues that the training unit must take into consideration when conducting training activities? Describe how these issues might create challenges for HRD.
4. Describe ways in which training units can go about meeting the challenges they face, which were described in this chapter. Provide a rationale for your answers.
5. Define and provide an example that was not used in the text for each of the following:
   a. Each of the three types of knowledge
   b. Each of the two levels of skills
   c. An attitude

WEB RESEARCH

Each year a number of companies are identified as the "Best Companies to Work For." Conduct a Web search to find a company that has recently made the list. See if there is information about the company's training. Conduct a second search to find any articles that have been written about this company's training. Write a one-page report summarizing your findings. Include a separate page with your references.

Aligning Training with Strategy

Learning Objectives

After reading this chapter, you should be able to:

➤ *Describe the strategic planning process, its components, and their relationships.*

➤ *Describe how the external environment influences strategic choices.*

➤ *Identify the major factors influencing the alignment of internal strategies with external strategies.*

➤ *Distinguish between an organization's external and internal strategies, and describe their relationship and the value of each.*

➤ *Describe the benefits of including a human resource development (HRD) perspective in strategy development.*

➤ *Describe the differences, similarities, and relationships among human resource (HR) and HRD strategies.*

➤ *Describe the field of organizational development (OD) and its relationship to training activities, including the value of cross training between the two.*

➤ *Identify possible HRD strategic alternatives and situations in which they might be appropriate.*

CASE: Hershey Aligns Training with Strategy

Hershey Foods is the leading North American manufacturer of chocolate-related grocery products and exports those products to over 90 countries. Hershey sells its products to distributors (such as large grocery and drug store chains, small retailers, wholesalers, and brokers) who then sell these products to their customers. Hershey's success depends on those retailers doing a good job of promoting Hershey products in their stores. Knowing the importance of product promotion, Hershey participates in a practice known as "trade funding." This practice has the manufacturer reinvest some of its profits back into joint promotional programs with its distributors. For

(continued)

example, Hershey might provide financial support to a grocery chain to create displays promoting Mother's Day specials or to promote "three for the price of two" specials. At the beginning of 2002, Hershey senior executives decided that significant changes were needed in this strategy.

Prior to 2002, Hershey's "trade funding" was done on a promotion-by-promotion basis with each customer. The customers felt that the promotional strategies were too complex, and Hershey executives felt that it was difficult to decide how to allocate the funds to maximize mutual benefit. In addition, there was no connection between a customer's sales of Hershey products and how much funding they received. Other aspects of the way the customers marketed Hershey's products, such as pricing, shelf space, and location, were not connected to the funding discussions with customers. On the basis of these issues and a customer satisfaction survey, Hershey decided to revise its strategy. The key elements of the new strategy were as follows:

- Hershey and each customer would develop an annual promotional plan for which Hershey would allocate funds.
- The annual plan would include a negotiated agreement on issues such as pricing, shelf space, and other marketing issues outside of "special" promotional events.
- The amount of funding customers would receive would be based on their past sales record and ability to execute the agreed-upon annual plan.

The new strategy was called "Blue Chip" and was introduced at their two-day Sales Summit held in May 2002. Not only was it introduced, it was the main event, and its focus was to provide the entire sales force with the knowledge, skills, and attitudes (KSAs) needed to implement the Blue Chip strategy. Interestingly, this event came at a time when Hershey's first-quarter financial numbers were down; they were in the middle of a management reorganization; the union workers in the largest factory were on strike; and the sale of the company was being quietly explored. Most companies would put the implementation of the new strategy on hold until they had a clearer picture of how everything would "shake out." What made Hershey decide differently? This wasn't just sales training; it was a change in strategy that signaled to both Hershey employees and customers that they were changing how they did business. As Bernie Banas, VP of sales at the time, said, "We were going through a transition. . . . It is critical to both Hershey and our customers that we execute the transition flawlessly." This wasn't just training focused on skill gaps; it was training that connected directly to Hershey's business goals and strategy.

So what did the training focus on? Before any specific training, it put the need for change into a context that all the sales force could understand and then provided a new strategy that would address the needs. This was followed by delivery of training, which focused on the key KSAs the sales force would need to implement the new strategy. The discussion of Hershey's strategic business needs included discussions of the following:

- Areas of customer dissatisfaction with current processes
- A shift from a relationship-based selling process to one that was more data driven
- The new pay for performance–based approach for working with customers

(continued)

- The increased sophistication of customer buyers in terms of purchasing and negotiating knowledge and skill
- The need to include all sources of value and negotiating leverage in discussions with customers

The Blue Chip strategy was then described in terms of 1) its benefits to customers, 2) its ability to motivate customers to do better planning and to incorporate all aspects of product promotion in the plan, and 3) Hershey's ability to gain compliance to the annual plans. The training was kicked off by the senior executives, who directly connected the training objectives to the business needs. These training objectives were based on what was going to be needed in terms of KSAs to effectively implement this new strategy. In other words, a future-oriented performance gap was evident based on the KSAs employees would need to implement the new strategic plan, making them highly relevant. The content of this training was based on the technical aspects of the Blue Chip program as well as negotiation skills. The negotiation skills helped the sales force effectively balance Hershey's interests with the maintenance of a collaborative relationship with the customer. All the training was focused on the practical application of the new KSAs. Experiential and discovery learning techniques were used to deliver this training.

The new strategy proved very successful for Hershey as its financial numbers have improved, and so have its surveys of customer satisfaction. The new strategy would not have been successful if the sales force didn't implement it correctly. The training provided at the "Summit," as well as the follow-up training and coaching of the sales teams, was key to the strategies' successful implementation. But just as critical were the changes to the internal reinforcement systems at Hershey that supported the changes that were required of the sales force.

As a side note, Hershey has an interesting training philosophy. They believe that visible short-term victories lead to credibility and future funding for long-term training and development projects. One rule of thumb is that every year's training budget should include at least one key strategic initiative that is "close to return on investment (ROI)." This could not be made clearer than the June 2008 announcement that Hershey is once again reshaping its market strategy. Details regarding internal training were not available as this was being written, but given the history, you can bet that they have that base covered.

Sources: Adapted from Strange, L., and Hennessey, P. "Training sweetens Hershey's core strategy." *Training and Development* (May 2003), 84(11). Hershey announces new consumer-centric approach and allocates resources behind core brands to drive long-term net sales and earnings growth. Hershey Foods Web site, June 21, 2008. http://www.thehersheycompany.com/news/release.asp?releaseID=1166722

OVERVIEW

As indicated in Chapter 1, aligning training activities with the goals and strategy of the organization has been the top priority of HR and HRD leaders for many years. The Hershey Foods case presented above exemplifies this process. Hershey realizes that doing this ensures that training dollars are put to the best use. This chapter provides a general explanation of business strategy and ways to make sure that training is aligned with that strategy. To understand how to align training with strategy, it is first necessary to understand the strategic planning process.

STRATEGIC PLANNING

Formalized **strategic planning** is a process used to determine how best to pursue the organization's mission while meeting the demands of the environment in the near (e.g., next year or two) and long term (e.g., next 5 to 10 years). A **proactive strategy** focuses on the longer term, and its process is more formalized, typically involving sophisticated analytical and decision-making tools. This is the process Hershey used. Its purpose is to build a good fit between the organization and its future environment. However, strategy can also develop in a more reactive fashion, responding to short-term business conditions. In a **reactive strategy,** less formal analysis and planning occur and more attention is focused on the immediate future. Many suggest that both reactive and proactive strategies are necessary for an organization to be effective.[1] The proactive process uses a best guess about what the future will bring, whereas the reactive process addresses how operations will confront what exists now and in the next year or two. A strategic plan that positions the firm for long-term expectations but is modified by the firm's experience as it moves forward is preferable to either having a rigidly held long-term plan or reacting only to short-term experience.

To be effective, strategic planning should occur throughout the organization, with each higher level of the organization providing direction to the lower levels. Once a strategic plan has been developed, organizational units develop or are given objectives by higher-level units that, when combined, will implement the strategy. The units develop their own strategies and tactics to achieve the organizational strategies. Individuals within the unit are given or develop objectives that will help achieve the unit's objectives. Thus, from the HR unit's perspective, the **organizational strategy** provides the direction for HR's strategic objectives. HR develops supporting tactics that provide the HR staff with a set of objectives to achieve (see Figure 2-1). In this way, plans for implementing the organization's strategy are developed and coordinated throughout the organization.

What role should the HRD unit have had in shaping strategy in the Domtar (Chapter 1) and Hershey cases? In both cases, the success of the strategy depended heavily on the competencies of the workforce. Without knowing the current capabilities of these individuals, the company does not know whether it has the capacity to successfully implement the strategy. HRD can and should be involved with strategic planning at the following three levels: organizational strategy, HR strategy (tactics), and HRD strategy (more tactics). We will review the factors that go into developing a strategic plan before covering these areas. Our goal here is to provide you with the basics needed to understand strategy development, so we will not cover the area in depth. For the sake of brevity and general understanding, we have simplified many of the concepts and principles.

Figure 2-1
Linkage between Strategy, Tactics, and Objectives

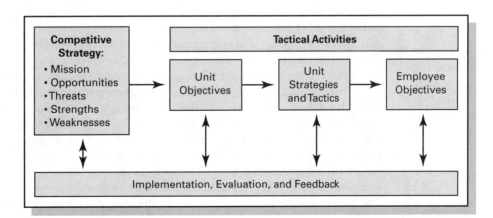

Organizational Mission

Strategies are created to achieve the organization's mission. A mission statement articulates why the organization exists. The mission is the focal point for strategy development because it outlines what the strategy is designed to achieve. Here are examples of relatively short and clear mission statements from two different types of organizations.

MISSION OF OZONE HOUSE (A SOCIAL SERVICE AGENCY)
Ozone House is a community-based, not-for-profit agency that seeks to help youth lead safe, healthy, and productive lives through intensive prevention and intervention strategies.[2]

MISSION OF HERMAN MILLER
Herman Miller, Inc., is a leading global provider of office furniture and services that create great places to live, learn, work, and heal.[3]

These statements, though different, show many similarities. A good mission statement is a fairly general description of what the organization seeks to accomplish. It describes the products or services the organization provides, to whom it provides them, and what it wishes to accomplish.

Strategic Choices

Strategies reflect choices that the organization makes about how to pursue its mission. An organization must choose from among a large number of often contradictory strategies. The strategic choices a company makes have significant implications for where HRD should focus its resources. To effectively align her unit's activities with the strategies, a manager will need to understand the factors that have led the organization to its strategic choices. The literature dealing with strategy contains a great many categorizations and terms that refer to different types and levels of strategy. For simplicity, we choose the term "competitive strategy." **Competitive strategy** focuses on positioning the company's products or services in the marketplace. This important strategy encompasses the internal and external choices the company makes to improve or retain its competitive position.

Two types of competitive strategy are market leader and cost leader. Firms that choose the **market leader** strategy are also referred to as prospectors[4] and innovators.[5] Their strategy is to find and exploit new product and market opportunities. Success depends on their capacity to survey a wide range of environmental conditions, trends, and events and to move quickly into windows of opportunity. Market leaders typically use multiple technologies capable of being used in many different ways.

Companies that adopt the **cost leader**[6] strategy, also referred to as the defender strategy,[7] represent the opposite end of the continuum. This strategy's main goal is to be the low-cost provider in the industry. Success depends on pricing competitiveness and having a product that is acceptable to (but not necessarily the best in) the market. Success is achieved by producing a standardized product or service efficiently, using economies of scale low-cost labor, and introducing innovative production methods.

Most organizations with multiple products or services will have different strategies for each product or service. Additionally, there are many ways to pursue a single strategy. For example, one way to pursue a cost leader strategy is to aggressively pursue competing bids from as many suppliers as possible, then accept the lowest bids from as many suppliers as are needed to meet requirements. A different tactic is to develop long-term relationships with a few suppliers with capacity to meet your requirements, guaranteeing sole supplier status in return for meeting a specified price target. For the HRD unit looking for outside training, this might mean choosing between having a large number of external training contractors or a single contractor who guarantees a low price. Both tactics can reduce the cost of needed goods and services, but they result in different effects on the purchasing activities of the organization and on supplier relationships. Among the feasible alternatives, the company seeks to choose the one that will best achieve the mission. Which will be "best" depends on how the organization addresses the strategic contingencies described in the following sections.

External Environment

An organization's **external environment** consists of elements outside the organization that influence the organization's ability to achieve its mission, such as competitors, the economy, societal norms and values, laws and regulations, raw materials, suppliers, and technological innovation. Each organization must determine the threats and opportunities that exist in its environment and address those that are critical in the strategy. What kinds of environmental factors might be important in the Hershey Foods case? In addition to identifying the critical threats and opportunities, the organization must assess how stable these will be in the future.

   Environmental uncertainty is determined by two factors: complexity and stability. **Environmental complexity** refers to the number of factors in the environment and the degree to which they are interrelated. **Environmental stability** is the rate at which key factors in the environment change—the more rapid the change, the more unstable the environment. When the environment is more complex and unstable, it is more uncertain. When it is simpler and more stable, it is more certain. Figure 2-2 depicts this relationship.

   In more uncertain environments, the organization must be flexible and adaptable if it is to respond effectively. A market leader strategy is consistent with this situation. More certain environments reward "getting it right and sticking to it." A more standardized operating system can minimize costs and maximize profitability, a situation consistent with the cost leader strategy. Uncertain environments generally favor strategies using more decentralized decision making, whereas centralized decision making is usually more effective when the external environment is more certain. Given two similar organizations, the one choosing the market leader strategy will, by definition, compete in a more uncertain environment. The cost leader competes best in established and more stable markets. This environment may be more hostile, but it will experience a slower rate of change.[8]

Internal Alignment with Strategy

Once a company has chosen a competitive (external) strategy, it needs to align its internal environment with that strategy. It needs an **internal strategy** (such as becoming more flexible) that provides direction for internal systems. For example, in the

Figure 2-2
Factors Influencing
Environmental
Uncertainty

		Complexity	
		High	**Low**
Stability	**High**	Moderate Uncertainty	**Low Uncertainty**
	Low	**High Uncertainty**	Moderate Uncertainty

Hershey Foods case, the Blue Chip program was the external strategy. Internally, this meant that salespeople would be required to negotiate effectively with their customers and that trade funding allocations would be based on new criteria. Thus, some of the internal changes required were the development of negotiating competencies for the sales force (training needs), the reward system that acted to reinforce the appropriate behavior of the sales force, and the decision-making system for allocating the trade funding dollars (nontraining needs). Two key factors in the internal strategy are the organization's core technology (how the principal products or services are created) and its structure (e.g., division of labor, policies, and procedures). Since the Hershey case didn't require changes in the product, but only in the behavior of employees, it was only the structure that needed to be changed to align with the new strategy. Figure 2-3 represents the relationships among environment, strategy, structure, and technology.[9] As the figure indicates, strategy is the process of making internal adjustments to accommodate the demands of the external environment while remaining true to the mission. Note, however, that the arrow between strategy and environment shows influence in both directions, reflecting the fact that the choice of competitive strategy may change the environment in which the firm operates.

Technology

Technology is how the work is done in the organization. Each unit in the organization uses technology to accomplish its tasks. **Core technology** refers to the main activities associated with producing the organization's principal products and services. Technology can be categorized in a number of ways.[10] Taking some liberties with these approaches, we use a simple continuum of "routine" to "nonroutine" technologies. At one end, the **routine technology** label is applied to tasks with outcomes that are highly predictable, demonstrate few problems, and use well-structured and well-defined solutions when problems do occur. High-volume assembly lines, such as in a garment factory or some automobile plants, are examples of routine technology. Such operations consist of highly specialized tasks and well-defined rules for coordinating activities. Decisions are usually top-down and highly formalized, leaving little discretion to the line employee. Routine technology is most often seen in the cost leader strategy. Even though the initial infrastructure required to put this technology in place can be expensive, its efficiency in high-volume production provides low production cost per unit.

A task using **nonroutine technology** is characterized by results that are difficult to predict, problems that occur often and unexpectedly, and solutions to problems that are not readily available and need to be developed on a case-by-case basis. With this type of technology, management needs to provide lower-level managers and line employees with more decision-making authority to meet the challenges encountered. This responsibility, of course, means that the firm needs employees with a higher level of KSAs. This technology also requires greater task interdependence, which increases the need for coordination and integration. Managers and workers

Figure 2-3
Mission, Strategy, Technology Structure Relationship

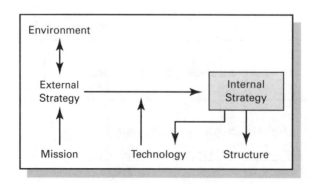

need decision-making authority within their own areas, but their activities must also be coordinated with the activities of others. Thus, employees must be given clear goals and parameters for their work outcomes but also be allowed to determine the best way to meet them. This type of technology is more typical of market leader strategies, in which the development and production of new products is key. The cost of the nonroutine technology might be high, but new products can command high prices in the marketplace.

Structural Choices

The internal strategy should also address the ability of the organization's structure to carry out the competitive strategy. **Organizational structure** refers to how a firm is organized (how labor is divided) in addition to the rules, policies, and procedures used for making decisions and coordinating its various activities. The organization's structure defines how the internal operations interact with the external environment. To be most effective, the organization's structure should funnel environmental input to those units best able to take advantage of opportunities and avoid threats. At the same time, it must facilitate the core technology. Although there are many structural components, we will examine only these three: organizational design, decision autonomy, and division of labor.

Organizational Design   The number and formality of rules, policies, and procedures created to direct employee behavior is the essence of **organizational design.** An organization's design can lie somewhere on a continuum ranging from mechanistic to organic.[11] A highly **mechanistic design** reflects an organization with highly defined tasks, rigid and detailed procedures, high reliance on authority, and vertical communication channels. A highly **organic design** reflects an organization that has flexibility in its rules and procedures, loosely defined tasks, high reliance on expertise, and horizontal communication channels. Few organizations operate on the extremes of this continuum; most lean more toward one end or the other.

The organic design places more emphasis on KSAs, whereas the mechanistic focuses more on technical and financial systems and resources. In the mechanistic design, employees' technical and interpersonal skills and behaviors are prescribed. In the organic design, these skills and behaviors are permitted to evolve (within broad parameters) to supplement and complement the unit's technology. As you might suspect, the organic design is most appropriate for nonroutine technologies, whereas the mechanistic design is more appropriate for routine technologies.[12]

Decision Autonomy   **Decision autonomy** is the amount of authority given to employees in deciding how to complete a task and the degree to which they are able to influence goals and strategies for their work unit.[13] Individual or small-group decision autonomy is a function of whether decisions are centralized or decentralized. Cost efficiencies are associated with more centralization, whereas flexibility/adaptability is associated with decentralization.[14] Thus, centralized structures are more appropriate for cost leader strategies and decentralized structures for market leaders.

Division of Labor   The way in which the work of the organization is divided among the units and organized is called **division of labor.** One way in which labor is divided is between line (those working directly with the core technology) and staff (everyone else); another is between management and labor. Some organizations divide their tasks by products, some by customers, and others by geography. Some divide work into functional areas, while others organize work around the processes in their core technology. Even though each of these divisions is important, our focus is on the degree to which duties and responsibilities within the organization are specialized. We place organizations on a continuum from narrowly defined (specialized) to generally defined (nonspecialized) duties and responsibilities. The more specialized the duties and responsibilities, the more centralized the decision making and the more mechanistic the organization. This results from the need to closely oversee and coordinate the activities of employees whose scope of responsibility is fairly narrow. In organizations with duties and responsibilities that are nonspecialized, a more organic and decentralized structure is appropriate. This allows employees to coordinate their activities less formally and provides more flexibility and adaptability for the organization. Again, you can see the close relationship between an organization's core technology and division of labor.

Aligning HR and HRD with Strategy

The HR function must support and enhance the organization's corporate strategy. This is accomplished by making sure that the various components in the HR system—such as staffing, HR planning, performance appraisal, compensation, health and safety, employee and union relations, and, of course, training—are aligned with the strategic plan. Each of these systems has a direct impact on the organization's effectiveness. Integrated under the HR umbrella, each can enhance the organization's ability to mobilize the necessary HRs to carry out the competitive strategy.

Why should companies invest in developing a strategic HR management capability? The evidence indicates that firms that do so will significantly increase their market value.[15] Data collected from more than 2,400 firms show that when HR systems achieve operational excellence and are aligned with the firm's strategic goals, the market value of the firm increases by about 20 percent. So investing in HR excellence and bringing HR systems into alignment with business strategies provides a clear competitive advantage.

HR should contribute to the development of the organization's competitive strategy and of course support those strategies once they are adopted. Decisions about competitive strategy need to be reflected in HR strategy, and vice versa. For example, if the company's operations are labor intensive and a strong union consistently demands high wages and restrictive work rules, it would be foolish to adopt a cost leader strategy without addressing these issues. Similarly, once the company makes the decision to adopt a cost leader strategy, HR must develop its own strategies for supporting cost leadership. Assume that a cost leader strategy requires a change in production technology that adds more automated equipment. This change would eliminate many labor-intensive jobs and add some technical jobs, thus providing a net labor saving. Such a change could be successful only if HR can fill the new technical positions with qualified people. Other HR factors would also need to be considered, such as the effect on labor relations and the financial costs associated with eliminating the old and staffing the new jobs. The HR department's input into the strategy formulation process would be to assess the HR issues critical to the strategic alternatives. Failure to address the HR side of the strategy could lead to the purchase and installation of a new technology that, among other things, is too costly to staff, creates labor conflict, produces conflicts in the existing culture, or requires lengthy training, thus delaying the implementation of the technology. What were the critical HR issues at Hershey Foods and Domtar?

We are not suggesting that HR issues should be the only, or the most important, influence on the strategic direction taken by an organization. However, they should be part of the equation. The relative importance of strategic variables such as technology, financial assets, product mix, and HR varies from one context to the next. Likewise, the importance of HRD issues to competitive strategy depends on how central employee competencies are related to successful implementation. Figure 2-4 shows how HR and HRD are related to the organization's business strategy.

Training in Action 2-1 describes the experience of Hewlett-Packard Canada in strategy reformulation. As illustrated in this example, the external strategy must be

Figure 2-4
Strategy
Development at
Different Levels

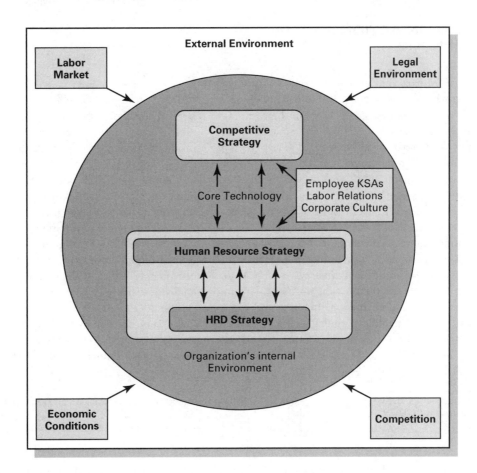

supported by internal strategies that bring the structure and core technology into proper alignment. HR and HRD are typically key players in the development of these internal strategies.

HRD is a part of the HR unit and contributes to the development of new strategy by providing an assessment of employee strengths and weaknesses relating to the competitive strategy being developed. Unfortunately, many organizations do not think of HRD in this strategic sense. Business strategies are often formulated with little consideration of employee capabilities, and it is only after implementation problems surface that HRD considerations arise. These problems often result in costly delays in implementing the strategy, and in some cases, even doom the strategy to failure. If the competitive strategy requires increasing the competencies of employees, the various methods of approaching this task would need to be examined. As a part of this, HRD would make an estimate of the time and resources required for employees to be ready to implement the strategy. This allows the strategic planning group to determine the feasibility and cost/benefit of the strategy.

You might think that hiring from outside the organization to improve the competency base of the organization wouldn't involve HRD much. In this approach, competencies are imported through recruitment and hiring. Even here, however, HRD needs to be involved in orientation and any other new employee training. If current employees are to be terminated or reassigned, HRD is likely to be involved in outplacement or training for the new job.

In the Domtar case, it became clear that no one had the knowledge and skills to implement a Kaizen approach to quality management. Domtar brought in an expert from outside to oversee the implementation process, but he would not be able to

In the early 1980s, Hewlett-Packard (HP) Canada was considered to be a slow-moving, inefficient company compared with its new competitors in the computer equipment business. Although it had state-of-the-art printers and other computer-related equipment, it was slow to get these products to the market, and its prices were comparatively high. Business results were poor and projected to worsen. Furthermore, a recession was in full swing. A rethinking of the competitive strategy was necessary. Top management performed the normal strategic planning activities, but it also formed teams to target companies in need of computer equipment and to determine what HP Canada needed to do to win their business. After analyzing their environment and internal strengths and weaknesses, the HP strategic planning team adopted a strategy combining elements of both quality and cost leadership.

To address the internal weaknesses related to this strategy, HP Canada cut staff and streamlined operations. The sales force, for example, had been organized into separate groups specializing in one or a few products. Under the new structure, the groups were merged into a sales force organized around customers but familiar with all products. HP Canada also relied on developing economies of scale in the production of its printers and pricing them competitively rather than taking large profit margins on their popular models. This strategy of getting a smaller unit profit from a larger volume of units, combined with improvements in product quality, vaulted Hewlett-Packard Canada back into a market leadership position. Profits increased in spite of a continued Canadian recession. By the late 1980s, HP Canada positioned itself to be one of the toughest competitors in a competitive industry.

Source: Information derived in part from Yoder, S. "A 1990 reorganization at Hewlett-Packard already is paying off." *The Wall Street Journal* (July 22, 1991), pp. AI, AID.

train the workforce by himself. The company wanted to improve customer service skills throughout the organization. It also needed to instill the Domtar values in the new employees it had inherited from mergers and acquisitions. Clearly, HRD needed to be a part of these strategic discussions.

Of course, the HRD unit's primary responsibility is to align itself with and support the organization's strategies. It does this by developing training that focuses on critical competencies that are needed to meet strategic performance objectives and delivering that training to the right people. HRD can better align itself with the organization's strategy by maintaining close connections to the product development area. Every business, whether it delivers goods or services, develops and delivers a product. New products are often a part of new strategy and require training for one or more of the following: the sales force, customers, and production employees. The earlier the training unit is able to understand the training needs relating to the new product, the better able it will be to meet those needs.

The HRD unit also plays a key role in identifying and assisting in the removal of barriers to desired performance. This last role is addressed in more depth in the next section.

OD, STRATEGY, AND TRAINING

The very best outcome that training, by itself, can achieve is the increase in trainee capabilities, that is, the trainee's ability to perform. The value of this comes from the transformation of this capability into improved job performance. Getting improved performance from improved capability is a performance management challenge. The HRD unit is focused on achieving the "capability," and **organizational development** is focused on the management of performance. Thus, the two should go hand in hand. The planning and implementation of strategy involves change—both in the way the organization interacts with its external environment and in how it manages its internal operations. OD deals with creating and implementing planned change. Thus, strategic planning and OD should go hand in hand. Unfortunately, in many organizations, these three sides of the organizational effectiveness triangle are not always aligned. In the sections below, we discuss what OD is and how it relates to strategic planning and training.

OD provides a research base and set of techniques related to organizational effectiveness and managing change. As the organization's objectives and strategies change, the KSAs required of employees also change. However, it is not enough simply to provide new KSAs. The organization's systems and procedures must change to support the use of the new KSAs if the desired change in performance is to occur. In the Hershey Foods case, what types of systems and procedures needed to change to make the new strategy successful? The reward system? The way Hershey is organized? The HRD process? The field of OD provides processes for identifying when systems and procedures need to change and how to manage the change. So let's examine the strategic planning process and the ways that HRD and OD can support each other in the implementation of a strategic plan.

OD and Strategy

Whether an organization's strategies are developed proactively or reactively, they require support from the internal systems. Organizational change is an inherent part of the process of developing and implementing strategy. Organizations must resolve the following three core issues in developing and implementing strategy:[16]

1. *Technical design issues.* These issues arise in relation to how the product or service will be determined, created, and delivered.
2. *Cultural/ideological issues.* These issues relate to the shared beliefs and values that employees need to hold for the strategy to be implemented effectively.
3. *Political issues.* These issues occur as a result of shifting power and resources within the organization as the strategy is pursued.

These three issues are critical to the organization's ability to achieve its objectives. In developing strategy, decisions such as what products to develop, how to manufacture them, and what marketing techniques to use will signal shifts in organizational values, power, and resources. These issues will need to be managed effectively to create support for, rather than resistance to, the strategic plan. The field of OD can help organizations manage change effectively. OD techniques provide methods for change to occur in an objective, goal-directed manner that addresses the needs of both the organization and the employees affected by the change. OD uses an open-system, planned-change process that is rooted in the behavioral sciences and aimed at enhancing organizational and employee effectiveness. A model of a generic planned-change process is provided in Table 2-1.

The strategic planning process, if done properly, is an OD approach to change. The first step, establishing a compelling need for change, occurs in strategic planning during the environmental scanning phase. The need for change is made apparent when the strategic planners identify the threats and opportunities in the external environment and compare that information with what the organization is currently doing. A need for change is established when a gap exists between what the organization is doing and what the external environment requires (or will require). Next, the company's business objectives are set (step 2 in the change model). The company's current strengths and weaknesses are analyzed to determine what internal

Table 2-1
Steps in a
Generic Planned
Change Model

1. Establish a compelling need for change.
2. Develop, in collaboration with the concerned parties, the goals to be achieved.
3. Determine what is causing the need for change.
4. Identify and evaluate alternative approaches for addressing the need for change.
5. Select an approach for addressing the need for change.
6. Implement the approach.
7. Evaluate the results.
8. Feedback the results to the organization.
   a. If results are favorable, go to step 9.
   b. If results are unfavorable, go back to step 4.
9. Internalize the change. The changes made become routine and the normal way the organization conducts its business.

changes are necessary (step 3). This information provides the compelling need for internal change, and internal strategic objectives are developed for these areas. The rest of the steps in the OD model concern the development of tactical activities to achieve the strategic objectives.

Levels of Change and Resistance

Whenever internal change is planned, the plan should address the following three levels in the organization:

1. *The organization itself:* The way the organization is put together (i.e., what we call structure and design) must be examined to ensure that work is allocated appropriately and organizational systems are supportive of the change. This level of analysis identifies how labor is to be divided and what rules and procedures will govern operations.
2. *Groups and their interrelationships:* The way work is performed in the organizational units (i.e., the sociotechnical systems) and how the outputs of the various units are integrated are the focus of this level of analysis. The issues here concern the design of jobs within units of the organization and the interrelationships of the jobs to one another.
3. *Individuals within groups:* The changes in performance that will be required of employees must be identified and mechanisms—facilities, machines, equipment, and KSAs—put into place to enable the desired performance to occur.

Resistance to change is a common occurrence. Without sufficient motivation to change, resistance is natural. Change requires effort, new learning, and possible shifts of resources and outcomes. Often, those satisfied with the status quo can create enough resistance to derail the change effort, even to the point that the business fails. A major factor in this resistance is the failure of the change process to address all three levels of change. For example, instituting a work-team system in the organization without addressing the performance-appraisal system will naturally cause resistance to the new approach. People may ask, "Why should we work as a team if we're getting evaluated as individuals?" Training in Action 2-2 provides a good example of what can happen if all three levels are not addressed in the change strategy.

Achieving successful change at one level, then, requires analysis and possibly interventions at all three levels. Consider the effect of a change in the organizational structure. Work would be allocated differently so that some units might get work they have not done before while others might have certain jobs taken away. The affected units would need to change their work processes because they would have different amounts or types of work to do. These changes would require OD interventions at the group level. Here, the OD practitioner is involved in the design or redesign of jobs and work systems

A southeast Michigan automotive parts manufacturing plant was divided into three manufacturing areas (Areas A, B, and C). The Area B manager, after some initial research, decided to install self-managed work groups (SMWGs). An outside consultant was brought in by the manager to assist in the change. The activities below were carried out in the order presented:

1. A steering committee was formed consisting of the plant bargaining committee chairperson, and two other United Auto Workers (UAW) representatives, the area manager, the plant industrial relations manager, two area superintendents, and the consultant. This group developed and managed the change process.
2. An analysis of Area B employees, supervisors, and production systems was conducted to identify areas for piloting the SMWG concept. Three production processes were selected on the basis of employee and supervisor interest and on the ability of the production process to create natural groupings of employees. While the equipment in these areas would remain the same, some of the tasks, and how work was assigned to individuals, would change as a result of the team concept.
3. Training was provided as described here, with duration indicated in parentheses.
   a. All Area B employees received a general orientation to SMWGs. This orientation included an overview of the changes that would occur in the pilot groups, the process of determining how those changes would occur, the role of staff support functions (e.g., engineering, accounting, etc.), and a question-and-answer period. (2 hours)
   b. Supervisors and line employees in the SMWGs were provided with the following:
      • A more in-depth orientation, including the goals, roles, and expectations for the SMWGs and the salaried coordinator (formerly supervisor).
      • In addition, each SMWG developed a team mission and set team goals. (4 hours)
      • Basic team skills: interpersonal communication, interpersonal relations, conflict management, and problem solving. (16 hours)
      • Team-building training for each group consisting of both instruction and trainer-facilitated application. After each component of training (e.g., development and assignment of roles), the team would apply the concepts and principles to their team. For example, after presentation of the team procedures material, the team developed an "operating plan," describing how work would be assigned, how team meetings would be conducted, how coordination between shifts would occur, and so on. (20 hours)
      • Training in information management, group facilitation, meeting management, and stress management to prepare supervisors for their new roles as salaried coordinators. Time was also provided for them to identify problems in carrying out their new roles and to develop potential solutions. (8 hours)
   c. Consultation for SMWGs and salaried coordinators was ongoing for a year after completion of the training.

This applied example demonstrates elements of effective change management at the group and individual levels. However, problems were encountered at the organizational level.

Group Level All SMWGs were informed of why the change was desirable and understood what the change would mean to them personally and how Area B and the plant would benefit. Their representatives on the steering committee (UAW representatives for the line employees and management for the supervisors) ensured that all voices would be heard. Each work group helped shape the way the change was implemented in that group by developing the team mission statement, goals, operating procedures, and so on.

Individual Level Prior to implementation, each individual could choose to remain in the work group or move to a different work group in the plant. Only a few individuals chose to leave their work groups. Extensive training provided each individual with the KSAs needed to be successful in the SMWG concept.

Organizational Level This effort ran into problems in two areas. First, no changes were made in the performance appraisal system, so salaried coordinators were

(continued)

still evaluated on the criteria used for supervisors. Thus, coordinators began reverting to their old supervisory behaviors, telling SMWGs what to do rather than helping the groups learn what to do. Second, no changes were made in support systems such as engineering and accounting. Accounting would not furnish the SMWGs with cost and operating efficiency information in a form they could understand. Without this information, the SMWGs were unable to determine whether they were meeting their goals. Equally troublesome was the relationship with engineering. Engineers were used to coming into an area and telling the employees what was wrong and how to fix it. The new system required them to work with the SMWG to determine both the problem and the solution. Engineers saw this process as a waste of their time as they already knew what to do. As a consequence, engineers frequently would not show up at team meetings and would implement changes without consulting with the SMWG that was affected by the changes. Because the engineers did not report to the area manager, he had little control over how the engineers interacted with the SMWGs.

These problems could have been prevented if organizational systems had been addressed as a part of the steering committee's change management plan. The plant manager needed to be a part of the steering committee as he was the only one with the authority to make systemwide changes.

and the associated interpersonal relationships. In addition, changes in how these work groups interact with others would be required because they would now be producing something different. Employee resistance to new procedures would need to be addressed as jobs are being redesigned. At the individual level, employees would also need to acquire the knowledge and skills necessary to perform their redesigned jobs.

You might think that these three levels of change are intertwined only if the change occurs at the organizational level. However, they are integrated no matter where the initial change takes place, which is why it is important to take a systems perspective. Suppose you want employees to increase their skill at integrating quality control (QC) into their production work. Of course, training at the individual level is required. But is it the only thing necessary for the change to be successful? Even if employees' KSAs are developed, the job itself and the organizational systems must support using the KSAs. The company will need to ensure that the design of the job supports the performance desired from its employees. For example, the equipment and tools might need to be changed. Also, if employees feel that QC is just a way for management to eliminate their jobs, they might resist this intervention, and providing new KSAs will not be enough. Work group norms (i.e., attitudes) will need to be changed to be consistent with QC objectives. At the organizational level, reward and appraisal systems would need to support the desired performance outcomes and work procedures. If the focus of the appraisal system does not assess the quality of the employees' work but only the quantity produced, employees will not be likely to sacrifice quantity for quality. The appraisal system needs to reflect the importance of quality as well as quantity. The point is that the components of the organization (structure and design, jobs and employees) are interdependent, and changes in one need to be addressed as part of the overall change effort. The training needs analysis process (Chapter 4) provides a model for determining not only what training is needed, but also what other changes are necessary to manage performance so that increased capabilities get transformed into increased job performance.

Training and OD

Using OD's principles-of-change management will increase the probability that your organization's strategic plans will be effectively implemented. But training also focuses on change, so change principles also apply to training efforts. By including an analysis of organizational issues as an integral part of the training needs analysis, the organization ends up not only with programs that address the KSA needs of employees, but also with an increased awareness of what other problems (these are the nontraining needs) have to be solved by other means. Trainers also use organizational information to better design programs so that problems related to applying the training are addressed in the training rather than becoming surprises after training ends.

Despite the seemingly obvious advantages of collaboration between OD and training professionals, a gulf sometimes seems to separate the two. Consider the following examples:[17]

- An executive complains that his training and OD people cannot seem to work together.
- Training staff complain at length about a manager they consider unreasonable and attribute her faults to her background in OD.
- A training staff member objects strongly when told that training needs analysis data could be used to identify performance problem solutions other than training.

Table 2-2 provides some insight as to why conflict such as in the preceding examples exists. OD practitioners are typically strategic, and executives are usually their clients. Trainers are typically tactical, and their clients are lower in the hierarchy (see Figure 2-1 for differences between strategy and tactics). It is the nature of the OD practice to challenge assumptions underlying organizational practices. Trainers typically take organizational procedures and practices as givens, trying to make people more effective within those practices. For example, suppose that the needs analysis data show that the problems in a work unit are a result of its manager acting inconsistently and arbitrarily. OD professionals more than training professionals would be willing to be guided by the data and confront the manager. Training professionals might be willing to say that no employee training needs were identified, but they are less likely to tell the manager that his or her behavior needs to change. OD professionals, however, are much more likely to get tagged with the "analysis paralysis" label than are trainers, who are seen as "doers." Yet as Table 2-2 suggests, each would benefit by working closely with the other because one's apparent weakness is the other's strength.

Why Trainers Need OD Competencies

Trainers can benefit from using OD, if only because its planning procedures help clarify what is needed in a given organizational situation. We believe that training programs will also benefit from the application of many other OD concepts and principles. The emphasis OD places on participative approaches to problem solving suggests that training is better when trainees take an active role in selecting their training opportunities and in the training itself. When trainees are involved in the planning stages, they are less likely to demonstrate resistance. This learner-focused orientation opens communication channels and results in higher levels of motivation during the training program. A participative orientation also ties line managers directly to the training process

Table 2-2
Differences
Between OD
Practitioners and
Trainers

Issue	OD Practitioner	Trainer
Role	Strategic	Tactical
Client	Top management	Middle-to-lower-level management
Response to problems with organizational politics, structure, etc.	Challenge and confront	Work around or within the system
Organizational perception	Overly analytical	Gets things done

by involving them in assessing their employees' needs, developing the training, and developing support systems for applying the training back on the job.

In Chapters 4 and 5, we emphasize an open systems approach. Chapter 4 focuses on understanding training needs in the context of organizational systems. Chapter 5 emphasizes connections between the training program and other organizational systems. These connections help ensure transfer of the training to the job. Many trainers told us of their frustrations when trainees were excited about what they learned, but at the conclusion of training, nothing had changed. The design chapter describes why this can happen and how to avoid this type of training disaster.

Force-field analysis is one among a multitude of OD techniques but can serve as an example of how these techniques can be of substantial benefit to trainers. The underlying concept is that any situation can be explained by the sets of counterbalancing forces that hold it in place.[18] Force refers not only to physical forces but also to psychological forces that influence individual behavior. For example, if you wanted to understand why a work group is not following the new company procedures, you might examine the forces acting within and outside the group that influence the members' behavior. Tradition, reward systems, and group norms are forces that often exert strong pressure on group members, preventing them from trying new ways of doing things. Other forces that can influence group behavior are economic factors; individual KSAs; stereotypes of race, gender, and religion; and group conflict.

To understand a particular situation, first you must identify all the factors that exert influence on that situation. Then you must determine whether each factor is exerting force toward change (drivers) or against change (restraining). All the steps for using the force-field analysis are listed in Figure 2-5. The arrows show forces that are driving and restraining change. In this figure, the restraining forces are more numerous and larger than the driving forces, a combination that would create resistance to change in the people operating within the force field. The line of interaction, where these forces meet, symbolizes the current state: This line reflects the array of forces on either side, which have created the current situation you are trying to change. Thus, for change to occur, actions must be developed to shift the force fields so that the forces for change are larger than the restraining forces.

This model helps trainers understand the actions needed to overcome resistance to change. As we detail in Chapter 3, training is often met with resistance, as it is one of the

Figure 2-5
Force-field Analysis Model

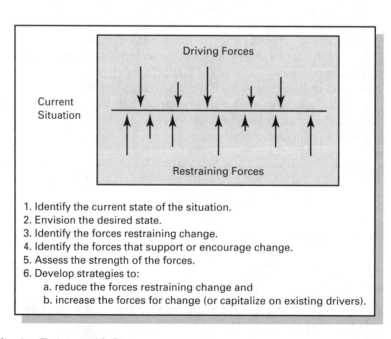

1. Identify the current state of the situation.
2. Envision the desired state.
3. Identify the forces restraining change.
4. Identify the forces that support or encourage change.
5. Assess the strength of the forces.
6. Develop strategies to:
   a. reduce the forces restraining change and
   b. increase the forces for change (or capitalize on existing drivers).

most personal types of change. Research indicates that change occurs more smoothly and quickly if the forces that are restraining change are reduced before or at the same time as driving forces are increased. Simply increasing the driving forces (putting on more pressure) often results in escalated conflict. This conflict then becomes another force for resisting change as individuals become more defensive and positions harden.

Why OD Professionals Need Training Competencies

Although generally successful, OD has experienced some glaring failures, many of which could have been avoided with more attention to training principles.[19] Earlier, we identified the types of training required as a prerequisite or supplement to various OD techniques. OD interventions nearly always involve groups of employees in structured activities such as planning, problem solving, and intergroup conflict management. It is naive to assume that one can bring people together to solve new problems, in new relationships, in new situations, with new processes, and without prior training. These employees need to

- have a common KSA base in these areas,
- understand group dynamics and be skilled at working in groups, and
- understand and be skilled at using a common problem-solving model.

If OD practitioners are not skilled in designing and implementing training programs, they must develop collaborative relationships with trainers who are. Such collaboration provides an excellent opportunity for involving internal training resources in change efforts. It is especially helpful when an OD consultant, familiar with good training practices, is retained from outside the organization. When HRD and OD work together in a collaborative fashion, they will go a long way toward defusing any conflict between external consultants and the HR function.

If OD is to be a long-term effort, the change must be institutionalized into the way the company does business. In one study, only about one-third of the OD efforts examined lasted more than five years.[20] This finding indicates that training is a critical component to institutionalizing the change. Three situations are identified as key times for training:

1. When the OD process is started, training is needed to provide education about the change process and to provide the necessary KSAs.
2. After the process has been in place for a while, some retraining or upgrading of KSAs is required to sustain the process.
3. As new employees enter the organization, they need an understanding of the process and the KSAs.

Although most organizations provide the initial training, few conduct follow-up training or modify their new-employee training to include the new process and the related KSAs.

PUTTING IT ALL TOGETHER

Recall from Figure 2-1 that it is not enough for the organization to develop competitive strategies—these strategies must be followed with action. The strategies are implemented through a tactical action plan consisting of the actions required and the unit(s) responsible for those actions. The process begins with assigning objectives to the different work units of the organization. The units must then develop strategies and implementation tactics to achieve the objectives. Eventually, they are translated into individual employee objectives. The objectives for the HRD unit, as for all functional areas, must be tied directly to organizational strategies. Of course, for HRD, these will be filtered through the strategies the HR unit developed to achieve its objectives.

Developing an HRD Strategy

Without a strategic plan, training is likely to be managed in a haphazard manner, its resources underutilized, and its full strategic value not realized. At the most basic level, the training function must make strategic decisions about where it will focus its resources and energies. It also depends in part on the environment in which training operates, the resources available (financial, material, and personnel), and the core competencies contained within the training function. Analysis of these areas leads to strategic decisions about the technology that should be used to develop necessary employee competencies. The organization and its HR unit form the bulk of HRD's environment. Thus, in developing an HRD strategy, these areas must be analyzed. How to conduct this analysis, and sources from which data can be obtained, are detailed in Chapter 4. For now, we will provide some examples of how HR and HRD strategy might be developed based on the competitive strategy of the organization.

Organizational and HR Strategy

The market leader strategy depends on innovation; therefore, employee knowledge and skills are critically important. Highly skilled and knowledgeable people must be hired and developed. They need to work under a structure that allows them latitude in how they go about their work. Reward and feedback systems must focus on long-term rather than short-term performance. Some amount of failure must be expected as employees try out new ideas. The failure of an experiment can be positive if it brings the organization closer to realizing its objectives through the learning that occurs. If failure is punished, employees will be reluctant to attempt new things. Hewlett-Packard, Raytheon, and PepsiCo illustrate this philosophy by selecting highly trained and skilled employees, being committed to their long-term development, and developing systems that evaluate and reward employees for their contributions to the company's objectives.[21] HRD in the market leader organization must adopt a strategy that builds on the already high level of competency brought into the organization.

Cost leader organizations, in contrast, emphasize tight fiscal and management controls. Because their leadership position is dependent on their ability to produce high volumes at low cost, efficiency and productivity are critical. Strategies for reducing costs include reducing the number of employees, reducing wages and salaries, using part-time and contract labor, and improving work methods. Conforming to standardized procedures is emphasized in these organizations, and training helps ensure conformance. On-the-job training (OJT) techniques are used more frequently for line employees. It is only at the middle-management levels and above that more autonomous decision making occurs and that higher-level competencies are emphasized. In these organizations, training is more likely to be focused on management.

Integrating HRD and OD Activities

Most organizations' competitive strategy calls for some type of performance improvement, both for the organization as a whole and for individuals. Perhaps the most effective way to ensure the seamless implementation of performance improvement plans is to integrate HRD and OD. Trainers and OD professionals have legitimate differences in the nature of the change they are responsible for, but their interests are intimately connected. Each can provide valuable service to the other. Nonetheless, as we noted, they are often at odds with each other. One reason for the division between them is that companies typically organize around their different functional activities, and OD and HRD departments are often separated.[22] This separation increases the differences in perspective, role, value of service, clients, and so on. An obvious solution is to house them together in something like a performance improvement department within HR. This would be an example of a structural change to align the organization's internal structure with its strategic direction.

Of course, this type of organizational change effort will require attention to critical change management issues. For example, such a department would need different measures of success than either currently uses. Success could be measured by contribution to business results, rather than by the number of bodies passing through training courses or the number of teams built and facilitated by OD staff. This overarching goal would require trainers to identify system deficiencies that are likely to interfere with training, and OD staff to identify KSA deficiencies that are likely to interfere with system changes.

Companies such as Andersen Consulting Education, AT&T, and Universal Card Service made these changes and improved their business operations.[23] These companies found that integrating OD and training activities requires sponsorship from the top HR and other executives. One way toward full-scale integration of these activities is to develop pilot collaborations focusing on a particular business problem. This approach allows staff from each discipline to learn more about how the other operates and where the synergy exists. In addition, the HR executive needs to encourage people in both disciplines to learn as much as possible about the other. Another process that should lead to better integration of training and OD activities is having the staff in both areas work together to identify both barriers to collaboration and ways to remove those barriers. This activity not only creates familiarity but also uses the OD principle of involving those affected by the change in the change process. By integrating the two activities, the organization also has the potential benefit of cross-functional training, increasing the KSAs of both groups. At Domtar, Claude Belley is the senior vice president of human resources and organizational development. Do you think he understands the importance of this type of integration? Might this have contributed to Domtar's success?

Some Strategic Training Alternatives

The number of possible strategic choices an HRD unit might make is far too large to cover them all. We will look at one key strategic decision: whether to outsource training, keep it in-house, or some of both. This example will show you how HRD strategy is tied to both the HR and competitive strategies of the business.

Internal Provider Strategy   Large organizations in a stable environment, where training needs do not change rapidly, often choose to do most of the training themselves. The "in-house" strategy directs all, or nearly all, training to be developed and provided by the internal HRD unit. The types of training needs that will be addressed, the development of programs to address those needs, and the evaluation of those programs are typically determined by a centralized HRD function in consultation with the HR executive. Because it is most effective in a stable environment where training needs do not change rapidly, it is most appropriate for cost leader companies. The principal advantages of this strategy are the control over the training content, consistency in delivery across the organization, and reduced training costs. In this strategy, a single program is developed to meet a particular training need across many groups of employees. As a result, the content and delivery can be controlled for consistency across the organization. Because in-house specialists develop the content and design of the program, it is tailored to the company's needs. Because the cost of development can be spread across a large number of employees, the cost per employee is reduced.

This strategy requires a fairly large centralized training staff. Core competencies for HRD departments using this strategy include all those necessary to identify training needs; design, develop, and conduct training programs; evaluate the programs; and manage the training processes and systems. Because of the resource requirements, typically only larger companies adopt it. This is not to say that all large companies adopt this strategy, only that they are more capable of adopting it.

A way to reduce centralization but maintain a low cost is to have training developed by the corporate HRD staff but delivered by other employees or electronically. This system places a higher reliance on train-the-trainer and self-learning methods (e.g., videos and computer-based training). In this approach, after the training programs are developed and handed off to the various business units, the training is completed by the trainee alone or facilitated by a business unit representative (e.g., supervisor or in-house technical expert). Those programs with face-to-face components will need to go through a train-the-trainer course to familiarize themselves with the content and methods.

Suppose Hershey identified "listening skills" as a problem area for the sales force in dealing with customers. In response, HRD developed a listening skills training program and decentralized the training so it was conducted by team managers within the division. This type of training includes many experiential exercises and some behavior modeling. These managers would, therefore, need to demonstrate effective listening skills, be familiar with the exercises and skilled at facilitating them, and be skilled at providing constructive feedback. Because there are differences in managers' training capabilities, different locations would receive different levels of training. For this reason, evaluation would become especially important. Often the strategic KSAs that training is intended to provide are subverted through modifications in the training content and design at the work unit level. One solution to this problem is to provide extensive training and develop reward systems that motivate the work unit trainer to be consistent in presenting the material and applying the methods built into the training. However, this level of monitoring can substantially reduce the cost advantage.

Outsourcing Strategy   This strategy employs outside training vendors for all, or almost all, training activities. The HRD unit's role is to select and manage training suppliers. Suppliers may be training firms, consultants, professional seminars, college/university courses, and the like. A full commitment to this strategy would use outside vendors to conduct all aspects of the training process from the training needs analysis through evaluation.

The outsource strategy is appropriate for larger organizations whose training needs vary dramatically over short periods of time and for small businesses and organizations with a small or nonexistent training function. Large market leader firms, for example, will find many advantages in this strategy. Small businesses adopt outsourcing primarily for budgetary reasons. This strategy provides a flexible way of meeting changing and diverse training needs with professionally developed and administered programs. It also fits well with a decentralized HRD structure. A small central HRD staff is involved in the budgeting process, monitoring of training-related policies, and providing consultation and support to the various units. For example, compilation of lists of approved vendors, payment of vendors, and mandated training are decisions that might be made by the central HRD group. In a decentralized organization, the different operating units of the organization (business units, divisions, geographical units, and the like) are then free to select from the list of approved vendors and programs those best suited to their needs and within their training budget. In a more centralized structure, the HRD unit would select and manage the vendors for each location. Program selection would derive from mutual agreement between the central HRD unit and the operating unit.

The core competencies required of the HRD unit in this strategy include a thorough understanding of the training process, skills in evaluation and selection of appropriate training providers, and general management KSAs. As a large number of firms and

Table 2-3
Questions to
Assess Training
Provider
Capabilities

What is the trainer's background (education, experience, etc.)?

Has the trainer ever provided these particular training programs or services before?

Has the training been evaluated? If so, what levels of outcomes were evaluated, and what have been the results?

Can the trainer give you the names of people in these companies who could speak knowledgeably about the trainer's products and services?

Can the trainer give you names of and permission to contact the following people?
- Trainees who received the training
- The person who was the trainer's primary contact in the client organization
- The person who monitored or coordinated the training

How does the trainer go about developing a program, delivering training, or providing a training service? Can the trainer provide examples or an outline of his approach or process? Will this fit your organization's culture and budget?

If the training is already developed, can the trainer show you materials, such as handouts, exercises, and videos?

If these materials are not specific to your organization, how will the trainer alter them to make them appropriate for your situation?

individuals offer training services, the manager must carefully screen potential providers. Obviously, cost is one factor to consider. Typically, the low-cost providers are those who recently entered the field. However, the fact that a provider is more expensive or experienced does not mean that its quality is higher. Within your budgetary limits, the primary criterion should be the ability to provide the desired KSAs to your employees. Some key questions for making this determination are listed in Table 2-3. Of course, this list is not sufficient to evaluate the provider fully, but it provides a good start for making comparisons. These issues will be discussed more completely in Chapter 8.

Managing the training providers requires typical management competencies. The provider must be given clear direction—that is, the goals and expectations must be clearly spelled out. The various training providers and their programs need to be organized in a logical flow with minimal disruption to the activities of the company. The providers' activities need to be monitored to ensure that they are acting to plan and that goals are met. An open communication system must be established between the training function and the training providers so that both parties can access the needed information.

Even though flexibility is a key advantage, the outsourcing strategy can also reduce costs. It can translate into substantial savings on HRD staff salaries, benefits, and taxes. The cost per training session is usually higher because the cost for training vendors is almost always higher than the comparable cost of internal training staff (even including benefits and taxes). However, the vendor is paid only for the contract period. With this strategy, no layoffs or staff relocations are required when the need for training slacks off. Also, because vendors can spread program development costs across clients, the company typically pays less for program development.

To reduce costs further, a train-the-trainer approach can be used with the outsourcing strategy. In this case, a training vendor (rather than HRD staff) trains one or more employees to use the vendor-developed program. For example, it might be too costly and disruptive for a small business (of, say, 15 employees) to send all its employees to a customer service seminar and workshop. Instead, the company might send the general manager to the workshop and then to a train-the-trainer session conducted by the workshop provider. When the general manager returns to the company, she can train the rest of the employees as time allows and for little additional cost (such as paying a fee for using the materials, etc.). The general manager can also modify the training, customizing it for the specific needs of the organization.

The Mixed Strategy   Most firms use some combination of the two preceding strategies, providing some training internally and contracting some to external providers. Decision making is centralized for some training activities and decentralized for others. Different philosophies suggest where centralization should take place and what training should be developed or conducted internally. One approach is to conduct ongoing training internally and contract to external providers all new training. New training is usually required when some aspect of the environment changes. This strategy allows the firm to be adaptable to changing aspects of the environment while focusing its internal efforts on ongoing training. If uncertainty surrounds the training that is required or how quickly the need will change, this strategy puts the company in a more flexible position to respond. In addition, less of the development costs of new training are borne by the company. A negative aspect, however, is that training developed by outside vendors can be less directly relevant to the employees, and additional resources might have to be allocated to tailor the training to the organization. Also, if the training need becomes ongoing, plans should be developed to provide it internally, an action that will require agreement from the external provider. Another approach is to develop all new training internally and contract out ongoing training.

The mixed strategy reduces the size of the organization's training staff somewhat. Typically, trainers are individual consultants who are willing to work as contract employees for the firm. This strategy ensures the fit between the training and the training needs, but the organization must shoulder all the development costs. These costs may be offset by the reduced staffing needs. A careful break-even analysis would determine whether reduced staffing would adequately compensate for increased development costs. Many companies find they do, as the use of vendors for training has been increasing. For example, General Motors doesn't provide "Mr. Goodwrench" training, an outside vendor does. Firms such as Avaya, Cisco, Nokia, and Hewlett-Packard all have outsourced significant amounts of their training.[24]

The mixed strategy might be appropriate for organizations with training needs that are extremely diverse from one sector of the organization to another. MASCO Corp., a home improvement and building products company, is a good example. MASCO consists of an assortment of divisions producing different products and services. The corporation has adopted elements of both the market leader and cost leader strategies. The training needs of the different divisions are unique for the most part. It would be expensive for MASCO to hire a centralized HRD staff to handle all the training needs for its divisions. It makes more sense for the HRD function to be decentralized to the divisions. On the other hand, when MASCO was in the process of redefining its culture after a period of strong growth, the company instituted an executive development program that was centralized in its corporate headquarters. This centralized program, in which key executives and high-potential managers are given the opportunity to earn an MBA, is provided by an outside vendor (Eastern Michigan University [EMU]). The company's HR executives and training staff worked closely with EMU to ensure that course materials met MASCO's strategic KSA needs while reflecting the breadth and rigor of a traditional MBA program. Materials were customized to reflect problems and issues MASCO faced. It wasn't the only training that the company centralized. As part of its strategy to realize synergies among its divisions, it instituted a training program in logistics in which the content was customized by a different outside vendor (Michigan State University) to meet MASCO's strategic needs. Again, sets of employees from all divisions take part in the program. Thus, MASCO's mixed training strategy takes advantage of centralized programming for some of its strategic training while decentralizing the rest.

We have looked at just one of the myriad HR and HRD strategy implications. The most important point is for you to understand that the organization's competitive strategy and the supporting HR strategies determine HRD's strategic direction.

Table 2-4
Small Business Owners' Reasons for Not Planning Strategically

Not enough time	Too busy with day-to-day operations and concern about tomorrow are the excuses for not planning for next year.
Unfamiliarity	Lack of awareness of strategic planning or failure to see its value. See it as limiting flexibility.
Lack of skills	Do not have the skills or time to learn them. Do not wish to spend money to bring in consultants.
Lack of trust	Want to keep key information confidential. Do not wish to share this information with other employees or outsiders.

FOCUS ON SMALL BUSINESS

Is it necessary for small businesses to get involved in strategic planning to be successful? The answer is yes. Strategic planning is positively related to small business performance.[25] In spite of this benefit, many small business owners and managers do not engage in strategic planning.[26] Some of the reasons are outlined in Table 2-4.[27]

What can be done to encourage small businesses to become more involved in such planning? First, education about the advantages of such efforts would be useful. Even large organizations use the excuse that they are too busy fighting fires to find time for planning. However, if they spent time planning, they might see fewer fires. Bringing small business owners and managers in touch with those who use strategic planning successfully in their small businesses is a good start for this education.

The skills issue can be addressed by using a less formal and rigorous process. Evidence indicates that small businesses that use a more informal strategic planning process can be more effective than those using more formal processes.[28] Additional evidence suggests that, at the very least, a formalized process produces no better results.[29] The emphasis on structured written plans in strategic planning might be dysfunctional for the small business. A less formal way to approach strategic planning for the small business is provided in Table 2-5. By researching and answering these questions, the small business owner will be well on the way to a strategic plan.

What about the issue of lack of trust? Research suggests that when faced with threats, small firms benefit by going outside the organization for help. Unlike large organizations, they are unlikely to have the necessary internal resources to address these threats.[30] Without a source that they trust, they simply will not obtain the necessary information or assistance. Small businesses need to seek out possible resources and establish appropriate relationships in "good times" so that they can be drawn on for help in "bad times."[31] The small business owner can evaluate the relationship during times when threats are not creating a crisis.

Will an increase in strategic planning result in a corresponding increase in the attention that small businesses give to training? We believe that it will focus attention on the "right" training. Training is often ignored as a strategic initiative because owners and managers do not have a clear model for making decisions about whether training activities will lead to a competitive advantage.[32] Involvement in strategic

Table 2-5
Strategy Questions for Small Business

1. Why are we in business?
2. What are the key things we are trying to achieve?
3. Who is our competition, and how can we beat them?
4. What sort of ground rules should we be following to get the job done right?
5. How should we organize ourselves to reach our goals and beat the competition?
6. How much detail do we need to provide so that everyone knows what to do? How do we make sure that everyone gets the information?
7. What are the few key things that will determine whether we make it? How do we address and keep track of them?

TRAINING IN ACTION 2-3
Stories Along the Road to ISO

Rivait Machine Tools, which provides electrical discharge machining of steel, employs 14 people. The president, James Rivait, made an important strategic decision to diversify into the aerospace industry. To even be considered as a supplier in this industry, a company must be ISO 9000 certified. Eighteen months later and $100,000 poorer, Rivait achieved certification.

Early in 1993, Grace Specialty Polymers set out in a new strategic direction that required ISO 9000 certification. The strategic plan set a target of achieving certification for four separate locations by the end of 1994. To accomplish this goal, an executive steering committee was assembled, consisting of the general manager and employees who reported directly to him. The committee was to provide the direction, commitment, and resources needed. Next, an ISO implementation team was set up. Department managers made up most of this cross-functional team. Although successful, the members of the team indicated that it is not an easy process. Their assessment was that a company must be committed to getting it done. You can't have less than a full effort.

Reelcraft Industries embarked on an ISO certification program to improve processes. It took the company two years to achieve certification, and the paperwork it produced was awesome. The main difference is that Reelcraft now "builds quality in rather than inspects errors out." Among the chief benefits are increased knowledge, skills, and communication.

Cavalier Tool & Manufacturing examined the ISO process and determined that it did not make strategic sense for them at that time. Sometimes a customer faces a short-run emergency and needs a "down and dirty mold." "If we were ISO 9000 certified, we would not be allowed to take on that business. All your work must follow the ISO process, and so I would have to turn down this customer. I am not ready to do that," President Rick Jannisse said. Furthermore, he is not disposed toward the discipline required to be ISO certified. Examining the external environment, he realizes that he may be forced to become certified eventually, but not now. At least he is aware of the implications of the decision he is making.

Sources: Benson, R., and R. Sherman. "A practical step-by-step approach." *Quality Progress* (October 1995), pp. 75–78. Bible, R. "Implementing ISO has made us better." *Industrial Distribution* (April 1996), p. 128. Williamson, D. "ISO rating: The sign of the times." *Windsor Star* (July 16, 1997), p. F1.

planning will provide such direction. As we discussed earlier, when the need for training emerges from the strategic planning process, it is clearly tied to the mission and objectives of the small business. For example, in companies that include International Organization for Standardization (ISO) certification in their strategy, training is clearly value added because certification will not be granted without it.

One final point should be made about small businesses. Because they are small, communicating a strategic direction and implementing the plan should be considerably easier than with a large firm. The evidence indicates that in implementing strategic plans, small companies needed to anticipate and prevent fewer problems than larger firms.[33] Some problems still do exist, however. For example, the small business that seeks to become a preferred supplier to a company doing business must receive ISO certification. Metro tool and die, a small manufacturer in Ontario, for example, became ISO certified in 1999, in order to be able to supply parts to the auto industry.[34] Many small companies used the strategic planning process to determine whether becoming certified is worthwhile. The planning process allows them to see how certification fits their overall competitive strategy. Training in Action 2-3 shows how different companies used the strategic planning process to make the decision.

SUMMARY

Training activities need to be aligned with the organization's strategy to be effective. Part of the alignment process is the development of training unit strategies in support of the organizational strategies. So it is important for training professionals to understand the basics of the strategic planning process. Two examples of competitive strategy—market leader and cost leader—were presented to illustrate how differences in strategy influence the internal operations and lead to different training needs. The organization's strategic choice will depend, in part, on key factors in the external environment and on the general level of environmental uncertainty. The organization's core technology influences not only external strategy, but also the alignment of internal operations with those strategies. Organizations must develop internal strategies to align their operations with the external strategies. For example, whether a company adopts a market or a cost leader strategy will have different implications for how HR and HRD go about their business. The HR department needs to be involved in the strategic planning process to provide information about workforce readiness to implement various alternative strategies being considered. HR also provides input in relation to managing change arising from new strategic directions. From this and other information, a sound strategic choice can be made.

The choice of strategic direction will also help determine the way HRD is structured. Cost leader organizations operate in a stable environment, and more training can be centralized. Market leaders, conversely, operate in an uncertain environment, and the HRD department needs to be more decentralized. Competitive strategy will also influence the degree to which HRD will outsource training.

OD focuses on improving the effectiveness of the organization through planned change. Strategic planning and training can benefit from the concepts, principles, and techniques used in OD. While training is focused on improving employee capabilities, OD is focused on managing performance. Improved capabilities do not translate into improved performance unless the performance management system is aligned to support those capabilities. Conversely, no matter how good the performance management system, employees will not perform if they don't have the capabilities. For this reason alone, the HRD and OD units need to work closely together. While there are differences in the focus of these two units that often create friction, their ultimate objectives are the same.

KEY TERMS

- Competitive strategy
- Core technology
- Cost leader
- Decision autonomy
- Division of labor
- Environmental complexity
- Environmental stability
- Environmental uncertainty
- Force-field analysis

- HR strategy
- HRD strategy
- Internal strategy
- Market leader
- Mechanistic design
- Nonroutine technology
- Organic design
- Organizational design
- Organizational development (OD)

- Organizational mission
- Organizational strategy
- Organizational structure
- Proactive strategy
- Reactive strategy
- Routine technology
- Strategic planning

CASE ANALYSIS

CASE: Strategic Planning at Multistate Health Corporation

As you read this case, think about the relationship among competitive strategy and both the HR and HRD functions at Multistate Health Corporation (MHC). The case was written in 1994 and is real, but the corporation asked that its name not be used. The federal and insurance environment for health care has changed substantially since that time; however, the strategic planning issues faced by MHC remain relevant today. The information provided here reflects the organization in 1993 as it was completing its strategic planning process.

(continued)

The Organization

MHC is a health care provider owned and operated by a religious order. MHC owns 30 hospitals and four subsidiary corporations employing more than 10,000 people. Its headquarters are in Michigan, with hospitals located in 17 states across the country. The overall organizational structure and the corporate HR structure are depicted in Exhibits 2-1 and 2-2.

Competitive Strategy

In line with its mission, which is rooted in the tenets of the order's religion, MHC focused on providing care to the indigent and less able members of the community. It was reasonably successful until 1989, when the health care industry began to experience considerable change in governmental regulations and insurance procedures. At the time of their strategic planning, hospitals were reimbursed on the basis of a preset, standardized price for treatment rather than the "cost-plus" method used previously. The federal and state governments were putting increasing pressure on health care

Exhibit 2-1

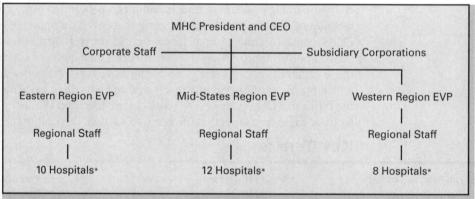

*Each hospital has a CEO reporting to the regional executive vice president (EVP). Hospital are referred to as divisions within MHC and have a CEO as well as a functional staff (including HR) for conducting divisional operations.

Corporate HR is included as part of corporate staff, as desicribed in Exhibit 2-2.

Exhibit 2-2

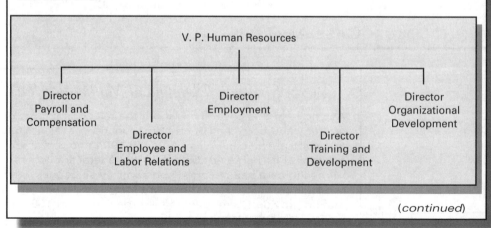

(*continued*)

institutions to reduce costs. In addition, new medical technologies and procedures being developed were expensive to acquire and implement. MHC recently acquired subsidiary corporations to develop or acquire new procedures and technologies. The subsidiaries were to work in partnership with the regions to implement new procedures and technologies.

MHC has lost money every year since 1987. Currently, it is experiencing an oversupply of bed space in most of the communities with MHC hospitals. Projections indicate that the need for inpatient services will decline while the need for outpatient services will increase. Nontraditional health-related services are also projected to increase (e.g., services in which patients and their relatives are trained in self-care or care of relatives). In short, the market is becoming much more competitive while products and services are rapidly changing.

MHC just finished its corporate strategic planning process and planned to develop a two-pronged market strategy to deal with its changing business environment. One major area of focus is technology. The strategic planners departed from the previous strategy, opting to become a leader in the development of new health care technologies and procedures. They felt that the new developments would allow quicker recovery times, thus reducing the hospitals' costs. In addition, the technology could be marketed to other health care providers, generating more revenue. The drawback was that new technologies and procedures were expensive to develop and were often subject to long waiting periods before being approved by the insurers and government agencies.

The second prong of the strategy was directed toward the hospitals and was focused on improving efficiencies in basic health care and outpatient services. This would allow them to continue to provide for the basic health care needs of the less fortunate. The substantial governmental fees, grants, and other revenues tied to this population would provide a profit only if efficiencies could be developed throughout the corporation.

Implementation Issues

Carrie Brown, hired six months earlier as corporate vice president of human resources, listened to several days of strategy discussion, without participating much. She now felt that it was time to address the HR implications of these strategies.

"While I agree that these are good strategies," Carrie said, "I don't know if we have the right people in the right places to carry them out. A few of our regional and divisional executives are already doing some of the things you're talking about, but most of them have grown up in the old system and don't know how to go about cost cutting in a way that doesn't diminish the quality of our service. Many of our divisions are in rural areas and haven't kept up with technology. We do have some middle- to upper-level managers who are up to date in cost cutting and technology implementation, but they are scattered throughout the organization."

Mitchell Fields, president and chief executive officer (CEO), suggested, "Why don't we just move those people who can implement our strategies into positions where they have the power to make it happen?"

"Unfortunately," Carrie said, "we have no accurate data about which of our people have the capabilities. It would be a mistake to move forward unless we're sure that we have the knowledge and skills on board to be successful. What I've discovered in the short time I've been here is that we have

(*continued*)

grown too large for our human resource information system (HRIS). We're still doing most of the data collection on paper, and the forms used are different in each of the divisions, so we can't consolidate information across divisions, and even if we could it would take forever to do it by hand. We have different pay scales in different divisions, and you can't get a VP in Boston to take a CEO position in Iowa because he'd have to take a cut in pay. Basically, what I'm saying is that we don't have a coherent HR system in place to give us the information we need to put the right people in the right places.

"Another issue is that our current structure isn't conducive to setting up partnerships between the subsidiary corporations and the regions. The corporations developing the technology are seen as pretty distant from the regions and divisions. While the subsidiary corporations will bear the developmental or acquisition costs, they are going to want to pass those along to the regions and divisions. The divisions will then have to bear the costs of implementing the new technology and working out the bugs. Once all the kinks are worked out, the subsidiaries will be selling the technology to our competitors at lower prices (due to volume) than they charged the divisions. The corporation and subsidiaries are likely to profit from this arrangement, but the divisions are likely to show losses. As you know, our compensation of division executives is based on profitability. They are likely to resist cooperation with the subsidiaries. Our current systems don't let all of our businesses come out winners."

"I understand what you're saying," Mitchell said. "Our competitive strategy is for the big picture and the long term. If these HR issues are going to be a problem, we have to fix them right away. We are going to have to work out some way for both the subsidiaries and the divisions to come out winners in moving new medical technology forward. Assuming we are able to put our HR house in order . . . get the right systems and people in place. . . . Are there any other concerns about adopting our strategies?" Hearing no additional objections, he said, "Okay, then, let's get to work on putting an implementation plan together, and first on the list is our HR system."

(The MHC case is continued at the conclusion of the chapter. As you read the chapter, we identify concepts and principles that apply to this case.)

HR Follow-Up to Strategic Planning at MHC

MHC determined that it needed to address the HR implications of the new climate in health care and that some type of planning system was in order, so it hired an outside consulting firm. The consultants agreed that some type of system would likely be appropriate, but they were not ready to stipulate what that system would look like. They conducted some initial diagnostic interviews, lasting one to two hours, with all of the divisional CEOs, the regional executive vice presidents (EVPs), the corporate CEO, and the corporate VPs, including the VP of HR and the VP of OD. The interview format is shown in Exhibit 2-3. The following information was obtained from the interviews.

The current HR activities conducted at the corporate level are as follows:

1. To collect and store résumé-type information for all employees. This information includes demographic data, employment history, and performance evaluations.
2. To select divisional CEOs, regional EVPs, corporate officers, and staff professionals, and to assist at the regional and divisional levels in the selection of management-

Exhibit 2-3
Agenda and
Clarification of
Issues for Human
Resource Planning
System

I. What is the purpose of this meeting?
   To enhance and develop the objectives of the human resource planning system (HRPS).
II. What is HRPS?
   HRPS is a business planning system designed to provide quality data to enhance individual and organizational decision making in all aspects of human resource management.
III. Why was I asked to participate in this meeting?
   Because you are a key decision maker, we want to ensure that HRPS fits the needs of your organization.
IV. What specific information should I provide?
   We want your input regarding the following:
   1. Should administrative access to the data in HRPS be local, regional, or only at the corporate level?
   2. Who in your organization would use and benefit most from this system?
   3. What, if any, problems are there with current information used in human resource management decisions (i.e., recruiting, training, appraising, etc.)? For example, do you lack information as to which people are capable successors for certain jobs, and do you know what recruiting sources produce the best employees?
   4. What values of the corporation should be incorporated into HRPS? How might these values be incorporated?
   5. As you see it, ideally, what job responsibilities will change in your organization as a result of HRPS?

level employees, primarily through posting the position and through word-of-mouth about who is competent and available.

3. To sponsor occasional management development programs at the corporate level, although no system is in place to determine whether these are perceived as valuable or necessary. Most management development is done externally with tuition reimbursement, and some is done by individual divisions.

The interviewees expressed varying degrees of dissatisfaction with the following:

1. No system for comparing internal candidates for positions. Performance evaluation is decentralized.
2. No system for making known the criteria for positions. People do not respond to posted openings because rejection is a block to future promotion. Recommendation from a higher-up is known to be necessary. A related complaint was that many CEOs will not recommend their best people either because the CEOs rely on them heavily or because the bright young people might eventually be competition.
3. No system for evaluating the KSA required of a CEO in one part of the corporation compared to that of another. For example, the CEO in Grand Rapids has different responsibilities compared with a CEO in Detroit, but no one at the corporate level knows what the differences are.
4. No corporate HR philosophy or strategy guides the organization in its HR activities.

Individuals at the corporate, regional, and divisional levels reported slightly different perceptions of the priority of needs for an HRPS. See Exhibit 2-4.

Although monitoring equal employment and affirmative action is in the company's mission statement, it was considered important by only one respondent. The various levels disagreed on what job classifications should be in the HRPS: Corporate and regional personnel preferred to include only executive-level personnel, and divisional personnel wanted to include data down to the first-level supervisor. As an interviewee stated, "The MHC value statement says that we respect the dignity of all individuals. To exclude people below the executive level tells them they are worth less." On the issue of control and administration of the HRPS, corporate and regional executives preferred corporate- or regional-level administration, while divisional

Exhibit 2-4
Rank Order of Top
HRPS Objectives by
Organizational Level

ORGANIZATIONAL LEVEL	IMPROVE SELECTION/ SEARCH PROCESS	DEVELOP A SUCCESSION PLAN	FORECAST CRITICAL HR SKILLS	DEVELOP CRITICAL HR SKILLS	CREATE AND UTILIZE CAREER DEVELOPMENT
Corporate	2	4	3	5	1
Regional	1	3	4	5	2
Divisional	1	5	4	3	2

executives had a strong preference for direct access. Some expressed concern that corporate administration would reduce divisional autonomy in human resource decision making. The degree of centralization had been a sore point for several years. The divisions previously operated individually as profit centers, but corporate headquarters was discussing the need for a more integrated approach.

After reviewing the consultants' report and meeting with the consultants, the executive committee (representing the three levels of management) arrived at a consensus on the following HRPS objectives:

1. Improve the selection/search process for filling vacant positions.
2. Develop a succession plan.
3. Forecast critical skill/knowledge and ability needs.
4. Identify critical skill/knowledge and ability deficiencies.
5. Identify equal employment and affirmative action concerns.
6. Create a career development system that reflects the organizational mission.

The following HR philosophy was developed and approved by the MHC board of directors:

As an employer committed to the value of human life and the dignity of each individual, we seek to foster justice, understanding, and a unity of purpose created by people and organizations working together to achieve a common goal. Therefore, we commit ourselves to the following beliefs:

1. People are our most important resource.
2. The human resource needs of the organization are best met through the development of employees to their maximum potential.
3. Justice in the workplace is embodied in honest, fair, and equitable employment and personnel practices with priority given to the correction of past social injustices.

CASE QUESTIONS

1. Describe MHC's strategy in terms of market position. Also, identify the type of external environment MHC is operating in and the degree to which the strategy matches the environment.
2. Identify the type of structure MHC currently uses in its primary businesses. Describe the fit between the structure and the competitive strategy. Describe any structural adjustments MHC should make to maximize the effectiveness of the strategy.
3. Identify any areas where current management KSAs are not aligned with effective implementation of the competitive strategy.
4. Describe how MHC should go about addressing the KSA deficiencies you have identified in the previous question. Your answer should be consistent with the mission and values of MHC.
5. Assume that you are the HRD manager and the competitive strategy was given to you prior to its adoption. Using principles and concepts from the chapter, what recommendations would you give to the strategic planning team?

6. Given the strategy, what tactical activities can the HR unit in general, and HRD specifically, develop to support the strategy (be sure to include the implementation of the HRIS)? Identify sources of support and sources of resistance to these tactical activities and point out any areas in which collaborating with the OD unit would be advisable.

EXERCISES

1. Conduct an analysis of HRD's environment at the company you work for (if you're going to school and don't work, use the school's environment). What are the opportunities and threats to HRD in that environment? What demands does the environment make on the HRD department?

2. Form groups of three to five people, one of them having been provided with training by their employer within the last two years. Have this person explain the company's mission to the rest of the group. Then have the person describe the type of training that was received. The group's task is to determine the linkage between the training and the mission.

3. Identify two organizations with different environments and core technologies. Describe these differences. Indicate how the HRD strategies of these companies might be similar or different. Provide a rationale for your conclusions using relevant concepts from the chapter.

4. Examine the mission at the institution you are attending. Examine the one for your area of study (if it has one). Do the two relate? On the basis of the mission and objectives, do a SWOT analysis through interviews with administration or using your own expertise. What major changes are indicated? How will they affect the way courses will be taught? What training might be necessary to meet these changes?

5. Identify (through personal knowledge or research) an organization that uses HRD as a part of its competitive strategy. What role does HRD play in that strategy, and how is HRD involved in implementing the strategy?

QUESTIONS FOR REVIEW

1. What factors might inhibit HRD managers from developing a strategic planning approach to training? How might these factors be overcome?

2. Think of possible strategic training alternatives other than those described in the text. Under what conditions would these be important in developing a training strategy?

3. Why do training professionals need OD competencies, and why do OD professionals need trainer competencies?

4. What is the relationship between competitive strategy, external environment, and internal strategies?

Chapter 3

Learning, Motivation, and Performance

Learning Objectives

After reading this chapter, you should be able to:

➤ Explain the value and importance of understanding theory.

➤ Identify the major factors that determine human performance and their relevance to training.

➤ Describe how motivation and self efficacy relate to the effectiveness of training.

➤ Describe the cognitive and behavioral approaches to learning and their contradictory implications for instructional practices.

➤ Describe how social learning theory integrates cognitive and behaviorist perspectives.

➤ Describe how the processes and components of social learning theory relate to training.

➤ Describe the causes of resistance to learning.

➤ Explain the effect of group dynamics on learning and the transfer of training.

➤ Explain why different people need different training methods to learn the same things.

➤ Identify the characteristics of training design that motivate learning and accommodate trainee differences.

CASE: The Wilderness Training Lab

Claudia, a successful 33-year-old corporate marketing executive, found herself in the mountains preparing to climb a rope ladder attached to a tree. When she reached the top of the ladder, she would fall off backward. It wouldn't be an accident. No, she wasn't suicidal or deranged.

(continued)

She was participating in an executive development program called Wilderness Training Lab.

Back at the corporate office she was known as an independent, smart, and tenacious businesswoman. She quickly moved up the corporate ladder from product research assistant to brand manager. Claudia had a reputation for micromanaging her subordinates and for being a loner. When asked about these issues, Claudia replied, "When I was in college, I had a lot of group projects. At first I went along with group decisions and trusted others to do a good job. Even though I felt anxious about putting my grade in the hands of someone else, it seemed to be a good way to get along in the group. Those projects received mediocre grades, and I'm only satisfied with being the best. Then I started to take over the leadership of every group I was in. I developed the plan, decided who would do what, determined the timelines, and always took on the most difficult and complex parts myself, all the time making sure the others were doing what they were assigned. From then on my group projects always got an 'A.' I carried those lessons with me into the workplace and I've had good success here, too. Maybe it rubs some people the wrong way, but it works for me. The only trouble I'm having is keeping up with all my projects. Some of the other brand managers want to work with me on joint projects, but I do not have time. Besides, they probably just want me to do their work for them or steal my ideas. The VP of marketing will be retiring soon and only one of the seven brand managers will get that job. What's in it for me if I collaborate with them? Let each of us sink or swim on our own merits."

A few months ago, the VP of marketing, Sandy Cines, discussed career plans with Claudia. Sandy had always praised and encouraged Claudia's work, but this time he was a little reserved. He suggested, in rather strong terms, that she attend a wilderness executive development program. Claudia hesitated because of her workload and upcoming deadlines. Sandy said, "Well, I'll leave the decision up to you. The director of training and I have looked at your strengths and what you'll need for the next level as an executive. Technically you're very strong, but more important at the next level is building good interpersonal relationships. The training director recommended this program for you, but, as I said, I'll leave the decision up to you." Claudia wondered what he thought was wrong with her interpersonal relationships. She had great relationships with customers and outside vendors, and in her personal life. Relationships with her subordinates and peers needed to be different. She needed to be firmer and less flexible with them, did she not? She did not think she had bad relationships with her subordinates or peers. They never complained to her. However, Claudia decided it was pretty clear that Sandy wanted her to attend the wilderness program.

She found a diverse group of men and women executives from all over North America when she arrived for the training. Many confided that their organizations had sent them to "learn how to be more effective in groups." Most of them indicated they were interested and eager but a little nervous about what was expected of them. They soon found out. They were divided into groups of 10 and taken out on the "course."

The first training exercise was climbing the "trust ladder." Doug, the program director, explained that the group members would have to rely on each other quite a bit during the coming week. To demonstrate that the group could be trusted, each person was to climb to the top of the

(continued)

ladder and fall backward into the group, which would catch the person in the proper manner. Doug showed them how. After everyone had completed the exercise, they discussed risk taking, building and trusting one's support systems, being part of a support system, and communicating one's needs. Then came more challenging exercises, such as building and using rope bridges to cross a stream, white-water rafting, and—the most physically challenging of all—scaling a four-meter wall. The front of the wall was sheer and smooth. A platform was on the other side, on which two people could stand at about waist level with the top of the wall and from which extended a ladder to the ground.

Everyone had to scale the wall, and no one could stand on the platform until he or she had scaled the wall. It was a timed event, and the groups were in competition with one another. The first thing a group had to do was develop a plan. Strong and tall people were needed to boost the others to a point where they could pull themselves over. Some stood on the platform and helped those who were not strong enough to pull themselves over. It was clear that the first people over also had to be strong. Another problem was the last person over. Everyone, except the last pair, would have "spotters" in case of a fall. Also, the last person could not be boosted to the top. Someone would have to act as a human rope, hanging down from the top so that the last person could climb up the person and over the wall. Therefore, the last person would have to be strong enough to boost the second-to-last person up, but light enough to climb over the human rope. To determine the order, the group members needed to share with one another their strengths and weaknesses. Claudia wanted to be the last person so that she could make sure everyone was doing what they were supposed to, and also because, as the last person over the wall, she would represent the group's successful completion of this exercise. Two of the strongest men in the group confessed to having injuries that would hamper their performance. Claudia realized that her tennis elbow would be a great liability. When it came to her turn to discuss her strengths and weaknesses, she was honest about her injury and indicated that she would fit best somewhere in the middle where many people could help her.

When Claudia's turn to climb came, she called out to those on top what to expect—where she couldn't put much strain and how she would indicate that someone was pulling too hard. Then she was being pushed up with spotters all around her, and the next thing she knew she was over the wall.

Later, when the members discussed the event, Claudia asked what impact her limitations had caused in the group. Those who had been pullers replied, "None." They said they knew what to do because she had told them about her problem ahead of time.

While packing to go home, Claudia thought about how much she had learned about herself and her relationship to other people, especially at work. She recognized that she generally failed to trust others to do their part and so she was not as effective as she would like to be. Her success came at a high price because of the extra workload she imposed on herself. In addition, she wondered, "What is the price my subordinates pay? How have my actions affected their attitudes and performance? Do I need to be so competitive with my peers? Is that really in the company's best interest? Is it in my best interest?" She knew she would have a lot to think about on the trip home.

A Few Words About Theory

Theories are speculative road maps for how things work. In fact, most of us develop our own theories to explain how the world around us works. The child yells, "I want an ice cream cone." He is told, "No, not until you ask properly." After several such incidents, the child begins to see that when he says "please," he is more successful than when he says "gimme" or "I want." The child develops a theory of how to get things he wants; he must always say "please." "Good" theories assemble a number of facts, show the relationship among those facts, and develop a logical rationale for what is likely to be true, given those facts. From theory, predictions or hypotheses can be generated and tested. If the tests show that the predictions are correct, the theory is supported. If the new facts are inconsistent with the predictions, the theory is revised or discarded. Suppose the child in the previous situation takes his theory to the extreme. When he says "please" but is denied his request, he continues to badger the person, saying "pleeeease, pleeeease." If he soon finds that this approach does not work, he might revise the theory. The new theory says: "Please" works more often than not, but if you have to say it over and over, it does not work. In fact, it makes the person annoyed. This process of developing, testing, and reformulating a theory is the basis of science. It is how new knowledge is created. A good theory is also practical because it

- explains facts as simply as possible,
- predicts future events, and
- provides information on what can be done to prevent undesirable things from happening.

A **theory** is an abstraction that allows us to make sense out of a large number of facts related to an issue. Effective training practices are developed from theories and theoretical constructs that describe how learning occurs and what motivates people. This chapter is about theory, so it is necessarily somewhat abstract. Unfortunately, some people may see little value in wading through the complex logic and rationale of theories. It is easier to follow a set of instructions like a recipe. But, in training, as in business, a single recipe will not work. Recipes require standardized ingredients—businesses do not have standardized ingredients. Each organization is unique, with different missions, strategies, environments, technologies, and people. The interaction of these elements creates a different "chemistry" in each organization, thus making a "one best way for everyone" approach ineffective. Theories provide the guidelines, principles, and predictions that allow organizations to create the right recipe for their situation. Successful people in business pay attention to theory.

Firms in all industries from manufacturing to telecommunications, from energy production to health care (e.g., Ford, 3M, Microsoft, Motorola, Toshiba, Toyota, and Xerox), jumped ahead of the competition because they understood and applied theories. Some of these theories concern the product; others concern how the product is made, and still others how the firm is managed. Rather than copying others, these companies understood the underlying theories related to what they were trying to do and applied those theories to meeting their goals. As the quality guru W. E. Deming indicated, experience teaches nothing without theory.[1] He warned that unless you understand the theory behind someone's success, copying can lead to chaos.[2] A survey of *Fortune* 1000 companies engaged in programs to improve quality (e.g., total quality management, ISO 9000) and involve employees in decision making supports this view. The companies that applied the underlying models and theories correctly were getting the best results; those that simply put programs into place were getting the worst results.[3]

Consider pay systems. Suppose a company pays its employees on the basis of how much they produce (i.e., a piece-rate system). The company is successful and the employees make a high wage. You decide to institute the piece-rate system in your company. Will it work? It might, but it might not. Its success will depend on the total reward system, what the company is trying to accomplish, and what the employees value. For example, employees might turn out a high volume of the product but at the cost of many problems with quality. They might produce more than can be sold. Piece-rate systems can create a "norm" in the work group that prohibits them from producing more than a specified amount (to avoid increases in the product/money ratio or to protect slower workers). In other words, the differences in the people and work environments affect the success of the piece-rate system.

As a manager, your understanding of motivational theory allows you to improve employee performance levels by applying the principles of motivation to your firm's unique circumstances. The same is true with training. Whether one company's training program will work in another's will depend on the needs of each company, its employees, and the training system used. Copying without understanding is like taking someone else's prescription drugs. Even though they might have made someone else better, they could kill you.

What theories are important to the success of the training enterprise? If trainees do not learn, then training has failed, so theories of learning are certainly important. If trainees learn but do not try to transfer the learning to the job, then training has failed. Add theories of motivation to the list. If the trainees learn and try to transfer the learning to the job site, but obstacles in their work environment prevent them from making the transfer, then again training has failed. It failed because the changes in the work environment that needed to support the desired behavior were not considered. Thus, to design and implement effective training programs, you need to understand how people learn, what motivates learning and performance, and how the learning and work environment affect motivation and performance. This chapter focuses on these topics. The theories, models, and concepts discussed here serve as a foundation for the rest of the book. We will refer to these theories and their implications for training throughout the text because they are related to each phase of the training process.

UNDERSTANDING MOTIVATION AND PERFORMANCE

Your job performance and your behavior in general are a function of what you know, what you are able to do, and what you believe (knowledge, skills, and attitudes [KSAs]). If you do not have the requisite KSAs, you cannot perform. However, additional factors are important in determining your performance. Figure 3-1 depicts a general **performance model.** This model indicates that a person's performance (P) depends on the interaction of motivation (M), KSAs, and environment (E). Motivation arises from your needs and beliefs about how best to satisfy those needs. Both motivation and KSAs are part of your memory and thinking systems (i.e., **cognitive structure**). **Environment** refers to the physical surroundings in which performance must occur, including barriers

Figure 3-1
Factors Determining
Human Performance

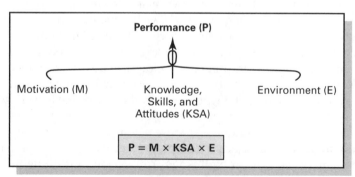

Performance (P)

Motivation (M)   Knowledge,   Environment (E)
                   Skills, and
                   Attitudes (KSA)

$$P = M \times KSA \times E$$

and aids to performance. Environment also includes the objects and events (cues) that you might see as indicating that your performance will be rewarded or punished.

Think back to the wilderness training case. Which of Claudia's KSAs allowed her to reach her current position? Recall that her boss felt that she lacked the interpersonal skills necessary for developing good relationships. Did she lack these skills or was she not motivated to use them? Apparently, she had the skills, because she was able to develop good relationships with others with whom she was not working directly. The training director probably understood this, because he suggested the wilderness training rather than an interpersonal skill-building workshop. The wilderness training did not teach people how to develop good interpersonal relationships as much as it broke down barriers that prevented those relationships from developing. The program worked on the motivation and attitudes of the trainees. What barriers in Claudia's work environment might keep her from developing these relationships? How about the upcoming retirement of the VP and that open position? What criteria could be used to evaluate managers that would encourage them to develop positive relationships with peers and subordinates?

Each of the factors M, KSA, and E in Figure 3-1 can influence performance, but the combination of these factors determines the person's performance. The weakest factor, then, limits the likelihood of engaging in any activity. For instance, no matter how knowledgeable or skilled you are, if you are not motivated to perform the activity—or worse, are motivated to not perform it—then you will not. If the environment does not support the activity or blocks it, then it does not matter how motivated or knowledgeable you are, you will not do it. For example, if necessary tools are not working or equipment is missing, you won't attempt the activity. Likewise, if the environment is sending signals that your performance will be punished, you won't perform. In Claudia's case, she seemed to want to stay at work and not attend the training. However, her boss gave strong indications that staying would be viewed negatively. Her environment changed, signaling that old ways of performing would not be rewarded and new ways would.

The model in Figure 3-1 is important for determining employee training needs. It helps us understand whether poor job performance is a result of KSAs or other factors. It is also important in the design of training. When putting together the learning modules and training methods, the trainer must consider how they will affect the trainees' motivation to learn. Similarly, when selecting the training facility and materials, we must consider how they will interact with trainee motivation. When we ask trainees to use their new knowledge and skills back on the job, we must make sure that the environment is supportive of this new way of performing. A deeper understanding of the three determinants of performance will increase your ability to design and implement effective training programs. First, we look at motivation, presenting the most prominent theories and clarifying their relationship to the training enterprise.

Motivation: Why Do They Act Like That?

Motivation is part of a person's cognitive structure and is not directly observable. Thus, it is typically defined in terms of its effects on behavior, which are observable. Most of the scientific literature defines **motivation** as the direction, persistence, and amount of effort expended by an individual to achieve a specified outcome. In other words, the following factors reflect a person's motivation:

- What need(s) the person is trying to satisfy
- What types of activities the person engages in to satisfy the need
- How long the person engages in the activity
- How hard the person works at the activity.

Go back to Claudia's situation. What need is she trying to satisfy: the growth need or the need to achieve and get ahead in the company? To answer this, look at the types of activities she is involved in. She takes on extra projects, volunteers to work on task forces, works late, and so forth. How long has she been doing it? For about two years. How hard does she work at it? Well, it seems pretty hard: She works 12-hour days and often goes in on Saturday.

Motivation is goal-directed and derived from both personal needs and the decision processes used to satisfy those needs. Separate theories evolved to explain the relationship between needs and motivation, and between decision processes and motivation. Needs theories attempt to describe the types of needs people have, their relative importance, and how they are related to one another. Process theories attempt to describe and explain how a person's needs are translated into actions to satisfy the needs.

Needs Theory

Our needs are the basis of our motivation and the reason for almost all of our activity. Understanding a person's needs helps you understand his behavior. From Maslow's early work,[4] Clayton Alderfrer developed a **needs theory** of motivation called **ERG theory**.[5] The initials ERG represent the three basic needs of the theory: existence, relatedness, and growth. **Existence needs** correspond to Maslow's lower-order physiological and security needs. They are the immediate needs required to sustain life—needs for food, shelter, and the like—and the need for some security in the future for a safe and healthy life. **Relatedness needs** reflect people's need to be valued and accepted by others. Interpersonal relationships and group membership (work, family, friends, etc.) act to satisfy these needs. **Growth needs** include feelings of self-worth and competency and achieving our potential. Recognition, accomplishment, challenging opportunities, and a feeling of fulfillment are outcomes that can satisfy these needs. Even though some disagreement exists in the scientific community about the relationships among these needs and their relative importance at any given point in life, few dispute the idea that these needs exist for everyone.

People work to satisfy their needs. Understanding the types and strengths of employee needs is important to the training process. It can help identify some of the causes of poor performance and therefore determine training needs. Consider the employee who has strong relatedness needs but whose job is structured so that he must work alone most of the time. He might be unable to complete the required quality and quantity of work because he spends too much time socializing with others in the workplace. Additional technical KSAs will do little to improve his job performance. Performance improvement would more likely result from some other type of training (perhaps time management) or some nontraining intervention (such as job redesign or counseling).

Understanding needs is also important in designing training programs and facilities. Trainers need to make sure that the environment and training methods—that is, how the training is conducted and where it takes place—meet the trainee's physical, relationship, and growth needs. We discuss these issues in depth in the chapters covering training design, development, and implementation. Think back to the wilderness training case to get a sense of how training methods, materials, and environment influence trainee motivation.

Although she was motivated to attend the training because of her boss's pressure, was Claudia motivated to learn when she first arrived, or was she skeptical about the value of the training? What if she had attended a series of lectures on the importance of developing strong interpersonal relationships instead of the outdoor group experiences? Would she have been as motivated to absorb the lessons and apply them to her work? How strong do you think Claudia's relatedness needs were? How effective would the training be if it focused on showing her how changing her behavior would result in increased acceptance by her peers? It seems apparent that Claudia did have high growth needs. The outdoor training presented her with a series of physical and psychological challenges, fitting in with her growth needs and motivating her to become an involved participant in the training.

The few empirical studies conducted on this topic tend to support Alderfer's notion that people can experience needs in all three areas simultaneously.[6] The relative satisfaction level in each area determines the importance of the needs. Unsatisfied needs motivate us, and motivation decreases as needs in an area are satisfied. However, needs in these three basic areas tend to renew themselves; they can also expand. Although you might have a good job that provides you with food, shelter, and security, you might start to feel the need for better food, a larger and more comfortable home, a larger savings account, or an investment portfolio. Similarly, even though your relationships with family, friends, and coworkers may at first satisfy your relatedness needs, you might begin to feel that you would like the relationships to be better or closer, or that you want to develop additional relationships.

Sometimes our needs conflict with one another, or one type of need might become more important than the others. Then we feel we must choose one over the other, which is what happened with Claudia. We cannot be sure how strong her relatedness needs are, but we do know that she saw them as conflicting with her ability to satisfy her growth needs at work. The wilderness training was designed to satisfy the trainees' needs for growth and relationships at the same time. Step by step, the training demonstrated how building strong interpersonal relationships could not only satisfy relationship needs, but also make greater accomplishments possible.

This example illustrates a central point about motivating trainees to learn. The best training incorporates opportunities to satisfy all three categories of needs. The training facility and accommodations address, in part, existence needs. How much trainees learn is affected by the trainees' physical comfort, level of hunger, and so on. Demonstrating how the training will improve the trainee's competencies and, in turn, increase job security and fulfill existence needs will also motivate the trainee. Building a network of positive relationships among trainees and between trainees and the trainer will address relatedness needs. Using methods that provide challenging experiences that lead to the attainment of the target KSAs will address growth needs. By having training address all three types of needs in some way, you can be assured that all trainees will find at least one need that can be satisfied. This will go a long way toward motivating all trainees, because you offer something for everyone.

Needs theory leads to implications for the training process even after completion of the training. Trainers must make sure that trainees can see how learning fulfills their needs. In Claudia's case, her boss provided some of that linkage when he told her how important relationship building is to her current and future job success (i.e., security needs). What could the trainers at the Wilderness Training Lab do to create these links? We discuss this issue more in the next section, because these links are the focus of the process theories.

Process Theories

Needs are only one part of the motivation equation. Deciding how to go about satisfying those needs is the other part. **Process theories** of motivation describe how a person's needs translate into action. Although many types of process theories exist, we will focus on the three with the most direct implications for training: classical conditioning, reinforcement theory, and expectancy theory.

Classical Conditioning   Classical conditioning is the association of a generalized response to some signal in the environment. It typically involves learning to emit a nonvoluntary response to some signal that in the past did not produce that response. For example, when an optometrist examines your eyes, she may put you in front of a machine that blows a puff of air into your eyes. This puff of air causes you to blink

Table 3-1
Classical
Conditioning
Process

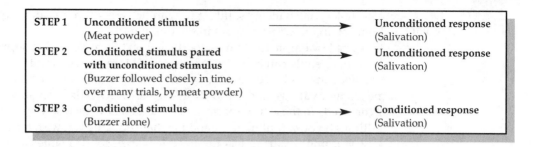

STEP 1	Unconditioned stimulus (Meat powder)	⟶	Unconditioned response (Salivation)
STEP 2	Conditioned stimulus paired with unconditioned stimulus (Buzzer followed closely in time, over many trials, by meat powder)	⟶	Unconditioned response (Salivation)
STEP 3	Conditioned stimulus (Buzzer alone)	⟶	Conditioned response (Salivation)

your eyes. If a red light came on just before the puff of air, you would probably learn to associate the puff of air with the red light and begin blinking whenever the red light comes on. At that point, you would have learned to blink (generalized response) in response to the red light (signal).

The most widely known example of this type of learning involves Pavlov's dogs.[7] Pavlov was not studying learning; he was examining the physiology of digestion by measuring the amount of salivation produced by various substances placed on the tongues of dogs. As the story goes, Pavlov observed that the dogs began to salivate on his entering the laboratory, thus playing havoc with his desire to determine the amount of saliva produced by various substances. He speculated that over time his entrance was followed so often by substances placed on the dogs' tongues that the dogs learned to salivate on his entrance.

Table 3-1 shows how the classical conditioning process works. Step 1 reflects the state of affairs before conditioning takes place. Certain factors in the environment (unconditioned stimuli) produce automatic responses (unconditioned responses) in animals and people. If we place an unconditioned stimulus such as meat powder on a dog's tongue, an unconditioned response would be the dog's salivation. That is, the dog need not be trained (conditioned) to salivate when meat powder is put on its tongue. However, this salivation response does not occur with every stimulus that might be in the dog's environment, such as a buzzer. If, however, you sounded that buzzer just before putting meat powder on the dog's tongue, over a number of trials the buzzer would become a conditioned stimulus. The dog is learning (being conditioned) to associate the buzzer with the meat powder. However, you are still putting meat powder on the dog's tongue, so the salivation is really a response to the meat powder and remains an unconditioned response. This situation is reflected in step 2 of Table 3-1. In step 3, you stop putting meat powder on the dog's tongue after sounding the buzzer. If the dog salivates at the buzzer, you have created a conditioned response (salivation) to a conditioned stimulus (the buzzer). Continually sounding the buzzer without offering the meat powder will extinguish (remove) this response. Over time, the conditioned response gradually disappears. Through conditioning, a response to one stimulus can be transferred to another, unrelated stimulus.

Classical conditioning occurs frequently in the workplace, though it typically receives little attention. The noon whistle blows at the factory, and the worker's digestive juices begin to flow. Sparks fly from the welding machine and your eyes blink, even though you are wearing goggles. As you will see later, this type of learning can affect the learning environment.

Reinforcement Theory   Reinforcement theory is relatively simple on the surface but can be difficult to apply. It does not provide all the answers for how needs are translated into action, but its major points are essential for understanding human behavior. The foundation for reinforcement theory comes from the work of E. L. Thorndike.[8] Thorndike's law of effect states that behavior followed by satisfying experiences tends to be repeated, and behavior followed by annoyance or dissatisfaction

Figure 3-2
Behaviorist Model
of Learning

Stimulus ⟶ Response ⟶ Consequence

tends to be avoided. B. F. Skinner used this principle in developing the operant conditioning model and reinforcement theory.[9]

The basic components of learning in **operant conditioning** are illustrated in Figure 3-2. A person is faced with an object or event in the environment (stimulus) and behaves in a certain way (response). That behavior results in an outcome (consequence) to the individual that is positive or negative. In the illustration, the man has seen a book of great interest (environmental stimulus) while on the way to work. He purchases the book and reads it (response) while continuing to walk to work. You can imagine the consequence. The environment provides stimuli that elicit behaviors and consequences that reinforce or punish them.

In similar situations, the consequences of past behavior affect future behavior. How will the man in Figure 3-2 respond to books while walking in the near future? Operant learning theory says that due to the negative consequence of falling into the hole, the man will learn to avoid reading and walking at the same time. A person's motivation (i.e., direction, magnitude, and persistence of behavior), then, is a function of her reinforcement history. Unfortunately, reinforcement theory provides no explanation of the processes involved in storing, retrieving, or using the lessons of past reinforcement. The model leaves us wondering how future behavior becomes influenced by previous reinforcement history. Nevertheless, the theory does convincingly predict the various effects on future behavior caused by the consequences of past behavior.

Skinner identified four types of consequences that can result from behavior:

1. Positive reinforcement
2. Negative reinforcement
3. Punishment
4. Extinction

When behavior results in either positive or negative reinforcement, the likelihood that the behavior will occur in similar future circumstances is increased. **Positive reinforcement** occurs when your behavior results in something desirable happening to you—either tangible (such as receiving money), psychological (such as feeling pleasure), or some combination of the two. **Negative reinforcement** occurs when your behavior results in removing something you find annoying, frustrating, or unpleasant. This "good" outcome increases your likelihood of repeating the behavior. For example, if you have a headache, take an aspirin, and the headache goes away, the "aspirin-taking response" is negatively reinforced. Nothing is inherently desirable about taking the aspirin; its reinforcing power comes from its ability to remove the pain. Either the environment or the person can provide reinforcement. For example, when a person receives his pay, the environment provides positive reinforcement (pay). When a person feels a sense of pride and accomplishment after completing a task, the person is positively reinforcing himself.

Your behavior is punished when it results in something undesirable happening to you. **Punishment** decreases the likelihood of the response occurring in the future. Like reinforcement, punishment can be tangible, psychological, or both and can come from the environment or be self-administered. In Figure 3-2, the environment provides the punishment. However, when we do things that violate our personal values and beliefs, and therefore experience negative feelings, we are self-punishing that behavior. Punishment exists when you receive something unpleasant or when you lose something desirable. The latter form of punishment is called **extinction.** For example, you might buy books by a certain author because of the positive feelings you experience as you read them. However, while reading the last two books by this author, you did not experience those positive feelings. Therefore you stop buying this author's books. When a person's behavior (like buying and reading the books) no longer produces the desired outcomes, the behavior is less likely to occur in the future. Figure 3-3 depicts the various types of behavioral consequences.

A few examples here should clear up any misunderstandings or confusion created by these definitions. First, think back to the Wilderness Training Lab case. What kind of reinforcement history did Claudia experience from working in groups? Her first group experiences in college resulted in the negative outcomes (for her) of mediocre grades. Because her cooperative behavior in groups was punished, she stopped it. When she changed her behavior to become more directive—monitoring and doing more of the important work—two consequences resulted: (1) she was positively reinforced by good grades and (2) she avoided the negative feelings of anxiety about the other group members not doing their assignments well and the resulting mediocre grades. Her new group behavior was both positively and negatively reinforced over a number of years. It is no wonder, then, that she continued to work this way in groups. Is it possible that Claudia avoided working in groups with her peers because she couldn't control those groups in the same way she could her subordinates? The training she received provided her with new group situations in which she was positively reinforced (e.g., recognition, accomplishment) for using a new set of group behaviors. This new set of outcomes seems to have changed her beliefs and attitudes about how to work effectively in groups.

Figure 3-3
Types of Consequences That May Follow Behavior

	Desirable Consequences	Undesirable Consequences
Trainee Receives	Behavior Positively Reinforced	Behavior Punished
Trainee Loses	Behavior Punished (Extinction)	Behavior Negatively Reinforced

In another example, after working for a few hours, Jon, a machinist, suddenly hears a loud unpleasant screeching noise coming from the exhaust fans near his work area. He finds the electrical switch and turns the fans off; he later switches them on again, and they work for the rest of the day. The same thing happens over the next two days. On the fourth day, when he takes his break, he turns the fans off before the noise begins. When he returns from his break, he turns them on, and they operate normally for the rest of the day. This behavior becomes a daily habit with Jon. Jon does not know that plant maintenance repaired the fan the evening before he began his "turning it off at the break" behavior. Jon maintained his behavior because it was negatively reinforcing. By "giving the fans a rest," he avoided the loud, unpleasant noise. As this worked every time, it was self-reinforcing. This is how superstitious behaviors develop.

Reinforcement versus Punishment   Punishment can eliminate undesirable behavior in the workplace. However, several problems make it undesirable as a management or training tool.

- It does not motivate people to do things, only not to do things. It does not indicate what the desired behavior is, only what is not desired.
- If the undesired behavior is punished only sometimes, people will learn the situations in which they can get away with it. The saying "While the cat's away, the mice will play" neatly captures one problem with this technique; punishment requires constant vigilance on the part of a supervisor and encourages employee efforts to "beat the system."
- If a person's undesired behavior is rewarding, the punishment must be severe enough to offset the behavior's reinforcing properties. Escalating negative outcomes to employees can raise ethical, moral, and commonsense objections.
- Someone must do the punishing. This person becomes someone to be avoided. Supervisors avoided by subordinates experience leadership problems.

Positive and negative reinforcement are better tools for motivating and especially for training employees. Negative reinforcement can cause the desired behavior to become self-reinforcing, like Jon's turning off the fans. When the person continually performs the desired behavior (avoiding the undesired behavior), negative outcomes are avoided. If the desired behavior is then also positively reinforced, the person not only avoids the negative outcome but also receives a positive outcome. As with Claudia in the opening case, the result is a strong maintenance of the behavior.

With reinforcement, the person doing the reinforcing does not always need to be present for the desired behavior to occur. The employee actively seeks to make the reinforcing agent (e.g., supervisor or trainer) aware of her behavior. When punishment is used as the motivational or learning mechanism, the employee attempts to hide behavior so as to avoid the consequences. Obviously, a trainer or supervisor's job is much easier when employees are attempting to communicate what they are doing rather than hiding it.

Thus, either positive or negative reinforcement is preferred over punishment as a strategy for motivating learning and behavior change. Used in combination, positive and negative reinforcement appear more effective than either used alone.[10] For those interested in finding out more about how to implement positive, humanistic, and effective work environments, we would encourage you to read Dick Grote's *Discipline Without Punishment.*[11]

Reinforcement theory suggests that any training must be concerned not only with teaching the KSAs but also with the consequences that are attached to the following:

- the learning process,
- the old way of doing the job, and
- the new way of doing the job.

These factors play a key role in determining how much is learned and how much is actually used back on the job.

As noted earlier, many unanswered questions arise when using reinforcement theory to describe the motivational process. Expectancy theory, however, provides some additional explanation and leads to many more implications for training.

Expectancy Theory   In 1964, Victor Vroom published a theory of work motivation called expectancy theory.[12] This theory describes the cognitive processes involved in deciding the best course of action for achieving our goals (i.e., satisfying our needs). A **cognitive process** is a mental activity such as information storage, retrieval, or use. Thinking and decision making are cognitive processes. In its most basic form, expectancy theory proposes that a person's motivation can be explained by the relationship among three conceptually distinct elements:

1. The level of success expected by the individual (e.g., how well she will be able to do what she sets out to do), which is termed Expectancy 1.
2. The individual's beliefs about what the outcomes will be if she is successful. The expected outcomes and their likelihood of occurrence make up Expectancy 2.
3. The individual's feelings about the various outcomes' positive or negative value. An outcome's subjective value is referred to as its **valence.**

In combination, these elements determine the individual's motivation (i.e., effort) to engage in a particular course of action. When situations allow different courses of action, as most do, the one with the highest motivation level is chosen. The motivation level for a particular course of action can be calculated mathematically with the following formula:

$$Effort = Expectancy\ 1_i \times \Sigma_{ij}\ (Expectancy\ 2_{ij} \times Valence_{ij})$$

Although this formula is useful for those conducting research on motivation, it is not particularly useful in the day-to-day activities of most people. It does, however, present some important implications for training and learning, which we discuss shortly.

To gain a better understanding of the expectancy theory framework, let's go back to Claudia at the point at which she was trying to decide whether to attend the executive development seminar as suggested by her boss. Today is the last day she can register for the seminar, which starts in two weeks. She postponed the decision as long as possible and now must decide. She feels confident about her ability to complete this training successfully, but she holds some doubts about whether it will teach her anything useful about running her marketing operation or working more effectively in a group. She knows that during her week of training, the marketing strategies for five important accounts will arrive on her desk, and she will need to review and finalize them before forwarding them to top management. They are due on the Wednesday following training. In addition, her normal work will continue to pile up. Claudia faces the choice between incompatible courses of action. Her cognitive processes, in expectancy theory terms, are illustrated in Figure 3-4.

Examining Claudia's situation in terms of expectancy theory, we see that her expectations of success (Expectancy 1) are high for both behaviors. The expectancy of 1.0 means that she is 100 percent sure that she would successfully be able to complete either course of action. The Expectancy 2 links reflect the outcomes that Claudia anticipates if she successfully completes the seminar or stays at the office and completes her workload. If she turns down the training and stays on the job, she believes that there is a 50 percent chance her boss will see her skills as inadequate. It would be higher, but she believes that if she can do a superior job on these strategies, he will not think that those relationship skills are so important. She believes that it's 90 percent likely that she will have feelings of pride and accomplishment for getting all her work completed on time. However, if she turns down the training,

Figure 3-4 Illustration of Expectancy Theory

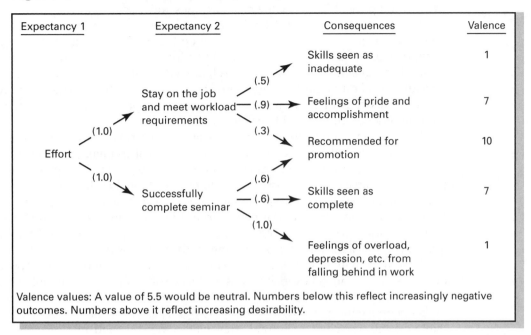

Expectancy 1	Expectancy 2	Consequences	Valence

Effort

(1.0) → Stay on the job and meet workload requirements

(1.0) → Successfully complete seminar

(.5) → Skills seen as inadequate — 1
(.9) → Feelings of pride and accomplishment — 7
(.3) → Recommended for promotion — 10
(.6) → Skills seen as complete — 7
(.6)
(1.0) → Feelings of overload, depression, etc. from falling behind in work — 1

Valence values: A value of 5.5 would be neutral. Numbers below this reflect increasingly negative outcomes. Numbers above it reflect increasing desirability.

she believes that there is only a 30 percent chance that her boss will recommend her for promotion.

Conversely, if she goes to the training, she believes that the likelihood is 60 per-·cent that her boss will evaluate her as having a more complete set of managerial skills. However, she will fall behind in her work, and it is a certainty (1.0) that she will feel harried, overloaded, and depressed. Yet she sees the chances of being recommended for a promotion increasing to 60 percent if she goes to training. As the valences in Figure 3-4 show, she values her boss's recommendation for promotion the most. She views having her boss evaluate her skills as being inadequate and the feelings associated with being behind in her work as the least desirable of the outcomes.

How would you use the formula to calculate Claudia's motivation to stay on the job rather than go to training? By multiplying each Expectancy 2 by its respective outcome valence and summing the values, you would get 9.8.

$$(Expectancy\ 2_{ij} \times Valence_{ij}) = (.5 \times 1) + (.9 \times 7) + (.3 \times 10) = 9.8$$

Then you would multiply that total by Expectancy 1, which is 1.0, and you would arrive at a force of 9.8 for nonattendance at the seminar.

Using the same procedure for the alternative goal—attending the seminar—you would arrive at a force of 11.2. Thus, for Claudia, the motivation to stay at work is less than the motivation to attend the seminar.

Even though the actual values of expectancies and valences are interesting from a scientific perspective, from a practical standpoint it is the relationships among the elements of the model that are useful. This example illustrates the cognitive processes that link a person's goals, possible courses of action, and likely outcomes. These connections determine the person's motivation and are what is missing from the reinforcement theory. Of course, we simplified the situation considerably from what Claudia would actually face in the real work setting. She had many other alternatives. She could delegate someone to cover most of the normal work coming across her desk (though she was not especially comfortable with delegating). She could arrange for the marketing strategies to be sent to her at the training facility and work on them at night, after training, and over the weekend. Each of these alternatives would present its own expected outcomes and associated valences.

Faced with the situation Claudia faced, what would you do? It is unlikely that you would place the same value (valence) on the outcomes or give them the same likelihood of occurring. You might identify more or fewer outcomes. One of the things that make this theory so useful is that it takes into account the fact that people view the world differently and are motivated by different things. The lesson from expectancy theory is that you need to know what the person expects and what they value in order to understand their motivation.

Few people would consciously go through the formal math or mapping of expectancy theory, but it is interesting to note that most training programs that teach decision making use a model similar to this one. More typically, we go through these processes unconsciously and in a less systematic fashion. We choose a particular way of behaving because of our expectations about the costs and benefits of that action. Relationships between our past behavior and its consequences are combined with current information to make inferences about the consequences of our future behavior. Some implications for training become rather obvious here.

First, to be willing to try, a person must expect that there is a reasonable chance of success. Expectancy 1 exerts the most influence on our behavior because we do not waste our time trying to do things we believe we cannot do. Sometimes this belief makes people reluctant to go to training, so trainers must demonstrate that success is likely for the participants. Second, and related to needs and reinforcement theory, trainers must make sure that the right outcomes are attached to the successful completion of training. Trainees should be able to see clear connections between the content of training and important organizational and personal outcomes. Third, the training outcomes must be made as desirable as possible for the trainees rather than just for the organization, the supervisor, or the trainer.

Self-Efficacy and Motivation

Feelings about our own competency are reflected in the concept of **self-efficacy,** which is one of the better-researched constructs related to motivation. High self-efficacy is associated with a belief that we can and will perform successfully. Individuals with low self-efficacy are preoccupied with concerns about failure.[13] Research supports the belief that the higher the self-efficacy, the better the performance.[14] Not only is performance better, but in difficult situations, those with high self-efficacy also try harder, while those with low self-efficacy tend to reduce effort or give up.[15] In a training context, research shows that those with high self-efficacy beliefs are more motivated to learn and are more likely to transfer that learning.[16]

Several factors combine to provide employees with an estimate of their ability to be successful:

- *Prior experience.* The person's past successes and failures and their consequences
- *Behavioral models.* Successes and failures of others observed attempting the behavior
- *Others' feedback.* The encouragement or discouragement provided by others
- *Physical and emotional state.* The physical or emotional conditions the person believes will affect their ability to perform.

Self-efficacy, therefore, is the primary factor in the person's Expectancy 1 evaluation. The employee's feelings of self-efficacy are translated into behavior. If success is expected, the employee works harder, longer, and more creatively, anticipating the positive consequences of a successful effort. If failure is expected, the employee acts to minimize the negative consequences of failure. For example, withdrawing from the activity (refusing to try) moves the person away from proven failure to simply "I did not try." It also allows the person to say, "At least I did not put a lot of energy into it," or make some other rationalization. The point is that the employee's self-efficacy sets up the person's behavior to fulfill the self-efficacy beliefs. In expectancy theory terms, if I do not believe that I can successfully do something, I won't exert the effort to do it; instead, I'll do something else.

What can be done specifically to improve an individual's self-efficacy? The supervisor can provide the employee with confidence through persuasion. Convincing her that she is quite capable of succeeding in the training will help. Also, seeing others who are similar to the employee succeed will improve the employee's self-efficacy.

Training can improve self-efficacy either directly or indirectly, as a by-product.[17] If the employee experiences low self-efficacy regarding her abilities to perform the job, but evidence indicates that she possesses the requisite KSAs, a program of improving self-concept and confidence is needed. When low self-efficacy results from a true lack of required KSAs, attaining competency in these KSAs should increase the employee's self-efficacy if the training allows the trainee to demonstrate mastery on a continuous basis. In this case, the training needs to be designed so that the trainee begins with easily mastered tasks and moves to more complicated tasks after the easier components have been mastered. Trainers can also emphasize what the objectives are and the success of similar sets of trainees in the past.

Self-efficacy is very powerful in terms of facilitating trainee success. It seems to be a good predictor of both learning in the training environment and transfer of the behavior to the job.[18] So determining a trainee's self-efficacy before training and, if low, providing means to improve the trainee's self-efficacy would seem to be a worthwhile endeavor.

UNDERSTANDING LEARNING

Theories of learning are important in the development of training. We examine the essential elements of learning theories and identify their relationship to training. Specific applications of the theories are provided in subsequent chapters.

What Is Learning?

To understand the differences among learning theories, it helps to understand the difficulties of simply defining the concept of learning. Learning is not directly observable, but it is something that almost everyone says they experience. People "feel" that they have learned. It is clear from physiological evidence that learning is related to changes in the physical, neuronal structure of the brain and its related electrochemical functioning.[19] However, how or why these electrochemical changes take place is still unknown. Learning is closely tied to memory; whatever is learned must be retained if it is to be useful. Electrochemical changes created during learning apparently create a relatively permanent change in neural functioning that becomes what is commonly termed *memory*. Again, relatively few definitive answers exist about how or where learning is stored in the central nervous system.

Two Definitions of Learning
Because we cannot observe learning, we must infer that it occurs by looking at its observable effects. What things, influenced by learning, can we observe? The answer is, the learner's behavior. For instance, in school, tests are given to determine what has been learned. The way questions are answered is the observable behavior. In the workplace, your supervisor might look for ways you perform your job differently after training. Because learning is measured in terms of relatively permanent changes in behavior, this becomes the operational definition of learning for many theorists. Behaviorists in particular adopt this definition.

Cognitive theorists, however, insist that even though learning can be inferred from behavior, it is separate from the behavior itself. By examining the ways in which people respond to information and the ways in which different types of behavior are grouped or separated, cognitive theorists developed theories of how information is learned. For cognitive theorists, learning represents a change in the content, organization, and storage of information (see the section, Example of Cognitive Theory). The term used to refer to the mental processing of information is **cognition.** For cognitive theorists, learning is defined as a relatively permanent change in cognition occurring as a result of experience. These theorists discuss learning in terms of mental infrastructures or schema rather than in terms of behavior. Learning is seen as the building and reorganization of schema to make sense of new information. Bruner,[20] Gagné,[21] and Piaget[22] are among the cognitive theorists.

Implications of Behaviorist versus Cognitive Approaches

At first, the differences in the definition of learning might not seem important. It might seem to be a simple difference of whether learning is synonymous with behavior or of how information is processed, organized, and stored. However, these differences create widely different approaches to how education and training are conducted.

One obvious and important difference is where control of learning is believed to occur. The behaviorist approach suggests that the environment controls learning. Certain external stimuli are present, the person responds to them, and certain consequences result. It is the model of learning implied in Figure 3-2 (page 67) and discussed earlier as part of reinforcement theory. In the behaviorist approach, the trainer controls learning by controlling the stimuli and consequences that the learner experiences. The learner depends on the trainer to elicit the correct associations between stimulus and response. Note that this model does not include the brain or any mental activity. B. F. Skinner's explanation of learning perhaps clarifies why he was sometimes referred to as a radical behaviorist. He defined learning as "a relatively permanent change in behavior in response to a particular stimulus or set of stimuli."[23] In other words, we perceive things a certain way because of the consequences of perceiving them that way. Learning occurs when new consequences are experienced.

In contrast, the cognitive approach suggests that the learner controls learning. Prospective learners come to training with their own set of goals and priorities. They possess a set of cognitive structures for understanding their environment and how it works. They even develop their own set of strategies about how to learn. The learners decide what is important to learn and go about learning by applying the strategies they developed and with which they feel comfortable. For cognitive theorists, the learner controls both what is learned and how it is learned. The trainer and the learning environment facilitate that process to a greater or lesser degree. Adoption of one approach or the other leads to implications for how training is conducted and the resulting atmosphere of the training environment. Table 3-2 lists some of the instructional implications of these two positions. For some learning situations, a behaviorist approach is better, and for others a cognitive approach works better.[24] We discuss this issue again later in the chapter.

Example of Cognitive Theory

Piaget identified two cognitive processes critical for learning: accommodation and assimilation. **Accommodation** is the process of changing our construction ("cognitive map") of the world to correspond with our experience in it. Piaget indicated that accommodation occurs through the creation of new categories, or schemata, to accommodate experience that does not fit into existing categories. **Assimilation** is the incorporation of new experience into existing categories. In cognitive map terms, accommodation changes the map, whereas assimilation fills in the detail. These two processes are most clearly evident in young children but exist in adults as well. Suppose Mike (age eight) is

Table 3-2

Some Training
Implications of
Cognitive and
Behaviorist Learning
Theories

ISSUE	COGNITIVE APPROACH	BEHAVIORIST APPROACH
Learner's role	Active, self-directed, self-evaluating	Passive, dependent
Instructor's role	Facilitator, coordinator, and presenter	Director, monitor, and evaluator
Training content	Problem or task oriented	Subject oriented
Learner motivation	More internally motivated	More externally motivated
Training climate	Relaxed, mutually trustful, respectful, and collaborative	Formal, authority oriented, judgmental, and competitive
Instructional goals	Collaboratively developed	Developed by instructor
Instructional activities	Interactive, group, project oriented, and experiential	Directive, individual, and subject oriented

in the rear seat of the car with his younger brother Brandon (almost two and learning to talk) as Dad drives through some farmland. As they pass a pasture where horses are grazing, Mike points and says, "Look Brandon, horses." Brandon responds hesitantly, "Horsies?" Mike excitedly replies, "Yes, that's right, horsies!" Dad glances back and says, "Good work, Brandon, you now know a new word!" Brandon is pleased and repeats the word several times to himself. As they continue driving, they pass another pasture with cows grazing. Brandon yells, "Look Mike, horsies!" Mike or Dad is now faced with teaching Brandon the difference between horses and cows.

What is the learning process that took place? Brandon started out with no understanding of horse or cow. When presented with a new perceptual experience and a label, Brandon created a new cognitive category that might include the following parameters: large, four-legged, brown, moving thing with a tail. So, when Brandon saw the cows, they fit enough of the parameters that he attempted to assimilate this new experience into the category "horsies." If Mike and Dad do a good job of teaching Brandon the differences between horses and cows, he will learn to discriminate between these two and create a separate category for cows (accommodation). What he does not know yet is that later in life he will be taught to create new categories such as mammals and species and that both horses and cows are included in some categories but not in others.

The processes of assimilation and accommodation reflect the way we organize our experience and the meanings we attach to the world as we encounter it. Our behavior depends on how we accommodated or assimilated previous stimuli.

Integration of Cognitive and Behavioral Approaches

We believe that the cognitive and behavioral approaches must be integrated to provide a full definition of learning. **Learning,** as we use the term throughout this text, is defined as a relatively permanent change in cognition resulting from experience and directly influencing behavior. A fairly obvious implication of this definition is that changes in cognition and related behavior that result from things other than experience (e.g., effects of drugs, fatigue, and the like) would not be considered learning. The definition also implies that changes in cognition and behavior that are short-lived have not been learned. For example, memorizing a phone number long enough to walk from the telephone directory to the phone and dial the number would not fit into our definition of learning. However, learning mnemonic techniques that allow you to do that would be learning, if they were retained over a relatively long period of time.

Learning, as defined here, is not dependent on behavior. Relatively permanent cognitive changes (new KSAs) can occur in the absence of observable behavior. However, only the learner would know whether the learning took place. For example, think of courses you took in which the material was presented in a lecture or audiovisual form. If it was effective, you changed your way of thinking about the topic or came to a deeper understanding of the material—even though you did nothing other than pay attention and think about what was presented. However, until you engage in some activity related to the topic, no one other than you would know that learning had taken place. This phenomenon could also happen with skills. Suppose you are a chef and you attend a seminar on preparing a dish. You observe the presenter enhancing the flavor of a dish using a technique of which you had no previous knowledge. You go back to your kitchen, try the technique, and are successful on the first try. You acquired the "flavoring" skill through observation rather than behavior. However, you might not be sure you had acquired the skill until after you engaged in the behavior. Additionally, the more you use the technique, the more permanent (i.e., resistant to forgetting) it would become. Thus, behavior is both an important measure and means of learning.

Each of these two approaches produces valuable insights about learning. Learning theories that integrate the substantiated aspects of both approaches explain learning more completely than either one alone. We discuss such a theory next.

SOCIAL LEARNING THEORY

Albert Bandura and his associates[25] developed a model of learning known variously as observational learning, vicarious learning, and, most often, social learning theory. One of the theory's most important contributions to the science of learning was demonstrating that learning could occur without any overt behavior by the learner. That is, the learner did not have to do anything except observe what was going on around her. No behavior pattern was produced, and no reinforcement was given.

The basic premise of **Social Learning Theory** is that events and consequences in the learning situation are cognitively processed before they are learned or influence behavior. The processing of information leads to learning and changes in behavior. Certainly, the consequences of behavior (reinforcement or punishment) influence the likelihood of that behavior in the future, but they do so as a result of how they are perceived, interpreted, and stored in memory. Thus, a person can learn by observing the behavior of others and the consequences that result. This theory contradicts the strict behaviorists, who claim that learning can occur only as a result of a person's own behavior and its consequences. The cognitive processes that are a part of social learning theory are motivation, attention, retention, and to some extent behavioral reproduction. Figure 3-5 illustrates the relationships among these cognitive processes. Let us examine this model in more detail.

Figure 3-5
Cognitive Processes Involved in Social Learning

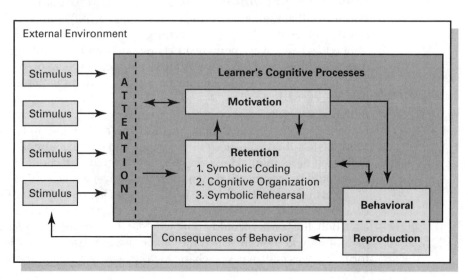

Motivation

Although motivation was discussed at length earlier in this chapter, it is useful to see how it fits in with social learning theory. As the model indicates, motivation both influences and is influenced by the other processes. The learner's needs determine what things receive attention and are processed for retention. As depicted in the model, social learning theory incorporates the operant conditioning concept of behavioral consequences affecting the likelihood of future behavior. Operant conditioning principles stipulate that the consequence can be learned only through the learner's behavior (consequence pairings), whereas social learning theory suggests that behavioral consequences can be acquired through anticipatory learning. **Anticipatory learning** occurs when a person learns what consequences are associated with a behavior (or set of behaviors) without actually engaging in the behavior and receiving the consequences. By observing someone else's behavior, the observer can learn something about how to perform the behavior and also something about the consequences of the behavior. Thus, this theory provides a model for learning through observation alone. For this reason, it is often referred to as a theory of observational or vicarious learning. However, the model of learning processes illustrated in Figure 3-5 is more than just observational learning. It combines cognitive and behaviorist concepts into a comprehensive set of integrated processes that are applicable to all types of learning, providing another set of tools for designing and implementing training. Additional motivational issues are discussed later in the Motivation to Learn section.

Attention

The learning process begins with the learner's **attention** becoming focused on particular objects and events in the environment (stimuli). Of the great multitude of objects and events in the typical environment, we notice many of them but pay attention only to some. The things we pay attention to are those that stand out for some reason (loud, bright, unusual, etc.) or those that we learn are important (e.g., lead to need satisfaction). This reaction is reflected in the fact that we are more likely to model the behavior of someone who is spotlighted in some way (highly publicized, unusually attractive, popular, etc.) than of someone who is not. Similarly, we are more likely to model someone who seems to receive a lot of reinforcement than someone who receives little.

The concept of attention is important in training. Learning is improved by making key learning points stand out so that the trainees will focus attention on them. Eliminating extraneous objects, such as cell phones and beepers, keeps trainees from becoming distracted during training. Making learning exercises fun and interesting keeps attention focused on the learning topic. However, exercises that are fun but do not relate to the learning objectives draw attention away from what trainees are expected to learn, making the training less effective. The training design chapter addresses issues related to capturing trainee attention.

Retention

Once attention is focused on an object or event, the incoming information is processed for possible **retention.** Some of the information will be retained, and some will be lost. The more training is designed to facilitate the retention processes, the more learning will occur. The initial phase of retention is the translation of the information into symbols meaningful to the individual, a process called **symbolic coding.** It transforms external objects and events into internal images and verbal symbols. These symbols are then organized into the existing cognitive structure through associations with previously stored information. This process is called **cognitive organization.** It can be facilitated in training by asking the trainees to provide examples of how the new information relates to what they already know. This exercise serves two purposes: It allows the trainee to code and store the information more easily, and it allows the trainer to see whether the desired associations are being made. Chapter 5 discusses additional ways in which training can facilitate retention.

To facilitate the retention process, the learner should "practice" the learned material through **symbolic rehearsal,** which involves visualizing or imagining how the knowledge or skill will be used. If the focus is on skill building, the trainee imagines using the skills in different situations. This exercise is usually fairly easy to do because the skill helps define the situations. When the focus of learning is knowledge, it is sometimes more difficult to imagine how it can or will be used. For example, think back to when you were learning the multiplication tables. Most of us memorized these through constant repetition over many months, and that repetition provided us with the experience of using multiplication to solve problems. Each year, as we advanced to the next grade, we were given more multiplication problems to solve. In contrast, storing information without any associations with personal use—in other words, just memorizing—typically results in only short-term retention. Students who have ever crammed for an examination are probably familiar with this phenomenon. Thus, associating information with its uses enhances the storage and retrieval processes. The symbolic rehearsal process can be thought of as mental practice. Observing others use the knowledge or skill provides additional opportunities for symbolic rehearsal because as you watch them, you can put yourself in their place. Symbolic rehearsal also increases the ability to generalize learning to novel situations. The discussion on training design in Chapter 5 discusses other ways to enhance retention through symbolic rehearsal.

Behavioral Reproduction

Behavioral reproduction is repeated practice. The more a person practices using new information, the more it is learned and retained. The effectiveness of practice depends on how the practice is designed and reinforced. This will be discussed in detail in Chapter 5. Figure 3-5 shows the behavioral reproduction process as being a part of both the learner's cognitive processes and the external environment. This duality reflects the fact that the person's cognitive processes initiate the behavior (retrieving the appropriate behavior from storage and directing the body to perform) and then the behavior actually occurs in, and becomes part of, the environment.

We already spent considerable time discussing the importance of behavioral consequences. One additional point is worth making, however. If consequences are to affect behavior, the individuals must be aware of these consequences. For example, assume that a supervisor recommends an employee for a bonus but has not yet told the employee. Subjectively, for the employee it is not a consequence of behavior, even though objectively it is. Even when aware of a consequence, the person may misinterpret its value. The supervisor who is disappointed in an employee's performance may sarcastically say, "Really nice job," but the employee may misinterpret this as giving praise. Thus, the person must be aware of and correctly interpret behavioral consequences if those consequences are going to have the desired effect. Effective training programs need to call attention to the desirable consequences of learning and of using the learning back on the job.

ALIGNING TRAINING DESIGN WITH LEARNING PROCESS

We have discussed various theories of how individuals learn. Gagné and his associates[26] suggest that for instruction to be effective, a "set of events" external to the learner must be designed to facilitate the internal learning process. So how can the

Table 3-3

Gagné-Briggs
Nine Events of
Instruction

INSTRUCTIONAL EVENT	THIS EVENT CAUSES THE TRAINEE
Gaining attention	To focus on trainer
Informing the trainee of goal (objective)	To begin to focus on the goal
Stimulating recall of prior knowledge (learning)	To retrieve prior learning to working memory
Presenting the material	To selectively perceive important parts of training
Providing learning guidance	To consider how the new material fits into the trainee's overall schema and clarify where it belongs for ease of retrieval
Eliciting the performance	To do it
Providing feedback	To perform effectively by reinforcing correct responses and assisting when incorrect
Assessing performance	To attempt a number of similar problems to determine if the trainee has the concept
Enhancing retention and transfer	To do more complex and varied examples of the concept and assess the success

Source: Gagné, R. M., L. Briggs, and W. Wager. *Principles of Instructional Design* (1992). Fort Worth, TX: Harcourt Brace Jovanovich.

sequencing of events in a training process increase the likelihood that learning objectives will be achieved?

Gagné and his associates provide a **Micro Theory of Instructional Design,** which is a guide for designing training events to achieve the learning outcomes (KSAs) that you want to create. The theory provides nine steps (sets of events) to follow in developing training for a learning objective.[27] To be most effective, this "set of events" should be arranged in a specific order, as depicted in Table 3-3. Gagné and his associates do not indicate that the nine steps are necessary for every learning objective, or that the sequencing must be exactly as indicated. They say,

> These events of instruction do not invariably occur in this exact order, though this is the most probable order . . . by no means are all of these events provided for every lesson. . . . Their role is to stimulate internal information processes . . . sometimes an event will be obvious to the learner and not needed . . . or provided by the learner themselves. . . . In using the checklist the designer asks, "Do these learners need support at this stage for learning this task?"[28]

To clarify the application of the model, we will go through each of the events using a learning objective related to teaching apprentice electricians.[29] You are the trainer, and the learning objective for the training is to determine the amperage of an appliance, given the watts and voltage. The first event, "gaining attention," is obtained by showing a short video in which a family is in a kitchen; the lights, radio, and toaster are all on. One of the children plugs in the blender and when she turns it on, the radio, lights, and toaster turn off. This gets everyone's attention (instructional event one). Now you ask, "What happened here?" When the answer is given (a fuse was blown), you discuss why it happened and move to the second event: "Inform the learner of the objective." The objective is to calculate the amperage of appliances so as to wire a room properly with the correct number and type of plugs on the basis of what will be used in that room. The next event is "stimulate recall of prerequisites." Here, you would ask apprentices to recall the typical voltage in a house (it is 120 volts, but for ease of calculation, here we will round it to 100). You then ask, "Where is the wattage for an appliance found?" The answer is on a label on the back or side of the appliance. Then ask, "What is the purpose of fuses?" The answer is to prevent circuit overload. Finally, ask how their size is measured (amperes).

"Presenting the stimulus" is done by providing the formula for determining amperage (amperes = watts/volts). Given the wattage of the blender (1000 watts), you ask, "What is its amperage?" You may give a few more examples. Next, for the "provide learning guidance" event, you ask the apprentices to go back to the example at the beginning of the discussion. Tell them that all the kitchen outlets were wired to one typical 15-ampere fuse and ask, "Would the fuse have still blown if the toaster was not plugged in?" They cannot give the correct answer because they need more information, so you discuss the need to have the wattage of everything in the kitchen to determine the total amperes. You then give the wattages to them (100-watt light, 1000-watt toaster, 10-watt radio) and ask for the amperes generated for each.

For the next event, "eliciting performance," you provide the apprentices with the wattage of a number of appliances (refrigerator, 1000 watts; television, 300 watts; space heater, 1400 watts; and so forth) and ask them to determine the amperes each will

Table 3-4 Example of a Lesson in Problem Solving

Objective: Given a drawing of a plot of land, the student generates a plan for a sprinkler system that will cover at least 90% of the land, using the least amount of materials (PVC pipe and sprinkler heads).

EVENT	MEDIA	PRESCRIPTION
1. Gaining attention	Live instruction and overhead projector	Show pictures of sprinkler coverage of a rectangular plot of ground. One highly successful (90% coverage), one unsuccessful (70% coverage), and one using too many sprinkler heads. Show these rapidly, inviting attention to their differences.
2. Inform the learner of the objective	Same	The problem to be solved is to design the most efficient sprinkler system for a plot of ground—one that covers at least 90% and uses the least amount of materials.
3. Stimulate recall of requisites	Overhead projector	Have the learners recall applicable rules. Since the sprinkler heads they will use spray in circles and partial circles, rules to be recalled are (1) area of a circle, (2) area of quarter and half circles, (3) area of rectangular areas, and (4) area of irregular shapes made by the intersection of circular arcs with straight sides.
4. Presenting the stimulus material	Same	Restate the problem in general terms, and then add specific details: (a) rectangular lot 50 by 100 ft; (2) radius of the sprinklers, 5 ft; (3) water source in the center of the lot.
5. Providing learning guidance, *and* 6. Eliciting performance	Same	Have the student design tentative sprinkler layouts, draw them out, and calculate the relative efficiency of each. Guide the learner through various options if it appears that rules are not being applied correctly. For example, "Could you get more efficient coverage in the corner by using a quarter-circle sprinkler head?" or "It looks like you have a lot of overlap; are you allowing for 10% non-coverage?" Ask the learner what rule he is following for placing the sprinkler.
7. Providing feedback	Oral review by instructor	Confirm good moves, when in a suitable direction. If the learner doesn't see a possible solution, suggestions may be made. For example, "Why don't you draw four circles that barely touch, calculate the area, then draw a rectangle around the circles and calculate the area of coverage to see how much you have?"
8. Assessing performance	Teacher	Present a different problem using the same type of sprinkler, with different lot shape and size. Check the efficiency of the student's solution in terms of coverage and amount of materials used.
9. Enhancing retention and transfer	Worksheet	Present several different problems varying in shape of lot, position of the water source, and area of sprinkler coverage. Assess the student's ability to generalize problem solving to these new situations.

Source: Gagné, R. M., Briggs L., and Wager W. (1992). *Principles of Instructional Design.* Fort Worth, TX: Harcourt Brace Jovanovich. p. 242.

require. To "provide feedback," you review the answers to the preceding questions and determine how well each apprentice understood the process. "Assessing performance" is done by providing the apprentices with a number of problems for which they need to calculate the amperes of appliances. For the final event, "enhancing retention and transfer," you provide them with the problem of wiring a workshop. The appliances to be used in the workshop include a table saw, router, planer, drill press, sander, four lights, radio, electric heater, and so forth. You also give the wattage for each of the appliances. Then you ask them to indicate how many 15-ampere circuits they would need to provide to be most efficient and what they would put on the same circuit.

Using the theory helps you design a series of events that are most likely to result in the learning that you want to occur. Table 3-4 provides another example.

MOTIVATION TO LEARN

In addition to designing training to align with learning processes, the design must also address the trainee's motivation to learn. **Motivation to learn** is defined as the intensity and the persistence of the trainee's learning-directed activities related to the content of the training program.[30] Figure 3-6 shows how various individual and organizational factors affect motivation to learn. The relationships shown in the figure have been supported by numerous research studies. While the relationships among all the variables are much more complex than depicted, we have taken a few liberties in the interest of clarity to show how individual characteristics and the organizational context interact to influence the trainee's motivation to learn. Motivation to learn has been shown repeatedly to influence the outcomes of training, such as knowledge and skill acquisition, in addition to transfer of KSAs to the job and resulting job performance. Thus, training professionals need to understand the factors affecting motivation to learn and how to address these in the design of training. In this chapter, we focus primarily on understanding the factors and only briefly touch on training design implications. We will cover the design issues more fully in Chapter 5.

Resistance to learning occurs when the trainee's motivation to learn is not high enough to overcome other forces acting on the trainee that discourage learning. Learning, like eating, is one of the most fundamental processes of survival, so why do trainees resist it? Trainers and managers continually complain about trainees who do not pay attention, are disruptive, and demonstrate a general resistance to learning new material. If learning is a basic human process, why are so many complaints of this type made?

Viewing learning as a performance outcome is the first step to understanding **resistance to learning.** Most learning is not something that happens automatically or unconsciously. It is an activity we decide to do or not do. From the performance model discussed earlier (see Figure 3-1 on page 62), we know that learning performance is determined by a person's motivation, KSAs, and learning environment. If the trainee doesn't have the prerequisite KSAs or the environment doesn't allow learning to occur, then resistance occurs. If trainees are not motivated to learn the material, they will also demonstrate various forms of resistance. As Figure 3-6 shows, the trainee's motivation will be determined by individual factors (self-efficacy, valence, anxiety, and cognitive ability) and environmental factors (organizational context such as climate for learning, peer and supervisor support). We turn first to the environmental factors.

Environmental Factors and Resistance

There are many organizational-context factors that influence how employees enter training. We will focus on three key factors: peer support, supervisor support, and the

Figure 3-6 Factors Affecting Motivation to Learn and Transfer of Training

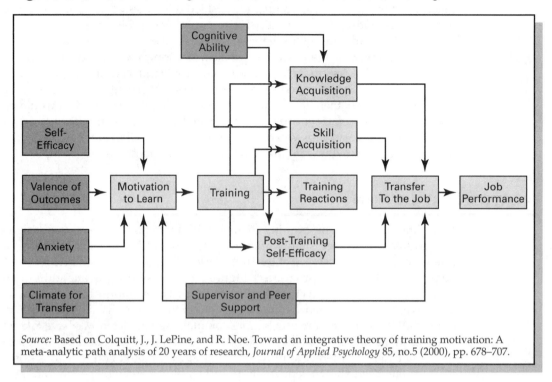

Source: Based on Colquitt, J., J. LePine, and R. Noe. Toward an integrative theory of training motivation: A meta-analytic path analysis of 20 years of research, *Journal of Applied Psychology* 85, no.5 (2000), pp. 678–707.

climate for transferring KSAs learned in training back to the job. These have substantial research support and are factors that can be addressed by the training design.

Peer Support

Peer support is the encouragement and assistance that trainees receive from their coworkers. The effect of **group dynamics** in the work unit on individual group member behavior and motivation is significant and is one reason trainees might resist new learning. The power and control of the group over its members was first noted in the Hawthorne studies of the 1920s and 1930s.[31] Even though members of the group were paid a piece rate, the output from members of the group was always within a certain number of units. Examination of this study revealed that the group set a standard, rewarded those who remained within the standard, and punished those who did much more or much less. Thus, the group norm of a certain number of units was generally followed.

The power of the group comes from rewards the group gives to members who follow group norms or the punishment for those who do not. These rewards or punishments can be as simple as talking to (reward) or shunning (punishment) a group member. Punishment can also be severe, such as slashing tires or physically threatening those who do not comply. Consider the following scenario. Sarah arrives at the training center early, excited to be attending a workshop on how to communicate with customers more effectively. Fellow trainees are talking among themselves, making fun of the training. One of them says, "They are going to tell us how to do our job; I bet the trainer has never even done our job, so how could he know?" Another responds, "Yeah, these workshops are put together by those who never worked in a real job, but at least we can enjoy this as a day off work." Then one turns to Sarah and says, "Hey, I see you managed to con your boss into sending you here for a rest too—good work." To be part of the "in group," Sarah will have to agree and, as a result, will be much less active in the training than she would really like. This will affect the amount she learns.

Let's say that in spite of her (and everyone else's) lack of participation in the workshop, Sarah did learn a few skills. Now she goes back to her workplace. There she hears coworkers (peers) comment, "Well, did you enjoy your day off? Wasn't that training the stupidest stuff you have ever seen?" and "Can you imagine using that 'active listening' stuff on a real customer?" With such comments, what is the likelihood that Sarah will want to try some of these new skills? Group dynamics is a powerful force that can drastically inhibit both learning and transfer of skills.[32]

Group dynamics can also be used to support high performance. The pajama factory experiments of the late 1940s compared employees in two groups where change was necessary in how the jobs were done.[33] In one group employees were told about the changes, and in the other the members provided input into the changes. The no-participation group showed a drop in productivity from the baseline, and the participation group showed an increase in productivity from the baseline. The most important factor in the difference was group norms that developed either to restrict output (no-participation group) or increase it (participation group). More recent research indicates that peer support for training is a strong predictor of the likelihood that trainees will transfer what they learned to the job.[34] The control the work group exerts over the individual member is a double-edged sword. It is a good thing if the norms are developed in line with the organizational goals, bad if they are not. One way of developing positive norms is to allow input from the work group on decisions that will affect them. The movement toward more teams and teamwork in organizations provides such opportunities, but to ensure that the right norms are developed, these work groups need to be nurtured and made to feel that they are a valuable part of the organization.[35]

Supervisor Support

Supervisor support is also a key factor influencing motivation to learn and resistance to training. Supervisors are the official source of rewards in most organizations. If your supervisor doesn't think that training is worthwhile and communicates this to you, what will your reaction be? Probably you will also think that the training is not worthwhile, and your attitude walking into the training will be negative. With this predisposition, you are likely to demonstrate one or more signs of resisting the training. For this reason, we advocate engaging the trainees' supervisor(s) early in the training design process. This allows the trainer to have input into the training and to see how the training will be of value to the work unit.

Climate for Transfer

For training to be successful, the learning must be transferred back to the job. This requires a positive climate for transfer. While a positive climate for transfer includes supervisor and peer support, it includes many other things as well. It requires aligning organizational systems and procedures to support the new job behaviors and the training process in addition to removing barriers. What sorts of systems and procedures need to be aligned? We will talk more in depth about this in the next chapter on the needs analysis phase of the training model. For now, it's sufficient to know that organizational reward systems, job materials and equipment, and job procedures are on the list.

Individual Factors and Resistance

Differences in personality and other individual characteristics are related to trainees' motivation and ability to learn and thus are also factors in resistance to learning. We have already discussed in some depth how a person's self-efficacy and the way she values the outcomes of training ("valence" in expectancy theory terms) will influence her motivation. The number of personality traits that influence a person's motivation to learn is far greater than can be discussed here. For the most part, an understanding of these personality traits provides little practical value for training design and implementation. This is true for several reasons. In most organizations, employee personality traits are not measured, as it is too costly and impractical. Even if these traits were measured, designing a training program that addresses all the individual differences among the trainees would be too complex and costly to be practical. The same is true for developing separate training programs for sets of trainees with unique combinations of traits. However, there are some individual characteristics that are fairly easily observed and which training can be designed to address.

Cognitive Ability

Cognitive ability refers to individual differences in information-processing capacity and the level of cognitive resources that a person can bring to bear on a problem. This is often referred to as general intelligence. It is clear that individual differences in cognitive ability relate to differences in learning.[36] Trainees with differences in cognitive ability will respond differently to goals set for training.

Goal Setting   Some interesting findings came from studies regarding the learning process for low- and high-ability individuals.[37] Goal setting as a motivational incentive does not always operate with the same magnitude for these two groups. When those with low ability are starting to learn a moderately difficult task, providing goals to them will inhibit, rather than enhance, learning. Although the same is true for high-ability individuals, it is not nearly as severe. High-ability individuals, it seems, have the additional cognitive capacity to focus on goals in addition to the new learning in the early learning stage. This difference disappears as the task is learned, and then goal setting enhances the performance of both low- and high-ability individuals. Even though a difference separates the two groups, results from this research suggest that generally, it is wise to design training so that difficult tasks are broken down into a set of simpler tasks that are more easily mastered. If this is not possible, then it is best not to introduce goal setting as a motivational device early in the training process.

KSA Base   Trainees with higher levels of cognitive ability not only process information more quickly but also typically have a larger store of knowledge. Although we indicate that it is desirable to consider diversity among trainees as an opportunity, this is true only up to a point. Substantial differences in the trainees' KSAs related to the training can create significant challenges for the design of training. Those with less knowledge will need to have more training material available to them than the others. It is not only differences in KSAs that can create problems in a training group. The speed at which trainees can process the training information can also make a big difference. Those with less cognitive ability might not be able to keep up with the material, or if the material is presented at a slower pace, the more knowledgeable trainees are bored to tears.

The logic of using different approaches for trainees with significant differences in cognitive ability and KSA base makes some sense here. One approach would be to design separate training programs for the two groups. Another approach would be to develop two phases for the training. The first phase would be for those with lower cognitive abilities. This phase would develop the KSA base and other prerequisite knowledge for the second phase. The idea here is to reduce the differences in ability to keep up with the material in the second phase. The second phase would include all trainees. Another approach would be to use electronic, self-paced training methods, allowing each trainee to move through the material at a pace consistent with their cognitive abilities.

Valences

If training is perceived as leading to attractive outcomes such as better performance and better pay, there is a higher probability that the learning will take place, and transfer to the job will occur.[38] This was demonstrated in a recent study showing that trainees who believed that the training was relevant to their job were more likely to learn and transfer that learning to the job.[39]

However, it is important to note that even when trainees acknowledge the value of the training, they might believe that the effort required to master the learning is just not worthwhile. In Piaget's terms, the accommodation process (developing new cognitive categories) is the most difficult, whereas assimilation (adding new things to existing categories) is relatively easy. Accommodation requires a learner to create new categories that then need to be linked to other related categories. The more categories that exist and the more developed they are, the more difficult the learning. When assimilating, the learner simply adds new elements and rearranges associations among elements within a single category. When accommodating, not only must learners create a new category and place elements into that category, but they must also associate this category with other categories. The elements within those categories must be modified to create the network of associations that appropriately incorporates the new information.

This type of situation occurs whenever a company changes the paradigms it uses for conducting its business. For example, think about what supervisors face when companies move from a traditional, centralized, hierarchical, autocratic decision-making system to a flexible, team-based, more consensus-based, employee-involvement system. From their experience and training in the traditional system, the supervisors developed a cognitive structure for getting things done. They learned how to make all the decisions for their subordinates and developed a system for communicating those decisions and ensuring that they were carried out effectively. These strategies were probably reinforced over many years. A new piece of equipment or a change in the work process brings new procedures that are learned and assimilated into the supervisor's decision-making structure relatively easily. Under the new team-based decision-making structure, however, the whole process of making decisions must be relearned because the underlying organizational assumptions have changed. For the supervisor, the focus is no longer on the quality of decisions but on the supervisor's ability to facilitate quality decisions by the team. Although some aspects of the supervisor's old decision-making process might still be useful, his cognitive structure must be changed to incorporate the new concepts, and the useful aspects of the old concepts must be reorganized and integrated with the new. For this reason, learning the new system will be more difficult for supervisors with a lot of experience than for a newly hired supervisor with little experience in the traditional system.

Anxiety

Anxiety is a heightened state of arousal related to feelings of apprehension or fear. High levels of anxiety interfere with other cognitive processes and cause the trainee to withdraw from or actively resist the learning process. Many trainees feel anxious as they enter training. Most trainees arrive at training with an elaborate and highly integrated cognitive structure. They already know a lot about themselves, their work, their company, and many other things.[40] The objective of training is to change some part of that cognitive structure so that the trainee's performance will be improved. Change creates anxiety, however, for the following reasons:

Fear of the unknown	"Right now I know how things work, but I do not know how this training will affect things."
Fear of incompetence	"I do not know whether I'll be able to learn this stuff."
Fear of losing rewards	"What will happen to my pay, status, and perks, among other things?"
Fear of lost influence	"Will this training make me more or less valuable?"
Fear or lost investments	"I've spent a lot of time and energy learning to do it this way. Why change?"

These concerns deal with the trainees' needs, their current competencies, and how training will change their current outcomes. Pretraining counseling, the set up of the training facility, and the way in which training is introduced can all reduce the level of anxiety trainees feel. Expectancy theory addresses these factors, and the trainees' motivation to learn will depend on the answers to these questions. To the degree that the answers indicate that learning is worth the effort, the individual will be motivated to learn.

The "fear of incompetence" issue deserves more discussion. In general, the more experienced employee has a more developed, integrated, and complex cognitive structure. A great deal of effort has gone into creating that cognitive structure. Now he is being told that his KSAs are not good enough and he has to go to training. Trainees also might feel that they are being told that the trainer knows more about how to do their job than they do. Both of these situations can contribute to the trainee feeling that his competence is under attack, leading to defensive behaviors. This is especially true if the training is mandatory. These defensive behaviors can take the form of trying to show the trainer, and the other trainees, that the training is inadequate or irrelevant and that their current KSAs are better than what training has to offer. They also might try to show that the trainer is incompetent. By degrading the training or the trainer, the trainee feels that he is protecting himself.

This generalization is not to say that more experienced people always resist learning new things or discarding old beliefs. They frequently do not. As adults mature, they appear to go through periodic episodes of cognitive reorganization in which concepts or principles of long standing are reevaluated. [41] During these cognitive reorganizations, knowledge that is of little functional value is discarded, and new KSAs are discovered and integrated into their cognitive structure, especially in times of transition such as job or career changes. For adults, the key factor in discarding old learning and acquiring new learning is its practical usefulness. Training that seems abstract, theoretical, or otherwise unrelated to doing the job will likely be ignored or resisted. Training that can demonstrate its value and practical utility will find trainees eager to learn. This needs to be built into the training design.

Goal Orientation

Goal orientation is a relatively new construct in the adult training literature and is not as well researched as factors contained in Figure 3-6. Nevertheless, it does seem to have a significant impact on motivation to learn. [42] Goal orientation is the degree to which an individual is predisposed toward either a "learning orientation" or a "performance orientation." [43] Those with a learning goal orientation focus on the learning process. They seek challenging tasks to increase their competence, see negative feedback as important information to help them master the task, and see failure as a learning experience. One result of this learning goal orientation is persistence when having problems doing a complex task; they are more motivated to continue to try and solve the problem.

Those with a performance goal orientation differ because they focus on the end result. They wish to be seen as competent and therefore desire favorable, not negative, feedback. They prefer easier tasks where they are able to demonstrate their competence rather than learning something new. A result of having this performance goal orientation is avoidance of complex tasks for fear of failure, limited persistence, and a tendency to be easily distracted.[44]

In an organizational setting, those with a performance goal orientation have a strong desire to impress others and focus on the outcome of their performance. Those with a learning goal orientation focus on mastery of the task to develop their competence, acquire new skills, and learn from their experience.[45] The research using goal orientation in an organizational/training setting has only been going on for a few years, but much of it concludes that it is better to have a learning goal orientation than a performance goal orientation in a training setting.[46] In other words, the focus should be on the process of learning new things rather than on some end product performance goal. The good news is that although there is evidence that goal orientation is a trait, the trait can be influenced by the situation. In fact, it seems that as long as there are situational cues suggesting a focus on learning rather than performance, the situational cues will override the goal orientation trait.[47] Furthermore, these findings tend to be supported when the task is complex and requires new knowledge and strategies.[48]

TRAINING THAT MOTIVATES ADULTS TO LEARN

Learning occurs quite frequently in adults when it appears to offer practical application immediately or in the near future.[49] For example, a study showed that IBM sales representatives averaged more than 1,100 hours a year in "new learning episodes." (A new learning episode was defined as a deliberate attempt to gain and retain some significant knowledge or skill for problem solving or personal change.) Professors, by contrast, averaged slightly more time (1,745 hours) on fewer episodes. Clearly, adults are not resistant to learning but they are sometimes resistant to training offered by their companies. Why?

Training Relevance, Value, and Readiness to Learn

Some of the most often mentioned reasons for adults engaging in new learning are problems on the job, job/occupational changes, home and personal responsibilities, and competency at some hobby or recreational activity. In the study mentioned previously, about two-thirds of the learning episodes were job-related. The need to know and the readiness to learn are critical aspects in the success of adult learning programs.[50] The need to know refers to the value of the knowledge to the learner. Adults most often seek to learn when the learning is life-, task-, or problem-centered.[51] Readiness to learn refers to the amount of prerequisite knowledge (KSAs) the trainees possess and the trainees' belief that they can learn the material. This aspect is consistent with the principles of self-efficacy and expectancy theory. People's motivation to learn a particular knowledge or skill set is directly influenced by their belief that if they put forth the effort, they will be successful in their learning (Expectancy 1). Beyond this expectation, they must feel that the benefits of learning the KSAs outweigh the benefits of not learning them (Expectancy 2).

The challenge is to provide instruction in a context that overcomes the natural resistance of adult learners to changing their cognitive structures. Making the relevance and value of the learning clear as it relates to the trainee and organizational goals addresses one source of resistance to learning.[52] Ensuring that the trainee believes she can successfully master the training content is another important motivator. Over time, adults might develop feelings of low self-efficacy in certain areas and feelings of high self-efficacy in others. For those with a low self-efficacy for learning in general or for the specific content area of the training, the trainer needs to change the self-efficacy beliefs so that trainees are more willing to attempt new learning. Doing so requires a careful match between the trainee's characteristics (e.g., KSA level, learning-style preferences) and the design of the training. Trainers can overcome a significant type of resistance to learning by demonstrating that learning in the subject area can be as easy as in areas in which trainees have high self-efficacy.

Allowing Trainees Control Over Their Learning

As we pointed out, trainees walk into training with well-developed cognitive maps that reflect their experiences. Since these experiences differ from person to person, any given training group is likely to differ considerably in the KSAs they possess and in their learning strategies. Trainees often view these differences as hindrances to their learning and resist training with others who are dissimilar. However, these differences can be viewed as a learning resource if the trainees are willing to share their experiences and strategies and if the training environment supports such an exchange. In fact, adult learners prefer sharing their learning experiences with others if the environment is supportive. Even though adults prefer to plan their own learning projects and to adopt a self-directed approach to learning, this preference does not imply a desire to learn in isolation. Rather, it reflects a desire to set their own pace, establish their own structure for learning, and employ flexibility in the learning methods. More often than not, adults seek learning assistance from others. In short, they do not mind learning from others but they want to maintain some control over the learning experience. These characteristics suggest that training that incorporates individualized components and also makes use of shared, relevant experiences will be most effective at overcoming resistance to learning.

Although it is true that many adults are able to learn new competencies even when they are not told the significance or usefulness of the training, they are much less likely to be able to apply these new competencies to their job. Research suggests that trainees receiving instruction on how to perform a set of skills show improved performance at the end of training but fail to use the skills on their own or to generalize the skill usage to similar situations.[53] Training that provides instruction on the "how to" and includes the "why and when" results in improved performance and continued use of the skill across appropriate situations.[54]

Involving Trainees in the Process

Training, then, should take into account the motivational and cognitive processes that influence the trainee's readiness and willingness to learn. Many writers emphasize the importance of participation, choice, personal experiences, critical reflection, and critical thinking as key characteristics of adult learning.[55] Involving the trainees in the learning process from needs assessment to design and evaluation addresses many of these issues.

Involvement is a key part of overcoming resistance to change. You might remember from the discussion of OD principles in Chapter 2 that involving those who are affected by change in planning and implementing the change creates a sense of ownership. The result is increased commitment to the change and better implementation of the change. Supervisors and trainees should be involved in determining the training needs because both are affected by the change. Supervisors have a clearer understanding of why new KSAs are necessary, how they fit in with the overall plans for the work unit, and the consequences of their employees learning or not learning the new KSAs. The trainees, in turn, see what KSAs they need to improve and understand why those KSAs will be of value. Involving trainees in needs analysis and other parts of the training process will be discussed in more depth in the relevant chapters.

Training design issues are discussed in more detail in Chapter 5. However, training professionals should consider the following nine principles in developing training programs for their employees:

1. Identify, where possible, the trainees' strengths and challenges relating to motivation to learn and design the training to address as many of these as is practical.
2. Align learning objectives to organizational goals and show how learning is important to trainee and organizational success.
3. Describe program goals and objectives clearly at the start of training.
4. Engage the trainee early, thus maximizing attention, expectations, and memory.
5. Use a systematic, logically connected sequencing of learning activities so that trainees master lower levels of learning before moving to higher levels.
6. Use a variety of training methods.
7. Use realistic job- or life-relevant training material.
8. Allow trainees to work together and share experiences.
9. Provide constant feedback and reinforcement while encouraging self-assessment.

The trainer can address the diversity of characteristics trainees bring to training within the context of a group-learning environment by applying these principles to training programs.[56]

SUMMARY

An employee's performance is a function of motivation, KSAs, and environment. This is true of performance in training in addition to job performance. Learning the content of a training program will depend on the motivation and KSAs the trainee brings to the training program and to the training environment. Examination of theoretical frameworks in the fields of motivation and learning provides us with practical insights for the design of training programs. Theories of motivation fall into two categories: needs theories and process theories. Needs theories, such as ERG, explain what it is that motivates an individual. Process theories, such as expectancy theory, explain how an individual's needs lead to goal-directed behavior. Self-efficacy, a person's belief in her performance capabilities, plays a significant factor in motivation.

Two historical approaches to understanding learning are the behaviorist perspective (Skinner) and the cognitive perspective (Piaget). The behavioral approach (reinforcement theory) focuses on the importance of the environment, and the cognitive approach (accommodation/assimilation) emphasizes the processes that lead to learning. Together, the two theoretical perspectives provide a more complete picture of the learning process than either can do alone. Bandura's social learning theory provides a more integrated approach through which we can more fully understand learning. The process of learning provides the foundation for designing effective training. Gagné and colleagues provide this foundation with their theory of instructional design (nine events of instruction).

A model (Figure 3-6) was presented showing individual and organizational factors influencing motivation to learn and the influence of motivation to learn on training outcomes. The factors influencing motivation to learn (self-efficacy, cognitive ability, anxiety, valence of outcomes, climate for transfer, and supervisor and peer support) were also discussed in terms of their relationship to resistance to learning. A number of reasons explain why trainees are hesitant to learn new material, such as fear of the unknown or of not being successful at learning the new material. The concept of learning goal orientation was introduced, and how it differed from a performance goal orientation was discussed, including the ramifications of each orientation to training.

Training design implications from the Motivation to Learn section were provided. To motivate trainees, the training needs to be relevant and valuable. Trainees need to feel confident of being successful in learning the training content. Goal setting will increase motivation in the later parts of the training program but will interfere with learning in the early stages for those lower in cognitive ability. Finally, trainee involvement with each phase of the training process will facilitate trainee interest and motivation in the training. The design of training will also need to consider differences in trainee traits and other characteristics within the context of what is practical. In some cases, separate training programs will be best; in other cases, counseling or prerequisite KSA training may be desirable.

KEY TERMS

- Accommodation
- Anticipatory learning
- Assimilation
- Attention
- Behavioral reproduction
- Classical conditioning
- Cognition
- Cognitive organization
- Cognitive process
- Cognitive structure
- Environment
- ERG theory
- Existence needs
- Expectancy theory

- Extinction
- Group dynamics
- Growth needs
- Law of effect
- Learning
- Learning goal orientation
- Performance goal orientation
- Micro Theory of Instructional Design
- Motivation
- Needs theory
- Negative reinforcement
- Operant conditioning
- Performance model

- Positive reinforcement
- Process theories
- Punishment
- Reinforcement theory
- Relatedness needs
- Resistance to learning
- Retention
- Self-efficacy
- Social learning theory
- Symbolic coding
- Symbolic rehearsal
- Theories
- Valence

QUESTIONS FOR REVIEW

1. Explain the behavioral and cognitive approaches to learning. Which is most relevant to training? Explain your answer.
2. You are a trainer explaining expectancy theory to a group of managers so they can better understand and deal with employee motivation problems. One of the managers says, "I do not have time for this theory stuff. I want real-world training that helps me in my job." How would you respond to the trainee? What is your rationale for your response?
3. List the nine events of instruction as outlined by Gagné and Briggs and indicate how you would use them in a training situation.
4. Explain why different people need different training methods.
5. How does a work group exert control over the performance of a worker? Provide a rationale for why this "power" is a positive or negative thing.
6. How can training be designed to motivate learning and accommodate trainee differences?

EXERCISES

1. The following steps provide practice in implementing a social learning strategy:
   a. Consult with a friend, coworker, or fellow student to identify a target behavior that the person does not currently have but would like to have.
   b. Develop a social learning strategy for the person to acquire that behavior.
   c. Implement the strategy.
   d. In small groups or with the whole class, describe what you tried to do and what happened.

2. In groups of four to six people, discuss the differences among you that would affect the kind of training you would prefer. Use Figure 3-6 on page 82 to start your discussion, but do not limit it to only those characteristics. What accounts for the differences and similarities among your group members?
3. Observe an introductory course in computer programming. Then observe an introductory course in art or music. Which course uses a more behavioral and which a more cognitive approach to learning? If possible, interview the instructors to find out why that is their approach. Describe the match between the instructional approach and the subject matter.
4. Use the following to see how expectancy theory explains differences in student motivation.
   a. In a small group, discuss the most important outcome that you want to achieve in this class (it may or may not be a letter grade). Have each person indicate how valuable that outcome is by using a scale from 1 = "not at all desirable" to 10 = "extremely desirable."
   b. Ask a group member to describe the most important outcome; then ask that person to describe how strong that motivation is compared with the other goals for this term (use a scale of 1 = "not at all motivated" to 10 = "extremely motivated").
   c. Ask that same person to describe the things that must be done (performance level) to achieve that outcome.
   d. Ask the person to indicate the Expectancy 1 level (the belief that he or she will reach the performance level). Then ask the person to describe Expectancy 2 (the likelihood that successful performance will result in the outcome). Use probabilities (e.g., 1 = "very unlikely,".5 = "50% chance of happening," and .9 = "very likely") to reflect expectancies.
   e. Now examine the expectancy linkages to see how well they conform to the person's level of motivation. Discuss any discrepancies and why they exist.
5. This exercise is for those who are working together on a project. Without conversation among members of your group, write a list of the group's norms for performance on the project. When you are done, indicate whether you follow each of the norms and why. Once everyone has finished the tasks above, collect all the responses and mix them up. Hand them out. Allow each person to read the responses they received and compile the responses on a flip chart. Once all responses have been read, discuss the implications of your group's perception of performance norms.

WEB RESEARCH

There are more theories of learning and motivation than have been described in this chapter. Do a search for a learning or a motivation theory that is not in the text. When you find one, write a summary of the theory and suggest how it could be used in training.

Conduct a search for how a business has applied one of the theories in this chapter. Write a summary of how the theory was applied and the results of the application, if this is available.

CASE ANALYSIS

Rick's New Job

Rick recently received an MBA. In university, he was known as smart, hardworking, and friendly. His good grades landed him an internship with Peterson Paper Products (PPP) to head their sales department. Near the end of the internship, Val Peterson, the president and founder of the company, asked Rick to meet him after work to discuss the future.

Peterson Paper Products

Val Peterson founded PPP 17 years ago. It purchases raw paper of varying grades and produces paper stock for business, personal stationery, and greeting cards. Its annual sales topped $15 million, and it employs 80 to 90 people, depending on demand. Sales gradually declined over the last two years after steady and sometimes spectacular growth during the previous seven years. Competition increased markedly over the last three years, and profit margins dwindled. Although PPP is known for the high quality of its products, consumers are shifting from premium-priced, high-quality products to products with higher overall value. Through all of these changes, PPP maintained a close-knit family culture. At least half of the employees have been with the company since the beginning or are friends or relatives of the Petersons or Mr. Ball, Val's partner.

Val Peterson, 53, holds the majority of stock in this privately held company that he founded. He began working summers in a paper company during high school. He supervised a shift at a paper plant while he went to college at night. After graduation, he worked at increasingly higher management levels, occasionally switching employers for a promotion. Eighteen years ago, he quit his vice presidency with a major paper product manufacturer to start his own company. Employees see him as charismatic, even-tempered, and reasonable. He spends most of his time and energy on company business, putting in 12-hour days.

Rosie Peterson, 50, is Val's wife and the controller for the company. She holds 5 percent of the company stock. Rosie never went to college, and her accounting methods are rather primitive (all paper and pencil). Nonetheless, she is always on top of the financial picture and puts in nearly as many hours as Val. She exerts a great deal of influence on the operations and direction of PPP.

Walter Ball, 61, is both Mr. Peterson's friend and business partner. He owns 25 percent of the stock and has known Val since before the start of PPP. He is VP of operations, which means that he oversees the computer information systems that run the paper production process and handles the technical side of the business. He is not current on the latest computer or manufacturing technology, but he loves the paper business. He says he will probably retire at 65, but most say they will believe it when they see it.

Diane Able, 41, is the customer service manager and is married to Steve Able, the chief engineer. Diane worked her way up in the company over the last 10 years. She is often asked to assist Mr. Peterson with projects because of her common sense, and he trusts her to keep information to herself.

Rick's Offer   When Rick met Mr. Peterson to "discuss the future," he was nervous. He knew that Mr. Peterson liked his work so far, but did not know if it was enough to extend his internship another six months. So far, he had worked with Mr. Peterson only on special projects and did not know the rest of the management group well. He was flabbergasted when Mr. Peterson said, "I was thinking that you might like to work here at PPP full-time and help us out with our sales department."

The two of them discussed the problems in the sales area and talked about what could be done to boost sales. Rick agreed to start the next Monday. During this conversation, Rosie walked in and suggested that they all go out to dinner. At dinner, Rosie emphasized to Rick that PPP was a family operation, down-to-earth and informal. "You probably shouldn't try to change things too quickly," she warned. "People need time to get used to you. You have to remember, you're an outsider here and everyone else is an insider." Then Val moved the conversation back to what the future could be like at PPP.

Rick's Awakening   During the first few days at work, Rick spent time getting to know the plant and operations, meeting all the employees, and familiarizing himself with the problems in sales. He met with Val each morning and afternoon. He also met with the key managers, not only to introduce himself but also to convey his desire to work collaboratively with them in addressing the problems in sales. He was conscious not to flaunt his university education and to convey that he recognized he was a newcomer and had a lot to learn. In the middle of his second week, Val told him that his reception by the other employees was going very well: "Your enthusiasm and motivation seem to be contagious. Having you join us shows them that things need to change if we're going to reach our goals."

Rick noticed, however, that the managers always went out in groups, and he had not been invited along. Also, he was not included in the informal discussion groups that formed periodically during the day. In fact, the conversation usually stopped when he approached. Everyone was friendly, he thought; maybe it would just take a little more time.

By his third week, Rick identified some of the problems in the sales department. Among the four salespeople, morale and productivity were moderate to low. He could not find any sales strategy, mission, or objectives. The records showed that Val was by far the leading salesperson. The others indicated that Mr. Peterson "always works with us very closely to make sure we do things right. If he senses there might be a problem, he steps in right away." After formulating a plan, Rick discussed it with Mr. Peterson. "First, I would like to institute weekly sales meetings so we keep everyone up to date. I also want to create a centralized sales database," he told him. Mr. Peterson smiled and agreed. Rick felt he was finally a manager. He did feel that he should have mentioned his idea for creating a sales department mission and strategy, but recalled Rosie's caution about not moving too fast.

Rick discussed with Mr. Ball the possibility of using the centralized computer system to run word processing and spreadsheet software on terminals. Mr. Ball was concerned that outsiders could access the data in the spreadsheets. Anyway, he did not think the system could handle that task because its primary function was production. Puzzled, Rick asked if a PC could be allocated to him. Mr. Ball said that no one in the company had one.

"Well," Rick thought, "I'll just have to bring mine from home." The next Monday Rick walked through the office carrying his computer. Several of the other managers looked at him quizzically. Making light of it he said, "I'm not smart enough to keep everything in my head and I do not have enough time to write it all down on paper." As he was setting up the computer, he got a call from Val: "Rick, that computer you brought in has caused a heck of a ruckus. Can you lie low with it until I get back late this afternoon?" Rick thought Val sounded strained but chalked it up to overwork. Rick agreed and left the computer on his desk, partly assembled. Five minutes later, Rosie walked into his office.

"Do you think it's funny bringing that thing in here? What are you trying to prove—how backward we all are? How much better you are with your big initials behind your name? You're still an outsider here, buster, and do not forget it."

Rick tried to explain how much more productive the sales department would be with a computer and that he had tried to use the company's computer system. However, Rosie was not listening: "Did you think about checking with me before bringing that in? With Val or even Walter? Don't you think we have a right to know what you're bringing in here?" Rick knew argument would do no good, so he apologized for not checking with everyone first. He said he had a meeting with Val later to talk about it. Rosie said, "Good, talk to Val, but don't think he calls all the shots here."

At the meeting with Val, Val agreed that the computer would certainly help solve the problems in sales: "But, you have to be sensitive to the feelings of Rosie and the other managers. It would be best if you did not use the computer for a while until things calm down."

The next day Walter walked into Rick's office. He told Rick that he had moved far too fast with the computer: "That's not how it's done here, son. Maybe you're spending too much time listening to what Val says. He isn't really the one to talk to about these kinds of issues. Next time you just ask old Uncle Walter."

Rick spent the next few weeks building the database by hand and conducting sales meetings with his staff. He tried to set up meetings with Mr. Peterson, but Val was usually too busy. One day, Rick asked Diane Able about not being able to see Mr. Peterson and she said, "You know, you monopolized a lot of his time early on. Those of us who worked closely with him before you came were pushed aside so he could spend time with you. Now it's your turn to wait."

"Are you the one who's been spending all the time with him?" Rick asked.

"Well, it's been me and some of the other managers. We've really been taking a beating in sales, so we need to figure out how to reduce our costs," Ms. Able answered.

A few weeks later, Rick was called in to Val's office. Val began, "Rick, you know we've been going through some bad times. We're reducing head count and I'm afraid you're one of the people we're going to let go. It has nothing to do with your work. You haven't really been here long enough to have either succeeded or failed. It's just that we had unrealistic expectations about how quickly things in sales would turn around. I feel terrible having to do this and I'll do everything I can to help you find another job."

After packing his things and loading up the car, Rick sat in his car and stared out of the window. "Welcome to the real world," he thought to himself.

CASE QUESTIONS

1. Why do you think Rick was let go? How does reinforcement theory apply to the main characters in this situation? How does expectancy theory apply?
2. Explain Rosie's and Walter's reactions to Rick's computer in terms of resistance to change. How might Rick have used the concepts in this chapter to approach the computer situation so as to gain acceptance?
3. Explain Rick's inability to "fit in," using social learning theory. Where did the breakdowns in his processing occur?
4. If Val hired you to develop a management training program for the senior managers at PPP, what are the key concepts from this chapter that you would use in designing the program? Provide appropriate theoretical rationale to support your position.

Chapter 4

Needs Analysis

ANALYSIS PHASE

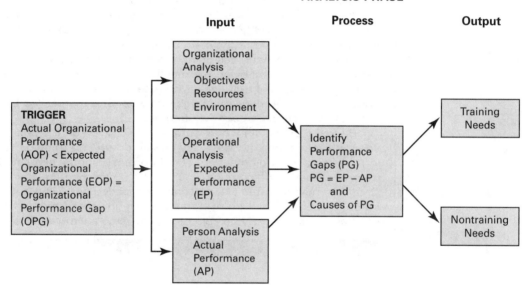

Input	Process	Output

TRIGGER
Actual Organizational Performance (AOP) < Expected Organizational Performance (EOP) = Organizational Performance Gap (OPG)

Organizational Analysis
Objectives
Resources
Environment

Operational Analysis
Expected Performance (EP)

Person Analysis
Actual Performance (AP)

Identify Performance Gaps (PG)
$PG = EP - AP$
and
Causes of PG

Training Needs

Nontraining Needs

Learning Objectives

After reading this chapter, you should be able to:

➤ Describe the purpose of a needs analysis.

➤ List and describe the steps in conducting a needs analysis.

➤ Explain what a competency is and why it is useful.

➤ Differentiate between proactive and reactive needs analysis approaches, and describe the situations favoring the use of one over the other.

➤ Outline the rationale for using performance appraisal information for a needs analysis, and identify what type of performance appraisal method is appropriate.

➤ Describe the relationship between needs analysis and the design and evaluation of training.

➤ List four contaminations of a criterion.

Chris is a human resources (HR) manager at Westcan Hydraulics, and Irven, the VP of HR, is her boss. One morning Irven called Chris into his office. "I just saw an old training film called *Meetings Bloody Meetings* starring John Cleese," he said. "It deals with effective ways of running meetings." Irven, a competent and well-liked engineer, had been promoted to VP of HR three months earlier. Although he had no HR expertise, he had been an effective production manager, and the president of the company had hoped that Irven would provide a measure of credibility to the HR department. In the past, employees saw the HR department as one that forced its silly ideas on the rest of the company with little understanding of how to make those ideas work.

"Well," said Chris, "I . . ."

"Oh, yes," Irven interjected, "I talked to a few managers this morning and they were enthusiastic about it. It's the first time I have ever seen managers enthusiastic about any type of training. Do we have such a training package available?"

"No, I do not believe so," Chris replied.

"Well," said Irven, "we need a one-day training session. It must be interesting, useful, and generalizable to all managers. Okay?" With that, Irven stood up, signaling that the meeting was over.

Chris went to work designing the training. She began by going to the local university and viewing the meetings film her boss had seen. After examining some books that dealt with meetings, she decided that she had a good idea of what made meetings effective. She then called Larry, a friend at Satellite Systems, to see what he had.

He faxed over a copy of a lecture he had given on the dos and don'ts of an effective meeting. It was nicely broken down into three parts: premeeting, meeting, and postmeeting. That information and a simulated meeting (to provide hands-on practice) could make up the one-day training program. Chris had never written a simulation and needed help. She put in a call to Karen, a subordinate who was fresh out of university and had majored in HR. Karen would surely be able to help develop a simulation, Chris thought.

WHY CONDUCT A TRAINING NEEDS ANALYSIS?

What is wrong with the situation at Westcan? It is a scene that repeats itself in some form every day. The boss wants some training, and the HR manager complies. After all, the boss must know what kind of training the employees need. Right? Maybe not. Recall from Chapter 1 that a **training needs analysis (TNA)** is a systematic method for determining what caused performance to be less than expected or required. Performance improvement[1] is the focus of training. This is obvious when you turn to the beginning of the chapter and look at the analysis phase figure. Note that the "trigger" for doing a needs analysis occurs when **actual organizational performance (AOP)** is less than **expected organizational performance (EOP).** We refer to this difference as the **organizational performance gap (OPG).** Does an OPG exist at Westcan? Perhaps. In this situation, we might consider the VP's suggestion that there is a need for training as the "trigger" to conduct a needs analysis. Are the meetings producing less than expected results? To answer this question, Chris would need to conduct a TNA.

If AOP is less than EOP at Westcan, Chris needs to identify where these differences exist in terms of the meetings. Once these are known, other questions need answering. How many meetings are ineffective? What is causing the problem? Is it the manager's knowledge of "how to run an effective meeting," or are other issues causing the meetings to be ineffective? How much do these managers already know about meetings, and how skillful are they at applying this knowledge? Chris needs to answer these and other questions by conducting a TNA before she begins to design the training program for effective meetings. Instead, Chris assumes that she knows what managers require and begins to develop the training on the basis of her assumptions. She does not conduct a TNA to determine exactly what the deficiencies are. Think about this scenario as we examine the process of a TNA. Would you want to be in Chris's shoes? We refer back to this example throughout the chapter, and at the end, we give you the rest of the story.

A TNA is important because it helps determine whether training can correct the performance problem. In some cases, the TNA indicates that employees lack the necessary knowledge, skills, and attitudes (KSAs) to do the job and that they require training. In other cases, employees have the KSAs to do the job, but there are roadblocks that prevent effective performance. These obstacles need to be identified and removed. As a training professional, you will use the TNA to ensure that you provide the right training to the right people. Chris at Westcan is overlooking a critical part of the training process by not completing a TNA. Instead, she is relying on what Irven says and jumping directly to the training design phase. If Chris were to conduct a TNA first, she could accomplish several important things:

- Increase the chances that the time and money spent on training is spent wisely
- Determine the benchmark for evaluation of training
- Increase the motivation of participants
- Align her training activities with the company's strategic plan

Why spend thousands of dollars, or more, on a training program no one needs? With increased concern about costs, it is important that all departments, including HR, use resources wisely.

A TNA will provide a benchmark of the performance levels and KSAs that trainees possess prior to training. These benchmarks will let you compare performance before and after training. This will allow you to demonstrate the cost savings or value added as a result of training.[2] We will say more about these evaluation issues in Chapter 9.

A TNA provides more than just evaluation measures. A good TNA ensures that only those who need the training attend and provides the data to show trainees why the training will be useful to them. Consider the employees who do not need the training but are sent by their supervisor anyway. Are they going to take the training seriously? Probably not. In fact, their lack of interest might be distracting to those who need and want the training. Worse, they might cause other trainees not to take the training seriously. Using a TNA also ensures that your training focuses on KSAs the trainees really need. The needs analysis allows the trainer to begin by explaining how the training will be useful. If trainees see the training as relevant, they are more likely to be interested in attending and maintain interest during the training.

As noted in Chapter 1, implementing a strategic plan requires careful analysis of the organization's HR capabilities. A TNA is one process for determining the degree to which employees possess the necessary KSAs to carry out the strategies. Training can then be designed in alignment with the strategic plan. The TNA also provides the human resources department (HRD) with information as to the relevance of training to the strategic plan. This information is helpful in determining which training needs are more important.

WHEN TO CONDUCT A TNA

There are times when a TNA might not be necessary. For example, if the organization is trying to communicate a new vision or address legal concerns, it might be advisable to train all employees. Suppose the company has concerns regarding sexual harassment. Everyone should be aware of how seriously top management considers breaches of their "sexual harassment" policy. Here, company-wide training on the issue might be necessary. Sending everyone to a workshop on sexual harassment ensures that management's expectations regarding this issue are clear. It also demonstrates an employer's position on sexual harassment to the courts, should an employee consider a sexual harassment lawsuit.

Another situation in which a TNA might not be necessary is if a team requires team-building skills. In this instance, the goal of training is to build the dynamics of the team so that the members work together cohesively and effectively, and also to provide the relevant KSAs. In this case, everyone on the team should be part of the training, even though they already might possess many team KSAs.

For most types of training, however, a needs analysis is beneficial and will increase the relevance and effectiveness of training. For example, team building for teams that have been working together for a while would benefit from a TNA. In this case, the needs analysis focus is on the team itself, not the individuals in the team. Only teams that demonstrate problems in effectiveness or cohesion would go through a TNA to determine if training is necessary. Teams already functioning effectively would not need to attend, so the overall cost of training is reduced.

THE TNA MODEL

Examine the model at the start of the chapter. The first part of the model is the triggering event that initiates the TNA. For example, when a key decision maker suggests that there is a performance problem now or in the future, a TNA is triggered.

The next step in the TNA model is the input, which consists of an organizational analysis, an operational analysis, and a person analysis. The **organizational analysis** is an examination of an organization's strategy, its goals and objectives, and the systems and practices in place to determine how they affect employee performance. An **operational analysis** is the examination of specific jobs to determine the requirements, in terms of the tasks required to be carried out and the KSAs required to get the job done. It is analogous to a job analysis, or a task analysis, as it is sometimes called. A **person analysis** is the examination of the employees in the jobs to determine whether they have the required KSAs to perform at the expected level.

In the process phase, the operational analysis provides information on expected performance (EP). **Expected performance** is the level of performance expected in a particular job.

The person analysis provides information on actual performance (AP). **Actual performance** is the current level of performance by an individual on a particular job. When AP is lower than EP, a more specific performance gap (PG) is identified. As noted in the model, this specific **performance gap*** is the difference between EP and the employee's AP.

The "output" phase is your conclusion as to whether the PG indicates either training or nontraining needs, and in some cases, both. This will be explained later.

So, as you can see from the model, a TNA is conducted when a key decision maker in the company notes an OPG (AOP is, or will be, less than EOP). A **reactive TNA** focuses on current performance problems (the OPG currently exists). A **proactive TNA** focuses on performance problems in the future (the OPG will exist at some point in the future). Let's look at an example of each.

A current OPG triggers a reactive TNA. For example, if the expected number of widgets produced per week is 5,000 and actual production is only 4,300, you need to investigate this gap.

As an example of the proactive approach, consider an organization's decision to implement statistical process control (SPC) to improve the quality of its widgets. Sometime in the near future, the employees producing widgets will begin using SPC methods. Potential for a future OPG exists (the trigger) because if the employees do not have the appropriate KSAs for SPC, they will have a PG that will lead to an OPG. This potential gap triggers a proactive TNA to determine whether employees will be able to perform as needed when the organization implements SPC. You conduct an assessment of employees' capabilities regarding SPC and find that they are not able to perform the arithmetic needed in the use of SPC. This PG will need to be addressed before SPC can be implemented. As this example illustrates, when you expect an OPG to occur at some point in the future, you should conduct a proactive TNA to verify that the gap will exist and identify the specific KSAs that need to be developed.

An OPG may occur for many reasons (see Figure 4-1), only one of which is a lack of KSAs. You need to conduct the TNA to discover why the gap exists and what can be done to correct it. Consider the problem at a regional telephone company a few years back. Sales revenue did not meet expected levels (AOP was less than EOP), triggering a TNA. The TNA identified that sales were indeed below expectations. The TNA narrowed the source of the less-than-expected sales to the installation and repair unit. The phone company had hoped to increase revenue by having their installation and repair employees make sales pitches to customers for additional services when on a service call. However, data on sales indicated that few such sales took place, so AP was less than EP. Note in Figure 4-1 that several possible causes of a PG are listed. If the cause is not a KSA deficiency, then some nontraining solution is required to alleviate the PG.

What caused the PG? It was not a KSA deficiency. Installation and repair employees' performance was based on the time it took them to complete a call. They had a certain amount of time to complete each call. If they took longer than the time allotted for a number of calls, their performance was rated as below average. The time allotment was not changed, even though employees were now expected to stick around and try to sell their products and services. So most employees simply did not spend any time selling. In this example, reward/punishment incongruities were causing the PG. We return to examine Figure 4-1 in more detail later, but now let's examine where we look for PGs.

---

*Note that for the TNA trigger, the difference between actual organizational performance and expected performance is called an "organizational" performance gap. The difference between actual and expected performance obtained from the operational and person analysis of the TNA is simply termed a "performance gap."

Figure 4-1   Model of Process When Performance Gap Is Identified

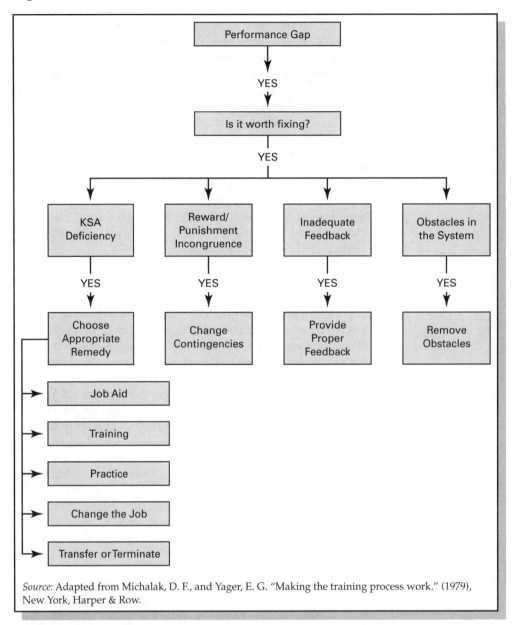

Source: Adapted from Michalak, D. F., and Yager, E. G. "Making the training process work." (1979), New York, Harper & Row.

Where to Look for OPGs

There are numerous places to look for OPGs. A company's archival data, such as its profitability, market share, grievance levels, productivity, and quality measures, provide indicators of how it is operating. These are included in Table 4-1, which provides a list of sources for gathering data related to potential PGs. Let's examine a few to see how the process works. The first data source, organizational goals and objectives and budgets, provides standards against which unit performance can be measured. Suppose, for example, that the triggering event was a loss in profitability because of excessive costs related to warranty work. A reactive TNA is implemented, which might lead you to examine the quality standard for rejects in the production department. The standard (EP) is less than 1 per thousand, but you see that the AP is 12 per thousand.

Table 4-1   Recommended Data Sources for Locating Gaps in Performance

SOURCES OF DATA	IMPLICATIONS FOR TRAINING NEEDS	EXAMPLES
1. Organizational Goals	This source suggests where training emphasis should be placed.	Maintain a quality standard of no more than one reject per thousand.
Objectives and budget	This source provides information on both standards and direction.	Achieve a goal to become ISO certified and allow $90,000 for this effort.
2. Labor Inventory	This source helps HRD identify where training is needed because of retirement turnover, age, etc.	30 percent of our truck drivers will retire over the next four years.
3. Organizational Climate Indicators	These "quality of working life" indicators at the organization level provide indicators of organizational performance gaps.	
a. Labor-management data, strikes, lockouts, etc.	These indicators relate to work participation or productivity and are useful in discrepancy analysis and in helping management set a value on the behaviors it wishes to improve through training.	
b. Grievances		70 percent of the grievances are related to the behaviors of six supervisors.
c. Turnover		
d. Absenteeism		High absenteeism for clerical staff.
e. Suggestions		
f. Productivity		
g. Accidents		Accident rate for line workers increasing.
h. Short-term sickness		Line workers' attitude toward teamwork is poor.
i. Attitude surveys	Surveys are good for locating discrepancies between organizational expectations and perceived results.	
4. Analysis of Efficiency Indexes		
a. Costs of labor		Labor costs have increased by 8 percent in the last year.
b. Quality of product		Number of rejects has increased by 30 percent since the new batch of workers began.
c. Waste		Wasted steel has increased by 14 percent since the company began using part-time workers.
5. Changes in System or Subsystem	New or changed equipment may require training.	The line has shut down about once per day since the new machinery was installed.
6. Management Requests or Management Interrogation	One of the most common techniques of identification of performance discrepancies.	Production manager indicates a drop in quality since the layoffs.
7. MBO or Work Planning and Review Systems	Provides actual baseline performance data on a continuous basis. From these measures, the company is able to determine improvement or deterioration of performance.	

Source: References for all at these methods can be found in M. Moore, P. Dutton (1978). Training Needs Analysis: Review Critique. *Academy of Management Review* 3, pp. 532–545.

The process is similar when you expect future performance to be less than what it should be. Here, a proactive TNA is initiated. Suppose the company's new strategic plan indicates a substantial modernization of the plant, including new computerized machinery. There is no OPG now, but the plant manager believes there will be when the new machinery arrives. This possible OPG in the future prompts a "proactive" TNA. As part of this TNA, the HRD department will need to assess the employees' current level of KSAs for operating the new machinery. If these current KSAs are not sufficient, a gap exists for the future.

The second data source, labor inventory, is also useful to determine an OPG in the future and the types of training necessary to prevent such a gap from occurring. Knowing that a number of senior engineers are retiring over the next few years can trigger the HRD department to start training those in line for promotion to obtain some necessary skills. Not being aware of these retiring employees could lead to an OPG because the company would lack enough senior engineers to manage the expected number of projects.

Finally, let's examine the third data source, organizational climate indicators. Identification of high absenteeism in a particular area, or an increasing accident rate, provides you with early signs of problems. The quicker you are able to identify problems, the quicker you will be able to find and implement solutions. This is one secret to an effective HRD department. Cindy Baerman, the human resource development officer of Miller Brewing Company, provides an example for this. She began attending production meetings a few years back. She received funny looks, as the meetings were held to focus on production problems. Why would HRD want to be there? As Cindy pointed out, "What better place to learn of the type of performance problems the line manager is having?"[3] For her, the focus was on performance management. Being able to react quickly to maintain and improve performance is the first step in a continuous performance improvement framework, which is so important in today's environment.[4]

THE FRAMEWORK FOR CONDUCTING A TNA

Recall from Figure 1-3 (on page 7 in Chapter 1) that all five phases of the training model have an input, a process, and an output component. The "input" for the analysis phase, as shown in the figure at the start of this chapter, is made up of organizational, operational, and person analysis. The "process" is where we determine the specific nature of any PGs and their causes. The "output" provides us with either training or nontraining needs—and in some cases, both. So, once a trigger has set a TNA in motion, the three levels of analysis—organizational, operational, and person—need to be completed.[5] In the section below, we provide an overview of the three TNA inputs. Following this we provide a detailed examination of each area.

Organizational analysis looks at the internal environment of the organization—influences that could affect employee performance—to determine its fit with organizational goals and objectives. It is this analysis that provides identification of the OPG at the organizational level. Imagine that company ABC decides one of its goals is to become team oriented in its production operation. Examining the various policies of the organization reveals an incentive system that pays up to 15 percent of base pay for individual productivity above quota. This focus on individual productivity is not in line with the new goals of a team approach and could cause team members to be more concerned with their individual performance. It needs to be removed or changed to align with the goals of a team-based approach. The organizational analysis is also an examination of how the internal environment affects job performance. In the ABC example, if both Bill and Mary again do not come to the team meeting, does it mean they are not interested? Perhaps, but it is more likely that they are working on beating their quotas so they will receive the bonus pay. Finally, the organizational analysis identifies constraints on training. Consider the small-business owner who employs unskilled assembly-line workers who are unable to read well. He wishes to move to a more team-oriented approach. The owner does not have the funds or time to develop a remedial reading course. This presents an organizational constraint and leads to the development of training that does not require reading.

Operational analysis examines specific jobs to determine the requirements (KSAs) necessary to get the job done (i.e., expected job performance). This process is generally called a **job analysis,** or task analysis, and it requires an extensive analysis of a job to determine all the tasks necessary to perform the job at the expected level. After all tasks are identified, the next step is to determine the KSAs necessary to perform each of the tasks. Each task needs to be examined by asking the question "What KSAs are necessary to be able to perform this task at the expected level?" The KSAs obtained from the analysis are the ones that an incumbent must have to perform at the expected level. There are several ways to obtain this information, such as interviewing incumbents and their supervisors, observing the job, and so forth.

Finally, **person analysis** examines those who occupy the jobs to see whether they possess the required KSAs necessary to do the job. Here we measure the actual job performance of those on the job to see whether they are performing at an acceptable level. This task might seem easy enough: Simply look at the supervisor's appraisal of the incumbents. As you will see later, however, many problems can arise with performance appraisals completed by supervisors, such as halo, leniency, and other effects. So, as a result, other methods are also used to obtain this type of information. For example, asking incumbents themselves and asking coworkers are two other methods. All methods have strengths and weaknesses that will be discussed in more detail later.

These "inputs" are conceptually distinct, but in practice, much of the information is gathered at the same time and is closely interrelated. For example, information related to all three types of analysis can be collected from the job incumbents. Questions would include, "Do any particular organizational policies or procedures that you must follow negatively affect your job performance?" (organizational analysis); "Describe for me the tasks you perform when you first arrive at work" (operational analysis); and "Do you believe you are lacking any skills that, if you had them, might enhance your ability to perform at a higher level?" (person analysis). Now that you have an overview of these TNA input factors, let's examine each in more detail. Then we will look at some specific issues surrounding the two types of TNA, proactive and reactive.

Organizational Analysis

An organizational analysis focuses on the strategies of the organization, the resources in the organization, the allocation of these resources,[6] and the total internal environment.[7] The internal environment includes an examination of structures, policies and procedures, job design, workflow processes, and other factors that facilitate or inhibit an employee's ability to meet job performance expectations.

An organizational analysis is necessary to help identify the cause of OPGs and, specifically, to determine whether OPGs are, in fact, correctable through training. According to Nancy Gordon, a TNA analyst at Ameritech, about 85 percent of all requests for training turned out to be related to issues that could not be addressed by training. They were, instead, incongruencies in the organizational environment that inhibited or prevented the appropriate work behaviors. Training in Action 4-1 provides an example of where this is the case. As you can see in this example, the bank manager neglected to consider the need to align the tellers' performance appraisal with the goals of the new training. So, even if the KSAs were learned, there was no incentive to use them. In fact, tellers would be penalized under the existing performance appraisal system.

A bank manager decided that to increase profits, he would send all his tellers to a training workshop about the products and services the bank offered. He wanted the tellers to provide such information to customers who came into the bank, thinking that this would increase the number of products and services sold.

The manager developed a method of tracking the number of products and services sold so he could have a measure of the success of the training. After a time, he noticed no increase in sales. Training did not result in an increase in sales. What went wrong?

Analysis revealed that when tellers returned from training, they also returned to the same appraisal system that had been in place before the training. Performance assessment was based largely on the number of customers the teller was able to process. Why would a teller risk receiving a low performance rating to spend time telling customers about the products and services being offered by the bank?

Source: Adapted from Johnson, C. "Making your training stick." *HR Magazine* (May 1995), pp. 55–60.

An organizational analysis, then, should be able to provide information about the following:

- The mission and strategies of an organization.
- The resources and allocation of the resources, given the objectives.
- Any factors in the internal environment that might be causing the problem.
- The effect of any of the above on developing, providing, and transferring the KSAs to the job if training is the chosen solution to the OPG. These would be considered to be organizational constraints. Should training become one of the solutions for the OPG, you will need to revisit these to determine how the training will be designed to deal with them. We will discuss this in more depth in Chapter 5.

Mission and Strategies

The organizational analysis helps the analyst align the training with the organization's mission and strategies. Consider the Windsor Ford Engine Plant mission statement: "Our mission is to continually improve our products and services to meet our customers' needs, allowing us to prosper as a business and provide a reasonable return to our stockholders." A strategy arising from that mission statement was to focus on the team approach for continuous improvement. Two types of training traditionally used to support this strategy are training in problem solving and negotiations. But what if the workers in the plant are offered training in traditional negotiation skills? Is this in line with the team approach? Perhaps not. Problem-solving training requires openness and trust to be effective. Traditional negotiations training often teaches that it is useful not to reveal all your information but instead to hold back and attempt to get the best deal that you can for yourself or your department. To offer such training would, at best, not reinforce an environment of openness and trust, and at worst, would impede it.

A company's mission and strategies also indicate priorities for training. Training resources are always finite, so decisions must be made as to where to spend the training budget. If, for example, "Quality is job one" at Ford, the analyst knows that development of KSAs relating to quality should receive priority. Thinking back to the Westcan case, can you identify how that company's priorities would be related to the need for effective meetings?

Capital Resources   A company's finances, equipment, and facilities are considered to be capital resources. During strategic planning, decisions are made as to where money should be spent. If a large expenditure is made on new equipment for the machinists, or toward becoming ISO 9000 certified, these strategic decisions will help determine the priorities for the HRD department. In the case of purchasing new equipment for machinists, HRD's priority would be the machinists' positions. You would need to assess the machinists' level of KSAs to determine whether they need training to operate the new machinery. This decision to focus on the machinist is based on the financial decisions made at the strategic level. Likewise, the strategic choice of becoming ISO 9000 certified should indicate to you that support in that area is needed. After all, significant company resources will be directed toward these strategic initiatives. If the employees cannot operate the new equipment or engage in the tasks required for ISO certification, the money put toward those initiatives will be wasted.

Another concern for HRD is its own budget. Decisions about how to provide the required training are a function of the money that HRD has available for training. The decision whether to use external consultants or internal staff depends on a number of issues, not the least of which is cost. In the Westcan case, Chris decided to develop the training herself. Hiring a consultant to provide the training might get better results, but Chris would have to weigh that decision against other training needs at Westcan, given her limited budget.

Human Resources   The other area of resources that needs to be addressed is **human resources.** Examination of the KSAs in HR occurs at two levels. It includes a general strategic needs assessment and a more specific training needs assessment. First, at the strategic level, HRD provides top management with an assessment of the current employees' ability and potential to support various strategies. With this information, top management knows its employees' capabilities and can factor those capabilities into its strategic decision making. Heinz Canada's Leamington plant decided several years ago that its strategic plan was to improve efficiency in producing ketchup. Heinz wanted to purchase a state-of-the-art automated ketchup maker. The HRD department provided top management with information on the KSAs of the current workforce. This information indicated that no one had the skills necessary, and, in fact, many had reading difficulties such that operating computer-controlled machinery might be a concern. Because the strategic planning group knew this information early in the strategic planning phase, they were able to make an informed decision about how to proceed. They considered the following choices:

- Abandon the idea of purchasing such equipment, and consider alternative strategic plans.
- Hire employees who have the skills to operate such machinery.
- Train current employees to operate the machinery.

Heinz chose to move forward with the plan and train the current employees. Since they addressed the issue early, Heinz had plenty of time to do this.

HRD's strategic needs assessment is more proactive and provides a great deal of information about the capabilities of the workforce to carry out various strategic alternatives. This information helps decision makers decide which strategic alternatives will be followed. Once managers approve a strategic plan, HRD can focus on areas where priorities are identified from the strategic plan.

At the second level, HRD focuses on those employees who are identified to be working in areas contributing to OPGs. This is really part of the person analysis, but an example will help clarify the difference. In our earlier example, it would be the machinist who had to learn to use the new computerized machinery. What about in the Heinz example? Recall that none of the Heinz employees has the required KSAs to operate the new ketchup equipment. As a result, although they are effective employees now, an OPG will develop when the new equipment arrives. The HRD department's priority is to provide the employees with the requisite KSAs so that when the ketchup machine arrives, they will be able to operate it effectively.

Organizational Environment   Another key objective of the organizational analysis is to examine the organizational environment. The **organizational environment** is made up of various structures (e.g., mechanistic or organic) and designs (e.g., workflow, division of labor, pay system, and reward policies). The environmental analysis determines whether or not these structures are aligned with the performance objectives of the department or unit in which OPGs have been identified. Identifying this lack of alignment early and aligning the environmental factors with the training will help ensure that when training is complete, the new skills will transfer to the job.

Consider two organizations:

Organization A decides to adopt a more team-oriented approach. The company's mission and objectives reflect this recent change in company policy. Present procedures include the use of a suggestion box and provide rewards for individual suggestions that improve the company's performance.

Organization B's mission and objectives can be summed up as "quality is most important." One of the organization's policies is that performance appraisals for first-line management provide a measure of how well these managers meet productivity quotas. However, the appraisals measure nothing related to quality of the product.

In the first scenario, do you believe that the individual incentive system would reinforce or hinder the team approach? If, after training and implementing the team approach, teams were not producing innovative ideas, would that mean that the training was not effective? You cannot really tell. The skills might be learned but not transferred to the job. Consider the reward/punishment incongruence (see Figure 4-1 on page 100) between rewarding for individual ideas (suggestion box) and instituting a team approach, which means sharing ideas with the team. If I can get a reward for my idea by putting it in the suggestion box, why would I want to freely share it with the team? Identifying this incongruence and removing it before instituting the team approach would facilitate transfer of the training. To go one step further would be to implement a team-incentive system, thereby aligning the incentive system with the team approach.

In the second scenario, would you expect training in quality issues to be effective, or is training even needed? Instead of training, it might be possible simply to redesign the appraisal system to emphasize quality, thus aligning it with the objective.

These examples illustrate the value of conducting an analysis of the organizational environment as it relates to performance problems. Consider one other point. The analysis at the environmental level should not be conducted until you have an idea of what jobs are targeted either for their performance problems or because of future changes. This targeting allows for a certain degree of focus when you are conducting the analysis; you gather data that are relevant only to those jobs. Otherwise, you might gather an enormous amount of information on jobs that may be irrelevant and therefore waste valuable resources.

To summarize, data gathered from the organizational analysis must be examined to determine if it is aligned with the training that is to be provided. In almost all cases of training, there are some environmental factors that need to be realigned to fit the new training. If they are not, transfer is highly unlikely.[8]

Where to Collect Data

Table 4-2 identifies potential individuals to be interviewed and points to raise with them. Once a gap in performance is identified in a specific department or location, the cause of the gap needs to be determined. You should not assume that training is required to alleviate the gap. Do not forget Nancy Gordon's words: "About 85 percent of training requests turn out to be solvable without training."

Table 4-2
What Do You Ask
and of Whom?

WHAT TO ASK ABOUT	WHO TO ASK
Mission Goals and Objectives	
What are the goals and objectives of the organization?	Top management
How much money has been allocated to any new initiatives?	Relevant department managers, supervisors, and incumbents
Is there general understanding of these objectives?	
Social Influences	
What is the general feeling in the organization regarding meeting goals and objectives?	Top management
What is the social pressure in your department regarding these goals and objectives, and regarding productivity?	Relevant department managers, supervisors, and incumbents
Reward Systems	
What are the rewards, and how are they distributed?	Top management
Are there incentives, are they tied to the goals and objectives?	Relevant department managers, supervisors, and incumbents
What specifically do high performers get as rewards?	
Job Design	
How are the jobs organized?	Relevant supervisors and incumbents, perhaps relevant department managers
Where does their work/material/information come from, where do they send it when done?	
Does the design of the job in any way inhibit incumbents from being high performers?	
Job Performance	
How do employees know what level of performance is acceptable?	Relevant supervisors and incumbents
How do they find out if their level of performance is acceptable?	
Is there a formal feedback process (performance appraisal for example)?	
Are there opportunities for help if required?	
Methods and Practices	
What are the policies/procedures/rules in the organization? Which if any inhibit performance?	Relevant department managers, supervisors, and incumbents

Operational Analysis

When an OPG is identified, an operational analysis is conducted in conjunction with the organizational analysis to fully understand the nature of the OPG. The operational analysis determines exactly what is required of employees for them to be effective. The typical technique for obtaining the task and KSA data that are required to meet expected job performance standards is the job analysis. Table 4-3 shows sources for operational analysis data. The most frequently used process includes questioning employees doing the job and their supervisors. Let's now examine this process of analyzing a job and the issues to consider.

Analyzing the Job

HR employees need to know how to conduct an effective job analysis. The following steps are useful in doing this.

Table 4-3 Recommended Data Sources for Operational Analysis

SOURCES FOR OBTAINING JOB DATA	TRAINING NEED IMPLICATIONS	PRACTICAL CONCERNS
1. Job Descriptions	This source outlines the job's typical duties and responsibilities but is not meant to be all inclusive.	Need to determine how developed. Often written up quickly by supervisor or incumbent with little understanding of what is required
2. Job Specifications	These are specified tasks required for each job. More specific than job descriptions and may include judgments of required KSAs.	May be product of the job description and suffer from the same problems
3. Performance Standards	This source provides objectives related to the tasks required and their standards in terms of performance.	Very useful if available, and accurate, but often organizations do not have formal performance standards
4. Ask Questions About the Job a. Of the job holders b. Of the supervisor	Asking both job holder and relevant supervisors provides accurate data.	Must be done correctly to be of value

What Is the Job?   The first step is to determine exactly what job is going to be analyzed. In today's environment, a common job title can mask real differences in the tasks that are carried out. An extreme example is at Honda Canada Manufacturing, where everyone from line workers to top management has the job title of "Associate." Other organizations use the same job title for employees who do different tasks because they work in different departments and geographical locations.

Where to Collect Data?   As Table 4-3 indicates, data can be gathered from a number of sources. Job descriptions and specifications are one source of data for understanding the job and its basic requirements. If this information was gathered through a job analysis, you can be confident of its value. Even if it was not, it provides a basic understanding of the job and is useful to have before starting to ask questions of these employees.

Who to Ask?   When analyzing a job, the incumbent needs to provide relevant information about the job; after all, she is the expert regarding how the job is done. Data should also be gathered from the incumbent's supervisor because

- This information provides a different perspective and helps yield a well-rounded concept of exactly what is required.
- When discrepancies are noted between what the supervisor and the incumbents say, an investigation into the reason for the discrepancy can provide useful information.

Earlier, we suggested that trainers need organizational development (OD) skills. In this instance, those skills provide an effective way of resolving differences between incumbents and supervisors regarding how the job should be performed. A more proactive approach is to avoid conflicting beliefs between subordinates and supervisors in the first place by implementing the **job expectation technique.**[9] This technique includes facilitating a meeting between subordinates and supervisors to discuss the job responsibilities of the subordinates. The goal here is to clarify job expectations. This process may sound simplistic, but it requires trust and respect between supervisors and their subordinates. In reality, many job incumbents learn about their job through working with other incumbents and through trial and error.

Who Should Select Incumbents?   The selection process should be carried out by the job analyst, not the supervisor or manager. If you let supervisors make the decision, they might choose on the basis of who is available at the time, to whom they prefer to give the opportunity, or any other reasons that quite likely would result in a biased sample. Perhaps more important, however, is that the incumbents might question the real purpose of the assessment and provide inaccurate data.

How Many to Ask?   Different jobs in any organization are filled with different numbers of incumbents. Exactly how many to ask is determined by your method of data gathering and the amount of time available. Let's say that a job has five classification levels with 20 incumbents in each level, for a total of 100 incumbents. You have chosen to interview in small groups. You might have four interview sessions, each with five incumbents—one from each level. If time allowed, you might want to double the sessions to eight for increased participation and a more representative sample.

How to Select?   The best way to select the participants is through representative sampling of all those incumbents who are performing "adequately or better" on the job. The incumbents need to be placed into subgroups on the basis of relevant characteristics, such as their level in the job (e.g., mechanic 1, mechanic 2). Once the categories are developed within the job, the job analyst should choose within these categories on the basis of other factors, such as years in the category, performance level, gender, and so on, to ensure that different views of the job are obtained. Note that we do not advocate random sampling. Random sampling is effective only when you have large numbers of incumbents who are similar, which is seldom the case in a particular job. One other issue needs to be considered. What if the number of incumbents is large and they are scattered across the country? Table 4-4 provides the process used to identify the tasks and KSAs for salespeople at a large computer firm in the United States with offices all across the country. Because of the breadth of the job—many different types of equipment (hardware) were sold—and the many different locations, the needs analysis was a major undertaking. The effort was worthwhile, however, because important information was obtained. For example, it was determined that irrespective of the type of hardware sold (cash register or computer), similar tasks and identical KSAs were required. It was also determined that the job was the same in Los Angeles as it was in Detroit. Finally, from the importance scale, it was determined that a number of tasks and KSAs, although performed, were not critical to effective job performance. For example, knowledge of computer operations, and program language, as well as the ability to write simple computer programs were beneficial but not necessary because it was possible to obtain such support in the field.

From these data, the company was able to refocus its selection procedures to include the KSAs necessary at the time of hire and to provide its training department with a clear picture of the training necessary after the salespeople were hired.

What to Ask About?   Several job analysis techniques are available for gathering information about a job. The two main categories are worker-oriented and task-oriented approaches. A **worker-oriented job analysis** focuses on the KSAs that are required on the job rather than on the tasks or behaviors. Incumbents are asked to rate how important a list of KSAs (e.g., far visual differentiation—the ability to differentiate details at distances beyond arm's length—use of precision tools, use of measuring devices) is to the job (see Figure 4-2). A drawback of this approach is that task statements are not available to show how the KSAs are linked to the tasks. Such a link not only provides justification for the KSA requirements but also can be used to develop scenarios for use in the actual training.

The **task-oriented job analysis,** as the name implies, identifies the various work activities (tasks) required to perform the job. After the tasks are identified, systematically examine these tasks to determine the KSAs necessary to perform them. Now you have justification for the KSAs and potential ideas for developing training. That is why this approach is preferred for a TNA.

One example of the task-oriented approach is the **job-duty-task method,** depicted in Figure 4-3. Note that the job is identified first, and then each of the duties is

Table 4-4   Assessment Procedure Followed by a Large U.S. Computer Firm

1. *Define the job in question.* The analyst met with management to discuss the scope of the assessment. It was determined that the assessment would include all salespeople in the company.

2. *Who to ask.* Because of possible differences between what was being done in offices in different states, incumbents who work in each state would need to provide input. Furthermore, because of the different types of equipment being sold by different salespeople, it would be necessary to have a representative number of incumbents from these subgroups.

3. *What method to use.* Because of the need to include a large number of incumbents who were located in different geographical regions and sold different equipment, the questionnaire method was chosen. This allowed a large number of incumbents to provide input that could be easily analyzed.

4. *Develop a questionnaire.* To develop a questionnaire relevant to the job, the analyst obtained job descriptions from the various locations and for the different types of hardware being sold. He then met with incumbents (in small groups) and with supervisors (in separate small groups) to obtain input on what tasks were done. After the tasks were identified, he asked them to indicate the KSAs that they believed were necessary to do the tasks. The small-group interviews were scheduled so that out-of-state incumbents who were to be at the head office for other reasons could attend, thus providing input from the various states.

5. *Rate importance of tasks and KSAs.* The questionnaire included all the tasks and KSAs that had been identified. Two ratings were requested for each task and KSA. The first related to how important the task (KSA) was to successful job performance (see below).

How Important Is the Task

   1 Not Very Important Poor performance on this task will not affect the overall performance of the job.

   2 Somewhat Important Poor performance on this task will have a moderate effect on the overall performance of the job.

   3 Important Poor performance on this task will have an effect on the overall performance of the job.

   4 Very Important Poor performance on this task will have a serious effect on the overall performance of the job.

6. *Rate task importance for new hires.* The other rating was related to how important it was to be able to do the task successfully at the time of hire. The scale for that rating is below.

Importance at the Time of Hire

   1 Not Important A person requires no specific capability in this area when hired. Training will be provided for an individual to become proficient in this area.

   2 Somewhat Important A person must have only a basic capability in this area when hired. Experience on the job or training is the primary method for becoming proficient in this area.

   3 Important A person must show considerable proficiency in this area when hired. There is time or training available only to provide "fine tuning" once the person is on the job.

   4 Very Important A person must be completely proficient in this area when hired. There is no time or training procedure available to help an individual become proficient in this area after being placed on the job.

7. *Send out questionnaire.* The questionnaire was sent to all incumbents and their immediate supervisors.

8. *Analyze data.* Returned data were analyzed to determine if there were any differences between states and between salespeople who sold different hardware.

9. *Display analysis data.* Those tasks that came up with a mean rating of 2.5 and above were placed in the relevant quadrants (see below).

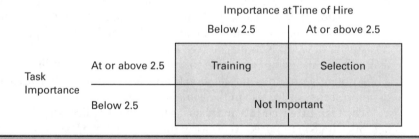

Figure 4-2
Worker-Oriented
Approach

Information Input

Note on Rating "Importance to This Job":

Rate each of the items in the questionnaire using the "Importance to This Job" scale. Each item is to be rated on how important the activity described is to the completion of the job. Consider such factors as amount of time spent, the possible influence on overall job performance if the worker does not properly perform this activity, etc.

	Importance to This Job scale
N	Does not apply
1	Very minor
2	Low
3	Average
4	High
5	Extreme

1. _____Far visual differentiation (seeing differences in the details of the objects, events, or features *beyond arm's reach,* for example, operating a vehicle, landscaping, sports officiating, etc.)

2. _____Depth perception (judging the distance from the observer to objects, or the distances between objects as they are positioned in space, as in operating a crane, operating a dentist's drill, handling and positioning objects, etc.)

3. _____Color perception (differentiating or identifying objects, materials, or details thereof on the basis of color)

4. _____Sound pattern recognition (recognizing different patterns or sequences of sounds; for example, those involved in Morse code, heartbeats, engines not functioning correctly, etc.)

5. _____Sound differentiation (recognizing differences or changes in sounds in their loudness, pitch, and/or tone quality; for example, piano tuner, sound system repairman)

written out. The writing out of the duties provides a stimulus to generate tasks and subtasks for each of these duties. From the duties, identify the relevant tasks and any subtasks each of these tasks might have. Once all the tasks are identified, identify the relevant KSAs required to perform each of these tasks. This provides the justification for requiring these KSAs. It is also possible to list all duties first, followed by tasks and subtasks for each duty, and then go back and identify the KSAs for each of the

Figure 4-3 Form for Recording Task Analysis Results Using the Job-Duty-Task Method of Job Analysis

Job Title: _____   Specific Duty: _____

Tasks	Subtasks	Knowledge and Skills Required
_____	_____	_____
1. _____	1. _____	_____
	2. _____	_____
	3. _____	_____
2. _____	1. _____	_____
	2. _____	_____
	3. _____	_____
3. _____	1. _____	_____
	2. _____	_____

Source: Adapted from Mills, Pace, and Peterson (1988).

tasks and subtasks. It is equally appropriate to go through each duty, determine the subtasks, and then identify the required KSAs before moving to the next duty.

Determining what the incumbents do in the job identifies the duties, tasks, and subtasks. This information is generally obtained by interviewing several incumbents and their supervisors. The list of tasks necessary to do the job is developed by systematically examining each duty and inquiring about the tasks. Identifying the required KSAs is carried out through the examination of each task and asking the question, "What KSAs are necessary to perform a particular task?"

Figure 4-4 depicts an example of a completed job-duty-task method for the job of a HR professional.

Another step in the process is to determine how critical each of the tasks is and how important it is to be able to perform the task at the time of hire. By determining this aspect, you can identify those tasks that new employees will be expected to be able to perform at the time of hire and those that new employees will not need at the time of hire (those that will require training). To obtain this information, ask those providing information to rate each of the tasks on a scale such as the one depicted in Table 4-4. This step not only documents the importance of the tasks but also provides valuable evidence for which KSAs will be used in selecting employees and which will not (and therefore require training). Finally, the KSAs necessary to perform each of the important tasks and subtasks are identified. These aspects should also be rated for importance to the job and importance at the time of hire.

Figure 4-4 Applying the Job-Duty-Task Method to the Job of Human Resource Professional

Job Title: HRD Professional		Specific Duty: Task Analysis
Tasks	**Subtasks**	**Knowledge and Skills Required**
1. List tasks	1. Observe behavior	List four characteristics of behavior Classify behavior
	2. Select verb	Have knowledge of action verbs Have grammatical skills
	3. Record behavior	State so understood by others Record neatly
2. List subtasks	1. Observe behavior	List all remaining acts Classify behavior
	2. Select verb	State correctly Have grammatical skill
	3. Record behavior	Record so it is neat and understood by others
3. List knowledge	1. State what must be known	Classify all information
	2. Determine complexity of skill	Determine whether skills represent a series of acts that must be learned in a sequence

Source: Adapted from Mills, Pace, and Peterson (1988).

Table 4-5 A Comparison of the Outcomes for Worker- and Task-Oriented Approaches to Job Analysis

Job	Task-Oriented Approach	Worker-Oriented Approach
Garage Attendant	Checks tire pressure	Obtains information from visual displays
Machinist	Checks thickness of crankshaft	Use of a measuring device
Dentist	Drills out decay from teeth	Use of precision instruments
Forklift Driver	Loads pallets of washers onto trucks	High level of eye-hand coordination

To understand the difference between the worker-oriented and task-oriented approaches, note the different results obtained using each of these methods, as depicted in Table 4-5.

If There Are No Incumbents Available   Incumbents are a critical group for obtaining information about the job in a job analysis. But what if no incumbents are available? In today's environment of fast-changing technology, jobs are constantly changing. In some cases, new technology creates a job that requires skills distinctly different from the job it is replacing. In the example cited earlier in this chapter, management at the Heinz plant in Leamington ordered a state-of-the-art ketchup machine. Previously, ketchup was made with low-technology equipment. This new machine required new skills, so the issue was to figure out how to perform a job analysis for a job that did not exist. Dr. Mitchell Fields was approached by Heinz Canada to assist in determining the selection and training requirements for the new job. Table 4-6 describes how Dr. Fields did this.

Table 4-6 Job Analysis When There Are No Incumbents

The H. J. Heinz Company in Leamington, Ontario, Canada, is unionized. The union contract stipulates that new jobs go to existing employees. The company was purchasing a new machine for making ketchup and wanted to be sure that those selected for this new job would have the KSAs to do the job. A person analysis indicated that most employees did not have much formal education and had very low reading levels. An operational analysis (job analysis) is necessary to determine future KSAs needed. But how do you do a job analysis when there are no incumbents, as the job does not exist? Dr. Fields outlines how he did the job analysis.

1. I contacted the manufacturer of the new equipment and asked if that or similar equipment was being used elsewhere, so that job analysis data could be obtained from another company. In this case, no other application existed.

2. I obtained specifications and operating manuals for the new machinery. The manuals were incomplete and difficult to understand. In fact, they were more complex than they needed to be. As a result, initially I thought that a high level of reading comprehension would be necessary.

3. I interviewed engineers who were responsible for designing the new machinery. This is where I received important information as to its operation. However, the engineers tended to overestimate the level of aptitude required. They believed that operators would be making modifications to the programming software. Further discussions revealed that for the operator's job, reading requirements were minimal. Operating manuals were needed only for maintenance and repair.

4. I obtained blueprints and layouts of the physical equipment and flowcharts of the operating software. This material indicated that the operators would be required to interface with a user-friendly, icon-driven software package (far less than the complex programming tasks envisioned by the engineers).

5. I identified two main tasks. First, the operators would be required to keep track of the mechanical operations of a number of different (but integrated) assembly operations. I determined, therefore, that mechanical aptitude was necessary. Second, the operators had to look at a two-dimensional video display terminal (VDT) and make decisions about the three-dimensional assembly-line operation. Having skill in spatial relations, therefore, would also be important.

6. On the basis of the skills identified, I suggested two subtests of the Differential Aptitude Test for use in selection of employees: mechanical comprehension and spatial relations tests. All operators were selected from current employees. The major advantage to these two tests is that reading level (which was determined not to be important) is not a factor.

What You Should Get from the Job Analysis (EP)

Using the task-oriented approach yields both the tasks and KSAs required to perform the job. KSAs are important, as it is the KSAs that need to be trained. But the tasks are also important for the following reasons:

- Identifying the expected behavior that needs to be performed on the job and performance deficits
- Developing actual training programs
- Making subsequent evaluations of the training.[10]

Knowing all the tasks that are necessary to be effective in a particular job provides justification for the KSAs that employees are expected to have. In the ketchup machine example, the machine operator was required to watch a video display (which is two-dimensional) and make decisions about the assembly line (which is three-dimensional). This justifies the need for spatial relations skills as a job requirement.

A list of job-related tasks would also help develop training. Once the tasks to be performed are known, training that closely resembles the real job can be developed. Consider the job of a customer service representative. We determined that one of the important tasks is to "deal with irate customers." We used this task to help develop role-plays that closely emulate the real job. The use of real-task behaviors in training makes the training more relevant and interesting to trainees and assists in the transfer of training.

Finally, we can use task information to develop tests that are reflective not only of the training but also of the job. These tests can be used in the person analysis phase to identify those with training needs and can also serve to evaluate the effectiveness of training.* Task identification leads to identification of the KSAs necessary to do the job.

Knowledge All jobs require some type of knowledge. The job analysis should provide a list of tasks that, when examined, will point to the knowledge requirements necessary to be successful. For example, if one of the tasks identified is to edit manuscripts using Microsoft Word, then an inferred declarative knowledge requirement would be knowledge of Microsoft Word edit functions. Going back to our customer service job, we find that knowledge of "steps in a conflict resolution model" would be important.

An Alternate Approach Assessing the need for declarative knowledge is possible using traditional methods of job analysis, as just discussed. Some argue, however, that with the increased complexity of jobs in today's workforce, analysis of tasks alone is not sufficient; we need to determine the knowledge requirements at the procedural or strategic levels.[11] The concern is that if the job is reduced to individual tasks, the interrelatedness and complexity of the job is lost.

The operational analysis for higher levels of knowledge would be accomplished by examining the mental models of experts. Here an "expert" could be a high-performing incumbent or someone who performs the same job in another context (e.g., computer programmer). These types of analysis would be useful when more advanced training is required. Techniques such as multidimensional scaling and link-weighted methods can be used to identify such structures.[12] Space does not permit us to explore this area in detail, but those interested in this approach should consult more advanced texts and research papers.[13]

Skill The job analysis should provide a list of all skills required to successfully perform the job. Consider again our customer service representative's task of "dealing with an irate customer." This task requires conflict resolution skills. The skills should

---

*More will be said about how to develop tests in the person analysis section below.

be identified as to the level of mastery required (e.g., compilation vs. automaticity). A completed job analysis will identify a complete list of required KSAs for the job, thus providing needs analysis with an understanding of all the job requirements.

Attitude   What are the attitudinal outcomes from the job analysis? Many job analysts do not incorporate attitudes into their model of job analysis.[14] The job analysis gives an understanding of the tasks that must be carried out. For each task required, knowledge and skills are inferred. However, many analysts stop here, and that is not a good idea. We believe that attitudes are important. They surface in our behavior, so an employee with a poor attitude toward customers is inattentive to customer needs.[15] To determine attitudes of importance to the job, simply ask the question, "Can you think of any attitudes or feelings a person could have that might facilitate or inhibit an employee from doing any part of this job well?"

What attitudes should a customer service representative have to be successful? Would a positive attitude toward helping people be useful? What about a job that requires working in teams? Here, a person should have a positive attitude toward the team approach or perhaps have a positive attitude toward working with others. Such data provide the analyst with information on what should be addressed in training. Just such an issue was of concern in the new Ford assembly plant (see Training in Action 4-2). In this instance, the incumbents were unavailable because the plant was not yet open. So the needs analysis was conducted using their supervisors, who were brought on board early to prepare the plant for opening.

Competency Modeling

Another approach to conducting an operational analysis is to identify key competencies of the job. Businesses are increasingly adopting competency models, as they have proven their value as an HR management tool.[16]

TRAINING IN ACTION 4-2
Changing Attitudes Toward the Team Approach

The Ford production plants have moved toward a team approach. The team approach is part of the "Ford Production System." The Windsor Engine Plant was new, and there was an agreement with the Canadian Auto Workers (CAW) stipulating that employees from other plants had first choice of the new jobs.

Employees transferred from other plants for many reasons: cleaner plant, closer to home, old job being phased out, and so forth. Few transferred to work in a team environment. In fact, it is well known that the CAW traditionally opposes such efforts. They made an exception in the case of the Windsor Engine Plant.

In the determination of the skills needed, it became evident that many of the employees would be older, and the concern was that they would be set in their ways and generally against the team approach. The training consisted of team skills such as communication, effective meeting, and problem-solving skills. Also, a component was added to influence attitudes toward the team approach.

This "component" consisted of an orientation to the team process. Modules were designed to show the advantages of teams for the company and workers. An exercise called "Best Job/Worst Job" allowed trainees to describe what they considered to be a "best job." Then trainees were asked to consider what teamwork provided in terms of what they would do. Trainees discovered that their own description of a "best job" looked quite similar to what their job would look like in a team environment. The training also provided a six-hour session on individual growth and self-fulfillment. It was assumed that helping employees to focus on these issues would improve their attitudes toward the team approach.

Did the training have a significant impact on attitudes? No one knows for sure. After all the time and money spent on the training, there was no formal evaluation of the process. This omission should not be a surprise, as you will see in Chapter 9 on evaluation.

A **competency** is a cluster of related KSAs that differentiates high performers from average performers.[17] This definition is specific to North America. Other countries, such as the United Kingdom and Australia, define competencies as simply "what someone needs to be doing to be competent at their job."[18]

Some disagreement arises as to whether deriving competencies is a process different from job analysis. Some experts in the HR field indicate that the process is the same, but the majority suggest that it is different.[19] To this majority, the major difference is that job analysis derives "tasks" or the "what" that is done on the job, leading to the determination of knowledge and skills but not attitudes. A competency-based approach focuses on all the characteristics that underlie successful performance,[20] not just on the knowledge and skills derived from the tasks. Competencies place equal weight on attitudes, feelings, and motivation, in addition to knowledge and skills. Because we incorporate attitudes into our job analysis model, we agree with both sets of experts. Although the data derived are somewhat different for competencies, the process for determining competencies is similar to the typical job analysis. Before discussing the "how-to" regarding competencies, let's look at the makeup of one.

Consider the competency "time management" for a manager. Skills for this competency include delegating work, prioritizing assignments, and making to-do lists. The knowledge required is "knowledge of the value of a manager's time." For example, if the manager knew that she was valued at $120 per hour, it would help her see the value of determining what she does and what she should delegate. Attitudes reflecting "I have no one I can trust to do this," "I cannot say no," or "It is quicker if I do it myself" all get in the way of effective delegation, which in turn affects time management.

Why Competencies?   When compared with KSAs, competencies exhibit the following characteristics:

- They are more general in nature.
- They show a longer-term fit.
- They include knowledge, skills, feelings, and motivation.
- They tie into corporate goals.[21]

Competencies tend to be of a more general nature and, therefore, applicable to several jobs. In some cases, competencies are applicable to everyone at a particular level no matter what department, such as all first-line supervisors, or even multiple levels of a job, such as all managers. Northern Telecom, for example, developed a set of competencies relevant to all their managers (see Training in Action 4-3). Note that for different levels of management, the competency remains the same, but the behaviors expected are different. In this way, the focus is always on the same set of key competencies but with a different behavior, depending on the management level.

In today's environment, jobs are always changing. Even shop-floor jobs are under constant change, in many cases requiring more decision-making and other new responsibilities. This constant evolving means that the specifics obtained in job analysis can become dated. A more general focus of competencies is advantageous to such ever-changing jobs.[22]

Using competencies makes it easier to identify the emotional aspects of work performance. For example, organizations increasingly focus on issues such as "meeting customer expectations." This area of the job, which requires dealing with people rather than producing goods, requires a broad view of good performance. Many argue that this broad view is easier to obtain using competency models.

Finally, in the process of developing the job competencies, a great deal of effort is made to understand the business context and competitive strategy. Competencies are

Northern Telecom developed a list of Core Values for the company.

Excellence: We have only one standard, excellent.
Teamwork: We share one vision and are a team.
Customers: We create superior value for our customers.
Commitment: We do what we say we do.
Innovation : We embrace change.
People: Our people are our strength.

Northern Telecom instituted a performance appraisal and development process based on the "People" value. In separate meetings with their supervisors, all employees had the opportunity to work on the development of objectives and their own development. The common competencies that are applicable to all managers are defined differently at each level.

One of these competencies and the relevant descriptions is listed below.

COMPETENCY	DEMONSTRATION OF THE COMPETENCY		
	FIRST LEVEL	MID LEVEL	SENIOR LEVEL
Customer Orientation	Develops customer consciousness in others	Understands customer needs and translates to the goals of the organization	Establishes a relationship at the strategic level
	Communicates and resolves conflict	Fosters process improvement and change with linkages to customer groups	Gains trust of customers
	Ensures work (own and team) exceeds customer expectations	Instills and maintains customer focus of work unit	Formulates strategies to meet identified and anticipated requirements
			Is considered by customers to be an extension of the organization

then developed with a focus on these broader goals of the organization in conjunction with the specific job in question.[23]

How You Develop Competencies Several methods have been used to develop competency models.[24] According to Maxine Dalton of the Center for Creative Leadership, some are not very effective. She indicated that about 70 percent of competency models are just a list of positive attributes obtained in a half-day meeting with senior management.[25]

Generally, more methodologically sound procedures entail the following process:

- Meet with upper management to
  - determine strategies, goals, specific challenges, or specific focus, and
  - generate some tentative competencies.

- Identify specific jobs.
- Meet with high performers of those jobs and their supervisors to
  - determine critical incidents that make "high performers" different from average performers,
  - focus on the aspects that tie into the strategic direction of the company, and
  - formulate some tentative competencies.

- Determine the competencies that overlap with upper-management competencies.

- Verify the preceding information with another group of high performers and their supervisors.
- Link this information to job analysis information obtained from the job to articulate specific KSAs that make up the competency.

Regarding the last point, competency models are more general and fit several jobs. Linking these competencies to the KSAs of the job will ensure that the competencies are not only valid but also able to stand up in court. This linkage also provides the information needed to develop training. Having the KSAs that make up the competency helps determine what the training should look like.

Concerns about Competencies   When carried out correctly, a job analysis is scientific and defendable in court. It reflects what is required to do the job, thus making selection, training, and performance appraisal relevant and valid. To date, there have been no challenges to competency models, but they are not typically developed with the same rigor as a job analysis.[26] Also, as often occurs with new ideas, organizations develop competency models with little understanding of the process outlined above (see Training in Action 4-4). Competency models, however, will continue to be developed, particularly for training and development, for the following reasons:

- Training based only on task analysis can become dated quickly as the nature of work undergoes constant dynamic change.
- Hourly paid employees are expected to participate much more in decision making and ensure customer satisfaction, rather than simply produce a product.
- Corporate downsizing forces a move away from tight job design to more flexible job design.
- Competencies help the HRD department focus its training.

TRAINING IN ACTION 4-4
Development of Competencies

Scott Parry is the chairman of Training House, Inc., a consulting firm. He was discussing some issues with a client when the topic turned to competencies. The client indicated to Mr. Parry that she had just completed a six-month survey of her company's managers to determine what the essential competencies were that would result in their having a world-class performance team. She indicated that so far she had gathered 78 competencies, and asked Mr. Parry if he would mind looking at them. Perhaps, she said, he could think of some important ones that they had not thought of. Of course Mr. Parry, whose training firm deals with these issues all the time, indicates that when done properly, somewhere between 10 and 14 competencies should result.

The problem is that most managers and many trainers do not understand what a competency is.

When an exercise such as the one above is set up to generate competencies, often what is obtained is a list of what managers believe is important to effective performance. The list below is a dozen that were obtained from the client in question.

Initiative	Negotiation	Analyticity
Self-esteem	Counseling	Intuitive
Decisiveness	Interviewing	Action Oriented

This looks like a list of what you would like a person to be like and not what is required to be effective on the job, and that is the problem. Too often the exercise is not done in a methodologically sound way to obtain the information you really want; and so you get wish lists of traits, characteristics, skills, and attitudes with little organization to them.

Source: Parry, S. "Just what is a competency?" *Training* (June 1998), pp. 59–64.

This latter point is particularly important. Competencies not only are related to each managerial level in the organization but also are tied to the strategic direction of the organization. Furthermore, by definition, competencies are what separates high performers from others. With limited resources, decisions related to what needs to be provided in the way of management training are clear.

In very well run organizations, the HR department has a human resource information system (HRIS). This system provides information on individual managers in terms of what positions they have held, what training they have received, their performance levels related to the competencies, and, of specific interest to the HRD department, required competency training for managers. This system makes the task of identifying what training needs to be offered much easier. Examination of the HRIS tells the HRD manager how many need training in each of the competencies. Use of competencies also makes it easier for managers to identify employee strengths and weaknesses, thereby facilitating the development goals for employees. The easier and clearer the process is, the more likely managers will take the time to do it.[27]

Some concern might be raised that competencies are not developed with the rigor of job analysis, and the lack of specificity might not be able to withstand possible court challenges. We argue that as with any tool, proper methodology will result in relevant and definable competencies. Organizations that decide to use competencies should not abandon job analysis, but use its methodology to demonstrate the link between the relevant KSAs and key competencies of the job.

Now let's go back and consider the total operational analysis process, whether KSAs or competencies are used. Data related to the job are gathered to determine standards for acceptable performance. From these standards, criteria are developed. Developing criteria is an important but complex process, so an examination of the issues involved in criterion development is presented in Appendix 4.1. Understanding this information will also help you understand the criterion issues related to evaluation presented in Chapter 9.

Person Analysis

The operational analysis determines the tasks (or competencies) and KSAs necessary to reach or exceed EP. A person analysis will identify those incumbents who are not meeting the performance requirements and will determine why. Here, each employee is examined to determine who does not have the necessary KSAs to meet performance expectations. Imagine that the EOP for a department that assembles widgets is five rejects per month. This department's AOP is 20 rejects per month. This triggers a TNA. The operational analysis identifies the KSAs necessary to build the widgets properly. A person analysis is conducted to determine which, if any, of the employees do not have these KSAs. Those employees will be sent to training. Recall from the needs analysis model at the beginning of the chapter that the formula for a PG is:

$$Expected\ performance - Actual\ performance = Performance\ gap*$$

A PG is most often thought of in the reactive sense, as the difference between EP and AP. For example, assume that the standard number of snowmobile trailers that a "Builder Class 2" is expected to produce is 1.5 per day. For the last three weeks, three employees in this class are averaging 0.6 trailers per day. The PG is 0.9 trailers per day (1.5 − .6 = .9).

---

*Recall that this "performance gap" is different from the "organizational performance gap" in that it is obtained through comparing the operational analysis (what is required) with the person analysis (how the person actually performs). It is the combination of PGs that create the OPG.

In the proactive analysis, the EOP is what is needed in the future and AOP is the likely performance level with current KSAs. Suppose that the trailer manufacturer in the preceding example decides to purchase equipment that will bend the trailer frame to the correct shape, eliminating several welds. The engineering studies indicate that this change in production process will increase the "Builder Class 2" output to three trailers per day. At the present KSA level, "Builder Class 2" employees are expected to produce 1.5 trailers per day. Here, the PG is the "future" required performance level (three trailers per day) minus their predicted performance level in the future, given their current level of KSAs. This PG will be 1.5 trailers per day. In addition to collecting information regarding the PG, you should also examine individual differences that might be present in the trainee population, which might affect the type of training you offer. Self-efficacy of trainees, for example, has been shown to be an important variable related to successful completion of training. Refer back to Figure 3-6 (page 82) for a number of areas to consider related to individual differences.

Where to Collect Data (AP)

Table 4-7 shows sources for person analysis information. We will discuss two of the more commonly used sources, performance appraisal and proficiency tests, in some detail. We will also address the less commonly used attitude survey.

Performance Appraisal   Supervisors are the ones who most often complete performance appraisals.[28] If supervisory ratings actually provided an accurate assessment of an employee's deficiencies, other assessment tools would hardly be necessary. But these ratings often suffer from a lack of reliability and validity for a number of reasons:

- Lack of supervisor training on how to use appraisals
- Lack of opportunity for the supervisor to see substantial amounts of a subordinate's performance
- Rater errors such as bias and halo and leniency effects, among others
- Poorly developed appraisals and appraisal processes

If appraisal instruments are developed properly and the process of completing them is followed conscientiously, performance appraisals can be a valuable source of employee training needs. The literature, however, suggests that this is not often the case.

Supervisor ratings provide less-than-accurate assessments of the incumbent's KSAs for both political and interpersonal reasons.[29] This inaccuracy is less likely to occur if performance appraisal information is gathered specifically for employee development, where the climate in the organization fosters such development.[30]

Several things can be done to minimize problems with supervisor ratings, such as:

- Have the appraisal system be relevant to the job. Sometimes appraisals are too generic to meet specific needs. Also, they need to be acceptable to both supervisor and employee.[31]
- Be sure that the supervisor has access to relevant information to make accurate appraisals. As noted earlier, in some cases, supervisors are not in contact with subordinates often enough on the job to be aware of their performance.[32]
- Provide incentives for supervisors to complete accurate ratings. One way to do this is to use the performance appraisal for the TNA only. As Murphy and Cleveland note,

  "It is likely that a supervisor experiences little conflict when information from a performance appraisal is being used for providing feedback to employees on their strengths and weaknesses and to recommend employees to training programs."[33]

Table 4-7 Data Sources for Person Analysis

Sources for Obtaining Data	Training Need Implications	Remarks
1. Supervisor Performance Appraisals	Useful if done specifically for TNA.	Supervisor ratings often not just for TNA, and often not done well.
2. Performance Data		Useful, easy to analyze and quantify for the purposes of determining actual performance.
a. Productivity		
b. Absenteeism and tardiness		
c. Accidents		
d. Grievances		
e. Waste		
f. Product quality		
g. Downtime		
h. Customer complaints		
3. Observation—Work Sampling	More subjective technique but provides both employee behavior and results of the behavior.	This is done effectively in some situations such as customer service where employees know that the telephone calls employees answer from customers can be monitored.
4. Interviews/Questionnaires	Individual knows her areas of training need. Also involvement in TNA motivates employees to learn.	Need to be sure employee believes it is in her best interest to be honest; otherwise, she may not be forthcoming as you would like.
5. Proficiency Tests	Can be tailor-made or standardized.	Care in the development of scoring keys is important and difficult to do if not trained in the process.
a. Job knowledge		
b. Skills	Care must be taken so that they measure job-related qualities.	
c. Achievement		
6. Attitude Surveys	Useful to determine morale, motivation, and satisfaction.	Important to use well-developed scales of employees.
7. Devised Situations	Certain knowledge, skills, and or attitudes are demonstrated in these techniques.	Useful, but again, care in development of scoring criteria is important.
a. Role-play		
b. Case study		
c. Business games		
d. In basket		
8. Assessment Centers	Combination of several of the above techniques into an intensive assessment program.	Although expensive, these are very good as they use multiple raters and exercises to assess employees. Also, criteria for performance are well developed.
9. Coaching	Similar to interview, one to one.	Must choose coaches carefully and train them if you want them to be effective.
10. Individual's objectives	Shows the relationship between performance data and the individuals' goals.	Good process when implemented properly.

One way to obtain better ratings is to provide training on how to complete such appraisals. Training should address how to avoid various types of rater bias, such as halo[34] and leniency[35] effects.

    Another concern is that for some jobs, such as teaching and sales, supervisors do not often get to see the employee in action. Sometimes the supervisor is unfamiliar with the job details. Perhaps the best way to deal with these concerns is similar to the method suggested for dealing with gathering job analysis data: The more the perspectives, the better the picture. For this reason, it is useful to consider additional potential raters of employee performance.

Self-Ratings   A possible way to determine employee needs is through self-ratings. Much of the research on self-ratings suggests that the individual tends to overrate her capabilities. However, evidence also indicates that the inflated ratings are a function of the rating instruments rather than the individual attempting to sound better.[36] Also, when self-raters understand the performance system, they are more likely to agree with supervisor ratings.[37] These findings suggest that self-ratings are accurate if subordinates are more involved in the development of the appraisal process.

McEnery and McEnery examined self-ratings and supervisory ratings gathered for a needs analysis related to training.[38] They noted that self-ratings were inflated but were also more discriminating in identifying different needs than were supervisory ratings. Furthermore, the results suggested that supervisory assessment of "subordinate needs" more closely resembled the needs of the raters themselves. More recent research noted that self-ratings actually have lower measurement errors than supervisor ratings on some performance dimensions.[39] In short, self-ratings are an important part of any needs assessment.

Generally, the more sources used to gather information, the higher the reliability and validity of the results. This tendency supports use of the **360-degree performance review,** by which an employee rates himself on a number of dimensions and receives ratings on these dimensions from his supervisor, peers, subordinates, and sometimes even customers.[40] This information is fed back to the individual. This broader view takes pressure off the supervisor, especially when others in the loop agree more with the supervisor than with the individual. Such data provide a springboard for dialogue between the supervisor and the subordinate regarding the subordinate's needs. Also, there is evidence that those being appraised view this process more positively than they do the traditional methods of appraisal.[41]

The advantages of this process are that the various groups see the person under different conditions, maintain different relationships with the individual, and also have different expectations regarding performance. Evidence indicates that ratees find feedback from peers and subordinates particularly useful in planning their developmental goals.[42] As noted before, the more the sources of such information, the better. The disadvantages of the 360-degree performance review are the amount of time it takes and the cost of implementation. If not properly integrated into the company's HR system, it can also lead to negative results.[43] So, for it to be effective, a supportive climate is necessary for development in general,[44] and, as always, support from top management is helpful.[45]

To summarize, performance assessments designed to focus on development are more likely to provide accurate data than are more generic or all-purpose appraisals. Also, to determine developmental needs, both supervisory ratings and self-ratings should be gathered. Both parties need to be involved in the assessment process. As McEnery and McEnery suggest, the supervisor provides a valuable perspective on the subordinate's needs. The subordinate gains insight into his needs through discussion with the supervisor. This process will also improve communication between the supervisor and the subordinate and will serve to improve the accuracy of the assessment. The 360-degree feedback data are also very useful in determining an employee's needs. These data will allow for an examination of the performance from a broader perspective. It is important, however, that if 360-degree feedback is being used, it must be incorporated properly into the organization. United Parcel Service, in Training in Action 4-5, seems to be doing it properly.

TRAINING IN ACTION 4-5
United Parcel Service Uses 360-Degree Feedback and Training

At United Parcel Service (UPS) in Louisville, Kentucky, about 1,200 management employees participate in an automated 360-degree feedback process. Managers are measured on a number of critical skills such as "customer focus," "people skills," "business values," and so forth. But, before any of this happens, HR trainers hold mini training sessions to explain the purpose and process of 360-degree feedback to those involved. At these sessions, training is also provided on how to give and receive feedback. This training uses role plays to help managers learn how to both give and receive, and how to respond.

After receiving training, peers, supervisors, and subordinates rate a manager once every six months, on the critical skills. They do this by completing a questionnaire. The manager then sits down with her supervisor and discusses the feedback. She then sets objectives for improvement over the next six months. The manager has the option of attending programs that provide skills training and practice in the areas requiring improvement. Six months later, the manager receives another round of feedback that indicates any improvement in the areas targeted. How is the process being received? Hope Zoeller Stith, trainer at UPS, indicates that the information sessions that incorporate discussion about the purpose of the process, along with the feedback training, have helped everyone see the benefits of the process. Stith says that employees have reacted very positively.

Source: Wells, S. "A new road: Traveling beyond 360-degree evaluation." *HR Magazine* 4 (1999), pp. 83–91.

Proficiency Tests   Rather than relying on ratings of job performance, an alternative is to test the individual under controlled conditions. Proficiency tests can measure both knowledge (cognitive) and skill (behavioral).

Cognitive Tests   Cognitive tests measure levels of knowledge. Plumbers need to understand government regulations for installing water and drainage systems in a house, supervisors need to understand the procedures for assigning overtime, and salespeople need to understand the procedures for accepting returned merchandise. Any job has a certain amount of knowledge attached to it, and a test to measure that knowledge can be developed. Tests of declarative knowledge can be paper-and-pencil. A concern in using such tests is that they might reflect the reading level of the participant when reading is not an important skill for the job. If you are concerned about the knowledge level of incumbents and reading is not a required KSA, paper-and-pencil tests would not be appropriate. In such cases, these tests could be given orally.

Paper-and-pencil tests offer several advantages, as they

- can be given to large numbers of individuals at once,
- can be scored easily, and
- provide an effective method of determining areas in which there is a lack of knowledge.

The disadvantages include the following:

- Time and effort are required to develop a comprehensive test that is both reliable and valid, and
- If the test format is other than true-false or multiple-choice, developing effective scoring keys takes a great deal of time.

A logical choice in developing a paper-and-pencil test is to use a multiple-choice format. They are easy to administer and score, highly reliable, and able to accurately measure declarative knowledge.[46] Some trainees indicate that they are not good at taking multiple-choice tests. However, evidence suggests that such tests consistently correlate highly with other forms of testing. A big advantage of multiple-choice tests is their reliability. Also, because of the number of questions that can be asked, it is possible to cover a broader range of the content than with other methods. The major difficulty with this type of test is in the construction of the items. A complete discussion on how to write good multiple-choice questions is beyond the scope of this text, but some general rules to consider in constructing questions are found in Figure 4-5. Figure 4-6 provides some examples of common errors in the development of multiple-choice tests and how to fix them. More comprehensive information can be found in *Evaluating Training Programs*, a book published by the American Society for Training and Development.[47] It might be wise to contact a local university and discuss the project with someone who has the appropriate background. Even small companies with limited budgets should be able to obtain such help from a supervised graduate student eager to get some real-world experience.

Behavioral Tests   Behavioral tests measure skills and are an important means of determining an employee's training needs. Such tests can incorporate **work samples,** which are simply work situations designed to reflect what actually happens in the workplace. Standardized rating methods are developed so that everyone is presented with the same situation and measured according to preset criteria. For example, a welder might be required to measure and cut three pieces of channel iron and then weld them at right angles to make a U; a salesclerk might be required to respond to an irate customer who provides standardized antagonistic responses to the salesclerk's handling of a situation; or a manager might be required to make a presentation to a boss on the advantages of going global. An important part of the development of these types of tests is determining the criteria for successful performance. In the case of the welders test noted above, what amount of error in measurement is still considered acceptable; 1/8 inch, 3/16, 3/8? Also, what error in terms of the 90 degree angles is acceptable? And finally how strong does the weld have to be? These data would all be used in grading the welders test, and where she was not up to standards would be the PG for that welder.

  Assessment centers are an expansion of the work sample approach. They often involve several work samples and other tests along with assessors who evaluate individuals in different situations. Although assessment centers are costly to develop and administer (they often require two to three days off-site), they provide a comprehensive analysis of needs, especially for managerial positions.

Attitude Measures   Attitudes are an important part of organizational effectiveness. If, for example, the team approach is an organizational objective, then attitudes toward this approach are important. Some organizations routinely conduct various attitude surveys. In such a situation, a scale related to the attitude toward teamwork could simply be included. If this practice does not exist, it might be useful to consider instituting one. At the very least, organizations could survey trainees before training to determine how they feel about teams and teamwork (if teamwork was a PG).

  Developing attitude scales requires a great deal of skill; therefore, it is much better to use well-developed scales found in the literature. Texts such as *Assessing Organizational Change*[48] and *The Experience of Work*[49] contain a number of attitudinal measures. Another source that publishes such scales is the Institute for Social Research at the University of Michigan.[50] Contacting a local university's psychology department or business school for help in this area would likely yield good results. Graduate students are always anxious to apply their knowledge in real-world situations.

Figure 4-5 Guidelines for Developing a Multiple-Choice Test

1. Examine objectives to gain a clear understanding of the content area to be tested.
2. Write the questions in a clear manner. Shorter is better.
3. Choose alternatives to the correct response that are plausible, take from typical errors made during training. Make alternatives realistic.
4. Do not consistently make the correct response longer than incorrect responses.
5. Limit the number of alternatives to the amount necessary to measure the knowledge or opinion. For measures of knowledge, it is difficult enough to write three reasonable alternatives along with the correct answer. For other types of measures (such as the one below), too many alternatives ask the respondent to make unnecessarily fine discriminations.

   Bad: What percentage of the time are you sure of what your compensation will be?

1	2	3	4	5	6	7	8	9	10
0%–10%	11%–20%	21%–30%	31%–40%	41%–50%	51%–60%	61%–70%	71%–80%	81%–90%	91%–100%

   Good: What percentage of the time are you sure of what your compensation will be?

1	2	3	4	5
0%–20%	21%–40%	41%–60%	61%–80%	81%–100%

6. Place the correct answer randomly among other options.
7. Avoid double negatives. And avoid as much as possible negatively worded questions and alternative. If it is necessary to use negatives, put the negative words in capital letters and underline them. For example, such a question might look something like this: Which of the following alternatives is **NOT** correct?
8. Try to avoid the use of alternatives such as "None of the above" and "All of the above." As much as possible, the alternatives should contain only the correct response.
9. Pretest items by giving the test to those expected to know the material. Ask them for feedback on clarity. Note any questions that many of them get wrong.
10. Give revised items to a group of fully trained (experienced) employees and a group of not trained (inexperienced) employees. The former should score well, and the latter should do poorly.
11. Write simply and clearly, and make the meaning obvious.

    Bad: To what extent do supervisors provide information regarding the quality of performance of people at your level?

    Good: How often does the person you report to give you feedback on your job?

12. Ask one question at a time.

    Bad: Both the organization's goals and my role within the organization are clear.

    Good: The organization's goals are clear.

    My role within the organization is clear.

13. Provide discrete response options.

    Bad: During the past three months, how often did you receive feedback on your work?

1	2	3	4	5
Rarely		Occasionally		Frequently

    Good: During the past three months, how often did you receive feedback on your work?

1	2	3	4	5
Not once	1–3 times	About once a week	More than once a week	Once a day or more

14. Match the response mode to the question.

    Bad: To what extent are you satisfied with your job?

1	2	3	4	5
Strongly disagree	Disagree		Agree	Strongly agree

    Good: To what extent are you satisfied with your job?

1	2	3	4	5
Not at all	A little bit		Quite a lot	Very much

Figure 4-6 Examples of Mistakes in Developing Multiple-Choice Questions

---

Example 1
The stem of the original item below fails to present the problem adequately or to set a frame of reference for responding.

Original	**Revised**
When you have a conflict?	Who should you go to when you have a conflict at work?
a. Superior/Supervisor	a. Superior/Supervisor
b. Subordinate	b. Subordinate
c. Colleague	c. Colleague
d. Customers/Stakeholders	d. Customers/Stakeholders

Example 2
There should be no grammatical clues to the correct answer.

Original	**Revised**
Barack Obama was a:	Barack Obama was:
a. senator from Illinois	a. a senator from Illinois
b. eastern European	b. an Eastern European
c. Arabic prophet	c. an Arabic prophet
d. Imam	d. an Imam

Example 3
Alternatives should not overlap (e.g., in the original form of this item, if either of the first two alternatives is correct, "C" is also correct.)

Original	**Revised**
How old were you when you first started smoking?	How old were you when you first started smoking?
a. While in grade school.	a. Less than 10 years old.
b. While in middle school.	b. Between 10 and 15 years old.
c. Before I graduated from high school	c. Between 16 and 19 years old.
d. After I graduated from high school	d. Over 19 years old.

Example 4
Example of how the greater similarity among alternatives increases the difficulty of the item.

Easier	**Harder**
Which of the following statements about training in different cultures is true?	Which of the following statements about training in different cultures is true?
a. Europeans will resist training that requires trainee involvement.	a. Europeans require training to be attention grabbing.
b. Russians require training to be attention grabbing.	b. Russians require training to be attention grabbing.
c. Asians look forward to the "flash" of North American–style training.	c. Asians require training to be attention grabbing.
d. Greeks require lots of technical components to be successful.	d. Greeks require training to be attention grabbing.

Gathering Data for the TNA: Final Thoughts

For a conceptual understanding of the types of data required to conduct a TNA, it is useful to divide the TNA input phase into three distinct stages: organization, operation, and person. Practically, however, they are highly interrelated and often conducted at the same time. The sources for each of these analyses, as found in Tables 4-1, 4-3, and 4-7, have a great deal of overlap. For example, if you were interviewing incumbents regarding operational analysis, you would at the same time obtain information regarding roadblocks to getting the job done, which is part of the organizational analysis. When you examine the performance data for the person analysis, it is useful to determine any structural reasons for the poor performance, which is part of the organizational analysis. This gathering of multiple levels of information at one time is again illustrated in the Fabrics, Inc. example at the end of this chapter.

Once the operational analysis data determine the KSAs for the job, the person analysis will define whether each of the relevant employees possesses these KSAs. For those who do not, the PG between what is required and what the employee has serves as the impetus for developing necessary training.

For the TNA to be effective, it is important that employee development be of high concern to both the individual and the organization. This is more likely to occur when an organization does the following:

- Puts procedures in place that allow for developmental appraisals to take place regularly and separately from appraisals used for other personnel decisions
- Allows the individual to provide input into the process through self-appraisal
- Places a high value on developing subordinates by rewarding supervisors who spend time doing so
- Provides systematic opportunities for employees to receive the training and mentoring necessary for development

Although having these procedures in place will serve the organization well, it is still not enough! Numerous stories recount supervisors who simply go through the motions of a performance appraisal and employee development and then get on with the "real work." Such attitudes on the part of supervisors are likely to undermine any employee development system. Subordinates' perceptions of the process must also be positive, and they must believe that training will be useful in their development, particularly when self-assessment is being used in the TNA.[51]

Recall from the analysis phase of the training model that the organizational, operational, and person analyses are the inputs. The process is the identification of the gap, which is done by comparing the AP with the EP. The resulting PGs become the output of the TNA.

OUTPUT OF TNA

As noted in the training model at the start of the chapter, outputs include both training and nontraining needs. Training needs are dealt with by designing appropriate training programs, which are discussed in the Chapter 5. Here, we examine nontraining needs.

Nontraining Needs

Nontraining needs include those that show no KSA deficiency and those characterized by a KSA deficiency but for which training is not the best solution. First, let's examine those that show no KSA deficiency, as depicted in Figure 4-1.

Nontraining Needs That Have No KSA Deficiency
These PGs are not a result of a lack of KSAs, but a result of

- Reward/punishment incongruencies
- Inadequate or inappropriate feedback
- Obstacles in the system

No amount of KSA development will improve performance in situations where these PGs exist. The causes of these PGs will be uncovered in the organizational and operational analysis.

Reward/Punishment Incongruencies   Can working at the expected level of performance be punishing? The answer is yes, it can. Consider Nancy, the employee who always has her work done on time and done well. The other three employees in the department often complete assignments late, and their work tends to be done sloppily. Now the supervisor has a very difficult assignment that must be done in record time. Whoever gets the job will need to work late for the next few weeks. Who is assigned to the job? Nancy, of course. Nancy's reward for being a good performer is to get the difficult assignments that require staying late to complete. Soon Nancy catches on and begins acting more like the rest of the employees in her department. When Nancy is not working at the expected level, training her will not help. Her lower performance is not a KSA problem. So is training going to help Nancy? No. Training her supervisor how to motivate all department employees might be useful. It would also be useful to have systems in place to motivate the supervisor to reward employees appropriately.

Inadequate Feedback   Another nontraining need comes from employees not receiving appropriate feedback. Numerous examples tell of employees who believe they are good performers, but their supervisors believe otherwise. Supervisors generally dislike providing negative feedback.[52] In fact, some suggest that it is the most disliked of all managerial activities.[53] So they simply do not say anything to the employees. Once again, the problem is not a training issue for the subordinate, but it could be for the supervisor.

Obstacles in the System   Conditions in the workplace that obstruct the desired performance level are a third reason for deficiencies in performance. Receiving material too late, using worn-out machinery, and being constantly interrupted are but a few of the possibilities that could hinder performance. Once identified, these roadblocks need to be removed, a complex task that, in some cases, might require high-level support. Suppose a supervisor has too many reports to file each week and this responsibility takes away from the time needed to help subordinates; however, middle management needs these reports. The only way to reduce the amount of paperwork is to request that middle management reduce the number of reports they receive or find another way to generate them. This problem is not an easy one to solve, but as you can see, providing the supervisor with training related to helping subordinates will not solve the problem.

Nontraining Needs That Have a KSA Deficiency
Nontraining needs where a KSA deficiency is present are also presented in Figure 4-1. Note that even when it is a KSA deficiency, there are solutions other than training.[54]

Job Aids   A **job aid** is a set of instructions, diagrams, or other form of providing information that is available at the job site. Its purpose is to provide guidance to the worker. A job aid is useful if the worker's task is complex, if it requires a number of steps, or if it is dangerous to forget a step. Airline pilots use job aids—a list of things they must do prior to takeoff—so that they do not forget any of the steps required. Another example of a job aid would be a diagram. Rather than teaching someone a number of steps in wiring an automobile, a picture depicting where the wires should go should suffice. It is often cheaper and more efficient to use job aids when practical, rather than developing elaborate training packages, as Bill Stetar notes in Training in Action 4-6.

Practice   Regarding tasks that are important but are performed infrequently, employees can easily forget or become less proficient at them. For this reason, police officers are required to practice on the firing range each month. Schools conduct fire drills as practice for an important incident that might never occur. In these cases,

A few years back, a *Fortune* 500 durable goods manufacturer decided to increase its design engineer complement by about 40 employees. They wanted to get these new hires up to speed as quickly as possible, so they called Bill Stetar, president of Performance Technology Group, to assist in the development of an appropriate training package.

On arrival at the company, Bill learned that the company had already decided that the training should consist of a series of lectures and seminars and other formal learning processes. However, Bill suggested that before deciding to use a particular type of training, it would be useful to do a TNA. The company was initially reluctant to do a TNA because they wanted to get the training set up as quickly as possible. However, Bill was able to convince them that it would be a useful step.

The TNA indicated that much of the required learning could be completed without any formal classroom training. Instead, job aids (task-specific job instructions) and supplementary self-help information was put online for access by the new hires at their convenience. Much of it was related to

- what the person needed to do
- how to do it (self-help instructions were provided), and
- where to go for help if you needed it.

The results were that new hires got up to speed faster, made fewer mistakes than in prior years, and did not have to spend any time in the classroom.

How much did the company save? Well first of all, they saved approximately 50 percent of what they had originally budgeted for the training. But there was more. Learning of the material was faster. Management expected it to take about 90 days for a new engineer to be up to speed; it only took on average about 45 days. Without the TNA, traditional training clearly would have been less efficient. So, as Bill would say: "Training is not always the answer, do a TNA first."

Source: Bill Stetar, President of Performance Technology Group. *Personal communication,* July, 2005.

providing the practice is meant to prevent a PG. If a PG in an infrequently performed task is discovered, periodic practice sessions should be considered to ensure that the gap does not continue to occur, particularly if its occurrence can have serious consequences.

Changing the Job Itself This approach might seem extreme, but it is sometimes worth considering. Several years ago, salespeople in automobile dealerships were completely responsible for the job of selling a car, from meeting the customer through to closing the deal. The most difficult part of selling is closing the deal, which requires certain KSAs that are difficult to impart through training. As a result, many car salespeople did not last long in the business. This deficiency led the dealers to change the job. They provided the salesperson with the skills to show the car, discuss various options, and negotiate to a certain extent. Then, when it came to closing the deal, the salesperson could send the customer to the sales manager. Thus, the job was changed so that the salesperson no longer needed to know how to close the deal.

Training Needs

For those PGs that result from the employees' lack of KSAs, and for which training is a solution, the KSAs need to be listed and described clearly and unambiguously. These KSAs will be used to develop training objectives (discussed in detail in Chapter 5).

It is important to understand that in most cases, even if a training need is identified, nontraining needs are usually also present. We cannot emphasize enough the importance of these nontraining factors. For training to be successful and transferred to the job, these "nontraining" factors must be aligned with the training. As Robert Brinkerhoff, an internationally recognized expert in training effectiveness said,

> The reality is that these non-training factors are the principle determinants [for transfer of training], if they are not aligned and integrated they will easily overwhelm the very best training [inhibit transfer]. . . . Best estimates are that 80 percent or more of the eventual impact of training is determined by performance systems factors [nontraining needs].[55](p. 304)

APPROACHES TO TNA

Now that we have examined the general approach of conducting a TNA, we examine more closely the distinction between proactive and reactive approaches.

Proactive TNA

The proactive TNA focuses on future HR requirements. From the unit objectives resulting from the organization's strategic planning process, HR must develop unit strategies and tactics (see Figure 2-1 on page 29) to ensure that the organization has employees with the required KSAs in all of its critical jobs. Two approaches can be taken to develop the needed KSAs:

1. Prepare employees for promotions or transfers to different jobs.
2. Prepare employees for changes in their current jobs.

An effective, proactive procedure used for planning key promotions and transfers is succession planning. **Succession planning** is the identification and development of employees perceived to be of high potential to fill key positions in the company as they become vacant. The first step in the development of a succession plan is to identify key positions in the organization. These positions, if left vacant for any length of time, would affect organizational functioning negatively. In practice, these positions are often high-level management positions such as vice president of finance or plant manager, but they could be at any level (e.g., mold maker, if the position is key to the operation and difficult to fill). Once the key positions are identified, employees with the potential to fill these key positions are identified. Then information is provided on employees' readiness to fill the position if it becomes vacant. Employee readiness, of course, is the difference between what is expected in the new job versus what the employee is currently capable of doing. Organizations with this type of system in place have a ready-made TNA.

When preparing employees for changes in their current jobs, it is important that the TNA identify the expected changes in performance. Once the performance expectations are determined, the new KSAs required for that job can then be identified. These future KSAs are compared with the incumbent's current KSAs, and any resulting PGs are addressed through training. Consider Heinz in Leamington, Ontario (see Table 4-6). When they determined that they would be moving to a high-tech ketchup machine, it was necessary to determine what KSAs would be necessary to operate it. Training in these KSAs occurred *before* the new equipment was in place.

Organizational Analysis

The proactive approach starts with expected changes and any new objectives. As an analyst, try to determine the best fit between the organization's current internal environment (structures, policies, procedures, etc.) and future expectations and objectives. As an example, questions regarding the formal structure might include the following:

- Are pay practices congruent with the new direction taken by the company? Example: Would a strict hourly pay structure fit if the plan were to treat each department as entrepreneurial?
- Is the emphasis of the new priorities congruent with the performance appraisal system? Example: If the priority is quality, does the performance appraisal have a dimension to measure this?
- Is the strategy congruent with the current practices? Example: The new strategy is to move to a more positive union–management relationship. Currently, a policy does not allow any union business to be conducted on company time. Should this policy be revisited?
- Are enough employees available to accomplish the objective? Example: The plan is to improve quality to meet ISO 9000 standards, but employees are constantly rushed because of a lack of personnel. Does the company need to consider massive hiring or training of current employees?

Informal procedures might be evaluated with the following questions:

- Do norms that would restrict output exist?
- Will workers believe that changes in performance are required?
- What formal procedures are short-circuited by informal procedures, and what are the implications (perhaps the formal procedure is inappropriate)?

These questions need to be asked at all levels in the organization, but specifically at the departmental level, where more meaningful data will be found. Often, those in higher levels of management take a different view of the effect of various policies on behavior.

Operational Analysis

Job analysts gather information not only on what tasks are carried out currently, but also on what tasks will be required in the future. **Strategic job analysis** is defined as the identification of the KSAs required for effective performance in a job as it is expected to exist in the future.[56] Data gathering is identical to that in traditional job analysis, with the addition of a section called "gather information on the future." For this section, it is necessary to look at changes in areas such as societal values, political and legal issues, economics, market, labor, and technology, and also how those changes would affect the job in question. In this case, input from more than just incumbents and supervisors is necessary. Information from the following people is necessary:[57]

- At least one person involved in corporate strategy and closely tied to the job in question
- Someone who is aware of how the competition structures the job (technologically and from an HR standpoint)
- An efficiency expert (internal technology/communication expert)
- Someone who worked his way up through the job in question
- A forward-thinking incumbent (one willing to suggest new ideas)

This list is not exhaustive and serves only as a guide. Once these data are gathered, a revision of the tasks and KSAs based on these changes can be determined. The training function then uses this information, coupled with person analysis, to determine future training needs. The previous discussion about what to do if no job incumbents are available is helpful here. In reality, no job incumbents exist if the job will change in substantial ways.

At first this task might seem rather daunting; however, it does not need to be. The first step is to identify the critical jobs. For example, if the primary function of the organization is writing software, the computer programmer's job will be more critical to the effectiveness of the organization than the file clerk's and should be examined first. Likewise, if the organization is making parts for the automotive industry, mold making might be a critical job.

Person Analysis

Assessment of the person (for the required KSAs) is identical for both the proactive or reactive TNA, so the information presented earlier on person analysis is applicable.

Let's Do It

In the Multistate Health Corporation (MHC) at the end of Chapter 2, a strategic plan was outlined, and from it a number of potential objectives were developed for HR related to developing a human resource planning system (HRPS). The main focus of the HRIS objectives was that MHC was having financial problems, and it seemed as if the trouble could be traced to the competency of the chief executive officers (CEOs) at their hospitals. Unfortunately, no clear documentation exists describing the required KSAs for the 30 CEOs; as a result, no one knows the KSAs needed to be successful or to be promoted to CEO. To deal with this lack of KSA documentation for CEOs and other key positions in the organization, the MHC executive committee developed six objectives. The first step in addressing these objectives (as they affect the position of CEO) is to conduct an operational analysis of the CEO position. Recall how the job analysis was conducted for the large computer firm (Table 4-4). You could use a similar process here and conduct interviews, given the small number of incumbents. You can interview all incumbents (four or five small group meetings), or hold one meeting with six CEOs: two from each region, one from the largest and one from the smallest hospital in that region.

At the meeting, ask the CEOs to list all the tasks and subtasks they perform, or prepare a partial list from previous conversations to use the time available most efficiently. Then, using a scale similar to the one in Table 4-4, ask each of them to rate each task on its importance for the job. On the basis of the ratings provided, determine which are important. You need to examine these tasks to determine whether any differences distinguish between geographical locations or large versus small hospitals. If any differences are noted, they need to be resolved. If a large number of critical tasks are different, the jobs themselves could be different and may need different titles. It might also be that the task was not identified as important by some because it never was required. The task of "effective cost cutting" might not have been identified in some smaller hospitals because it was not used. It is still an important task for CEOs (assuming that CEOs in larger hospitals indicated it as important), and would be included, although some CEOs might not have the KSAs to do it effectively, as noted in the case. Once you identify all the tasks, it is useful to classify them into broader duties, as outlined in Figure 4-3.

Next, you need to identify the KSAs necessary to perform each task. These KSAs will be used to make either selection or training decisions, depending on where they were classified concerning "need at the time of hire." Publishing the ones required at the time of hire for the recruitment process makes the selection criteria clearer to all.

A team of subject matter experts on the position of CEO (see the discussion of strategic job analysis in the "Operational Analysis" of the preceding selection) should be consulted to develop the strategic part of the job analysis (how the job might look in five years). This information, when compared with the information on current requirements, highlights what the future requirements would likely be. At this point, executive development programs could be put in place to develop the KSAs needed for the future job of CEO at MHC.

Let's look at one duty. From the job analysis, one duty might be defined as the "development of subordinates." You might identify the following tasks related to that duty:

- Initiates action to identify developmental needs
- Provides timely feedback to help subordinates improve
- Provides subordinates with opportunities to develop
- Meets with subordinates to discuss performance and development
- Coaches subordinates in a manner that allows them to improve their skills

Several other duties (and relevant tasks) would, of course, be identified. Finally, the KSAs necessary to perform the tasks would be identified. From the preceding list of tasks, KSAs that would be relevant include the following:

- Knowledge of the performance review process
- Knowledge of basic coaching skills
- Skill at providing feedback in an effective manner
- Skill at interviewing
- Positive attitude toward the participative approach to problem solving
- Positive attitude toward helping others

Based on the assessment of the skills of the 30 CEOs at MHC, some or all of these KSAs might be lacking, and training might be necessary. To determine which CEOs need which KSAs, the person analysis is conducted.

For the person analysis, let's just focus on the specific KSAs necessary to appraise performance. Here you want to know about CEOs' knowledge of the appraisal process and their skill in providing effective reviews. This information is obtained in part by asking CEOs directly (a subpart of your job analysis meeting). If managers have no confidence in a performance appraisal system, they will have no compunction about telling you that "it's not worth the time" or "it's never used anyway so why bother." If they do not believe that they have the skill, they might also tell you that. Another place to obtain such information is from the CEOs' subordinates. You might get information from the CEOs' subordinates such as "She really tries to do a good job but is constantly telling me what I need to do and never asks my opinion" or "He tells me I have a bad attitude. I'm not sure what he means but am in no mood to ask either." These types of comments suggest a lack of skills on the CEO's part, or it is possible that the CEO has a negative attitude toward the process. Again, asking the CEO directly could determine which it is. You can also use the option of behavior testing to assess the skills. Put CEOs in a role-play situation where they must provide feedback to an employee, and score them on how well they do.

For the organizational analysis part of the TNA, some information has already been gathered from interviews conducted by the consultants. One of the objectives based on those findings was the inclusion of a succession plan. It provides the mechanism for supplying instant information on who should be considered for the next promotion, rather than relying on individual CEOs to make that determination. Of course, you need a standardized performance review system in place to make such determinations.

The job analysis provides relevant data for developing standard performance appraisals necessary in both promotion and developmental decisions. With such a system in place, each CEO would be responsible for completing performance reviews on his subordinates and providing developmental plans for them. This process would help address the lack of interest in some CEOs for recommending their subordinates. Although not explicitly noted, one important measure of the CEOs' performance appraisal would need to be how well CEOs prepare and develop their subordinates for promotion. This measure, as part of their performance review specifically, along with the use of a succession plan in general, will serve to encourage all CEOs to work toward developing their subordinates for promotion.

Reactive TNA

The reactive TNA begins with an existing discrepancy in job performance. In this sense, Figure 4-1 represents a more complete picture of the reactive process. A middle manager might notice that production is dropping, a supervisor might see that a particular employee's performance has declined, or HR might note an increase in grievances from a particular department. Once you identify a discrepancy, you need to determine whether it is worth fixing. Although this decision may be based on financial implications, it does not have to be. For example, the company notes that one department has lower ratings of supervisory consideration (as rated by subordinates) than the organization expected. The cost of this lower rating would be difficult to assess. It might take a long time (if ever) to notice any significant effect on the company's bottom line. If the company makes a strong commitment to developing a good employee–management relationship, it may decide to try to alleviate the problem.

In the reactive TNA, you still conduct the organizational analysis, operational analysis, and person analysis, but the distinction among them is even more blurred, for the following reasons:

- The focus is primarily on the one department.
- Those who demonstrate the discrepancy (and their peers and subordinates) are the key persons to be interviewed about all three components.
- The discrepancy focuses the issue on a particular part of the job (e.g., interactions with subordinates, as previously noted).

Organizational Analysis
Organizational analysis deals with the three issues identified to the right of the KSA deficiency in Figure 4-1. A complete analysis of all four aspects of Figure 4-1 is necessary regardless of whether the issue is a KSA problem. Even if a lack of KSAs is identified as a problem, additional roadblocks might exist that would prevent performance even if the KSAs were learned.

Operational Analysis/Person Analysis
In the reactive approach, the performance discrepancy is already identified; it triggers the analysis. Operational and person analyses are aimed at identifying the cause of the current gap between EP and AP. These analyses are conducted in a manner consistent with our earlier descriptions.

Let's Do It
When a reactive performance discrepancy is identified, it is best to work from the discrepancy and deal only with those issues indicated from the analysis of the discrepancy. Instead of moving step by step through this analysis, let's look at Training in Action 4-7, an actual example of this process.

From the information provided in Training in Action 4-7, will training help? You cannot really determine the answer yet, although some factors identified suggest that few external forces are acting on the professors to change their teaching.

Students in a training and development class decided that for their class project, they would like to determine why some professors are interesting and informative, whereas other are not. The needs analysis of this performance discrepancy (PD) would help determine whether the issue is training or something else.

They examined the PD using operational analysis (expected performance) and person analysis (actual performance). As is noted in Table 4.3, one way of obtaining expected performance data is to observe the job. The group of students had observed the job (lecturing) of professors for two years, and also using data from other students they interviewed, they developed a list of behaviors that they believed made lectures interesting and informative.

For person analysis (actual performance), the students used observation and performance data (see Table 4.7). Using the observation method, the students identified six professors who were considered as having a performance discrepancy. These data were compared with OTHER performance data (published student surveys) about the professors' teaching skills, which verified the observations. An attempt to verify this information further was made by asking the dean to provide student (customer) complaints about professors over the past two years. The dean declined to provide such information.

The organizational analysis was then conducted. Because of the nature of the discrepancy (only business school professors were identified), the organizational analysis focused primarily on the business school.

Examining the university-wide mission and other documents was not necessary. From Figure 4.1, questions about the reward/punishment incongruence, inadequate feedback, and obstacles in the system were examined. This was done through an interview (management interrogation as noted in Table 4.1) with the dean of the business school. Questions related to adequate feedback were as follows: (1) Are there other performance ratings of professors? (2) Do the professors receive feedback on their performance? The dean's answer was that the only measure of their teaching performance is student surveys and any unsolicited complaints from students. Regarding feedback, the professors receive the student evaluations along with a ranking of themselves and all other faculty members based on these data. Any student complaints would also be made available to the professor. The dean noted that the same professors tended to be rated low each year but again declined to provide specifics. A question related to reward/punishment incongruence was as follows: What happens to those who are rated high and low? The answer was nothing; there are no extrinsic rewards or punishment for being a good or poor teacher. Finally, in response to a question about obstacles in the system, the dean emphasized the pressure for publications. "Publish or perish" were the words he used. Promotions, tenure, travel, and other rewards were all provided to those who were publishing on a regular basis. These were the overall findings of the needs assessment.

Let's suppose that you did talk to the professors, and they told you that they always teach this way and suggested that their job was not to entertain, but to teach. Through some subtle questioning, you determine that they do not seem to understand some basic skills about making a lecture interesting and effective. They evaded questions about how an effective overhead should be set up, how questions can be used to create interest, and so on. Thus a KSA deficit is revealed. Would training alone be enough? It might, if the training were designed in a way that was interesting and it motivated the professors to go back to the classroom to try some different ideas. They would more likely try these new ways of teaching if organizational changes were made that encouraged them to improve. For example, when they reached an average on teacher evaluations of 3.5 on a 5-point scale, the professors could be offered a bonus (in the form of travel money or computer equipment if a cash bonus were not possible). Changes in the way pay increases are offered, with heavier emphasis on the importance of student evaluations in getting tenure or promotion, would encourage professors to be more concerned about their teaching. Even personal interest by the dean could be effective. The dean might meet with the professor and indicate a concern with the performance; they could set goals for improvement and then meet on a regular basis to encourage the change. All these changes, combined with a well-designed training program that would also motivate the professors, should result in an improvement.

Reactive versus Proactive

From a systems perspective, it makes sense that a proactive approach would be better than a reactive approach. Obviously, anticipating needs is better than waiting until they cause problems. Companies that integrate the training function with strategic objectives are more readily able to respond to the rapidly changing technology and business conditions that are an everyday part of corporate life.[58] However, even when operating proactively, the organization will at times need to react to changes in the environment. Strategic plans are not cast in concrete but must be adapted to current events. Using a combination of proactive and reactive strategies allows an organization to be most effective. It is, in fact, possible that a proactive approach is more important for market leader organizations than for cost leader organizations.[59] Market leaders need to be much more aware of their environment and anticipate how they will respond to that environment; otherwise, they will not survive.[60] In reality, however, many organizations operate from a reactive perspective when it comes to training.

FOCUS ON SMALL BUSINESS

Some suggest that the small business is not simply a miniature large organization but a unique entity in itself.[61] So what is true for large organizations might not be relevant for small ones. This assessment might be true in some areas but not necessarily in the area of HR practices. Research has shown that small firms with high-quality HR practices are generally higher performers than those without such practices.[62] Also, small firms with higher amounts of training consistently demonstrate more innovativeness than those with lower levels of training.[63] What is unique about the small firm is that the HR procedures that management decides to implement are likely much more critical (compared with the large organization) because errors in judgment that create challenges for large companies (such as the building of the Edsel car by Ford) could destroy a small business. Therefore, the proactive approach to training would seem to be more important for the small business. Furthermore, in smaller organizations, it is easier to integrate a proactive approach because fewer employees are involved.

The top management of a small business is usually the owner, who is usually responsible for any training.[64] However, this person likely does not have any HR background and might not understand how a proactive approach to training can be advantageous.[65] In fact, much of the dissatisfaction with training in the small business sector is a function of the reactive approach, which responds to a crisis with a "quick fix." The small business owner/manager needs to realize that sound training practices tied to the strategic plan will pay off in the long run, as Metro Tool and Die discovered in Training in Action 4-8.

Other evidence indicates that more small manufacturing businesses are undertaking TNA. One reason for this is the wish to become ISO certified. David Alcock works for the Canadian Plastics Training Centre (CPTC) in Toronto, which provides training to many of the small mold-making companies in the region. He says that because of the investment required in becoming ISO certified, companies are requesting a TNA to obtain the maximum effect for their training dollars. He noted that in

Metro Tool and Die of Mississauga, Ontario, Canada, has 42 employees, most of whom have little education or training. Mr. Panteno, the owner, was interested in improving the quality and efficiency of his shop. He contacted Fabian Hogan, a consultant with the Ontario Skills Development Ministry. After an assessment, Mr. Hogan suggested that all employees receive training in basic literacy skills, blueprint reading, and instrumentation die setup. Doing this would entail a considerable expense, but the consultant convinced Mr. Panteno that the investment was, in the long term, a good one. At 3:30 every day, training sessions were held on company premises and company time. Was this commitment to training worthwhile? Since completion of the training, rejects dropped from 7,500 per million to 325 per million. The company won the prestigious Xerox Quality Award in a worldwide competition. Metro recently provided one of its customers with a $9,600 cost savings. In the owner's own words, "Training has paid for itself. There is no tool and die company like us. We are a small company using big-company tactics."

That was in the early 1990s. Today, the company has grown to 100 skilled employees, and their market expanded from business machines to the auto industry, appliances, computers, etc., and they have clients all over the world. They have become ISO 9000 and QS 9000 certified. These certifications were very time consuming and costly in terms of training, but as Anna Pentano said, "We are committed to having a highly trained workforce. One of our niches is being able to meet unreasonable deadlines and last minute changes to specs, while still meeting deadlines. This is accomplished because we believe in cross-training and have a number of our employees capable in more than one operation, making us very adaptable to last minute changes by our customers. On top of that each employee must receive a specific amount of training each year. Without the training commitment we have, that simply would not be possible."

Sources: Adapted from MacKinnon, D. J. "Training days at Metro Tool," *Toronto Star* (April 22, 1992); Anna Pentano, Human Resource Manager. Personel communication (June 24, 2008), 2.

the last few years, more than half of the company's customers, many of which are small businesses, requested a TNA.

The time factor is always a concern for any business, but particularly for small business. For small business, the TNA often seems a waste of time. Techniques can speed up the process of working through a TNA, but generally these techniques require using a trained analyst to be effective.[66] Here are some tips for the small business HR person or manager to consider when faced with conducting a TNA:[67]

- Be clear on what is to be done.
- Examine existing available data.
- Develop some ideas related to the issue and test them in the data gathering.
- Collapse the steps.
- Use technology.

The most important thing is to clarify what type of OPG you have, and then map out a plan of what to do for the TNA before venturing out to do it. Examine records, minutes, and any other documentation related to the gap. Determine who needs to be talked to and what questions will need to be asked. (A reexamination of Tables 4-1 and 4-2 might be helpful here.) Sometimes it is difficult to help employees understand exactly what is being sought.

Consider Fred, the only salesperson in the organization who consistently gets letters of praise from customers and high repeat business. When Fred is asked what he does that makes him so successful, his response is, "I do not know, I just treat them well." To explore this more, outline a scenario that you think might be correct. Such a scenario might look like this: When customers come in, Bill greets them by name, asks about the family, asks questions about themselves, then asks what he can do for them today, and so forth. Once Fred hears the scenario, he can correct or amend it so the scenario fits what he actually does. You provided Fred with a template from which to provide information to you. Clearly, one way to speed up the process is to collapse the steps. For example, meet with everyone at once and give them a possible solution to the problem. Now ask for candid responses to questions such as, "Is this an adequate description of the problem? Is the proposed solution the best one? What would you do differently?" or "What would prevent the successful implementation of this solution?" Of course, it is necessary to be sure that everyone at the meeting is willing to be open and honest. Finally, the use of e-mail, discussion boards, and so forth, can help to gather information from several employees, with minimum time spent actually meeting them. Place the problem or issue on a discussion board and ask for comments. Return to it from time to time to review comments and questions and pose new or follow-up questions. E-mail is also a way of soliciting input. Simply get a group on an e-mail list, and conduct meetings using the technology.

However, problems can arise when you do not do the full TNA, which can lead to less-than-ideal solutions. Still, the shortcut is better than not doing a TNA at all. Often the ramifications of not doing a TNA are time and money wasted on things unrelated to solving the problem. Even for a small business, it is important to do something, rather than nothing, even if it is less than ideal.

Assistance for Small Business

Small-business owners can access resources to aid them in training their employees. The different levels of government assist in various ways to help fund training. For example, most states have small business development centers (SBDCs) that provide assistance in training. In California, customized training programs assist companies in becoming ISO certified and are available from the California State Department of Education at no cost. Instructors with factory experience conduct a TNA and develop training on the basis of the analysis, making the training organization-specific. As a result, employees can see its advantages to their job. The major hurdle to these programs is convincing management of their value. Also, the training must be integrated into the overall plan of the organization, or it is not successful.

When the small business does not have time or expertise, government-sponsored consultants can provide support. Furthermore, in most universities, graduate students in psychology or business would welcome the opportunity to become involved. These individuals often operate under the watchful eye of highly trained professors and are willing to do the work, at a fraction of the cost a professional would charge, simply for the experience. In fact, if the situation provided research possibilities, the project might be done for free. Moreover, many business schools have professional training consultants associated with their continuing education or executive education programs who also provide seminars and/or consulting. For those who argue that small businesses simply cannot afford the time to do a comprehensive TNA, we argue the opposite; they cannot afford not to. It is better to do something rather than nothing.

TNA and Design

We return now to the opening case, Westcan. Remember that Chris was all set to begin developing an "effective meeting" training program. As you read the rest of the case, think about the things you learned about conducting a TNA. Note that the TNA Westcan uses is much simpler and less formal than some we discussed. However, the value of doing the TNA is quite obvious.

Chris told Karen about the conversation with Irven and what she had put together. Chris said, "What remains is to develop the simulation. Can you help?"

"Sure," said Karen, "but it's too bad you are so far along. I might have been able to help you design the training."

Chris indicated that she had not put a great deal of time into designing the training and was open to any suggestions.

Karen suggested that Chris consider doing a needs analysis. "In a way, you completed a partial operational analysis by determining what is required in running an effective meeting. What we do not know is where the managers are deficient; we call that a person analysis. One way to obtain that information is to ask the managers to describe how their meetings currently run and the areas they see as ineffective. Their answers should reflect the areas in which they are deficient. Also, by asking the managers what training they want, we could ensure that the training is relevant. Another method would be to sit in and observe how they run their meetings. It would allow us to identify deficiencies they might be unaware of," said Karen. Karen noted that in her brief time at Westcan, it seemed that premeeting information was well distributed and understood, agendas were given, and notice of meetings always contained the relevant information.

"You might be right," said Chris. "I simply never thought of asking them." Together they developed a questionnaire asking questions related to effective meetings, such as, "What would you like to see contained in a one-day effective meeting workshop?" and "How well do the meetings with your staff stay on track?" They also got permission to sit in on a number of meetings.

The returned surveys and meeting observations indicated that most managers understood the rules of effective meetings. All had, at one time or another, attended a lecture or read material on running an effective meeting. The problem was that they had never been able to turn the knowledge into action. They knew what to do, just not how to do it. They wanted practice, with feedback from a professional. They also wanted the training to be for the exact teams they continually operated in, which required that management and nonmanagement from a team attend the same training and learn the behaviors required for effective meetings together. After going through the TNA with Karen and documenting all the information, Chris said to Karen, "Well, it looks like the training I was going to provide was way off the mark compared with what we now know they need. I owe you a dinner."

The needs assessment at Westcan shows that training was required but not the training that Chris first imagined. Her problem was that she did not have enough information to understand the types of needs the managers had. Without this information, she began to design what she thought would be a good "effective meeting" training session. What would have happened if she had gone ahead with her original plan? After conducting the TNA, she is now in a much better position to design an appropriate training program. The next step is to develop a clear set of training objectives that will drive both the design and evaluation of training. The importance of sound training objectives cannot be overstressed. Chapter 5 provides a step-by-step procedure for developing these objectives and meshing them with training design issues and constraints.

SUMMARY

Training is a reasonable solution when a PG is caused by an employee's lack of KSAs. However, most problems identified by managers as requiring training actually do not require training. Most such problems are a function of a poor match between organizational structure (reward/punishment incongruities, inadequate feedback, or obstacles in the system) and performance expectations. A TNA will reveal the location and reason for the problem.

When a KSA deficiency creates a PG and training is required, the TNA ensures that the KSA deficiencies are identified. Training that is focused on these KSAs will be relevant and therefore more motivating for the trainees. The likelihood is higher that training will be successful when a TNA is conducted because

- the appropriate KSAs required to do the job are identified (operational analysis),
- the KSAs of the employees in that job are determined (person analysis) so that only those needing training are trained, and
- the roadblocks to transfer of the training are identified (organizational analysis) and removed.

The TNA consists of organizational, operational, and person analysis. The organizational analysis is designed to assess the capital resources, HR availability, and the work environment. It is important to understand the amount and type of resources available and what type of environment the affected employees work in. Often, employees are not performing at the expected level for reasons other than a lack of KSAs. The organizational analysis identifies these reasons so they can be rectified. Even where KSAs are the problem, other remedies (job aids, practice, and so forth) can be considered before training.

The operational analysis provides information pertaining to the KSA requirements for the job in question. Observing the job, doing the job, and examining job descriptions and specifications are some of the ways of determining this information. The method most often used, however, is to ask incumbents and supervisors what is required in a systematic way.

The person analysis provides information on each employee's specific level of competence regarding the KSA requirements. Several methods can be used to determine competence levels, such as examining performance appraisals, testing, or simply asking employees where they encounter problems. Each of these approaches offers advantages, and the one you choose depends on factors such as time and availability.

There are two types of TNA: proactive and reactive. With proactive TNA, the focus is on planned changes to jobs and performance expectations. Typically, these changes evolve from strategic planning, but also might occur from other processes. Because the proactive TNA anticipates future changes, it also must anticipate the KSAs required to meet or exceed performance expectations in the future. As a result, some of the types of information collected are different from those collected for the reactive TNA.

The reactive TNA is far more common and is a response to a current PG. Here, the TNA needs to be completed more quickly because the gap is already affecting productivity. An effective organization uses both proactive and reactive types of TNA.

This section is the beginning of a step-by-step process for developing a training program for a small fabrications company. Here, we examine the TNA for the program, and in subsequent chapters, we will continue the process through to the evaluation.

Fabrics, Inc., once a small organization, recently experienced an incredible growth. Only two years ago, the owner was also the supervisor of 40 employees. Now it is a firm that employs more than 200. The fast growth proved good for some, with the opportunity for advancement. The owner called a consultant to help him with a few problems that emerged with the fast growth. "I seem to have trouble keeping my mold-makers and some other key employees," he said. "They are in demand, and although I am competitive regarding money, I think the new supervisors are not treating them well. Also, I received some complaints from customers about the way supervisors talk to them. The supervisors were all promoted from within, without any formal training in supervising employees. They know their stuff regarding the work the employees are doing, so they are able to help employees who are having problems. However, they seem to get into arguments easily, and I hear a lot of yelling going on in the plant. When we were smaller, I looked after the supervisory responsibilities myself and never found a reason to yell at the employees, so I think the supervisors need some training in effective ways to deal with employees. I only have nine supervisors—could you give them some sort of training to be better?"

The consultant responded, "If you want to be sure that we deal with the problem, it would be useful to determine what issues are creating the problems and, from that, recommend a course of action."

"Actually, I talked to a few other vendors and they indicate they have some traditional basic supervisor training packages that would fit our needs and, therefore, they could start right away. I really want this fixed fast," the owner said.

"Well, I can understand that, but you do want to be sure that the training you get is relevant to the problems you experienced; otherwise, it is a waste of money. How about I simply contract to do a training needs analysis and give you a report of the findings? Then, based on this information, you can decide whether any of the other vendors or the training I can provide best fits your needs in terms of relevancy and cost. That way, you are assured that any training you purchase will be relevant," said the consultant.

"How long would that take?" the owner asked.

"It requires that I talk to you in a bit more detail, as well as to those involved; some of the supervisors and subordinates. If they are readily available I would be done this week, with a report going to you early next week," the consultant replied. The owner asked how much it would cost, and after negotiating for 15 minutes, agreed to the project. They returned to the office to write up the contract for a needs analysis.

The interview with the owner (who was also the manager of all the first-line supervisors) was scheduled first and included an organizational and operational analysis. What follows is an edited version of the questions related to the organizational analysis.

The Interview
Direction of the Organization

Q: What is the mission of the company? What are the goals employees should be working for?
A: I do not really have time for that kind of stuff. I have to keep the organization running.
Q: If there is no mission, how do employees understand what the focus of their job should be?
A: They understand that they need to do their jobs.
Q: What about goals or objectives?
A: Again, I do not have the time for that, and I have never needed such stuff in the past.
Q: That may be true, but you are much larger now and do need to communicate these things in some fashion. How do employees know what to focus on: quality, quantity, customer service, keeping costs down?
A: All of those things are important, but I get your point. I never actually indicated anything

(continued)

about this to them. I simply took it for granted that they understood it.

Q: What type of management style do you want supervisors to have, and how do you promote that?

A: I assumed that they would supervise like me. I always listened to them when they were workers. I believe in treating everyone with dignity and respect and expect others to do the same. I do not have any method to transmit that except to follow my style.

HR Systems

Q: What criteria are used to select, transfer, and promote individuals?

A: I hired a firm to do all the hiring for me when I was expanding. I told them I wanted qualified workers. As for the promotion to supervisor, I picked the best workers.

Q: Best how? What criteria were you using?

A: Well, I picked those who were the hardest workers, the ones who always turned out the best work the fastest, and were always willing to work late to get the job done.

Q: Are there formal appraisal systems? If yes, what is the information used for promotion, bonuses, and so forth?

A: I do not have time for that. I believe that people generally know when they are doing a good job. If they are not, I will not keep them.

Job Design

Q: How are supervisors' jobs organized? Where do they get their information and where does it go?

A: Supervisors receive the orders for each day at the beginning of the day and then give it out to the relevant workers. They then keep track of it to see that it is done on time and out to the customer.

Reward Systems

Q: What incentives are in place to encourage employees to work toward the success of the organization?

A: Well, I think I pay them well.

Q: Does everyone receive the same amount of pay?

A: At the present time, yes, because they are all relatively new supervisors. I do plan to give them raises based on how well they are performing.

Q: But you indicated that you do not really have a method of informing them what you are measuring them on. How are they to know what is important?

A: Well, I will tell them. I guess I need to be considering that issue down the road.

Performance

Q: How do the supervisors know what their role is in the company?

A: I told them that they needed to supervise the employees and what that entailed.

Q: How do they find out how well they are doing in their job? Is there a formal feedback process?

A: I talk to them about how they are doing from time to time, but I get your point and will think about that.

Q: Are there opportunities for help if they are having problems?

A: Take this problem with the yelling and getting employees angry at them. I have talked to them about it and have offered to get them training.

Q: How do they feel about that?

A: Actually, they thought it was great. As I said, none of these supervisors have had anything in the way of supervisory training.

Methods and Practices

Q: What are the policies, procedures, and rules in the organization? In your view, how do they facilitate or inhibit performance?

A: I really do not think there is anything hindering their performance. I am always willing to help, but I also have work to do. That is why I promoted employees to supervisors, so I would not have to deal with that part of the business.

After gathering information on the organization, the consultant gathered operational analysis data from the manager (owner). The consultant used the method provided in Figure 4-3. What follows is a portion of the completed form.

(continued)

JOB TITLE: SUPERVISOR

SPECIFIC DUTY: BE SURE WORK IS COMPLETED AND SENT TO THE CUSTOMER ON TIME

TASKS	SUBTASKS	KSAs
Organize jobs in manner that ensures completion on time	Examine jobs and assess time required	Knowledge of types of jobs we get Knowledge of times required for jobs to be completed
	Sort and give jobs to appropriate employees	Organization and prioritizing skills Knowledge of employees' capabilities
Monitor progress of work	Talk to employees about their progress on jobs	Knowledge of proper feedback Effective feedback skills Helping attitude
	Examine specific job products during production to ensure quality	Knowledge of quality standards Quality assessment skills
Listen effectively	Provide feedback to employees about performance	Knowledge of effective listening skills Knowledge of conflict styles Conflict resolution skills Knowledge of proper feedback Effective feedback skills Positive attitude for treating employees with respect

And so forth . . .

Next, the consultant met with the supervisors, first as a single group of nine to do an operational analysis and then individually to discuss individual performance. He chose to use a slightly different approach to the operational analysis because he expected that they might have some problems working from the form used with the owner. The following excerpt comes from that interview.

To begin the meeting, the consultant said:

I am here to find out just what your job as supervisor entails. This step is the first in determining what training we can provide to make you more effective in your job. First, we need to know what it is you do on the job. So I am going to let you provide me with a list of the things you do on the job—the tasks. Let me give you an example of what I mean. For the job of a salesperson, I might be told a required task was to "sell printers." This description is too general to be useful, or you might say you must "introduce yourself to a new client," which is too specific. What we need is somewhere in between these two extremes, such as "make oral presentation to a small group of people." Are there any questions? OK, let's begin.

Q: Think of a typical Monday. What's the first thing you do when you arrive at work?
A: Check the answering machine.
Q: That is a little too specific. Why do you check the answering machine?
A: I need to return any important calls from suppliers or customers.
Q: What do these calls deal with?
A: Complaints usually, although some are checking on the status of their job.
Q: Anybody else do anything different from that?
A: No.
Q: What do you do next?
A: Examine the jobs that have come in and prioritize them based on their complexity and due date.

(continued)

Q: The task, then, is organizing and prioritizing the new jobs you received. What next?

A: Meet with each subordinate, see how they are doing, and distribute the new work.

Q: Tell me what "see how they are doing" means.

A: I make sure that they are on schedule with their work. I check their progress on the jobs they are working on.

Q: OK, so check on progress of subordinates is the task. What next?

A: After all the work is distributed, I check to see what orders are due to be completed and sent out today.

Q: OK, but I guess that assumes everyone is on schedule. What do you do if someone is behind in their job?

A: Depends how far behind the job is. If it is serious, I may simply take the job away and give it to someone I think can do the job faster.

A: I do not do that. I find out what the problem is and help the person get back on track.

Q: So you spend some time training that person?

A: Well, sort of. It is not formal training, but I will see why the person is having problems and give some of my "tricks of the trade" to speed things up.

Q: Anybody deal with this issue differently?

A: I do not usually have the time to do any training. I will give it to someone who can do it, or in some cases, just do the job myself. Sometimes that is faster. After all, we have all this useless paperwork that we have to do.

Q: I want to come back to the paperwork, but first, are you saying that no standard exists for dealing with employees who are having problems with particular jobs?

A: Sure there is. The boss expects us to train them, but with the pressure for production, we often do not have time to do that.

A: Well, I agree with that. Even though I do stop and spend time helping, I often feel the pressure to rush and probably do not do a good job of it. I do try and tell them what they need to do to improve in the particular area.

Although the format used in the session starts first thing in the morning and continues through a typical day, clues often emerge as to other tasks that are done. The mentioning of "tell them what they need to do to improve" causes the consultant to focus on that task and what other tasks are related to it, because the owner did indicate that providing feedback was an important task.

Q: OK, let's look at the issue of telling them how to improve. We could think of that as giving feedback to employees. What other tasks require you to discuss things with subordinates?

A: We are supposed to deal with their concerns.

A: Yeah, that's right, and also we are supposed to meet one-on-one with them and discuss their performance. Trouble is, these new employees are know-it-alls and not willing to listen.

A: You're right about that. On more than one occasion, many of us resort to yelling at these guys to get them to respond.

A: Boy, is that ever true.

Q: What about the paperwork?

A: Well, it is stupid. A clerk could do it, but we are expected to do it. If we do not, then billing and other problems come up, so we have to do it or else. . . .

A: Yeah, it takes away from us being out here where we are needed.

And so forth. . . .

Other questions that might be asked:

What is the next thing you would do in the afternoon?

The next?

What is the last thing you do in the day?

That pretty much describes a typical day (Monday in this case). Is there anything you would do at the beginning of the week (Monday) that is not done at other times?

How about at the end of the week? Is there anything you do then that is not done during the rest of the week?

Is there anything that you do only once or twice a week that we missed?

Now think about the beginning of the month. What do you do at the beginning of the month that is not done at other times?

How about the end of the month?

(continued)

Is there anything that is done only a few times a month that we might have missed?
The beginning of the year?
The end of the year?
Are there any tasks that we may have missed because they occur only once in a while?

You will note that often it is necessary to redefine the task statements for the incumbent. This art comes with practice. The following list contains some of the tasks and relevant KSAs obtained from the TNA.

TASKS	KSAs
Deal with customer complaints	Knowledge of effective listening processes Knowledge of conflict resolution strategies Listening skills Conflict resolution skills
Organize and prioritize jobs	Knowledge of types of jobs received Knowledge of time required for various jobs Organization and planning skills
Check on progress of subordinates' work and provide feedback on performance	Knowledge of proper feedback processes Communication skills
Deal with concerns of employees	Positive attitude toward treating employees with respect Knowledge of effective listening processes Knowledge of communication strategies Positive attitude toward helping employees

Next, for the person analysis, individual meetings with supervisors and one with the owner (supervisor of the supervisors) were conducted. The questions came right from the job analysis and asked about the supervisors' knowledge of the areas identified, the skills needed, and their attitudes toward issues identified as important in their job. The introduction to the interview was as follows:

From the interviews, I have listed a number of knowledge, skills, and attitudes that are necessary to be an effective supervisor here at Fabrics, Inc. I would like to ask you how proficient you believe you are in each of them. By the way, do not feel bad if you have no understanding of many of these concepts; many do not. Remember, the information gathered will be used to determine how to help you be a better supervisor, so candid responses are encouraged. In terms of having knowledge of the following, indicate to me if you have no understanding, a very low level of understanding,

some understanding, a fair amount of understanding, or complete understanding.

The results of the TNA identified a number of KSAs (training needs) that were deficient, as well as some nontraining needs.

Addressing Nontraining Needs

The following nontraining issues need to be addressed to help ensure that supervisory training will be transferred to the job:

- Have owner (either with others or on his own) determine the goals and objectives of the company and which aspects of performance should be focused on.
- Set up a formal appraisal system where, in one session, the owner sits down with each supervisor to discuss performance and set objectives. In another session, performance development is discussed.
- Use objectives set for the year and clarify how rewards (bonus, pay raises, and so forth) will be tied to the objectives.

(continued)

- Set up similar sessions for supervisors and subordinates in terms of developmental performance review (at a minimum). Also, consider incentives based on performance appraisals.
- Hire someone to relieve the supervisors of some of their paperwork so they can spend more time on the floor.

And so forth. . . .

Training Needs

Several training needs were evident from the needs analysis beyond what was indicated by the owner. Specific to those issues, however, supervisors were particularly candid in indicating that they had never been exposed to any type of feedback or communication skills. They had no knowledge or skills in these areas. Attitudes in this area were mixed. Some believed that the best way to provide feedback is to "call it like it is." "Some of these guys are simply not willing to listen, and you need to be tough" was a typical comment from these supervisors. Others believed that treating subordinates the way you would like to be treated goes a long way in gaining their support and willingness to listen.

A partial list of training needs includes lack of knowledge and skill in:

Effective listening
Communication
Conflict resolution
Effective feedback
Employee performance measurement
Employee motivation . . . and so forth

At this point, we will leave "the training program" with the needs identified. The next step is the design phase. We will return to Fabrics, Inc. at the end of Chapter 5.

KEY TERMS

- Actual criterion
- Actual organizational performance (AOP)
- Actual performance (AP)
- Assessment center
- Behavioral test
- Bias
- Bias in performance ratings
- Capital resources
- Cognitive test
- Competency
- Content validity
- Criteria
- Criterion contamination
- Criterion deficiency
- Criterion relevancy
- Error
- Expected organizational performance (EOP)
- Expected performance (EP)
- Group characteristic bias
- Halo effect
- Human resources
- Job aid
- Job-duty-task method
- Job expectation technique
- Knowledge of predictor bias
- Operational analysis
- Opportunity bias
- Organizational analysis
- Organizational environment
- Organizational performance gap (OPG)
- Performance gap (PG)
- Person analysis
- Proactive TNA
- Reactive TNA
- Reliability
- Self-ratings
- Split half reliability
- Strategic job analysis
- Succession planning
- Task-oriented job analysis
- Test retest reliability
- 360-degree performance review
- Training needs analysis (TNA)
- Validity
- Work sample
- Worker-oriented job analysis
- Ultimate criterion

QUESTIONS FOR REVIEW

1. What is the purpose of a TNA? Is it always necessary?
2. What is the difference between proactive and reactive TNA? When is proactive better?
3. What are competencies, and why are they popular in training departments? How are competency models related to job analysis?

4. Describe how you would go about analyzing the future training needs of your university.
5. To obtain person analysis data, why not just use the performance appraisal completed by the supervisor? How can you obtain the best information possible if performance appraisal data must be used? How do self-ratings fit into this approach?

EXERCISES

1. In a small group, analyze the job of "student." What are the duties and tasks required? From these tasks, list the KSAs that students need. Are any in your group deficient in any of these KSAs? Now identify and list the workshops offered to students to help them be successful. Are these relevant to the KSAs you identified? What additional programs would you recommend be offered?
2. Do the same job analysis for students in another field, and compare it with yours. Are the KSAs the same for a student in science and arts? In law or engineering? What, if anything, is different?
3. Talk to someone you know who is currently working and see whether it would be possible to do a TNA on a particular job classification or on that person's job. Even interviewing only a few employees would provide enough information to give you an idea of how to conduct the TNA.

FABRICS, INC., QUESTIONS

1. Compare the information provided in the Fabrics, Inc., case with the sources for locating gaps in performance in Table 4-1 and identify which sources were used. Are there any other sources that would provide useful information?
2. In collecting information, did the training analyst ask the correct people for the relevant information? Explain your answer. Hint: Examine Table 4-2.
3. How would you go about dealing with the nontraining needs? Why is this important?
4. What sources of data were used in the operational analysis? Indicate how closely they correspond to the ideal model presented in the text.
5. What sources of data were used in the person analysis? Indicate how closely they correspond to the ideal model presented in the text.

WEB RESEARCH

Conduct an Internet search to identify a needs analysis model that is different from the one presented in this chapter. Summarize the two models and describe how they differ. Provide a critical analysis of these differences.

CASE ANALYSIS

Fred recently became a manager at a local hardware store that employs six managers and 55 nonmanagement employees. As new, larger chains such as Home Depot come to the area, the owner is concerned about losing many of his customers because he cannot compete on the basis of price. The management team met and discussed its strategic response. The team determined that the hardware store would focus on particular items and make personalized service the cornerstone of its effort. Fred's responsibility was to train all nonmanagement employees in good customer relations skills; for that he was given a budget of $70,000. Over the past six months, Fred has received a number of training brochures from outside organizations.

One of the brochures boasted, "Three-day workshop, $35,000. We will come in and train all your employees (maximum of 50 per session) so that any customer who comes to your store once will come again."

Another said, "One-day seminar on customer service skills. The best in the country. Only $8,000 (maximum participants 70)."

A third said, "Customer satisfaction guaranteed on our customer satisfaction training for sales clerks. Three-day workshop, $25,000. Maximum participants 25 to allow for individual help."

Fred liked the third one because it provided personalized training. He called the company to talk about its offering. The consultant said that by keeping the number small, he would be able to provide actual work simulations for each of the trainees. He also indicated that he would tailor the simulations to reflect the hardware store. Fred noted that they would need two sessions and asked the consultant if he could take a few more per session to accommodate the 55 employees. The consultant agreed. The training went ahead, and the cost was under budget by $20,000.

CASE QUESTIONS

1. Do you agree with Fred's decision to use the third vendor? Using concepts from the chapter, explain your answer.
2. What else might Fred do before choosing a training package? Use information provided in Chapter 2 and 3 to describe your approach. Make sure to provide enough detail to demonstrate your understanding of the key issues and approaches to determining how to proceed once a triggering event has occurred.
3. If training went ahead as indicated, how successful do you think it would be? Explain your answer using concepts from this chapter.

Appendix 4.1

One of the most critical components of training is the development of appropriate tests (criteria) to accurately measure success in training. These criteria can be used for assessing KSAs during the TNA, providing feedback during training, and evaluating the training once it is completed. This section provides both a conceptual framework for understanding criterion measures and a practical guide for developing sound criteria.

Criteria

Criteria are measures of expected performance. The data gathered in the operational analysis describe what the expected performance is for the job. From this, ways to measure both the level of job performance and the employees' KSAs will have to be developed. Development of sound criteria is important, as they will be used not only to measure how employees are doing but also as a measure of training success. So let's examine this issue of criteria development in more detail. Two critical components of good criteria measures are that they should be both reliable and valid.

Reliability

Reliability is the consistency of a measurement. It is often calculated using a correlation coefficient. It can be measured in the following two ways: across similar measures **(split half reliability)** and across time **(test-retest reliability).**

For the **split half** method, let's assume that 100 multiple-choice questions are used to test students' knowledge of this course. To determine the reliability of the test, the instructor splits the test into two sections: even-numbered questions and odd-numbered questions. He considers them as separate tests, even though the 100 questions are given at the same time. Adding up the score of the odd-numbered and even-numbered questions provides two scores for each student. Correlating the two scores, the instructor determines how reliable the test is. A high correlation would suggest that the test is highly reliable.

In the **test-retest** method, the instructor gives the test today and again in three days. He correlates student scores from the two time periods. Again, a high correlation between the two sets of scores would indicate a reliable test.

Highly reliable criteria measures are important. Consider a criterion for a machinist who has completed training. He must produce a shaft exactly four centimeters thick. A test is constructed requiring the trainee to produce a shaft with the correct specifications. To pass the test, the trainee must produce a shaft with a measurement that can be off by no more than 2/1,000ths of a centimeter. The evaluator measures the shaft with a micrometer (a measurement instrument able to detect differences in thousandths of centimeters). She finds it 1/1,000th of a centimeter too large. If she measured it tomorrow, she would find the same results. If another instructor measured it using the same procedure, he would find the same results. This criterion is highly reliable. If a ruler is used instead of a micrometer, the results still might be reliable but less so, because the less accurate ruler makes judgment errors in reading the scale more likely. Developing well-designed instrumentation, therefore, is important to obtaining a reliable measure, whether it is for a machinist or a measure of interpersonal skills.

Although developing a reliable instrument is important, the reliability in the *use* of the instrument is of equal importance. Both the instrument and the procedure used in applying it affect the reliability of the results. Without training, the evaluator in the example above would not know how much to tighten the micrometer around the shaft before obtaining the measurement. If one evaluator tightened it as much as he could and another tightened it just until she felt the first sign of resistance, the difference in results could be more than the 2/1,000ths of a centimeter tolerance allowed.

Validity

Validity is the degree to which a measurement actually measures what you say it measures. Compared with reliability (the consistency of a measure), validity is more difficult to assess. Consider the question, "Has training resulted in learning?" Learning is a physiological process that takes place in the brain. We cannot assess this process directly, so we test individuals and, on the basis of their scores, we infer whether learning takes place. It is not a direct measure of the learning process but an inference based on behavior.

To better understand the problems associated with validity, let's look at what we call the **ultimate criterion.**[1] The ultimate criterion is what we would like to be able to measure if it were possible to do so. It would include the exact indicators of the object being

Figure 4-7 Diagram Illustrating the Criterion (Constructs) of Deficiency, Relevance, and Contamination

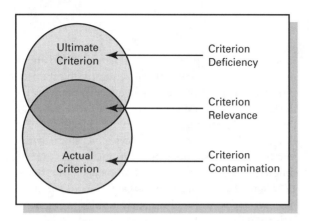

measured. However, we are never able to measure the ultimate criterion, because it is simply a theoretical construct. We must settle for what we are able to measure, which is the **actual criterion.**[2] Examining the relationship between the ultimate criterion and the actual criterion provides us with insight into the problems associated with criteria development. The actual criterion, what we settle for, can be thought of in terms of its relevance, deficiency, and contamination in relation to the ultimate criterion (see Figure 4-7).

Criterion Relevancy Criterion relevancy is the portion of the actual criterion that overlaps the ultimate criterion (see Figure 4-7) and represents the validity of the actual criterion. However, given that we can never measure the ultimate criterion, an empirical measure of this validity (a correlation between the ultimate criterion and actual criterion) is not possible. This problem illustrates the need for logical and rational analysis in developing the actual criterion to obtain the best approximation of the ultimate criterion.

Let's look at an example in which training is designed to improve interpersonal relationships. Raters evaluate the learning by rating a trainee's behaviors in a scripted role-play. The degrees to which the raters are trained, to which the scales to be used in rating are well developed, and to which examples of acceptable and less acceptable behavior are clear to the raters are all factors that contribute to the validity of the criterion (overlap of actual with ultimate). Because these will never match the ultimate criterion perfectly, deficiencies and contamination will always be factors. The more rigorous the development of criterion measures and processes, however, the more the actual criterion will approach the ultimate criterion.

Criterion Deficiency Criterion deficiency is the part of the ultimate criterion that we miss when we use the actual criterion or the degree to which we are not measuring important aspects of performance. The factors that make up a trainee's ability to produce parts with a tolerance of a few thousandths of a centimeter are more complex than simply being able to do it under ideal testing conditions. Factors such as noise in the plant, climate in the plant, different types of parts that need to be machined, and supervisor–subordinate relationships contribute to making a machinist successful. Our measure of success (producing one part in a training room) will obviously be deficient when compared with an ultimate measure of a successful machinist, which takes into consideration all the above factors (the ultimate criterion).

Criterion Contamination Just as any measure will miss some important aspects of true success (criterion deficiency), so too will it contain some part that measures aspects not related to the true measure of success **(criterion contamination).** This part of the actual criterion does not overlap with the ultimate criterion.[3]

The two main categories of contamination are error and bias. **Error** is random variation. It is, by definition, not correlated with anything, and, therefore, not as great a concern as is bias. Error lowers validity but does not cause misrepresentation of the data unless the error is too large. Then, of course, error can be a problem. Poorly trained evaluators, poorly developed instruments, or other factors could also cause high error content.

When the contamination is **bias** rather than error, it means you are measuring something other than what you want to measure. A large amount of contamination will lead to erroneous conclusions about the object you are measuring. Four sources of such bias are opportunity bias, group characteristic bias, bias in ratings, and knowledge of predictor bias.[4]

When certain individuals have some advantage that provides them with a higher level of performance, irrespective of their own skill level, **opportunity bias** occurs. Suppose, for example, you wanted to know if knowledge gained during training predicted performance on the job. To do this, you would correlate the scores on the training exam with performance one year later. If the correlation is positive and strong, this suggests those scoring highest on the training test also produced the most product and best quality (i.e., a high correlation between success in training and overall performance after training). However, those who scored the highest in training received the newest machines to work on as a reward. The relationship between the two scores was contaminated by the fact that the better trainees received the better machines. These machines might have provided the opportunity for success.

If something about the group creates higher (or lower) performance, irrespective of an individual's capability, that is called **group characteristic bias.** For example, trainees who did well in training are placed with Supervisor A, who is progressive and participative in her approach. Those who did less well in training are placed with a more authoritarian supervisor, Supervisor B, who will "keep an eye on them." Once again, those who did better in training might produce more and better-quality products as a function of the climate created by Supervisor A, not the training they received.

Bias in performance ratings is another possible contaminant. Bias in performance ratings is that portion of the actual criterion which is not correlated with the ultimate criterion but correlated with variables used by raters in their subjective judgments. Supervisors often use subjective ratings in evaluations. These ratings can be tainted because even in areas where objective data are available, it might not reflect the actual skill level of the worker. Some workers have better territories (sales), better equipment (machinist), or a better (clean, well-lit) environment. In many cases, the supervisor does not take these differences into account when rating subordinates. One of the most frequent biases in performance ratings is the **halo effect.** This is a powerful force in rating subordinates. It occurs when a supervisor rates a subordinate on all dimensions of performance on the basis of knowledge of only one dimension. For example, Susan is well organized, so she is rated as a great performer. Supervisors need to be trained to avoid these biases.

The final possible contaminant is **knowledge of predictor bias.** The criterion for success in training could be thought of as a predictor of later performance on the job; successful training should contribute to successful performance. But knowing each employee's success level in training could influence the supervisor's ratings at some time in the future.

Relationship Between Reliability and Validity Reliability is the consistency of a measure, and validity is the degree to which you are measuring what you want to measure. As an example, imagine that a rifle manufacturer has two new rifles he wishes to test for their ability to hit the bull's-eye. He places the first rifle in a vise-like mechanism to prevent deviation, which occurs if a person were doing the shooting. For the purpose of this discussion, we will change the terminology for validity slightly. We will say that validity is "doing what you want it to do" rather than "measuring what you want to measure." Conceptually, these notions are the same. In the vise, the first rifle is aimed at a target 50 yards away, and five shots are fired. Each shot hits the target (see Figure 4-8A). Is the rifle (instrument) consistent (reliable)? As you can see, the five bullets struck the target but they are all over the place. The rifle is not reliable. Nor is it valid (doing what you want it to do: hit the bull's-eye). There is no point trying to make the rifle valid (doing what you want it to do) because it has no reliability; you need reliability before you can have validity. The next rifle is placed in the vise. This time the five shots are all in the upper left-hand corner of the target (Figure 4-8B). Is the rifle reliable? Yes, because it consistently hit in the same place for all five shots. Is it valid? No, it did not hit the bull's-eye. We now adjust the sight and fire; all five hit the bull's-eye (Figure 4-8C). Is this rifle reliable? Yes, the bullets were all in relatively the same place (consistent). Is it valid? Yes, all five hit the bull's-eye as well.

From this example, it should be clear that you can have a reliable test that is not valid, but you cannot have a valid test that is not reliable (Figure 4-8). You need consistency of a measure before you even consider expecting all the bullets to hit the bull's-eye. Reliability, therefore, is a primary concern, but only because you need it to have validity.

Figure 4-8 A Comparison Reliability and Validity

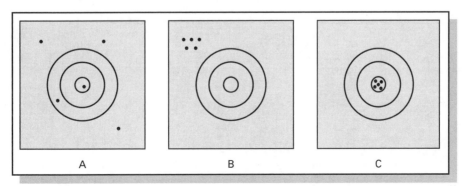

Development of Criteria It might seem that developing sound criteria is impossible. Not so. As we discussed previously, the operational analysis identifies the level of acceptable performance and the KSAs required to meet this performance level. From this analysis, criteria can be developed. Once criteria are established, the next step is to carefully develop instruments to measure the criteria. The instruments should leave as little as possible to the judgment of the rater.

Consider the job of internal auditor. One of the tasks identified from the operational analysis is "knowledge of which reference books to use for auditing problems." A part of the knowledge required, then, is to know what is contained in the various reference manuals. Training would require the trainee to learn what was contained in the various reference books. A criterion for success would be demonstrating this knowledge.

If you want to develop a reliable and valid measure of the criterion "understanding what is contained in the reference manuals," an excellent method would be a multiple-choice test of the material. The advantage of a well-designed multiple-choice test is that minimal judgment is necessary. So no matter who scores the test, the outcome will be the same, making it highly reliable. Taking care to choose a cross section of questions from all the material will provide a level of validity. Given that well-designed multiple-choice tests can accurately measure any type of knowledge,[5] we strongly suggest their use when possible.

Developing sound criteria for skills is more difficult and may not be as reliable. However, instruments to measure skills, if carefully developed, can still meet reliability requirements. Some examples of such measuring instruments are presented in the discussion of evaluation in Chapter 9, under "Fabrics, Inc."

In the internal auditor example above, an expected behavior might be "calm an irate department head." The skill required to accomplish this behavior could be "active listening." A measure of the criterion would be how a trainee behaves in a role-play situation in which the role-player becomes angry at something the auditor says.

In the case of measuring the criterion "calming an irate department head," it is critical to develop clear rules and examples of what is and is not acceptable. Also, it is important to train raters in the use of the rules and to provide examples. The more familiar the raters are with good, average, and poor responses, the more reliable the measure can be.

Validity in such instances is called **content validity,** when an expert examines the criteria on the basis of her knowledge of the TNA.[6] It is important, therefore, to conduct a good TNA, for everything that follows from it (both training content and evaluation instruments) is based on that analysis.

The time and effort spent developing a sound criterion are critical to the training process. Once developed, the criterion is used to determine the

- Expected level of performance (operational analysis)
- Likelihood that the incumbent can reach it (person analysis)
- Training needs for those who cannot reach it (a training objective)
- Measure of training effectiveness (training success).

Chapter 5

Training Design

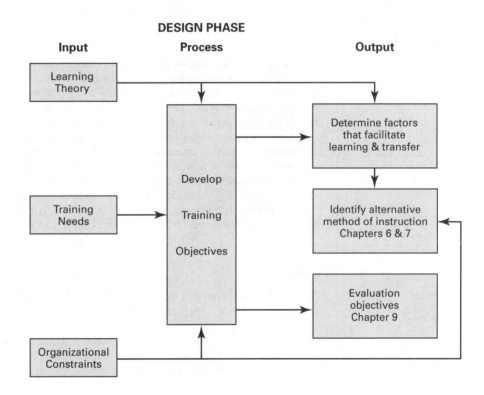

DESIGN PHASE

Input	Process	Output

- Learning Theory
- Training Needs
- Develop Training Objectives
- Organizational Constraints
- Determine factors that facilitate learning & transfer
- Identify alternative method of instruction Chapters 6 & 7
- Evaluation objectives Chapter 9

Learning Objectives

After reading this chapter, you should be able to:

➤ *Identify three constraints a human resources department (HRD) might face in the design of training, and what might be done to deal with each.*

➤ *Describe the purpose of learning objectives, the criteria for evaluating such objectives, and the advantages of developing these objectives.*

➤ *List the reasons that learning objectives are a benefit to the trainee, training designer, trainer, and training evaluator.*

➤ *Use expectancy theory to explain how to motivate a trainee to attend training.*

153

➤ Describe social learning theory and how it helps in the design of training.

➤ Identify what to include in training to facilitate transfer of training to the workplace.

➤ Identify the help that supervisors, peers, and trainers can provide back on the job to assist in the transfer of training.

➤ Explain the relationship between the Gagné-Briggs theory of instruction and social learning theory.

➤ Use elaboration theory and the Gagné-Briggs theory of instructional design to design a training session.

➤ Describe the advantages a small business has when considering the transfer of training.

CASE: The Real World of Training . . . What Is Wrong Here?

Case 1

A large government-operated training establishment offered a course in which trainees learned how to operate and repair a large, complex electronic system. The goal of the course was simple: to develop trainees' ability to operate and maintain the electronic system. It was impossible to provide an individual system to each trainee for practice, so the instructor decided to increase the amount of troubleshooting experience by providing classroom exercises on troubleshooting. The instructor posed various problems for the trainees to solve. For a specific problem, such as a burned-out capacitor, he asked the trainees to identify the symptoms that would appear (e.g., the control board would not operate). After the training, the instructor was surprised to learn that many trainees were not doing well on the job. They seemed to be able to operate the equipment, but when it came to troubleshooting, they were not performing well.

Case 2

The chief instructor of a 32-week military course examined the grades of the last four groups that completed the course. He noted an unusual trend. Trainees did poorly on the first exam but then did considerably better on the second and third exams. Then the trainees did poorly on the fourth, but improved on the fifth and sixth. This trend continued throughout the 32 weeks, even for the brightest trainees. What was going on here?

Source: Mager, R. *Preparing Instructional Objectives* (1975). Belmont, CA: Pitman Learning. CEP Press Center for Effective Performance, Inc.

INTRODUCTION TO THE DESIGN OF TRAINING

The design phase of training is a process of identifying the set of specifications that will be used in the development phase for creating the training modules. In the simplest terms, the design phase answers the following questions:

- Why is training needed?
- Who will be trained?

- What are the training objectives, and what methods will be used?
- When and where will training take place?
- What are the principles that will be used to facilitate the learning of the material and its transfer to the job?

The model of the design phase at the start of the chapter provides an overview of the process and guides our discussion in this chapter. The training needs analysis (TNA) results, along with organizational constraints and learning theories, are the inputs into the design phase. Once training needs have been identified, additional research is needed to determine what constraints exist that must be accommodated and how learning theory applies to the training. These inputs are used to determine the **learning objectives**—the process part of the model. The first of the three outputs for this phase is to determine the factors that facilitate learning and transfer of training, which is what this chapter is about. The two other outputs that come from the design phase are discussed in separate chapters. Identifying the most appropriate method of instruction is discussed in Chapters 6 and 7. Determining the methods for evaluating the training is discussed briefly here, and in much more detail in Chapter 9.

In summary, training needs, learning theories, and an understanding of the constraints placed on the training process are the inputs into the first step of the design phase—developing objectives. These objectives are then used to drive the rest of this phase and subsequent phases (development, implementation, and evaluation). Decisions we make about training design integrate what we know about *how* people learn (learning theory) with *what* they need to learn (training objectives). From there, we develop the appropriate training, taking into consideration any constraints (money, time, facilities, etc.) we face. Suppose that an HRD department completed a TNA that identified that supervisors need training in effective communication skills. The next decisions to be made include the following:

- What will the training achieve
- What methods of training will be used
- How much time will be allotted for the training
- How many trainees will be trained at the same time
- Whether this training will be conducted on company time or overtime
- Whether this training will be voluntary or mandatory
- Where to locate training

Organizational constraints will influence many of these decisions. For example, if the HRD department does not have the resources to develop the program, or if supervisors cannot be off the job for more than a half-day, then these factors will help shape what the training will look like and how it will be offered.

ORGANIZATIONAL CONSTRAINTS

In a perfect world, it would be possible to develop the perfect training program for every training need identified. For supervisors who need effective communication training, you could develop a two-week intensive training package using the most effective methods with plenty of practice built in. Reality prevails, however, and you must consider the constraints on training design. Many of these constraints influence the type of training that can be offered. Table 5-1 provides a list of some of these constraints and various ways to approach training design on the basis of these constraints. This list is not exhaustive and serves primarily as an example of the ways in which organizational constraints affect the methods and approaches used to meet the training needs. We discuss two major categories of constraints: organizational/environmental and trainee population. Each affects the issue of whether to train and the type of training that can be offered.

Table 5-1 Some Organizational Constraints and Ways of Dealing with Them

CONSTRAINT	SUGGESTION FOR HOW TO HANDLE
Need high level of simulation[a] because:	
Law (fire drills)	
Task is critical to the job (police firing a gun)	Incorporate longer lead times to prepare simulations/role-plays.
Mistakes are costly (airline pilot)	Purchase simulators.
Trainees vary in amount of experience	Consider modularization.
Trainees have large differences in ability levels	Use programmed instruction—Have high level of trainer–trainee interaction.
Mix of employees and new hires trained on a new procedure	Consider different training programs because of possible negative transfer for employees but not for new hires.
Long lag between end of training and use of skill on the job	Distribute practice through the lag. Provide refresher material or models for the employees to follow.
Short lead time	Use external consultant or packaged training.
Bias against a type of training (e.g., role-play)	Develop proof of effectiveness into the training package. Use another method.
Few trainees available at any one time	Use programmed instruction.[b]
Small organization with limited funds	Hire consultant or purchase training—Join consortium.

[a] This constraint results if you are forced to provide a more costly training program involving simulators or costly practice sessions, and so forth.
[b] This method of instruction is discussed in Chapter 7. It provides self-paced learning.

Organizational/Environmental Constraints

Budgets generally are limited, so choices must be made about who gets trained and what type of training they receive. One way of making these decisions is to use the strategic direction of the organization to set priorities. The strategic plan provides a rationale for determining who gets how much of what kind of training. Recall the Domtar case presented in Chapter 1. The "Domtar difference" was "tapping the intelligence of the experts, our employees." The tactic for doing this was the introduction of Kaizen. Clearly, then, training dollars will be marked for such training given that it is a primary operating principle. The next decision is to determine whether Domtar plans to use internal resources for the training or hire outside consultants. Here, they decided to hire someone with the expertise and bring them in-house to oversee a major undertaking—the training of all employees in the Kaizen method.

Even if the organization does not have a clear strategic plan in place, the top managers in human resources (HR) can establish priorities by meeting with senior executives. Such meetings help define HR and HRD priorities and determine how to put resources in line with the direction of the company. A side benefit is that the process might stimulate top management to engage in strategic planning.

The technological sophistication of the organization affects the type of training that can be offered. If, as in the Domtar case, there are many locations, and each location has access to computer networks or videoconferencing, the type of training you can offer will be different from that offered by an organization without these capabilities.

Decisions about training priorities also must follow the law. As discussed in Chapter 1, some training is mandated by law. For example, one study noted that 29 percent of organizations surveyed provided safety training on a weekly or monthly basis and another 36 percent on a quarterly or yearly basis.[1] How much of this training is a function of legal requirements is not clear, but it is likely that it plays an important part.

Budgeting for Training

The budgeting process presented here is from the perspective of the HRD department that charges its customers (departments in the organization) for the services that HRD provides. Charging for services is occurring more frequently in organizations because HRD departments are being asked to justify their existence just like other departments. In fact, in some cases, they are expected to market their training outside and inside the organization.[2] This budgeting process is, for the most part, similar to that used by an outside consultant bidding on a project. So, when providing estimates, understand that departments are competing for resources and that the estimate must be as accurate as possible. Otherwise, the department could lose the training to an outside consultant or have the training put off until later.

In creating a budget for a particular training program, estimates of training cost can be difficult to determine accurately. Because the estimate is often expected before a needs assessment is completed (or even begun), providing budgets for several scenarios is helpful to decision makers. Before a TNA, there is not really a clear idea of what, or how much, training is required. So how to start? Begin with the triggering event, as explained in Chapter 4. Provide budget estimates for different training scenarios or deal with this issue the way it was done in the Fabrics, Inc., example presented at the end of Chapter 4. Recall that the consultant offered to do a TNA at a given cost, providing the company with a clearer idea of what would be required. To avoid any ethical issues the consultant offered to bid on any training that might result from the TNA in competition with any other consultants Fabrics might consider. The resulting bids would be more accurate because the issues were identified and the type of training required would be clearer.

Once the objectives of training are determined, it is necessary to estimate the amount of time it will take to design and develop the training for delivery. The more accurate this estimate is, the more accurate the costing will be, and the more credibility the department will have with clients. The length of the training program (how long it takes to actually deliver the training) is a good guide for estimating the length of time to prepare. The ratio of preparation time to training days varies a great deal, however. It can range from 12:1, if much of the material is in some form of readiness, to 300:1, if it is computer-based training with little already prepared. In many cases, when training is requested, the client wants a proposed training solution and its associated costs quickly.

To respond quickly, Brooke Broadbent, a training consultant, developed a method for estimating how long it will take to develop training. This guide is shown in Table 5-2. It is possible to make a rough calculation of the length of time it will take to develop the training. First, circle low, medium, or high for each of the 12 variables related to the questions on who, what, and how. Count up the numbers that were circled in each column, and put that number at the bottom of the table. Multiply as instructed in the table, and add the totals from the three columns together. That is the approximate number of days it will take. The calculation will depend on many factors, including the trainer's expertise in developing training programs.

Imagine calculating a bid on a one-day workshop on effective communication. Using Table 5-2, you check "low" for all but the last factor (degree of interactivity). You rate "high" for this item because of the extensive interaction within the training program. On the basis of the table, the training will require 14 days to prepare $(11 \times 1) + (0 \times 2) + (1 \times 3)$. A simple calculation on overall cost could be done on the basis of this information, but it might seem high to those not knowing what is involved in the development of training. So it is useful to have some sort of breakdown, as depicted in Table 5-3. With such estimates, it is a good idea to build in a contingency fund of about 10 percent, to help cover unforeseen costs. This portion is indicated under "miscellaneous." The "rate" should include both the trainer's

Table 5-2
Estimating the Time
Required to Design
and Develop
Training

Designer Competencies	Level
Instructional Design Competency	1 = high 2 = medium 3 = low
Understanding of Subject Matter	1 = high 2 = medium 3 = low
Size and Diversity of Participant Group	1 = small or medium and homogenous 2 = medium and moderately diverse 3 = medium and very diverse 4 = large and very diverse
Amount of Material to be Covered	1 = 1 to 3 modules 2 = 4 to 6 modules 3 = 7 to 10 modules 4 = 11 to 13 modules
Complexity of Material to be Covered	1 = simple 2 = moderate 3 = complex 4 = very complex
Level of Professionalism Required in Appearance	1 = low 2 = moderate 4 = high level
Level of Completion (draft, pilot, or full delivery)	1 = draft 2 = up to pilot 4 = complete to ready for delivery
Amount of Client Collaboration and Input	0 = none 1 = minimal 2 = approval at each level 3 = at each juncture
Degree of Participant Engagement Required	0 = none 1 = some 2 = a moderate amount 3 = a great deal

Circle the number in each cell that represents the training you are developing. Then add up the numbers that are circled, and that represents the approximate number of days it will take to provide the training.

Assess each of the areas in the left-hand column by putting an X in the appropriate box. For each item that is rated low, put a "1" next to the X; for items rated medium, put a "2" in the box; and for items rated high, put a "3" in the box. Now total your numbers, and this is an estimate of the number of days it will take to develop the training program if you are starting from scratch. Obviously, if you already have similar programs, the time will be reduced, based on how similar the program is.

Source: B. Broadbent, "The Training Formula," *Training & Development,* 1991, 52: 41–43.

fee and overhead costs. In the example depicted in Table 5-3, if the training were presented only once, the cost of the total training package would be $15,400 plus the cost of the one-day training session. If it is to be offered 10 times, then the total cost of the development can be amortized over the 10 sessions, making its cost per session or per employee much less.

So far, we have dealt only with the developmental costs associated with training. Direct costs associated with delivering the training (trainer compensation, travel, facilities, food and beverages, and so forth), indirect costs, overhead costs, participant compensation, and evaluation costs must also be included to determine the total

Table 5-3   Proposal for Developing a One-Day Workshop on Effective Communication

Action	Time (Days)	Rate ($)	Total Amount ($)
Prepare			
Interview relevant employees to determine issues and context to develop training	1	1,000	1,000
Develop objectives and plan for developing training, including identifying appropriate strategies (methods) to be used in instruction; also develop evaluation objectives	2.5	1,000	2,500
Develop training materials on the basis of objectives	8	1,000	8,000
Develop visual aids and evaluation material	2.5	1,000	2,500
Miscellaneous			1,400
Total			15,400

Table 5-4
Training Costs
for Grievance-
Reduction Training

Developmental Costs	
1. 20 days of director's time at $50,000 per year	$ 4,000
2. 5 days of trainer's time at $30,000 per year	$ 600
3. Materials	$ 1,000
Direct Costs	
1. 5 days of trainer's time at $30,000 per year	$ 600
2. Training facility rental for 5 days at $150 per day	$ 750
3. Materials and equipment	$ 2,000
4. Coffee, juice, and muffins	$ 600
Indirect Costs	
1. 1 day of trainer preparation at $30,000 per year	$ 120
2. 3 days of administrative preparation at $20,000 per year	$ 240
Participant Compensation	
1. 30 supervisors attending 5-day workshop (average $35,000/year)	$ 21,000
Evaluation Costs	
1. 6 days of evaluator's time at $30,000 per year	$ 720
2. Materials	$ 800
Total Training Costs	**$ 32,430**

Note: Calculations for the personnel costs are based on a 250-day work year.

cost. For an example of a more inclusive estimate of the total costs associated with delivering a training program, see Table 5-4.

Trainee Population   What if the TNA identifies two or more subgroups with the same learning objectives but different levels of knowledge, skills, and attitudes (KSAs)? It is difficult to develop a single training program to meet all their needs. Going back to our supervisors who need the communication training, what if the TNA indicated that half of them previously received training in active listening and were reasonably proficient in it? The effective communication model we plan to use in the training of supervisors involves five steps, the first of which is active listening. The training could be designed in a modular manner to provide only the relevant modules to each subgroup. In our supervisor example, the first module would be skill building in the active listening process, and only those not already proficient would need to attend. Then all of the supervisors would receive the effective communication training, with the understanding that all were proficient in the active listening portion of the model.

Sometimes the needs analysis identifies a wide variability in the KSAs of the target population. In this case, the training design could provide individualized instruction, accomplished through computer-based or video instruction, although both take a long time to develop. Another alternative would be to allow for small classes and a high level of interaction between the instructor and each trainee.

In some instances, trainees hold negative feelings about a particular training technique. If this attitude is known during the design stage, a different technique can be considered. Alternatively, the design could build in attitude-change modules at the beginning. We found, for example, that many managers do not want to role-play in training. We often hear arguments such as "This is silly," or "These never work." One way to handle this resistance is simply to call it something different. The term *play,* for some, suggests that it is not serious learning. Sometimes when we present the technique, we suggest it is time for some "behavioral practice." This simple change in terms causes the exercise to be received more positively. The point here is that if, through the needs analysis, it is discovered that a particular method of training is disliked because of past experience or word of mouth, the training design should include a way of changing the perception or another method should be used.

While organizational constraints influence most aspects of the training process, they can have a real impact on the development of the training objectives. As stated earlier, it would be wonderful if we could always deliver the perfect training to satisfy the training needs. Unfortunately, we face constraints on what we are able to do, thus the objectives we set for training must be realistic, reflecting what is achievable. The budget available, the nature of the employees needing training, and so on, will place limits on what can be achieved. Once you have a general understanding of what can be achieved, you will need to refine that into clear objective statements.

DEVELOPING OBJECTIVES

The term *training objectives* refers to all the objectives that are developed for the training program. There are generally four types of training objectives: reaction, learning, transfer of training, and organizational outcome (see Table 5-5). Reaction objectives refer to the objectives set for how trainees should feel about the training and their learning environment. Learning objectives describe the KSAs that trainees are expected to acquire throughout the training program and the ways that learning will be demonstrated. Transfer of training objectives describes the changes in job behavior that are expected to occur as a result of transferring the KSAs gained in training to the trainee's job. Organizational outcome objectives describe the outcomes that the organization can expect from the changes in the trainees' job behavior as a result of the learning. Ideally, a training program would develop objectives in all four areas.

Creating Objectives

The TNA is a critical part of determining what the objectives of training should be. To summarize briefly, integrating the organization, operation, and person analyses results in the identification of performance gaps. With this information, you determine the following:

- Which performance gaps can and should be addressed by training
- Which KSAs need to be learned so that job behavior is changed and performance deficiencies are reduced or eliminated

Table 5-5   Types of Training Objectives

Trainee Reaction Objectives	Describes the desired attitudinal and subjective evaluations of training by the trainee
Learning Objectives	Describes the type of behavior that will demonstrate the learning, the conditions under which the behavior must occur, and the criteria that will signify that a sufficient level of learning has occurred
Transfer of Training Objectives	Describes the job behaviors that will be affected by training, the conditions under which those behaviors must occur, and the criteria that will signify that a sufficient transfer of learning from training to the job has occurred
Organizational Outcome Objectives	Describes the organizational outcomes that will be affected by the transfer of learning to the job and the criteria that will signify that organizational outcome objectives were achieved.

From the performance gaps, we set the learning objectives, transfer of training objectives, and organizational outcome objectives. Trainee reaction objectives can be linked to the person analysis but also might include areas not addressed in the needs analysis. For example, consider that you determined in the person analysis that a group of line employees do not like training. A reaction objective here might be, "At the end of training, trainees will respond to questions about their experiences in the training environment with either a positive or very positive response."

Although the content of the various types of objectives differs, the structure and process of developing good objective statements is the same. Objectives are statements about what is expected to be accomplished. A good objective has three components:[3]

1. *Desired outcome:* What should be expected to occur?
2. *Conditions:* Under what conditions is the outcome expected to occur?
3. *Standards:* What criteria signify that the outcome is acceptable?

It is difficult to write good objectives. You must take care to ensure that the three components are specified in unambiguous terms and that the full range of expectations is addressed.

Writing a Good Learning Objective

We focus attention on learning objectives for two reasons:

1. Learning objectives are often the most difficult to write.
2. Learning is the central purpose of the training.

Clearly articulated learning objectives are a critical first step in developing an effective training program. Learning can be observed only through its influence on behavior. Thus, when writing a learning objective, think not only about what will be learned but also about how the learning will be demonstrated.

Desired Outcome: Behavior

The desired behavior must be worded clearly and unambiguously. Anyone reading the objective should be able to understand what the learner will be required to do to demonstrate that she learned the KSA. A learning objective that states, "After completing the training, the trainees will understand how to splice electrical wire" is ambiguous. It fails to specify what trainee behavior will indicate that the trainee "understands." Recall that just a few sentences ago we said—think not only about what will be learned but also about how the learning will be demonstrated. A clearer learning objective would be: "will be able to splice electrical wires of any gauge." This statement indicates what the learner should be able to do at the end of training. Consider another example: "The trainee will demonstrate how to differentiate (by sorting into two piles) between computer chips that are within specification and those that are outside of specification." Here the behavior is clear, but not how the trainee is expected to differentiate between the computer chips. Will the trainees have gauges to work with? Will he have to be able to tell by simply looking at the chips? The conditions under which the person will sort the chips are not stated.

Conditions

Explaining the conditions under which the behavior must occur further clarifies exactly what is required. In the preceding example, it is not clear what, if any, aids will be available to the trainee to determine whether the computer chips are within specifications. Providing the conditions makes the objective even clearer: "Using an ohmmeter and a chart, the trainee will be able to differentiate (by sorting into two piles) between computer chips that are within specification and those that are outside of specification."

A description of the conditions (assistance or barriers) under which the desired behavior will be performed should be provided when creating objectives. For example, the statement "Using an ohmmeter and a chart" indicates the help that is provided. If the objective began with the phrase "Without the use of reference material," it is clear that the trainee must discriminate between the chips without using any aids.

Writing in conditions is necessary in some cases but not in others. In the following example, it is critical to know that the pie charts must be developed using a specific software package: "Present the results of an accounting problem in pie chart form, using the Harvard Graphics software." Objectives often begin with the phrase, "After completing the training, the trainee will. . . ." This is condition, as it states when the behavior will occur. However, it isn't always necessary to include this statement, as it is typically understood that the objectives for the trainees are measured at the end of the training. However, for transfer of training and organizational objectives, the point at which the objectives are achieved typically doesn't occur until sometime after training has ended. For example, a transfer of training objective might read as follows: "Six weeks after the completion of training, the rate of incorrectly sorted computer chips will drop from the pretraining rate of 3 percent to less than 0.01 percent." Conditions should be included only if they help clarify what is required.

Standards

Standards are the criteria for success. Three potential standards are accuracy, quality, and speed. For example, a learning objective might define accuracy as "being able to take a reading off an altimeter with an error of no more than three meters." A quality standard might be indicated by the statement "is within engineering specifications 99.9 percent of the time." Or, if speed is a critical concern, "will be completed in 15 minutes or less."

Here are a few examples of learning objectives for a telephone repairperson. The desired behavior is **bolded,** the conditions are *italicized*, and the standards are <u>underlined</u>.

> *Using a drop wire, bushing, and connector, but without the use of a manual,* **the trainee will splice a drop wire** <u>meeting the standards set out in the manual</u>.
> *Using a standard climbing harness and spikes,* **the trainee will climb a standard telephone pole** <u>within five minutes, following all safety procedures</u>.
> **The trainee will splice,** <u>according to code,</u> **six sets of wires** <u>in ten minutes</u> *while at the top of a telephone pole wearing all standard safety gear*.

The Formula for Writing the Objective

The outcome specifies the type of behavior; the conditions state where, when, and what tools will be used; and standards describe the criteria for judging the adequacy of the behavior. Remember that a learning objective should state clearly what the result of the training will be. Here are the steps to follow:

- Write out the "desired behavior." Here, the verb needs to describe clearly what will be done: A "doing" verb is used to indicate some action. Do not use the word *understand*. Always make sure that the verb describes an action. Examples of "doing" verbs are provided in Table 5-6 below.
- Now add the conditions under which the behavior must be performed. This description encompasses the use or nonuse of aids. So "using an ohmmeter," "using reference material provided," "using a standard climbing harness and spikes," "while at the top of a telephone pole," "without the use of a manual,"

Table 5-6
Types of Doing
Verbs

Knowledge	Analyze, cite, compare, define, describe, distinguish, explain, identify, list, provide, name, quote, reproduce
Skills	Assemble, compute, construct, count, design, demonstrate, eliminate, install, list, measure, operate, place, recite, replace, solve, sort
Attitudes	Align, belong, choose, commit, criticize, decide, praise

"without the use of a calculator" are all examples of conditions that would be expected in certain situations.

- Finally, it needs to be clear what standards for success will be used. How will the trainee know that he successfully completed the training? What level of accuracy is required? Is quality or speed an important part of success? "According to code," "following all safety procedures," "within five minutes," "according to the manual" "within 15 minutes," "with no more than three errors," and "obtaining a score of 80 percent" are all possible standards.

Now, to test whether the learning objective is effective, ask someone to read it and explain exactly what she believes a trainee needs to do, under what conditions, and how the trainee will know if she is successful. If the person can articulate these factors, the learning objective is a good one.

Table 5-7 provides some examples of poorly written learning objectives followed by an improved version. For some practice in writing a good learning objective, cover the right column of Table 5-7 and read the poorly written learning objective on the left side of the table. Improve this objective using the formula. Now check the right side for an example of how the objective can be improved. How did you do? Now do the remaining objectives, as this will provide good practice for writing effective learning objectives.

Table 5-7   Learning Objectives Improved

BEFORE	AFTER
Upon completion of training, the trainee	*Upon completion of training, the trainee*
Will be able to apply theories of motivation to different situations.	Will be able, after reading a scenario of an unmotivated trainee, to identify orally what she would do to motivate the trainee, and explain which theory she used and why. The explanation must identify at least three motivators and tie them to correct theory. The trainee must do the above on four of five scenarios, without the use of any outside material.
Will be able to recognize and identify different personalities, and know how to motivate them.	Will be able to watch a fellow trainee role-play a situation and correctly explain in writing what type of personality is being exhibited and what to do to motivate the trainee. Trainee must be 100% correct on the personality and identify at least two motivators.
Will understand what is necessary to have an effective team.	Will be able to correctly tell the trainer five things that are necessary to have an effective team.
Will have knowledge of three types of active listening, and will be able to use the appropriate one in a particular situation.	Will be able to correctly identify, at the end of training and in writing, three of the active listening techniques that were identified in training.
	In a role-play, will be able to respond verbally to an angry comment using one of the appropriate active listening types, and orally explain which was used and why.
Will be able to say no to boss and peers when asked to do extra work.	In a role-play, will be able to correctly use one of the ways of saying "no" from the training, and orally explain which was used and why, with 100% accuracy.

The other three types of objectives listed in Table 5-5 require similar components. For example, a transfer of training objective might read as follows:

After completing training, participants, *at their regular job station* and *using an ohmmeter and a chart*, **will be able to separate acceptable (within specifications) from unacceptable (outside specifications) computer chips** <u>with an accuracy of 99.99 percent</u> *while sorting a minimum of 10 chips per minute.*

Attitudes

Sometimes attitudes, in addition to knowledge and skills, are the focus of training. How do you write a learning objective for an attitude? When the goal of training is attitude change, the focus of training activities is to provide the trainees with information that contradicts inappropriate attitudes and supports more appropriate attitudes. Thus, training does not focus on changing attitudes specifically, but rather on providing new knowledge. This new knowledge might consist of alternative views and information related to attitudes. Therefore, learning objectives for attitude change should focus on acquisition of the relevant information rather than on the resulting attitude change.

Consider training that is attempting to improve attitudes toward teamwork in a group of trainees who all scored below the midpoint on a TNA teamwork awareness survey. In this case, the learning objective might read as follows: At the end of training, trainees will demonstrate an increased awareness of the positive aspects of teamwork (new knowledge) as demonstrated by a 50 percent improvement on the team awareness survey.

Recall that the reason we want to affect an attitude is to influence behavior. In this example, we want trainees to have positive attitudes so that once they are back in the workplace, they will participate fully in team meetings and provide input. The transfer of training objective in this case might be "Eight weeks after completing training, the participants will have attended all team meetings and, using the skills taught, provide ideas and suggestions in those meetings." Another might be "Eight weeks after completing training, the participants' performance rating in team meetings (as rated by other team members) will average one point higher than before training."

Purpose Statements

At times you will need to communicate only a short statement of what the training is intended to accomplish. This is called a purpose statement. The purpose statement is used to synthesize the individual training objectives into one clear statement regarding what the training will be all about. This can be useful when first communicating with trainees or others about an upcoming training program (invitations, announcements, and the like). In these initial communications, you want to convey the overall purpose of the training without getting into the detail of the individual objectives. So, the purpose statement should describe what the trainee will be able to do as a result of the training but should not contain all of the detail in the formal objectives. For example, if the previous section of this chapter were to be converted into a training workshop, some of the formal training objectives might be those described below.

Given a set of training needs, organizational priorities, and constraints, the trainees, at the end of training, using notes and materials from the training, will be able to

1. Identify the needs that should be met by the training
2. Write learning objectives for each of the needs that meet the guidelines specified in the training for good objectives (i.e., behavior, standards and conditions)

3. Write transfer of training objectives for the needs that meet the guidelines specified in the training for good objectives (i.e., behavior, standards and conditions)
4. Write organizational objectives for the training that meet the guidelines specified in the training for good objectives (i.e., observable changes in outcomes, standards, and conditions)

The purpose statement might read as follows: "The purpose of the Writing Training Objectives workshop is to provide participants with the ability to construct training objectives that effectively facilitate the design, development, and evaluation of training." This conveys the essential purpose of the training in a simple and straightforward manner. However, as we indicate in the following section, there are significant advantages to communicating the specific objectives to various audiences.

WHY USE TRAINING OBJECTIVES?

Developing good learning objectives takes time, effort, and careful thought. Why not spend that time constructively developing the actual training? In fact, some HRD specialists seriously question the value of specific learning objectives.[4] Some concerns about the use of objectives include the following:

- Waste of valuable time
- Inhibited flexibility
- Focus moved from other areas
- Unrealistic for management training and other soft areas of training
- Not practical in today's workplace

We respectfully disagree with those HRD specialists regarding the first concern; the argument is that resources are often scarce and the time taken to develop the objectives takes away from more important endeavors. On the face of it, this generalization might be true, but the objectives guide the development of training. They might even result in less time to develop the training because of the clear guidelines objectives provide. Go back and look at the objectives in Table 5-7. Note in the "After" column how much clearer the focus is regarding "what will be trained" as compared with the "Before" column.

Some suggest that objectives inhibit the trainer's flexibility to respond to trainee needs. The counterargument here is that a comprehensive TNA is designed to determine trainees' needs and that the objectives focus specifically on those needs. They do, perhaps, inhibit the trainer's flexibility to go off on tangents that she might like to pursue, but adhering to a focused direction is a positive thing. Moving the focus from other areas is again the point of having objectives. The idea is to keep the focus on the topics identified in the TNA.

Some argue that concrete objectives are not possible in management training or areas such as time management or interpersonal skills.[5] We note that whatever the training, the goal is to achieve certain outcomes, and those outcomes need to be translated into objectives. With time management, for example, you want trainees to gain some cognitive knowledge about strategies for time management. The purpose is for them to develop skills to use in the workplace. Trainees must know the skills before they can transfer them into the workplace. So articulating an objective that states, "At the end of training, trainees will demonstrate time management skills by completing an in-basket exercise within 45 minutes and be able to provide an appropriate time management rationale for each decision" makes perfect sense.

Finally, some say that objectives have outlived their usefulness, and they are too specific for today's complex jobs.[6] They say that we need to find methods that are better at determining what is required for effective performance. Although this reasoning might be true at a more macro level, the purpose of objectives as a guide for training development is still valid. The complexities of the job will surface during a TNA, but it is still necessary in any job to have competence in specific KSAs to be an effective performer.

The majority of HRD specialists agree with us that training objectives are important from the following stakeholders' perspectives:

- Trainee
- Designer of training
- Trainer
- Evaluator of training

The Trainee

Trainees benefit from training objectives because the training objectives

- Reduce anxiety related to the unknown
- Focus attention
- Increase the likelihood that the trainees will be successful in training

High levels of anxiety can negatively affect learning.[7] Not knowing what to expect in a situation creates anxiety. Training objectives provide a clear understanding of what will be taking place over the training period. This reduces the anxiety felt from not knowing what to expect. The objectives also focus attention on relevant topics to be trained, which, recalling social learning theory in Chapter 3, is the important first step to learning. Thus, from a learning theory perspective, it is important to let the trainee know what the performance expectations are and be able to refer to them throughout the training. Also, as was indicated in Chapter 3, this information will assist the learner in both focusing attention and cognitively organizing the new information. A key here is to make sure that your objectives are easily understood. Recall the formula for writing good objectives: you should check to make sure the objectives are clear and understandable. Finally, learning objectives increase relevant learning[8] and the likelihood that trainees will be successful in training. This makes sense according to goal-setting research,[9] which indicates that when specific and challenging goals are set, the probability is higher that these goals will be achieved than when no goal is set or an instruction to "do the best you can" is given.[10] A goal is what a learning objective is.

The Training Designer

The learning objectives guide the designer of the training or the purchaser of a training package. The objectives directly translate the training needs into training outcomes. With clear objectives, training methods and content can be checked against the objectives to ensure that they are consistent. Furthermore, evidence shows that following learning objectives results in the development of better lesson plans.[11]

Suppose the designer is told to "design training to provide salespeople with skills in customer service." Does the designer design a course in interpersonal skills so that salespeople learn how to be friendly and upbeat? Does the designer design a course in product knowledge so that the salesperson can provide information about the various products and their features to customers? Does the designer design a course in technical expertise so that salespeople can assist customers in getting the product to work effectively? Consider the learning objective that reads, "After completing training, participants will, using paraphrasing or decoding and feedback (desired outcome), respond to an angry customer (conditions), suggesting two alternative remedies judged by the customer to be appropriate for resolving the problem (standard)." This learning objective provides a clear, unambiguous goal for the designer. The designer can then design a course in active listening (paraphrasing, decoding, and feedback), with the focus on dealing with angry customers. Without that guidance, the training might not be designed appropriately.

The Trainer

With clear learning objectives, the trainer can facilitate the learning process more effectively. Clear, specific objectives allow the trainer to more readily determine how well the trainees are progressing and thus make the appropriate adjustments. In addition, the trainer can highlight the relationship of particular segments of the training to the objectives. Some trainers might see objectives as infringing on their freedom to train the way they want to. It is probably for those trainers that objectives do the most good, keeping the trainer on the right track.

The Evaluator

Evaluating training is much easier when objectives are used, because these objectives define the behaviors expected at the end of training. With no clear indication of what training is supposed to accomplish, an evaluator has no way to assess whether the training was effective. It is analogous to the army sergeant who tells the private, "Dig a hole here." The private starts to dig and the sergeant walks away. After digging for a few minutes, the private begins to worry because he knows he's in trouble. He doesn't know how deep the hole should be, how long, wide, or anything else. When the private sees the platoon leader walk by, he asks him, "How am I doing on this hole, sir?" The platoon leader, of course, says, "How should I know?" When good objectives are developed, the evaluator simply needs to assess whether the stated outcomes and standards are met.

FACILITATION OF LEARNING: FOCUS ON THE TRAINEE

Recall from Figure 3-1 on page 62 the formula for factors influencing performance ($P = M \times KSA \times E$). Many issues exist within each of these factors that will make it easier or more difficult for the trainee to achieve the learning objectives.

Individual Differences in KSAs

The TNA supplies information not only on the need for training but also on the trainees' readiness for such training. Let's take the example of employees recently hired or promoted. They were selected for their new job because of their KSAs, but they need some initial training to get them ready to perform in their new job (processes, procedures, and the like). Perfect selection techniques would ensure that these people have the requisite KSAs to be successful in training, but few selection techniques are perfect. Even the best selection practices result in a certain number of individuals who are selected but subsequently are not successful. If these false positives—those who are predicted to be successful but are not—can somehow be identified in the TNA, the design of training might be able to address the issues that would prevent them from being successful.

For example, some who are identified as in need of training might not have the requisite KSAs to make use of the training methods and materials that would be effective for 90 percent of the other potential trainees. Providing a preliminary training module for this group prior to the regular training might increase the likelihood of them successfully completing training.

The selection process sets minimum criteria (based on a job analysis) that individuals must meet to be selected. Even here, however, if all met those criteria, some individual differences in abilities would be evident. Some will show higher levels of the KSA in question, and others might not possess the minimum skills (e.g., false positive). Needs assessment data that show large differences among the potential trainees indicate that the training design must be adjusted to address the differences, which relates back to organizational constraints (Table 5-1). If the variance in KSAs is large, you need to consider a design that allows those with lower levels of the KSAs to "catch up." Otherwise, the training is demotivating by being too boring for some and too complex for others.

By not accounting for trainee differences, companies can be the losers. For example, there was an insurance company that hired a number of older workers for its call center.[12] The company believed that an older voice could relate to older customers better. The older workers were sent through the company computer-training program. Many of them quit before completing training, and those who did stay were substandard performers. The company decided that it was simply a bad idea to hire older workers, as they were not capable of learning the new technology. After discussions with a consultant, the company decided to try again. This time, the training was extended. Trainers were able to work more closely with the older trainees. As a result, performance on the job after training was on par with that of the younger employees.

Just how important is the individual difference issue? Consider the following:

- Increased ethnic diversity—Hispanics will become the largest minority group in the U.S. workforce by 2016.[13]
- A very large portion of the workforce is made up of older workers.[14]
- Women will continue to increase as a percentage of the workforce.[15]
- New technology and government legislation in North America is making it easier for people with disabilities to enter the workforce.

These facts suggest a very different workforce emerging in North America. With this increase in diversity will come an increase in individual differences in more than just KSAs. Different cultures and ethnicities mean different ways of viewing the workplace and its norms and values. Care in the needs assessment to understand the special requirements of some individuals will help tremendously in designing a successful training program.

Differences in Learning Styles

Individual differences also exist in how people learn.[16] There are a number of different learning style models to choose from. A recent Google search turned up over 80 different inventories. While each has a slightly different perspective based on the particular research premises of the authors, they do have much in common. We chose the Felder-Silverman model to use as an example of how different trainee learning styles can influence the effectiveness of the training. We chose this model because it is consistent with many other models and the scale has reasonable reliability and validity.[17] In this model, there are four different dimensions of learner preference. Within each dimension, the learners will differ in their preference for how they like to learn. The different learning styles are described below.

Sensing versus Intuitive Learners

Your preference for one style or the other may be strong, moderate, or mild. Everybody is sensing sometimes and intuitive sometimes. To be effective as a learner and problem solver, you need to be able to function both ways. If you overemphasize intuition, you may miss important details or make careless mistakes in calculations or hands-on work; if you overemphasize sensing, you may rely too much on memorization and familiar methods and not concentrate enough on understanding and innovative thinking.

- Sensing learners don't like training that doesn't connect closely to practical application, tend to like learning facts, and prefer solving problems by well-established methods. They dislike complications and surprises. They are good at memorizing and patient with details. They like hands-on learning opportunities. Sensors are more likely than intuitors to resent being tested on material that has not been explicitly covered in training.
- Intuitive learners often prefer discovering possibilities and relationships, like innovation, and dislike repetition. They seem to be better at grasping new concepts and are often more comfortable than sensors with abstractions and mathematical formulations. Intuitors don't like "plug-and-chug" courses that involve a lot of memorization and routine calculations.

How Can Trainers Help Sensors?   Sensors remember and understand information best if they can see how it connects to the real world. If you are training in an area where most of the material is abstract and theoretical, you may have difficulty. You can be helpful by providing specific examples of concepts and procedures and how they apply in practice.

How Can Trainers Help Intuitors?   If your training requires primarily memorization and plugging in formulas, you may have trouble with these trainees. Provide interpretations or theories that link the facts, or ask these trainees to find the connections. You should also create incentives for memorizing details and correct solutions (reinforcing the trainee for checking her completed solutions). Some type of competition (either among a group or individual improvement) might work well when the content of the training doesn't match the intuitor's preferred approach.

Visual versus Verbal Learners

Visual learners remember best what they see—pictures, diagrams, flowcharts, time lines, films, and demonstrations. Verbal learners get more out of words—written and spoken explanations. Everyone learns more when information is presented both visually and verbally.

How Can Trainers Help Visual Learners?   The simple answer is to find diagrams, sketches, schematics, photographs, flow charts, or any other visual representation of course material that is predominantly visual. Even showing a short video of someone else presenting the material will help the visual learner. Prepare a concept map showing key points, enclosing them in boxes or circles, and drawing lines with arrows between concepts to show connections.

How Can Trainers Help Verbal Learners?   Have trainees write summaries or outlines of course material in their own words. Put trainees into groups where they can gain understanding of material by hearing others explain the concepts. The most learning will occur when the trainee does the explaining.

Sequential versus Global Learners

- Sequential learners tend to gain understanding in linear steps, with each step following logically from the previous one. They are able to absorb and use material even though they do not understand the big picture, but the material has to be presented in a logical order.
- Global learners are not able to absorb the details until they understand the big picture. Even then, they may not be great with the details. They tend to learn in large jumps, absorbing material almost randomly without seeing connections, and then suddenly "getting it." They tend to be able to solve complex problems quickly or put things together in novel ways once they have grasped the big picture, but they may have difficulty explaining how they did it.

How Can Trainers Help Sequential Learners? One useful technique here is to provide trainees with a copy of the lecture material with blank spaces in place of key terms and definitions. Ask trainees to fill in the blanks as the training progresses. At the end of the module, as a review, go through the blank spaces and ask the trainees to tell you what should be in the space. You can help strengthen the trainees' global thinking skills by asking them to relate each new topic to things they already know.

How Can Trainers Help Global Learners? Before beginning each module, indicate how that module fits into the overall purpose of the training. Follow this up with how the module fits into the world of the trainees. As indicated above, one way to do this is to get the trainees to make the connection between the new topic and things they already know. This helps the global learner to put the new topic into a familiar context and see the connections. Fortunately, there are steps you can take that may help you get the big picture more rapidly.

Active versus Reflective Learners

- Active learners tend to retain and understand information best by doing something active with it—discussing or applying it or explaining it to others. These trainees want to try it out and see how it works because that's how they most effectively process the new information (e.g., symbolic coding, cognitive organization, and symbolic rehearsal). Because they process information externally, these trainees like working in groups.
- Reflective learners prefer to think about the new information before applying it. They are more comfortable processing the new information internally, before using it externally. These trainees prefer working alone so that they can complete their internal processing of the information.
- Sitting through lectures without any activity except taking notes is hard for both learning types, but particularly hard for active learners.

How Can Trainers Help Active Learners? Create time for group discussion or problem-solving activities as part of the training. If training requires work outside the classroom, have the trainees work in teams.

How Can Trainers Help Reflective Learners? Before moving to group activities, have the trainees engage in individual thinking. At the end of each module, ask trainees questions about the content. Also, ask them to think of possible applications. It will also help this type of learner if you allow some time at the end of the module for them to write down a summary of the material in their own words.

What's a Trainer to Do?

Typically, a training class is filled with trainees that have a mix of preferred learning styles. If the training is of short duration, this will not matter too much. As noted

Figure 5-1 No Trait and Treatment Interaction

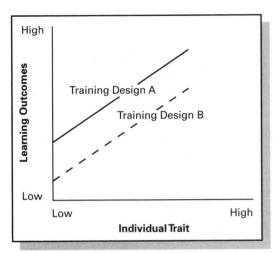

Figure 5-2 A Trait and Treatment Interaction

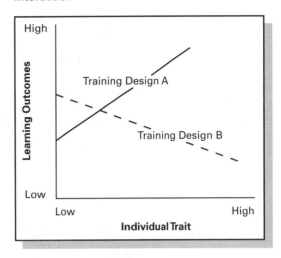

earlier, everyone has the ability to learn material presented in their nonpreferred style. However, if the training is more extensive, this becomes a problem as learners will "turn off" and stop learning because the cognitive load becomes too great (too much stress on the trainee's cognitive processes). The most effective approach in this instance is to design the training to tap into the whole brain. That is, design in components to each module that cater to each of the learning styles. For example, your lecture covering the content of each module should be accompanied by lots of diagrams, graphs, charts, and such. Organize the lecture so that you start out with the big picture and then begin covering the details in a sequential manner. Create sets of exercises that ask the trainees to use memorized facts and details and other sets of exercises that ask them to identify relationships and possibilities. Some of these exercises should have the trainees actually using the material, and other exercises should have them thinking and reflecting on the material. As you can see, our advice here is to design the training to accommodate all styles of learning unless you have the luxury of limiting the trainees to a certain learning preference.

The individual difference issue is complex, and interactions are not easily generalizable to different situations.[18] Note in Figure 5-1 that training design A produces better results for those at all levels of the particular trait, suggesting that training design A is the method of choice. In Figure 5-2, however, design A provides positive results for those high in the trait but not for those low in the trait. In contrast, training design B provides positive results for those low in the trait but not for those high in the trait. Ideally, those low in the trait should receive training design B, whereas those high in the trait should receive training design A. When you are not able to create separate programs for differences in traits, we are suggesting that you will want to design the training to accommodate the different traits as much as possible. This method offers the advantage of covering the same learning point in different ways, thus facilitating the learning process for everyone. Disadvantages include increased time to complete training and higher costs to design than the time and costs involved in simply providing one mode of instruction. However, this expense must be weighed against the cost of putting people through training who cannot learn the required KSAs.

An alternative is to create separate training programs designed around the learning style preferences of each group. Here, the training is tailored to the preference of the training group, but multiple training programs need to be designed, developed, and implemented. Time for everyone to complete training is minimized, but the cost of development remains high.

Motivation of Trainee

As the performance formula ($P = M \times KSA \times E$) indicates, if motivation is lacking, no learning is likely to occur. Thus, training should be designed not only to provide KSAs but also to motivate trainees to learn those KSAs and apply them to their jobs.

Expectations toward Training

Those who come to a training program with positive expectations are more successful. Trainees who agree with such statements as

- "Even if I fail, this training will be a valuable experience"
- "I will get more from this training than most people"
- "I have a better chance of passing this training than most others"
- "If I have trouble during training, I will try harder"

are more likely to meet the objectives than those who do not.[19] Those with positive expectations are more motivated. If such expectations were determined during the needs assessment, an intervention could take place for those with unfavorable expectations. These interventions might include:

- Showing the trainee that he or she has the ability to complete training,
- Clarifying the outcomes associated with completed training, and
- Showing that if training is completed, positive outcomes are more likely to occur.

Evidence indicates that doing these things increases motivation to learn.[20]

Suppose one of your supervisors has poor relations with her subordinates. Sending her to training to provide her with better interpersonal skills is fruitless unless she sees the value in such training. If, in the TNA, it is determined that she has low expectations and sees no value in the training, she could be asked to attend a pretraining workshop. You design the workshop to show the advantages of a positive relationship between supervisors and subordinates. The workshop also previews the training, showing that participants can learn the skills if they put forth the effort. After attending such a pretraining workshop, the supervisor would more likely be motivated to learn the skills.

Expectancy Theory Implications

Let's return to the intervention we suggested previously. We have trainees who we believe have negative expectations regarding training. By intervening before training and providing those trainees with information that shows that they can succeed in the training, we are influencing Expectancy 1 (E1, the belief that effort will lead to desired performance). By clarifying the positive outcomes of training, we make trainees aware of what can be achieved by being successful in training. Finally, by showing that training increases the positive outcomes, we influence Expectancy 2 (E2, the belief that desired performance will lead to desired outcomes). Increasing the expectancies (1 and 2) and also the number of positive outcomes will have the net effect of increasing motivation to be successful in training.

No one consciously goes systematically through all the steps suggested in expectancy theory to make a decision, but unconsciously, such a process does occur. Understanding the process helps focus on an important process that influences motivation. An example will illustrate the point. A TNA in the area that Bill supervises found lower than expected productivity. It was also found that Bill's subordinates were afraid to talk to him about problems they experienced doing their work. An interview with Bill revealed that he believed that the best way to supervise was

What are the outcomes Bill sees and their attractiveness (valence) to him (on a scale of 1 to 10) if he is successful in training versus if he is unsuccessful?

Outcomes if Successful	Valence	Outcomes if Not Successful	Valence
Promotion	7	Does not have to change behavior	10
Better at job	8	Employees still afraid of him	8
Less tension between Bill and subordinates	6	Not ridiculed by coworkers for being a nice guy	9
Less feeling of stress	4		
Better relationship with union	7		
Fewer grievances	9		

How likely is it that if Bill is successful or unsuccessful, these outcomes will actually occur (Expectancy 2)? These expectancies are based on Bill's belief that they will occur and range from 0.0 (not at all likely to occur) to 1.0 (guaranteed to occur).

Outcomes if Successful	Expectancy 2	Valence	Outcomes if Not Successful	Expectancy 2	Valence
Promotion	0.2	7	Does not have to change behavior	1.0	10
Better at job	0.6	8	Employees still afraid of him	1.0	8
Less tension between Bill and subordinates	0.7	6	Not ridiculed by coworkers for being a nice guy	1.0	9
Less feeling of stress	0.8	4			
Better relationship with union	0.4	7			
Fewer grievances	0.6	9			

Finally, how likely does Bill think it is that he could learn the new skills if he really tried (Expectancy 1)? This likelihood is also expressed as a probability (0 to 1.0).

In this case, Bill believes that the skills will be difficult for him to learn, and he also believes that "leopards cannot change their spots." Therefore, Bill believes that if he really tries, there is only a 0.5 chance that he will be successful. On the other hand, if he does not try, he definitely (1.0) will not learn or change his behavior.

to be tough. "If they are afraid of what I might do to them if they screw up, they will work harder," he said. Bill seemed to like the idea that subordinates were afraid of him. On the basis of this information, Bill was encouraged to attend a training workshop. The workshop covers active listening, effective feedback, and other skills designed to teach supervisors how to interact better with subordinates, peers, and superiors. Will he be motivated to learn these skills? Let's look inside Bill's head, as represented in Training in Action 5-1.

To answer the question of whether Bill will be motivated to learn, we need to examine the factors in expectancy theory. What does Bill consider to be possible outcomes of successful training, and what is the attractiveness (valence) of each of the outcomes? An examination of Training in Action 5-1 indicates that he sees promotion as one outcome, and it is a fairly attractive outcome (7 on a 10-point scale). Less stress is another outcome, but that is not especially attractive (4 on a 10-point scale). Altogether Bill identified six outcomes that might occur if he is successful at training. If he is unsuccessful, he identifies three outcomes, and all three are attractive; the lowest is an 8 on a 10-point scale. Notice that Bill does not perceive that his training can have any effect on the productivity of his workgroup.

Now examine the likelihood that Bill believes that the outcomes he identified will actually occur (E2) if he is successful or unsuccessful in training. If successful in training (improves his interpersonal skills), the likelihood of his being promoted is low (0.2, or a 20 percent probability). The likelihood he will feel less stress is quite high at 0.8. All others are somewhere in between. If he is unsuccessful (does not learn the new skills), the probability that he will not have to change his behavior (he will behave in the same manner as before) is 1.0, or absolutely guaranteed. If he is not successful in training, no one would expect him to change his behavior. Similarly, because he has not changed his behavior, employees will still be afraid of him (probability of 1.0); he will be the same old Bill, and his peers will not ridicule him. As for Bill's belief about his ability to complete training successfully, he believes that if he really tries, it (E1) is 0.5. If he does not try, he believes that the likelihood of being unsuccessful is 1.0, or guaranteed to happen. Let's determine whether he is likely to try in training through the following calculations:

Formula

$E1[(E2_{outcome1} \times V_{outcome1}) + (E2_{outcome2} \times V_{outcome2}) + \ldots + (E2_{outcome6} \times V_{outcome6})]$

where V is the valence or attractiveness of the outcome.

Will try in training

$$0.5[(0.2 \times 7) + (0.6 \times 8) + (0.7 \times 6) + (0.8 \times 4) + (0.4 \times 7) + (0.6 \times 9)] = 10.9$$

Will not try in training

$$1.0[(1.0 \times 10) + (1.0 \times 8) + (1.0 \times 9)] = 27.0$$

On the basis of these calculations, it is clear that Bill will not be motivated to learn in the training. The motivation to not try is substantially higher than the motivation to try. What can be done to influence Bill to learn? A number of approaches can be taken. First, recall from Chapter 3 that expectancies are beliefs about the way things are. They can be influenced in many ways (e.g., past experience, communication from others). If Bill heard from other supervisors that the training was not difficult, he might change his belief about how difficult it would be to complete the training successfully (Expectancy 1). If Bill learned that supervisors who were successful in training were promoted more often than others, this information would influence Bill's belief that if he completed training, he would get promoted (Expectancy 2). If those who go to training generally receive higher pay raises and Bill is not aware of this fact, make him aware of the relationship between training and the raise (Expectancy 2). This relationship will add an additional positive outcome to Bill's calculations, with a high probability of occurring.

It is also possible that Bill did not consider some potentially positive outcomes such as "Improved productivity in his area," "Respect from upper management,"

"Better relationship with family and friends" (because he also will be able to use the skills in his personal life), and "Better able to persuade others of his point of view." Once made aware of these outcomes, depending on their attractiveness, the motivation may be altered to try rather than not. For example, "Respect of upper management" might be a given (E2 = 1.0) for all those who successfully complete the training. If this outcome were highly attractive to Bill, it would go a long way toward changing the decision to "try."

Other ways to influence Bill's motivation to learn can focus on enhancing Expectancies 1 and 2 and clarifying the types of outcomes that will result from successful training. As Bill's supervisor, you could[21]

- Discuss Bill's job performance and job-related goals and reach agreement that he needs to improve some set of KSAs to achieve those goals. Providing focus on goals presents specific outcomes that the trainee might not have considered.
- Agree that this particular training program is the best alternative available for achieving the desired improvement (Expectancy 1).
- Agree that demonstrated improvement in the identified KSA area will result in desirable outcomes for him (Expectancy 2).

These steps should result in Bill's realizing the advantages of successful training and should make his attitude more positive. In the design of training, therefore, it is important to include such pretraining interventions. An integral part of a training design might be working with the supervisors to ensure that the suggested discussions take place. In large organizations with well-organized HR functions, the trainee-supervisor discussions might take place in the formal performance review. A portion of any thorough review is the developmental aspect, which is useful for the supervisor to use with subordinates in determining training needs and increasing the motivation to learn.

As noted earlier, it is not likely that anyone consciously goes through the expectancy model process since many of the factors are not known. But the model is still useful. It provides evidence of the complexity of the motivational process and what factors to consider when meeting with a subordinate to discuss their development and motivate them to improve. Discussion regarding his desired outcomes, his belief in achieving them, and his beliefs about successfully completing training can assist in helping change the person's perceptions and improve motivation, without resorting to the complex analysis above.

Implications from Conditioning and Reinforcement (The Environment)

Classical Conditioning   Recall from Chapter 3 that classical conditioning takes place without awareness. We salivate when we smell something we like cooking because of prior learning. Emotional responses can be conditioned in a similar manner. A trainee who had bad experiences in school might feel anxious and even sick on entering a training room set up like a school classroom. Trainees who experience high stress in their jobs become conditioned to feel stressed when they arrive at work. Eventually, just seeing the building begins to create the stress because the two events are so often paired. Having someone in such an emotional state does not facilitate effective training, which might be a good reason to hold the training off-site for employees of this type. The point here is that some situations are associated with unpleasant emotional conditioned responses. Pleasant emotional responses are conditioned to other situations. When designing training, in most circumstances, you want to create situations that are pleasant. When the trainees are comfortable both physically and emotionally, they are better able to focus their attention on training. For these reasons, it is useful to know in advance as much about the trainee as possible.

Operant Conditioning   Recall from Chapter 3 that if a particular behavior is immediately followed by a reward, the behavior is likely to be repeated. Also, punishment that immediately follows a particular behavior will decrease the likelihood of that behavior continuing. The following are important points to consider in the design of effective training:

- Know the things your trainees will see as rewarding and those that will be seen as punishing.
- Plan to reward at lower levels for effort and at higher levels for success using successive approximations.
- Use both tangible and intangible rewards. Do not underestimate the power of trainees learning how to self-reward. Sometimes trainers will give coupons to trainees as a recognition and reward for participating in training exercises. These coupons are then redeemed at the end of the day for prizes such as books and/or other mementos related to the training.
- Do not forget that feedback is a reinforcer and key element in learning. Design feedback to show what the trainee did well and what needs improvement.

The following example illustrates these points.

Some trainees are reluctant to role-play. However, the role-play is an effective method for achieving behavior change. If role-plays are incorporated into the training design, it is important to ensure that positive reinforcement, rather than punishment, follows. For example, the two trainers might first act out a simple role-play to demonstrate how it is done. After it is over, the trainers thank each other and point out some positive things that each did during the role-play. They might then indicate that they would like someone to volunteer to do another simple role-play; when the trainee is finished, the trainer and the other trainees applaud the efforts. Of course, this approach is successful only if the applause is seen as both real and reinforcing. You might then give the trainee feedback, highlighting the positive things done, and present the trainee with a "participation ticket" that can be exchanged later for a training memento.

Goal Setting

Goal-setting research consistently demonstrates that specific, challenging goals result in higher motivation levels than do no goals or the goal of "do the best you can." Specific goals direct the individual's energy and attention toward meeting the goal. Several conditions related to goal setting affect performance:[22]

- Individuals who are given a specific, hard, or challenging goal perform better than those given specific easy goals, "do the best you can" goals, or no goals.
- Goals appear to result in more predictable effects when they are given in specific terms rather than as vague intentions.
- Goals must be matched to the ability of the individual so the person is likely to achieve it. Being able to achieve the goal is important for an individual's self-efficacy, for that is how individuals judge their ability to perform well on the tasks. For this reason, the analyst will need to design intermediate goals that reflect progress.
- Feedback concerning the degree to which the goal is being achieved is necessary for goal setting to have the desired effect.
- For goal setting to be effective, the individual needs to accept the goal that is set.

What is the application of this goal-setting research to training? Well, what better way to capture the interest and attention of trainees than to provide them with individual goals? Learning objectives, discussed earlier, are a form of goal setting and could provide challenging, specific goals. These goals provide the measuring stick against which trainees can evaluate their progress and from which they derive self-satisfaction as they progress.

Goal Orientation

Goal orientation, although studied in children for years, has only recently been researched in an organizational context. It is the degree to which an individual is predisposed toward a learning goal orientation versus a performance goal orientation.[23] Those with a learning goal orientation focus on the learning process. They seek challenging tasks to increase their competence, see negative feedback as important information to help them master the task, and see failure as a learning experience. One result from this learning goal orientation is persistence when having problems doing a complex task.

Those with a performance goal orientation differ because they focus on the end result. They wish to be seen as competent and, therefore, desire favorable feedback. They prefer easier tasks where they are able to demonstrate their competence rather than learning something new. A result of having this performance goal orientation is avoidance of complex tasks for fear of failure, limited persistence, and a tendency to be easily distracted.[24]

In an organizational setting, those with a performance goal orientation have a strong desire to impress others and focus on the outcome of their performance. Those with a learning goal orientation focus on mastery of the task to develop their competence, acquire new skills, and learn from their experience.[25] The research using goal orientation in an organizational/training setting has only been going on for a few years, but much of it concludes that it is better to have a learning goal orientation than a performance goal orientation in a training setting.[26] In other words, the focus should be on the process of learning new things rather than on some end product performance goal. The good news is that although there is evidence that goal orientation is a trait, the trait can be influenced by the situation. In fact, it seems that as long as there are situational cues suggesting a focus on learning rather than performance, the situational cues will override the goal orientation trait.[27] Furthermore, these findings tend to be supported when the task is complex and requires new knowledge and strategies.[28]

What has this to do with design of training? First, it provides support for designing the training of complex tasks with the simple examples before moving to the more complex. You will see how to do this later in the chapter, when we discuss elaboration theory (ET), a macro theory of training design. The use of simple tasks at the beginning will help negate the influence of goal orientation. Also, getting trainees to experience success early in training will lessen the effect of goal orientation. The use of practice and feedback will be useful in this regard. In active listening, for example, using the easiest situation possible for beginning to practice a new skill, providing positive feedback, and suggesting alternative methods of response keep the focus on learning. In summary, goal orientation seems to be a personal trait that is influenced by cues in the training environment. A training design that starts with the simplest examples and provides positive feedback should negate the negative effect of a performance goal orientation.

So far, we have discussed getting and keeping trainees interested in the training. Now let us examine how to facilitate the learning process. In this regard, a number of important factors need to be addressed when you are designing a training program. These factors will be presented under two headings: facilitation of learning and facilitation of transfer. Facilitation of transfer, of course, also helps facilitation of learning.

FACILITATION OF LEARNING: FOCUS ON TRAINING DESIGN

To develop effective training programs, it is important to understand learning theory, or more specifically, how individuals learn.[29] As noted in Chapter 3, we choose to focus on social learning theory. This theory provides a broad understanding of the process of learning yet is relatively easy to understand.

Social Learning Theory

Let's examine the parts of social learning theory as they relate to training. Specific training events that correspond to the specific learning processes are illustrated in Table 5-8.

Attention/Expectancy

Social learning theory (see Figure 3-5 on page 76) indicates that the trainee's motivation influences where attention is directed. Trainees attend to things in the environment that are most important to them. Thus, the environment and process should be structured so that the most important things are the learning events and materials. Attention distracters need to be removed and creature comforts attended to.

Eliminating Distractions   The room should be at a comfortable temperature, not too hot or too cold. People are generally comfortable at a temperature between 71 and 73 degrees Fahrenheit, with a humidity level at about 50 percent. The walls should be a neutral but pleasant color, free from distracting objects (e.g., posters, notices, and pictures unrelated to training). The room should be soundproof. The room should have no view to the outside, but if the room has windows, close the shades or curtains. Ideally, the learning facility will be away from the workplace, so trainees can concentrate on learning rather than be sidetracked by what might be going on at work. If the training must be conducted at the work site, establish a rule that no interruptions are allowed (from bosses, subordinates, or others who "just need a few minutes with . . ."). This rule also means no phones, beepers, or other communication devices while training is being conducted. Communicating with the work area can be important, so the training facility should have a system for incoming messages that can be delivered to trainees during breaks and after completion of training.

Table 5-8 Learning Processes and Corresponding Training Events

Attention/Expectancy	Learning environment, pretraining communications, statement of objectives and process, highlighting of key learning points
Retention	
Activation of memory	Stimulation of prior related learning
Symbolic coding and cognitive organization	Presentation of various encoding schemes and cognitive images, associations with previously learned material, order of presentation during training
Symbolic rehearsal and cues for retrieval	Case studies, hypothetical scenarios, aids for transfer of learning (identical elements and principles)
Behavioral Reproduction	Active and guided practice (role-plays and simulations)
Reinforcement	Assessment and feedback (positive and/or negative)

The seating should be such that trainees will not become uncomfortable over a two-hour period, but not become so comfortable that they must fight off sleep. Choose comfortable, flexible, cloth-covered chairs with armrests. Trainees will also need a surface on which to place their training materials and for writing.

Schedule training activities with the following rule in mind: "The brain can absorb only as much as the seat can endure." Breaks should be scheduled so that trainees do not have to sit for too long at one time. Provide refreshments if trainees are likely to be hungry at the start of or during training. A growling stomach is a significant force in taking the trainee's mind off the learning. Remember, food is a reinforcer, so it is important to create positive associations for training while keeping trainees attentive. If lunch is provided, it should be light and not contain large amounts of carbohydrates, which tend to make people drowsy. Also avoid turkey, because it is sleep inducing. Remember how you feel after a turkey dinner? Obviously, alcohol should be avoided.

Attracting Attention   The first steps in motivating the employees and setting their expectations are to notify them that they will be participating in the training, inform them of the nature of the training, and explain its job-related benefits. This communication should, at a minimum, indicate the learning objectives and agenda. State the objectives again at the outset of training, and review them at strategic points throughout. Reiterating the objectives helps keep the focus of training on the desired outcomes and attention on the important training activities. However, it is not enough for the trainer simply to state the objectives from time to time. The trainees must accept those objectives. To this end, ask trainees to describe how accomplishing the objectives will lead to resolving job-related problems. This exercise not only focuses trainees' attention on the learning objectives but also builds commitment that will facilitate the transfer of new KSAs back to the job.

In addition to accepting the learning objectives, trainees must also feel that the objectives are achievable. This principle comes directly from both expectancy theory and goal setting. Here is how achievable goals can be designed into the training. At the start of training, the overall objective might seem difficult, if not impossible, to achieve. Point out that the overall objective is just the final step in a series of obtainable subobjectives. Research on goal setting suggests that following these procedures will result in higher levels of trainee learning.[30] Suppose the purpose of a one-day seminar was to "use the conflict resolution model to calm an irate customer, without giving in to his request." The thought of calming an irate customer using a method (conflict resolution model) that the trainees know nothing about could create a high level of anxiety. An intermediate objective that stated, "Respond to a single angry comment using active listening," does not seem as imposing and would provide a view of one of the steps toward reaching the overall objective.

Finally, the trainees' attention should be focused on the critical aspects of each step in the learning process. Techniques for highlighting the important points should be built into the learning activities so that the appropriate material is processed into permanently stored information.[31] The method of highlighting will vary according to the instructional method (e.g., case study, lecture). In the example of conflict resolution training discussed previously, suppose the training included a videotape of the correct steps. As the video progressed through the various stages of the conflict resolution model, these steps would flash on the bottom of the screen. This model begins with active listening, so as the video shows the person using active listening, "Active Listening" will be flashed on the bottom of the screen. This device would give the trainee an idea of how to perform each step and how the steps integrate into the total model.

Retention

An individual goes through four stages in the process of retaining something she is taught:

1. Activation of memory
2. Symbolic coding
3. Cognitive organization
4. Symbolic rehearsal and cues for retrieval

Activation of Memory   The Social Learning model does not identify the activation of memory as a separate process but includes this as a part of the symbolic coding process. We have separated these two processes to show how each is an important consideration in the design of training. Information that is attended to is transformed into symbolically coded (typically as language) long-term memory. From there, it is called up when the appropriate cues are present.[32] Before the symbolic encoding process can begin, relevant prior learning must be stimulated, so connections between the new information and the old can be established. The trainer, through stimulating the recall of the relevant prerequisite learning or prior supportive learning, can facilitate this process.

Assume that the trainer wants the management trainees to learn the "relevant employee characteristics" for matching managerial behavior to the needs of the subordinate. The trainer can stimulate the recall of the prerequisite learning by asking the trainees, "Try to remember the names of the relevant employee characteristics and what things differentiate them from irrelevant characteristics." Recalling supportive prior learning can be stimulated by asking the trainees to draw on related experience. In this case, the trainer might say, "Think back to employees you've dealt with in the past. How would you determine which of their characteristics would be relevant to the management style you adopt with them?" This activity would recall information supporting the new learning, providing a context for the new learning to occur.

Symbolic Coding and Cognitive Organization   Once the appropriate prior learning is recalled, the trainee is ready to encode the new information. The trainer can facilitate the encoding process through the technique of **guided discovery.** Typically, the trainer makes statements and then asks a question. Assume that the trainees just watched a video of a supervisor and a subordinate discussing the subordinate's work performance. After watching the video the trainer might say, "Remember, certain employee characteristics are more closely related to how the employee approaches the work situation. In the video, how did the employee approach the work situation and what characteristics are most likely to influence this approach?" The statement is intended to stimulate relevant prior learning, and the question is designed to allow the trainee to discover the appropriate rule from the cues provided. The question should not contain all the information needed for the answer but should suggest a strategy for discovering the answer. The trainee develops a coding scheme that relates the new learning to prior learning by engaging in guided discovery.

Encoding can be enhanced through the use of images, in addition to being coded as verbal propositions. When **symbolic coding** incorporates both verbal propositions and images, retention of the information is improved, probably because image retention and language retention occur through different cognitive channels.[33] The addition of visual material in support of the oral and written language increases the trainees' ability to remember the information.

Cognitive organization is intimately tied to symbolic coding. The way information is organized during training and the prior learning that supports learning the new information shape the way the new information is organized into the cognitive structure. Likewise, the visual images used in training provide suggestions for how information fits together. When you develop the materials and the flow of a training program, you should make sure the new learning builds on relevant older learning. The flow of training should help the learner organize the new material by providing various organizational strategies.

Symbolic Rehearsal   **Symbolic rehearsal** is a type of practice. It is practicing in your mind, as when the trainer asks the trainees to imagine a hypothetical situation and discuss how they would behave. At this point, the trainees are not actually doing what they have learned to do—they are thinking, talking, or writing about it. Case studies provide one form of symbolic rehearsal. Trainees read about a situation and describe how they would handle the situation.

Behavioral Reproduction

Behavioral reproduction is the transformation of the learning into actual behavior. Pilot training provides a clear example of the difference between behavioral reproduction and symbolic rehearsal. Pilots go through an extensive training process in learning how to fly a new aircraft. They read manuals, attend lectures, watch videos, and engage in computer-assisted, self-paced learning modules. Once a sufficient amount of learning occurs, the pilot trainees demonstrate their knowledge of procedures through discussions with the trainer and one another about what they would do in specific situations. Trainees are given written or visual scenarios and asked how they would respond. All of these activities are symbolic rehearsal. When trainees demonstrate sufficient cognitive command of the aircraft's systems, procedures, and capabilities, they are put into flight simulators, which allow them to practice flying the aircraft. After they demonstrate competence flying the aircraft in simulation, they fly the actual aircraft under the supervision of an experienced pilot. The simulation and supervised flights are behavioral reproduction activities.

Strategic Knowledge

In the past, training was designed to provide trainees with only the KSAs needed for their particular job. Many organizations found that more broadly based training leads to greater organizational effectiveness. In many cases, physical work is being replaced by knowledge work. An examination of some of North America's best-managed companies found that the use of management teams was a common approach. This use of teams is on the increase all over Northern America. The Center for Study of Work Teams at the University of North Texas indicates that about 80 percent of the *Fortune* 500 companies use teams with half or more of their employees. To be effective in the team approach, employees need a broad understanding of how their jobs interact with other jobs. In these companies, job-specific training is supported with information about the job's relationship to other parts of the organization. This type of training incorporates aspects of strategic knowledge development because it allows trainees to understand when and why to use their new KSAs.

Strategic knowledge development increases the breadth of what is learned by extending the training content to include learning when and why KSAs are appropriate and developing strategies for their use. The strategies that are developed revolve around the planning, monitoring, and modifying of behavior. The trainee learns not only how to perform the task but also how to behave strategically and adaptively. Table 5-9 compares a traditional skills training format with a strategic knowledge training format. You can see that the main difference is that the strategic

Table 5-9
Comparison of Traditional and Strategic Knowledge Training

TRADITIONAL TRAINING	STRATEGIC KNOWLEDGE TRAINING
Step 1.	Step 1.
Declarative knowledge (what) is presented.	Declarative knowledge is presented the same way as in traditional training.
Workers are told that the materials are designed to teach them to read and interpret quality control charts used throughout their organization.	
	Step 2.
	The context of the procedures (why and when) is added by instructing workers about the importance of the skill and the appropriate time for its use.
	It is explained that if the assembly-line workers could read and interpret quality control data, mistakes would be caught earlier and the product saved because traditionally quality control measures are taken after a specific number of items have been produced.
Step 2.	Step 3.
Procedural knowledge (how) is presented.	Procedural knowledge (how) would be presented the same way as in traditional training.
Workers are assisted in recalling specific mathematics skills. Then stimulus materials and information required to master the task are presented. Examples of charts with various readings are provided, and the workers are shown how to record charts during production and interpret the data	
Step 3.	Step 4.
Workers practice using the charts and interpreting the results.	Workers practice using the charts and also practice determining when and why to use them.
	Workers are provided opportunities for rehearsal and reinforcement of both conditional and procedural knowledge.
Step 4.	Step 5.
Workers are given feedback.	Workers would be given feedback (same as in traditional training).

Source: Adapted from Schmitt & Newby, "Metacognition: Relevance to instructional design." *Journal of Instructional Development,* 9 (1986), pp. 29–32.

knowledge training provides information as to when the skill is used and why it is important. Trainees are also provided with practice sessions in determining when to use the skill.

FACILITATION OF TRANSFER: FOCUS ON TRAINING

Transfer of training refers to how much of what is learned in training transfers to the job. Training can result in the following transfer outcomes:[34]

- **Positive transfer:** A higher level of job performance,
- **Zero transfer:** No change in job performance, or
- **Negative transfer:** A lower level of job performance.

The goal is to have training result in positive transfer to the job.

Research into factors that influence transfer of training focuses on three areas: conditions of practice, identical elements, and stimulus variability. The research also provides evidence that the nature of feedback, the strategies used for retention, and goal setting can influence how well the training is transferred back to the job.

Conditions of Practice

Opportunities for trainees to practice can be designed in several ways. Each will facilitate the transfer of training more or less effectively depending on the nature of the KSAs to be learned.

Massed versus Spaced Practice

Which is more effective—having trainees practice continuously for four hours, for one hour on four different days, or for a half hour on eight different days? Research demonstrated that material learned under the latter approach, **spaced practice,** is generally retained longer than is material learned under the first approach, **massed practice.**[35] This finding is one of the most replicated in psychological research,[36] and additional support was found for simple motor tasks in a recent meta-analytic review of the research.[37] However, spaced practice requires a longer training cycle, and management generally resists it. Training departments need to become more creative in developing their training to allow for spaced practice. Instead of the traditional one-day workshop, eight one-hour sessions at the beginning of the workday might be possible. Instead of a five-day workshop, consider once a week for five weeks. This approach also gives trainees time to think about and even practice the knowledge or skill on their own.

Regarding more complex tasks, the research is less clear. A recent meta-analytic review suggests that using spaced practice for complex tasks is not as critical.[38] Tasks that are difficult and complex seem to be performed better when massed practice is provided first, followed by briefer sessions with more frequent rest intervals.[39] More recent work suggests that although there is no difference between the two with regard to acquisition of the complex task, spaced practice seems to inoculate trainees against skill loss over extended periods of nonuse.[40]

Whole versus Part Learning

First we need to be clear that in most instances it is important to provide an explanation of the whole before getting into the details of the individual parts of the training material. The learner needs to understand the "big picture" to see how the facts, principles, and concepts that will be presented in each of the "parts" of the training relate to each other and to the job. A wall chart that visually depicts the overall structure and individual parts of the training will be useful to trainees as a reference as the training moves through its individual modules.

Once the big picture is understood, the question still remains, should the training be designed to teach everything together or should it be separated into its component parts? From the learner's perspective this is termed **part learning** and **whole learning.** Whether trainees should learn parts of a task separately or learn the whole task all at once depends on whether the task can be logically divided into parts. In many cases, it is just too difficult to design part training.[41] Whole training devices are much easier because the design can be modeled after the real device (e.g., pilot-training simulators). James Naylor suggests that even when the task can be divided into parts, the whole method is still preferred when

- The intelligence of the trainee is high,
- The training material is high in task organization but low in complexity, and
- Practice is spaced rather than massed.[42]

Task organization relates to the degree to which the tasks are interrelated (highly dependent on each other). For example, in driving a car, the steering, braking, and acceleration are highly interdependent when you are turning a corner (high organization). Starting a standard-shift car, however, requires a number of tasks that are not as highly organized (pushing in the clutch, putting the gear shift in neutral, placing the foot on the accelerator, and turning the key to start). **Task complexity** relates to the level of difficulty of performing each task.[43]

In the design of training, it is often not practical to attempt to subdivide the task into meaningful parts. If it is possible to subdivide them, use the whole method if the task organization is high and use the part method if task organization is low.

As an example of high-task organization, imagine training a backhoe operator to dig a hole by first having her practice raising and lowering the boom, then moving the outer arm in and out, and finally moving the bucket. This sequence simply does not make sense. Ultimately the trainee has to learn how to open each of the valves concurrently and sequentially in the digging of a hole. An example of low-task organization is the maintenance of the backhoe. Here a number of tasks (check the teeth on the bucket, check the hydraulic oil, and inspect the boom for cracks) are not highly organized, so each could be taught separately.

A third option, **progressive part training,** can be used when tasks are not as clear in their organization. Consider the training of conflict resolution skills. Imagine that the model to be taught involves four steps (actively listen, indicate respect, be assertive, and provide information). These tasks are interdependent but might also be taught separately. In this case, a combination of the two types may make sense. The process is as follows:

1. The trainees learn and practice active listening.
2. Then the trainees learn and practice active listening and indicating respect.
3. Then the trainees learn and practice active listening, indicating respect, and being assertive.
4. Finally, the trainees learn and practice the whole model.

Whole, part, and a combination of the two (progressive part) learnings are represented in the following diagram:

| | PHASES | | | | |
TRAINING TYPE	PHASE 1	PHASE 2	PHASE 3	PHASE 4	PHASE 5
Whole	A+B+C+D	A+B+C+D	A+B+C+D	A+B+C+D	A+B+C+D
Part	A	B	C	D	A+B+C+D
Progressive Part	A	A+B	A+B+C	A+B+C+D	A+B+C+D

As mentioned previously, "whole learning" is generally preferred. However, you will need to take into consideration the **cognitive load** that is being placed on your trainees. Cognitive load refers to the amount of mental processing that is needed for the trainee to learn the material. The less familiar the trainee is with the material, the more complex the material, and the more material there is to learn, the higher the cognitive load. Other factors such as stress, fatigue, low self-efficacy, and so forth, can also increase the cognitive load. Perhaps you've experienced the situation in which the instructor just presented a constant stream of facts, principles and concepts until you felt that you just couldn't take anymore. At that point you probably shut down your processing of the information, feeling that your brain was overloaded. As a trainer you can avoid this type of situation by designing the material to be presented in organized and "right sized" chunks. Getting trainees to master smaller tasks (overlearning) leads to better learning of the whole.

Overlearning
Overlearning is the process of providing trainees with continued practice far beyond the point at which they perform the task successfully. The more a task is overlearned, the greater the retention.[44]

Overlearning is particularly valuable for tasks that are not used frequently or if the opportunity to practice them is limited. In a study of soldiers assembling and disassembling their weapons, the overlearning group received extra trials equal to the number of trials it took them to learn the task. The other group, called the refresher group, received the same extra number of trials as the overlearning group, but at a later date. The third group received no extra trials. The overlearning and refresher groups both outperformed the third group, but the overlearning group also retained more than the refresher group.[45] Even when information or skills are overlearned, however, it is important to put mechanisms in place to reinforce the use and practice of the learned behaviors on a continual basis, especially when it is a newly learned knowledge or skill.[46]

When trainees practice a skill beyond the ability to simply do the task, the responses become more automatic and eventually do not require thinking. For this reason, overlearning is most valuable for tasks performed in high-intensity or high-stress situations such as emergencies. For example, one trainee recalls that numerous times during initial pilot training in the air force, the instructor would pull back the throttle of the aircraft and yell, "Emergency!" He did it frequently, and soon the trainee discovered that thinking was not even required—the emergency procedures became automatic. This reflexive nature is important in a situation where correct responses are critical.

In Chapter 1 we defined the concept of automaticity, a concept closely related to overlearning. It could be thought of as an outcome of overlearning, although it could also occur after a great deal of on-the-job practice. It is a shift to a point where performance of a task is fluid, requires little conscious effort, and, as the name implies, is "automatic." Automaticity, through overlearning, should be designed into training when the task will be performed in high-stress situations, or those that are encountered infrequently but must be performed correctly.

Maximize Similarity

Maximizing similarity is also known as **identical elements.** The more the elements in the training design are identical to the actual work setting, the more likely it is that transfer will occur.[47] Two areas of similarity are possible: the tasks to be performed and the environment in which they are to be performed. How to increase similarity? A newscaster reading the news on television must use a teleprompter (the task) while someone is talking to him via an earphone (environment). After the basic skill is learned, the trainees practice the skill in an environment similar to their actual workplace environment to ensure transfer. A machinist is exposed to the background noise of the factory floor and the interruptions common to the job. The secretary is exposed to the office noise and to the interruptions that occur in the office.

Vary the Situation

It is much easier to use the concept of identical elements for motor or technical skills, where most of the elements required for learning are in the job situation. When conceptual or administrative skills are required, as in management training, a great deal of variability often characterizes typical situations, and the use of identical elements simply is not effective. In such cases, the general principles approach is more useful.

General Principles

For much of management training, it is impossible to provide specific training for what to do in every situation that might arise. It is necessary, therefore, to provide a framework or context for what is being taught, which is what strategic knowledge training attempts to do. Training through general principles will better equip trainees to handle novel situations.

Suppose that in teaching managers how to motivate employees, you tell them that praise is a good motivator. A manager goes back to the job and begins praising workers. Some workers are not motivated and, in some cases, they even become less motivated. The manager is at a loss. If, however, the managers were taught some general principles about motivation, they would understand the responses they get and alter their own behavior. The principles related to expectancy theory suggest that certain reinforcers are attractive to some and not to others. Furthermore, it indicates that praise must be a function of performance to be motivating. The manager could think through these principles and identify what change was required to motivate those not responding to the praise. For some of these employees, the attractive outcome might be for the manager to say nothing and stay away when they perform at an appropriate level.

Other Considerations to Facilitate Transfer

Knowledge of Results

Providing feedback (**knowledge of results**) to a trainee is important to learning and the transfer of training back to the job. Feedback performs three functions:[48]

1. It tells trainees whether their responses are correct, allowing for necessary adjustments in their behavior.
2. It makes the learning more interesting, encouraging trainees to continue.
3. It leads to specific goals for maintaining or improving performance.

When providing such feedback, it is better to indicate that the trainee can control the level of performance. Sometimes inexperienced trainers will try to be supportive by suggesting that the task is difficult, so any problems in mastering it are understandable.[49] This approach reinforces low self-efficacy. Feedback indicating that a trainee can master the task improves a person's self-efficacy, and trainees with high self-efficacy tend to be more motivated and achieve more.[50]

Frequent opportunities to provide feedback should be part of the training design. Providing feedback takes a rather long time if the group is large because the trainer needs to get to all trainees and monitor improvements. To help overcome this problem, other trainees can be used to provide feedback. For example, three-person groups can be used in interpersonal skills training. One of the three acts as an observer of the behavior and provides feedback to the person who is practicing.

Combination of Relapse Prevention and Goal Setting

A major reason that training does not transfer to the job is that, once back on the job, the trainee faces many of the same pressures that caused reduced effectiveness in the first place. Marx[51] instituted a system of **relapse prevention** into his training, modeled after a successful approach to assisting addicts to resist returning to their addictive behavior.[52] The strategy sensitizes trainees to the fact that relapse is likely, prepares them for it by having them identify high-risk situations that will result in relapse, and helps them develop coping strategies to prevent such a relapse.

Goal setting has also been shown to increase the likelihood of transfer.[53] With goal setting, the trainees are required to meet with fellow trainees to discuss the goals and how they will accomplish them. Furthermore, trainees are required to keep a record of their goal accomplishments, return these records to the trainer, and promise to meet at a later date to discuss these accomplishments publicly. This public commitment, through documentation of behavior, discussions with fellow trainees, and monitoring by trainers, further increases the likelihood of transfer.

Some evidence shows that relapse prevention without goal setting is not always successful,[54] so Marx incorporated both the goal setting and public commitment into his relapse prevention training.[55] This revised relapse prevention training is presented in Table 5-10. Table 5-11 presents some of the relapse prevention strategies (step 4 in Table 5-10) used in training. In preparation for relapse prevention training, trainees complete a relapse prevention worksheet (Figure 5-3) to get them thinking of the issues involved.

This combination of relapse prevention and goal setting is a powerful tool for encouraging transfer. The relapse part uses both cognitive and behavioral components to facilitate long-term maintenance of the newly learned behaviors.[56] Trainees leave the training expecting that relapse is a strong possibility, but possessing a repertoire of coping responses to deal with it. The addition of the goal setting and public commitment further provides an incentive for transfer. Recent research indicates this method is particularly effective where the climate for the transfer is not supportive.[57]

Table 5-10 Seven-Step Relapse-Prevention Training

STEP	PURPOSE
1. Choose a skill to retain	Helps manager to identify and quantify the skill chosen. Goal setting and monitoring of the skill require clear definitions of the skills, so this is an important step and often requires help from the trainer. "Be nice to my employees" is not clear enough and needs to be revised to something more concrete such as "Provide praise to employees when they meet their quota."
2. Set goals	Once a skill has been defined and quantified, then appropriate definitions of what a slip (warning that goal is in jeopardy) and relapse (more serious disengagement from goal) are. From this, goals are set as to what is desired. For example, the goal might be to praise at least five employees a minimum of once a day when they meet their quotas. Then define what a slip is: "Two consecutive days where five employees are not praised"; and what a relapse is: "A week where targeted behavior is not met."
3. Commit to retain the skill	Need to think about the reasons for maintaining the skill. Trainees write out advantages of maintaining the skills.
4. Learn coping (relapse prevention) strategies	These strategies help increase awareness of potential trouble spots, how to respond emotionally and behaviorally, where to get help, and so forth.
5. Identify likely circumstances for first relapse	The trainees are asked to think of a situation that would most likely cause them to slip back to old behavior. Prepares them for when it really happens and provides a nice transition to the next step, which is practice.
6. Practice coping (relapse prevention) strategies	With an understanding of what will cause a slip, trainees work in small groups practicing (using role-plays, and so forth) how to maintain the skill in such situations.
7. Learn to monitor target skill	Develop feedback mechanisms to help you monitor the frequency of using the specified skill. Use of whiteboard in office or notepad where you can check off each time you use the skill.

Source: Adapted from Marx, R. D. "Relapse prevention for managerial training: A model for maintenance of behavior change." *Academy of Management Review* 7 (1982), pp. 433–41.

Table 5-11 Coping Strategies for Relapse Prevention

STEP	PURPOSE
Understand the relapse process	By understanding that relapses are common and can be expected, it better prepares the trainee for such events. When a slip or relapse occurs, it is expected.
Recognize difference between training and the work setting	In training, there is often lots of positive feedback from peers and the trainer. This creates some overconfidence about how easy it will be to continue with the new skill when back on the job. However, you need to think about the likelihood that this attention and feedback will not happen back on the job, so realize that the transfer will be more difficult.
Create an effective support network on the job	Identify and enlist others who can support you back on the job. Peers who have also attended the same training and superiors who are supportive can be asked to provide you with needed feedback on how you are doing.
Identify high-risk situations	Determine times and situations where you are likely to slip back to old behavior. These cognitive "fire drills" help you determine cues that signal a potential slip.
Reduce emotional reactions that interfere with learning	Understanding that there will be slips and not reacting with feelings of failure, or tendency to blame the poor training. These responses are self-defeating, and being aware that they are likely to occur prepares you to take them in stride. Realize that it is a part of the learning process and does not reflect poorly on you or the training
Diagnose specific support skills necessary to retain new skill	Determine what support skills are necessary to assist in the transfer of the trained skill. Consider the skill of allowing the team, rather than the supervisor, to make the decisions. This is difficult to change, and the skill of time management is an important collateral skill. If you are always running behind, the tendency to make the decisions yourself or push the team to hurry will interfere with the taught skill. You need to be aware of this and, if necessary, also get training in the collateral skills.
Identify organizational support for skill retention	Determine who in the organization will support the skill, and actively seek them out for assistance in providing feedback. Ask supervisor to give feedback even if initially, the supervisor is not that interested in doing so.

Source: Adapted from Marx, R. D. "Relapse prevention for managerial training: A model for maintenance of behavior change." *Academy of Management Review* 7 (1982), pp. 433–41.

Figure 5-3
Relapse Prevention
Worksheet

A Plan to Apply Skills Back on the Job

1. What skill/technique: (be specific) _____

2. What will using skill/technique look like: (be specific) _____

3. What are the positive and negative consequences of using and not using this skill?

	Positive (+)	Negative (−)
Using Skill		
Not Using skill		

4. What will a "slip" look like? _____

5. How will you feel if you slip back to old techniques? _____

6. Under what circumstances is a slip likely to occur? _____

Source: Noe, R., J. Sears, and Fullemcamp, A. "Relapse training: Does it influence trainee's post training behaviors and cognitive strategies?" *Journal of Business and Psychology* 4 (1990), pp. 317–28.

FACILITATION OF TRANSFER: FOCUS ON ORGANIZATIONAL INTERVENTION

In Chapter 4, we noted that once a performance gap is identified, the next step is to determine how much of the gap is a function of inadequate KSAs and how much arises from other factors. Remember what Nancy Gordon from Ameritech said, that many of these gaps are a function of organizational forces and not a lack of KSAs. Just as these forces can interfere with effective performance, they can also interfere with new learning and inhibit transfer. To increase the likelihood of transfer, therefore, it is useful to harness as much help as possible back on the job.

Supervisor Support

Supervisor support is one of the key determining factors for the transfer of training.[58] Supervisors need to understand the behaviors being trained and provide support for trainees who use these new behaviors back on the job. In addition, research indicates that transfer is more likely when supervisors provide trainees with desired outcomes upon successful completion of training.[59] These actions on the part of supervisors will go a long way toward facilitating transfer.

Supervisors also can affect their employees' learning and transfer of training in other ways. If employees who are motivated to improve (involved in their own development) receive support from their supervisors for such developmental activity, this support enhances their motivation.[60] Also, motivation to learn can be enhanced when employees understand realistic information regarding the benefits of their development activities.[61] Two other factors that affect motivation to learn are the employee's perception of training relevance and reduction of negative side effects (like work that piles up) of attending training.[62] These two factors can also be controlled, to a great extent, by the supervisor.

Peer Support

Research indicates that peer support can also have a positive effect on transfer of training.[63] If the trainee is the only one from a department who receives training, peers back on the job might not understand how to provide social support. In some climates, this situation could result in pressure from more experienced peers to "forget all that stuff." With the right climate, however, peers can provide the proper support to use the training. What is the right climate? Learning must be considered an integral aspect of the organization's ongoing operation, becoming part of the employees' and managers' responsibilities. If everyone is involved in the learning process, it continues beyond the classroom. Most important, all employees must understand and support overall organizational objectives. By involving the entire workgroup in training, the resulting peer pressure will support company goals and objectives. With this type of climate, it is possible to use peer support in a more formalized manner. Peers could be considered potential coaches. Although it is the supervisor who is generally thought of as a coach to help recently trained employees transfer their skills to the workplace, experienced peers can also take on this role.[64] The peers would receive training as coaches and be provided with specific checklists to evaluate trainees periodically on their performance. In addition, more experienced peers can serve as mentors, willing to answer questions and provide advice, guidance, and support to remedy the difficulties trainees may encounter in applying the new skills to the work situation.

We discuss strategies for dealing with different climates in a later section. For now, it is sufficient to note that it is the training department's responsibility to inform upper management of the advantages of creating such a climate if the goal is to encourage transfer of training.

Trainer Support

Conventional wisdom is that the trainer's job is done when training is over. More recent research, however, demonstrates the value of continued trainer involvement in the transfer of training. Trainees who commit to meet the trainer and other trainees at some later date to discuss transfer of training use the training more effectively.[65] Thus, value derives from the continued involvement of the trainer, who can be a useful resource in helping trainees work through any problems encountered in the workplace.

In this regard, one idea is to have trainers monitor trainees at some point after training to assess how they are doing and provide feedback.[66] The trainer sits in and observes the trainee in a situation where she is required to use the trained behavior. To be effective, the **sit-in** must be

- Voluntary on the part of the trainee
- Confidential between the trainer and trainee
- Only for developmental purposes, not administrative

During the sit-in, the trainer must not interrupt the interaction between the trainee and others and provide feedback only after the session is over. After all, "Who is better to be coaching the trainee on behaviors that were learned in training than the trainer?"[67]

Using the trainer in a follow-up to facilitate transfer of training might spread the trainers rather thin. However, it is important to consider the investment already made in training. If transfer does not occur, the investment is lost.

Reward Systems

As noted earlier, valued outcomes contingent upon successful training enhance training transfer.[68] Operant conditioning is a powerful regulator of behavior. Employees are quite adept at determining which behaviors can get them in trouble, bring them rewards, or result in their being left alone. If trained behaviors are not reinforced, then the likelihood is small that such behaviors will be exhibited. Part of the trainer's responsibility is to work with the supervisor and other parts of the organization to align reward systems to support the behaviors learned in training.

Climate and Culture

Using a systems approach to training, you facilitate transfer of learning by focusing as many forces as possible on reinforcing the learned behaviors. Although supervisors, peers, and reward systems all influence an organization's climate and culture, these factors need to be discussed in their own right.

Climate

Climate can influence the transfer of training.[69] Climate is generally conceptualized as the perception of salient characteristics of the organization.[70] Such salient characteristics as company policies, reward systems, and management behaviors are important in determining the organizational climate. Supervisor support and peer support are part of the total climate that will reinforce the use of the trained skills, but they alone do not make up an organization's climate. Other climate factors such as company policies and the attitudes reflected by upper management regarding training, if positive, will also support the transfer of training. Consider how trainees perceive training. If they believe adequate resources (time and money) went into the development of training, trainees are more motivated to attend and learn. The message here is that the company cares enough about this training to devote valued resources. If these characteristics do not describe the climate, it might be better not to offer training at all.[71] Cultivating such a supportive climate toward training is important and does facilitate transfer.[72]

Climate is related to, and in many ways reflects, the culture of an organization. When asked, "What is useful in promoting transfer of training?" HR specialists and supervisors responded that it is critical to have a culture that supports training.[73]

Culture

Culture is defined as a pattern of basic assumptions invented, discovered, or developed by a group within the organization. It can be considered a set of shared understandings about the organization.[74] One type of culture—a continuous learning culture—evidenced by the shared understanding that learning is an important part of the job, shows a positive effect on the transfer of training.[75] A continuous learning culture is influenced by a variety of factors such as challenging jobs, social support (peer and supervisor), and developmental systems that allow employees the opportunity to learn continually and receive appropriate training.

Influencing Climate and Culture

Given the importance of climate, what can be done if the climate is nonsupportive or neutral regarding training? Changing climate and culture in an organization is a long and difficult process and must be done from the top. Issues related to the mismatch of the training goals and organizational climate and culture should surface in the organizational analysis part of the needs analysis. This information would then be provided to the top HR manager.

Evidence in North America indicates that the HR departments of organizations now carry more influence in organizational decision making than in the past[76] and that employees in these departments are better trained in HR issues.[77] With this increased influence and training, HR professionals are responsible for helping the company leadership to understand and resolve conflicts between organizational strategies and objectives and the existing climate and culture. Training in Action 5-2 provides an example of things that, incorporated into the training process to facilitate transfer, help change the learning climate and culture.

TRAINING IN ACTION 5-2
Helping Ensure Transfer

Dr. Richaurd Camp is a consultant to many organizations in the United States and abroad. A few years back, an executive search firm hired him to train its employees on effective interviewing techniques. This was a key part of their work. Dr. Camp, in a meeting with the firm's management, discussed the importance of approaching the training as an organizational intervention and the need to consider several organizational factors to ensure that the training transferred to the job. The client would be spending a great deal of money on the training and was willing to do what was necessary to ensure transfer, which would be especially difficult because the international company is highly decentralized.

After a number of meetings with management, Dr. Camp designed a three-day workshop to provide the interviewing skills requested. The first group to go through the training consisted of all the top managers, including the president. This not only provided them with the necessary skills but also garnered their support for the process throughout the organization. He then began training of all the other employees, from the top down. At the beginning of each training session, to indicate the importance of the training to the trainees, a video of the president of the company was shown. In the video, the president indicates the importance of the training and how it would make them a more effective organization. Furthermore, a senior manager who also verbalized support for the training was in attendance at each training session. The manager was also able to provide real-life examples of

(continued)

when employees had used old versus new training skills, and he answered questions that arose about using the training back on the job. This put the training in a real organizational context for the trainees.

In each local area, "stars" were identified (those using the process very effectively) and used as a resource people to facilitate transfer. After training, employees were also assigned coaches (recall that everyone has received the training, so experienced coaches were available). To reinforce the importance of using the skills on the job, Dr. Camp developed a "one-day refresher" training and went to the various offices to provide this. Part of the "refresher" training was to share concerns about the difficulties in implementing the process and to generate ideas on how to make transfer easier. At the end of this training, Dr. Camp encouraged trainees to send him copies of the "outcome of an interview process" so he could provide them with feedback to again facilitate effective transfer to the job.

Dr. Camp then suggested that the company develop a task force to examine how effective the transfer of training was and consider other steps that could be taken to ensure that what trainees were learning was being transferred to the job. A representative of the task force began meeting with employees (while they were at different training sessions) to explore ways of facilitating the transfer. One of the ideas to come from these meetings was that each trainee team up with another trainee who was at the training session. When they got back to their respective offices throughout the world, they would stay in contact, providing support, feedback, and ideas for dealing with obstacles to using the trained skills.

How successful has the training been? Management has looked at some bottom-line results and has determined that the training has helped them become more profitable. Does everyone use the skills as effectively as they could? No, but the organization continues to work on ideas to encourage the transfer. Recently, the task force has begun discussing the possibility of videos and online information to introduce the skills and to reinforce their correct use.

DESIGN THEORY

With an understanding of the factors that facilitate learning and transfer, we now provide two **design theories** that incorporate much of this information. There are several theories related to the effective design of training. Some, such as component display theory,[78] are specific only to cognitive learning, and others focus only on attitude change.[79] For more information on these and many others, you should consult *Instructional Design Theories and Models* by Charles Reigeluth.[80] For our purposes, we will examine two design theories with a broader application: ET,[81] a macro theory of design, and the micro theory of Gagné and Briggs.[82]

Theories of training design are not theories in the traditional sense, because they do not predict cause-and-effect relationships. They prescribe methods of presenting material (what is to be learned) in a way to enhance the likelihood that the material will be learned. So instructional design theories offer guidelines as to what techniques to use in what situations to design effective training.[83]

Elaboration Theory

Elaboration theory is a macro theory of design. It is based on a holistic alternative to the part/whole sequencing that is usually followed in training. This holistic approach is more meaningful and motivational for learners, because from the start they see and get to practice the complete task.[84] It is relevant only for complex tasks (and is not applicable for the design of attitudinal training). To understand when to use ET, it is necessary to understand the issue of sequencing. **Sequencing** is the process of how to group and order the content of training. It is directed at facilitating the "cognitive organization" aspect of social learning theory.

If you are training employees in the use of several software packages (word processing, spreadsheet, e-mail use), sequencing is not important, and it does not matter which you teach first. If the operating system is Windows and it is a part of the training, it would be necessary to present it first (because all other programs require its use). In this case, sequencing is important. Sequencing is important only when a strong relationship exists among the topics of the course. So, if your training included producing charts from the spreadsheet program and integrating them into a necessary word processing document, some sequencing would be necessary.

For the purposes of training different topics, two sequencing strategies are possible: topical and spiral (see Figure 5-4). Topical sequencing requires the complete learning of one topic before moving to the next task. Spiral sequencing requires learning the basics of the first task, then the basics from the second task, and so on. After completing the basic understanding of all tasks, the learner moves to the second level of the first task to do the same thing. The advantages and disadvantages to each of these strategies are depicted in Table 5-12.

A training program is seldom all one or the other, but a combination of the two, depending on the relationships among the tasks being taught. Consider a weeklong workshop for supervisor training on topics such as effective feedback,

Figure 5-4
Comparison of
Topical and Spiral
Sequencing

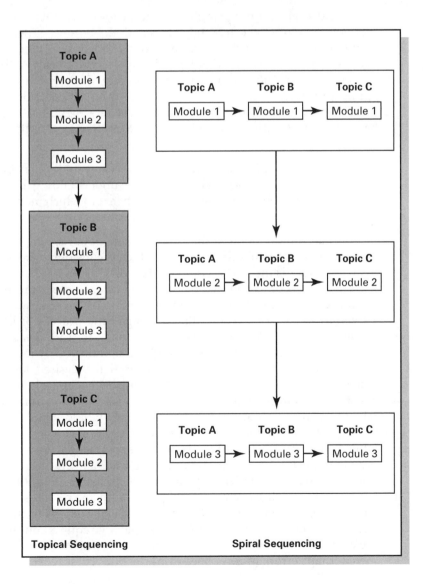

Table 5-12 Comparison of Topical and Spiral Sequencing

	Advantages	Disadvantages
Topical	Concentrate on topic, no interference from other topic	Once learned, move to the next topic, and the first is forgotten
Spiral	Built-in synthesis and review, interrelationships are more obvious and understood	Disruption of learner's thought processes when moving to the next topic

effective communication, providing performance reviews, running an effective meeting, problem solving, and so forth. In sequencing these topics, it makes sense to have feedback and effective communication before performance reviews, because they will provide help in doing an effective performance review. They can also be taught separately, using topical sequencing strategy. Consider another topic—problem solving. If you were teaching a six-step problem-solving process, you might combine the methods of sequencing. Learning to define a problem correctly and brainstorming might be taught topically before the problem-solving model is presented because they are stand-alone topics. Then the six-step model could be taught using the spiral method. The learning process is facilitated, because some tasks are learned independently. The complexity of the overall problem-solving process and interrelationship among the steps suggest the use of the spiral approach.

Here is where ET comes in. Recall that it is only applicable to complex tasks and is based on what Charles Reigeluth calls the **Simplifying Conditions Method (SCM)**. As he states:

> Regarding complex tasks, the SCM sequencing strategy enables learners to understand tasks holistically. . . . Holistic understanding of the task results in the formation of a stable cognitive schema to which more complex capabilities and understanding can be assimilated.[85]

SCM is based on the notion that for all complex tasks, simple and more complex versions exist. Consider driving a car, which is considered a complex task. Driving in an empty lot is much less complex than driving on a freeway during rush hour.

The SCM is based on two parts, epitomizing and elaborating. **Epitomizing** is the process of identifying the simplest version of the task, which is still representative of the task as a whole. **Elaborating** is the process of identifying progressively more complex versions of the task. In the design of training, the epitomizing version of the task is taught first, followed by increasingly more complex (elaborating) versions of the task until the desired level of complexity is reached. Consider the job of air traffic controller. The task is complex; they must assist several aircraft landings under various weather conditions. Training would take place in a simulator when the computer would simulate aircraft landing at the airport. First, determine the epitome: the simplest version of the task possible while still representative of the complex task. It would be where only one aircraft is on the screen, no wind or other adverse weather conditions are present, and the pilot is responding perfectly to the trainee's instructions (when told to turn to heading 040 and descend at 100 feet per minute, the pilot response is exactly that). Once this epitome is mastered, a number of elaborations of the task must be mastered, each more complex, until the complexity required on the job is reached. In the air traffic trainee's situation, the first elaboration is to add a light crosswind, then perhaps errors in responses from the pilot (first regarding the heading, then both heading and descent). The final elaboration would be matched to the expectation of air traffic controller in the field.

The major advantage of this approach to training is that the more complete tasks are presented immediately, which should foster better understanding and motivate trainees as they immediately see the relationship between what they are learning and the job-related tasks. Evidence indicates that ET is not only effective but also appealing to trainees.[86] Students wanting to know more about the theory and see actual examples of its use are referred to work by Carson and Curtis and others.[87]

Gagné-Briggs Theory

The Gagné-Briggs theory of instructional design,[88] discussed in Chapter 3, is applicable to cognitive, behavioral, and attitudinal learning. As a micro theory, it provides a set of procedures to follow for each instructional event to enhance learning. The theory identifies nine events of instruction, which are tied to social learning theory (see Table 5-13). Note that the first event in the theory of instructional design is "attention," which parallels that of social learning theory. The next event, "informing of the objectives," further activates a process of getting the trainees' "attention" focused. Stimulating recall of prerequisite learning ties into activation of memory. Let's examine the nine events of instruction in more detail. Typically a training program consists of multiple modules that are integrated to meet the training objectives. It is important to remember as you go through the nine events that they apply to each module of a training program. As we do so, we will refer back to relevant sections of social learning theory for additional information.

Gain Attention

Attention can be gained in several ways (raise voice, clap hands, or a comment such as "Now watch me carefully"), but is best when tied to the training at hand. If the training was in problem solving, for example, ask the question, "How do

Table 5-13 Gagné-Briggs Nine Events of Instruction

Instructional Event	Relation to Social Learning Theory
Gain attention	Attention
Informing the trainee of goal (objectives)	Attention
Stimulate recall of prior knowledge	Retention: Activation of memory
Present the material	Retention: Activation of memory/symbolic coding/ cognitive organization
Provide guidance for learning	Retention: Symbolic coding/cognitive organization through guided discovery
	Retention: Symbolic rehearsal
Elicit performance (practice)	Behavioral reproduction
Provide informative feedback	Reinforcement
Assess performance	
Enhance retention and transfer	Reinforcement

Source: Adapted from Gagné, R. M., L. Briggs, and W. Wager. *Principles of Instructional Design* (1988). Fort Worth: Harcourt Brace Jovanovich.

you go about solving a problem?" or "We have high absenteeism; what should we do about it?" These types of questions focus discussion on the types of problems trainees face and their typical problem-solving approaches. This initial focus leads nicely into the introduction of the problem-solving objectives. Another way to gain attention is to have the CEO/president welcome the trainees and indicate how important the training is to the future of the company. This approach was effective for the training developed by Dr. Camp in Training in Action 5-2. High-level support for training is always important, and when a key decision maker takes time to convey this support, it is especially effective in getting trainees' attention.

Inform the Learner of the Goal or Objective

We covered learning objectives and their importance in depth. Clearly, this step is important in getting the trainee focused and aware of not only what needs to be learned, but also what will be required when training is complete. Also, it is useful to tie the training back to the job and how it will help trainees be better performers. Having done a TNA, you will find this an easy task.

Stimulate Recall of Prior Relevant Knowledge (Learning)

This step is important to ensure that the trainee has accessed the information/knowledge necessary for the learning that is about to take place. At the moment of learning, all relevant prerequisite capabilities must be highly accessible to be part of the learning event.[89] Suppose "team problem solving" training is to be conducted. Previously, some brainstorming training and problem-definition training had been completed. Now trainees should be thinking about these topics so that the previous learning will be accessible to the problem-solving training. Ask for an explanation of brainstorming from a trainee, or focus a discussion on these two topics and show how they are related to the present learning task. Or simply review the two topics with a high level of participation from trainees.

Present Material to Be Learned

Material is presented in a logical and understandable format. This point seems obvious, but recall that what the trainer might think is obvious might not fit in the trainees' schema. To ensure understanding, the method of instruction should include several questions designed to elicit responses from trainees regarding their level of understanding. Highlight important points with verbal emphasis (raise voice, slow down presentation for effect). Use easel sheets with bold print to highlight important learning points. Also, eliciting examples from trainees serves to ensure that trainees understand the material. The trainer in team problem solving should list the steps on an easel board for all to see, with the substeps provided under each of the main headings. Some simple examples of problems and the procedures to solve them could be on a video for effect. The video could be stopped at each step to highlight the step and the preparation for the next step. These examples reflect ways in which the organization and presentation of material assist the trainee in their symbolic coding and cognitive organization.

Provide Guidance for Learning

The key here is to guide the trainees to the appropriate answer/conclusion, not just to tell them the answer. Get trainees to examine the possibilities related to the topic, both right and wrong. When the solution is reached, the overall discussion will have helped trainees obtain an in-depth understanding of the topic. Provide them with a problem and ask for possible alternatives. For example, in problem-solving training, give trainees a problem such as "absenteeism is high" and ask them to "define the problem" (the first step in problem solving). This task gets trainees thinking and providing different perspectives. These different perspectives are shared, and all can assess (depending on whether the response was correct) their own level of understanding. Providing numerous examples allows the trainees to see the generality of the material to many situations. Asking for their examples confirms that the material is being put into the correct context.

Elicit the Performance

Here, trainees actually do it. For example, in the case of learning a problem-solving model, they now would work in teams to solve a real problem. The problem should be similar to or even the same problem they have been discussing all along. It should also be the simplest type of problem they are likely to come across. Until now, working through the solution was piecemeal; now, as a team, they do it as a whole integrated process without interaction with other teams or the trainer. Once they are successful, provide a more complex problem to solve—even suggest that they use one they previously encountered in their workplace.

Provide Feedback

Once the team completes a process, a feedback session as to how they did is essential. Feedback can be provided in numerous ways. Videotaping the session and going over it with the team (time-consuming), sitting in on parts of each meeting and providing feedback, or having another team watch and provide feedback are all methods used to provide feedback. The type you use will, to some extent, be a function of the time available and the number of trainees. Of course, designing a program in which training is spread over a number of weeks would allow for more individual feedback between training sessions, but the benefits must be weighed against the cost of trainer time. The important thing is that trainees know what they are doing right and wrong, and that they can make corrections before training is complete.

Assess Performance

The Gagné-Briggs theory indicates that learning should be assessed after each topic is taught. So, after training on effective feedback skills and before moving to performance appraisal training, you need to assess the learning that took place regarding feedback skills. The assessment need not be formal, especially when a formal evaluation may be planned for the end of the training program. But some method of determining whether the trainees learned the material is necessary. Questioning (for cognitive knowledge) is one way to assess this. Asking trainees for a behavioral response (a skill) is also a form of assessment. This approach has two purposes: It confirms that learning took place and provides for additional practice at recalling the knowledge or performing the skill.

Enhance Retention and Transfer

An important part of any training program is the transfer of the training to the job. Designing the program to facilitate retention and transfer is one of the more critical components of the training design. If the purpose of the training is cognitive knowledge, the opportunity for review (retrieval of the information) needs to be provided at spaced intervals after the training is complete. The same applies to skills. All of the support processes discussed earlier are relevant here. For an example of using the Gagné-Briggs design theory to develop training, see Table 5-14 on page 198. This is an example of an introductory module of a multimodule training program designed to teach supervisors how to give feedback.

Table 5-14 Cognitive Module of "Giving Effective Feedback" Using the Gagné-Briggs Nine Events of Instruction

A sample training design using the Gagné-Briggs model:

EVENT	FEEDBACK TRAINING
Gain attention	Ask questions of trainees to initiate interest in topic of feedback: "Who has received constructive feedback that they actually appreciated?" If some have, ask them what it was about the feedback that made it better than other feedback they received. If no one has, ask what it was about previous feedback that made them not appreciate it. Have a brief discussion about what is wrong with the typical feedback received and what would make it better.
Inform of goal	Show objectives and discuss; tie to previous discussion.
Stimulate recall of prior knowledge	Ask "How do you behave when you are trying to help someone versus when you are disciplining them?" "How do you behave toward someone you are trying to help (helping is what feedback is all about)?" Get trainees to verbalize things they do such as "provide it in private," "do it as soon as possible," and so forth, to put them in a helping frame of mind with their rules for helping in their "working memory."
Present material	Share a list of what makes for effective feedback—be specific, not general; be descriptive, not evaluative; and so forth. Present it on an easel sheet in bold. Provide examples for each item.
Provide guidance	Provide trainees with multiple examples (some good, some poor) and ask for input as to effectiveness. Give a handout sheet with a number of feedback statements, and ask trainees to rate their effectiveness. Get trainees in small groups to discuss their results and come up with a group consensus as to which are good and which are not so good. Have them provide a rationale. Now go through each and ask trainees to discuss this in terms of their responses.
Elicit performance	Performance here is cognitive knowledge about what is effective, and not effective feedback. Ask trainees to form groups of three. Have one of the three teach the others the rules of effective feedback with examples. Then switch, so each trainee has the opportunity to show that they know the information well enough to teach it to others and provide their own unique examples.
Provide feedback	The other two trainees receiving training complete an evaluation form giving feedback to the one doing the training (in the groups of three). The trainer also goes around to each group and provides feedback.
Assess performance	Conduct a quiz that asks trainees to recall the rules for effective feedback. Go through a list of feedback examples (similar to the ones earlier), and indicate which are effective, which are not effective, and why they were not effective.
Enhance retention and transfer	Trainees will be back to learn the behavioral component of training in a week. At that time, review will take place to facilitate retention.

FOCUS ON SMALL BUSINESS

Small businesses follow more sophisticated HR policies today than in the past.[90] In fact, a recent study suggests that many of their policies and practices are not much different from those of large businesses.[91] Furthermore, like larger businesses, effective HR practices have been shown to have a positive effect on quality[92] and productivity.[93] These findings suggest that small businesses are beginning to realize the importance of sound HR practices. The major difference between small and large business is the effect that successful training can have on the organization as a whole.

Much of what was discussed earlier is relevant for any size organization. Ensuring that employees are highly motivated to learn, and presenting interesting and relevant training, is the goal no matter what the size of the company. Again, the major problem in many training programs is not the learning of the skills but the transfer of these skills to the job. We believe that given the requirements necessary for transfer of training, the small business enjoys a definite advantage. We see that climate and a continuous learning culture go a long way toward ensuring the transfer of training. Although any organizational change is difficult, a small organization should be able

The Sandwich Community Health Centre is a service-oriented organization with about 35 employees located in Sandwich, Ontario, Canada. The executive director and assistant executive director of the organization wanted to integrate the two areas of the organization (clinical and health promotion) and develop a team approach to much of the community care they offer. After a discussion on the issue, a consultant conducted a TNA and provided training on communication skills and conflict resolution.

Everyone attended training, even the executive director. This involvement by top management conveyed an important message about the importance of the training. Top management also insisted that the training be evaluated. Knowing that an assessment would be made at some future date kept everyone focused on the need to change. Finally, although no formal culture assessment was made, the interviews conducted in the TNA clearly indicated a climate of continuous learning.

to accomplish climate and culture change faster and more easily than a large one. Furthermore, in the small business, it should be easier to obtain and demonstrate top management's commitment. In many of the large company interventions conducted by the authors, top management provides written or verbal support for the intervention, but little else. Most of our dealings are with the HR manager, rather than with the CEO or president. Although we stress the continued involvement of upper management, we often have little interaction with top management once the intervention has begun. Top management typically feels they must spend their time on more important things.

In the small firm, it is often the CEO or owner who makes decisions about the type of training and development that will be provided.[94] Access to these individuals is much easier and provides a greater opportunity for you to influence them. Because of their greater involvement, they often develop a clearer understanding of their role in making training successful. An example of this involvement is shown in our Training in Action 5-3.

Will the training in Training in Action 5-3 transfer? According to the research, it stands a good chance. The fact that the organization is small enough that all could attend the same training at the same time and experience the same things will help the transfer process. This situation simply could not occur in a larger company.

OUTCOMES OF DESIGN

As noted at the start of this chapter, to develop effective training programs you need to understand the various factors that facilitate learning and transfer. This is one of the three outputs of the design phase. Table 5-15 provides a summary of some of these factors and how they are related to the Gagné-Briggs theory of design presented earlier.

The other two outputs are the development of evaluation methods and the identification of alternative methods of instruction.

Evaluation

The design of the evaluation for your training has already begun if you have been following our training process model. The methods you used to determine the organizational and person performance gaps are the same methods you should use to evaluate whether the training has reduced those gaps. The objectives you set (reaction, learning, etc.) define the behaviors, standards and conditions for evaluating the

Table 5-15 Learning and Transfer Factors as Related to Social Learning Theory and Gagné-Briggs Theory of Design

	SOCIAL LEARNING THEORY	GAGNÉ-BRIGGS NINE EVENTS OF INSTRUCTION	FACTORS TO CONSIDER
Training Module (name of module)	**Attention/Expectancy**	**Gain attention**	
Beginning	Create/reinforce positive attitude toward training		Provide introductory comments to develop a relaxed atmosphere.
		Inform trainee of goals	Describe the objectives for this module and discuss usefulness on the job; draw examples from trainees.
During Module			
	Retention		Focus material on training objectives.
	Symbolic coding	**Stimulate recall of prior knowledge**	Develop links between previous learning and the new learning (activation of memory).
		Make relevant	
	Cognitive organization	**Present material**	Use multiple media and make interesting.
		Make interesting	Ask questions to obtain trainee involvement.
	Symbolic rehearsal	**Provide guidance for learning**	Get trainees involved (symbolic rehearsal). Use relevant examples, and offer many of them.
	Behavioral Reproduction/ Reinforcement	**Elicit performance**	Provide relevant activities that allow practice with the material (including maximum similarity and/or different situations).
		Encourage learning	
		Provide feedback	Provide time to evaluate performance level accomplished and provide feedback. Tell trainees how they are doing or design activity to provide feedback
Ending of Module	**Reinforcement**		
	Ensure that trainees see results of training	**Assess performance**	Use an assessment tool (written or oral to determine if trainees have the KSAs). Allow trainees to indicate their comfort with the material. Ask for any questions.
	Sensitize trainees to difficulty in transfer training	**Enhance retention and transfer**	Review objectives to show what was accomplished. Ask trainees to describe how this could apply to the workplace.

effectiveness of the training. These become one set of inputs to the evaluation process discussed in Chapter 9. Recall the learning objective from earlier in the chapter:

> *Using a drop wire, bushing, and connector, but without the use of a manual,* **the trainee will splice a drop wire** according to the standards set out in the manual.

This objective assists us in development of the evaluation. From the objective it is clear that we need to develop a behavioral test that will assess how well the trainee will splice a drop wire compared with the standards set out in the manual. Ideally, you would have developed such a test when you were assessing employees to determine their needs. Chapter 9 discusses evaluations strategies when this is not the case. In any case, you should begin the design of your evaluation strategy once you have addressed the other design issues. Once you have completed the development phase you should finalize the evaluation strategy (develop the evaluation instruments, determine the time frame and location and so on). Note in Fabrics, Inc. (which begins on page 203), how we use the learning objectives in the development of the evaluation. You should find it useful to re-read this portion of Fabrics, Inc., just prior to reading Chapter 9 on evaluation, so that the contiguity between design and evaluation remains clear.

Identification of Alternative Methods of Instruction

In addition to developing the evaluation for the training, you also begin developing the training. To do this, you first need to understand the various methods available and what their effectiveness is in terms of training KSAs. So the next two chapters (Chapters 6 and 7) provide that information. Then in Chapter 8 we return to the development of training, which, as noted earlier, is done in tandem with developing the evaluation.

CASE: The Real World of Training . . . What Is Wrong Here? (Conclusion)

Were you able to figure out what went wrong in the two cases at the beginning of the chapter? Both deal with the need to develop good training objectives.

Case 1

Recall the incidents discussed in Case 1 at the beginning of the chapter. Training in troubleshooting did not transfer well. What went wrong? Would more training have helped the employees become better troubleshooters? Reexamine the training that took place. The instructor provided a problem, and the trainees indicated the symptoms that would result from the problem. This problem/symptom sequence was the exact opposite of what they would have been required to do on the job, which involved seeing a symptom and then determining the problem. Had proper learning objectives been developed before the design of the training, the instructor would have realized this mistake. For example, consider the learning objective, "Upon describing what is wrong with the system (a symptom), the trainee will immediately be able to describe all the possible problems that might cause these symptoms." Had this objective been developed before training, the type of training required would have been more obvious.

Case 2

In Case 2, all the trainees followed a cycle of doing poorly on tests 1, 4, 7, 10, and 13, and much better on the other exams.

Further analysis revealed that the 32-week course was divided into five subsections, each of which had three tests. Also, a different instructor taught each subsection. On the very first test, the trainees did not know what to expect and so did poorly. Once they understood what to expect on the tests, they improved on the remaining two tests. When a new instructor arrived, they prepared as usual, only to find the type of test had changed; once again they did poorly. When they understood what the new instructor wanted, they did better. It was "getting used to what the instructor wanted" that caused the cycle. Objectives were vague, and trainees did not know what to expect. The chief instructor then developed learning objectives for all subsections, which provided guidance to both instructors and trainees as to what exams would be about. The problem disappeared.

Source: Mager, R. *Preparing Instructional Objectives* (1975). Belmont, CA: Pitman Learning.

Table 5-16 provides a tool to use in reviewing design phase activities and whether the design is ready to be moved into the development phase. In the design of training, several constraints need to be considered, such as how much time will be given to prepare and present training, how much of a priority it is, and how much money can be spent. These will all place constraints on the type of training offered. Once these questions are answered, it is necessary to determine the type of trainees, their current level of KSAs, their motivation to learn, and the degree of homogeneity for the group. Answers to these questions will provide you with a framework that will be used to develop the objectives for training.

Learning objectives provide clear, unambiguous goals for the training. An effective objective contains three parts: (1) desired behaviors, or what the trainee is expected to be able to do; (2) conditions, or what help/environment trainees will have when performing the expected behavior; and (3) standards, or what will be required to be successful. Learning objectives should be developed for reaction to training, learning, transfer to the job, and organizational outcomes. These objectives provide guidance for designing and developing the training. They also provide the trainer with clear instructions on what to train and how to do it. Finally, they inform the trainees about what to expect.

Table 5-16 Design Matrix

Design Component	Activities and Issues	Ready to Move to Development?
Organizational Constraints	Review analysis data, and then identify any additional constraints that might relate to the "who, what, when, where and how" of the training program.	All constraints are identified, and accommodation strategies developed.
Training Objectives	Trainee reaction, learning, transfer, and organizational results objectives need to be developed. These must have a clear description of the desired outcome, the conditions under which that outcome will occur, and the standards that will signal that the outcome has been achieved.	All objectives have been reviewed and approved by the appropriate parties. The evaluation instruments are developed, and decisions about when and where to evaluate have been made.
Learning Theory **Focus on the trainee**	• Individual differences (KSAs, learning style, etc.) must be addressed. • Trainee motivation issues must be addressed.	The issues to the left have been completed and documented. This document will drive the development and implementation of the training.
Focus on training design	Review Social Learning theory, the Nine Events of Learning model, Elaboration theory, and other learning theories to arrive at the rules, policies, and procedures that will guide the development of the training and facilitate learning.	
Focus on Transfer	• Appropriate use of whole/part practice, maximized similarity, varied situations, and general principles to maximize transferability from the classroom. • Using data from the analysis phase, develop strategies for addressing organizational impediments to transfer.	
Alternative training methods	With the learning objectives in mind, identify the methods most suited to achieving those objectives and which fit within the constraints that have been identified are selected to be used for the training	

In the design of training, consider two aspects: learning and transfer. To facilitate learning, the design must address the motivation of the trainees and the environment in which training will take place. Social learning theory and the Gagné-Briggs micro theory of design provide a framework for setting up each instructional event in a manner that is most effective. To facilitate transfer, consider issues such as type of practice, whole or part learning, overlearning, and similarity to the job. Also, using a combination of goal setting and relapse prevention helps trainees transfer the KSAs to the job.

The support of the supervisor and peers in the work group is just as important to transfer, and sit-ins by the trainer will help too. Finally, congruent reward systems and a supportive climate/culture need to be present to ensure transfer.

ET, a macro theory of design, is useful for determining the sequencing of events and just how to present them in a training context. This theory argues that one should focus on whole rather than part learning, but to make the whole as simple as possible at the beginning and then make it more difficult in stages until it reaches the level of complexity found in the workplace.

This chapter sets the stage for showing the link between the learning objectives and the methods used to provide training. Understanding what makes a good learning objective and the groundwork in terms of what facilitates learning and transfer on the basis of theory allow for an examination of the methods of training and the link between these methods and the learning objectives.

THE TRAINING PROGRAM (FABRICS, INC.)

This continues the description of the Fabrics, Inc., training program that we began in Chapter 4. Recall that Fabrics, Inc., grew quickly and experienced problems with its supervisors. In Chapter 4, we described how the consultant completed a needs analysis. From this TNA, the consultant determined a number of areas in which supervisors could use training. A partial list included a lack of KSAs in the following areas:

Effective listening
Communication
Conflict resolution
Effective feedback
Measuring employee performance
Motivating employees

For the purpose of this exercise, we deal with only one, conflict resolution. The first step will be to develop the learning objectives.

The Learning Objectives

Some of the learning objectives are as follows:

- The trainee will, <u>with no errors</u>, **present in writing the four types of active listening, along with examples of each of the types,** *with no help from reference material.*

- When, in a role-play, the trainee is presented with an angry comment, **the trainee will respond** <u>immediately</u> **using one of the active listening types.** The trainee will **then explain orally the technique used and why,** *with no help from reference material.* <u>The trainee will be presented with five of these comments and be expected to correctly respond and explain a minimum of four.</u>

- The trainee will, <u>with 100 percent accuracy,</u> **provide in writing each step of the conflict resolution model, along with a relevant example,** *with no help from any reference material.*

- In a role-play of an angry customer, the trainee/employee **will show concern for the customer by listening and providing alternative solutions, using the steps in the conflict resolution model,** *with help from an easel sheet that has the steps listed on it.* <u>The trainee must use all the steps and two types of active listening in the role-play.</u>

- *After watching a role-play of an angry person and an employee using the conflict resolution model,* **the trainee will,** *without reference to material,* **immediately provide feedback as to the effectiveness of the person using the**
(continued)

conflict resolution model. <u>The trainee must identify four of the six errors.</u>

Reaction Objective

The trainee will upon completion of training **respond to a 15-item reaction questionnaire with** <u>minimum scores of 4 on a 5-point scale.</u>

Transfer of Training Objective

When an angry customer approaches the employee and begins speaking in an angry tone of voice, **the employee will,** *immediately,* **use the conflict resolution model to** <u>calm the customer down.</u>

Organizational Objective

Three months after training, <u>there will be a 75 percent drop</u> **in letters of complaint from customers.**

Design Issues

We turn now to design issues. The conflict resolution model has four steps and requires attending to cues at verbal, vocal, and visual levels. From an ET perspective then, it is a complex task. The four steps in the model are as follows:

1. Use active listening.
2. Indicate respect.
3. Be assertive.
4. Provide information.

Further examination of the model reveals that the first part, active listening is a complex task by itself,[95] as is the total model. So the first decision is what mix of spiral/topical sequencing to use in the training of this model. Active listening, being a skill that can also be used on its own, suggests the use of topical sequencing to train employees in active listening first. Then we will use spiral sequencing to train the total conflict resolution model.

Teaching of the cognitive component of each of these skills will be completed before the skills training, but for brevity we will discuss only the behavioral component. Using SCM, as proposed by ET, we first determine the epitome (simplest version of the task that still embodies the whole task). For active listening, it will be to use the skill in an everyday situation, such as discussing which movie to see. In this situation, the initiator (person in the role of disagreeing with the trainee) will simply disagree regarding a movie the trainee wants to see. This situation has minimal emotional content and should require minimal monitoring of the initiator by the trainee, as it will not result in an argument. The same epitome used for active listening can also be used for the conflict resolution model because the latter simply takes the discussion to a different level.

The most complex task will require dealing with a great deal of anger on the part of the initiator of the discussion. Once these two extremes are conceptualized, those in between can be determined.

Let's now examine this training at a micro level using Gagné-Briggs theory. For the module related to teaching active listening, we want to begin by getting trainees' attention, as suggested by Gagné-Briggs design theory. This can be accomplished by showing a video of two people in a heated argument and then asking, "Has that situation ever happened to you? Would you like to have a better way of responding in such a situation so tempers do not flare?" This would allow you to introduce active listening. The next step in the theory is to inform the trainees of the goal. Presenting the learning objective related to active listening accomplishes this. The training would continue to be designed paying close attention to the steps in the design theory.

Now let's turn to the evaluation component as an output from the training design. To consider these, we turn back to the learning objectives, which are as follows:

- The trainee will, <u>with no errors</u>, **present in writing the four types of active listening, along with examples of each of the types,** *with no reference material.*
- The trainee will, <u>with 100 percent accuracy</u> **provide in writing each step of the conflict resolution model, along with a relevant example,** *with no help from any reference material.*

These, along with a number of similar objectives not shown, will require a paper-and-pencil test of declarative knowledge.

(continued)

Regarding the behavioral component of the evaluation, consider these objectives:

- *When, in a role play, the trainee is presented with an angry comment,* **the trainee will respond** <u>immediately</u> **using one of the active listening types. The trainee will then explain orally the technique used and why,** *with no help from reference material.* <u>The trainee will be presented with five of these and be expected to correctly respond and explain a minimum of four.</u>
- *In a role-play of an angry customer* the trainee/employee **will show concern for the customer by listening and providing alternative solutions, using the steps in the conflict resolution model,** *with help from an easel sheet which has the steps listed on it.* <u>The trainee must use all the steps and two types of active listening in the role-play.</u>
- *After watching role-play of an angry person and an employee using the conflict resolution model,*

the trainee will, *without reference to material, immediately* **provide feedback as to the effectiveness of the person using the conflict resolution model.** <u>The trainee must identify a minimum of four of the six errors.</u>

These objectives will require carefully developed standardized role-plays. The role of the initiator will be scripted and standardized to provide each trainee with similar situations to respond to. In addition, a standardized scoring key, which will guide the scoring of a trainee in the behavioral tests, will be developed. These scoring keys will provide examples of acceptable and unacceptable behavior of the trainee, and a rating scale for different responses. There will also be a scoring key provided for the explanations (oral test) that follow the behavioral part of the test.

We will return to Fabrics, Inc., in Chapter 8, to provide a look at the development process.

KEY TERMS

- Behavioral reproduction
- Climate
- Cognitive load
- Cognitive organization
- Conditions
- Culture
- Design theory
- Guided discovery
- Identical elements
- Knowledge of results

- Learning objectives
- Massed practice
- Negative transfer
- Overlearning
- Part learning
- Positive transfer
- Progressive part training
- Relapse prevention
- Sit-in
- Spaced practice

- Standards
- Symbolic coding
- Symbolic rehearsal
- Task complexity
- Task organization
- Transfer of training
- Whole learning
- Zero transfer

QUESTIONS FOR REVIEW

1. What is a learning objective? List and explain its three components.
2. What can be done long before the trainee attends training to ensure that the trainee will be motivated to learn?
3. How does knowledge of classical and operant conditioning assist you in designing effective training?
4. How would you present training material in a manner that facilitates retention?
5. If a particular task were critical to saving a life (police officer shooting a gun, pilot responding to an emergency), what factors would you build into the design

of training to ensure that the behavior was both learned and transferred to the workplace?

6. To help ensure transfer of training, what would you do outside the training itself? Who would you involve and how? What would you do about the organizational structure/environment?

7. Suppose you are designing a training program for a group of 40 employees. These employees come from a wide range of ethnic and cultural backgrounds and have different educational and experience backgrounds relative to the content area of the training. What training design features would you use to address these constraints?

8. Discuss the Gagné-Briggs theory of design and its relationship to social learning theory.

9. Explain ET and how it would help you design a training program.

EXERCISES

1. You perhaps already noted that the learning objectives at the beginning of each chapter do not completely follow the three criteria we identified. They all describe the outcome in behavioral terms but do not identify the conditions or standards, which vary with the instructor. Assume you will be the instructor for this chapter and will rewrite each of the learning objectives at the beginning of the chapter in complete form. Your trainees are corporate HRD employees, and you are training them on the contents of this chapter. Additionally, write an objective for each of the other types of training objectives (trainee reaction, transfer of training, and organizational outcome).

2. What is your grade point average since you started your education at this institution? How hard do you work to maintain that average: 3 (very hard/hard), 2 (about average), and 1 (enough to get by)? Now ask yourself why. Tie your answer into Expectancies 1 and 2 and the valence of outcomes. Break into groups that contain a mix of 1s, 2s, and 3s. Discuss what makes the person in your group a 3. Is it attractive outcomes (valence), confidence in ability (Expectancy 1), or belief that it will result in the positive outcomes desired? From that information, is there any way you believe you could influence the 2s or 1s to be more motivated? What would you try to influence? Explain your approach in terms of Expectancies 1 and 2. How does this process relate to trainee populations in the workplace?

WEB RESEARCH

Conduct an Internet search to identify two companies that provide training design consulting services. Identify the design process for each. Compare and contrast each in terms of their approach.

Some Interesting Sites

Conditions of Learning (R. Gagné)
http://tip.psychology.org/gagne.html
Zenon Environmental, Inc. (small business with efficient HR management)
www.zenonenv.com

CASE ANALYSIS

1. Review the Domtar case from Chapter 1, and answer the following questions:
   a. In the implementation of Kaizen, what groups of employees are likely to need training? How should the trainees be organized? Think of this issue from a training design perspective and from a training content perspective.
   b. For the type of training envisioned, what are the learning objectives? Write these objectives in complete form.
   c. For each group of employees that will need training, what are the organizational constraints that need to be addressed in the design of the training? What design features should be used to address these constraints? Be sure to address both the learning and transfer of training issues.

2. Review the Multistate Health Corporation case from Chapter 2, and answer the following questions:
   a. In the implementation of the HRPS, what groups of employees are likely to need training? Think of this from a training design perspective and from a training content perspective.
   b. For the type of training you envision for each group, what are the learning objectives? Write these in complete form.
   c. For each group of employees that will need training, what are the organizational constraints you will need to address in the design of your training? What design features will you use to address these constraints? Be sure to address both the learning and transfer of training issues.

Chapter 6

Traditional Training Methods

Learning Objectives

After reading this chapter, you should be able to:

➤ *Describe the purposes, procedures, strengths, and limitations of the following training methods:*

◆ *Lectures, lecture/discussions, and demonstrations;*
◆ *Games and simulations; and*
◆ *On-the-job training (OJT).*

➤ *Describe the types of learning objectives for which each method is most suited.*

➤ *Identify the various audiovisual (AV) options and their strengths and weaknesses.*

CASE: *Training at Blockbuster, Inc.*

Blockbuster, Inc., the provider of in-home movies and game entertainment, chose a mix of methods to train its 38,000 field employees, but the central focus was on simulations. The training was to focus on how to work a shift, how to run a shift, how to manage a store, and how to manage a district. The training focused on participants learning what should be done, seeing how to do it, and then practicing doing it. About 25 percent of the learning came from computerized instruction, and the rest came from practice, application, and knowledge assessment. The knowledge components of the training were put into an e-learning format, allowing participants to learn at their convenience. During the practice sessions, they engaged in simulations where they were observed and given feedback. Once they completed a module, the participants took an online assessment. Participants had a minimum score they had to achieve to move onto the next module. If they did not pass, then they could go back

(continued)

through the module and retake the test. Blockbuster believes that there is much to learn through failure, and the simulations allow the failure to occur in a safe environment.

How has the training worked? Employee feedback has been very positive. More importantly, Dan Satterthwaite, senior V.P. of human resources (HR) and administration says, " . . . we committed to a five-year payback . . . we paid it off in a fraction of the time."

Source: Adapted from Dolezlek, H. "Focus on games and simulations." *Training* (October 2007), pp. 40–46.

OVERVIEW OF THE CHAPTER

This chapter provides a basic understanding of traditional training methods in terms of their strengths and limitations related to cost, suitable learning objectives, and other factors related to their effectiveness. In Chapter 7, we will discuss the same issues as they relate to computer-based training. The effectiveness of each training method for meeting various learning objectives is summarized in a table at the start of Chapter 8. We placed it there because that is (development and implementation) where final decisions about the methods to be used are made.

MATCHING METHODS WITH OUTCOMES

The material in this chapter and the next will provide the principle methods and delivery systems used in training. The designer of a training program needs to understand each of these to determine the best method for meeting the specific training objectives (given the organizational constraints). Instructional methods differ in their ability to influence knowledge, skills, and attitudes (KSAs), so the training designer must be able to evaluate a method's strengths and weaknesses to make good decisions about its use. Before we move into that discussion, a brief review of the KSA definitions might be helpful. Refer to the definitions in Chapter 1 for more detail. **Knowledge** is an organized body of facts, principles, procedures, and information. **Skills** are the capacities needed to perform a set of tasks. **Attitudes** are employee beliefs and opinions that support or inhibit behavior.

Think about what some of the KSA objectives might have been in the opening case. Like many training programs, there were learning objectives in more than one area. Most training requires a combination of methods because no single method can do everything well. For example, among the methods used in the opening case are lecture (printed form), role modeling, and simulation. Each method is used to accomplish different parts of the training objectives, but it is the combination of methods that allows the full set of training objectives to be achieved.

Training methods can be divided into cognitive and behavioral approaches. The primary focus of these approaches differs, although cognitive methods contain behavioral elements, and behavioral methods have cognitive elements. **Cognitive methods** focus on knowledge and attitude development by providing information that demonstrates relationships among concepts or provides rules on how to do something. These methods stimulate learning through their effect on the trainee's cognitive processes. Though these types of methods can influence skill development, it is not their focus. Conversely, **behavioral methods** focus on the trainee's behavior in a real or simulated fashion. They are best used for skill development and attitude change. Thus, both behavioral and cognitive learning methods can be used effectively to change attitudes, though they do so through different means. Now let's examine the methods in each of these approaches, their strengths and limitations, and when they are most appropriate.

LECTURES AND DEMONSTRATIONS

The lecture is one of the most frequently used and oldest forms of training. Nearly all training programs contain some lecture component, and a great many provide some type of demonstration. Although lectures and demonstrations have similar characteristics, they are appropriate for different objectives. We will discuss the lecture first.

The lecture can be in print or oral form. The oral lecture can be live or presented on video. In any form, the lecture is best used to present information. It is used to create understanding of a topic and to influence attitudes related to the topic. In its simplest form, the lecture is merely telling someone about something.[1] It is difficult to imagine training that does not use the lecture format to some extent. When the trainer begins a training session by telling the trainees the objectives, the agenda, and the process that will be used in training, the trainer is using the lecture method.

Several variations in the lecture format allow it to be more or less formal or interactive.[2] The clearest difference is the role that trainees are expected to play. The straight lecture does not include trainees interacting with the trainer. Adding discussion and a question-and-answer period invites the trainees to be more interactive in the learning process.

Straight Lecture/Lecturette

The **straight lecture** is a presentation of information by the trainer. The trainee's role is to try to absorb the information.[3] The lecture is typically thought of in terms of a lecturer speaking to a group (the trainees) about a topic. However, the lecture also might take the form of printed text, such as this book. The only differences between a straight lecture and the same material in print are the lecturer's control of the speed at which material is presented, voice inflections, body language used to emphasize points, and, of course, the visual image of the lecturer.

A good lecture is well organized and begins with an introduction that lays out the purpose of the lecture and the order in which topics will be covered. If it is an oral lecture, the introduction should cover any rules about interrupting the lecture for questions and any opportunity for clarification. The main body of the lecture—the topic content—follows the introduction. These parts of the topic area should be logically sequenced so that trainees are prepared for each topic by the content of the preceding topics. The lecture should conclude with a summary of the main learning points or conclusions.

Lectures require trainees to be fairly inactive, which, after 20 minutes or so, begins to reduce the amount being learned. A shorter version of a lecture, the **lecturette,** is often used to counter this problem. It has the same characteristics as the lecture but usually lasts less than 20 minutes if done orally. In print, the lecturette would be a shorter amount of printed text to read (e.g., this section on lecture/discussion compared with the whole chapter).

During an oral lecture or lecturette, the trainee listens, observes, and takes notes. Even when done well, it is not an especially effective technique for learning. However, it is useful when a large number of people must be given a specified set of information. The oral lecture should not contain too many learning points unless printed text accompanies the lecture, as trainees tend to forget information provided orally. A major concern about the straight lecture method is the inability to identify and correct misunderstandings.

When the training objective is to acquire specific factual information, increased learning can often be achieved at less cost by putting the information into text. This way, employees can read or view the material at their leisure, which minimizes lost productivity because of training. The added value provided by the oral lecture is the credibility the lecturer can give to the material by his or her personal presence and the attention commanded through presentation skills. Obviously, the oral presentation also presents the opportunity for discussion and questions, which are not possible in written form.

How to Use the Straight Lecture Effectively

If an oral lecture is used, the trainer must be clear and articulate. He must be familiar with the use of a microphone if a large number of trainees will be present. Table 6-1 provides a number of common errors made by lecturers and ways to avoid them. Of course, these will also apply to the lecture/discussion method.

Lecture/Discussion Method

The **lecture/discussion method** uses a lecturette to provide trainees with information that is supported, reinforced, and expanded on through interactions among the

Table 6-1
Typical Lecture Presentation Errors and Ways to Avoid Them

ERRORS	WAYS TO AVOID
Talking with back to trainees while writing on board or flip chart	Don't talk and write at the same time. Prepare flip charts ahead of time when possible. If considerable board work is required, use a document camera to project what you are writing while facing the trainees.
Using highly technical words, unfamiliar jargon, or complex sentences	If technical words or jargon must be used, provide definitions. Simplify the language and sentences so meaning is clear. Pilot test at least part of the lecture with an audience similar to the trainees.
Providing examples or asides without much relevance to the trainees	The lecturer need not provide all the examples. Ask trainees to provide some of the examples or illustrations. In preparing the lecture, go to the trainee's supervisor to get relevant examples.
Reading rather than lecturing	Prepare an outline of points to be covered rather than a word-for-word script. Be familiar with each point on the outline so that you are able to talk about it without reference to notes.
Speaking in a monotone	Listen to TV and radio commentators, paying close attention to when and how they change the tone and pitch of their voice. Practice fluctuating the tone and pitch of your voice on tape and in everyday conversation. Use pauses in your lecture so you can think about how you want to say something.
Making distracting gestures	Videotape a lecture you are giving, and observe your gestures. If they are distracting or irritating to you, the trainees probably feel the same way. Some gestures are useful and keep trainee attention. Don't stand stiff as a board either. The gestures you use are habits and can be practiced out or in.
Leaving projector on with no image or an irrelevant image	Get in the habit of glancing at the projected image as you are talking about the material it displays. When you are at the end of the material, you will see that it is time to turn the projector off or change the image.
Losing your place in the lecture	Not being able to find your place happens most frequently because your notes are too detailed. To deal with this, see ways to avoid reading above. Another technique is to check off topics completed.

trainees and between the trainees and the trainer. This added communication has much greater power than the lecture. Trainers can achieve more complex learning objectives—such as problem solving—through the use of logically sequenced lecturettes followed by immediate discussion and questioning.

The lecture/discussion method provides a two-way flow of communication. Knowledge is communicated from trainer to trainees, and communication from trainees back to the trainer conveys understanding. Verbal and nonverbal feedback from trainees enables the trainer to determine whether the material is understood. If not, the trainer might need to spend more time on this area or present the information again in a different manner.

Both the trainees and the trainer can ask questions. When the trainees volunteer questions, they demonstrate their thinking about the content of the lecture. A trainer who asks questions stimulates thinking about the key areas that are important to know. Questioning (by trainees or the trainer) and discussions are beneficial because they enhance understanding and keep trainees focused on the material. Furthermore, discussions allow the trainee to be actively engaged in the content of the lecture, an activity that improves recall and future use.

How to Use the Lecture/Discussion Effectively

Training that requires trainees to understand and integrate material before moving forward also requires two-way communication. Two-way communication, including questioning, is accomplished through the lecture/discussion method.

Questioning   Questioning is a powerful tool for starting discussions. It can help trainees discover for themselves the answers to questions asked. Questions also help the trainer determine whether trainees understand the information correctly, and help create a common understanding. Trainers should be familiar with a number of question types. First, let us examine closed- versus open-ended questions.

The **closed-ended question** asks for a specific answer. "What are the five strategies for dealing with conflict?" "What is the next step in the procedure?" This type of question is useful to assess learning or review previous material.

The **open-ended question** requires no specific response. In this case, no answer is incorrect—you are seeking an opinion. "What do you think about this method of problem solving?" "How would you approach this issue?" "What did you learn from that exercise?" These types of questions are useful for obtaining trainee involvement, generating discussion, and demonstrating the trainer's willingness to listen to the trainees' point of view.

Both types are useful. Closed-ended questions are useful to regain control of the discussion or to assess understanding of specific points. Open-ended questions are useful to relax the trainees or explore their beliefs and opinions about issues.

Two additional types are overhead questions and direct questions. **Overhead questions** are either open- or closed-ended and are directed at the whole group rather than at one person in particular. They are nonthreatening because they do not require any particular person to respond. This type of question is useful when trainees are highly involved and respond readily. If no one responds, tension can mount. Increased tension, however, is not always negative. Some trainers become anxious if their overhead question is not answered within 10 to 15 seconds. To relieve their tension, trainers answer the question themselves. Effective trainers understand that unanswered questions create tension in the trainees, which is a good thing because it helps focus trainee attention on the material being presented. This topic is discussed further in the "Encouraging Trainees to Respond" section. When only a few trainees are answering the questions, and it is the same trainees over and over, it is wise to revert to the direct question.

The **direct question** is asked of a particular trainee. It is used to draw out non-participators and to obtain differing points of view. As any trainer knows, a few trainees will often willingly answer any and all questions. If the same few trainees prevail over and over, many other trainees will tire of hearing from them and will withdraw. Keeping everyone involved in a discussion is an important skill required of an effective trainer. Most trainees begin responding to questions once they see that answering a question is a safe and rewarding experience.

Sometimes when asked a question by one of the participants, the trainer will want to hear how the rest of the participants would answer it. As the trainer in such a situation, you would need to repeat the question so everyone can hear it and then ask the trainee group to answer it. This is the **relay question** technique. For example, a trainee might ask, "How would this concept work in a unionized shop?" As the trainer, you might respond by repeating the question and following up with a statement such as, "An interesting issue. Does anyone have any ideas?" Redirecting questions to the trainee group allows you to hear the trainees' views and then reinforce appropriate responses. It can lead to interesting discussions about the issue that otherwise might not arise.

The **reverse question** is similar, except that the person asking the question is asked to answer it. Again, as the trainer responding to the same question, you might say, "Interesting question, Bill. Your area is unionized; how do you think it would work there?" Use this approach when you believe that the questioner really wants to provide an answer but is hesitant. This technique is also helpful to get a feeling for how deeply the trainee wants to delve into the question. Be careful in redirecting a question back to the questioner, however. If overused, it could inhibit trainees from asking a question for fear of having to answer it themselves.

Encouraging Trainees to Respond   Asking questions is only half of the equation in an effective discussion. Trainees must also respond. Here are some tips on how to encourage responses:[4]

- Do not rush to fill the silence. Trainers tend to show less tolerance for silence than do trainees. Sometimes waiting them out will work. Remember, the trainees are just learning the material, and it may take them a bit of time to process through the material mentally to arrive at an answer with which they feel comfortable.
- Ask them to write out an answer. Say, "Pick up your pens and write down a few reasons why workers are not motivated." Then allow them time for this task. Trainees are much more willing to read what they write than answer off the top of their heads.[5] This method also allows the trainer to ask specific trainees to respond, as the pressure of the "unknown" question is alleviated. A variation is to ask trainees to share their responses with one or two other trainees and come up with a common answer. This technique further diffuses the accountability problem.
- Use the **guided discovery** method when faced with no response to a question. As the trainer, you would not answer the question but would ask a new question that addresses much more basic material that the trainees should already understand. When the correct answer is given, move to a slightly more complex question. Each question is designed to bring the trainees closer to "discovering" the answer to the question themselves. It encourages trainees to respond because the questions are easy at the beginning and also the answer to the last helps answer the next.

Demonstrations

A **demonstration** is a visual display of how to do something or how something works. To be most effective, a demonstration should be integrated with the lecture/discussion method. Whether demonstrating how to do something or demonstrating how something works, the principles of an effective demonstration are the same. The demonstration is most useful when your training objectives are to increase knowledge and skills (technical or interpersonal).

The most effective demonstrations provide each trainee with the resources (equipment, materials, etc.) needed to actually do what is being demonstrated. Each trainee is then able to copy the demonstration process immediately after watching. As trainees are performing the demonstration, the trainer can move around the room giving feedback. Even having teams of four to five trainees sharing the demonstration resources provides opportunities for them to watch others and to do it at least once themselves. While one trainee is performing the demonstration, fellow trainees can recall the steps in the sequence and provide feedback. This approach also presents opportunities for questions, instructor clarification, and group discussion, all of which contribute to a common understanding of what should be done, the order in which it is done, and why it is done that way.

How to Use the Demonstration Effectively

To conduct an effective demonstration, first prepare the lesson plan by breaking down the task to be performed into smaller, easily learned parts. Then sequentially organize the parts of the task and prepare an explanation for why each action is required. There are two main components to the demonstration—present and try out. The following steps are part of the "present" component. Complete each of the following steps for each part of the task:

- Tell the trainees what you will be doing so they understand what you will be showing them. This focuses their attention on the critical aspects of the task.
- Demonstrate the task, describing what you are doing while you are doing it.
- Explain why each part of the task should be performed in that way immediately after you demonstrate a part of the task.

Just as in the lecture, the level of involvement of the trainee can vary in a demonstration. As with the lecture, more trainee involvement leads to more learning. The following steps increase the value of the demonstration.

After the trainer completes the demonstration, it is time for the trainee to "try out" the demonstration by doing the following:

- Ask the trainee to "talk through" the task before actually doing it.
- Give the trainee an opportunity to do the task and to describe what he or she is doing and why.
- Provide feedback, both positive and negative.
- Let the learner practice.

The temptation is not to spend much time on this process, as it seems so easy and obvious. But remember that what is being demonstrated might be easy for someone who is familiar with it, but not so for a novice. The demonstration process is used in the job instruction technique (JIT) discussed later as part of on-the-job training.

Strengths and Limitations of Lectures and Demonstration

In examining the strengths and limitations of the various methods, we focus on four major issues:

1. The cost of both financial and other resources required to achieve the training objective(s)
2. The amount of control the trainer has over the material that will be covered

3. The type(s) of learning objectives addressed
4. The ways in which the method activates different social learning theory processes

Costs

The financial costs typically associated with developing and implementing lectures, lecture/discussions, and demonstrations include the following:

- Development costs related to creating the content and organization of the training
- Cost of ancillary materials to facilitate learning
- Compensation of trainer and trainee time spent in training
- Cost of the training facility for the program
- Travel, lodging, and food for the trainer and trainees

In terms of development and delivery, printed lectures are the most time-efficient. Oral lectures followed by discussions and demonstrations require increasingly more time. Of course, the more questions, discussion, and participation allowed, the greater the amount of time required. If the training objective focuses on factual information, and interaction is not important, printed text, video lecture, or demonstration will be more efficient and equally effective. The advantage of the live lecture is that it guarantees that everyone is exposed to the information. Printed or video lectures rely on trainees following instructions.

Control of Material and Process

Lectures, discussions, and demonstrations provide a high degree of trainer control over the training process and content. The material covered is predetermined by the trainer, as are the processes used to present the material. The trainees have little, if any, influence other than whatever involvement was allowed in the TNA and program design process. However, as the training becomes more interactive, trainees are able to exert more control. Trainee questions or answers to questions shape the content of what is covered. The group dynamics help shape the processes used by the trainer in presenting the information.

For example, in lecture/discussions, the order in which issues arise is determined partly by the lecture content, the types of questions raised, and the results of the discussion sessions. Discussions can move into tangential areas not specifically addressed in the lecture material but which are of interest to the trainees. This is, in fact, what occurred in the opening case. Managers were concerned about a number of issues not specifically addressed by the training that had occurred so far. This was taking their attention away from the training at hand. Being able to address these concerns early on in training and provide the appropriate information helped refocus attention on the training material.

Learning Objectives (KSAs)

The lecture is most useful to fill gaps in trainee knowledge or address attitudes that conflict with the training objectives. The printed or video lecture is effective because it can be studied in more depth and retained to refresh learning over time. The lecture/discussion method is more effective than the straight lecture for learning higher-level knowledge such as concepts and principles. The lecture/discussion method is also more effective than the straight lecture at producing attitude changes. Because attitudes consist of a person's beliefs and feelings about an object or event, new learning can modify them. The lecture, especially combined with discussion, can change employee attitudes by providing new insights, facts, and understanding, as illustrated in the opening case. Lectures and discussions do not provide opportunities for behavioral reproduction, so they should not be used for skill development objectives, except to provide the knowledge base for the skill.

If the training objective is skill improvement, the demonstration might be appropriate. When training objectives include both knowledge and skill development, more than just a demonstration is needed. For example, the training objective might be to improve managers' ability to conduct effective meetings. First, the managers would need to know the components of effective meetings (facts) and when and how to use them (procedures). The lecture/discussion method might be appropriate to meet these objectives, but the skill development objectives should be addressed through methods that show trainees how to conduct meetings and allow them to practice these skills. The demonstration may also influence attitudes. For example, a new product demonstration is intended not only to show how the product works but also to generate enthusiasm in the sales force about the product.

Learning Process

In describing the effects of the various methods on learning processes, we return to social learning theory. Review these learning processes (attention, retention, and behavioral reproduction) by returning to Chapter 3 and specifically Figure 3-5 on page 76.

Lectures, lecture/discussions, and demonstrations can be good at capturing trainee attention, at least in the short term. They show some strength in the area of retention, especially discussions and demonstrations. Even though only demonstrations are good at facilitating behavioral reproduction, lectures and discussions can develop attitudes that are supportive of the desired behavior.

Table 6-2 lists the basic components of the lecture/discussion, and, using social learning theory, indicates the learning process affected. Table 6-3 provides the same information for the demonstration.

Attention   Done properly, lectures and demonstrations attract and maintain the attention of trainees. In fact, of the three learning processes (attention, retention, and behavioral reproduction), attracting attention is what the lecture does best. Demonstrations, when combined with lecturettes, are better at covering all the learning processes than either is alone. It is easy to gain the attention of the trainees at the start, but trainees' attention wanders, especially in longer lectures and demonstrations. Thus, these methods have a limitation in this regard. Printed and video lectures offer the advantage that the trainee can put down the lecture when attention begins to wander and come back to it when in a more receptive mental state.

For live lectures, a good lecturer will speak at about a rate of 125 words per minute, but the average person processes information at a rate equivalent of 400 to 500 words a minute. Thus, a trainee's attention can fluctuate dramatically during a one-hour lecture. Attention begins to decline after 15 to 20 minutes and begins to pick up again only near the end.[6] This phenomenon is a primary reason for the use of lecturettes. Likewise, demonstrations should be short enough to maintain trainee attention while providing the necessary information about how to complete the task. Discussion, if properly managed by the trainer, acts to heighten attention and refocus thought processes.

Retention   Retention involves the processes of symbolic coding, cognitive organization, and symbolic rehearsal. The lecture's strongest link in the retention process is the first step of symbolic coding. A symbolic coding system is provided during the lecture while the trainer is describing, explaining, and illustrating the learning points. The trainer symbolically codes the material by using the appropriate words and images. Likewise, in the demonstration, the actions of the trainer are symbolic coding. The learners translate the trainer's words and actions into their

Table 6-2 Basic Lecture/Discussion Components and Effects on Learning

LECTURE/DISCUSSION COMPONENTS	LEARNING PROCESS AFFECTED
1. Orientation Presenting information so that trainees understand the direction the lecture is headed and how it is organized.	Attention
2. Enthusiasm Presenting information in a manner that conveys the topic's importance and inherent value.	Attention
3. Variety Using voice, gestures, various components listed in this table, and audiovisual aids. For printed lectures, this component is minimized.	Attention Retention Symbolic coding
4. Logical organization Presenting information in a logical order and providing logical transitions between topic areas	Retention Cognitive organization

5. Explanations
Describing facts, concepts, and principles in a clear and easily understood manner.
	Retention
	  Symbolic coding
	  Cognitive organization

6. Directions
Providing instructions in a manner that allows trainees to understand what they are to do and how to do it.
	Retention
	  Cognitive organization
	  Symbolic rehearsal

7. Illustrations Providing clear, interesting, and relevant examples of how information can or has been applied (both correctly and incorrectly).	Attention Retention All areas
8. Compare and contrast Articulating the similarities and differences, advantages and disadvantages, and so on, of relevant topic areas.	Attention Retention All areas
9. Questions and discussion Seeking information from the trainees regarding their comprehension, their content-related ideas, and stimulating the trainees' thought processes (e.g., Socratic questioning). This component is not possible in printed lectures.	Attention Retention All areas
10. Summarize Highlighting important concepts covered in a manner that links the topics/ideas together.	Retention Cognitive organization

Table 6-3
Basic Demonstration Components and Their Effects on Learning

DEMONSTRATION COMPONENTS	AREAS OF LEARNING AFFECTED*

Present
• Tell
• Demonstrate
• Explain
	Attention
	Retention
	  Symbolic coding
	  Cognitive organization

Try Out
• Trainees talk through the task
• Trainees do task while describing what they are doing and why
• Trainer provides positive/negative feedback
• Trainees practice
	Retention
	  Symbolic rehearsal
	  Behavioral reproduction

Source: Adapted from Gold, L. "Job instruction: Four steps to success." *Training and Development Journal* (September 1981), pp. 28–32.

*From social learning theory, as illustrated in Figure 3-5.

individual symbolic coding schemes. The challenge for the trainer is to present the material in a way that ensures that the symbolic codes used by the trainer hold the same meaning for the learner. Discussions and questions help align the trainee's symbolic coding with the training objectives. Putting the lecture into print or creating a video for a demonstration facilitates the trainee's symbolic coding process by allowing the trainee more time to adjust her coding to that used by the text or video. This adjustment increases recall of the information at a later date (e.g., back on the job). Using visual aids, such as graphics in a text or projections in a live lecture, will facilitate the trainee's coding process by providing additional cues. The more varied the stimuli used to present the same material, the more accurately the information is coded.

Organizing the coded information into already existing or new cognitive structures is what social learning theorists call **cognitive organization.** The organization of information determines the ease of recall and its appropriate use when recalled. When trainees become actively engaged in integrating concepts and principles into their cognitive structures, the cognitive organization process is facilitated. Thus, demonstrations allow more opportunity for cognitive organization than does the straight lecture. Discussion and questioning allow trainees to clarify their understanding of the lecture and organize it appropriately. Better cognitive organization occurs when the trainees are free to discuss various aspects of the new knowledge and its relationship to already existing knowledge, and to question the trainer about actual or hypothetical situations in which they might use the knowledge.

Demonstrations, by their very nature, stimulate symbolic rehearsal. By simply watching the trainer demonstrate the task, the learner is encouraged to think about doing it, especially if the learner knows that he will be asked to do the task when the trainer is finished. Lectures present greater difficulty in this area. The lecturer can, and should, stimulate symbolic rehearsal by making suggestions about how the knowledge could be applied. However, these suggestions are not as powerful as the trainee herself seeing how the knowledge is applicable to her specific situation.

Properly managed, a lecture/discussion session can facilitate this symbolic rehearsal. For example, as a trainer you might ask the trainees to think about ways in which the knowledge could be used in their work area and write their ideas on a flip chart. Trainees could then be organized into small groups, and each individual encouraged to report her thoughts to the group. You might say to the group members, "As you listen to others describe how they could apply this knowledge, imagine you were applying it that way in your work area. When the person is finished, discuss the application idea and how it would apply in your area." This process would not only bring misunderstandings to the surface and possibly clarify them but also would assist in the cognitive organization of the information. The primary value, however, would be that each trainee was getting a chance to practice mentally (i.e., symbolic rehearsal) using the new knowledge in a variety of ways and situations.

Behavioral Reproduction   The lecture/discussion approach does not provide for practicing actual behaviors, so it is not appropriate for skill development objectives. Conversely, the demonstration incorporates behavioral reproduction into the training through practice. Remember, however, that it is important for the trainer to monitor the learner's performance, providing appropriate feedback to ensure that the correct behavior is learned.

Training Group Characteristic
The Trainees   For any type of lecture to be effective, trainees should be at about the same general level of intellectual ability and possess about the same level of

related content knowledge. If the trainee group is widely divergent in either of these areas, it is difficult to aim the lecture at the appropriate level of understanding. If the lecture is in other respects a satisfactory method, the best approach then is to train such groups separately.

Discussions allow more diversity in a training group because the discussion period provides an opportunity for more active learning. Trainees who learn better in a more active mode have the opportunity to do so. Trainees also have the opportunity to learn from their peers as they participate in the discussion and ask questions.

The training group can be fairly diverse for demonstrations. However, the trainer must be able to observe each trainee performing the task. As with lecture/discussion, the trainees in a demonstration learn not only by observing the trainer but also by observing other trainees performing the task and the type of feedback the instructor gives.

Size of Training Group   Lectures or lecturettes can be given to groups ranging from just a few to hundreds of trainees. This is not true of the lecture/discussion method. In general, class size should be small enough to allow all trainees ample opportunity to participate in discussions and questioning. The appropriate size depends on the complexity of the material and the amount of time allocated. More complicated material requires more time for more questions, so fewer trainees can be accommodated in a given amount of time. The dynamics of large groups make it difficult or impossible for all to participate in a meaningful way. When trainees cannot participate meaningfully, they will inevitably become less involved and withdraw their attention. So when using lecture/discussions in training, make sure that groups are small enough to allow all to participate within the time constraints of the training.

As with lecture/discussion, many of the advantages of the demonstration are lost when the group is too large. To capture all the advantages of a demonstration, it should be limited to small groups. A way to allow for larger groups is to provide additional trainers to monitor trainee practice on the task and provide feedback. A good rule of thumb is to have no more than five trainees per trainer when the demonstration involves hands-on practice by the trainees.

GAMES AND SIMULATIONS

Training games and simulations are designed to reproduce or simulate processes, events, and circumstances that occur in the trainee's job. Thus, trainees can experience these events in a controlled setting where they can develop their skills or discover concepts that will improve their performance. Equipment simulators, business games, in-basket exercises, case studies, role-plays, and behavior modeling are the primary examples of this method. We discuss each of these separately and then describe the strengths and limitations of simulations in general.

Equipment Simulators

If technical skills in the operation or maintenance of equipment are the focus of training, then one of the best instructional methods is the equipment simulator. **Equipment simulators** are mechanical devices that require trainees to use the same procedures, movements, and decision processes they would use with equipment back on the job. Simulators train airline pilots,[7] air traffic controllers,[8] military officers,[9] taxi drivers,[10] maintenance workers,[11] telephone operators,[12] ship navigators,[13] and product development engineers.[14]

It is important that the simulators be designed to replicate, as closely as possible, the physical aspects of the equipment and operating environment that trainees will find at their job site. This resemblance is referred to as the **physical fidelity** of the simulation. In addition, psychological conditions under which the equipment is operated (such as time pressures and conflicting demands) must also be closely matched to what the trainees experience on the job. This similarity is called **psychological fidelity.** Training in Action 6-1 describes what can happen when the match between simulation and work setting is less than adequate. The events described in this example were reported by one of the new sales clerk trainees.

The organizational development literature provides guidelines for the design or redesign of equipment.[15] Human resource development (HRD) professionals engaged in the design of simulators and their pretesting should involve those who will be using the equipment, as well as their supervisors. Users' input helps reduce potential resistance to the equipment and, more importantly, increases the degree of fidelity between the simulation and the work setting. In Training in Action 6-1, if trainers had brought in experienced sales clerks or their supervisors to pilot the simulation, they might have identified the fidelity problems, which then could have been corrected.

TRAINING IN ACTION 6-1
Sales Simulation

Twenty-five retail sales clerk trainees were learning how to operate the company's electronic sales register system. The trainees each stood in front of a sales register that was an older-model sales register refitted to serve as a training device. On a screen facing each trainee, a video depicted a customer waiting to make a purchase. The items this customer wanted to purchase were automatically brought on a conveyor belt to the trainee. The trainee entered specific keystrokes to activate the register for a new sale, picked up each item, and scanned it into the register. When all the items were entered, the trainee entered more keystrokes to total the sale. When the sale was totaled, the conveyor brought forward cash, a check, or a credit card, simulating the customer's payment choice. The trainee entered different keystrokes denoting a check, credit, or cash sale. If cash was used, the cash drawer opened. The clerk was to deposit the customer's payment and remove the correct amount of change, if any. Credit cards were scanned and automatically debited for the total of the purchase. Payment by credit card or check also required the customer's identification to be documented. Once payment was received, any change and the receipt were to be given to the customer. This was simulated by placing the change in a bin on the counter. The purchased items were then bagged and given to the customer (again simulated by placing in the bin).

This simulation might be fairly good. Unfortunately, when the trainees were placed at the real registers the next day, things were quite different from their training experiences. First, the registers they used were a newer model than those used in the training, so some of the keys were in different places. Second, people were standing in line impatiently. Some wanted to purchase items, and others needed help with merchandise or wanted to know the location of items in the store. The clerks couldn't concentrate only on working the register; they also had to interact with the customers. The scanner wouldn't read some customers' credit cards. Some customers argued about the price of items, insisting that those items were on sale for a lower price whereas the scanner indicated a higher price. Some customers had their items totaled and then decided that they did not want one of the items or that they wanted additional items. Needless to say, the simulation training proved less than helpful, and many considered it to have lowered their capabilities. They felt that they made many keystroke errors because of the training. If they just were allowed to learn on the job, they would not now be unlearning portions of the previous day's training.

How to Use the Equipment Simulation Effectively

When the simulator is used, it often occupies the bulk of the training time. Tasks are attempted on the simulator, feedback is provided, and then more simulator time is taken. Learning by doing is the major focus. At the same time, the instructor is available to provide feedback.

In the development of a simulation, there might be a temptation to use out-of-date equipment to reduce costs. After all, why take a piece of equipment off-line to use for training when it could be in use and contributing to organizational productivity? This issue was part of the problem in Training in Action 6-1. When we reduce the fidelity of the simulation, we also reduce the likelihood that training will result in appropriate changes in job behavior (transfer of training). Productivity will be lost and training time and costs will be wasted if the required skills do not transfer back to the job.

Psychological fidelity is just as important as physical fidelity. Imagine a pilot learning how to fly a simulator that did not have a wind factor built in. Suppose in landing a real plane, the pilot lines up with the runway and heads straight in, as taught, when suddenly a 35-mile-per-hour crosswind appears. This type of thing happened in Training in Action 6-1, when customers suddenly appeared with different requests, and events occurred that had not been part of the simulation.

The simulation should first be designed to allow the learning of the job skills without complications from other factors, such as wind in the case of the pilot and customers in the case of the clerks. Once the trainee acquires these basic skills, outside factors can be introduced into the training. Increasing levels of complication are added to the simulation until the trainee reaches the required levels of physical and psychological fidelity.

Business Games

Many decades ago, the University of Washington debuted a board game, *Top Management Decision Game,* as a way for business students to see the theories in their textbooks put into action.[16] Today trainers have moved to computer-based simulations that use interactive multimedia and virtual reality for the same purpose. **Business games** are simulations that attempt to represent the way an industry, company, or unit of a company functions. Typically, they are based on a set of relationships, rules, and principles derived from theory or research. However, they can also reflect the actual operations of a particular department in a specific company. Trainees are provided with information describing a situation and are asked to make decisions about what to do. The system then provides feedback about the effect of their decisions, after which trainees are asked to make another decision. This process continues until some predefined state of the organization is reached, or a specified number of trials are completed.

Games can also be used to review information presented in other forms. Often this uses a quiz show format such as the popular television (TV) show, *Jeopardy*. For example, recent titles of off-the-shelf games that can be customized with the information from your training session include *Quiz Show, Game Show Presenter, Gameshow Pro,* and *My Quiz Show*. Some of these types of games can handle up to 180 players at one time, making it useful for training with large groups.

Depending on the objectives, you will choose either an intercompany or an intracompany game. The intercompany games require trainees to compete in a marketplace. The more complex games require decisions about where to build factories, what product to advertise, what level of quality to be built into the product, how many salespeople to hire, how to pay them, and so on. Trainees are assigned to teams that compete against one another in the simulation game. As a result, the decisions made by each team affect the environment they all share.

These business games involve an element of competition, either against other players or against the game itself. Some of the purposes for which business games have been developed and used are listed below:[17]

- Strengthen executive and upper-management skills
- Improve decision-making skills at all levels
- Demonstrate principles and concepts
- Combine separate components of training into an integrated whole
- Explore and solve complex problems in a safe, simulated setting
- Develop leadership skills
- Improve application of total quality principles
- Develop skill in using quality tools

Games that simulate entire companies or industries provide a far better systems perspective than do other training methods. They allow trainees to see how their decisions and actions influence not only their immediate target but also related areas. Training in Action 6-2 describes how one company combined simulations, games, and lectures to improve performance.

Intracompany business games require teams or individuals to represent different functional areas in a single company. The process is similar to that of the intercompany game but without the competition. In fact, cooperation is usually required for success in the game.

TRAINING IN ACTION 6-2
Product Launch Training at Kimberly-Clark*

Kimberly-Clark is a global consumer-products company, based in Dallas, Texas. Launching new products is at the heart of Kimberly-Clark's business strategy, but many attempts at teaching employees about the process had failed. The director of Organizational Effectiveness was told by the senior executive group that an effective training program was needed immediately, that they didn't want to spend a lot of additional money, and that it had to bring the approximately 15,000 employees up to speed on how the process worked.

The training program that was developed to meet this need combined a business game with simulation and video presentations. The program was called "Go To Market" and began with a four-hour simulation that taught them about Kimberly-Clark's supply chain. Small teams discussed key customers and other supply chain issues that were presented visually on a "discovery map." Each member of a team then received a role in a fictional company that was bringing a new product to market. The role-play ended with their company being beaten to the market

by a competitor. This gave them an experiential understanding of the problems and issues with supply chain management. This experience was followed by a second discovery map that taught them how the Kimberly-Clark supply chain of the future would work. Teams were given assignments to find information, and winning teams were awarded prizes. The final phase of the program had the presentations from the CEO down to the local leaders in which progressively more specific information was provided about how to "Go To Market" and how employees could contribute to it.

After training, comments were all pretty much the same: "Now I understand for the first time how our supply chain really works." The director of Organizational Effectiveness knew he had a winner when he put the senior executive team through the training and, by the end, they were standing up cheering and giving high-fives. Another measure of how well the trainees understood the system came when they were asked to suggest ways to improve the supply chain process. They found $275 million in cost savings.

---

*Source: Adapted from Dolezalek, H. "Pretending to learn." Training (July/August 2003), pp. 20–26.

If it is decided to use a business game, first find one that meets the training objectives. A wide variety of business games and simulations are available. They cover a wide range of topics such as marketing, accounting, finance, and general management. A good source for exploring new games and learning how to develop your own games is the Association for Business Simulations and Experiential Learning. Its publication *Developments in Business Simulation and Experiential Learning* describes new business games and simulations. The association also sponsors an annual conference where new exercises, games, and simulations are demonstrated and discussed.

How to Use the Business Game Effectively

Business games should not be used as a stand-alone training method. A typical training program would alternate methods (such as readings, lecture, discussion) with trials on the simulation, continuing in this way to the end of the game, at which point a general discussion would take place. Initial interest needs to be created in the game. However, as the game progresses, trainees often become quite involved, spending a great deal of time determining their strategies and plotting moves.

Business games can take between a few hours and several weeks to complete. Unless the training objectives are fairly simple, expect to need at least a few days for trainees to complete the game. Before beginning the game and at its conclusion, point out to the trainees what the learning objectives are and how the game relates to the objectives. These briefings will help keep trainees focused on the key learning points. Before beginning the game, trainees will need to read the instruction manual. Once trainees are familiar with the objectives of the game and its rules and procedures, they meet in teams to make decisions about strategy, roles, and such. Once the game begins, the team's decisions are transferred to the trainer (game administrator) or computer. Results are tabulated and fed back to the teams. Teams examine the feedback and any new information in light of the previous decisions and then make another decision. This process continues over a number of decisions. Dr. Tony Faria, an expert in the field, suggests that a minimum of 12 decisions need to be made for trainees to benefit from the exercise. The first four decisions provide trainees with a general understanding of the game and how the various factors interact; the second four provide a framework for competing; and the final four allow strategic decisions to be made with enough knowledge to be meaningful.[18] After the final decisions are in and results tabulated, trainees meet to discuss the results and the logic and criteria they used to make their decisions. These discussions regarding how and why decisions were made, and their consequences, are a very important part of the training, as this is where a great deal of learning takes place.

In-Basket Technique

The **in-basket technique** provides trainees with a packet of written information and requests, such as memos, messages, and reports, that typically would be handled in a given position such as sales manager, staff administrator, or engineer. This popular quasi simulation focuses primarily on decision making and allows an opportunity for both assessing and developing decision-making KSAs. This technique is most often used when preparing employees for promotion or transfer to a new work environment.

Typically, the trainee's decisions are simply written down rather than carried out. Thus, the technique is good at teaching trainees what decision to make but not at developing the skills needed to carry out the decision. A few in-basket exercises require the trainee to "call" someone and communicate the decision or request additional information. In these cases, interpersonal skills can also be developed.

In-baskets are not as readily available commercially as simulations. One reason is that they are relatively easy to develop. Simply examine current jobholders' in-baskets for the material. Take papers from the in-basket, including filler material that requires no action (flyers, memos copied to the person) and follow the scenario from Training in Action 6-3. Use the trainee's current position as the position in the scenario. To provide the stress of real-life management, the amount of information that needs attention should be more than can be expected to be completed in the allotted time. To determine the appropriate actions that should be taken, choose high performers from the job in question and ask them what they would do. The attraction of the in-basket is that it is developed from real information from the trainees' organization.

How to Use the In-Basket Effectively

Typically, trainees are given a type of job to role-play. They receive a description of their role and general information about the context in which the role is being carried out. See Training in Action 6-3 for an example. Trainees are then given the packet of materials that make up the in-basket and asked to respond to the materials within a certain time period. After all the trainees complete the in-basket, a group discussion with the trainer follows in which the trainees describe the rationale for their decisions. For example, a trainer might ask about strategies the trainees used to prioritize the information, asking questions such as, "What criteria did you use to determine which person to contact first when you arrived on the job?" "How did you determine the order in which you addressed the issues?" The discussion will gradually become more specific and address how trainees

TRAINING IN ACTION 6-3
Typical Instructions for an In-Basket Exercise

Salesperson In-Basket Instructions

Your name is Lee. You have been with Bennett Corporation for one and a half years as a salesperson in the business machines marketing force on the east coast. A position opened up in the Midwest region a few weeks ago when the salesman, John Quitt, left the company and his customers without notice. The other salespeople in your new office were unable to cover the calls coming in from the accounts you are taking over, so you must do some catching up. Your transfer is still a week away, but the company flies you out to the Midwest office to go through your predecessor's overflowing in-basket. It is Sunday evening, April 13, and no one else is in the office. In 75 minutes, you must leave to catch a plane to the training center, and you will not be available for the coming week.

Read through the items in the in-basket, and decide on a course of action for each. It is imperative that you respond immediately, because you will not be back for a week. All responses must be in writing so you can leave them for the other office personnel. Responses may include writing letters, writing memos to others or yourself, scheduling meetings, making

phone calls (outline what is to be discussed), and so on. You may write your responses on the same memo you received or on the memo pad provided. Writing paper is also provided if you wish to write a letter. Be sure to attach any memos or letters to the appropriate item. It is your first trip to the Midwest, and you have not yet met any of your new co-workers.

An organizational chart and a calendar are provided for your reference.

Remember, every action you take or plan to take must be in writing. If you don't write it down, the assessor will have no way of assessing your performance.

It is advisable to read through the entire in-basket before taking any action.

TIMETABLE	
5 minutes	Read instructions.
75 minutes	Read and respond to in-basket items.

Please do not proceed until told to do so.

responded to specific items, such as "What did you do about the complaint that was three weeks old?"

The group discussion highlights the advantages and disadvantages of different approaches to the exercise. This allows trainees to see different strategies and approaches to the same set of issues. During or immediately following the discussion, the trainer provides a summary of the alternative approaches to making the various types of decisions. The training concludes with a discussion of the lessons learned and how these can be applied on the job.

The majority of the learning with the in-basket technique occurs during the discussion session. It can take a half-day or more to complete the in-basket and the discussion that follows. If the training objectives allow trainees to complete the in-basket materials before the start of the training session (perhaps the evening before), the actual time spent in training can be reduced. In such cases, the time constraint on the trainee to complete the in-basket is removed. If you can create the in-basket electronically, the time limit can be retained. The extra time you gain could be used to provide individual feedback on each trainee's decisions before the discussion session. This will help focus the trainees' attention on the areas most important to their individual development. It will also allow you to develop more targeted and effective questions to ask during the group discussion.

A variation on the technique is to run multiple, simultaneous in-baskets in which each trainee receives a different but interrelated set of information. The trainees must interact with one another to gather all the information necessary to make an appropriate decision. This activity allows development of communication and decision-making skills. It also includes elements of role-play and business games training.

Case Studies

The **case study** attempts to simulate decision-making situations that trainees might find on the job. The trainee is usually presented with a written (or videotaped) history, key elements, and the issues faced by a real or imaginary organization or organizational unit. The trainer should convey that no single solution is right or wrong and that many solutions are possible.[19] The learning objective is to get trainees to apply known concepts and principles and discover new ones. The solutions are not as important as is trainees' understanding of the advantages and disadvantages that go along with the solutions.

A written case study can range in length from a few pages to over 100. A series of questions usually appears at the end of the case. Longer ones provide a great deal of information to be examined and assessed for its relevance to the decisions being made. Others require the trainee to conduct the research themselves to acquire the appropriate information. The trainee must then analyze the situation, identify the key issues, and then identify ways to address the issues. Typically, the issues revolve around threats and opportunities to the organization in relation to its strengths and weaknesses. Smaller cases are often called scenarios and can only be a paragraph or two in length. The purpose of these smaller cases is to provide trainees with a very limited situation in which they are able to test out their new knowledge. These are typically used as exercises following a lecture/discussion segment of training.

Another variation of the case study is the **incident process,** in which trainees are given only a brief description of the problem[20] and must gather additional information from the trainer (and perhaps others) by asking specific questions. Because managers gather most of their information from questioning and interacting with others, this activity is meant to simulate a manager's work more closely. In all case study methods, the information sorting and gathering process can be as much a learning focus as the nature of the problem being worked on. In such instances, the focus is on understanding the criteria that separate relevant from irrelevant information, and learning where and how to gather relevant information.

If the decision is to use a case, it is necessary to find or develop one that will achieve the objectives. Harvard University and the University of Western Ontario are good sources. Their cases are based on real organizations' experiences. The advantage of "real" cases is that they can be enriched with up-to-date information from the organization and can describe "what the outcome of the case really was" and how it affected the company.

Writing a case requires a special skill, and if you can find a case that fulfills your objectives, it is probably preferable to use it. However, there are inherent advantages to trainers who can write a case about their own company. The case can be written with the learning objectives in mind and therefore be truly focused on the company's needs. Additionally, trainee interest and transfer of training will be high because it is about the trainees' own organization.[21] If you do decide to write a case, refer to guides such as the *Handbook of Creative Learning*.[22]

How to Use the Case Study Effectively

Cases reflect the typical situation faced by most managers—incomplete information about many of the factors that influence how an organization should move forward. For most cases, the trainees are given time to digest the information provided individually. If time permits, they may be allowed to collect additional information and integrate it into their strategy and action plan. Once individuals complete their case write-up, they may meet in small groups to discuss the different analyses, issues, strategies, and action plans. Then the trainees meet with the trainer, who facilitates and directs further discussion.

The trainer guides the trainees in examining the possible alternatives and consequences without actually stating what they are. The guided discovery method is especially important in this situation. The trainer's analysis of the case and action plan to address the issues are irrelevant to that process; in fact, they hinder it. The trainer must also direct the discussion of the case toward achieving the training objectives. Suppose problem analysis is the objective of the training. Here you allow the case to go in the direction the trainees wish it to go, as long as they are pursuing a problem and analyzing it.

The role of trainer also requires facilitation of group discussion, keeping the communication climate open while ensuring that the focus remains on important learning points. The trainer becomes the catalyst for discussion by calling on trainees for opinions and encouraging others to confront aspects of a position they do not support. In this role, the trainer must remember to deflect requests from trainees to give her own "solution" to the case. Instead, use relay or reverse questioning techniques.

One major concern for trainers when using the case method is making sure that participants read the case and prepare for the discussion. Using training time for case reading and preparation ensures that work will be done, but it cuts into discussion time. If several training days are to be used, especially if the training is off-site and trainees are staying at a hotel, structured assignments can be built into the evenings. This option reduces the downtime of the training day. Of course, with a one-day training period, you can always provide the case and ask that trainees read it and answer questions ahead of time. However, this technique is advisable only when you can be sure that everyone will in fact read it ahead of time. Trainees are more likely to read the case if they realize they will be required to meet in small groups to discuss it.

Role-play

Role-play is an enactment (or simulation) of a scenario in which each participant is given a part to act out. Trainees are provided with a description of the context—usually a topic area, a general description of a situation, a description of their roles (e.g., their objectives, emotions, concerns), and the problem they each face. For example, the topic area could be managing conflict, with the two parties in conflict being the supervisor and subordinate, and the situation might revolve around scheduling vacation days. The problem could be that the subordinate wants to take a vacation during the first week of August, and the supervisor knows that a big project comes due that week. Once the participants read their role descriptions, they act out their roles by interacting with one another.

The degree to which a scenario is structured will depend on what the learning objectives are. **Structured role-plays** provide trainees with more detail about the situation and more detailed descriptions of each character's attitudes, needs, opinions, and so on. Sometimes, structured role-plays even include a scripted dialogue. This type of role-play is used primarily to develop interpersonal skills such as communication, conflict resolution, and group decision making.

Spontaneous role-plays are loosely constructed interactions in which one of the participants plays himself while the other(s) play people with whom the first trainee interacted in the past or will in the future. This type of role-play focuses on attitudes. It is typically used to develop insight into our own behavior and its effect on others rather than to develop specific skills.

In a **single role-play,** one group of trainees role-plays for the rest, providing a visual demonstration of some learning points. Other trainees observe the role-play, analyzing the interactions and identifying learning points. Although this format provides a single focus for trainees and feedback from a skilled observer (the trainer), it does have some disadvantages. Those chosen to act as the characters might experience acute embarrassment at being the center of attention. They also do not have the advantage of watching others perform the roles. In addition, they might not clearly portray the behaviors that are the focus of training. Having people other than trainees act out the role-play eliminates these problems but adds some cost to the training.

A **multiple role-play** is the same as a single role-play except that all trainees are in groups, with each group acting out the role-play simultaneously. Following the role-play, each group analyzes the interactions and identifies learning points among themselves. Each group may report a summary of its analysis and learning to the others. This format allows a rich discussion of the issues because each group will play the roles somewhat differently. It also reduces the amount of time required to complete the process but also might reduce the quality of feedback. Trainees are generally reluctant to provide negative feedback to peers. Even if they are willing, they might not have the experience or expertise to provide constructive feedback. Videotaping the role-play is another option. The trainee uses the tape for self-evaluation, and the trainer can examine the tapes between sessions and provide individual feedback.

The **role rotation** method begins as a single role-play. After the characters interact for a period of time, the trainer will stop the role-play and discuss what happened so far and what can be learned from it. Then different trainees are asked to exchange places with some or all of the characters. These trainees then pick up where the others left off. This format allows a common focus for all trainees (except those in the role-play) and demonstrates several different ways to approach the roles. It keeps trainees more active than the single role-play and allows for feedback from a skilled observer. However, it requires the progress of the role-play to be interrupted frequently, creating additional artificiality. Again, trainees might be inhibited from critiquing the behavior of their fellow trainees publicly, and they might be embarrassed to play a role in front of everyone else.

How to Use the Role-play Effectively

Role-plays are available in many textbooks and other sources, but they are also reasonably easy to write. The advantage of writing a role-play is that it can be tailored to the needs of the company and the trainee population. Role-plays can be strategically placed throughout the training to provide not only the skills practice but also a change of pace.

Feedback is an important component in the role-play. The manner in which feedback is given will depend on the amount of time available. Training is more effective when the trainer can provide individual feedback. However, time and financial constraints might limit the degree to which this is possible. When time is limited, trainees may be asked to provide feedback to other trainees. For example, if the role-play involves two people, you could put the trainees into groups of three: the two people acting out the role-play (initiator and responder), and the other providing feedback (observer). Ideally you would provide three sets of role-plays that are different but contain the same learning points. Also, provide sheets of "learning points to look for" regarding the three role-plays. Each of the trainees is given the opportunity to act out each position, but with a different role-play scenario. The advantage to this feedback approach is that it reduces the amount of time required to complete the process because the entire training group can be completed after just three role-plays. The disadvantage is in the quality of feedback provided by the trainees. Trainees are generally reluctant to provide negative feedback to peers. Even if they are willing, trainees are not experts, so feedback might not be accurate. Nevertheless, if the role-play is set up with clear instructions and an understanding of the requirements, it can be an excellent learning tool. Each trainee is able to practice the skills, see how the skills work on them (when in the role of the initiator), and watch and provide feedback (as the observer). It might be useful to have the instructor and two volunteers run through exactly what is required (using a different role-play) before starting. Another option is to videotape the role-play. The trainee can use the tape for self-evaluation, peers in small groups can use it to evaluate each other, or the trainer can use it between sessions to provide individual feedback.

It is important to avoid the following problems when selecting or writing a role-play:[23]

1. Reduced level of generalizability to the job; this results from problems addressed in the role-play that are not generally handled at the trainees' level in the organization
2. Confusion that results from incomplete, excess, or misleading information
3. Confusion about how to behave in the role-play because the interrelationships are too complex
4. Conflicts left unresolved because the script creates more than can be resolved in the allotted time
5. Unrealistic or trivial scripts

Some concerns might arise about the trainees' involvement in the role-play. For some trainees, the role-play can be considered "fun" but not real, which lessens the generalizability to the job. Others find it stressful to act out a role with others watching. Table 6-4 provides tips on how to develop and present a role-play.

Depending on the method used in providing feedback, the time frame for completing a set of role-plays could be from one hour to one day. Considering that just the preparation of trainees for the role-play (along with a demonstration) could take 20 to 30 minutes, the complete session could take a whole day if everyone were to role-play in front of everyone else.

Table 6-4
Tips for Developing
and Presenting
Role-Plays

Developing

- Create your characters carefully to prove your point. Provide two characters who are going to clash in exactly the way you want. For example, use one player to force another player either to use the skills taught or to illustrate what happens when those skills are not used. Do not write a script (unless you are teaching rote responses), but provide detailed background on habits, attitudes, goals, personalities, and mood of your characters and on the business restrictions that motivate or restrain them.
- Use role-playing to illustrate one key problem. Do not try for more than one topic; otherwise, you will diffuse the impact and distract the learners with too much information.

Presenting

- Take the time to introduce the situation. Give trainees enough background to understand what's at stake; then assign the roles.
- Both the role-plays and the discussions can get off topic. To prevent digression, make sure that participants understand your instructions. For example, tell them, "The customer service representative must (1) use the customer's name three times; (2) organize, clarify, and confirm the nature of the customer's problem; (3) empathize with the customer; and (4) offer to do something for the customer." If you plan to use observers to provide feedback, have each of them use an observation sheet to look for key behaviors and to respond to key aspects of the performance.
- If the role-play gets off topic, stop the performance and ask, "What are the problems here? Why isn't the conversation moving in the right direction?" Be assertive to ensure that the participants stay in character and on topic.
- After the performance, always discuss what happened. This is how learning takes place. Ask questions of each player, and have the group advise the players.
- Encourage discussion. Challenge them with alternatives: "What would have happened if . . . ?"

Source: Adapted from Mitchell, G. *The Trainer's Handbook* (1993). New York: AMACOM.

Behavior Modeling

Behavior modeling uses the natural tendency of people to observe others to learn how to do something new. This technique is most frequently used in combination with some other technique. For example, the modeled behavior is typically videotaped and then watched by the trainees. We include it in the Games and Simulation section because once the trainees observe the model, they typically practice the behavior in some form of simulation or role-play. However, the behavioral modeling process itself is distinctly different from these methods. Only minor differences exist among the various descriptions of behavior modeling in the literature.[24] The behavior modeling process can be summarized as follows:

1. Define the key skill deficiencies.
2. Provide a brief overview of relevant theory.
3. Specify key learning points and critical behaviors to observe.
4. Use an expert to model the appropriate behaviors.
5. Encourage trainees to practice the appropriate behaviors in a structured role-play.
6. Provide opportunities for the trainer and other trainees to give reinforcement for appropriate imitation of the model's behavior.
7. Ensure that the trainee's supervisor reinforces appropriate demonstration of behavior on the job.

Develop a training module comprising all seven steps for each skill to be learned. An overview module should also be provided, as well as a separate workshop, to those who supervise the trainees back on the job.

Behavior modeling differs from both role-play and simulation by first providing the trainee with an understanding of what the desired skill level looks like. This method is based on Bandura's social learning theory and is focused on developing behavioral skills. However, steps 2 and 3 reflect the cognitively oriented learning features of the technique, and steps 5 to 7 reflect behaviorist/reinforcement theory features.

Behavior modeling is useful for almost any type of skill training. It can be used to provide interpersonal skills, sales skills, interviewee and interviewer skills, safety skills, and many other skills.[25] One method of behavior modeling makes extensive use of video modeling and feedback. The trainee first observes the behavior being performed by a model and then attempts to reproduce the behavior (step 5) while being videotaped. Through split-screen devices, the model and the trainee can be shown side by side, and the trainee can see exactly where his performance does or does not match the model's.

How to Use Behavior Modeling Effectively

Although a live model can be used, a video is better for two reasons. First, it will be an accurate, standardized depiction of the required behavior. The action can be re-done until it is exact. Using a live model leaves room for variations or inappropriate behaviors. Second, scripted learning points and steps being followed can be inserted into the video. These descriptions allow the trainee to see the behavior and the specific point being highlighted at the same time. The best results are obtained when both positive and negative models are used. This allows trainees to see both what should be done and what should not.[26]

One difficulty is finding or developing a video for the desired behavior. Many videos are available covering various types of skills, but the quality varies considerably.[27] It is important to preview them before purchase because the video must match the learning objectives. Videos developed for general sale typically do not model the behavior exactly the way the company would like. Developing a video is also a possibility, but cost, ability to make a professional product, and the time needed might rule out that option. Table 6-5 provides several suggestions if the decision is made to use behavior modeling.

A behavior modeling training session starts with trainees watching the modeled behavior. Trainees would then perform the behavior and receive feedback on it. If the trainee is videotaped while performing, the trainee would watch the video and receive feedback while watching the video. If video recording of the trainee is used, the number of video cameras and VCRs available limits the number of concurrent sessions that can take place. This method is highly dependent on effective feedback; thus, a sufficient number of trainers must be available to provide feedback.

Strengths and Limitations of Games and Simulations

Even though games and simulations come in many different formats, they share a number of common strengths and limitations. When a specific format differs from others in this regard, we discuss it separately; otherwise, our discussion of strengths and limitations applies to all formats.

Costs

The development costs of games and simulations vary from format to format. In general, equipment simulators are the most expensive to develop, but cost will depend on the nature of the equipment that is simulated. For example, millions of dollars are spent on aircraft simulators used to train commercial and military flight officers. Conversely, retail clerks and bank tellers can be trained on the actual equipment they will use on the job. The equipment can be moved back and forth from training to the job site. Even if the development costs of equipment simulators are high, they are often the best alternative. For example, pilot trainees taking test flights in an airplane will not be exposed to all the possible situations they might encounter in flying thousands

Table 6-5
Things to Consider
When Implementing
Behavior Modeling

- Use care in selecting the trainer/program administrator who will set up and conduct the sessions. This person must be skilled and experienced with this technique.
- Consider carefully whether this technique will meet your needs within your constraints of time and money. Unless you can accomplish the following, you probably should not use this technique:
  - identify specific skill deficiencies,
  - present a positive model of the appropriate behavior,
  - provide time for each trainee to practice the behavior under the watchful eye of the trainer, and
  - arrange for the manager of each trainee to reinforce correct behavior back on the job.
- Identify real skill deficiencies in advance of training, and involve the potential trainees and their bosses in this process. This activity will gain the key people's attention and their ownership of the objectives of the training sessions.
- Break the skills into small behaviors. Build a module around each small behavior, and progress one step at a time, starting with a simple behavioral element, to gain confidence.
- Do not emphasize more than seven learning points during any one training module.
- Ensure that the trainees can easily identify with the model used to demonstrate the correct way of handling a certain situation and that the model has sufficient status to be credible.
- Use a video of a model performing the correct behavior to ensure that all groups of trainees will see a positive example. A video might reduce costs because it is reusable. However, this advantage may be negated because it is difficult to find a model and a situation that is highly relevant and identifiable across diverse groups of trainees.
- Ask trainees to verbalize the behavioral cues demonstrated by the model and then to visualize their pending performance before they actually practice the desired behavior. Verbalization may help improve generalization and use of the behaviors in new situations.
- Establish a supportive climate that encourages experimentation for the practice sessions. Emphasis on positive reinforcement rather than criticism increases self-confidence and learning.
- Provide a wallet-sized card that outlines the key learning points and critical steps, after each session, as some experts suggest. This reminder acts as a security blanket for the trainees to reassure them that they will know the crucial features as they attempt to apply the training back to their jobs.
- Conduct a review session after the completion of several modules to reinforce the learning points and to demonstrate the progress attained by the trainees.
- Manage the consequences of attempting the newly trained behaviors in the actual job situation. Work with the trainees' manager to ensure that attainable goals are set for their subordinates, obstacles that may prevent trainees from attempting the new behaviors are removed, and incentives for attempting the new behaviors are provided.

Source: Camp, R., Blanchard, P., and Huszczo, G. *Toward a More Organizationally Effective Training Strategy and Practice* (1986). Upper Saddle River, NJ: Prentice Hall.

of hours a year, so the trainees would not learn as much from this method as they could from a simulator. Also, pilots will need to know how to respond in dangerous situations, which is best practiced in the safety of the simulator. In addition, the cost of "flying" a simulator is a small fraction of the cost of flying an actual aircraft. The total costs of using the simulation can be lower than alternative methods, even when the development cost is quite high.

At the low end of development costs are role-plays. A wide range of role-plays are already developed and published, including instructions and suggestions for their use. Many of these publications are free. However, a role-play tailored to the company's needs can be created at little cost.

Business games are somewhat more complicated and thus usually more expensive than role-plays. Multimedia or computer-based games or simulations will be more expensive but have the advantage of being reusable, so the cost can be amortized across the number of trainees. Behavior modeling costs can range from moderately low to high, depending on the format used. Using an expert to model the desired behavior live (e.g., welding two plates together) simply involves the cost of the model. Since the model is typically an employee of the company, the cost is just the lost production while the expert is modeling. Using professional actors as models for interpersonal skills training, for example, will add to the cost, but could be worth it in terms of improved quality. The use of live models is more expensive than using videotaped models because the cost is incurred each time the model is used. Videotaping the model allows the videotape to be used again but adds the cost of creating it. Professionally developed videos can be fairly expensive. This will be discussed more fully in the audiovisual section of this chapter.

Two things to consider when examining the cost of a game or simulation are

- the degree of flexibility built into the simulation or game, and
- the cost of making mistakes while in training.

Regarding flexibility, a cockpit simulator that is programmable to reflect the characteristics of many different aircrafts will be more cost-effective than one that can simulate only one type of aircraft. The same is true of business games and other types of simulations. A business game that is programmed to create different economic situations and business conditions will have a wider audience base and a longer useful life than one that is not.

One of the primary strengths of games and simulations is that they allow trainees to develop and practice skills in a safe setting. Mistakes in business decisions can be financially disastrous. Mistakes in equipment operation can cause damage to the equipment and physical harm to the operator and others. Mistakes in interpersonal behavior can also result in financial losses to the company through lost customers, resentful employees, and misinterpreted instructions. Mistakes can result in psychological harm to the trainee, such as lowered self-esteem and confidence or increased defensiveness. Simulations and games allow trainees the opportunity to develop their skills in a situation where the costs of making a mistake are low or nonexistent.

Control of Content and Process

When games and simulations are used, both the trainer and the trainee influence the content of what is learned and the processes used in learning. The game or simulation provides a set of information that focuses on a particular content area. The Kimberly-Clark simulation and game (Training in Action 6-2), for example, focuses on integrating business decisions across functional areas to improve company profitability and growth. Games and simulations also provide instructions and guidelines that strongly influence the learning process. By selecting an existing game or simulation or developing a new one, the trainer exerts control over the learning content and process. Many games and simulations are structured so that situations occur in a predetermined order, providing the trainer with greater control over both content and process. This control is desirable if all trainees will be exposed to the same situations back on the job. Arrest procedures for police, or machine maintenance and troubleshooting for equipment operators, are examples of such jobs. Other games and simulations allow the situation to change according to how trainees respond, enabling the trainee to exercise greater influence on what is learned and how. These types of games and simulations are useful when trainees must learn how to deal with a wide range of situations and how to apply general principles in areas such as business and financial planning, decision making, and military battle tactics.

The format providing the least built-in structure is the unstructured role-play in which only a general set of guidelines is given to the participants beforehand. How the trainees interact while playing out their roles is under their own control. Although the trainer controls the choice of situation and roles, the trainees control how they are carried out. By asking the role-players to focus on certain steps in the learning process, such as saying "First try to identify the cause of the conflict, and then try to generate win-win alternatives," the trainer exerts more influence. In the case of role-plays, reduced structure allows the trainees to imagine the situation as it might occur on the job. The potential danger is that it might be so unstructured that they do not take their roles seriously, or they are unable to imagine how it could possibly apply to their job.

Cases provide more structure, particularly in setting the situation (i.e., characteristics of the organization). However, the trainees' process of analyzing the case is largely internal or influenced by the interaction within the training group. Through the manner in which trainers facilitate discussion of the case, they can exert more or less control over what trainees learn and how.

Equipment simulators generally provide the most structure. They must replicate the physical and psychological characteristics of the equipment and the environment in which it is operated. The simulator itself controls the content and process of learning. To the extent that the simulation is programmable, the trainer can manipulate the content.

Learning Objectives (KSAs)

Games and simulations provide opportunities to learn through concrete experiences that require both theory and application. Theory provides the general principles that guide action. Application provides the opportunity to test those principles and understand them at a behavioral level, not just as abstract intellectual knowledge. As the philosopher Confucius said, "I hear and I forget. I see and I remember. I do and I understand."

Some types of knowledge enhancement and attitude change are achievable through games and simulations, but usually supplemental methods are required. Games and simulations generally require some background knowledge and provide a context in which this knowledge is applied. For example, a business game in which several teams of trainees compete for product market share makes some assumptions about the knowledge that trainees have about basic marketing strategies (e.g., product, pricing, promotions, and location). It allows them to apply their knowledge and see the consequences of that strategy.

For these and numerous other reasons, games and simulations do a good job of developing skills. First, they simulate the important conditions and situations that occur on the job. Second, they allow the trainees to practice the skill. Finally, they provide feedback about the appropriateness of the trainees' actions. Each of the formats is most suited to particular types of skills, as illustrated below:

- Equipment simulators are best at teaching people how to work with equipment.
- Business games are best for developing business decision-making skills (both day-to-day and more strategic) and for exploring and solving complex problems.
- The in-basket technique is best suited to development of strategic knowledge used in making day-to-day decisions.
- Case studies are best for developing analytic skills, higher-level principles, and complex problem-solving strategies. As trainees do not actually implement their decision/solution, their focus is more on the "what to do" (strategic knowledge) than on the "how to get it done" (skills).
- Role-plays provide a good vehicle for developing interpersonal skills and personal insight, allowing trainees to practice interacting with others and receiving feedback.
- Behavior modeling is a good technique for developing skills, especially when learning points are used as rules and when there is sufficient time for practicing the behavior.[28]

Role-playing is an especially effective technique for creating attitude change.[29] It allows trainees to act out behavior that reflects their attitudes and to experience others' reactions and their own feelings about the behavior. The experience and feedback allow the trainee to make proper attitudinal adjustments. The role reversal is even more powerful, as it requires the trainee to take a position opposite to their attitude. It allows the trainee to better understand why others may hold differing attitudes. One such situation would be the supervisor with a negative attitude about union officials being asked to play the role of union steward defending an employee who had been treated unfairly. As an old role-playing saying goes: "Seeing is believing, but feeling is the truth." Although trainees might see the logic of a principle through a lecture and see its application in a video, they can feel its personal value only when they use it themselves.

Learning Process

Attention   One of the strengths of games and simulations is their ability to gain the attention of the learner. The active learning process used by these training methods is generally more compelling to trainees than is sitting through a lecture or reading a text. In most games and many simulations, the aspect of competition against ourselves or others increases attention and enthusiasm. Many also use clever gimmicks that capture trainees' interest, but these aspects can also distract trainees from the real learning objectives of the training. Sometimes trainees get so engrossed in the competition or "figuring out" the gimmick that they fail to learn the principles or develop the skills the game/simulation was intended to produce. It is important for trainers to build modules into the training that prepare trainees to use the game or simulation by identifying the desired learning outcomes. Modules might also be planned for breaks during the simulation to capture learning that occurred and to refocus trainees on the learning objectives. In general, a debriefing module should always be included so that trainees can reflect and elaborate on what they have learned.

Another important factor affecting trainee attention is the credibility of the game or simulation. When the game or simulation does not realistically represent the key characteristics of the trainees' job, trainees will not take it seriously and will give it less attention. Consider a role-play or simulation designed to improve union-management problem solving. It asks trainees who are members of union-management committees to work on resolving certain issues. If these issues are, in reality, already contractually mandated in the company, both sides must pretend that part of the labor contract does not exist. When this happens, trainees are likely to consider the training irrelevant and not take it seriously.

Retention   Games and simulations are best at developing trainees' skills in applying or using knowledge. This approach assumes that the knowledge needed to play the game or use the simulation was already learned. This information exists as symbolic codes in the trainees' cognitive structure. Games or simulations do not do a good job of teaching facts or procedures, but they are especially good at enhancing this knowledge through the repeated recall and use of the information during the training. Thus they serve to refine and reinforce symbolic coding. Games and simulations focus primarily on the cognitive organization and symbolic rehearsal processes. Because the trainee must use many different areas of knowledge to complete the game or simulation, the trainee can see the connections and relationships between the different areas. Learning these new connections and relationships allows trainees to solve problems and develop strategies for achieving goals. Most games and simulations require trainees to engage in symbolic rehearsal by having them plan their action steps and anticipate their consequences.

Behavioral Reproduction   Of course, the real strength of games and simulations is their focus on learning by doing. Creating realistic situations in which trainees can apply their knowledge to goal-directed actions and receive fairly immediate feedback is critical for skill development. Behavioral reproduction is a significant part of the learning process when games and simulations are used. For the desired learning to occur, the training design must include feedback to the trainees about their actions. This requirement follows from the principles of reinforcement and shaping discussed in Chapter 3.

Training Group Characteristics

Only one person at a time can use an equipment simulator, so to some extent, differences in trainee readiness are addressed. As with all games and simulations, however, trainees must possess the prerequisite knowledge and skill to use the method effectively. Equipment simulators limit the number of trainees who can be trained, so this becomes a problem when a large number of trainees must be trained in a short period of time.

Business games and simulations, including behavior modeling, typically use small groups ranging in size from three to eight trainees. Differences in trainee characteristics can be both an advantage and a disadvantage, depending on the goals of the training. Differences in content knowledge or experience can be an advantage if one of the goals of training is to increase the awareness of how different people approach the situation. In a business game or simulation, for example, constructing a group of trainees from different functional areas of the business allows each trainee to learn how decisions in their area affect other areas. Thus, all trainees learn a more integrative framework for decision making. However, such groups generate more conflict and require more time for discussion and decision making. Other differences in content knowledge can be more troublesome. When some trainees in the group are more knowledgeable in basic business concepts than are others, they can become irritated at having to educate the rest of the group. In general, it is best to make sure that groups are formed so that everyone shares relatively the same level of basic knowledge—unless, of course, the goal is to have more knowledgeable trainees educate those less knowledgeable. The trainer must take care to identify how trainee group composition matches the training objectives.

Exercises and Activities

Most well-crafted training programs include exercises and activities that allow the participants to work with and explore the implications of the training content. These include paper-and-pencil self-assessment instruments, written assignments, and small-group activities. While some of these may fit into the methods we have discussed above, usually it is not a very good fit. For example, an activity commonly used in communication training is the Three Person Interview. In this activity, one person is the interviewer, one is the interviewee, and the other is an observer. The interviewer is given two minutes to learn as much as possible about some aspect of the person (her accomplishments, for example). After each two-minute interview, the roles rotate until everyone is done. When all the interviews are completed, each person then describes what they have learned to the rest of the training group. While there may be multiple objectives for this activity, one is to demonstrate the difficulty of effective listening. How would you categorize this activity in terms of the methods we have described? You might say it was an unstructured role-play, but that wouldn't exactly fit. Another activity used in creativity training is to organize the trainees into small groups and have them list as many possible uses for a brick as they can think of. This doesn't fit into any of the methods we have previously discussed. These types of activities often do not fit our definitions of the training methods. We think of these as supplements to the training that allow the participants to engage with the material that was delivered through the method (lecturette, case study, simulation, etc.). There are literally thousands of these activities and exercises available. For example, *101 Great Games and Activities* is over a decade old and contains many useful ideas.[30] A recent Web search showed over 250,000 sites related to this topic.

The most frequently used training method, especially in smaller businesses and among manufacturers, is **on-the-job training (OJT).** A recent study of the National Manufacturers Association found that 77 percent of the members used OJT as the primary form of training. OJT is the preferred method for training employees for new technology and increasing skills in the use of existing technology.[31]

OJT uses more experienced and skilled employees, whether co-workers or supervisors, to train less-skilled or less-experienced employees. OJT takes many forms and can be supplemented with classroom training. However, many organizations do not follow a structured approach.[32] Instruction by co-workers or supervisors at the job site often occurs on an informal basis and is characterized by the following:

- It has not been carefully thought out or prepared.
- It is done on an ad hoc basis with no predetermined content or process.
- No objectives or goals have been developed or referred to during training.
- Trainers are chosen on the basis of technical expertise, not training ability.
- Trainers have no formal training in how to train.

Formal OJT programs are quite different. Those chosen to be the trainers for OJT are not necessarily the ones with the best technical knowledge and skills. These trainers need to have a solid understanding of the job and be able to use one-on-one instructional techniques effectively. One-on-one training is not a skill most people develop on their own, so organizations with formal OJT programs provide "train the trainer" training for these employees.

Formal OJT programs should follow a carefully developed sequence of learning events. Learning is usually achieved through the following steps:

1. The trainee observes a more experienced and skilled employee (the trainer) performing job-related tasks.
2. The procedures and techniques used are discussed before, during, and after the trainer has demonstrated how the job tasks are performed.
3. The trainee begins performing the job tasks when the trainer determines that the trainee is ready.
4. The trainer provides continuing guidance and feedback.
5. The trainee is gradually given more and more of the job to perform until he can adequately perform the entire job on his own.

The generalized instructional process just described is formalized in more detail as the job instruction technique.

Job Instruction Technique (JIT)

The **job instruction technique (JIT)** uses a behavioral strategy with a focus on skill development. However, as with most jobs, some knowledge objectives are usually involved. JIT was developed during World War II and continues to be a standard in evaluating OJT programs.[33] JIT consists of four steps—prepare, present, try out, and follow-up—as shown in Table 6-6.

Prepare
Preparation and follow-up are the two areas most often ignored in OJT programs. Preparation should include a written breakdown of the job. The person responsible for the OJT might believe that, because of a familiarity with the job, written documentation is unnecessary. To ignore this step, however, is to miss seeing the job through the eyes of the trainee. A trainer who knows the job well is likely to be able

Table 6-6
JIT Instruction/
Learning Sequence

BASICS OF INSTRUCTION	AREAS OF LEARNING AFFECTED*
Prepare	Attention and motivation
1. Break down the job.	
2. Prepare an instruction plan.	
3. Put the learner at ease.	
Present	Retention
1. Tell.	Symbolic coding
2. Show.	Cognitive organization
3. Demonstrate.	
4. Explain.	
Try Out	Retention
1. Have the learner talk through the job.	Symbolic rehearsal
2. Have the learner instruct the supervisor on how the job is done.	
3. Let the learner do the job.	Behavioral reproduction
4. Provide feedback, both positive and negative.	
5. Let the learner practice.	
Follow Up	Behavioral reproduction
1. Check progress frequently at first.	
2. Tell the learner whom to go to for help.	
3. Gradually taper off progress checks.	

Source: Gold, L. "Job instruction: Four steps to success." *Training and Development Journal* (September 1981), pp. 28–32.
*From social learning theory as illustrated in Figure 3-5.

to do several things without thinking, and these tasks might be overlooked in training. A systematic analysis and documentation of the job tasks will ensure that all the points are covered in the training.

The next step is to prepare an instructional plan. As a trainer, first determine what the trainee already knows. The person analysis portion of a needs assessment provides this information (see Chapter 4). Next, review any data available from a completed TNA. If no TNA is available, checking personnel records and interviewing the trainee are ways for you to find out what the trainee knows and what training should focus on.

Finally, putting the trainee at ease is just as important in OJT as it is in the classroom. Care must be taken to create a comfortable learning atmosphere. One way to create such an environment is to provide the trainee with an orientation to the OJT/JIT learning process. This orientation may or may not be provided by the JIT trainer. In this orientation, help trainees understand their role and the role of the trainer in the process. The importance of trainee listening and questioning should be emphasized. Familiarizing trainees with the steps in the JIT process will reduce their anxiety because they will know what to expect.

Present
The four activities of this stage are tell, show, demonstrate, and explain.[34] First, tell and show. As the trainer, provide an overview of the job while showing the trainee the different aspects of the job. You are not actually doing the job but pointing out where buttons are pushed, where materials are located, where to stand, and so on. When finished, demonstrate how to do the job, and explain why it is done in that manner. If the job involves many components or is complex, cover only one segment at a time, in the same order in which segments occur when the job is performed. During the demonstration, indicate why the procedure is performed in that particular way, emphasizing key learning points and important safety instructions.

Try Out

Before actually trying the behaviors, the trainee describes to the trainer how to do the job. This step provides a safe transition from watching and listening to doing (symbolic rehearsal). The trainee then attempts to perform the job, and the trainer is able to provide instant feedback. Any errors that take place are probably a function of the training and not the fault of the trainee. With this in mind, the focus will be on improving the method of instruction rather than on the inability of the trainee to comprehend. In any case, it is useful to allow the trainee to learn from mistakes, provided they are not too costly. Allowing the trainee to see the consequences of using an incorrect procedure (such as having to scrap the product) reinforces the use of the correct procedures. Such an occurrence becomes a form of negative reinforcement because using the correct procedures avoids the scrap. Questioning the trainee about her actions while she is performing the job and guiding her in identifying the correct procedures will help her organize and retain the processes.

Follow-Up

There is a tendency for informal OJT programs to consider training completed after the previous step. That is not correct. The trainer must check the trainee's work often enough to prevent incorrect or bad work habits from developing. It is important that trainees feel comfortable asking for help during these initial solo efforts. Every opportunity should be taken to reinforce trainees in areas where they are performing well. As trainees demonstrate proficiency on the job, progress checks can taper off until they are eventually eliminated.

How to Use JIT Effectively

Trainers are chosen from those already knowledgeable about the job, so they often see the first step, preparation, as unnecessary. Ignoring the preparation step can result in missing something important, because for the trainer, it is automatic. Refer to Table 6-7 for an example of the preparation step for the job of press feeder. If it looks similar to the operational analysis in the chapter on needs assessment, it is. If an operational analysis was previously completed, the majority of the work outlined in Table 6-7 is already done.

The follow-up step may also be ignored because it is not considered important. This step, however, is critical to ensure that the trained skills continue as they were taught. During the try-out step, the trainee may demonstrate her capabilities in doing the job, but as with anything freshly learned, shortcuts, poor work habits, and incorrect procedures can creep into performance. Periodically dropping by to follow up can catch such performance gaps and correct them before they become habitual. Following up becomes less important as the trainee's performance becomes consistently acceptable.

Structured OJT is effective when done properly and supported by the organization. The seven steps provided in Table 6-8 help ensure successful OJT.

Focus on Small Business

Although any of the training methods described in this chapter are appropriate, OJT is the training method of choice for the small business. Many small businesses use peer training because they lack a budget for any formal training. The value of following the procedures outlined in the JIT, whether the supervisor or a peer is to be the trainer, cannot be overemphasized. An up-front investment of time to train the OJT instructor and prepare the proper plan will ensure an optimal return on investment. Research suggests that structured OJT such as that described in JIT can get workers up to speed on their jobs in half the time regular training takes.[35]

Table 6-7
Job Breakdown
Sheet for OJT

Dept.: Metal Decorating Job: Press Feeder			Prepared by: J. Smith Date: June 8
MAIN STEPS	KEY POINTS	TOOLS/EQUIPMENT MATERIAL	SAFETY FACTORS
Part I (Start of shift)			
1. Check level of fountain solution, and refill if necessary.	Ask pressman what solution to use. Scratch mark shows minimum and maximum capacities.	All solutions are kept in metal containers in storeroom.	Do not spill on walkway
2. Check level of varnish in wet varnish machine, and refill if necessary.	Check card for type of material being used, and determine the amount of thinner necessary to obtain proper viscosity.	Same as 1	Very volatile and flammable
3. Wash sponges, bucket, and gum containers.	Use same thinner as in 2.	Same as 1	Do not wash in enclosed area because of fumes.
Part II (Start a new bundle in press)			
1. Request lift driver to bring over new bundle.	Do not wait until bundle on press is almost finished.		
2. Check new bundle to be sure that it is the correct one and is in good condition.	Pull the job ticket and check order number; examine top sheets and sides and corners of bundle.	Leather-palmed gloves	Always wear gloves when handling sheets to prevent cuts.
Part III (Whenever press is stopped)			
1. Lower elevator with bundle on it, and cover with master sheet.	Lower only until top of bundle is at a convenient height.	Leather-palmed gloves	Wear gloves
2. Unless otherwise instructed by pressman, wet the plate on front unit.	Be sure entire plate is wet; dry spots can oxidize and damage the plate.	Use sponges and clear water	Be sure that press is clear before wetting the plate.

Source: Adapted from Gold, L. "Job instruction: Four steps to success." *Training and Development Journal* (September 1981), pp. 28–32.

Apprenticeship Training

Apprenticeship training, another form of OJT, is one of the oldest forms of training. Its roots date back to the Middle Ages, when skilled crafts- and tradespeople passed their knowledge on to others as a way of preserving the guilds (similar to unions). Many similarities characterize today's North American apprenticeship programs. Apprenticeship programs are partnerships among labor unions, employers, schools, and government. Most apprenticeships are in skilled trade and professional unions such as boiler engineers, electrical workers, pipe fitters, and carpenters. In general, an apprenticeship program requires about two years of on-the-job experience and 180 hours of classroom instruction, though requirements vary from program to program.[36] An apprentice cook, for example, might require a year of OJT and a week of

Table 6-8
How HRD Can
Support Effective
OJT

1. Create effective OJT process document.
   A. Create a document that does the following:
      i. States the rationale for using OJT.
      ii. Links OJT to the overall strategy of HRD (how it fits with HRD's general approach in the organization.
      iii. Identifies supervisory responsibilities with respect to OJT, such as what support will be provided to OJ Trainers, and how the OJ Trainer's regular job is affected in terms of reducing responsibilities and/or workload. It should also provide for a process of including the OJ Trainer's responsibilities in her performance appraisal.
2. Develop a job description and specification for the job of OJ trainer to aid supervisors in the selection of appropriate candidates for the job.
3. Develop a training program for OJ trainers.
   A. To the extent possible, this should be e-training to ensure the consistency of the information and provide convenience to those learning how to be an OJ trainer. This training will need to have a good evaluation component built in. Preferably, the assessment would consist of an OJT expert watching the trainee role-play the OJT process.
4. Make sure that a system is in place to keep track of how well those selected and trained in the OJT process are doing.
   A. This should be part of the performance appraisal process, but special attention needs to be paid to this particular dimension so those not effective in providing OJT are helped to improve or are removed from that responsibility.
   B. As jobs change over time, those responsible for providing OJT will need to update their OJT competencies with respect to those jobs.
5. Provide support for OJ trainers.
   A. Create materials such as lesson plans, checklists, manuals, and so on, for those who are providing the OJT training. Periodically, hold focus groups of your OJ trainers to see what tools and materials would be of value. This keeps the HRD unit connected to the OJT process and enhances the perception of HRD as a partner.
6. Think large, but begin small.
   A. Start implementing your OJT process in areas where supervisors are supportive. Build on your successes there to expand to other areas. Your goal is to have the entire organization using your structured OJT process, but this will be much easier after you are able to show how effective it is.

Source: Adapted from Rothwell, W., and H. Kazanas. "Planned OJT is productive OJT." *Training and Development Journal* (October 1990), pp. 53–56.

classroom training, whereas a moldmaker might require four years of OJT with three 8-week classroom sessions.[37]

Journeymen provide the training on the job, and adult education centers and community colleges typically provide the classroom training. An apprentice must be able to demonstrate mastery of all required skills and knowledge before being allowed to graduate to journeyman status. These programs are regulated by governmental agencies, which also set standards and provide services.

How to Use Apprenticeship Training Effectively

Although formal apprenticeship programs are strictly controlled by the Department of Labor, nothing would stop an organization from setting up its own informal apprenticeship programs. The journeyman rank provided to employees upon successful completion will not be transferable to other organizations, but it is possible to take advantage of the process nonetheless.

One way to do this is to find and examine a comparable job with an apprenticeship program and use it as a model. The classroom training could take place at a local community college, school of technology, or similar institution. Apprentices are usually off the job for their classroom training, but in designing a program it might be possible to arrange night-school classes, weekend classes, or some combination of the two. Correspondence-school training is sometimes substituted for classroom training.

Before venturing out to develop an apprenticeship program, check with local government agencies regarding the programs available. Given that government is usually willing to help pay for the classroom training part of the apprenticeship program, it might be advantageous to make the program official.

Coaching

Coaching as used here is the process of providing one-on-one guidance and instruction to improve knowledge, skills, and work performance. The term *coaching* is also commonly used to refer to the use of an outside consultant to assist upper level managers with specific challenges such as public speaking, a particular type of business problem, and so on. This will be discussed in Chapter 11. Although some of the general concepts are the same, there are substantial differences in the coaching process for lower levels of management, which is the focus here.

Coaching is usually directed at employees with KSA deficiencies, but it can also be used as a motivational tool for those performing adequately. Although co-workers can be coaches, especially in team-based organizations, more typically the supervisor acts as coach. One analysis suggests that in the past, supervisors spent, on the average, only about 10 percent of their time coaching subordinates. In today's organizations, supervisors typically spend more than 50 percent of their time in such activities.[38] The following outline looks at the process from the coach's perspective:

1. Understand the trainee's job, the KSAs, the resources required to meet performance expectations, and the trainee's current level of performance.
2. Meet with the trainee, and mutually agree on the performance objectives to be achieved.
3. Arrive at a mutual plan and schedule for achieving the performance objectives.
4. Show the trainee how to achieve the objectives, observe the trainee perform, and provide feedback. This process is similar to JIT and is conducted at the work site.
5. Repeat step 4 until performance improves.

The main difference between coaching and traditional OJT is that in coaching, the supervisor continues to analyze the subordinate's performance, plans mutually acceptable action, creates a supportive climate, and motivates the subordinate to improve.[39] Effective coaching requires a relationship between the coach (supervisor, peer) and player (employee) that motivates the employee to seek help from the coach to become a better performer.[40] Therefore, the role of the supervisor must change from controlling to collaborating with the trainee.

Even though coaching is clearly a skill-focused method, it can also be used for knowledge development, although other methods are better for transmitting knowledge. Like the OJT trainer, the coach must be skilled both in how to do the tasks and in how to train others to do them. HRD professionals typically do not perform the role of coach (unless they are coaching other HRD professionals). Rather, they train supervisors in the coaching process and develop the supervisors' interpersonal skills to make them more effective.

How to Use Coaching Effectively

For coaching to be effective, a needs assessment should be conducted. Figure 6-1 outlines the basic questions that the supervisor should ask. Note the similarity to Figure 4-1 (page 100) in the discussion of needs analysis.

Once it is decided that coaching is necessary, follow the five steps laid out in the previous section. Skills required to be an effective coach are similar to those for an effective trainer. Good questioning techniques, active listening skills, and good feedback skills are all essential when coaching.

Figure 6-1
Assessment of
Need for Coaching

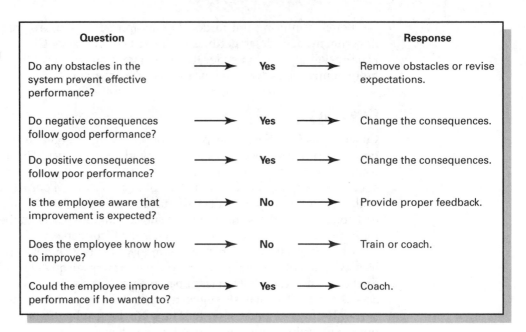

Question		Response
Do any obstacles in the system prevent effective performance? → **Yes** →		Remove obstacles or revise expectations.
Do negative consequences follow good performance? → **Yes** →		Change the consequences.
Do positive consequences follow poor performance? → **Yes** →		Change the consequences.
Is the employee aware that improvement is expected? → **No** →		Provide proper feedback.
Does the employee know how to improve? → **No** →		Train or coach.
Could the employee improve performance if he wanted to? → **Yes** →		Coach.

Mentoring

Mentoring is considered to be a form of coaching in which an ongoing relationship is developed between a senior and a junior employee. Mentoring provides the more junior employee with guidance and a clear understanding of how the organization goes about its business and how the person being mentored can be effective. Whereas coaching focuses on the technical aspects of the job, mentoring focuses more on improving the employee's fit within the organization. Thus, coaching emphasizes skill development, and mentoring focuses more on attitude development. Generally, mentoring is conducted only for management-level employees, though in some cases, it is applied at lower levels. In the past, mentoring was mostly informal, but more recently, some organizations have formalized the process.[41] The concerns about untrained OJT trainers discussed earlier also apply to mentoring. The value of mentoring programs was made evident in a recent article in which a management "headhunter" observed that banking firms without institutionalized mentoring programs were much more likely to experience dramatic defections of mid-level managers.[42]

At the core of the mentoring process is individual responsibility for learning. The mentor provides insights and guidance, but the person being mentored must accept personal responsibility for setting objectives, developing strategies for learning, and evaluating outcomes. These are shared with the mentor and discussed. Ultimately, agreement in these areas forms the basis for the mentoring relationship.

How to Use Mentoring Effectively

Several features characterize successful mentoring programs, all of which should be considered if mentoring is to be effective. These features include the following:[43]

- Top management support
- Integration into the career development process
- Voluntary involvement
- Assignment of mentees to mentors
- Relatively short phases to the program
- An established orientation
- Monitoring of the process

As in any organizational intervention, top management support is essential. Allowing mentoring activities to take place on company time is one way of sending the signal that these activities are important. Providing rewards to successful mentors is also a way of indicating that mentoring is a valued behavior.

Also, mentoring needs to be integrated into the overall career development process. It must be seen as an extension of the mentee's development process. Internal access to training is needed, along with development programs and materials to supplement mentor–mentee activities. The mentor program must be voluntary. Forcing managers to take part in mentoring activities will do more harm than good. A reluctant mentor cannot provide the interest and motivation needed to assist someone in the organization.

It is helpful to assign mentors to mentees. Most formal mentor programs require a nominating procedure. Mentees are nominated by their supervisors and matched by the director of training to a mentor. It is a good idea to allow for switching, particularly if a match does not seem to be working.

Keeping each phase of the program short will help prevent potential mentors from being reluctant to take on mentoring responsibilities. Six-month cycles are enough time for a mentor to help a mentee in a significant manner while not being tied to him indefinitely. Mentors who find the process successful will sign up for another stint.

Provide an orientation for mentors and mentees. This is a formal process by which they can meet and hear about what worked in the past and the role expectations for both parties in the mentoring relationship. The mentors should be allowed to work within their style and not be forced to follow a strict format. The orientation can feature successful past mentors who can describe how they took on and carried out the role. Presenting a few different approaches will reinforce the idea that it is not necessary to follow a specific process.

Finally, it is important to monitor the mentoring process, as this is critical to its success. At specific checkpoints, both parties can be surveyed about the progress of the mentee. This survey could take the form of a meeting to discuss what has happened, a request for minireports on progress, or simply phone calls to ask how the process is working. Use this information to highlight successful mentoring relationships in company newsletters and other communications. This publicity will keep individuals motivated and the program visible. Plotting the career paths of mentees is another method of showing the success of the program.

Strengths and Limitations of OJT

OJT is clearly a useful method for skill enhancement. Trainees learn their KSAs in the actual job situation; thus, transfer of training occurs naturally. An additional benefit is that the OJT process will provide new employees with a rapid orientation to how the company operates. It also has the potential to develop a more positive relationship among older and newer employees and between supervisors and their subordinates.

A major concern in OJT is the competency of the trainer. The trainer must possess the technical competence, training competence, and motivation to train. Without all these characteristics, training is not likely to be successful. In addition, the organization must provide the trainer with enough time away from her regular job to do the training. This accommodation not only leads to better training but also demonstrates the organization's commitment to its OJT program.

Cost

OJT offers some clear cost advantages if it is done effectively. Both trainees and trainers are at the job site performing job activities. Although neither the trainee nor the trainer will be producing at full capacity, they are at least producing something. With other techniques, neither the trainer nor the trainee is engaged in producing the organization's products or services while training is going on. Also, OJT does not require the purchase of expensive training materials such as simulators, games, or computer-based training modules. All the materials are part of the normal work equipment.

OJT also speeds up the learning process. No delay separates training from its application to the work situation. In addition, some evidence indicates that one-on-one training produces faster learning that is more resistant to forgetting.[44] The more efficient the training, the less costly it is.

One cost concern in implementing OJT is the cost of training the trainers. Unlike other methods, for a start-up OJT system, most, if not all, of the trainers will need training. In addition, whereas other methods have one trainer for many trainees, this method uses one-on-one training. The drop in productivity from having the more skilled employees conducting training must be added into the cost. In addition, companies should expect some increased waste, breakage, and downtime because of inexperienced trainees operating the equipment. There is more about training trainers in Chapter 8.

Control of Content and Process

The trainer primarily controls the content and process of learning in OJT during the "prepare" and "present" stages of training. As training progresses to the "try out" and "follow-up" stages, the trainee and trainer jointly control the content and process, because the trainee's actions determine what the next learning module will be. The training moves as quickly or as slowly as necessary for the trainee to master the learning. Thus, if the trainee is in the "talk through" portion of trying it out and misses some steps, the trainer might again demonstrate how the job is done. If the trainee is able to "talk through" the steps correctly, the trainer might be ready to move to the "instruct the trainee" portion. However, if the trainee were to say, "You know, I was just guessing on some of those steps," the trainer might repeat the "talk through" portion until the trainee feels confident of knowing all the steps.

Learning Objectives (KSAs)

The primary focus of OJT is skill development, but OJT can also enhance the knowledge base of trainees and influence their attitudes. Through discussions with the trainer and through questioning and restating of techniques, the trainee can learn facts and procedures that are required on the job. However, classroom techniques and individual reading assignments are more efficient at this type of learning.

The attitudes that new employees hold about their jobs and their company come from observing and interacting with others. OJT provides a great opportunity to get employees off on the right foot by clarifying the norms, expectations, and culture of the work unit. Of course, accomplishing this task will depend on the ability of the OJT trainer to convey these properly to the trainee.

On a final note, if knowledge acquisition is required to perform the job, OJT techniques should be supplemented with other techniques—such as apprenticeship training—that are more suited to knowledge acquisition. For skilled trades, it is important to develop the skills of the trade; however, certain knowledge is a prerequisite for that skill development. For that reason, a significant amount of classroom training is also required as a part of the training. Computer-based training, role-playing, reading of texts and manuals, and other techniques can all be combined successfully with OJT.

Learning Process

Trainees are likely to be relatively more attentive and more motivated during OJT, because it is easier to see a direct relationship between the training and job performance. Verbal and visual stimuli direct attention to key learning points. Periods of active practice require the trainees to attend to what they are doing and what is being said, thus increasing the learning potential.

The visual, auditory, and tactile cues in OJT assist in the symbolic coding process, providing many relationships among objects and actions in the work environment. Through observation, practice, and discussion, the trainee cognitively organizes these relationships into easily recalled patterns of behavior.

By asking the trainee to describe the steps in the operation (before letting the trainee perform the operation), the trainer is facilitating the symbolic rehearsal process. The trainee must imagine himself going through the operations as he describes the procedures.

Behavioral reproduction, of course, is a strong point of this method. The trainee practices small portions of the operation until they are mastered. The trainee then moves on to larger portions until command over all the tasks that make up the job reaches the level needed to perform the job alone.

SUMMARY OF METHODS AND WHEN TO USE THEM

While we have covered the different traditional methods in detail in the preceding sections, we thought it would be useful to provide a summary of the purpose of each of the methods and when it is appropriate to use them. Table 6-9 provides this summary.

Table 6-9 List of Methods, Purpose, and When to Use

METHOD	PURPOSE	WHEN TO USE
Lecturettes	• To convey knowledge	• To provide declarative or procedural knowledge • To provide instructions or other types of process information • Following a module or "chunk" of training to highlight the key learning points
Open Discussion	• To generate participation • To find out what participants think or have learned • To stimulate recall of relevant knowledge	• Following or during a lecturette • Following any experiential activity or small-group discussion • To facilitate participant symbolic coding and cognitive organization
Demonstrations	• To show how to do something or how something works	• When a visual display and/or hands-on manipulation of objects is required • When both knowledge and skill are learning objectives
Small-Group Discussions	• To generate and/or provide a safer place to test out ideas • To make use of collaborative learning related to the topic • To work through problems, issues, and concerns • To develop group cohesion	• When participants need an opportunity to explore or test ideas • After a lecturette to assist participants with integrating and organizing the new material into their existing cognitive structure • After an experiential exercise to allow participants to explore lessons learned as they relate to the topic • To build relationships among the participants
Games and Simulations		**The methods below should be used in conjunction with the methods listed above and not as stand-alone methods.**
Equipment Simulators Business Games	• To provide the skills needed for the operation and/or maintenance of equipment • To enhance management skills • To improve decision-making skills • To explore and solve complex problems in a safe setting • To provide strategic knowledge	• When using the actual equipment is not feasible (too expensive, dangerous, etc.) • After required declarative and procedural knowledge has been acquired • When the complexity of the issues is relatively high • To motivate participants to learn

(continued)

Table 6-9   List of Methods, Purpose, and When to Use (*Continued*)

Memory Games	• To provide participants with a review and/or refresher of key learning points	• As an alternative fun way to review information • As a way to assess if the participants seem to be acquiring the knowledge
In-Basket and Case Studies	• To develop decision-making skills that the participant will need on the job	• When preparing employees for a new assignment (promotion or transfer) • When written information is sufficient to convey the key aspects of the situation in which the decision must be made
Role-Play	• To develop and provide practice with interpersonal skills appropriate to specific situations • To experience what it feels like to be in a particular situation	• After required declarative and procedural knowledge has been acquired • Only if quality feedback can be assured • If an opportunity to debrief the experience can be provided
Behavior Modeling	• To show participants what the appropriate and/or inappropriate behavior looks like • To allow participants to compare their behavior to that of the model. • To increase participants' observational and critiquing skills	• When skills are the object of the training • When a good model of the behavior is available or can be developed. • When there is ample opportunity for feedback • When feedback is of high quality • When there is ample opportunity to practice
Task-Related Exercises or Activities	• To allow participants to work with the material individually or in small groups • To enhance the likelihood of transfer to the job	• At every opportunity. The key is to ensure the quality of the task/exercise and to provide an opportunity for debriefing when it is completed
On-the-Job Training Job Instruction Technique	• To provide a systematic process for teaching a new employee how to perform the job	• Primarily used for skilled trades and clerical and technical jobs
Coaching	• To enhance managerial or executive competencies in specific areas	• When a manager needs individual assistance of a specific nature
Mentoring	• To provide general advice to newly placed managers	• When a manager needs periodic advice and someone to discuss issues with. Care needs to be taken in selection of the mentors.

AV ENHANCEMENTS TO TRAINING

Audiovisuals (AVs) can be useful enhancements for meeting all three types of training objectives (knowledge, skills, and attitudes) and are easily applied to any of the other methods discussed. **Audiovisual aids** consist of any physical, mechanical, or electronic media used to provide or assist instruction. Typically, they are used as a supplement to other methods of training rather than as a stand-alone means of instruction, though some are effective training devices by themselves.

The range of AV alternatives is quite large, from simple chalkboard or whiteboard text and images to interactive multimedia presentations. They can be grouped under the headings of static or dynamic media. **Static media** are presentations of fixed (stationary) text or images such as printed matter, pictures/slides, and computer-generated projections. An AV is considered static if the material presented is stationary. **Dynamic media** create sequentially moving stimuli, where the information is presented in a continuously moving progression from beginning to end, as with audiotapes and videotapes, computer-generated presentations, and moving film.

Static Media

Static media are generally not suitable for training as a stand-alone method. Rather, they are used to augment and enhance other methods—in particular the lecture method—but they also are adaptable to other training techniques.

Newsprint, Charts, and Posters

Newsprint, charts, and posters display information through words or images. They range from handmade, with felt markers and newsprint, to professionally prepared glossy prints. An advantage of these presentations is that they can be posted on walls or other vertical surfaces so the information is visible to trainees while other training methods are in use (e.g., lecture, role-plays, video). For example, these media are frequently used to post an outline of the day's training and to display procedural steps related to the training material. They allow trainees to place the material that is presented at any time into the context of the total program. Figure 6-2 shows a poster that could be used during conflict resolution training. It might be left up during the entire training so that trainees are constantly reminded of the six steps the training focuses on. Posters and charts that the trainer knows will be used during training should be prepared before training and checked for accuracy. The credibility of the training and the trainer will suffer if errors exist.

Projected Text and Images

Creating slides for projection requires text and images to be presented in a way that is visually pleasing while conveying the desired information. Computer-generated text and images, and those copied from published materials, can be pasted together to create attention-getting and informative projections.

Many popular office software packages, such as those produced by Microsoft and Corel, contain presentation software components that create projections, discussion notes, and other training aids that can be integrated into the presentation. Once the projections are created and placed in proper order, they can be downloaded onto a portable storage device such as a USB drive or stored on a hard drive. During the training, the

Figure 6-2
Example of a Poster That Might Be Used in Conflict Resolution Training

SIX STEPS TO CONFLICT RESOLUTION

Solutions
- Actively Listen
- Indicate Respect
- Be Assertive
- Provide Information
- Reconsider Problem
- Brainstorm Possible Solutions

trainer will require a computer (typically a laptop or notebook) and a high-intensity digital projector. Most projectors will also project video images from a VCR, CD, or DVD player. The presenter can control the display of the projections with a mouse, clicking to move from one projection to the next, or time the presentation so that the image automatically advances to the next projection after a specified period of time.

The purpose of static projections is to focus trainees' attention on specific content. In addition to displaying information, projections can aid the trainer in moving systematically through the components of the training. This feature is especially useful in training methods where the interaction between trainer and trainees might cause the trainer to stray from the training outline; the trainer can simply look to the displayed projection to get back on track.

Effective Use of Static Visuals

Trainers tend to put too much information on slides. Guidelines for creating effective slides are as follows:

- Present one idea or concept.
- Print in large letters.
- Limit to six or seven lines with six to eight words per line.
- Use color for effect.
- If using a pointing device, make sure to keep your focus on the trainees.
- Make sure that the right image is being projected at the right time.
- Make sure that everyone has a good line of sight to the screen.
- Face the trainees, not the screen, when speaking. If necessary, turn to the visual aid to identify a point, and then turn back to the trainees to speak.

When using flip charts or posters, you should keep the following in mind:

- Remove or cover a visual aid when it is no longer being discussed.
- When writing on newsprint, look at the trainees from time to time as you are writing; do not stand in front of the easel or face it.

For effective static visuals, the room setup must allow easy viewing by all trainees. Seating should be arranged to allow a clear sightlines, and the projector should not block the trainees' view of the screen. Line of sight should also be clear for newsprint information. Here are some additional considerations:

1. Rehearse the presentation using the static visuals on the equipment in the room where training will occur. Doing so will reveal all the things forgotten about and the things not known (e.g., the circuit breaker for the outlet won't handle the computer projection unit and the video equipment at the same time).
2. Bring extra equipment accessories such as extra projector bulbs, cables, extension cords, and easels to the training facility before training begins. Remember, Murphy's Law applies to trainers, too. In fact, trainers face the following addendum: The more important the event, the more likely it is that things will go wrong. Extra precautions are always wise.
3. Arrive at the training site early, and check that all equipment is in working order. Make sure that visuals are ready to operate when training starts (overheads are in the correct order, right side up, computer-generated projections are ready, etc.).
4. Bring along an extra copy of your slide show for emergencies if using computer-generated projections.

Dynamic AV Methods

Dynamic AVs include audiotapes, moving picture film, videos, and computer-generated presentations. Dynamic visuals can also serve as aids to enhance other methods of training. However, unlike static visuals, these methods can be, and frequently are, used as the sole method of training.

Audiotapes

Audiotape has the same characteristics as the straight lecture. The only differences are that the audiotape is exactly the same each time it is used and provides no accompanying visual stimulus. Even though advances in video and computer-generated presentations reduce the popularity of audiotapes as training tools, they have an advantage in some situations. They are effective when the content of the training is primarily auditory recognition or auditory response. Almost 50 percent of companies with more than 50 employees use audiocassettes in their training.[45] One obvious instance is if the material to be learned requires specific responses to auditory cues. Telephone and radio operators of all types (e.g., 911 emergency operators, taxi dispatchers, and customer-service line operators) can receive beneficial training through audiotape playback that closely simulates the work environment. Learning a foreign language is also a fairly common use of audiotapes.

Audiotapes are also useful when other forms of training are not available. For example, audiotape training can be a productive use of the long hours that sales representatives spend in their cars.

Advantages of the audiotape over the lecture are its portability and its ability to be reused both for training additional people and for easy review and clarification by trainees. Also, if it is important that all trainees receive exactly the same information, an audiotape will be better than a lecture.

Videos

Videos are good ways of both showing and telling trainees how to do something. They can present conceptual or factual information by integrating narration with visual illustrations, graphics, and animated depictions. In more sophisticated applications, they can be used in an interactive fashion. This medium is relatively portable and generally can be made available to trainees at their convenience through wireless devices. The many advantages offered by videos make it clear why 96 percent of companies with 50 or more employees used video for training in some fashion, second only to classroom instruction.[46]

Videos can be used as a stand-alone training technique or in combination with other more interactive techniques. Many firms use videos to enhance training in ways similar to those described in Training in Action 6-4, featuring Home Depot and APC. In the APC case, the video is used to show engineers how to perform specific tasks. In the Home Depot example, video is blended with other training methods, some of which allow the trainee to interact with video.

Computer-Generated Dynamic Presentations

With the ability to project computer screen images onto a large screen and the increasing ability to digitize sound and images electronically, the computer is rapidly becoming a critical training tool. Multimedia software allows computers to store, modify, and reconfigure sound, images, and text, to create nearly any combination of audio and visual presentation. Developing a computer-generated dynamic presentation (CGDP) does require considerably more hardware and software knowledge than do the presentation software packages discussed earlier. The development process is similar to that of producing a video but also includes converting all the components into digital media. As with video productions, it is advisable to use professionals to ensure the quality of the presentation. This method is discussed in more depth in Chapter 7 under "Interactive Multimedia Training."

Following are two examples of how videos are used to train employees working in two vastly different work environments.

The Home Depot, Inc.

Most retailers have to keep employees up-to-date on rapid product change, but The Home Depot has an added challenge: Frontline workers also are expected to provide customers with information on how products can be used to complete home improvement projects. Basic product and project information is provided through e-learning modules. With store employees ranging in age from 18 to 70, the e-learning modules come with both audio and text onscreen. The ability to listen to key lessons, rather than read them, is helpful to all the generations as well as the multiethnic groups the company employs. To provide the skills needed to interact effectively with customers, the coursework has to have components where trainees are able to apply what they're learning. This hands-on approach allows workers to actually touch, feel, and do things with the products. The delivery of training is speeded up through what it calls "Rapid Web-Based Training." It is video-based e-learning in which the screen is divided into three sections. One part of the screen features a video, the second a PowerPoint presentation, and the third a program options menu. Customer interaction is simulated with all the products. Each module takes about 15 minutes to complete, so it's very convenient in the fast-paced retail world where learners can be scheduled to take that training before or after their shift.

American Power Conversion Corp. (APC)

APC is a global provider of network-critical physical infrastructure solutions and is based in West Kingston, Rhode Island. Field-service engineers provide maintenance and implement procedural changes. In the past, a training team at APC would compose lengthy text-based technical information bulletins for the maintenance and procedural changes and communicate these to field-service engineers. Though these text-only bulletins met stringent criteria, the field-service engineers had a difficult time comprehending and visualizing the recommended solution. They would frequently call in to request additional information and clarification. To address this problem, APC implemented the Video Information Bulletin program in June 2006. In each bulletin, trainers would demonstrate the skills and tasks required to perform each procedure. The videos were then incorporated into Flash-based e-learning modules that are supplemented by more detailed, text-based bulletins—both of which can be accessed from the field via wireless-enabled laptops. In tying this program back to corporate goals, APC has seen return on value in three areas: customer satisfaction, employee satisfaction, and profitability. The number of calls to the training team from those in the field asking for help and further explanation regarding how to perform new and/or complex procedures also decreased significantly.

Source: Adapted from Weinstein, M. "The Home Depot: Products and Projects." *Training* (July/August 2007), pp. 30–31.

Source: Adapted from Boehle, S. *Training* (September 2007), pp. 30–35.

Effective Use of Dynamic Media

How close to the AV equipment should trainees sit to view the material adequately? A rule of thumb (whether static or dynamic visuals are used) is one foot of trainee distance from the screen for every inch of screen size. Thus for a 32-inch TV screen, the maximum distance that trainees should be from the screen is about 32 feet. Sound can be a problem if the room is not wired and the TV is not adaptable to external speakers. Adequate volume for those who are seven feet from the TV will be too low for those who are 32 feet away, and making the sound adequate for those who are furthest away can make it too loud for those in the front. One solution is to create a semicircle around the TV, although this arrangement limits the number of people who can be seated comfortably. Learning to operate the equipment is also more difficult than with the other methods. Little skill is required to operate an overhead or slide projector. Significantly more skill is required to operate computer- or image-projection equipment.

As with anything mechanical, it is important to try the system before training begins. Arrive early to check out all the equipment. Be sure that remote controls for lights, video, and so on, are operating and that you understand how they work. Put the equipment through a trial run. Have a backup for any video or disk that will be used. Video machines do eat tapes, and disks do crash. Most training facilities have more than one VCR and computer, which can be critical if an important part of training requires their use. Find out where the extra VCR is kept, carry a portable computer as a spare, or arrange for backup overheads. Breakdowns do happen. When you are using dynamic visual aids, keep these points in mind:

- Turn off or blank the screen of the TV, computer, or other visual aid when it is not in use.
- Keep the line of sight to visual aids unblocked. If the group is large, use two TVs placed in strategic locations, connected to the single VCR.
- Turn the lighting up when talking about or discussing an issue (even for a short time) between the visual presentations. Do not attempt to discuss issues in a darkened room.

Strengths and Limitations of AVs

Static AVs are one-way communication techniques and should rarely, if ever, be used as stand-alone training tools. The only exception is printed material such as books or pamphlets, that can be used alone if the material is simple and straightforward. This use typically occurs as self-study material and not as part of a formalized training program. Static media cannot demonstrate how to use the material, answer questions, or allow for interaction between the trainee and trainer, so their value is greatest as a supplement to other methods. As they are generally not useful as a stand-alone training method, we will compare static visuals with each other and with dynamic AV methods.

Cost

Static AVs   An advantage of static AVs is their lower development costs. Costs range from low (flip charts, and computer-generated projections) to moderate (photographic slides and professionally prepared posters). Implementation costs range from low (flip charts) to high (computer-generated projections). The high implementation cost is entirely a result of the cost of equipment. Overhead projectors are relatively inexpensive (several hundred dollars), slide projectors are slightly more, and computer image projectors (requiring a relatively sophisticated system) can range from $1,500 to $10,000. Of course, all this equipment is amortized across the training sessions in which it is used, so even the most expensive projection devices might be only a minor factor in the total cost of training.

Static visuals are reusable, so a trainee who did not understand something the first time can look at it again and again. It is not necessary, however, for the trainee to use the original materials. For a minimal cost, computer-generated projections can be copied to paper and given as handouts; slides are more expensive to convert. Providing these handouts will help address any moderate-to-small differences in learning readiness among trainees.

Computer-generated projections provide a unique advantage because they are stored electronically. Any given display can be modified easily by adding or removing text and images. This reduces the cost of program modifications or adaptations. Slides, on the other hand, would need to be completely redone. For example, assume that 30 photographic slides are produced for training human resource clerks in the proper procedure for processing a worker's compensation claim. It is not likely that these slides would be much use in training supervisors about how to handle a workplace accident, even though worker's compensation claims are closely related. If computer-generated projections had been used, the original projections could be easily modified to delete irrelevant material and include the new material. Likewise, if six months later, the government rewrites the worker's compensation laws, it will probably be necessary to replace most of the slides for the HR clerks rather than modifying the existing slides. Technological advances in computer imaging and projection make slides less and less viable as static visual aids.

Dynamic AVs   Using a professional video production company is expensive. A completed video can cost from $700 to $1,200 per minute[47] or more, but it is often worth the cost because of the professional appearance of the video. Even developing in-house videos is fairly expensive, given the cost of labor, equipment, and so on. Developing an original CGDP can require even greater up-front costs than producing a video, because each component of the multimedia package must be developed, digitized, and then integrated into a coherent, logically flowing package. The cost of development is reduced if the training components can be developed digitally in the first place.

Although the up-front cost is high, the per-person cost of producing a video can be low if the trainee population is large enough. Videos, film, and CGDP are portable and reusable. Videos and CGDPs are easily and cheaply duplicated, enabling many trainees in different places to see them at any time, or one trainee to see them many times. This capability is valuable for refresher courses or for trainees who learn at a slower pace. Because of their reusability, the development cost can be spread over a large number of trainees, thus reducing the per-trainee costs.

When they are used for stand-alone training, the biggest advantage of videos and CGDPs is that trainees can view or study at their convenience. This capability can have significant cost and time savings because the trainees and trainers do not have to travel to the presentations. For example, ADC Communications estimated that it would cost about $150,000 to bring the company's 60 salespeople to the Minneapolis headquarters for a week of sales training.[48] By using stand-alone video training, this cost was eliminated. Since most employees can use VCRs and TVs in their homes, the company is not required to buy much equipment. The company should, however, provide on-site equipment to those employees who do not own the equipment or whose home environment is not conducive to learning. CGDP does not offer this equipment cost advantage because the employees do not likely own the necessary hardware and software.

Finally, if employees view the tape at home or during free time at work, the productivity savings are substantial. If trainees must travel more than 200 miles to reach a centralized training location, they lose not only their productivity for the time at training but also one or two days of travel time.

One way to cut the cost of video training is to rent or buy a video from commercial producers. A large number of commercially available training videos cover a wide variety of topics. Also, some videos and films produced primarily for entertainment can be used effectively in training. We used segments of the classic film *Twelve Angry Men* (a film about a jury's deliberations during a criminal trial) to illustrate the problems and benefits of consensus decision making. Small portions of the movie *Falling Down* can illustrate various risk factors and warning signs for workplace violence. TV broadcasts can be used in a similar fashion. For example, textbook publishers now provide, as accompaniments to their textbooks, videocassettes containing segments of news programs and TV specials that relate to the content of the text.

Equipment costs vary across the media used. A film requires a projector and a screen for presentation, and a video requires a VCR and a TV. Videos can also be projected onto large screens with a video projector. The technology is rapidly improving, and state-of-the-art projectors (costing about $4,000) can display large-screen images. This capability overcomes one of the disadvantages of the TV video, which is that only a small group of trainees can easily see it at the same time.

Control of Material and Process

Static AVs   Generally, computer-generated projections are more easily controlled by the trainer than are other static visuals. The sequence of projections can be structured so that material is displayed only when the presenter begins to discuss it. Text can be programmed to fade into and out of the projection with a click of the mouse. The mouse can also be used to point to or highlight particular parts of the projection. Finally, worry about slides or overheads getting out of order, being upside down, and the like is eliminated. The whole visual presentation is contained on a single floppy disk, so it is more easily transportable than slides or overheads.

Although computer-generated projection offers many advantages, it also comes with a major disadvantage—it suffers all the potential problems of computer technology. Hard drives crash at inopportune times, floppy disks are not readable by the operating system, viruses abound, and software and disk-formatting compatibility issues must be solved. To avoid most of these problems, take a portable computer to the training site, but make sure that a compatible backup is available. Of course, carrying a laptop reduces the convenience of having to carry only a single floppy disk.

Dynamic AVs   The disadvantage of acquiring a commercially made video is that the information might not be specific to the company or the training content, but rather must appeal to the largest audience. Such videos will likely need to be augmented with additional training relevant to the trainees. You can control the content and process of learning by selecting the appropriate video and creating the supplemental materials yourself.

The portability of dynamic AVs means that trainees can take them off the shelf and use them when convenient. To this extent, the trainee controls the learning process. However, many distractions may disrupt watching a training video or multimedia presentation at home. Here the training process is completely in the hands of the trainee, who can stop the presentation at any point and do something else. The desired level of learning might not be attained.

When video and CGDP are used as stand-alone techniques, the content and presentation format are controlled, but not the manner in which the trainee goes through the material. Especially with video, trainees may fast-forward over parts they do not understand or find boring, making evaluating learning particularly important when this training technique is used.

Learning Objectives (KSAs)

Appropriately prepared and displayed AVs will enhance almost any training and are especially effective for techniques in which the trainee is less active, such as lecture/discussion and some types of computer-based training. However, the nature of the learning objective will determine which type of AV is best.

Knowledge   Both static and dynamic AVs facilitate the trainee's knowledge development through their ability to activate or enhance learning processes. AVs focus trainee attention and provide visual stimuli that aid symbolic coding and cognitive organization. They are also useful for highlighting cues that will stimulate appropriate recall. AVs are most effective at enhancing declarative knowledge but can also be useful in developing procedural knowledge. Dynamic AVs are more suited than are static AVs for developing procedural knowledge because they can model the steps required to perform the task and display several different situations in which the task is appropriate.

Skills   Static presentation of information is not especially useful for skill building because it does not lend itself to facilitating development or practice of skills. Dynamic presentations, however, can be useful in skill development and practice, and foreign language audiotapes use this approach. Dynamic AVs can also make it easier to simulate the work environment. Police departments might use a film or video to place the trainee in the position of searching a building for an armed and dangerous suspect. The trainee must make decisions about what to do in several different situations, such as the sudden appearance of objects and people or entering a room that has a closed door.

Another AV technique increasingly being used is videotaping the trainee's performance during practice and using the video as feedback for skill improvement. Even though dynamic AVs can provide good models and instructions for skill development, they usually are not capable of providing feedback, so they should not be used as stand-alone methods. Interactive videos and CGDP provide the exceptions to this rule.

Attitudes   Static and dynamic AVs, used in conjunction with other techniques, can facilitate attitude change by visually clarifying the relationships among objects and events that are the basis of trainee opinions and evaluations. For example, the Domtar plant in southern California used static visuals to display the consequences of not following correct safety procedures. This manufacturer of construction products used graphic displays of eye injuries in a safety training program to develop positive attitudes about wearing safety goggles. It also used pictures of employees working on various equipment. Some pictures showed employees wearing goggles, and some showed employees not wearing safety goggles. Trainees were asked to identify the potential hazards to the individual in each picture. The process allowed the trainees to make the proper links between wearing the goggles and protecting themselves from injury. It is interesting to note that this plant won many safety awards from both the company and the state. The ability to provide visual documentation of the relationship between objects and events is a powerful source of learning and attitude change. Beliefs such as "Wearing goggles is uncomfortable and unnecessary" are often reinforced by cognitive distortions and rationalization. Statements such as "If you're careful, you don't need goggles" and "I'm too experienced to get an eye injury" are examples of the kind of rationalizations heard at the Domtar plant before training. The trainer's words alone might not be sufficient to change attitudes. Visual displays allow the trainees to see that their distortions and rationalizations are inaccurate, making a change in attitudes easier to accomplish. Dynamic AVs can produce even more powerful images because the connection among objects, actions, and consequences can be made even more explicit.

Learning Process
Attention   The saying, "A picture is worth a thousand words," reflects the importance of visual representation in the learning process. Static visuals provide the trainee with a visually based message, even if the image is simply enlarged text. Visual stimuli focus the trainee's attention when they represent a change in the environment. No matter how professional a trainer's voice and image are, they can become familiar to the trainees after a period of time. When familiarity occurs, it becomes easier for the trainee's attention to wander. The periodic presentation of new visual stimuli activates the attention process. If the visuals are consistently similar in format (e.g., all text, black print, same font size), they too will lose their ability to attract attention. Combining graphic images, charts, and text, and varying color to highlight key learning points, will add zest to the training and maintain trainee

attention. With dynamic AVs, the dynamic nature of the presentation itself attracts attention because it is constantly changing.

The trainer should be careful that all AVs are integrated with the content of the training. When they show little relationship to the content, they become distracting and can actually reduce learning. This distraction can also occur if the trainer fails to manage the presentation of the visuals properly, such as incorrectly moving to the next slide, standing in front of the screen, or otherwise interfering with the normal viewing of the visual. Trainees often begin to pay attention to the trainer's management of the presentation rather than to the content of the presentation, thus reducing learning.

Retention   Because different trainees learn more or less effectively through different media, the use of AVs provides additional modalities for learning. When several media are used to convey the same message, the message is more easily coded for storage and contributes more reference points. In general, visual communications are absorbed more quickly and retained for a longer time than are auditory messages. Visual images are also more readily coded symbolically and recalled in their original form.[49]

The symbolic coding process is enhanced when pictures or graphic images provide visual cues that supplement or complement auditory or written cues. Combining cues from different senses results in more accurate symbolic coding and thus better retention.[50] Showing several different images, all pertaining to the same issue, presents trainees with a wider base of common cues to use in storing the information. AVs are also extremely good for demonstrating events and effects not usually observable or noticed. For example, enlarged images of tiny or microscopic objects are useful in many training settings. In the safety training example discussed earlier, trainees could see the effects of not wearing goggles. Eye injuries are often not easily observable, but the visual projections used in the training allowed the trainees to see what actually happened to the eye and what damage tiny bits of material can do. By making objects and effects visible, symbolic encoding becomes much easier.

Cognitive organization can be facilitated by graphic images that demonstrate how the training relates to familiar concepts. Pictorially representing these relationships makes integrating the new with the old easier than using verbal descriptions alone does. Integration is likely to be easier and faster if the trainer is able to represent visually both the old cognitive organization and the new, showing the changes required. To the degree that the trainees' cognitive structures are different from one another, creating visual representations of them all is difficult. However, it can be accomplished by asking trainees to develop pictorial representations of their cognitive organization on flip charts. They can then compare these representations with the new organization being presented. For example, suppose that jobs in a work group were redesigned because of a change in how the product is produced. During training, trainees could map out how the old job was performed. Then, after presenting the new work procedures, the trainer could compare the old with the new and identify the areas for which the new KSAs provided by the training will be needed.

Using AVs in training provides a common reference for all trainees. When you ask the trainees to "picture this" or "imagine you are . . .," each trainee might hold a different image, but when you provide the image, they all receive the same sensory cues. When the trainees later recall the image, the frame of reference will be similar for all. Though a differential loss of information and detail is likely to occur across trainees, the basis of the recalled information is the initial image that is provided.

AVs can be somewhat useful in aiding symbolic rehearsal. They provide visual cues that trainees can use to practice hypothetical applications of the training material. This process works in much the same manner as behavioral reproduction (described next). The difference is that in symbolic rehearsal, the trainees are only imagining themselves applying the new learning. The AVs can help create the context in which the symbolic rehearsal takes place, and it provides cues to assist in the symbolic rehearsal (as in guided discovery).

Behavioral Reproduction   AVs can be used to enhance the learning of a new behavior. By illustrating what to do, AVs can provide a model of how to perform. This modeling is usually accomplished best with dynamic AVs. Static or dynamic AVs can also be used to provide the appropriate cues for when to perform. For example, sometimes cue cards are given to trainees when they are practicing new behaviors. These aids need to be present and visible when the new behavior is first being practiced. In the training facility, supplying these cues shouldn't pose a problem. However, to allow opportunities for reproduction outside the training environment, the visual images must be easily portable. Many training programs provide pocket- or wallet-sized cards (static visual aid) to help trainees practice the new material back on the job. As we mentioned earlier, videos and CGDPs are portable but require equipment that might not be compatible with the trainee's workstation (particularly line employees). AVs cannot observe the trainee's performance and provide appropriate feedback. Thus, although AVs can enhance behavioral reproduction, they are limited as stand-alone tools for this type of learning.

The big advantage of CGDPs is that each component of the training can provide the AV format best suited for meeting the objectives of that component. Some of these multimedia packages are now interactive, allowing the trainee to respond to and even pose questions, thereby partially eliminating the one-way communication limitation of standard videos and static AVs. With interactivity comes two-way communication, though the limitations discussed earlier about the quality and type of interaction should be kept in mind.

Limitations for Learning   The principal limitation of static visuals is that they are typically not stand-alone learning tools. They are best used as enhancements to other methods. Because they are static, they cannot capture the full range of material that is dynamic. Even though it is possible to capture the essence of some types of dynamic material, such as the "steps in conflict resolution" or "tips for providing constructive feedback," dynamic AV media generally will perform this task more easily and with higher quality. Except for the most sophisticated dynamic AVs (i.e., interactive CGDP), they cannot adapt to differing characteristics of the trainees or the situation. It is a "one-size-fits-all" technique. If trainees do not have the KSAs to learn from the AVs, they will not learn no matter how many times they reuse it.

Trainee Characteristics

Obviously, the trainees must be able to understand the AVs. This point may sound fairly trivial, but it is often overlooked. For example, the poster in Figure 6-2 assumes that the trainees can read. If the trainees are managers, it is a pretty safe assumption. However, if they are line employees in an assembly plant, problems may arise. Not only must trainees be able to read, but they must also be able to understand the terms. Even all managers might not know what the trainer means by "actively listen," "be assertive," or "reconsider the problem." Displaying this poster without defining all the terms might create confusion for the trainees. The issue of understandability applies to all AVs, both static and dynamic.

When wide differences in trainee readiness levels are present, AVs aimed at the highest level of KSAs might not be understandable to those at the lower level. If they are aimed at the lowest level, they will seem unnecessary and boring to those at higher levels. If a dynamic AV is being used as a stand-alone program, it is probably best to provide separate training AVs customized to the readiness level of each group.

SUMMARY

This chapter focused on non-computer-based training methods. We described the process of using the method effectively and the method's ability to meet KSAs learning objectives. These methods are included in a summary (Table 8-1) at the beginning of Chapter 8. Please note that this table represents a general guide. More specific information is provided in the relevant sections of this chapter and Chapter 7.

Learning objectives are a critical factor in designing a training program, but other factors such as cost, control of training content, and learning processes also need to be taken into account. This chapter discussed the non-computer-based training methods in terms of their advantages and disadvantages as they relate to the above factors. In most cases, organizations need to make trade-offs between effectiveness at meeting the learning objectives and the cost of the method or the time required to develop it into a usable training program.

KEY TERMS

- Apprenticeship training
- Attitudes
- Audiovisual aids
- Behavior modeling
- Behavioral methods
- Business games
- Case study
- Closed-ended question
- Coaching
- Cognitive methods
- Demonstration
- Direct question
- Dynamic media

- Equipment simulators
- Guided discovery
- In-basket technique
- Incident process
- Job instruction technique (JIT)
- Knowledge
- Lecture/discussion method
- Lecturette
- Mentoring
- Multiple role-play
- On-the-job training (OJT)
- Open-ended question
- Overhead question

- Physical fidelity
- Psychological fidelity
- Relay question
- Reverse question
- Role-play
- Role rotation
- Single role-play
- Skills
- Spontaneous role-play
- Static media
- Straight lecture
- Structured role-play

QUESTIONS FOR REVIEW

1. Supervisors often resist taking on the role of coach. What can organizations do to encourage supervisors to be effective coaches?
2. Go through the different instructional methods and sort them into those that you think would be most useful in training someone on the technical aspects of the job and those that would be most useful in the more social aspects of the job. Provide the rationale for your decisions.
3. Why are classroom-based training programs (lecture/discussion, role-play, games, etc.) used so much more than individualized approaches to training? Do you think this choice is appropriate?

EXERCISES

1. Your instructor will assign you (or your group) to one of the methods from the chapter. Contact the HRD department of a local business. Indicate that you are learning about training and would like to know whether the department uses the method in its training programs. If so, ask if you can schedule a time to observe the method being used. If the method isn't used or if you are unable to observe it, try other companies until you are successful. While observing the method, take careful notes on how it is used. On a date specified by your instructor, the class members will report their observations.

2. In small groups, develop a role-play. First, determine the objective of the role-play (a limited one that can be achieved in 15 to 20 minutes). Then develop all aspects of a role-play that will achieve your objective.

3. Take 10 minutes to think about your best classroom-based learning experience, and list the things that made it such a good experience. When the 10 minutes are up, use 10 additional minutes to think of your worst classroom-based learning experience, and list the factors that made it such a bad experience. At the end of this time, the instructor will ask you to share your experiences.

WEB RESEARCH

Do an Internet search to identify the types of games and business simulations that are available. From your research, select four that list different learning content objectives. Prepare a one- to two-paragraph description for each.

CASE ANALYSIS

Training for Customer Service Specialists

As a part of the president's initiative to remove "barriers to learning" at a regional midwestern university, an analysis of student services operations was conducted. The analysis revealed that the barriers deemed most important by students were those that would delay or prevent them from registering for classes. These barriers fell into three areas:

1. Resolving issues relating to fines accrued over the previous terms (e.g., library, parking, late fees)
2. Completing forms accurately and meeting processing deadlines for financial aid in time to enroll in classes
3. Acquiring appropriate advice so that they enrolled in the right classes (avoiding the problems associated with drops and adds)

As a result of this analysis, the university decided to create a new position called customer service specialist (CSS). The job description is presented here.

Classification Specification
Supersedes: New Classification
Title: Customer Service Specialist Grade: PT08

General Summary

Supervise, support, monitor, and assist with the continuous improvement of the work unit's customer service functions and related operational activities. Ensure quality customer service, both in person and over the telephone. These activities require a working knowledge of the work unit's program policies, procedures, and regulations and an understanding of other departments and systems that interface with the work unit's activities.

Essential Duties

Personally provide and ensure that customer support staff provide positive customer service practices throughout the work unit, including greeting departmental customers in person or over the telephone, identifying their needs, obtaining necessary and appropriate information, and processing customer requests in a manner that will best meet the needs of the customer.

Monitor staff and ensure that customers perceive customer service support staff as treating them with courtesy, respect, tact, and a sincere desire to meet their needs.

Provide mediation and resolution to customer complaints and requests within delegated authority limits and consistent with departmental policies.

Communicate to customers the departmental policies and procedures related to their needs, and provide customers with the appropriate forms and instructions.

Design and implement systems to ensure that forms turned in by customers are the correct forms for their service request and that they are complete and as accurate as possible.

Work with the appropriate departmental administrator to identify the training needs of designated support staff in the work unit who provide direct customer service. Where called for, provide on-the-job training and coaching. Work with the designated department administrator to identify suitable training experiences for customer service support staff.

Recruit, interview, and make recommendations in the hiring of customer support staff.

Identify processes and procedures in the department that are causing problems for groups of customers (not individuals), and work with department management toward their improvement. Where authorized, implement improvements in systems, processes, and procedures that will increase the customer satisfaction capability of the department.

Develop and maintain a network of contacts with other university departments that commonly interface with the work unit.

Interact with other university departments to resolve a customer's problem, or meet the customer's needs.

Interpret and reconcile account records related to area of assignment.

Receive, read, and interpret correspondence, and determine proper handling.

Perform other related duties as assigned.

Supervision Received

Supervision is received from the designated departmental administrator.

Supervision Exercised

Supervision may be exercised, as determined by the appropriate departmental administrator, over customer service representatives, clerical support staff, and student support staff in the work unit who provide direct customer service.

Qualifications

Ability to read, write, interpret instructions, perform basic arithmetic, and communicate orally and in writing at a level typically acquired through the completion of a college degree is necessary.

Personal computing skills sufficient to use word processing and spreadsheet applications and to perform file management and data input/retrieval functions are necessary. Knowledge of specific software applications and university information systems utilized in the work unit assigned is desirable.

Supervisory skills needed to provide direction to subordinates, monitor and manage subordinate performance, and to plan, organize, and coordinate the customer service activities are required, and supervisory experience is desirable.

Preference is given to those who master basic customer service and problem-solving skills as listed:

- The ability to communicate accurately and pleasantly with customers (across a wide diversity of cultural backgrounds) is necessary to identify customer needs and solve customer problems.
- The ability to communicate moderately to highly complex policies, procedures, and regulations and to ensure understanding of these while working under pressure (e.g., handling several requests at the same time) is required.
- Effective problem-solving abilities are required to (1) identify and prioritize customer service problems, (2) conduct a root cause analysis to determine the cause(s) of a problem, (3) develop a range of alternatives that will remove the cause(s) of a problem, (4) identify the alternatives that are most effective, and (5) develop an implementation plan for carrying out the alternative selected.
- Effective conflict management skills are required (e.g., defuse emotionally charged situations, clearly identify issues, and clearly communicate procedures for resolving the issue, and working with the customer to develop a resolution acceptable to the customer and the work unit).
- Knowledge and understanding of university, state, and federal policies, systems, procedures, and regulations as they pertain to the work unit's ability to meet customer needs and to areas of the university that interface with the work unit in meeting those needs.

Those hired without the preceding competencies will undergo training before assuming job responsibilities. During the training period, these individuals will be considered temporary employees. Upon successful completion of the training, the classification will be changed to permanent. Failure to complete training successfully will result in termination of employment or reassignment to another position, at the discretion of the university.

Working Conditions

Work is performed in a typical office environment.

After the position was posted and advertised, 25 applicants were selected. Unfortunately, only seven applicants were assessed as demonstrating the desired level of problem-solving and customer service knowledge and skills.

CASE QUESTIONS

You are assigned the challenge of designing the training program for the temporary CSS employees, who must complete training before they become permanent CSS employees.

1. What are the training objectives for the CSS training program? Indicate how these objectives are tied to the KSA requirements. Assume that all trainees have college degrees but need KSAs in all other areas listed in the Qualifications section.
2. On the basis of the training objectives, provide a training agenda and indicate the time allocated and order of modules in your program.
3. For each module, describe the goals of the module and the training methods you will use to accomplish it. Provide your rationale.
4. How will you evaluate whether each person in your training program has mastered the knowledge and skill levels needed to perform as a CSS? Describe the types of questions you would ask of those supervising the CSS employees graduating from your program.

Chapter 7

Computer-Based Training Methods

Learning Objectives

After reading this chapter, you should be able to:

➤ *Describe the relationship between computer-based training (CBT) and e-learning.*

➤ *Identify the components required to develop and deliver CBT.*

➤ *Describe the various formats, procedures, strengths, and limitations of the following CBT methods:*

◆ *Programmed instruction*
◆ *Intelligent tutoring systems*
◆ *Interactive multimedia*
◆ *Virtual reality*

➤ *Describe the types of learning objectives for which CBT is most suited, and indicate to what degree each method is applicable.*

➤ *Indicate the impact of each CBT method on the learning process.*

➤ *Evaluate CBT as stand-alone training.*

CASE: Evolution of Training at Mr. Lube

In 1979, Clifford Giese had become so frustrated with the amount of time it took to get his fleet of vehicles serviced that he created a drive-through oil change system. His first store opened that year, and by 1984, there were 45 stores. Shortly thereafter, Mr. Giese sold the rights to the Mr. Lube trademark to Imperial Oil Limited (Esso), and by 2003, the number of corporate stores and franchised outlets had grown to 87. However, this growth has created new challenges for maintaining the consistent high quality and customer-focused service across the widely distributed network.

The success of the Mr. Lube operation depends on a high level of competence from a relatively young and geographically dispersed workforce.

(continued)

The technical aspects of the industry are becoming increasingly sophisticated, making training a key component in Mr. Lube's strategic thinking. In 2002, Senior Vice-President Bill Tickner did not feel that the paper-based training system that had developed over the history of the company could meet the demands of the current workforce and company configuration. The training manuals contained all the correct information about how to service a vehicle properly, but he didn't feel that employees were actually reading the voluminous training manuals and technical bulletins distributed to each of the stores and franchises. Additionally, there was no reliable and easy way to ensure that the employee actually understood and retained the information. How could he ensure that every employee across the country had the competencies needed to meet Mr. Lube's standards, while keeping the cost within reasonable limits?

OVERVIEW OF THE CHAPTER

The material in this chapter will provide you with an understanding of the various **computer-based training (CBT)** methods, how to use them effectively, their strengths and limitations in terms of cost, suitable learning objectives, and other factors related to their effectiveness. Following that, we will examine the various delivery systems available for use with these methods.

OVERVIEW OF COMPUTER-BASED TRAINING (CBT)

Today's competitive business environment requires more knowledge and skill from employees than ever before. This translates into more training for more employees than ever before. At the same time, business success requires companies to lower costs, so companies are looking for ways to provide low-cost training to their employees. Compared with the traditional training methods discussed in Chapter 6, CBT offers the following advantages:[1]

- Reduced trainee learning time,
- Reduced cost of delivering training,
- More instructional consistency,
- Privacy of learning (errors can be made without embarrassment),
- Easy tracking of trainees' learning progress,
- Time to allow the trainee to master learning,
- A safe method for learning hazardous tasks, and
- Increased in employee access to training.

CBT uses many of the methods described in Chapter 6 but converts those methods into electronic form and delivers the training through a computer. CBT is so varied in its forms and applications that it is difficult to describe in concise terms. We stay with convention and use the term *CBT* to refer to any training that occurs through the use of a computer.[2] It is different from traditional training because face-to-face interaction with a human trainer is not required. Under this definition, CBT may include many different techniques and processes for providing the training experience. Table 7-1 lists and briefly describes some of these in order of technological sophistication.

The growth of electronic technology and connectivity has made the use of CBT feasible for most companies. By 2001, about 75 percent of organizations surveyed

Table 7-1 Names and Descriptions Used for Computer-Based Training Approaches

CBT	*Computer-based training* is the term most often used in private industry or government for training employees using computer-assisted instruction. It is a general term referring to training provided in part or whole through the use of a computer.
PI	*Programmed instruction* is used in computer-based programs consisting of text, graphics, and multimedia enhancements that are stored in memory and connected to one another electronically. Material to be learned is grouped into chunks of closely related information. Typically, the trainees are presented with a chunk of information and then tested on their retention of that information. If the trainees have not retained the material, they are referred back to the original information. If they retained the information, they are referred to the next chunk of information to be learned. PI may be computer-based but is also found in printed material and interactive videos.
ICAI	An *intelligent computer-assisted instruction* (ICAI) system is a CBT system that is able to provide some of the primary characteristics of a human tutor. It is a more advanced form of PI. Expert systems are used to run the tutoring aspect of the training, monitor trainee knowledge within a programmed knowledge model, and provide adaptive tutoring on the basis of trainee responses.
ITS	*Intelligent tutoring systems* make use of artificial intelligence to provide tutoring that is more advanced than ICAI-type tutoring. ITS "learns" the best methods of facilitating the trainee's learning on the basis of the trainee's responses.
Simulations	*Simulations* in CBT provide a representation of a situation and the tasks to be performed in the situation. The representation can range from identical (e.g., word processing training) to fairly abstract (e.g., conflict resolution). Trainees perform the tasks presented to them by the computer program, and the computer program monitors their performance.
Virtual Reality	*Virtual reality* is an advanced form of computer simulation, placing the trainee in a simulated environment that is "virtually" the same as the physical environment. This simulation is accomplished by the trainee wearing special equipment, such as head gear, gloves, and so on, that controls what the trainee is able to see, feel, and otherwise sense. The trainee learns by interacting with objects in the electronic environment to achieve some goal.

indicated that they provided training to employees through the Internet or an intranet (accessible only to those in the particular organization).[3] And by 2007, about 20 percent of employee "self-study" training was provided through e-learning.[4] An additional 10 percent received training through the virtual classroom.[5]

E-Learning and Delivery Systems

Often, CBT and the systems used to deliver CBT are used interchangeably. They are two distinct systems that require different types of expertise to create, manage, and maintain. Innovation in CBT and associated learning management and delivery systems occurs so rapidly that confusion often exists regarding terms and their usage. In this section, we provide a description of the process used in creating a CBT program and delivering it to trainees. This will clarify our use of terms throughout the rest of the chapter.

Figure 7-1 shows the basic components for creating and delivering a CBT program. E-learning is often used as a synonym for CBT. In practice, however, **e-learning** refers to the delivery of training or education through electronic media. The training itself is distinct from the **delivery system.** The Internet and intranets are common means of delivering training, but they are not learning systems or training programs. As Figure 7-1 shows, the training content is developed from a **knowledge base** created by subject matter experts. Once the content is developed, it is translated into some type of electronic format through the use of authoring and learning development tools. The design of the training is discussed in more detail in the sections on CBT methods. In the late 1990s, some predicted that e-learning would become the primary delivery method for training within five years. That has not yet happened, but e-learning is gathering momentum. Large firms, in 2007, indicated that they provided 37 percent of their training via either e-learning (25%) or virtual classroom (12%).[6]

Figure 7-1
Basic Components
for Creating and
Delivering CBT

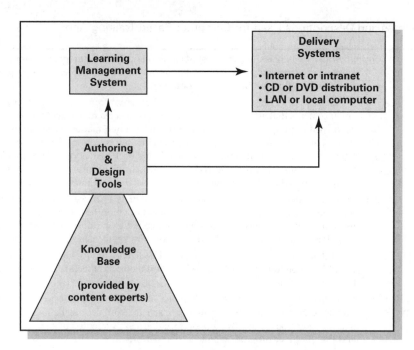

Once developed, e-learning may or may not be integrated into a **learning management system (LMS),** depending on the sophistication of the company's e-learning systems. An LMS is software that manages the content of the training and records the progress of trainees. An LMS can be more or less sophisticated and may or may not include features such as

- authoring,
- class management,
- competency management,
- knowledge management,
- certification or compliance management,
- mentoring,
- chat,
- threaded discussion, and
- video conferencing.

A set of standards called the Sharable Content Object Referenced Model (SCORM) has been created to encourage the standardization of LMSs.

As Figure 7-1 indicates, the final step is delivering the CBT to the trainees. The most common delivery methods are

- local computers and local area networks (LANs),
- CD-ROM and DVDs,
- Internet and intranet, and
- iPods and MP3 players.

Regarding the latter, some companies have been experimenting with iPods or MP3 players to distribute their training programs. Usage of podcasting for *training* purposes grew from 5 percent in 2006 to 15 percent in 2007.[7] Many learners like to listen to podcasts not only on the road, or while jogging, but also while at their desks or at home. By giving employees iPods, they can now provide them with training as they drive, ride the subway, or simply walk to work. Alexis Conelias, a learning consultant with IBM Learning in Piscataway, New Jersey, began creating podcasts for sales and solutions education and training for the global sales team. The podcasts use interviews and discussions with internal experts to teach and inform the team about competitors, products, customers, information management, new initiatives, and sales solutions. "This was the perfect solution for trying to get information to our sales team," Conelias says. Because the global sales force is so mobile, it's difficult to find a good time for face-to-face education or even conference calls. This way, the sales team can download the latest segment on a train, in a car, or even waiting for a meeting at the client site.[8] Training in Action 7-1 provides another example of the value of iPods in training.

E-learning vendors are becoming a part of a larger approach to knowledge management. Companies are now linking their portals to a vendor's LMS. This creates a single location for corporate information, learning, and collaboration. Web-based training programs are being used extensively for mandatory or compliance training. This is because this type of training is easier to deploy, measure, and report.[9]

The next step for human resource departments is the integration of their LMS with other human resource functions. Performance Management Systems (PMS) is software that does just that. It links an employee's competencies from the LMS to annual performance reviews, compensation-based performance, succession planning, and so forth. Although this sounds like a great idea, it does require a great deal of money and commitment to make it work properly.

Converting Programs to E-Learning

Not all training programs should be converted to an e-learning format. Neither should conversion be done on a piecemeal basis. The entire curriculum should be analyzed to determine which content areas can be converted to an electronic format effectively. These content areas then should be analyzed to identify similarities and overlap in content. Converting these areas of similarity and overlap into a standardized electronic format reduces the workload that would be required if each course was done separately. "Yes," you might say, "but each program might have a somewhat different purpose and context for that content." You would be right. So, when integrating the content back into the original course, it will need to be customized.

TRAINING IN ACTION 7-1
iPods at Capital One

Steve Arneson, senior vice president of learning and development at Capital One, in McLean, Virginia, was inspired by Duke University's decision to provide all its students with iPods. He decided to try a pilot program at Capital One. The company provided 50 iPods to a random sampling of Associates and loaded the devices with material generated by Capital One University, the financial services corporation's training organization. Buoyed by positive feedback generated from surveys on the pilot program, the company purchased 3,000 iPods for distribution to Associates who had signed up for the 20 most popular instructor-led courses offered at Capital One University. Has it been successful?

In an employee survey, 94 percent of the respondents said that they would recommend the company's audio learning to others, 92 percent said that it's a worthwhile investment for Capital One, and 93 percent said that it's a worthwhile use of their time.

One employee commented in the survey report: "I love audio learning because I can listen to lectures or speeches while driving, jogging or working in the yard that I simply wouldn't access another way." Another said: "One of the biggest advantages of the iPod is that you can learn at your convenient open times and not lose an entire day (or more) from deliverables."

Source: Agnvall, E. "Just-in-time training: With MP3 players, iPods and other mobile devices, employee training is truly on the go." *HR Magazine* (May 2006), pp. 66–72.

However, using a standardized format, it becomes easier and more efficient to make the customization than to create the electronic content separately for each course. At the same time, you have captured a set of knowledge that can be stored and later used by programs that are developed in the future. Another benefit of doing the curriculum analysis is that you can identify content that can be considered to be prerequisite knowledge for other courses. Once these are identified, they can then serve as "pretraining work" for trainees who might not be quite ready for the main program. A sophisticated system would assess the trainee's readiness for the training program by administering a pretest. The results of the pretest would then be linked to pretraining modules that the trainee needs to be ready for the main program.

Off-Line Delivery Systems

Local computers are individual computers that are available to the trainees. The CBT is loaded onto each computer's hard drive and can be accessed by the trainee. This is not a very efficient delivery method if more than a few trainees are to be trained. A more efficient process is to use the organization's **local area network (LAN).** A LAN is simply the electronic connection among the various computers and a central server. With a LAN, the CBT is loaded onto the server, where it becomes accessible from any authorized computer on the network. This saves memory in the individual computers and the time and inconvenience of trainees loading the program onto their own computers.

The CBT can be reproduced on CDs or DVDs and delivered to individual trainees. This method of delivery allows trainees to access the training outside the LAN and without downloading the program onto the computer. The development of small, portable DVD players allows trainees to access the training even in remote locations where computer connections do not exist. CDs and DVDs are small, easy to package, and inexpensive to reproduce and distribute.

Internet and Intranet

The Internet and intranets are also rapidly becoming methods for transmitting standardized training to trainees who are in many different locations. Companies using an **intranet** provide access to training through a company portal. The portal allows only authorized employees' access to training. Training over the Internet or intranet will require the use of an LMS to monitor who is accessing the training, record trainee progress, and perform other training management functions. An advantage to this delivery approach is that the time that trainees spend on the training, and any evaluation of trainee learning, can be recorded in a central location. With the development of Web 2.0, dynamic person-to-person and group-to-group interaction was possible. This will allow Web-based training to become a more instantaneous collaborative experience.[10]

CBT METHODS

Programmed Instruction

Programmed instruction (PI) is a method of self-paced learning managed by both the trainee and the learning system. **Self-paced learning** means that the trainees move through the training as fast as they are able to learn the material. The program determines the trainees' learning through trainee responses to questions. Higher forms of CBT, such as intelligent tutoring, are much more than PI, but the principles of PI are the basis on which these other techniques operate. PI is the process of leading a trainee systematically through new information in a way that facilitates the most efficient learning. At its most basic level, PI provides the trainee with information, asks a question, and, on the basis of the response, goes to the next bit of information. Table 7-2 describes the PI principles while at the same time providing an

Table 7-2 Programmed Instruction for Programmed Instruction

LEARNING STEM	QUESTIONS	INSTRUCTIONS
1. Many people think that it is impossible to learn without making a large number of errors. Because *trial and error learning* is time consuming and creates frustration for the learner, most people don't like this method. After making a large number of errors, people begin to *lose their desire* to learn. Many trainers feel that if learning is carefully *programmed* to occur in a specific manner, people can learn without making a large number of errors.	1.a Learning by making a number of errors until the right response is discovered is called: 1.b What is likely to happen to people's desire to learn when they must use the trial and error method? 1.c When the material to be learned is prepared so that the trainee makes few errors, it is said to have been carefully:	Compare your answers with the following: 1.a trial and error learning. 1.b It decreases. 1.c programmed. If your answers closely match those listed above, go on to section 2. If not, re-read section 1, paying close attention to the italicized concepts. Then answer the questions again.
2. Programmed instruction (PI) operates on the principle that if *learning is programmed to occur in small steps*, few errors will occur. Another principle of PI is that if trainees are *given immediate feedback* regarding the appropriateness of their response, they will learn more quickly and complete a greater amount of material.	2.a If the goal is to reduce the number of trainee errors before the material is learned, how should learning be programmed? 2.b To increase the amount learned and the speed of learning, when should feedback be given?	Compare your answers with the following: 2.a In small steps 2.b Immediately If your answers closely match those listed above, go on to section 3. If not, re-read section 2, paying close attention to the italicized concepts. Then answer the questions again.
3. Trainee learning is enhanced if the trainee is active in the learning process. PI asks trainees to *respond to questions putting the trainee in an active learning mode*. Because trainees learn at different rates, *they will learn best if they can move through the material at their own pace*. PI allows people to learn at their own pace. Finally, *frequent review of material helps trainees retain* the material for longer periods of time.	3.a Programming questions into the material enhances learning because it places trainees into a(n)_____ mode of learning. 3.b At what pace should trainees move through the material to be learned? 3.c Frequent review of material results in:	Compare your answers with the following: 3.a active 3.b their own pace 3.c longer retention of the material. If your answers closely match those listed above, go on to section 4. If not, re-read section 3, paying close attention to the italicized concepts. Then answer the questions again.
4. In summary, PI allows trainees to learn more material quicker and retain it longer with less frustration by: a. programming small learning steps resulting in fewer response errors, b. requiring frequent active responses by the trainees, c. providing immediate feedback to trainee responses, d. allowing trainees to move through the material at their own pace, and e. reviewing the material frequently.	4.a What are five principles that PI uses to improve the ease, amount, speed, and retention of learning? 4.b PI increases the trainees' desire to learn by reducing the number of _____the trainee is likely to make.	Compare your answers with the following: 4.a i. Small learning steps ii. Frequent and active response by the trainee iii. Immediate feedback iv. Self-paced learning v. Frequent review 4.b response errors If your answers closely match those listed above, you have successfully completed the section on PI. If not, review section 4 again.

example of the PI approach. Working sequentially through the questions shows how this method works and what principles of learning it uses.

In its most sophisticated form, PI consists of a set of branches that might be activated depending on the answer provided to a question. If the trainee provides a correct answer, one branch moves the trainee forward to new information. If the answer is incorrect, a different branch is activated, taking the trainee back to review relevant information in more detail. This format allows trainees to move through the material as rapidly as they are able to. Trainees who show a better grasp of the material (on the basis of their responses) move rapidly through the material. The branches taken by those for whom the material is more difficult are different and will depend on the types of errors they make.

CBT applies PI techniques within a computerized format to create the learning experience. However, PI can also come in book, interactive video, or other formats. We will focus on the computerized application, but keep in mind that the principles are the same regardless of format.

How to Use PI Effectively

Development of PI is a difficult and expensive process and might not justify the cost and effort needed. However, when a large number of people require training, especially if they are geographically dispersed, it can be a viable option. Once developed, PI can be transferred to whatever medium is appropriate for the training (CD-ROM, DVD, or Web site). Trainees are then able to complete the training at their own pace, on their own time (if desirable), and from different locations around the world. PI can automate the less interactive components of training.[11] In a blended approach, you can use PI to provide the required knowledge base and then use classroom and on-the-job training for the hands-on practice. PI can be used to teach some skills (e.g., computer) in addition to knowledge. PI can be a stand-alone type of training, or it can be integrated into a multimethod training program.

Intelligent Tutoring Systems

An **intelligent tutoring system (ITS)** is a more sophisticated form of PI. It uses artificial intelligence to assist in tutoring or coaching the trainee. An ITS provides guidance and selects the appropriate level of instruction for the trainee. In addition, an ITS can learn from its own process what worked and what did not in the training process. On the basis of this information, the ITS improves its methods of teaching the trainee. Intelligent tutoring can be a text-based system or a combination of text with graphics and other types of audiovisual (AV) aids.

ITS has five components: an expert knowledge base, a trainee model, a training session manager, a scenario generator, and a user interface.[12] The **expert knowledge base** is the set of knowledge about what is correct (e.g., the best way to perform a task, or the knowledge needed to be effective). This corresponds to the "knowledge base" triangle in Figure 7-1. The **trainee model** component stores information about the trainees' performance during training, keeping track of what they seem to know. As the trainees respond to items, the information is used to tutor or coach them. The **training session manager** is the component that interprets the trainees' responses and responds either with more information, coaching (helping the trainee explore the topic), or tutoring (guiding the trainee toward the correct answer). This component also determines how and when to send the trainee back to more basic material and what strategy to use in the remedial work. For example, the session manager may act simply as a reference source (providing sources for the trainee to look up needed information), it might decide to provide a demonstration, or it might tutor or coach (suggesting an appropriate response) the trainee.[13] The **training scenario generator** is the component that determines the order and level of difficulty of the problems that are presented to the trainee. The **user interface** is the equipment that allows the trainee to interact with the ITS. It commonly includes a computer keyboard, mouse, or joystick.

ITS sets itself apart from simple PI because it can do the following:[14]

- Generate instruction that matches the individual trainee's needs
- Communicate and respond to trainee questions

Figure 7-2
Student Modeling
Example

Student A	22 + 39 51	46 + 39 75
Student B	22 + 39 161	46 + 39 185
Student C	22 + 39 62	46 + 39 83

- Model the trainee's learning processes (assess current level of knowledge and identify misconceptions, learning problems, and needs)
- Determine what information should follow based on previous trainee responses
- Determine the trainee's level of understanding of the topic
- Improve its strategies for teaching the trainee on the basis of the trainee's responses

An examination of Figure 7-2 illustrates how trainee responses allow the system to interpret the response and provide the trainee with specific training to address the problem.[15] Note that the three trainees depicted in Figure 7-2 all provided the wrong answer to the addition questions, but each made different errors. The intelligent tutor determines that trainee A never carries over, trainee B carries over but sometimes inappropriately, and trainee C has trouble with simple single-digit addition. The tutor will then provide a different type of instruction to each of the trainees on the basis of the diagnosis of the errors. This process continues, with the tutor constantly reevaluating and providing new instruction until the learning objectives are achieved.

Advances in ITS continue. Presently, there is work being done to have the intelligent tutor identify when the trainee is bored, confused, or frustrated and to have the system respond accordingly.[16] At North Carolina State University, scientists are working to have ITS determine a trainee's self-efficacy.* Enabling ITS to determine a trainee's self-efficacy could lead to improved pedagogy.[17]

How to Use ITS Effectively

ITS is even more expensive to develop than PI. It requires specific expertise not likely found in the organization. With electronic training technology changing so fast, however, it is difficult to make recommendations that will hold even a short time into the future. ITS is definitely worth considering, given the enormous advantages over simple PI. Numerous vendors offer relevant PI and ITS training that is available for purchase. Whether to buy off the shelf or to develop one will depend on a cost/benefit analysis.

Interactive Multimedia Training

Interactive multimedia training (IM) integrates the use of text, video, graphics, photos, animation, and sound to produce a complex training environment with which the trainee interacts. Typically, PI methodology is applied to learning chunks that are converted into a multimedia format to facilitate learning. For example, the trainee is put into a real-life job situation and asked to solve a specific problem. Once the trainee

---

*Recall, trainees with high self-efficacy learn differently from those with low self-efficacy.

interacts with the program to solve the problem, he can receive immediate feedback as to the effectiveness of his decision.[18] Typically, trainees become very engaged in this type of learning because they are immersed psychologically into the situation.

The development of CD, DVD, and networking technology has allowed IM to grow rapidly over the last few years. In the early 1990s, few firms used this technology for training. About 45 percent of those responding to a 2008 training survey indicated that they used IM as a training tool.[19]

Examples of IM Usage

IM training systems can provide training related to almost any training objective. The training can be as simple as providing some basic knowledge or as complex as teaching how to diagnose heart disorders or improve communication skills. Companies across many industries are using this technology for training in widely differing content areas. Below are some examples of the types of training for which IM is used.

Nugget Brand Distributors developed a certificate in food safety training, which it markets to restaurants.[20] Jackson Hewitt Tax Service, with its huge number of part-time workers (in the tax season), needed a way to bring employees up to speed regarding tax changes. CD-ROM technology allowed them to distribute the information more easily and cheaply than did printed material. It provides training just when the new employee needs it, and a trainer does not have to be there.[21] Training in Action 7-2 describes the success of Aeronett, a company that specializes in the development of IM training for the airline industry.

IM technology is also used to provide medical training.[22] This training, delivered via the Internet, allows a medical student to take the medical history of a hypothetical

TRAINING IN ACTION 7-2
Aeronett Corners Airline Training

Aeronett Technologies Limited is in the business of developing courseware for a new generation of aviation training. Development of courseware comes from their team of subject matter experts, instructional designers, graphic designers, 3D animators, multimedia programmers, and sound engineers. Air Canada, Pan Am International Flight Academy, Jetway Aeronautics, and Star Airlines have selected Aeronett's CBT for their employees.

Training packages can be delivered over the Internet. They include initial pilot training and transitional and recurrent ground school training. Other CBT training packages for pilots include flying dangerous goods, cold weather/winter operations, Pacific operations, and minimum equipment. But Web-based training has been developed for more than just pilots. Aeronett has developed training for maintenance personnel and flight and cabin crews. Pan Am International Flight Academy's (PAIFA) Gary LaGuardia indicates that Aeronett's course will enable PAIFA to offer state-of-

the-art training "that is specifically designed to meet the needs of our commercial airline clients who come to our training from around the world." Air Canada selected Aeronett because its integration of 3D simulation, 2D digital images, and interactivity provides a realistic portrayal of the flight deck. The courses motivate the learner, improve retention of new information, and allow for effective transfer of knowledge, skills, and attitudes to aircraft operation.

As a result of their advances in CBT, Aeronett was named the 2001 Leading Edge Training Innovator by the Aerospace Industry Association of British Columbia. Training times have dropped 50 percent to 70 percent from previous methods. Their technology-based training programs have lowered costs associated with travel and time spent in training centers. Because the system provides learners with the ability to study anytime and anywhere, trainees are enjoying the flexibility this training provides.

Source: This case was developed from information contained in the Aeronett Web site: http://www.aeronett.com

patient, conduct an examination, and run laboratory tests. For example, as part of the examination, the medical student may choose to examine the patient's chest. The student clicks the "examine chest" button and is then asked to choose a type of examination to conduct (visual inspection, palpation, or auscultation). The trainee might click on "auscultate" (listen to sounds made by the lungs) and hear the chest sounds that would be made by a particular patient. On the basis of the interpretation of the sounds, the trainee would make a diagnosis and click the button that represented a diagnosis. The trainee would then be informed of the accuracy of the diagnosis. If the diagnosis were incorrect, the trainee would be given an explanation and moved to supplementary materials designed to provide the knowledge needed to make a correct diagnosis. The previous examples show how useful IM can be in developing knowledge, psychomotor, and decision-making skills. What about improving interpersonal skills? Training in Action 7-3 describes a training program developed by Marriott International to develop their employees' interpersonal skills. Another application, Virtual Leader, was developed by SimuLearn, Inc. It utilizes artificial intelligence (fuzzy logic) to render graphics and dialogue dynamically to give the user a simulated real-life environment for learning and practicing persuasive leadership skills. In this example of high-end IM, the system can simulate realistic situations, interpret trainee responses within the logic of the leadership model, and show how trainee interactions will

TRAINING IN ACTION 7-3
Marriott International Uses Multimedia Training for Soft Skills

Marriott International, a widely recognized name in the lodging industry, is noted for their people-oriented high-touch culture, so their strategic plan indicating a commitment to growing from 900 properties to 2,000 in only a few years raised a concern regarding their ability to train such large numbers of new employees. Analysis indicated that in the next five years, Marriott would be hiring about a million employees, and all would need training.

A training transformation team was struck to study the problem and find a solution. The solution that made the most sense was a set of multimedia training packages that use CD-ROM technology and operate from a traditional personal computer. One of these, Front Desk Quest, provides soft-skills training. To begin the training, the trainee logs on with an ID and a password. An on-screen person greets the trainee, walks her through the training, and is always available for help (by pressing the Help button). The trainee is presented with a series of different training modules, the culmination of which is a simulation in which the trainee plays an active role in combining the skills and knowledge learned earlier. In the simulation, trainees are presented with a situation in which

they are required to determine, from a set of choices, what is the correct thing to say or do. They then click on what they believe to be the correct response, and the computer program responds by playing out the scenario to show the student what happens if they make a correct or incorrect decision. If the trainee was correct, she sees the customer on the screen saying something positive. If the choice was not correct, the video might show an angry customer responding. The trainee can make alternative responses and see the customer reaction.

Trainees can sign on to the training at any time and start up where they left off in the previous session. They can go over previous exercises as often as they want and can track their progress. Management can also sign on and note the progress of employees.

Do employees like the new training format? Reactions are consistently positive, so the answer must be yes. Even those with minimal skill in the use of a computer find it easy to use and are going full speed in only a few minutes. As Starr Shafer, a manager at Marriott, says, "They immediately give better service with greater self-assurance. And they say, 'Wow, I felt so comfortable doing it.'"

Sources: Stauffer, D. High-tech training a huge win in Marriott's high-touch culture (1999). Available at http://www.traininguniversity.com
Jensen, E. Personal communication (January 31, 2002).

influence employees to behave. The simulation's intent is to teach people to monitor and appropriately balance power, tension, and ideas to align the work of employees with business goals (financial performance, customer satisfaction, and employee morale). The authors received training in the use of the simulation and found it to be challenging and engaging. As with any off-the-shelf training product, the trainer will need to carefully evaluate the product's fit with the firm's training objectives.

How to Use IM Effectively

As always, the effectiveness of the program will depend on how closely it meets the learning objectives. With IM, trainees are likely to enjoy their experience and give the training high marks because it is so much fun, even if many of the training objectives are not met. Thus, it is especially important to verify the match between the IM program's outcomes and the training objectives. Although this sounds logical and straightforward, our discussion a few years ago with Nina Adams, president of Adams I Solutions (a firm that designs IM training), suggests that it is often not the case. She told us

> If I had one message to give people considering the use of IM training, it is this: Understand the goals of the program you're going to develop before you do anything else. I recently worked on a project where the client was converting a live presentation to multimedia. The major problem was pulling out of the client what they wanted to accomplish . . . what they wanted people who went through the training program to think, do, or feel. It's amazing how many people develop a program without knowing what they're trying to accomplish. How do you know the program is "successful" if you don't know what you're trying to do?

To be most effective, your IM should accommodate multiple learning styles and make it easy for trainees to organize the new KSAs into their existing knowledge base (cognitive organization). Any target group of trainees is likely to have a variety of learning styles and cognitive organization systems. Thus, it is necessary to ensure that the IM uses a variety of audio and visual cues to communicate the information and the many ways of connecting new KSAs to old. Attention to self-pacing, interactivity, and the sophistication of the multimedia will address these issues and improve its effectiveness.[23]

Self-pacing allows trainees to learn on the basis of what they already know. It is important that the self-pacing be designed to accommodate multiple ways of organizing and using information (cognitive organization). The better your design is in this area, the better the learning that will be realized by your trainees. Interactivity is the program's ability to allow trainees to respond to situations and to receive feedback. The more interactive the CBT, the more the trainees will retain the training. It is important to make sure that the CBT has a sufficient level of interactivity for trainees to retain the learning. The sophistication of the multimedia, in this context, refers to audio/visual integration and realism of the program. The more ways the same information is communicated, the easier it will be for trainees to learn it. At the same time, the various ways of presenting the information must be connected realistically and reinforce each other. A good IM program should rate high on all three factors. Table 7-3 provides points to consider when evaluating IM training.

The degree to which the IM training will result in the transfer of new KSAs back to the job will depend on the physical and psychological fidelity that the programming creates. This fidelity can be accomplished by having the program developers visit the operational areas that will be involved in the training and by having a representative from these areas consult with the development team. The more closely the IM program reflects the kinds of situations faced on the job, the more the KSAs will transfer back to the job.

It is a good idea to consider blending IM with other methods. This blending allows each method to provide unique learning opportunities while reinforcing learning from

Table 7-3
Points to Consider in Development of Interactive Multimedia

FACTOR	HIGH IF	LOW IF
Self-pacing	• The pace of the program is entirely controlled by the learner.	• The only way to control the pace of the presentation is by using a special key.
	• Trainees can select menu options to determine the order of modules.	• It is not menu driven, i.e., the trainee can't select a particular lesson segment or skip segments.
	• Trainees can skip lessons or segments at will and can exit the program from any screen.	• Trainees can exit the program only at certain points.
	• Additional practice and more in-depth material are available on request.	
Interactivity	• Trainees' responses follow instructional segments.	• The program has long, uninterrupted lesson segments that offer no chance for the trainee to ask or answer questions.
	• The program tests skills and judgments, not just facts.	• The program tests recall instead of skills.
	• The orderly sequence of topics is apparent to the learner.	• Segments do not build on one another.
		• The learner's answers are tagged right or wrong with no further explanation.
Multimedia Sophistication	• The voices are distinct and natural.	• The sound or visuals are of poor quality.
	• A voice provides program instructions so that the trainee doesn't have to read them.	• There is no direct connection between the audio and visual material (the sound is limited to irrelevant music, for example).
	• Sound and visuals reinforce one another.	• The sound is restricted to a voice saying, "You are correct" or "Try again."
	• Visuals use color and motion to reinforce the audio message and illustrate the idea presented.	• The visuals don't reinforce instructional points.

Source: Anonymous. "Put SPIMM in your CBT." *Training* (February 1993), pp. 12, 14.

other methods. Blending has been shown to improve the transfer of the training to the job.[24] Instructor-guided discussion will generally be helpful as a supplement to IM. One thing that was evident after going through the SimuLearn leadership training was the energy it creates for discussing the experience. Some of our conversation focused on the balance of realism and artificiality, some on the relation of the leadership model to other models in the literature, and some on our rationale for our personal scores. All of these topics, guided appropriately by a trainer, can provide valuable insight to the trainees. Other advantages to blending guided discussion with IM include the following:

• The trainer's enthusiasm for the training content encourages learning.
• The trainer provides assessment and accountability that is missing in IM alone.
• Trainees' questions and comments raise issues not addressed in the IM programming.
• Trainees acquire a deeper understanding through social interaction.

Although significant learning can occur without it, guided discussion can lead to additional learning and greater understanding. Another approach is to supplement the IM with manuals and other material. This was Duracell's approach, as described

Duracell needed to develop a training program to support its battery manufacturing plant in China. The program had to provide a training process that was highly visual. The program that was developed relied heavily on graphics, animation, digitized photos, video, and Chinese text. These components were integrated into a multimedia presentation that was supplemented with "hard copy" materials. These included manuals that trainees could take with them to use as a reference and printed job aids to assist in the recall of the more complex manufacturing processes. Most importantly, the multimedia program was followed by "hands-on" practice sessions. It was felt that these backup methods were necessary to aid the trainee in retention and transfer.

The training was comprehensive. It included health and safety, operations, quality, and causal analysis. The goal was to create a standardized training process that would promote a safe work environment and help the workforce become as productive as possible, as quickly as possible. Employees were excited about the program, and a crowd immediately formed around the workstations of the first employees to use the program. Employees were anxious to be next in line to get their personalized training session. As motivation is a critical component of successful training, this program was off to a positive start.

Source: Marquardt, M. *Technology-Based Learning: Maximizing Human Performance and Corporate Success* (1999). Boca Raton, FL: CRC Press.

in Training in Action 7-4. This method also seems to increase learning beyond what was gained in the IM training.

Virtual Reality

Virtual reality (VR) training is the next best thing to being there. It allows training for dangerous situations (police car chases, hostage situations) and situations for which using the real thing is very expensive (flying, operating heavy equipment). VR puts the trainee in an artificial three-dimensional environment that simulates events and situations that might be experienced on the job. The trainee interacts with these images to accomplish specific goals. In these respects, VR is not much different from the more advanced forms of IM. The difference is in how the trainee experiences the simulation. In VR, the trainee experiences a physical involvement with and a presence in the simulated environment.[25] That is, the trainee psychologically experiences the environment as real. To experience a computerized VR, the trainee must wear devices that provide sensory input. Such devices include a headset that provides visual and audio information, gloves that give tactile information, and treadmills or other types of motion platforms for creating the sense of movement. Some can even supply olfactory information.

Many advanced forms of IM use artificial intelligence to portray situations more realistically and manage interactions with the trainee. They do not, however, reach the level of creating a sense of physical presence. The creators of these advanced IM programs wish to distinguish themselves from the less advanced IM training, and they have taken to referring incorrectly to their products as VR. So when reading about VR in trade journals, be aware that much of what is called VR is in reality IM. For some good reasons that are discussed later, few actual VR training systems exist.

VR provides trainees with an understanding of the consequences of their actions in the work environment by interpreting and responding to the trainees' actions in the simulation. Sensory devices transmit to the computer how the trainee is responding in the virtual workplace, allowing the VR program to respond by changing the environment accordingly. For example, a police academy trainee sitting in a simulated

Taking a molten bar of steel and placing it in a stamping die correctly, quickly, and most important safely is critical to running an effective forging plant. Vulcan Forge, realizing this, was on the lookout for less harsh methods of training employees in the use of their stamping machines. The on-the-job training was dangerous and inefficient, in terms of use of the machinery and waste.

That is where virtual reality (VR) came in. The trainee dons the glasses and other peripherals, and he appears to be in the plant with the stamping machine and all the other environmental factors present. He picks up the molten steel bar and places it under the hammer. The hammer comes down hard stamping the steel, he picks it up and rolls it to the next mold, and again the hammer comes down hard. He drops the newly stamped part into the bin and gets another molten steel bar to complete the task again. When he takes off the glasses, he is back in the training room. This VR training is safe and results in no waste. But is it realistic? According to trainees, the weight of the molten bar is very similar, as is the hammer weight coming down on the bar. Trainees suggest that it is very close to the real thing. Furthermore, the trainees like the idea of learning in a safe environment, where mistakes are much more forgiving.

But what about the effectiveness of VR training? A one-day evaluation of employees trained using VR and those who were trained on the job determined that those trained using VR were 10 to 20 percent more productive than those who were trained on the job.

Source: Ohio Supercomputer Center, Columbus, Ohio (2008). http://www.osc.edu/research/video_library/ford.shtml

driver's seat of a police car can see the speedometer and all the gauges on the dashboard; looking to the right, the trainee sees an empty seat; when the trainee turns the steering wheel, the view through the windshield provides a visual representation of the car turning along a corner. VR has been used to train police officers how to stop a speeding car safely, without the danger of using real people and automobiles. To date, VR has been used for training complex and dangerous skills, such as flying outside the earth's atmosphere,[26] and more traditional skills, such as teaching someone to speak in front of large audiences.[27] More recently, it has been expanded to organizational training such as the one in Training in Action 7-5.

Using VR Effectively

The points raised for effective use of IM apply even more strongly to VR. A concern unique to VR training, "simulator sickness," has limited the growth of VR. Prolonged immersion in the VR environment has caused some people to experience vertigo and general motion sickness. Because people show different tolerances in terms of how long they can last in such an environment, and because of the cost and long lead time, VR training is a risk not many companies are willing to take. For the most part, VR remains in the entertainment industry.[28] If it is being used, a number of organizations are available to provide assistance, but you should expect a long development period and possible problems when trainees are using it. It is necessary to do extensive pilot testing, as the complexity of this type of programming leads to bugs in the program that are not readily apparent.[29]

As with all these technologies, change is the one constant. For example, VirtuSphere, Inc., has developed a system that consists of a large hollow sphere that sits on top of a base, which allows the sphere to rotate 360 degrees. The trainee wears wireless goggles. When inside the sphere, the trainee can move in any direction, walk, jump, roll, crawl, and run over virtually unlimited distances without hitting a wall.[30] Another breakthrough at the University of Pennsylvania has a VR system that does not require those bulky, sometimes vertigo-producing, glasses.[31]

Strengths and Limitations of CBT Methods

Costs

Arguments are made both supporting and criticizing the cost effectiveness of CBT. The costs of developing and implementing a CBT program are related to the following factors:

- Number of trainees taking the course per year
- Cost of wages per hour for trainees while they are taking the course
- Cost of wages per hour for course developer
- Amortized cost of hardware to support the CBT
- Amortized cost of software used in the CBT
- Hours needed to complete the CBT program
- Hours needed to develop CBT course content
- Stability of the course content
- Cost of not addressing the training need sooner with some other method

The development cost of CBT is not usually justified for a small number of trainees. On average, an hour of CBT instruction is reported to require about 220 hours of development time.[32] This of course is not for complex multimedia and VR development. This can be much higher and has been estimated as high as 1300 hours per 1 hour of instruction.[33] But as with all technology, there have been advances, and some rapid development tools have made it easier and faster to create CBT training. Compared with the 220 hours required for 1 hour of less complex CBT, some rapid-development tools can do a similar job in 33 hours—a substantial savings.[34] So, CBT is definitely becoming more affordable.

An ITS consists of a shell that houses an LMS and a knowledge base. The LMS is the engine that delivers the knowledge to the trainee. The knowledge base is the information that needs to be learned. Development of the LMS is fairly expensive, but the development of the knowledge base is less so.[35] Using the same shell, a knowledge base that is used for one application (training a salesperson to sell an automobile) can be quickly and easily changed to fit another application (training the HR manager to explain why a grievance cannot be allowed).[36] Thus the shell engine, once developed, can be used across many training programs. Many e-learning companies have developed very sophisticated shell engines that they lease or license. Many companies acquire access to a shell engine and develop the knowledge base in-house to keep the cost of ITS and IM down.

Multimedia training is also initially costly to develop but is easy to deliver and convenient to use. CDs or DVDs are inexpensive to reproduce and distribute to trainees across geographically dispersed locations. If the topic to be trained is generic, various programs are available at a reasonable cost. Consider the health and safety training programs offered by Comprehensive Loss Management of Minneapolis, presented in Table 7-4. They offer a number of reasonably priced canned CD-ROM training programs in safety. Likewise, companies can share in the development costs for common types of training, as was the case with LearnShare (see Training in Action 7-6). Its charter members can access more than 500,000 online development courses.[37] This concept is a great idea for small companies to consider in the pursuit of all types of training, but particularly the more expensive types of CBT.

Unless there is access in the organization to a technology unit with specific skills related to the development of IM, it will probably be more cost-effective to use outside vendors. The more sophisticated and complex the material, the more likely it is that it will be necessary to contract with an outside provider. Although many generic "off-the-shelf" programs can be useful, many vendors will customize the content to fit the objectives of the company. In addition to the organizations discussed

Table 7-4
Some Health and
Safety Training
Using CD-ROM
Technology

Accident Investigation

Prevents costly accidents from recurring by investigating to find causes and implementing steps to prevent them.

Length of video 12 minutes. Price $449

Office Ergonomics

Helps workers understand injuries caused by repetitive motion and how to prevent them.

Length of video 17 minutes. Price $319

Blood-Borne Pathogens

Helps workers understand the cause of hepatitis B and HIV, the virus that causes AIDS. This course uses 30 interactions to teach workers what blood-borne pathogens are and the precautions to take to prevent being infected.

Length of video 13 minutes. Price $449

Confined Space Entry

This training teaches workers concepts essential for a safe work environment when in a confined space. Twenty-nine interactive activities assess the level of understanding of the key learning objectives and let trainees apply what they learned in a safe environment.

Length of video 17 minutes. Price $449

Note: All videos come with administrative materials, trainee handbooks, etc.

Source: Information available at http://www.clmi-training.com

TRAINING IN ACTION 7-6
The High Cost of Multimedia Training

A software developer was extolling the virtues of multimedia training. "It will alter the learning landscape for the next millennium," he said to 200 training executives at a Boston conference. Rick Corry, newly appointed training executive from Owens Corning, listened with mild annoyance. He recently had been told by one of these people that they would develop a nice CD-ROM training program for Corning for $150,000. The software developer went on to say that Corry's division would not be able to share the program with other business units in Owens Corning. In fact, the corporation would not even own the copyright on the program for two years, during which time the developer could sell it to anyone else who was interested.

When the speaker asked if there were any questions, Corry looked at all the others in the audience and said, "I'm just wondering, why don't we get together and share what we have and fund what we need? After all, most companies have similar training needs in a number of areas: basic sales skills, time management, leadership skills, and interpersonal skills." The room went silent. The speaker did not say a word. As the session ended, Corry was surrounded

by training executives, and he collected 27 business cards from people who wanted to explore the idea. From that encounter came a consortium of nine large non-competing manufacturing companies; it is called LearnShare. One of its goals is to develop partnerships with vendors of multimedia training, "but in a manner that is as good for us as it is for them," said Corry. With the consortium's combined revenues of more than $100 billion and 2.2 million employees, they are likely to carry some real clout with vendors.

One of LearnShare's first objectives was to determine similarities in the training needs across the different companies. LearnShare conducted a survey in all nine companies of the training material that was not related to processes or products. The result: 74 percent of the training was addressing the same needs. In other words, diversity training is diversity training, no matter where it is taught.

The companies are already sharing non-multimedia training information and programs. Furthermore, they are sharing training space. Motorola, for example, allows managers at Owens Corning who are stationed in the Pacific Rim to sit in on some training Motorola is conducting in its facility there.

Source: Blumfield, M. "Learning to share." *Training* 34 (1997), pp. 38–42.

previously, Michelin, IBM, Motorola, Volvo Heavy Truck, and Duracell use IM training. Applications range from the start-up and shutdown of a production line to verbal interaction skills.[38] Some of these programs are developed in-house, and others are purchased.

A VR unit can cost as little as $20,000, and even with the cost of designing, the training could make the total cost reasonable compared with something like an equipment simulator.[39] Keep in mind that the time to build a VR program can be eight months or longer. The potential health risks will also need to be weighed when using VR.

Although all CBT technologies generally involve more expensive start-up costs than does classroom training, they offer a major advantage: CBT delivery systems make it possible to eliminate many of the costs incurred with other methods, such as trainers, facilities, and trainee travel and lodging.

Research shows that CBT reduces training time and, in most cases, travel and lodging costs related to training. Several studies examining various types of CBT (programmed instruction and multimedia) indicate that CBT learning takes less time.[40] In a more recent study, Air Force trainees were taught troubleshooting of the hydraulic subsystems of F-15 aircraft using ITS and CBT-programmed instruction. Evaluation of the two teaching methods indicated that the ITS trained group not only learned the material in less time, they also learned more.[41]

As mentioned earlier, there is typically a significant lag time between the point at which a training need is identified and completion of a relevant CBT program. The cost of not immediately addressing the training need through some other method must be factored into the cost of developing the CBT.

Control of Material and Process

CBT software determines the content and process of the training. Perhaps the most important advantage of CBT is its control over the content of the material, method of presentation, and movement of the trainee through sequentially structured learning episodes based on previous trainee responses.[42] The pace of learning is controlled by the interaction between the software and the trainee.

The above features are both strengths and weaknesses of various CBT compared with instructor-based training. The advantages are that CBT ensures consistency of topic coverage and topic mastery across all trainees. Sometimes, however, learning opportunities are lost if trainees cannot diverge from prescribed topic areas to clarify understanding. A live trainer can identify when such divergence is necessary. CBT programs have tried to address this issue by providing instant messaging and other communication tools that allow trainees to communicate with one another and a live trainer. Of course, this adds to the cost of training. Pilot testing of the CBT can attempt to identify these issues ahead of time and incorporate appropriate segments to deal with them.

CBT has the advantage of being portable, allowing the trainee to learn at times and places that are most convenient and to control the pace of learning. Trainees can start and stop training whenever they wish. Unfortunately, we could not find any studies that looked at the effects of such interrupted learning. Frequent interruptions in the learning process might lead to increased time to learn the material, as trainees must go back and review previously covered material to catch up to where they left off when the training was stopped. In Chapter 5, we cited research showing that whole rather than part learning is more effective when the task to be learned is highly organized but not complex. Spaced practice of the learning is more effective than when done all at once. It is important then for CBT to provide guidance to the trainees about when and when not to interrupt their learning.

Most CBT programs lack control over who is actually taking the training. A few years ago, a professor of an introductory MBA accounting course decided to use an online learning program to teach basic accounting principles. Each student got a personal password to sign on to the system. Students could complete lessons at their convenience, as long as they completed the 10 modules within a three-week period. The modules were linked so that the students were required to complete module 1 before they could begin module 2, and so on. According to the records generated by the program, everyone completed all the modules by the end of the third week. At this point, the professor began his lectures and discussions about contemporary accounting practices. It soon became clear that many of the students did not understand the basic principles covered in the CBT. Further investigation revealed that several students had recruited others to use their password and complete their CBT modules. The professor abandoned the CBT approach the following year.

This could also happen when training is mandated (e.g., safety, sexual harassment) and the trainees are not particularly motivated to complete it or when there are no rewards for actually using the KSAs on the job. For example, employees in "pay for knowledge" systems have been known to divide the training among the members of the group so that one or two people complete the training for all the other members. When it is important to ensure that the target population is completing the training, it is necessary to develop appropriate control mechanisms for the CBT.

Learning Objectives (KSAs)

CBT is a useful method for enhancing trainees' knowledge base. It can do so through repeated presentation of facts in several different formats and presentation styles. It can do an excellent job of describing when and how to apply the knowledge to situations relevant to the training objectives. CBT can document the appropriateness of the trainee's application and provide additional practice modules to improve areas of weakness.

Skill development is also possible with CBT when task simulations are highly consistent with the actual job. For example, CBT software training employees in the use of word processing, spreadsheet, and other computer-based programs can easily replicate situations they will face when back on the job. Evidence exists that even more complex skills that require the use of natural language (e.g., interpersonal or conflict resolution skills) or psychomotor development (driving a forklift) can be developed through IM and VR, though not to the level of mastery. Recall the Marriott hotel chain in Training in Action 7-3. Although Eric Jensen, director at Marriott headquarters, was initially hesitant about the ability of multimedia to train soft skills, he changed his mind. The Marriott soft skills focus on improving the interaction between two or more people. Developing these skills requires trainees to engage in the interaction and receive immediate feedback about their performance. It is extremely difficult for computers to simulate these situations in a fully realistic manner. That is why we recommend a blended approach combining CBT with instructor-led training that allows the trainee to practice with the feedback and guidance of an expert. As Eric Jensen noted regarding the training at Marriott, "There is no 'intelligent tutoring' in terms of the system 'knowing' what kind of tutoring an individual needs. The program simply branches in certain areas, but the branching is also limited, because of the enormous cost in trying to take many different options into account."[43] Although the interaction is far from perfect, it does provide one-on-one feedback, and learning does occur.

What about training of psychomotor skills? Well, we have the Vulcan Forge Training (Training in Action 7-5) example. Another example is the National Guard. They train members on how to troubleshoot and repair Bradley tanks. In many situations, the tanks are not available; having members train in an IM-simulated environment is less expensive and still effective. Of course, the Aeronett example (see Training in Action 7-2) also demonstrated that CBT can improve psychomotor and decision-making skills for pilots, flight crew, and aircraft maintenance personnel.

What do all these examples mean? CBT can be a useful tool in developing skills, including more complex skills such as those that can be simulated electronically. However, other methods are required to develop those skills to higher levels. For instance, unless a VR program is highly sophisticated, it will not be able to observe the person and provide feedback on such things as standing too close when talking to someone or not maintaining good eye contact.

Attitudes and motivation can be positively or negatively influenced through CBT by showing connections among objects, events, and outcomes. The opportunity to experience or interact personally with the objects and events, however, is limited by the CBT's ability to simulate reality. As a result, the emotional or affective side of attitudes might not be strongly activated. This might partially explain why most adult learners prefer CBT when it is blended with some form of instructor-based training.[44]

Learning Process

Attention   CBT is generally seen as more interesting and motivating than instructor-based training, such as the lecture. Trainees cite reasons for this, such as feeling less threatened by the machine and having more control over the pace of instruction. In addition, CBT can integrate audio and visual effects that draw the learner's attention to the material. For these reasons, CBT is good at capturing and retaining trainee attention.

Retention—Symbolic Coding   CBT can provide multiple cues that can be used in the symbolic coding process. Textual, auditory, and oral cues can be integrated to allow trainees to use those that fit best with their learning style to code the content of the training. Audiovisuals (AVs) are also effective in facilitating trainees' cognitive organization. The programming of the CBT creates a specific organization of the material, with each learning segment broken down into small steps. This makes it easier to integrate with the trainee's existing cognitive organization. Through the accumulation of these small steps and their repetition, CBT is able to shape the cognitive organization of the trainee in the desired manner. The ease with which the trainee can do this will depend on how closely the organization of the CBT matches the cognitive organization of the trainee. The more self-paced the CBT, the more it facilitates cognitive organization.

Retention—Symbolic Rehearsal   Symbolic rehearsal is a strong feature of the CBT approach, especially IM and VR. The trainees are first moved through mastery of the facts; then they are provided application segments in which to apply the facts to specific situations. For example, suppose trainees were learning to take photographs. The CBT would provide a simulated situation such as the inside of a room with artificial lighting, objects that are closer or farther away, and a description of what should be photographed. The trainees would then indicate the camera settings for taking the picture. The CBT could even provide feedback that shows what would happen in a real situation. Using the photography example, the CBT program could show what kind of photograph would be produced. It allows each trainee to continue to practice while providing immediate feedback, until the trainee masters the simulation. This type of symbolic rehearsal borders on behavioral reproduction and is valuable for retaining the material.

Behavioral Reproduction   CBT is effective at modeling appropriate behavior and providing simulations in which the trainee can apply knowledge. These components facilitate the development of skills but do not provide the opportunities to actually reproduce the desired behavior and receive feedback. For example, CBT can be used to learn a foreign language. The trainee can learn the meaning of words, correct usage, and proper pronunciation, but she will not master the language conversationally until actually interacting with an expert and receiving feedback. Likewise, the photography example is not true behavioral reproduction because the trainee is not using a real camera or a real scene. Pilots do not complete their training until they fly under the guidance of experts. Physicians are not certified to practice medicine until they have trained under the guidance of experts. Blending CBT with some form of on-the-job training will allow trainees to master the more complex skills.

Training Group Characteristics

Typically, only one trainee can use a computer at a time, so the number of computers available limits the number of trainees who can be trained at the same time. However, because training is available virtually all the time, this is usually not much of a problem. If the CBT is online or on a CD, then trainees can take it anywhere they have access to a computer and, in the case of online situations, the Internet.

Because CBT can take into account many differences in trainee readiness, there are few trainee limitations. As with most methods, trainees must be able to read and understand the text and AV components presented. Trainees must also have basic computer skills. If you are considering CBT as a training method, it will be necessary to assess the trainees' reading levels, computer literacy, and attitude toward CBT. Some type of pretraining orientation or preparation program can address these issues. It might also be possible to build the considerations into the design of the CBT program.

Blending CBT and Other Methods

Blending instructional methods allows the benefits of instructor-led training to be incorporated with those of CBT. Advantages of blending are that it can foster learning communities, extend training time, provide follow-up resources, provide access to guest experts, and offer timely mentoring or coaching via either face-to-face or online laboratory and simulation activities.[45] There is substantial evidence that blended learning is more effective than either method alone, for training focused on declarative and procedural knowledge. To attain this advantage, however, the design of the CBT should include a high level of control by the learner. By learner control, we are referring to control of the content, sequencing of training events, and pace of the learning. The trainee should also have an opportunity to practice the material and receive feedback.[46] So, although each type of CBT can stand alone and in some cases be sufficient, you should consider integrating CBT with other methods when possible. For example, training supervisors in active listening skills through an interactive video would provide the trainee with some level of skill. Coupling the video with some instructor-led, active listening role-plays with real people, followed by trainee–instructor discussions of the experience, will lead to a richer learning experience. Remember, all the previously discussed advantages related to guided discussion apply to any training conducted by an instructor. Combining CBT with these other methods, therefore, can only enhance the learning experience.

SUMMARY

Computer-based training (CBT) is delivered to trainees through e-learning systems such as LANs, CDs, DVDs, intranets, and the Internet, as well as iPods and MP3 players. CBT methods integrate the content to be learned (knowledge base) into a training design such as programmed instruction (PI), intelligent tutoring system (ITS), interactive multimedia (IM), or virtual reality (VR). The content and design are transformed into electronic media through the use of authoring and design tools. A learning management system (LMS) is sometimes used to integrate training management functions and learning tools with the training program.

PI is a method of self-paced learning managed by both the trainee and the program software. Although typically delivered electronically, this training can also be delivered via print, multimedia, or other formats. ITS utilizes PI and artificial intelligence to diagnose and deliver the kind of training the trainee needs. IM training integrates the use of text, video, graphics, photos, animation, and sound to produce a complex training environment with which the trainee interacts. Typically, PI or ITS methodology is applied to learning chunks that are converted into a multimedia format to facilitate learning. VR puts the trainee in an artificial three-dimensional environment that simulates events and situations that might be experienced on the job. The trainee experiences a physical involvement with and a presence in the simulated environment. To experience a computerized VR, you must wear devices that provide sensory input. This method is relatively new and has not caught on as rapidly as some had predicted. This method also raises some health concerns.

CBT can provide training to more employees, in more locations, and at a lower cost than other training methods. However, development costs for CBT are typically higher than for other methods, so a careful cost/benefit analysis is necessary to determine whether a CBT method is appropriate. The more sophisticated the CBT, the higher the development costs and the longer the time it will take to develop the training. CBT maintains very good control of the learning process. In most cases, this is an advantage, but it can become a disadvantage when the software does not allow needed clarification or discussion that addresses trainee concerns. Because CBT can take into account many differences in trainee readiness, there are few trainee characteristics that would limit its use. CBT can do an excellent job of activating the learning processes of attention, symbolic coding, cognitive organization, and symbolic rehearsal, making it a good method for addressing knowledge and attitude training objectives. It does a fairly good job of developing skills up to, but not including, the mastery level. It is recommended that, where possible, CBT be blended with other training methods to maximize learning.

CASE: Evolution of Training at Mr. Lube (Conclusion)

Senior VP Bill Tickner had decided that his paper-based training system was not an effective tool for ensuring that the geographically dispersed workforce had the competencies required by Mr. Lube. After investigating many alternatives, Mr. Tickner found his solution in partnering with the e-learning company, Acerra Learning, Inc., and Q9, a provider of outsourced Internet infrastructure and managed hosting services. Mr. Lube now conducts its training over the Internet, using a learning management system (LMS) developed by Acerra. Mr. Tickner says he is sure that the system is working because employees are completing oil changes and safety checks more quickly now that they are being coached with an LMS. For Mr. Lube, e-learning presents a compelling business proposition. It provides training on a just-in-time basis to employees anywhere in the world. It allows on-the-job training and self-paced learning. For Mr. Lube, an important component is that the LMS can monitor the progress of each employee and administer and score online tests to ensure that each employee has the required competencies. Mr. Lube blends computer-based

(continued)

training with worksite mentors assigned to the trainees. The LMS data are complemented by online progress reports from these worksite mentors.

Mr. Lube plans to eventually integrate its LMS with other corporate information systems such as payroll and human resources. Mr. Tickner sees an advantage to having all employee information stored in one place. This would allow the mining of these data to improve systems and make better decisions. For example, he believes that such a system would allow Mr. Lube to get a better understanding of how new recruits respond to the training programs.

Sources: This case is based on information contained in the following Web sites: www.globeandmail.com/servlet/story/RTGAM.20030710

welearn.0710BNStory/Technology/; www.mrlube.ca www.newswire.ca/en/releases/archive/july2002/

KEY TERMS

- Computer-based training (CBT)
- Delivery system
- E-learning
- Expert knowledge base
- Intelligent tutoring systems (ITS)
- Interactive multimedia training
- Intranet

- Knowledge base
- Learning management system (LMS)
- Local area network (LAN)
- Performance Management Systems (PMS)
- Programmed instruction (PI)

- Self-paced learning
- Trainee model
- Training scenario generator
- Training session manager
- User interface
- Virtual reality (VR) training

QUESTIONS FOR REVIEW

1. How is CBT different from e-learning?
2. What are the basic components of CBT and its delivery?
3. How does programmed instruction allow the trainee to work at his or her own pace?
4. How does ITS differ from programmed instruction?
5. What learning processes are most influenced by interactive multimedia? Which are influenced the least?
6. What is the most expensive part of developing a CBT?
7. What are the factors associated with calculating the cost of CBT?
8. How effective is CBT in maintaining control over learning processes and training content? Provide your rationale.
9. What is the purpose of an LMS?
10. How are ITS and LMS related to each other?

EXERCISES

1. Your instructor will assign you (or your group) to one of the CBT methods from the chapter. Conduct an Internet search to find a company in your area that uses the method. Contact the HRD department, and indicate that you are learning about training and would like to know how they use the method in their training

programs. Schedule an interview with your contact person, meet with that person, and find out the following information:

a. How long has he or she been using this method?
b. Approximately how many people get training with this method each year? What are the advantages of using this over other methods?
c. What are the disadvantages of using this over other methods?
d. Does he or she blend this type of training with other methods? If so, why?
e. Does he or she have any evidence of whether trainees are responding positively or negatively to the method?
f. How is the method delivered to the trainees (e.g., LAN, Internet)?

WEB RESEARCH

Conduct an Internet search to identify two companies that provide some type of CBT service (e.g., develop training, learning management, training delivery, etc.). For each service that is provided, identify where it fits in Figure 7-1.

CASE ANALYSIS

Science and Technology, Inc. (STI) is a high-tech consulting firm. The core business is helping firms and individual scientists transfer basic scientific discoveries into practical applications. Their 40 consultants provide consulting and training services for developing strategies and implementation processes for the commercialization of new technologies. These employees are grouped into teams that operate from offices in different cities, from coast to coast. These teams are frequently on the road, and individual employees often work from home.

In addition to its work with private companies and individual scientists, STI recently was awarded a grant by the government to provide training to 150 small-business owners awarded governmental grants to pursue the development of businesses based on new technology. Each of these business owners has a different set of circumstances that must be addressed in making the business a success. Also, there are widely differing types of technology that need to be commercialized. The basic training has already been developed by STI, but the consulting will require the expertise of different STI consultants on the basis of the small-business owners' needs and situations.

STI has several challenges to overcome to fulfill the government grant and successfully move its core business forward. Your tasks include the following:

- Provide basic technology commercialization training to the 150 small-business owners and ensure that they have learned the material.
- Provide customized consulting to each of the 150 small-business owners.
- Develop a method for small-business owners to be able to get the appropriate consultation and be able to document that the consultation was provided.
- Develop a system that would capture the learning provided by each of the STI consultants and make that available to all STI consultants. This would allow STI to develop their consultants' knowledge base.
- Ensure whatever is developed is as cost-effective as possible, because government grants leave little room for profit.

CASE QUESTION

Develop a business solution for STI that addresses all of the challenges they face. Indicate any assumptions you are making that are not directly addressed by the case.

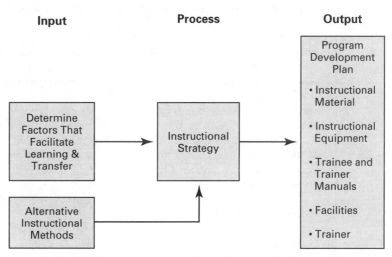

Chapter *8*

Development and Implementation of Training

DEVELOPMENT PHASE

Input	Process	Output

Determine Factors That Facilitate Learning & Transfer

Alternative Instructional Methods

Instructional Strategy

Program Development Plan

• Instructional Material

• Instructional Equipment

• Trainee and Trainer Manuals

• Facilities

• Trainer

Learning Objectives

After reading this chapter, you should be able to:

➤ *Identify the elements in an instructional strategy*

➤ *Identify the factors to consider in choosing a trainer*

➤ *Choose the most effective seating arrangement on the basis of the nature of the training*

➤ *Examine a room, and determine whether it meets training requirements*

➤ *Describe the alternatives to developing training "in-house"*

➤ *Describe the mechanisms that should be put in place to assist in the transfer of training.*

➤ *Explain how you would deal with each of the four types of difficult trainee*

CASE: Jack Goes to Training

Jack, a 43-year-old machinist, had worked for Scanton Industries for 23 years. It seemed that the need to learn something new was constant, and Jack was getting nervous about his job. The nervousness grew last week when he saw a new batch of equipment arrive. It looked something like the machinery he uses now, but it was hooked up to computers. Bill, his foreman, said, "It looks like you'll be going back to school for a couple of days, Jack. You're going to have to learn how to program your work into the computer." Jack smiled but felt sick to his stomach. He always had been good with his hands, but he had never done well in school.

All Jack thought about that weekend was the training he would be going to. He fell asleep Sunday night thinking about it. The phone awakened him at 7:00 the next morning. It was Bill telling him that training had been switched from the local training center downtown to the local school because of a sudden strike at the training center. The school was the only place available on short notice.

As Jack walked up the steps of the school, he felt sick to his stomach again. He entered the hall and then the classroom. Everything was similar to what he remembered about school, except that now there was a computer on each desk. Even the smell was the same, and it brought back memories. Some were good (the guys getting together between classes), but most were bad (being yelled at, taking tests, and doing poorly). As he sat in the wooden chair in the back where he used to sit, he looked out of the window and began to daydream, just as he had done in high school.

The other 20 trainees were sitting quietly at their desks. All of them seemed as nervous as Jack. Suddenly someone burst through the door. "Hi, my name is Jason Reston. I'm your instructor for this course. You're here to learn some basic computer skills and how to program the machines that you will be using at work. I realize that you come from different companies and will operate different machines, but the process for all of them is similar. First, I am going to show you how to get signed on and into the program you will be running. . . ." Jack was back from his daydream. Well, here we go, he thought.

At lunch, Jack and his classmate Murray went to a local deli. "Are you keeping up?" Jack asked.

"Are you kidding? Are we going to be tested on this stuff?" asked Murray.

"I have no idea. If we are, I'm dead," said Jack.

The afternoon went slowly. The trainer simply gave an instruction, and the trainees entered the information into the computer. Then he gave another and they entered that as well. "How are we supposed to remember all this?" Murray whispered. The second day was worse. On a few occasions, Jack was jolted out of his daydream while staring out of the window. "Jack," yelled Jason, "are you with us?" At 3:00 P.M. on the second afternoon, Jason announced that they would be tested to see what they had learned. Jack looked at the test questions. Was he that stupid? He did not even understand many of the questions. Would he lose his job if he failed this test? He could almost hear his boss yelling at him, "You are fired! Get out, get out!"

This case is an example of how not to conduct training. The training room and the training itself exacerbated the anxiety that Jack felt about going to training. As we go through the chapter, think about what you would do to make the training more conducive to adult learning.

DEVELOPMENT OF TRAINING

The first step in the development phase of training consists of formulating an instructional strategy. The focus of the instructional strategy is on achieving the training objectives that were created in the design phase. The chosen alternative instructional methods and the factors related to learning facilitation and transfer (inputs from the design phase) are used to shape the strategy so that it will achieve the objectives. The **instructional strategy** is a listing of all the elements of the training program, including the individual modules, their organization, timing, methods, and materials to be used. The outputs of the development phase are all of the things needed to deliver the training program to the participants.

These include the specific content of the training, materials to be used, any slides, videos and such that are needed, presentation equipment, manuals, and so forth. All these outputs will serve as inputs to the implementation phase. The relationship of these inputs, processes, and outputs is shown in the model of the development phase at the beginning of the chapter.

Choosing Instructional Methods

In Chapters 6 and 7, we discussed a variety of training methods. Our discussion included the strengths and weaknesses of each method. Many of them, such as role-play, behavior modeling, and case study, are not meant to be stand-alone methods, but rather, they facilitate learning by providing alternative mechanisms for providing practice. A summary of these methods and their effectiveness in developing knowledge, skills, and attitudes (KSAs) is presented in Table 8-1.

Although the method's effectiveness in meeting the learning objective should be the major criterion for selection, other considerations are costs, time needed to develop the material, and time allotted for the training session. For example, if cost prevents you from using the best method, then choose a different method that meets the budget but still provides the necessary KSAs. The workforce's literacy is another issue to consider. Methods such as programmed instruction and computer-based instruction rely on trainees' ability to read and understand. If they are not skilled in these areas, alternative approaches are necessary, particularly if reading is not an important skill for the job.

The knowledge gained from Chapter 5 provides an awareness of the factors that facilitate learning and transfer of KSAs back to the job so that you can meet your training objectives. Of course, you will also need to operate within the organizational constraints that you have identified. Keeping all of this in mind, we now turn to the instructional strategy.

Instructional Strategy

The instructional strategy is a written document, often called a **training plan.** We will use these terms interchangeably. This plan details all aspects of the training, including the methods, materials, equipment, facilities, and trainers. The following sections indicate *what* should be included in the documentation, *rather than the form* that it should take. An instructional strategy should first identify the target population, the overall training objective (purpose), the location of the training, and the initial configuration of the training space. It should then provide a listing of the learning objectives for the training. These objectives should be organized into modules that encompass related topics. For each learning objective, a list of key learning points should be developed. The training methods to be used to achieve these objectives, the materials and equipment needed, and the trainer who will deliver this module

Table 8-1 Training Method Effectiveness at Meeting KSA Objectives

| | OBJECTIVES OF TRAINING | | | | | |
| TRAINING METHODS | KNOWLEDGE | | | SKILLS | | |
	DECLARATIVE	PROCEDURAL	STRATEGIC	TECHNICAL	INTERPERSONAL	ATTITUDES
Lecture						
Straight[a]	3	2	1	1	1	3
Discussion	4	3	2	1	1	4
Demonstration	1	4	2	4	4	3
Computer-Based						
Programmed Instruction	5	3	3	4	1	3
Intelligent Tutoring	5	4	4	5	2	4
Interactive Multimedia	5	4	4	5	4	4
Virtual Reality	3	5	3	4	4	4
Simulations/ Games						
Equipment	1	3	2	5	1	2
Case Studies	2	2	4	2	2	3
Business Games	2	3	5	2	2[b]	2
In-Basket	1	3	4	1	2[c]	2
Role-Play	1	2	2	2	4	5[d]
Behavior Modeling	1	3	3	4	5	3
OJT						
JIT	3	5	4	4	2	5
Apprentice	5	5	4	5	2	5
Coaching	3	5	4	4	4	5

Scale: 1 = not effective, 2 = mildly effective, 3 = moderately effective, 4 = effective, 5 = very effective.
[a] This rating is for lectures delivered orally; printed lectures would be one point higher in each knowledge category.
[b] If the business game is designed for interpersonal skills, this rating would be a 4.
[c] If multiple in-baskets were used, this rating would be 3.
[d] This rating applies specifically to role reversal.
Note: These ratings are consistent with earlier research by Shoenfelt, E. L., and N. Eatman. "The relative effectiveness of training methods for attaining training objectives: Current opinion of training practitioners." Paper presented at the Annual Conference of the Southeastern Psychological Association, March 1991, New Orleans, LA. Neider, L. "Training effectiveness: Changing attitudes." *Training and Development Journal* 35 (1981), pp. 24–28. Carroll, S. J., F. Paine, and J. J. Ivancevich. "The relative effectiveness of training methods: Expert opinion and research." *Personnel Psychology* 25 (1972), pp. 495–509.

should also be identified. Sometimes the configuration of the training space needs to be changed to accommodate a different training method. For example, with a large number of trainees, the appropriate configuration for a lecture will be different than that for a small-group exercise. Your plan should identify any points in the training where the seating configuration needs to change. After all the components of the training are identified, a brief statement as to what actions will be taken to assist transfer of training to the job should be listed. Mechanisms used to assist transfer must be documented so it is clear what will occur once training is completed. It is generally expected that transfer of training will occur, but often little is done to ensure that it does. When no one person is responsible, the feeling of responsibility is diffused, and transfer is soon forgotten.

Finally, a short description of how the training will be evaluated should be included. It is important to include the evaluation process and time frames as these items need to be included in the time allocation for training if evaluation occurs at the end of training. This also helps ensure that each component of the training is focused on achieving the desired outcomes.

Table 8-2 can serve as a guide for developing your instructional strategy. The instructional strategy will help you systematically examine what is required and what ordering of the material makes the most sense. Each component of the instructional strategy is discussed in more detail in the following sections.

Objectives and Learning Points

As stated, the instructional strategy should contain all of the learning objectives, organized into the modules in which these objectives will be addressed. Each learning

Table 8-2 Components of Instructional Strategy

INSTRUCTIONAL STRATEGY/TRAINING PLAN

Name of Program: Pipe Fitting I
Location: Classroom 101 next to Field simulation site no. 2

Classroom configuration: 15 seats in "U" shape with open end facing projection screen.

Evaluation: conducted at the end of training (Correct connection of furnace to a gas meter, in a simulation, with no assistance from readings or instructor.)

Target Population: Apprentices who successfully passed the gas fitters exam

Overall Training Objective: Trainees will be able to examine a work project and with appropriate tools measure, cut, thread, and install the piping according to standards outlined in the gas code.

TIME	TOPIC	LEARNING OBJECTIVE	LEARNING POINTS	METHOD	MATERIAL AND AUDIOVISUALS
12:05–12:25 (20 min) Trainer: Mr. XX	Introduction; Welcome ground rules, agenda, etc.		• Get individuals in newly formed groups used to each other • Create a warm environment conducive to learning	Icebreaker activity Small-group discussion	Training manual Projector
12:25–1:00 (35 min) Trainer: Mr. XX	Determining number and length of pipes needed	1. Using a tape measure, determine the length and number of pipes necessary to connect the furnace to the gas meter in a manner that meets the gas code	1. The extra length necessary because of the threading 2. That length is reduced by different fittings, e.g., street elbow, union elbow, etc. 3. Method for constructing appropriate drop for furnace	Lecture and simulation	Training manual Projector Assortment of 1-inch and 3/4-inch fittings, elbows, street elbows, and unions Mock meter and furnace setup Tape measure, note pads
1:00–1:45 (45 min) Trainer: Ms. YY	Cutting and threading pipe	2. Using a threading machine, cut and thread length of pipe required	1. Length of thread required 2. Importance of cutting and reaming, measuring, and use of threading machine oil	Lecture and simulation	Trainee manual Videocassette recorder and television Threading tape Threading machine Steel pipe Oil Tape measure
Measures to assist transfer:	Mentor assigned on work crew.				

objective should have the list of key learning points required to achieve the objective. A **learning point** is an important piece of information that a trainee must acquire to accomplish a learning objective. Each learning objective provides specific information as to what needs to be learned, and that helps identify the key learning points. Consider this learning objective: "Solder twenty feet of half-inch copper pipe, using elbows and unions, in 20 minutes or less with no leaks." To ensure that there are no leaks, the trainee must pay specific attention to the cleaning of the copper pipe, the proper heating of the pipe, and the correct application of the solder. These factors would be key learning points, which the trainer would need to be sure that the trainee had mastered in order to achieve the objective.

Other Content

As each learning objective is considered (along with its learning points), the most effective configuration of methods, material and equipment, facilities, and trainers is determined. In Table 8-2, the lecture method provides the cognitive information, and the simulation provides the actual practice. If the training is to teach supervisors how to deal effectively with conflict, the methodology might be lecture and discussion to provide information, and role-play or behavior modeling to provide practice. Once the methods to be used and the sequencing of the training are established, it is necessary to determine time frames for each of these activities. In most cases time is limited, and the inexperienced training developer tends to overload the material to be covered. Always allow for a reasonable amount of time for discussion and interaction, which is where much of the learning occurs.

On the basis of the type of training, the next step is to decide on the configuration of the room. Clearly, documenting this information reduces the likelihood of mistakes. For example, a problem might develop if the training requires a great deal of face-to-face interaction among the trainees, but the training facilities are too small to accommodate those interactions. This is discussed in more depth later, under the heading "Furniture Setup."

After agreement is reached on a carefully constructed instructional strategy, the next step is to obtain or develop the instructional material, instructional media and equipment, and so on, that you have identified as needed. This is your **program development plan** and consists of the checklist (derived from your instructional strategy) of all the components of the training that need to be developed or acquired. The output from the development phase (as shown in the development phase of our training model at the start of the chapter) is development or acquisition of all the items on your program development plan. Methodically completing the program development plan should make it possible to identify and develop everything required for training. We discuss each of the development plan components in more detail below.

Materials and Equipment

Once your training plan is completed, document all the necessary material you will need such as printed material, slides, and the like, and the time frames for their completion. Allow sufficient time to prepare materials properly. Order equipment and anything else provided by others at off-site locations well in advance. Important charts, posters, and easel sheets can be professionally printed depending on cost and time constraints.

Trainee's Manual

The trainee's manual is an important learning tool for training. The instructional strategy provides you with an outline of what needs to be included in the manual. To keep the trainees' interest and their complete involvement in discussions, provide notes on all the key information that will be presented. The trainees will then be able to pay more attention to what is being said and done, rather than being concerned about taking notes. The manual often includes all lecture materials, learning points, and supplemental readings. It may also include exercises and some blank sheets for jotting down notes and lists in small-group meetings.

A good choice for holding the manual's material is a three-ring binder, because the trainee can add information as the training continues. If you will be using handouts, have them printed on paper with the holes already punched so they can easily be inserted into the manual. It is sometimes better to hold back certain information—for example, exercises—from the trainees until it is time to use it. Trainees should not be distracted from the current topic by trying to figure out various problems ahead of time.

Trainer's Manual

The trainer's manual provides all the information in the trainee's manual and information on what the trainer needs to do and how to do it. It is a visual aid for the trainer. One format is to have the lecture notes on the right-hand side of the page and the instructions for the trainer on the left-hand side. These instructions range from indicating when to generate lists on newsprint to what some of the expected information on the list might be and how the trainer might want to respond. A well-prepared trainer's manual will provide everything a trainer needs to know to conduct the training.

Facilities

If training is taking place in the company's facility, be sure that the room is available by reserving it. If training will be off-site, be selective as to the design of the room. Be sure that the site can accommodate breakout rooms if they are needed and that the seating can be appropriately configured. If movable dividers separate the room from others, inquire about the events scheduled next door. Attending a training session when a motivational speaker or sales rally is next door can be distracting. If nothing is scheduled, get assurance that the booking office will be sensitive to your concerns if they book the rooms next door. Check the soundproofing of the panels that separate the rooms. Avoid booking rooms that lead directly to the kitchen unless it is certain that the walls are soundproofed.

Some Advantages to Off-Site Training Facilities
Although a certain pride can come from having your own training facilities, they can be expensive. Off-site training offers several advantages.

First, being off-site provides more assurance that trainees will not be interrupted. It is simply too easy to contact the trainee if he is on the same floor or even in the next building.

Another advantage is the change of pace off-site training offers. Going to a hotel or conference center is not the same as going to work. Many trainees will associate staying in a hotel with a vacation (unless they are traveling salespersons). This change of pace is even more important if a great deal of stress is associated with the job. Recall the discussion of classical conditioning. Regular pairing of work with stress will result in a feeling of stress upon arrival at the workplace. Off-site training in this situation might be more suited to the learning process. However, choose the off-site facility with care. Remember Jack and his training at the old school?

Going off-site also allows the trainer to choose a facility compatible with the needs of the particular training event. If breakout rooms, a classroom, U-shaped setup, or all three are required, you can choose the location that best fits the requirements.

The Training Room

Whether you are designing a training facility or going off-site to train, many factors contribute to making the training room a learner-friendly environment. The following describes the type of training room that is ideal for most types of training.

A windowless room is best. Windows can distract the trainees, as was evident in the case at the start of the chapter. Jack was easily distracted from the training for many reasons, but the window gave him a way to avoid the training. If the room does contain windows, be sure that they are fitted with shades or curtains that you can close. Unblocked windows, even on upper floors of a building, can be distracting when the weather turns bad. Also, light coming through the windows can create glare. The walls should be blank—neither decorated with pictures nor brightly painted—and a neutral color, such as beige. The point of this is to eliminate things that will distract trainees from the training. Material that is related to the training can and should be posted on walls and easels. Lighting should be adjustable so it can be dimmed for slide shows or video presentations and can be made brighter for the lecture, discussions, and exercises. Ideally, the room should be close to square in shape. Rectangular rooms limit the type of seating arrangements possible. A rule of thumb is to avoid a training room whose length exceeds its width by more than 50 percent.[1] The room should be carpeted and should have a sound-absorbing ceiling. As noted earlier, a soundproof facility, whether on premises or off-site, is very important.

The room should be equipped with its own temperature control and quiet heating/cooling fans. This point might sound trivial—after all, who would build a training room with noisy fans? The problem is that contractors are good at constructing buildings but do not specialize in any particular type. When the University of Windsor Business School was being built, a team of faculty members provided input into the design of the classrooms. This input helped tremendously in the development of user-friendly classrooms, but the team did not think about fan noise. The result: One of the few complaints about the building is fan noise. When the fans are on, it becomes difficult to hear the questions being asked.

Under the heading "nice to have," consider the following for a multipurpose training room:

- Have tracks built onto the walls with a slot into which newsprint can be pushed, allowing for the hanging of charts and posters anywhere in the room.
- Have whiteboards built into the walls at strategic locations to allow easy access to large writing surfaces.
- Have built-in consoles that control lighting, audiovisuals (AVs), and computers, to provide easy access to the operation of these training aids.
- Have a working remote control so trainers can operate the lights and AVs from anywhere in the room.
- Have an interactive whiteboard (e.g., SMART board) for developing models or listing points generated in discussions, and be able to provide copies to trainees easily.

If AVs are built into the facility, make sure that they are situated so that all trainees can view and hear them. Also make sure that AVs are not built into places where the equipment itself blocks sight lines.

Furniture   Use tables and chairs rather than classroom-type desk chairs. Tables should be movable so they can be set up in any configuration. An ideal table size is 5 feet long and 2½ feet wide, as this allows two people to sit comfortably on one side. Many configurations are possible by arranging the tables. Putting two of these tables together makes a 5-foot square where eight people can hold a group discussion.

If possible, use padded swivel chairs that are cloth covered (not vinyl) and have casters and armrests. Trainees will be required to sit for extended periods of time, and comfort is important. In addition to providing overall comfort, the swivel and casters allow for ease of movement when trainees must form small groups or turn to work with another trainee. Being able to lean back and rest your arms creates a relaxing environment conducive to learning.

Furniture Setup   Seating arrangements depend on the type of training being conducted. The typical configurations are classroom, U-shape, conference, and circle. The arrangement determines the degree of formality, focus of attention, and level of two-way communication.[2] To appreciate this point, consider the two extremes, circle and classroom (Figure 8-1 styles A and B). The classroom style (B) places the focus

Figure 8-1   Different Seating Arrangements for Training

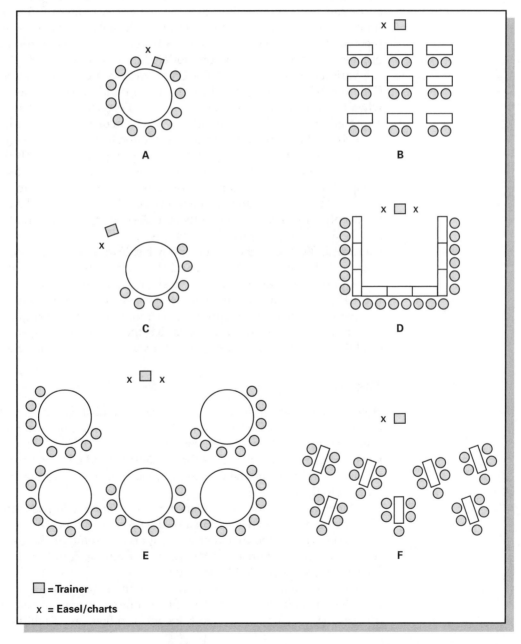

□ = Trainer

x = Easel/charts

on the trainer and limits two-way communication between trainees because the trainees are all facing one direction. If no tables are used, more trainees can be accommodated. This arrangement is called theater style. When a trainee sees such a setup, her role is clearly defined in her mind: She is there to listen. In the circle setup (A), the focus is evenly distributed; no single person is being looked at. A trainee sees this style and his role is also defined: She will be a part of the discussion. Furthermore, this lack of focus makes it easier for trainees to debate and discuss issues among themselves.

To provide employees with information on the company's position regarding sexual harassment, for example, the classroom configuration is appropriate. Here the goal is to provide information, and the focus should be on the trainer. Most two-way communication involves question-and-answer exchanges between the trainer and the trainee. Suppose the goal is to train managers to deal with sexual harassment. A circle is chosen because the goal is to generate discussion about managers' experiences and ways of handling them. In the circle, trainees face one another and the trainer is just one of the members of the circle; the focus on all members of the group is equal. Another obvious difference between these two configurations is that a larger number of trainees can be accommodated in the classroom setup.

Various modifications of these two extremes can also be used. The semicircle (Figure 8-1C) encourages trainee discussion and allows trainees to be face-to-face when the trainer is not talking. In this situation, the trainer stands when presenting information and sits with the trainees when encouraging discussion.

Perhaps the configuration used most often is the U-shape (Figure 8-1D). It is similar to the semicircle but allows for a larger group of trainees. The U-shape places the main focus on the trainer, allows a fair amount of face-to-face discussion among the group members, and accommodates a reasonably large group (30 to 35 trainees). However, the U itself can become too large. The trainer must be careful not to move too deeply into the U and cut off those at the end. Also, if flip charts are used, two sets may be needed to make reading them easy for all participants, particularly if the number exceeds 30. Placing the charts slightly inside the open end of the U (see Figure 8-1D) ensures that they are not blocked and all participants can see the material easily.

Another alternative is to have trainees sit at round tables in a semicircle (Figure 8-1E). This arrangement facilitates easy switching from lecturette to small-group exercises or discussions. Figure 8-1F is similar but with rectangular tables. The other advantage of these configurations is that they set up small groups where members can interact, making the training less threatening at the beginning.

The Trainer

How is the trainer chosen? One of the reasons most commonly cited for ineffective training is its lack of relevance to the trainee's situation. Comments such as "The training is great but it will not work in our plant," "You do not understand the problems we have," and "My boss is the one who should be here, because the boss makes the decisions" indicate the concern trainees perceive as to the transferability of the training to their jobs.

One way to ensure the relevance of the training is to use managers as trainers.[3] Their involvement alleviates most of the preceding concerns, but some other problems may arise. If the manager also supervises some of the trainees, his presence could dampen the trainees' enthusiasm for training. Additionally, the manager may not have the skills needed to be an effective trainer.

Larger organizations can overcome the supervision issue by not having managers train their immediate subordinates. Smaller organizations would need to assure such trainees that they will be treated the same as others (although this assurance doesn't always work). As long as trainees do not perceive any different treatment, the word would get out that this system was okay. Another concern is the potential that the middle manager may spend too much time dealing with organizational issues rather than the training topics. Solid training objectives would help prevent this conflict.

Another way to develop a successful training program is to use a seasoned trainer (e.g., outside or internal consultant) and a manager to team-teach the training program. The two could work from each other's strengths. An advantage of this approach is that the manager receives good on-the-job training on how to be an effective trainer. The disadvantage is cost, and for this reason it is not often chosen. The larger issue of the trainer's competence is addressed below.

Trainer KSAs

The KSAs of an effective trainer are presented in Table 8-3. Note that many of the requirements are similar to those suggested for an effective lecturer. This is important because almost all training includes a lecture component.

Just how much knowledge of the subject matter does the trainer need? The level of knowledge required depends on the complexity of the subject matter. Highly technical subject matter requires a high level of such knowledge. Is the high level of knowledge more important than being a skilled trainer? Perhaps that question is not the correct focus, because both subject-matter knowledge and trainer skills are important. We know that trainer skills are critical to trainee learning, so the better question is, "Which is more advisable, to train the trainer in the technical skills or to train the expert in training skills?" The answer, especially if the subject matter is highly technical or complex, is the latter. In the short term, it may be necessary to pair a technical expert with a training specialist until the technical expert acquires sufficient training skill.

The trainer should possess a reasonable knowledge of the organization and trainees. Such knowledge increases the credibility of the trainer and helps her answer questions that come up regarding integrating the training back into the workplace.

Although most of the knowledge and many of the skills required of a trainer are trainable, it would be best to be able to begin with individuals who already possess the attitudes identified in Table 8-3, because attitudes are more difficult to change.

Table 8-3
Knowledge, Skills, and Attitudes Required of an Effective Trainer

Knowledge
Subject matter
Organization
Adult learning process
Instructional methods
Skills
Interpersonal communication skills
Verbal skills (ability to explain clearly)
• Active listening
• Questioning
• Providing feedback
Platform skills (ability to speak with inflection, gesture appropriately, and maintain eye contact)
Organization skills (ability to present information in logical order and stay on point)
Attitudes
Commitment to the organization
Commitment to helping others
High level of self-efficacy

Experience and Credibility

How important is it to have experience related to the training topic? The more experience a trainer has in the topic area, the more credibility for the trainer. Consider, for example, one successful trainer's early run-in with trainees because of a perceived lack of experience. The trainer was part of a corporate training staff. The course he was asked to teach was called "Nonfinancial Motivation Techniques." The trainees were first-line supervisors with an average of six years' experience in their positions and more than 10 years with the company. Ten minutes into the first training component (the lecture), one of the older trainees raised his hand and said, "Sonny, have you ever supervised a group of unskilled laborers?" The answer, of course, was "no," but he qualified it with the fact that he had supervised white-collar employees. Several knowing smirks around the room made it clear that the trainer's credibility had been destroyed. Throughout the rest of the program, trainees were inattentive, lethargic, and occasionally rude. This trainer learned early on that trainer credibility is a key factor in the effectiveness of classroom training.

How could the trainer handle such a situation more effectively? One approach would be to set the context of the training at the beginning. He might say something like the following: I will be presenting a number of nonfinancial techniques that you might be able to use to motivate your employees. These techniques worked for other supervisors in a variety of situations. First, I will explain the technique, and then we will discuss how it might work for you or how it might be adapted to work for you. You know your work units better than anyone else, so I'm counting on everyone to help identify ways that these techniques can be applied.

A trainer does not need to have the same work experience as the trainees to be credible. However, a trainer needs to be seen as having something worthwhile to offer. Here the trainer is offering some new ideas and expertise in facilitating the discussion of these ideas, but—and this point is important—the trainer does not dismiss or diminish the expertise of the audience. In effect, the trainer says, "Let's merge our separate areas of expertise to arrive at something we both want—more motivated employees."

Acknowledging the differences in experience at the beginning of training is also important. It allows the trainees to see that the trainer is aware of the differences and is taking them into account. For example, in the previous situation the trainer might say, "My experience has been supervising white-collar employees. How do you think the motivations of these employees differ from those you supervise?" After some differences are noted, the trainer might then ask, "At one time, most of you were unskilled workers. What were the things that motivated you when you were an unskilled worker?" This question would allow the supervisors to see that while individuals may differ in the things that motivate them, general categories of motivators apply for all individuals. The questioning process allows the trainees to test their assumptions and learn through self-discovery, provided the trainer has the skill to translate the participant responses into learning opportunities. We will discuss other issues that affect trainer credibility in the chapter section "Implementation Ideas for Trainers."

On-the-Job Trainers

On-the-job (OJT) trainers are different from the traditional trainer. OJT trainers are usually classified as jobholders or supervisors for the jobs for which they are providing training. As a result, there are some unique issues to consider. For OJT programs to be effective, the trainers need to[4]

- know the job to be trained,
- be knowledgeable in the interpersonal skills necessary to interact effectively with those they train,

- be skilled as trainers, and
- be motivated to be trainers.

OJT in general uses co-workers and supervisors as trainers. None of these people started out to be a trainer, and likely none has formal training in how to be an effective trainer. The OJT trainer does need to know the job to be trained, but the best trainer is not necessarily the person who can best do the job. The OJT trainer should have a solid understanding of how the job is performed and an ability to interact effectively with others. But given that they did not sign on as trainers, it should not be expected that they would understand specifics related to teaching others how to do the job. To be effective, therefore, such training is necessary and should include[5]

- the company's formal OJT process (e.g., JIT) and the policies and support provided by the organization,
- interpersonal skills and feedback techniques, and
- principles of adult learning.

Motivating the OJT trainer is also a key factor in making the OJT method effective. Trainers need to observe the trainee closely to ensure adequate skill development and to prevent the trainee from causing damage to equipment and property or injury to self or others. For this to happen, OJT trainers must be rewarded for conducting the training while doing their jobs. This can be done in many ways, but there are several things to remember. Someone who is training another employee and performing his own job should not be expected to perform at the same level of productivity as someone who is not training others. Rewards must be provided for giving effective training. Think back to the proper process of OJT. It requires the trainer to go through the steps of particular tasks methodically and then observe as the trainee does the same. This process requires time, which will take away from the productivity that would be possible if the trainer were doing nothing but his own job.

One way to motivate the OJT trainer would be to institute a different (higher) classification for someone who was capable of training other employees. This designation would provide prestige (and perhaps more money) for the position. At the same time, the measure of performance for the trainer could be how well the trainee performs at the end of the formal OJT. Here the motivation would be to turn out good trainees. If this is not done, and trainers are expected to perform their regular jobs at a similar level as nontrainers, then the result might well be similar to what happened in the following example. A food service and vending company used experienced vending machine service route drivers to train new route drivers. The company attributed a history of high turnover among trainee drivers to the nature of the job, the low starting wage, and the hours required. The arrival of a new human resources manager led to a reexamination of this problem. Discussions with current trainees and trainees who had voluntarily terminated their employment in the recent past revealed that many of the trainers would do all the easy work (restocking the machines) and make the trainees do the "dirty" work (performing maintenance on the machines). Others would not let the trainees do any of the work because it "slowed them down." As the drivers were paid on the basis of the number of machines they serviced, rather than on an hourly rate, they were essentially doing the training for free.

Alternatives to Development

For several reasons, an organization may choose not to develop its own training. A small business might not have the resources; a large company might not have many individuals to train or simply might have too many other projects in the works. In such situations, alternatives are available. The company could hire a consultant and use one of their prepackaged programs or look to outside training seminars. The option to hire a consultant to do all the work is an expensive alternative but would result in a program tailored to the company's needs, much as if the organization did it all itself.

The Consultant

If the training required is not specific to the organization but more generic (e.g., conflict management, interviewing skills, or computer skills), find a consultant with a training package that can be adapted to fit the company's needs. Using the consultant's prepackaged program without any alterations would reduce the overall cost.

The advantage of prepackaged programs is that they are ready to go. The disadvantage is that they are not specific to a company. This trade-off may be more acceptable for a session on conflict resolution than for a session on team development. In fact, many prepackaged programs can be used to supplement a company's own program. They can be less costly than hiring a consultant, but some are still expensive. Some consulting firms offer prepackaged programs and also provide training for the trainers. This option adds to the cost, but the training is usually quite good. If a great deal of training will be taking place in the organization, this option may be worth the extra expense if it is amortized over multiple sessions.

In deciding whether to use a consultant, consider questions such as the following:

- How many employees are to be trained, and will they need constant retraining?
- Can advantages be realized from involving a neutral third party (e.g., union–management cooperative ventures)?
- Is there a rush to get the training done?
- Is there in-house expertise?

If the decision is to use a consultant, consider the following:

- Ask for references, ask who they have trained, and be sure to follow up on this information (consultants vary in their expertise).
- Determine how much the consultant knows about the industry.
- Review some of the training objectives in the consultant's training packages.
- Find out how the consultant evaluates success in training.
- Make sure you know who will be doing the work. Often you meet the salesperson, not the trainer.

Outside Seminars

The outside seminar is training offered from time to time at local hotels, conference centers, and universities. These seminars are the least expensive and best alternative if only a few employees need training. For a sufficient number of attendees, these seminars may be brought to your site. On-site seminars can be tailored to the organization for a moderate extra cost. They can also include an evaluation component.

When choosing a seminar, consider the following questions:

- What are the training objectives? Skills require practice, and seminars often are too large to include practice sessions.
- Is any form of evaluation used? (Evaluation is rarely done.)
- How well does the content focus on the training objectives?
- Can someone be sent to preview the seminar and report back on its potential value?

If the decision is to purchase training, assess how it fits into the overall training strategy. Many companies have implemented team training in the past because it was "the thing to do." Spending money on team training simply because others were doing it wasted money. Training should be seen as a mechanism to support the organization's mission and goals. Other mechanisms must also be in place to support the training if it is to transfer effectively.

Focus on Small Business

In Britain, organizations with fewer than 100 employees reported a 25 percent increase in training with about 60 percent reporting financial benefits from the training.[6] Another study in Britain noted that the payoff of more training seems to be a higher level of innovation from employees.[7] So formal training is a valuable commodity for the small business. In North America, a study of small businesses (fewer than 100 employees) indicated that most (83 percent) had some form of formal training.[8] The cost of this training is unknown, but knowing how important costs are for the small business, it is useful to consider options that could reduce these training costs. To achieve the benefits of formalized training, the small business might find it advantageous to hire a consultant or purchase prepackaged training. If so, it is important that they follow the same suggestions mentioned previously when choosing a consultant or packaged training.

Small businesses should also examine the feasibility of developing a consortium of small businesses that could all use the same training. LearnShare (see Training in Action 7-6) discovered that 74 percent of their training is not specific to a particular organization's process or products.[9] The same is likely true for small companies. Why not take advantage of this commonality and work together to identify training needs and share in the cost of developing or purchasing relevant training? This is what LearnShare does. LearnShare developed an online training program called the Leader Survival Kit.[10] The total cost of the program was $285,000, but sharing the cost among companies made it only about $22,000 each. If this shared development expense can be done for e-learning, it can also be done for any type of training development; thus, it can be affordable for smaller businesses. Also, given the increasing number of small businesses, the expense could be shared among more, making the cost of development even less.

E-learning is now an option for the small business. Numerous businesses are providing a template for developing online learning. This way, the small business gets affordable training that can be tailored to its needs. There are several e-learning opportunities now available. Quelsys is a company that allows trainers from other companies to use its authoring tools to build training programs. No cost is charged until employees begin to take the course, and then the cost is on a per-employee basis.[11] The Small Business Administration's training network provides several training courses via the Web for free.[12] Some companies are even more adventuresome and develop an online learning university (see Training in Action 8-1).

Small businesses often belong to industry-specific associations that can provide a venue for discussing this idea to determine the level of interest. The associations themselves could develop a consortium for their constituents. If a consortium is too complex a project to consider, why not simply purchase a few prepackaged training programs? If a small business located three other companies with similar training interests, it would save 75 percent of the cost.

Western Learning Systems of California is a variation on the consortium idea. It develops courses for larger companies but retains the copyright. It then markets these courses to small companies at a more affordable rate. They offer a one-year membership for $5,000 that entitles a company to 75 classes at the rate of $195 per class.[13]

Another inexpensive way to train in some areas is to require trainees to read a particular book and then participate in a discussion group on the topic. The person most knowledgeable about the subject leads the group. A company preparing for ISO

Walker and Associates, a telecommunications equipment distributor, has just under 300 employees. A new president came on board who strongly believed in the training and development of employees. He formed a partnership with GeoLearning, Inc., a Web-based learning provider, to create the Walker Institute of Training and Development, an online corporate university.

To facilitate using the Internet for training, Walker's president offered employees an interest-free loan to purchase a home computer. At the same time, he purchased several laptops for employees to check out for home or travel. Some employees were still a bit reluctant to use the Internet for fear of misusing it.

To help encourage e-learning, Frank Russell, president of GeoLearning, provided some much-needed advice to Walker's president. "Start small, with a pilot program of a few employees, and get feedback from the naysayers," was his advice. This approach helped to launch the program. To further encourage its use, supervisors made its use one of the goals for employees in their performance review. They also integrated e-learning and its use into their orientation.

Note that these practices, starting with a pilot program integrating the use of the Web training into an employee's first experience in the organization (orientation) and building it into performance appraisal, are all practices for any effective training, Web-based or not.

Source: Adapted from Tyler, K. "E-Learning: Not just for e-normous companies anymore." *HR Magazine* 46 (2001), pp. 82–88.

certification asked a group of employees to read a book written by one of the quality gurus, Philip Crosby. After they read each chapter, they met to discuss it. The manager prepared questions in advance to keep the discussion going.[14] Earlier we indicated how important trainee involvement is for adult learning. These discussion groups are the epitome of involvement. The informal training in this company became more formal after this initial orientation.

Although this method does not follow all the criteria that we suggest for an effective training program, it might more than compensate for this by motivating participants. No single best way to train has been established, especially when the variations in cost-benefit for different training alternatives are considered. Training in Action 8-2 provides examples of various methods being used by small businesses.

At Staffmasters, a small temporary service provider in Louisville, each of its 10 employees specialize in a particular area (e.g., safety) and attend outside seminars to gain relevant knowledge. On return, each is responsible for teaching others about the particular issue.

At Rivait Machine Tools, Inc., a 14-person operation in Windsor, Ontario, Canada, only one basic type of work is done . So, instead of providing training in job procedures, a "job aid" was developed consisting of a checklist of tasks to be performed. The employee goes through the list, checks off each task as completed, and then moves to the next task. This means that training, except at the basic level, is not necessary.

You do not have to be big to win prestigious awards, but you do need training. Custom Research, Inc., is a market research company based in Minneapolis. Each of its 105 employees received a minimum of 130 hours of training in 1995. In 1996, it became the first professional service company and the smallest company ever to win the Malcolm Baldrige National Quality Award.

Steve Braccini, president of Profastener, a small business in California with about 150 employees, suggests that it is a good idea to send two employees, rather than only one, to a specific type of training. A single trainee might return with a skewed view of

(continued)

what took place. Sending two, who discuss the training with each other, ensures a common understanding. Braccini believes that this system results in a better overall product. He also makes sure that these employees have "train the trainer" skills before sending them off to the training.

Sources: Adapted from O'Brien, K., Rivait Machine and Tool. Personal communication, July 24, 1997, Oldcastle, Ontario, Canada. Zemke, R. "The little company that could." *Training* (January 1997), pp. 59–64. Filipczak, B. "Training on the cheap." *Training* (May 1996), pp. 28–34.

IMPLEMENTATION

At this point, you are ready to implement your instructional strategy. This phase of the training model is depicted below. Note that the outputs from the development phase are brought together and become the inputs for the implementation stage. Next, the "process" phase contains two steps that are important to take before your training is ready for general use.[15] They are, first, a dry run, and then a pilot program. The former is a "first test" of new material; here, the training package may not be presented in its entirety. The latter is the first full-blown presentation of the training using finished materials.

Before discussing the dry run and pilot program, let us examine some ideas for implementing training, first in terms of the structure of training, and then in terms of what the trainer should do.

Implementation Ideas for Training

There are several things you can do to ensure that trainees become, and remain, interested in training.

Icebreaker

Have an **icebreaker** to start the training. An icebreaker is a game or exercise that prompts trainees to get involved in meeting and talking with others. It is designed to be fun but at the same time generate energy that will transfer to the rest of the training. Would an icebreaker have been a useful way for Jason Reston to start his training? We believe so. The

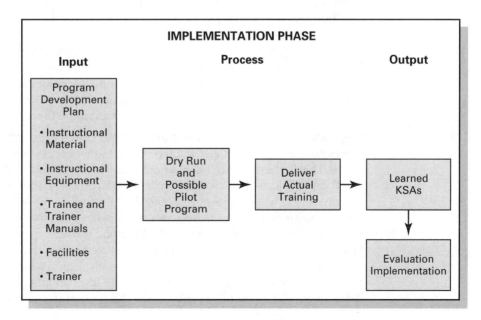

major reason given for not using an icebreaker is that it takes up too much time, but this assumption is a mistake.[16] Without the icebreaker, training starts off fast, but because of the lack of "getting to know others" and making discussion a legitimate part of training, it soon slows down and loses the race.[17] The choice of icebreaker depends on the size of the group. Suppose the focus of training was on listening and communication skills. One approach, if the class is not too large and trainees do not know one another, is to group trainees into triads. If possible, set up these groups ahead of time so that group members do not know each other. Each trainee interviews one member of the triad, with the third as an observer. The questions should be simple but should help in getting to know the person. For example, ask for the following information:

- The person's name (for obvious reasons)
- The organization the person is from and title (learn about the type of work he or she does)
- The amount of time in his or her present job (learn about his or her experience)
- The best aspects of the job (learn about "work person")
- The person's hobbies (learn about "home person")

Once the interviews are complete, each trainee in turn introduces the interviewed person to the total group. This activity gets everyone talking to the entire group, provides information on trainees, and releases a great deal of tension, while at the same time relating to the focus of the training. Later on, the trainer can come back to the icebreaker for examples of issues related to effective listening and communicating.

Provide Variety

Provide variety during training to maintain interest. Recall from Chapter 6 that trainees' attention begins to decline after 15 to 20 minutes of lecture,[18] so be sure to provide breaks, activities, and the like to keep trainees interested in what you are saying. Keep a watchful eye on the trainees to signal time for a break. Even a five-minute stretch can help.

Exercises or Games

Exercises or games (not to be confused with business games) are also valuable for gaining and maintaining interest, assuming that the games are relevant. They are especially useful if they provide an entree to, or an example of, the training objective. These tools should be used with a clear and definite purpose. We emphasize this point because of the experience of a colleague at a training workshop a few years ago (see Training in Action 8-3).

Several models incorporate exercises into the learning process.[19] One such model is exhibited in Figure 8-2. This modification of an earlier model from Pfeiffer and Jones[20] allows trainees to experience first-hand a process related to the current training, then hear some information about the topic for comparison with what they did. Then they process the new information, generalize it to their situation, and attempt to apply it in a more relevant situation. Let's examine this process more closely.

Step 1: The Experience   The learning experience begins with some sort of activity that ties into the training topic. In this way, all trainees begin by sharing a common experience. This first experience should not be related too closely to the actual work setting.

For example, when managers are being trained to be better interviewers, one of the objectives is to teach them how to develop appropriate interview questions. The first thing to realize is that most managers already believe that they are good interviewers. So how does the trainer convince them that training is necessary? To emphasize the importance of sound question development, the exercise (experience) is for them to help a committee select the new leader of a scout troop. Trainees take 10 minutes to develop their own interview questions. Then they meet in small groups and develop an overall list of questions and the rationale for each. This list is posted on newsprint and discussed.

A few years ago, Helen went to Amelia Island for a seminar that was heralded as an Advanced Seminar in Process Consultation. She even called the instructor to be sure that it would be advanced—not "an introduction to."

At the seminar, Helen soon realized that the other 11 attendees were from prominent companies across North America and possessed a great deal of experience as trainers. However, they were not as advanced as she was at process consultation. About halfway through the five-day seminar, they were put in two groups to learn about the different ways of intervening in a team's process. After receiving the information, the two groups were told to go off separately and develop a game for training the other group.

Each of the participants in Helen's group told of a game that was used in previous training and how much everyone liked it. Helen suggested developing a role-play whereby they could demonstrate the various components of process intervention. One of the other trainees said, "No one likes role-plays." "That's right," agreed another, and the group moved on to the more enjoyable games they were discussing. When they finally decided that they would play the spiderweb game, Helen asked how they would tie the training into the game. Unanimously, they said that it was not necessary.

"The professor did not say we needed to do that," was the reply. "The game is to get the group interested in training. We'll move to the training after the game is finished," was another reply. Helen insisted that they somehow tie the game to the process consultation training they had been given, and reluctantly two of the group worked with her to accomplish this connection.

Back in the training room, the other group went first, getting Helen's group to play a game. After the game was completed, the professor asked, "But how does this activity tie into the training?" They all looked puzzled, and everyone in Helen's group looked at her rather sheepishly. When it was their turn, Helen's group did tie the training to the game, but the professor commented, "It looks like you first decided on the game you wanted to play, and then tried to work the training around the game; it should be the other way around. First understand what the training is trying to accomplish, and then find a game to meet that requirement."

The point of this story is that exercises and games that do not tie into the training objective are a waste of valuable training time. Although games are fun, their main value lies in their ability to reinforce the learning while providing a break in the routine.

Figure 8-2
Experiential
Learning Model

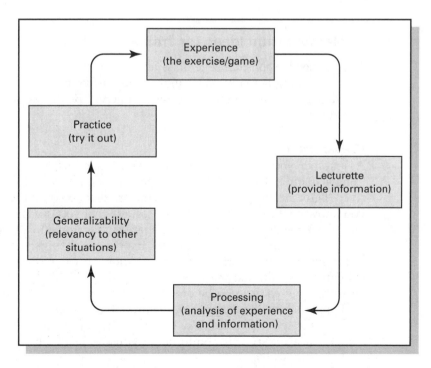

Step 2: The Lecturette   After the experience, the trainer provides information (e.g., concepts and principles) related to the topic at hand. This can be a lecture, a video, or some other form. In our example, a lecture would describe how to develop interview questions related to job requirements. Here the trainer shows how important it is to examine the job to determine what is needed, rather than simply making up questions that sound good.

Step 3: Processing the Information and Experience   After the experience and lecturette, trainees work in small groups to discuss their experience based on the information they just received. In our example, the trainer might ask the groups to analyze the questions they developed and answer the question "What criteria did we use to develop these questions?" Another question might be, "How are these questions related to the job of scout leader?" Then each of the small groups could report to the entire group what they discovered about how they developed interview questions.

Step 4: Generalizability   At this point, it is important for the trainees to see how the learning is relevant to situations outside the training. According to Pfeiffer and Jones, the key question here is "So what?"[21] The goal is to have trainees consider how this new information fits with the things they do back on the job. From the analysis and learning that took place, trainees should infer that scout leader interview questions can be developed in a better way and be able to generalize this to other similar situations. In our example, the trainees should decide that the use of job-related information for developing interview questions is appropriate for all jobs. This point would be an opportunity to provide another lecturette on how to examine a job to determine the relevant questions to ask.

Step 5: Practice   The trainees receive another task similar in nature to the first so that they can practice the newly found skill. Note that in this step, the task should be more closely related to the actual job. In our example, the trainees could be asked to develop interview questions for selecting someone for a job in the area they manage.

Table 8-4 shows how this model ties into the Gagné-Briggs nine events of instruction.

Implementation Ideas for Trainers

Trainers need to consider several issues for training to be effective. They must ensure that everything is ready on time, that they provide an initial positive impression, and that they gain and maintain trainee interest. Below are some things to consider in that regard.

Preparation

As a trainer, you need to arrive at the training site early enough to ensure that everything is in order. Check seating arrangements and make sure that materials have arrived. Before trainees begin arriving, ensure that all equipment is working and that you know how to operate it. Do not assume that you can turn it on. Try it and find out. Check the projector to see that a spare bulb is stored inside. If not, find a spare (if you don't, you are tempting the fates). If a video will be used, try out the remote control to ensure that it works and that you know how it operates. Ensure that there are enough newsprint and markers available. As the trainer, you need to be sure that everything is ready to go before the trainees arrive; otherwise, you can lose your credibility before you get started. In addition to preparation of the room and equipment, the trainer needs to make sure that she is prepared. This means that she has completed a dry run, is comfortable with the materials and their use, and is at

Table 8-4 Relationship between the Experiential Learning Model and Gagné-Briggs Nine Events of Instruction

EXPERIENTIAL LEARNING MODEL	GAGNÉ-BRIGGS NINE EVENTS OF INSTRUCTION[a]
Experience: Exercise/game	**Attention:** The exercise provides a task that gets trainees sharing their experiences and becoming very involved in the process.
	Stimulating recall of prior knowledge: Through the exercise, trainees are required to generate ideas and information that is based on prior knowledge.
Lecturette: Providing information	**Informing trainee of the goal or objective:** Prior to providing information, it would be useful to reiterate the objective even if it had been done before the start of the training session.
	Presenting stimulus material: Lecture material
Processing: Analysis of experience and information	**Providing learning guidance:** Discussions allow for the trainees to explore the previous experience and tie it into what they have learned. Assess performance and provide feedback.
Generalizability: Relevancy to other situations	**Providing learning guidance:** Discuss how the learned information fits similar situations, and see where the new information fits in their schema. This discussion will clarify where it fits into the individual trainee's schema for ease of retrieval in different relevant situations.
Practice: Try it out	**Eliciting Performance:** Practice the new learning.
Experience[b]**:** More complex or varied example of the new learning	**Enhancing retention and transfer:** Practice on different situations provides increased likelihood that the new learning will not only be retained but transfer to the job.

[a]As noted in the text, this exact order of the events need not always occur.
[b]Note that Experience both begins and completes the Gagné-Briggs nine events.

ease facilitating exercises and activities. She has rehearsed her presentation of the material to the point where she appears to be engaged in normal conversation rather than regurgitating memorized material. Finally, preparation means that the trainees have been prepared. They have been provided with information about where the training will be held and the time it begins. They should also have been informed of the purpose of training (the overall training objective) and perhaps even a summary of the agenda. By providing the participants with this information ahead of time, you help reduce their anxiety and increase their comfort levels.

First Impression

Earlier we discussed the impact on trainer credibility of factors such as topic knowledge and experience as well as trainer competencies. Those effects occur after the trainer has had an opportunity to interact with the participants for a while. Some things a trainer does can impact the participant's perception of the trainer's credibility right at the start of training (or even before). Typically, the favorable (or unfavorable) impression that a job candidate makes in a selection interview is made in the first few minutes. The same is true of the impression that the trainer makes on trainees. Since this issue is so critical to effective training, the first few minutes need to be managed well. In the case at the beginning of the chapter, what kind of first impression do you think Jason Reston made? Did he establish any credibility with the trainees? Did he demonstrate a concern for their needs? Did he seem approachable?

What should a trainer wear? The answer is: know the audience. If unsure, ask. In many situations, a business suit is a safe bet. Training accountants, who all come to work in conservative business attire, suggests that a business suit is a good idea. This same attire, however, could create distance from some other groups. Training line workers from a manufacturing plant, for example, might require more casual dress—not wearing the uniform of management. Remember, the trainees should perceive the trainer as someone able to help them in their job. To gain this credibility, the trainer needs to dress accordingly. The right dress for training line workers might be casual dress—tasteful casual, but casual nevertheless.

It is equally important that the clothes are clean, pressed, and fit well; that shoes are shined; and that accessories match the outfit. Hair style and coloring should be appropriate. This first impression will help establish your credibility. In one instance, one of the authors was using a graduate student to assist in a project at a major automobile manufacturer. They were to arrive on site the day before to meet with representatives of the company to go over the activities that would begin the following day. The author picked up the student for the four-hour drive to the company only to discover that the student had purple and orange hair cut in a "monk" style. What type of credibility do you think the author would have had if he had shown up with his "assistant"? Needless to say, a trip to the hair salon occurred prior to arrival at the client's offices.

If the dress code is a suit, and you are not as comfortable conducting your training in this attire, you can always take off the jacket and roll up your sleeves after the training gets underway. Trainees also need to feel comfortable, and the trainer can signal a more relaxed atmosphere by removing his jacket and loosening his tie. The trainer might say, "I think I need to loosen up a bit; please feel free to do the same." For training spread over several days, at some point on the first day, the trainer should ask the trainees to decide on a suitable dress code.

The Start of Training

Greet Participants and Make Them Comfortable   First impressions begin when trainees walk through the door of the training room. When trainees begin to arrive, greet them individually. Small talk with individual trainees before the session helps make them comfortable and, in turn, will facilitate discussion once the training begins. If there is assigned seating, show the participant where they will be sitting. Make sure to explain any materials that are at their seats and what to do with them. If you have refreshments available, point out their location and invite the participant to partake.

Start Up, Objectives, Expectations, and Ground Rules   Starting on time is important, but most trainers we know allow for some tardiness the first day, when trainees might not know exactly where the training room is, or simply did not give themselves enough time to get to the location. Whether you start on time or not, one reason for starting with an icebreaker is that it allows those who may arrive a little late to fit right in with little disruption and not miss any of the content of the program.

After the icebreaker, begin training by warmly greeting the participants (if you haven't done so prior to the icebreaker). Follow this with a description of the purpose of the training and a review of the learning objectives. This will help provide focus for the training, and, if the needs analysis was successful, it will mean that all trainees will understand the need to learn the KSAs. When going through the learning objectives, you will want to make sure that they are stated in easily understood language. If you have an extensive number of learning objectives, you will probably want to list major objectives only (ones that incorporate a number of lesser objectives).

Trainees might come with differing expectations about what the training will be about, and they also may have a variety of personal goals related to the training. After reviewing the objectives, it is useful to ask trainees if they have any additional expectations for training. You might ask each person to develop lists to present to the larger group or ask them to do this in small groups. Typically, this will not take long as your discussion of the learning objectives will have addressed most of the participant expectations. As participants report out their expectations, write these on a flip chart or whiteboard for future reference. Indicate to the trainees which of the points mentioned will be a part of the training and which will not. For any points that are not part of the training design, you might offer to try to fit them in if they coincide with your objectives. If not, explain why they are not appropriate for this training session and offer to meet with them during break time to discuss where they might go to address that need. This process clarifies for the participants what the training will and will not cover. Make sure to refer back to the list periodically as you move through the training to be sure that all the things you promised were in fact covered. At the conclusion of training, it is useful to review the list with the participants to ensure that you have not forgotten to address any of their expectations.

Following the discussion of expectations, go through the agenda to indicate what will be happening over the duration of the training. As you go through the agenda, indicate where the items on the list of expectations will be covered. Explain how breaks will be distributed and how messages for the trainees will be handled.

Following the agenda, initiate a discussion of the ground rules for training. This should cover things like starting and ending on time, breaks, leaving the training room while training is being conducted, use of cell phones, how messages from the office will be handled, and so on. You might start off the discussion by focusing on the issue of starting on time and why this is important. Recall reinforcement theory as discussed in Chapter 3. If those who arrive late discover that training has not begun, it reinforces the belief that showing up on time is not necessary. A late start also punishes those who do arrive on time. For the rule of starting on time to be effective, however, it is necessary to obtain commitment from the trainees. Thus, you provide the rationale and then ask for any discussion. Following the discussion, you can ask for a consensus vote of all in favor of starting and ending on time. You can use the same procedure for the other ground rules. The trainees are more likely to abide by these rules because they helped develop them. To expedite the process, prepare a set of suggested ground rules and explain why they are useful. Then ask the trainees for any suggestions to modify, add, or delete from the list.

The Podium

One of the authors was hired to assist a consultant in training automobile workers in a new plant. The consultant hired a number of local people because of the size of the project. Concurrent training sessions allowed opportunities for the trainers to observe one another. One trainer was in the habit of sitting behind a table while talking to the trainees, another stood behind a podium, and the rest stood and moved around, going back to their notes only occasionally. Which procedure is best? Again, it depends. Standing behind the podium or sitting at a desk is acceptable for one-way communication, but it is not the most effective style for training adults, for whom two-way communication is important. In these cases, any barriers (desk, podium) present nonverbal impediments to the communication process. Additionally, seeing someone who is teaching them sitting behind a desk might remind some trainees of unpleasant school experiences. Being out in front of a desk or podium and moving around helps make the trainer look more accessible and open to input. In any event, two-way communication is much more important in the lecture/discussion method, whereas for the straight lecture, a podium is perfectly acceptable. A skilled trainer will use the podium to signal to trainees when interruptions and comments are acceptable and when they are not.

Communication Tips

Communicating with trainees occurs continuously in face-to-face training programs. We provided several trainer tips earlier in our discussion of the lecture/discussion method. We need to elaborate a bit here on how trainers should respond to trainees when they make comments. Trainers may think that they are encouraging trainees to talk, but, in reality, trainer responses often do not facilitate learning or encourage the trainee. For example, comments following a trainee's response such as "yes," "OK," "thank you," and so on, do little other than acknowledge that the trainee has spoken. Examine the following exchange between a trainer and a participant:

> PARTICIPANT: "At the company where I used to work, we made product changes based on customer feedback."
> TRAINER: "That's very interesting. Does anyone else have a comment?"

The trainer's response, while acknowledging the comment doesn't indicate why the response is of interest or how it fits into the topic. A better response would have been to say

> TRAINER: "That's very interesting since it relates to our discussion of how to meet or exceed customer expectations. Can you tell us how you were able to get the customer feedback and the process that was used for integrating that into your workflow?"

Trainee comments and dialogue need to be encouraged by the trainer, but the trainer needs to do more. The trainer must use those comments and dialogue to foster learning. That can only be done if the trainer understands the content of the training well enough to incorporate the comments into learning opportunities.

Below are some other things to consider as you respond to participants in your training.

Listening and Questioning   Good listening and questioning skills separate good trainers from average or poor trainers. This statement is not to demean presentation skills but rather to stress the importance of listening and questioning. The techniques discussed earlier cannot be emphasized too strongly. If you are using the lecture/ discussion method, use the experience and information provided by the trainees. Control the urge to tell them continually about your experiences. Remember that trainees relate to one another and their experiences more often than to yours. In the beginning, it might be helpful to share your relevant experiences to establish credibility and to show that sharing of experiences is desirable and useful. As training moves on, you will want to encourage trainees to begin sharing their experiences that are related to the training.

This requires being a good listener. Good listening is difficult for several reasons, including the ones listed below:

- We can process information much faster than someone speaks, which gives us opportunities to do or think of other things.
- We often believe that we know what the person is going to say, so we interrupt to respond.
- We believe that speaking, not listening, is where the power and control are.

Therefore, listening requires practice. Active listening, originally developed for clinical counseling, involves three steps:

1. Listen carefully to what is said.
2. Summarize in your mind what was said.
3. Feed the summary back to the individual.

Following this process helps keep us focused, but more important, it confirms to the speaker (and all other trainees) what has been said, and leaves little room for misunderstandings. Training in Action 8-4 provides an example of active listening.

Dialogue between trainer and trainee at the training workshop on decision making:

> TRAINEE: This is training in decision making, but I am in sales. What I want to know is how will this training help me?
>
> TRAINER: You want to know how this training will help you improve your sales?
>
> TRAINEE: No, not necessarily in sales . . . Just help me do my job better.
>
> TRAINER: So you would like to know what the benefits of this training are and how these benefits will help you do your job.
>
> TRAINEE: Yes, that's right.

Providing Instructions   It is important to provide clear instructions with each exercise used. Many role-play exercises are wasted because trainees do not understand exactly what is expected. Oral instructions certainly need to be provided, but a handout containing the same information is also a useful resource for trainees. Even then, it is helpful to provide an example of what is expected. Once the exercise has begun, it is too late. It is discouraging both to the trainer and to the trainees if the trainees are confused and embarrassed because they misunderstood what they were supposed to be doing.

Moving Around While Talking   This technique does not imply methodically pacing back and forth, but rather moving out from behind the podium. If a podium must be used, step away from it at times. If possible, stay away from it altogether. Moving around while lecturing shows knowledge of, and comfort with, the material. Approaching trainees from time to time and talking specifically to them sets up a friendly atmosphere. The movement also requires trainees to follow the trainer with their eyes, preventing the "glazed stare" that can occur if the trainer is stationary.

Using Nonverbal Communication   Everyone is always sending out **nonverbal cues,** so it is important that these cues are the correct ones. Keep eye contact on a trainee who is asking a question; do not turn and walk away while the trainee is talking. Give a head nod when a trainee answers a question, and hold eye contact. Also, maintain eye contact with the trainee group as a whole while talking to them. Avoid talking to the image on the screen, or the lecture notes. Avoid folding your arms, as it can suggest displeasure or that the discussion is over. If writing on the board or flip chart, turn your head to the trainees while talking.

The key to nonverbal behavior is to convey enthusiasm about the information being discussed. If the enthusiasm is real rather than feigned, it will show in nonverbal expressions. Think of someone passionately arguing a point of view. Are her arms out in front and her palms up? Perhaps she is moving her hands up and down in short gestures. In any case, it is unlikely that her arms are folded across her chest.

What if the trainer is not enthusiastic about the material that must be presented? This lack of energy can develop after presenting the same material a number of times. What to do? First, realize how important enthusiasm is to effective training. Recall training sessions in which you were the trainee. It is easy to distinguish a good trainer from a not-so-good trainer. The good one was enthusiastic. So the trainer needs to psych himself up to generate enthusiasm. The trainer needs to give himself reasons to be enthusiastic about the material. Remember, the trainees are not as familiar with the material as the trainers. Starting off enthusiastically will be infectious, for both the trainees and the trainer.

Getting Rid of Dysfluencies   **Dysfluencies** are those "and uh," "like," "um" space fillers injected into speech. Everyone uses them occasionally, but some use them far too often. This tendency is usually more prominent when a trainer is nervous or unsure. It becomes immediately noticeable, and trainees tend to focus on these utterances rather than on the material. Videorecording lectures, or simply asking others to inform you when you use dysfluencies, can help you get rid of them.

Tips on Dealing with Different Participant Personalities

A successful trainer needs to understand how to deal with the various types of trainees that might be encountered. Some will need to be encouraged to become more involved in discussion, while others are far too involved.

Quiet Trainee   In Chapter 6, we discussed methods for encouraging quiet trainees to become more involved (small group discussions, writing their answers first), and these approaches are usually successful. What if they do not work? If there are several small groups for discussion sessions, one way to encourage the quiet trainee is to ask each group to rotate the person who is responsible for reporting back to the larger group. The quiet trainee will then take a turn reporting to the larger group, thus increasing his participation. However, too much pressure to become involved is not a good idea. If a quiet person is speaking up during the small group sessions, he is providing input. Do not attempt to get these trainees to participate at a level equal to others if they are not so inclined. Doing so can create too much tension in the environment. If all these methods are tried with little change in the quiet trainee's behavior, do not push any further. Further attempts will only create barriers to the trainee's learning.

Talkative Trainee   The talkative trainee is usually far more of a problem than the quiet one. No matter what question is asked, this trainee wants to answer. Usually the answer involves a long story, and soon other trainees are rolling their eyes and tuning out. The trainer loses the trainees' attention, and valuable training time is wasted on irrelevant stories. It is important to tone down that trainee's input but not embarrass anyone. One approach is to ask others for their opinion. Say something like "We have been making Lex do all the work here so far—how about someone else responding?" Or use the direct questioning technique to get the focus away from the talkative trainee. It may be helpful to speak to the talkative trainee in private, suggesting that her comments are appreciated, but there is a concern that others are not participating as much as they should. In this context, asking the talkative trainee to hold back on participation usually works.

Angry Trainee   Some trainees who come to training simply do not want to be there. They set out to ruin the session for everyone. Such trainees must be dealt with early on before they disrupt the class. One of the authors was training line workers in team concepts, and although the union executive and most union members were supportive of the training, some were violently opposed. In the first session, one of these trainees said, "I really do not want to be here; this training is management propaganda designed to weaken the union." The author's response was "I have heard that said before; how do others feel about the training?" At that point, a number of others indicated support for the training, and although the angry trainee did not participate much in the rest of the training, he did not disrupt it either.

If in such a situation most trainees felt the same way, it would be wise to spend some time discussing the issue because such an attitude will certainly affect training. The important point is to focus on how training can benefit them. One way to accomplish this task is to ask trainees to identify ways they would be able to use the training.

The Comedian   These trainees are a gift and a curse. They are a gift because when their jokes work, and if they are not put forth too often, they will do wonders to set a positive tone. Laughter is good medicine, and a comedian is able to provide it. The potential curse is in the nature and frequency of the jokes. Some jokes are clearly out of place. In other cases, it is difficult to know what is offensive. However, it is not productive for even a small number of trainees to feel that a particular joke was offensive. Also, if the comedians do get a lot of laughs, they are likely to continue to joke around. This behavior can disrupt the timing of the sessions and put the trainer behind.

What to do? If the joking gets out of hand or some jokes are inappropriate, you can talk with the comedian at a break. Indicate a concern that some of the humor is offensive to some of the other trainees or is distracting from the focus of training. In taking this approach, you need to indicate appreciation of the comedian's intention to contribute to the training, but reach an agreement about how often the jokes can be offered and what types of jokes are acceptable. This conversation should be enough to curb such behavior. Sometimes the comedian's jokes are directed at the trainer. In these cases, the trainer must have a tough skin and be willing to laugh without taking it personally. This reaction will defuse any tension that may have been created, reduce the amount of distraction, and show that the trainer is not "too full of herself." It is only when the jokes become distracting or offensive that action needs to be taken.

Dry Run

In the training model, the process component of the implementation phase contains two important steps that should be completed before training is ready for general use:[22] the dry run and the pilot program. The former is a rehearsal of the training program to test out new material, work out delivery issues, and firm up the timing of different segments. In some situations, the training package might not need to be presented in its entirety. The pilot program is the first full-blown presentation of the training using finished materials.

The **dry run** is not designed to actually train participants who assume the role of trainees. Instead, it is designed to determine the value and clarity of the various pieces of the training program, identify and correct any delivery problems, work through timing issues and otherwise make sure that the training is ready for delivery. The dry run provides a controlled setting in which these issues can be discussed and resolved. In general, the dry run will take much longer than the actual training, so enough time should be set aside to not only deliver the material but also make necessary adjustments. To this end, it is necessary to get as many key perspectives as possible to view the training. The trainer should be the person(s) who will actually deliver the training. For a really effective dry run, use some potential trainees but choose them carefully; consider their diverse backgrounds, their general supportiveness of the value of training, and their willingness to provide feedback. More seasoned employees will be able to help evaluate the transferability of the training back to the job. Include some content experts who can provide feedback on the validity of the material and its usage. Some members of the training design and development team should also participate in the dry run, assuming the role of trainees or observers. They can provide feedback as to how well the various pieces of the design fit together.

The dry run might not require that all the training modules in the program be tested. If a previously used specific exercise, case, or role-play has been used with a similar target population, the dry run for this exercise might simply involve the participants reading through the exercise and providing feedback as to its relevance. However, you should make sure that the exercise or activity has enough history to provide you with an accurate estimate of the time it will take during an actual training session. Newly developed or occasionally used exercises and activities require the dry run participants to go through the full process, providing feedback after it is completed.

It is important to ask participants and observers a list of questions after each exercise or module that is tested. For example, after participants complete a role-play, you ask the following:

- Is the situation realistic for this organization? If it is not, future trainees might dismiss the training as being irrelevant.
- Is the information and direction for the exercise clear enough for trainees to do the exercise?
- Is the time allocation too long or too short?

After the dry run is completed, examine the feedback carefully, and revise the training where applicable. Then it is time for the pilot program.

Pilot Program

The **pilot program** is different from the dry run in that trainees are there to be trained. It will be a full-fledged training program. The dry run refines the training to eliminate any major glitches. In the pilot program, trainees are again chosen carefully, as you want people who are generally supportive of training and who are not likely to be disruptive. Trainees will spread the word about training to others in the organization quickly. That word should be as positive as possible so that when new trainees come into the program, they bring positive expectations. The pilot program will provide additional input to further refine the training (if necessary), and disruptions are not conducive to this process. To evaluate how the training comes across to different groups, it is desirable to have a good cross section of those who will be in the later training sessions.

The main goals of the pilot program are as follows:

- To provide the trainees with the relevant training
- To assess further the timing and relevance of modules and various training components
- To determine the appropriateness, clarity, and flow of material

The pilot program provides valuable responses and viewpoints that are inserted in the trainer's manual. These inputs will help guide new trainers in what to expect. Another use of the pilot program is to provide an opportunity for future trainers to attend the training and experience what takes place firsthand. Finally, the pilot program will provide valuable feedback to designers regarding the effectiveness of the training.

After the pilot program, any revisions are documented in the training plan and trainer's manual and implemented in future training sessions. If new material or activities are added, these should be perfected in a dry run. Thus it is possible that a training program might have a dry run, followed by a pilot program, followed by another dry run that would be followed by the actual training. One final note: Although a dry run and a pilot program will help improve the program, evaluation and appropriate revisions should not stop here. Training evaluation goes on continuously. The primary objective of training is the transfer of the training to the job to positively affect organizational results. Training should continue to be modified until desirable outcomes can be reliably achieved.

Going back to the model, the output of the implementation phase is the learned KSAs and evaluation (discussed in Chapter 9). When trainees are back on the job, it is expected that the new learning will be transferred to the job. This issue of transfer was discussed in Chapter 5 and will be further elaborated on here.

Transfer of training to the job can be simple and easy, or, at the other extreme, complex and next to impossible. Consider training on how to complete a new requisition form. Once training is complete and the form is available, transfer of the new behavior should be relatively easy. However, consider the supervisor training that teaches a supervisor to take time to use conflict resolution skills to deal with subordinates. Back on the job, the supervisor is measured by the units his subordinates produce. In the past, being angry and yelling at them resulted in high productivity. Here, transfer of the new behaviors is less likely. Figure 8-3 helps us examine this more difficult type of transfer in more detail.

First, because the new behaviors are more difficult and not part of the trainee's regular behavior, he will need to practice these new behaviors on the job. Examining Figure 8-3, there are two inputs that specifically influence this: trainer support and relapse prevention/goal setting. Trainer support can come from a sit in. The design phase is where you would obtain the trainers commitment to do a sit in. Recall from chapter 5 that in a sit in the trainer follows the trainee around for a while noting how he is using the skills, and then provides feedback. Providing the trainee with the relapse prevention/goal setting process will help him when relapses do happen. These two inputs along with the other non-shaded inputs in the model are factors that the trainer can directly influence. The shaded factors also affect transfer back on the job but are not directly controlled by the trainer. All these inputs will increase the likelihood that transfer will occur.

Other inputs into the transfer of training not directly controlled by the trainer, such as supervisor and peer support, will provide an incentive for the trainee to practice the new behaviors. The supervisor and peers should be encouraged to support these new behaviors as part of regular job performance. The supervisor in

Figure 8-3
Transfer of Training

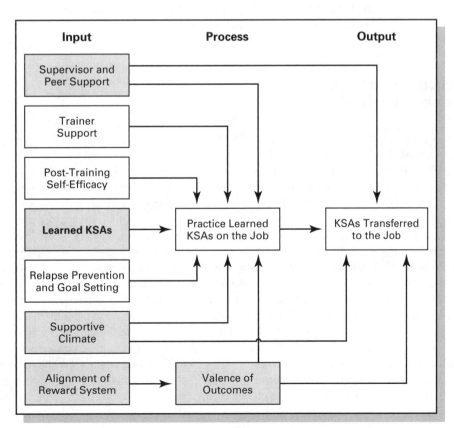

particular needs to help the trainee by providing support and feedback as to how the trainee is doing. Trainers hope for supportive climate and culture, as these will increase the likelihood that the new behaviors will be practiced and maintained during and after transfer. Recall from Chapter 3 that successful completion of training should have a positive impact on the trainees' posttraining self-efficacy. This, in turn, should encourage them to practice the learned KSAs on the job. Finally, alignment of the reward systems to encourage the new behaviors will add to the likelihood that the transfer will take place and be lasting, provided they have a high enough valence.

From the training needs analysis, any reward systems that were not aligned, or supervisor and peer attitudes toward the training that were dysfunctional, should have been identified. Plans to make needed changes in these areas should have been addressed in the design phase and implemented prior to training. The output of Figure 8-3 is the complete transfer of the KSAs to the job. The degree to which this is achieved depends on how many of the input factors are aligned to support the transfer.

Of all the forces that are important to ensure transfer, peer support can be the most problematic. Peer pressure from those who have been around for a long time and who are comfortable doing things the "old way" can do a great deal to inhibit a trainee's ability to change, even if she wants to. In many cases, this peer pressure for the status quo is very difficult to change. Training in Action 8-5 provides an example where Ford was successful in dealing with potential peer pressure. However, this involved a new plant, new relationships, and training focused on changing attitudes. It is very different in an older plant where employees are set in their ways and there are strong relationships among the workers. In cases like this, change management skills are required to help employees see the advantages of new ways and obtain their support. A review of Training in Action 5-2 provides a reminder of just how much can and should be done to ensure that transfer of training takes place. After all, without it, the training was a waste of money.

TRAINING IN ACTION 8-5
Peer Pressure and New Skills

Ford needed a new plant and was determined to implement a more flexible work system that included teamwork in this new plant. So, before agreeing to build the plant in Windsor, Ford management insisted that the Canadian Auto Workers union sign a "special operating agreement" to allow such changes. However, the union was strong, and many of those who transferred to the new plant were strong union members who believed in the old way of working. They laughed at the idea of teamwork. Peer pressure in such a situation was a concern. It could derail any effort to institute this major change to the way work was done. If peers on the shop floor were making fun of the idea of teamwork, it would be difficult to get others interested and willing to be involved.

At the opening of the plant, all workers who had transferred to the new plant were required to attend a week of training. To deal with this potential negative impact of peer pressure, Ford incorporated information designed to change attitudes toward this more flexible system of working into this training program. In the beginning, some trainees were openly hostile to the training. One said: "The company pays me to come here, but they cannot force me to learn this stuff." Others, by their lack of participation, were likely feeling the same but were not as vocal. However, by the end of the week, many were actively involved, and when asked at the end of training what they thought of the more flexible work systems, most indicated a positive response. Was there transfer to the job? There was no formal evaluation, but most did become actively involved back on the job. Although there were still those actively opposed to it who did not get involved, there were not enough of them to create the pressure on peers to stay uninvolved.

CASE: Jack Goes to Training. . . (Conclusion)

"Get up. Get up, you're going to be late for the training!"

"Huh," grunted Jack. "What time is it?"

"It's 7:30 and you have to go downtown to the training center today, remember?" said his wife.

Wow, what a dream, thought Jack, feeling a little nervous as he walked up the steps of the training center. The training room was not at all like a schoolroom. No windows, no blackboards. As he entered the room, a nicely dressed man approached him and said, "Hi, my name is Doug, welcome to the training center. Have you ever been here before?" The name tag indicated that Doug was the trainer. He seems like a nice guy, thought Jack.

"There's some coffee and doughnuts over there—help yourself," said Doug. This might even be enjoyable, thought Jack, although he still felt a little apprehensive.

With introductions out of the way and the objectives and agenda explained, Doug summed up by saying, "So at the end of the two days you will be expected to take a set of specifications and program them into the machine. Are there any questions?"

"So there are no tests?" asked Jack.

"Well," responded Doug, "that is the test."

Jack was a bit confused. "But that is what we do at work—I don't see it as a test. A test is where I have to write down an answer to some question you pose about all this stuff."

"There are no paper-and-pencil tests, just behavioral tests," said Doug.

Suddenly it was lunchtime. Jack thought, "It's true, time does go fast when you are having fun. This sure isn't like school." All 23 trainees went to another room where lunch was served.

"I can't believe it. This is nothing like I expected," said Ron. Ron was the fellow who Jack had to interview and introduce to the group in what was called an icebreaker. That icebreaker sure did a lot to get me relaxed and actually interested in the training, thought Jack.

Ron continued, "I always did poorly in school and was petrified about coming here." Jack responded, "Me too."

Ron said, "I like the idea of his periodically giving us mini-tests. Gives us an idea of how we are doing and provides us with extra help if we are falling behind."

"Tests . . . oh, yeah, I find it hard to consider them tests. They're hands-on, exactly what we will do on the job," said Jack.

Later Jack thought, "Wow, it's already over."

"Nice job, Jack. You are now certified on this piece of equipment," said Doug.

"Hey, Ron," said Jack, "do you believe how much fun learning can be?"

Ron agreed: "Doug was great. He kept getting our input and tying our experiences to the new stuff we had to learn. I never thought I would say this, but I would like to get more training like this."

"You bet," said Jack. "I still can't believe how great this was, especially after the dream I had."

First, we discussed the development of training. At this stage, creating a program development plan is crucial to ensure that everything that needs to be done is done. This plan outlines everything that must be done to prepare for training, from material and equipment to trainee and trainer manuals. Content learning points from each learning objective need to be highlighted to clearly identify what needs to be learned.

The type of training facility chosen is also important. Arrangement of the seating and closeness of the trainer to the trainees should be a function of the objectives of the training, not the design of the room. Also, noise levels from adjoining rooms or from outside the room need to be determined before choosing a training room. The proper training facility then allows the seating to be arranged in a manner that best reflects what type of training will be taking place.

We examined the factors to consider when choosing a trainer, and specifically an OJT trainer, because of the unique issues that revolve around OJT trainers.

Alternatives to development of the training were examined. After all, sometimes it is simply not viable to develop training. In cases like this, the use of consultants, prepackaged training, and outside seminars can provide a solution. This is especially true for the small business.

In the implementation of training, we first focused on some practical issues related to keeping trainees' interest in training. Use of icebreakers, learning objectives, variety, and an example of a type of exercise to keep training interesting was discussed. Next we provided some tips for trainers in the execution of the training program. Preparation, importance of the first impression, what to consider at the start of training, and how to use the podium were all discussed. Finally, some tips on communication and how to deal with certain types of trainees were provided.

The dry run and the pilot program were discussed. Before implementation of a large training program, it is useful to have a dry run in which the material is tested to see how effective it is. This dry run is not an actual training session but a process of going through the material and determining whether it is doing what you expect it to. The next step is a pilot program in which the first trainees go through the training, but with selected supportive trainees, so they can spread the word about the training program in a positive manner. Also, constructive feedback from the trainees is solicited to put the finishing touches on the program before it is formally launched.

FABRICS, INC., DEVELOPMENT PHASE

Recall that in the design phase for Fabrics, Inc., we developed objectives. The output from the design was an examination of the various methods of instruction and factors that affect learning and transfer. These outputs are now the inputs into the development phase of training. The process is to develop an instructional strategy, which leads to a program development plan. The program development plan includes developing instructional material, obtaining needed instructional equipment and facilities, creating or obtaining trainee and trainer manuals (if applicable) and selecting a trainer. Below are partial examples of some of these outputs, starting with the instructor's manual.

Instructor's Manual

First we will provide a section of the instructor's manual that will take you through the start of the active listening training. This will lead into the practice sessions for active listening followed by an example of that material.

(continued)

INSTRUCTOR'S NOTES	TIMING	POINTS TO BE COVERED	REFERENCE
The question being asked is to get the trainees' attention and involvement in determining the need to learn how to listen.	20 min	Ask the question "Why do we need to attend a training session on how to listen? After all, listening is a natural thing, right?"	Easel
As you get trainee involvement, record their responses on an easel sheet. When ideas have been exhausted, examine the sheet, compare it to the prepared easel, and discuss any that had not been thought of by the trainees. Tape both to the wall next to each other.		Easel points • tend to believe that we have the correct answer so why listen to others; they need to listen to us • message overload, too much going on at once • believe that talking is more important • listening is the responsibility of the listener • listening is a passive activity	
Now ask for a volunteer to play a peer of yours at a meeting. When you have someone, set up the scenario of you two sitting in a room waiting for others to show up for a meeting. Progress on the task has been slow but sure. Ask them to respond to what you say as they would in a real situation.		Say to the volunteer "I am tired of coming to all these meetings—we never seem to get anything done."	
The volunteer will answer as most people do in situations like this as they move directly to dealing with the issue. Responses will likely be something like the following: • So what should we do about it? • We have made some progress. • Its not as bad as all that		After they respond, point out to all that this is a typical response, as most people move toward trying to address the concern in some way. Point out that what you need to do is provide support through active listening first, then move to deal with the problem.	
Give volunteer the statement to read, and ask to reverse the roles and say that same statement to you.		When they read the statement, respond something like "So you are saying that we are wasting our time at these meetings?"	Handout with statement on it
Now ask for volunteers. To each one say one of the following statements. Then provide feedback as to its effectiveness regarding active listening. . . .		• I do not want to work with Bill on any more projects; he never does his share. • You are always giving me unscheduled work. I can't get it done. • We tried that last year, and it did not work, so let's not go there again.	
Now you are going to provide the trainees with the opportunity to practice their new skill. You will need Instruction Sheet 1 to read from and Handout 1 to give to trainees while you read the instructions from Instruction Sheet 1.		Say "OK, now it is time for practice. I am handing out instructions for the practice sessions using Person 1, 2, 3; it is titled Handout 1. Now go to Instruction Sheet 1, and read the instructions to the trainees.	

THIS IS THE END OF THE INSTRUCTOR'S MANUAL EXAMPLE

The above is a sample of what should be contained in an instructor's manual. Now let's turn to instructional material.

Instructional Material

Part of the training is going to involve trainees practicing active listening skills they have been taught. Below are the instructions for this (Instruction Sheet 1) and a sample of the exercise "Person 1, 2, 3," which is an exercise designed to provide trainees with practice situations where they can use the new skill.

(continued)

INSTRUCTION SHEET 1 (Instructor reads this to trainees)

"Now that you have seen how to use active listening in your response, we are going to give everyone an opportunity to practice this skill. To do this, we are going to put you into groups of three trainees. Each person in the triad will have a sheet labeled "Person 1," "Person 2," or "Person 3." Now look at the Active Listening Exercise Instructions I have just handed out titled Handout 1, and follow along while I read it out loud."

The trainer now reads the instructions from the sheet (Handout 1) going down to the third situation (Situation C) and then asks if everyone understands or has any questions. Once the trainer is satisfied that everyone understands their roles, she puts them in groups of three and hands out the Person 1, 2, 3 sheets, one to each of the three person groups, again asking "Are there any questions?"

Below are the instructions that are handed out for the exercise "Person 1, 2, 3."

HANDOUT 1 Active Listening Exercise Instructions

Initiator: Begins the exercise with a conflict-provoking statement.
Active Listener: Receives the statement from the initiator and provides an appropriate response.
Observer: Watches the interchange between the initiator and the active listener. After completion, the observer gives feedback regarding the appropriateness of the active listener's comment. NOTE: You have an example of an effective active listening response to that situation, so as an observer you can coach the active listener if necessary.

Each group member will be alternating among the three roles!

SITUATION	PERSON 1	PERSON 2	PERSON 3
A	Initiator	Active Listener	Observer
B	Observer	Initiator	Active Listener
C	Active Listener	Observer	Initiator
D	Initiator	Active Listener	Observer
E	Observer	Initiator	Active Listener
F	Active Listener	Observer	Initiator
And so forth			

(continued)

Below are the handouts for the three person groups. Each person in a group will receive Person 1, 2, or 3.

PERSON 1

Situation

A   Person 2 is the Active Listener
Person 3 is the Observer

YOU ARE THE INITIATOR
Your boss just finished
giving you a lecture for
not being at the job site.

You start. Say angrily: **"HOW COME YOU NEVER WAIT TO HEAR MY SIDE OF THE STORY. YOU JUST ASSUME I'M IN THE WRONG."**

B   Person 2 is the Initiator
Person 3 is the Active Listener

YOU ARE THE OBSERVER
The active listener is meeting
with a subordinate regarding
their performance. The listener
has just told the subordinate that
her performance is average.
Listen and provide feedback

Response example: **"YOU'RE SAYING I RATED YOU LOWER THAN WHAT YOU DESERVE."**

C   Person 2 is the Observer
Person 3 is the Initiator

YOU ARE THE ACTIVE LISTENER
A group of equal-level managers
are meeting on a project. You
believe that these meetings need
some structure, so you have taken
control of the meetings. Listen, then
respond to the comment by saying:

(continued)

PERSON 2

Situation

A   Person 1 is the Initiator
     Person 3 is the Observer

     YOU ARE THE ACTIVE LISTENER
     You just reprimanded your
     subordinate for not being at
     the job site. Listen, then respond to comment by saying:

B   Person 3 is the Active Listener
     Person 1 is the Observer

     YOU ARE THE INITIATOR
     You have just been told that your
     performance rating for the year
     is average. You are angry.

     Say angrily: "YOU ONLY RATED MY PERFORMANCE AS AVERAGE. THAT'S
                                     RIDICULOUS. I AM 10 TIMES BETTER THAN ANY OF THE
                                     OTHERS IN MY DEPARTMENT."

C   Person 1 is the Active Listener
     Person 3 is the Initiator

     YOU ARE THE OBSERVER
     A group of equal-level managers are
     meeting on a project. The active
     listener believes that the meetings needed
     some structure and took charge.
     Listen and provide feedback.

     Response example: "SO YOU ARE SAYING THAT WHEN I BEHAVE THIS WAY, I'M
                                     ACTING TOO MUCH LIKE A BOSS."

PERSON 3

Situation

A   Person 1 is the Initiator
     Person 2 is the Active Listener

     YOU ARE THE OBSERVER
     The active listener just
     reprimanded a subordinate for
     not being at the job site.
     Listen and provide feedback.

     Response example: "SO YOU'RE SAYING I NEVER GAVE YOU THE OPPORTUNITY
                                     TO PRESENT YOUR POINT OF VIEW."

(continued)

B   Person 1 is the Observer
Person 2 is the Initiator

YOU ARE THE ACTIVE LISTENER
You are meeting with a
subordinate regarding their
performance. You have just told
the subordinate that their
performance was average.

Listen, then respond using
decoding and feedback.

C   Person 1 is the Active Listener
Person 2 is the Observer

YOU ARE THE INITIATOR
A group of equal-level managers
are meeting on a project. One
of these people has just taken
control of the meeting, and you
don't like it.

You start. Say angrily: **"YOU'RE CONTROLLING THESE MEETINGS LIKE YOU WERE THE BOSS. WE ARE ALL EQUAL HERE AND I AM SICK AND TIRED OF YOU ACTING LIKE THE BOSS."**

And so forth

We will return to Fabrics, Inc., in the next chapter (evaluation) to complete the example. As you might expect, similar exercises appear in the evaluation chapter that are designed to measure how much learning took place.

KEY TERMS

- Dry run
- Dysfluencies
- Icebreaker

- Instructional strategy
- Learning point
- Nonverbal cues

- Pilot program
- Program development plan
- Training plan

QUESTIONS FOR REVIEW

1. You are asked to deliver a two-day workshop for managers on effective feedback skills. It is focused primarily on performance reviews. Approximately 100 managers need to be trained. Describe what the content of the training would entail, the methods you would use (e.g., lecture, case study, role-play), and the instructional media and equipment you would want, and explain why. Also, what type of room setup would you want, and why? Indicate how many sessions you would need for this number of managers, and explain why.
2. Describe how the experiential learning model relates to the social learning model.
3. What are some typical difficult trainees, and how would you deal with them?
4. How do the dry run and pilot training differ? Why?

1. Check the room where your class meets. Does it meet the requirements of a good training room? What changes would make it more amenable to effective training?

2. Assume that you are in training on conflict resolution. Think of a situation in which you got into an argument with someone, and write up the role of the person with whom you were in conflict. Follow the instructions in the chapter. Do not forget that you need to write the role of the other person, not you, because you will play yourself. Show the role to a classmate and ask her to play it. As you play your part, try to behave differently from the way you did in the original confrontation. Although you do not have any training in the area of conflict resolution, simply try to remain calm and not turn the situation into a confrontation. Now debrief. How did it go? Was the role-play useful in helping you practice being calm? Ask the classmate whether the role you wrote could be better in terms of providing information as to how the classmate is to act.

3. In a small group, each person takes a turn giving a three-minute impromptu speech (on anything). Have someone designated as the bell ringer. Each time the speaker uses a dysfluency (uh, and uh, um, etc.), the bell ringer will hit a glass with a spoon (or make some other sound). Keep score for each person. Over the next few weeks, ask friends to tell you when you use these dysfluencies, and try to reduce them. Then get together with your group and redo the exercise. Do you note any improvement?

4. In small groups, choose someone who worked in a particular job. Interview the person to determine the job requirements and develop a procedure for providing OJT for the job.

WEB RESEARCH

Conduct a search on the Internet to identify tips for trainers in dealing with difficult trainees. Compare the types you find with the types identified in the text. If different, compare those you found with those in the text, and offer an explanation as to why you think they were not included. If types are similar, compare how the text and Internet suggest handling these types, noting any differences and explaining which method you prefer.

CASE ANALYSIS

Jim worked as a laborer for a gas utility in Winnipeg, Manitoba. When the opportunity came to apply for a backhoe/front-end-loader operator job, he was excited. Three people applied. To select the one who would get the job, the company asked each of them to go out and actually work on the backhoe for a day. Jim felt his chance for the job disappear because he had never even driven a tractor, let alone used a backhoe. When he went out, he did not know how to start the tractor. One of the other backhoe operators had to show him. He managed through the day, and to his surprise, did better than the others. He was given the job.

On his first day at the new job, one of the other backhoe operators showed him where to check the hydraulic fluid and said, "These old Masseys are foolproof. You will be okay." Jim taught himself how to dig a hole by trial and error. He initially believed that the best way was to fill the bucket as much as possible before lifting it out of the hole and emptying it. He would wiggle the bucket back and forth until it was submerged and then curl it. When it came out of the hole, the earth would be falling off the sides. This job was not so difficult after all, he thought.

He cut through his first water line about two weeks after starting his new job. Going into a deep, muddy hole did not make the crew happy. After Jim cut through his third water line, the crew chief pulled him aside and said, "You are taking too much earth out with each bucket, so you don't feel the bucket hitting the water line; ease up a bit." Water lines were usually six to eight feet down, so Jim would dig until about four feet and then try to be more careful. It was then that he pulled up some telephone lines that were only about three feet deep.

Realizing that more was involved in operating a backhoe than he first had thought, he sought out Bill Granger, who was known to have broken a water line only twice in his 15 years. It was said that he was so good that he could dig underneath the gas lines—a claim that Jim doubted. Bill said, "You need to be able to feel any restriction. The way to do that is to have more than one of your levers open at the same time. Operating the bucket lever and the boom lever at the same time reduces the power and causes the machine to stop rather than cut through a line of any type." Jim began to use this method but still broke water lines. The difference now was that he knew immediately when he broke a line. He could feel the extra pull, whereas in the past, he found out either by seeing water gushing up or by hearing the crew chief swearing at him. He was getting better. Jim never did become as good as Bill Granger. In fact, two years later, he applied for another job as gas repairperson and was promoted, but the training as a gas repairperson was not much better.

CASE QUESTIONS

1. What are the potential costs to this lack of training? Why do you think the company operated in this manner?
2. What type of training would you recommend: OJT, classroom, or a combination? Describe what the training might entail.
3. What type of training environment would you provide?
4. Who would you get to do the training, and why?
5. Would you consider purchasing a training program for backhoe operators? Provide your rationale.

Chapter 9

Evaluation of Training

EVALUATION PHASE

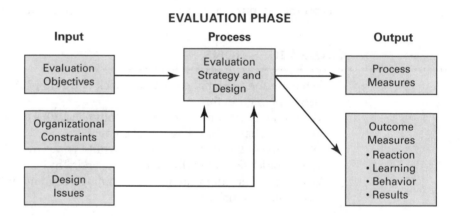

Learning Objectives

After reading this chapter, you should be able to:

➤ Describe the pros and cons of evaluation and indicate which way to go on the issue

➤ Explain what process evaluation is, and why it is important

➤ Describe the interrelationships among the various levels of outcome evaluation

➤ Describe the costs and benefits of evaluating training

➤ Differentiate between the two types of cost-effectiveness evaluation (cost savings and utility analysis)

➤ Describe the various designs that are possible for evaluation and their advantages and disadvantages

➤ Define and explain the importance of internal and external validity

The city of Palm Desert, California, decided to provide training to improve employees' attitudes toward their work and to provide them with the skills to be more effective on the job. The two-day seminar involved a number of teaching methods, including a lecture, films, role-plays, and group interaction. Among the topics covered were conflict control, listening, communicating, telephone etiquette, body language, delegation, and taking orders. Throughout the two days, the value of teamwork, creativity, and rational decision making was stressed and integrated into the training.

Before the training was instituted, all 55 nonmanagement employees completed a paper-and-pencil questionnaire to measure both their attitudes toward the job and their perception of their job behaviors. Supervisors also completed a questionnaire assessing each of their employees. All 55 employees were told that they would be receiving the same two-day seminar. The first set of 34 employees was chosen at random.

The 21 employees who did not take the training immediately became a comparison group for evaluating the training. While the first group of employees was sent to the training, the others were pulled off the job, ostensibly to receive training, but they simply took part in exercises not related to any training. Thus, both groups were treated similarly in every way except for the training. Both groups completed attitude surveys immediately after the trained group finished training. Six months later, both groups completed self-report surveys to measure changes in their job behavior. Their supervisors also were asked to complete a similar behavior measure at the six-month mark.

The data provided some revealing information. For the trained group, no changes in attitude or behavior were indicated, either by the self-report or by supervisor-reported surveys. This result was also true (but expected) for the group not trained.

---

*Source: Adapted from Miller, S. "Effects of municipal training on employee attitudes and behavior." *Public Personnel Management* 19 (1990), pp. 429–40.

Was training a failure in the Palm Desert case? Would the training manager be pleased with these results? Was the evaluation process flawed? These types of issues will be addressed in this chapter. We will refer back to the case from time to time to answer these and other questions.

RATIONALE FOR EVALUATION

Imagine a business that decided it would not look at its profitability, return on investment (ROI), or productivity. You are a supervisor with this company, but you never look at how well or poorly your subordinates are performing their jobs. This is what training is like when no evaluation is conducted. Good management practice dictates that organizational activities are routinely examined to ensure that they are occurring as planned and are producing the anticipated results. Otherwise, no corrective action can be taken to address people, processes, and products or services that stray "off track".

Nonetheless, many rationalizations for not evaluating training continue to exist, and evaluation of training is often not done. A 1988 survey of 45 *Fortune* 500 companies indicated that all of them asked trainees how much they liked training, but only 30 percent assessed how much was learned, and just 15 percent examined behavioral change.[1] Other evidence from that time suggested that only 1 company in 100 used an effective system for measuring the organizational effects and value of training.[2] But this is changing. In a 1996 study, 70 percent assessed learning, 63 percent assessed behavior, and 25 percent assessed organizational results.[3] Evaluation of training at all levels is becoming more common. Nevertheless, the evaluation of training is still not where it needs to be. A study of 140 businesses of all sizes and types shows that the things organizations view as the most important outcomes of training are still not being measured very often.[4]

But, as noted, over the course of 20 years, more organizations are evaluating training. The main reason for this is an increase in accountability. Top management is demanding evidence that training departments are contributing positively to the bottom line.[5] Dave Palm, training director of LensCrafters, knows firsthand about this trend. A frantic regional manager called Dave and told him that executives were looking to improve the bottom line and could not find enough evidence that training programs were providing a quantifiable return on the company's investment. Yes, they knew that trainees were satisfied with training, but was the company getting the bang for their buck? The conversation ended with the regional manager saying, "So, Dave, what are you going to do about it?" Dave got his wake-up call.[6]

RESISTANCE TO TRAINING EVALUATION

Training managers can come up with a surprising number of reasons for not evaluating training, including the following:

- There is nothing to evaluate.
- No one really cares about it.
- Evaluation is a threat to my job.

There Is Nothing to Evaluate

For some companies, training is simply a reward for good performance, or something that is mandated so everyone has to attend.[7] The argument here is that training is not expected to accomplish anything, so there is nothing to evaluate.

The Counterargument   The first thing we would question here is why the company is spending money on something that has no value. We would argue that even in cases where training is a reward, it is designed with some goals or objectives in mind. Some type of knowledge, skills, or attitude (KSA) change is expected from the participants even if it is just that they feel more positive about their job or the company. Once this goal or objective is identified, it can be measured. Evaluation is simply measuring the degree to which objectives are achieved. Even when training is mandated, such as safety training, there are still objectives to be achieved in terms of learning, job behavior, and the organization.

No One Really Cares About Evaluating Training

The most common rationale for not conducting training evaluations is that "formal evaluation procedures are too expensive and time-consuming, and no one really cares anyway." This explanation usually means that no one specifically asked for, demanded, or otherwise indicated a need for assessment of training outcomes.

The Counterargument   If an evaluation is not specifically required, this does not mean that training is not evaluated. Important organizational decisions (e.g., budget, staffing, performance evaluations) are made with data when data exist, but will also be made if the data do not exist. If no formal evaluations of training have taken place, the decision makers will decide on the basis of informal impressions of training's effectiveness. Even in good economic times, the competition for organizational budget allocations is strong. Departments that can document their contributions to the organization and the return on budget investment are more likely to be granted their budget requests. The question, then, is not whether training should be evaluated, but rather who will do it (training professionals or budget professionals), how it will be done (systematic and formally or informal impressions), and what data will be used (empirical studies of results or hearsay and personal impressions).

Evaluation Is a Threat to My Job

Think about it. According to the Industry Report conducted by *Training* magazine, training budgets in the United States totaled over 56 billion dollars in 2008.[8] Why wouldn't human resource development (HRD) departments be evaluating their results? Fear of the result is one reason. Football coach Woody Hayes, back in the 1950s, once said that he never liked to throw the forward pass because three things could happen and two of them were bad. The same could be said for evaluation. If time and money are spent on training, and an evaluation determines that no learning occurred, or worse, job performance declined, this doesn't reflect well on the training provided. Although most managers are not likely to admit this concern publicly, it can be a real problem. When we use the term *evaluation*, we too often think of a single final outcome at a particular point that represents success or failure—like a report card. This type of evaluation is called an **outcome evaluation.** When the focus is on this type of evaluation, managers naturally can be concerned about how documenting the failure of their programs will affect their careers. Consider Training in Action 9-1. It provides an example of an evaluation designed to provide feedback so that improvement (through training and practice) can take place. But when the focus shifted from "helping improve" (**process evaluation**) to a "measurement of success or failure" (outcome evaluation), the desire to participate in the process disappeared, and the airline threatened to discontinue it.

The Counterargument   Can the airline in Training in Action 9-1 be blamed for wanting to opt out of the program? It is easy to understand why someone would not want to participate in a program where the information could be used against them. While long-term results are important in making business decisions, the day-to-day purpose of evaluation should be used as a feedback mechanism to guide efforts toward success.[9] While trying to convince a client that the company's training should be evaluated, one trainer decided not to use the term *evaluation*. Instead, he chose the term *data tracking*. He emphasized tracking attitudes and behaviors over time and supplying feedback based on the findings to the training designers and presenters. This feedback could then be used to modify training and organizational systems and processes to facilitate the training's success. The term *data tracking* did not have the same connotation of finality as *evaluation*. Hence, managers saw it as a tool for improving the likelihood of a successful intervention rather than as a pass/fail grade.

Was the evaluation in the Palm Desert case outcome or process focused? It is difficult to say without actually talking to those involved. If it was used for continuous improvement, assessment of the training process as well as how much participants learned, it could be helpful in determining the reason that transfer did not take place. On the basis of this information, the city could design additional interventions to achieve desired outcomes.

For 30 years, British Airways maintained a system in all its aircraft that monitors everything done by the aircraft and its pilots. This information is examined continuously to determine any faulty aircraft mechanisms and to constantly assess the skill level of the pilots. When a pilot is flagged as having done "steep climbs" or "hard" or "fast landings," for example, the pilot is targeted for training to alleviate the skill deficiency. The training is used, therefore, as a developmental tool to continuously improve the performance of pilots. The evaluation is not used as a summative measure of performance upon which disciplinary measures might be taken. The result for British Airways, one of the largest airlines in the world, is one of the best safety records in the world.

In the past, one of the major ways of determining problems in the airline industry in North America was to wait until an accident occurred and then examine the black box to find the causes. The findings might indicate pilot error or some problem with the aircraft. This information was then sent to all the major airlines for their information. This form of summative evaluation met with disastrous results. Recently, six major American airlines began a program similar to the one at British Airways. After all, it makes sense to track incidents and make changes (in aircraft design or pilot skill level) as soon as a problem is noticed. In this way, major incidents are more likely to be avoided. In fact, airlines are using the evaluation information gathered as a feedback mechanism to ensure the continuous improvement of performance and not as a summative evaluation of "failure."

This seemingly effective way of ensuring high performance threatened to come to an end in the United States. The Federal Aviation Administration (FAA) wanted to access this information for possible use as a way to evaluate pilots. The airlines feared that the information given to the FAA could be used to punish both pilots and the airlines. Fortunately, these regulations were never put into place and both the airlines and the FAA continue to use this cockpit information as a means of continuously improving safety and pilot performance by improving the training of pilots.

Source: Adapted from: Orr, B. Toward safer skies. 2001. Available at http://www.cbsnews.com/stories/2001/03/05/eveningnews/main276466.shtml

So We Must Evaluate

On the surface, the arguments for ignoring evaluation of training make some sense, but they are easily countered when more carefully analyzed. However, perhaps the biggest reason for abandoning the resistance to evaluation is its benefit, especially today, when more and more organizations are demanding accountability at all levels. Managers increasingly are demanding from HRD what they demand from other departments: Provide evidence of the value of your activities to the organization.[10] Other factors that influence the need to evaluate training are competitive pressures on organizations requiring a higher focus on quality, continuous improvement, and organizational cost cutting.[11]

Sometimes, the image of the training function, especially among line managers, is less than desirable because they see this as a "soft" area, not subject to the same requirements for accountability as their areas. By using the same accountability standards, it is possible to improve the image of training. Furthermore, the technology for evaluating and placing dollar amounts on the value of training has improved in the last several years. However, let us be clear. We do not advocate a comprehensive evaluation of every training program. The value of the information gained must be worth the cost. Sometimes, the cost of different components of an evaluation is simply too high relative to the information gained.[12]

Let's go back to the evaluation phase figure at the beginning of the chapter. Recall from Chapter 5 that one of the outputs from the design phase is evaluation considerations. These considerations, or more specifically, what is determined important to evaluate, are inputs to the evaluation phase. Organizational constraints and design issues are also inputs to evaluation. Remember that evaluation processes and outcome measures should be developed soon after the design phase output is obtained. The two types of outputs from the evaluation phase are process and outcome evaluation. Process evaluation compares the developed training to what actually takes place in the training program. Outcome evaluation determines how well training has accomplished its objectives.

Process Data

One of the authors has a cottage near a lake, and he often sees people trying unsuccessfully to start their outboard motors. In going to their assistance, he never starts by suggesting that they pull the plugs to check for ignition or disconnect the float to see whether gas is reaching the carburetor. Instead, he asks if the gas line is connected firmly, if the ball is pumped up, if the gear shift is in neutral (many will not start in gear), and if the throttle is at the correct position, all of which are process issues. He evaluates the "process" of starting the engine to see whether it was followed correctly. If he assumed that it was followed and tried to diagnose the "problem with the engine," he might never find it.

It is the same with training. If learning objectives were not achieved, it is pointless to tear the training design apart in trying to fix it. It might simply be a process issue—the training was not set up or presented the way it was intended. By examining the entire training process, it is possible to see all the places where the training might have gone wrong. In the examination of the process, we suggest segmenting the process into two areas: process before training and process during training.

Process: Before Training

Several steps are required in analyzing the processes used to develop training. Table 9-1 identifies questions to ask during the analysis of the training process. First, you can assess the effectiveness of the needs analysis from the documentation or report that was prepared. This report should indicate the various sources from which the data were gathered and the KSA deficiencies.

Next, you can assess the training objectives. Are they in line with the training needs? Were objectives developed at all levels: organizational, transfer, learning, and reaction? Are they written clearly and effectively to convey what must be done to demonstrate achievement of the objectives? It is important that you examine the proposed evaluation tools to be sure that they are relevant. On the basis of the needs assessment and resulting objectives, you can identify several tools for assessing the various levels of effectiveness. We discuss the development of these tools later in this chapter. Then evaluate the design of the training. For example, if trainees' motivation to attend and learn is low, what procedures are included in the design to deal with this issue?

Would a process evaluation prove useful in the Palm Desert case? Yes. In that situation, as it stands, we recognize that training was not successful, but we do not know why. The process that leads to the design of training might provide the answer. Another place we might find the answer is in the training implementation.

Process: During Training

If your outcome data show that you didn't get the results you expected, then training implementation might be the reason. Was the training presented as it was designed

Table 9-1
Potential Questions
to Be Addressed in
a Process Analysis
(Before Training)

Were needs diagnosed correctly?
- What data sources were used?
- Was a knowledge/skill deficiency identified?
- Were trainees assessed to determine their prerequisite KSAs?

Were needs correctly translated into training objectives?
- Were all objectives identified?
- Were the objectives written in a clear, appropriate manner?

Was an evaluation system designed to measure accomplishment of objectives?

Was the training program designed to meet all the training objectives?
- Was previous learning that might either support or inhibit learning in training identified?
- Were individual differences assessed and taken into consideration in training design?
- Was trainee motivation to learn assessed?
- What steps were taken to address trainee motivation to learn?
- Were processes built into the training to facilitate recall and transfer?
- What steps are included in the training to call attention to key learning events?
- What steps are included in the training to aid trainees in symbolic coding and cognitive organization?
- What opportunities are included in the training to provide symbolic and behavioral practice?
- What actions are included in the training to ensure transfer of learning to the job?

Are the training techniques to be used appropriate for each of the learning objectives of the training?

Source: Adapted from Camp, R. P., Blanchard, P. N., and Huszczo, G. E. *Toward a More Organizationally Effective Training Strategy and Practice* (1986). Upper Saddle River, NJ: Prentice Hall.

to be? If the answer is yes, then the design must be changed. But, it is possible that the trainer or others in the organization made some ad hoc modifications. Such an analysis might prove useful in the Palm Desert case.

Imagine, for example, that the Palm Desert training had required the use of behavior modeling to provide practice in the skills that were taught. The evaluation of outcomes shows that learning of the new behaviors did not occur. If no process data were gathered, the conclusion could be that the behavior modeling approach was not effective. However, what if examination of the process revealed that trainees were threatened by the behavior modeling technique, and the trainer allowed them to spend time discussing behavior modeling, which left less time for doing the modeling? As a result, it is quite plausible that there are problems with both the design and the implementation of the training. Without the process evaluation, this information would remain unknown, and the inference might be that behavior modeling was not effective.

Examples of implementation issues to examine are depicted in Table 9-2. Here, it is up to the evaluator to determine whether all the techniques that were designed into the program actually took place. It is not good enough simply to determine that the amount of time allotted was spent on the topic or skill development. It must also be determined whether trainees actually were involved in the learning activities as prescribed by the design. As in the previous behavior modeling example, the time allotted might be used for something other than behavior modeling.

Putting It All Together

Actual training is compared with the expected (as designed) training to provide an assessment of the effectiveness of the training implementation. Much of the necessary information for the expected training can be obtained from records and reports developed in the process of setting up the training program. A manual would provide an

Table 9-2
Potential Questions
to Be Addressed in
a Process Analysis
(During Training)

- Were the trainer, training techniques, and learning objectives well matched?
- Were lecture portions of the training effective?
  - Was involvement encouraged or solicited?
  - Were questions used effectively?
- Did the trainer conduct the various training methodologies (case, role-play, etc.) appropriately?
  - Were they explained well?
  - Did the trainer use the allotted time for activities?
  - Was enough time allotted?
  - Did trainees follow instructions?
  - Was there effective debriefing following the exercises?
- Did the trainer follow the training design and lesson plans?
  - Was enough time given for each of the requirements?
  - Was time allowed for questions?

Source: Adapted from Camp, R. P., Blanchard, P. N., and Huszczo, G. E. *Toward a More Organizationally Effective Training Strategy and Practice* (1986). Upper Saddle River, NJ: Prentice Hall.

excellent source of information about what should be covered in the training. Someone could monitor the training to determine what actually was covered. Another method is to ask trainees to complete evaluations of process issues for each module. Videotape, instructors' notes, and surveys or interviews with trainees can also be used. Keep in mind that when you are gathering any data, the more methods you use to gather information, the better the evaluation will be.

When to Use It

Table 9-3 depicts those interested in process data. Clearly, the training department is primarily concerned with this information to assess how they are doing. The customers of training (defined as anyone with a vested interest in the training department's work) usually are more interested in outcome data than in process data.

Providing some process data is important, even if it is only the trainer's documentation and the trainees' reactions. The trainer can use this information to assess what seems to work and what does not. Sometimes, more detailed process data will be required, such as when training will be used many times, or when the training outcomes have a significant effect on the bottom line. If, however, it is only a half-day seminar on the new computer software, collecting process information might not be worth the cost.

Table 9-3
Who Is Interested
in the Process Data

Training Department	
Trainer	Yes, it helps determine what works well and what does not.
Other trainers	Yes, to the extent the process is generalizable.
Training manager	Only if training is not successful or if a problem is present with a particular trainer.
Customers of the Training Department	
Trainees	No
Trainees' supervisor	No
Upper management	No

Source: Adapted from Camp, R. P., Blanchard, P. N., and Huszczo, G. E. *Toward a More Organizationally Effective Training Strategy and Practice* (1986). Upper Saddle River, NJ: Prentice Hall.

Once training and trainers are evaluated several times, the value of additional evaluations decreases. If you are conducting training that has been done numerous times before, such as training new hires to work on a piece of equipment, and the trainer is one of your most experienced, then process analysis is probably not necessary. If the trainer was fairly new or had not previously conducted this particular session, it might be beneficial to gather process data through a senior trainer's direct observation.

To be most effective, we believe that evaluations should be process oriented and focused on providing information to improve training, not just designed to determine whether training is successful. Some disagree with this approach and suggest that process evaluation ends when the training program is launched.[13] We suggest, however, that the evaluation should always include process evaluation for the following reasons:

- It removes the connotation of pass/fail, making evaluation more likely.
- It puts the focus on improvement, a desirable goal even when training is deemed successful.[14]

Outcome Data

To determine how well the training met or is meeting its goals, it is necessary to examine various outcomes measures. The four outcomes measures that are probably the best known are reaction, learning, behavior, and organizational results.[15] These outcomes are ordered as follows:

- Reaction outcomes come first and will influence how much can be learned.
- Learning outcomes influence how much behavior can change back on the job.
- Behavior outcomes are the changes of behavior on the job that will influence organizational results.
- Organizational results are the changes in the bottom line related to the reason for training in the first place, such as high grievance rate, low productivity, and so forth.

This description is a simplified version of what actually happens, and critics argue that little empirical evidence indicates that the relationships between these outcomes exist.[16] We will discuss this in more detail later.

Reaction outcomes are measures of the trainee's perceptions, emotions, and subjective evaluations of the training experience. They represent the first level of evaluation and are important because favorable reactions create motivation to learn. Learning may also occur even if the training is boring or alternatively, it may not occur even if it is interesting.[17] However, if training is boring, it will be difficult to attend to what is being taught. As a result, the trainees might not learn as much as they would if they found the training interesting and exciting. High reaction scores from trainees, therefore, assure the designers that attention was obtained and maintained, which, as you recall from social learning theory, is the first part of learning—getting their attention.

Learning outcomes are measured by how well the learning objectives and the overall training objective were achieved. The learning objectives for the training that were developed in the design phase specify the types of outcomes that will signify that training has been successful. Note the critical relationship between the needs analysis and evaluation. If the training process progressed according to the model presented in this book, the way to measure learning was determined during the training needs analysis (TNA). At that time, the employee's KSAs were measured to determine whether they were adequate for job performance. The evaluation of learning should use the same measurement techniques as in the TNA. Thus, the needs analysis is actually the "pretest." A similar measure at the end of training will show the "gain" in learning.

Job behavior outcomes are measures of the degree to which the learned behavior has transferred to the job. During the TNA, performance gaps were identified and traced to areas in which employees were behaving in a manner that was creating the gap. The methods used for measuring job behavior in the TNA should be used in measuring job behavior after the completion of training. Once again, the link between needs analysis and evaluation is evident. The degree to which job behavior improves places a cap on how much training can improve organizational results.

Organizational results occupy the highest level in the hierarchy. They reflect the gap in performance identified in the TNA. The organizational result is often what triggers reactive (as opposed to proactive) training. Here are some examples:

- High levels of scrap are being produced.
- Employees are quitting in record numbers.
- Sales figures dropped over the last two quarters.
- Grievances are on the increase.
- The number of rejects from quality control is rising.

Once again, if one of these organizational results triggered the training, it can be used as the baseline for assessing improvement after training. This process of integrating the TNA and evaluation streamlines both processes, thereby making the integration more cost-effective.[18]

Putting It All Together

If each level of the hierarchy is evaluated, it is possible to have a better understanding of the full effects of training.[19] Let's examine one of the items in the preceding list—a high grievance rate—as it relates to the training process and the four levels of evaluation.

The needs analysis determines that the high grievance rate is a function of supervisors not managing conflict well. Their knowledge is adequate, but their skills are deficient. From the needs analysis, data are obtained for later comparison with skill levels after training has been completed. Tools for evaluation are developed at this time if they are not already available from the needs analysis. Training is provided, and then participants fill out a reaction questionnaire. This tool measures the degree to which trainees feel positive about the time and effort that they have invested in the program and each of its components. Assume that the responses are favorable. However, even though the trainees feel good about the training and believe that they learned valuable things, the trainer recognizes that the intended learning might not have occurred. A test of conflict management skill is administered, and the results are compared with pretraining data. The results show that the trainees acquired the conflict management skills and can use them appropriately so the learning objectives were achieved. Now the concern is if these skills transferred to the job. We compare the behavior of the supervisors before training and after training regarding use of conflict management skills and discover they are using the skills so transfer to the job was successful. The next step is to examine the grievance rate. If it has declined, it is possible, with some level of confidence, to suggest that training is the cause of the decline. If it is determined that learning did not take place after training, it would not make sense to examine behavior or results, because learning is a prerequisite.

Let's examine each of these four levels of evaluation more closely.

Reaction Questionnaire

The data collected at this level are used to determine what the trainees thought about the training. Reaction questionnaires are often criticized, not because of their lack of value, but because they are often the only type of evaluation undertaken.[20]

Affective and utility are two types of reaction questionnaire.[21] An **affective questionnaire** measures general feeling about training ("I found this training enjoyable"), whereas the **utility questionnaire** reflects beliefs about the value of training ("This training was of practical value"). We focus here on the latter type because we believe that specific utility statements on reaction questionnaires are more valuable for making changes.

Training reaction questionnaires do not assess learning but rather the trainees' attitudes about and perceptions of the training. Categories to consider when developing a reaction questionnaire should include training relevance, training content, materials, exercises, trainer(s) behavior, and facilities.

Training Relevance   Asking trainees about the relevance (utility) of the training they experienced provides the organization with a measure of the perceived value of the training. If most participants do not see any value in it, they will experience difficulty remaining interested (much less consider applying it back on the job). Furthermore, this perceived lack of value can contaminate the program's image. Those who do not see its value will talk to others who have not yet attended training and will perhaps suggest that it is a waste of time. The self-fulfilling prophecy proposes that if you come to training believing that it will be a waste of time, it will be. Even if the training is of great importance to the organization, participants who do not believe that it is important are not likely to work to achieve its objectives.

Once trainees' attitudes are known, you can take steps to change the beliefs, either through a socialization process or through a change in the training itself. Think about the Palm Desert case. What do you think the trainees' reactions to the training were? Might this source of information help explain why no change in behavior occurred?

Training Materials and Exercises   Any written materials, videos, exercises, and other instructional tools should be assessed along with an overall evaluation of the training experience. On the basis of responses from participants, you can change the training to make it more relevant to participants. Making suggested modifications follows the organizational development principle of involving trainees in the process.

Reactions to the Trainer   Reaction questionnaires also help determine how the trainees evaluated the trainer's actions. Be sure to develop statements that specifically address what the trainer did. General statements tend to reflect trainees' feelings about how friendly or entertaining the trainer was (halo error) rather than how well the training was carried out. Simply presenting an affective statement such as "The trainer was entertaining" would likely elicit a halo response. For this reason, it is useful to identify specific aspects of trainer behavior that need to be rated. If more than one trainer is involved, then trainee reactions need to be gathered for each trainer. Asking trainees to rate the trainers as a group will mask differences among trainers in terms of their effectiveness.

Asking about a number of factors important to effective instruction causes the trainees to consider how effective the instructor was in these areas. When the final question, "Overall, how effective was the instructor?" is asked, the trainees can draw upon their responses to a number of factors related to effective instruction. This consideration will result in a more accurate response as to the overall effectiveness of the instructor. There will be less halo error. Note that the questionnaire in Figure 9-1 asks the trainee to consider several aspects of the trainer's teaching behavior before asking a more general question regarding effectiveness.

Facilities and Procedures   The reaction questionnaire can also contain items related to the facilities and procedures to determine whether any element impeded the training process. Noise, temperature, seating arrangements, and even the freshness

Figure 9-1
Reaction
Questionnaire for
the Trainer

Please circle the number that reflects the degree to which you agree or disagree with the following statements.

1 = Strongly disagree
2 = Disagree
3 = Neither agree nor disagree
4 = Agree
5 = Strongly agree

1. The trainer did a good job of stating the objectives at the beginning of training.	1	2	3	4	5
2. The trainer made good use of visual aids (easel, whiteboard) when making the presentations.	1	2	3	4	5
3. The trainer was good at keeping everyone interested in the topics.	1	2	3	4	5
4. The trainer encouraged questions and participation from trainees.	1	2	3	4	5
5. The trainer made sure that everyone understood the concepts before moving on to the next topic.	1	2	3	4	5
6. The trainer summarized important concepts before moving to the next module.	1	2	3	4	5

7. Overall, how would you rate this trainer? (Check one)

_____ 1. Poor—I would not recommend this trainer to others.

_____ 2. Adequate—I would recommend this trainer only if no others were available.

_____ 3. Average

_____ 4. Good—I would recommend this trainer above most others.

_____ 5. Excellent—This trainer is among the best I've ever worked with.

of the doughnuts are potential areas that can cause discontent. One way to approach these issues is to use open-ended questions, such as the following:

- Please describe any aspects of the facility that enhanced the training or created problems for you during training (identify the problem and the aspect of the facility).
- Please indicate how you felt about the following:
  - Refreshments provided
  - Ability to hear the trainer and other trainees clearly
  - Number and length of breaks

Facility questions are most appropriate if the results can be used to configure training facilities in the future. The more things are working in the trainer's favor, the more effective training is likely to be.

The data from a reaction questionnaire provide important information that can be used to make the training more relevant, the trainers more sensitive to their strengths and shortcomings, and the facilities more conducive to a positive training atmosphere. The feedback the questionnaire provides is more immediate than with the other levels of evaluation; therefore, modifications to training can be made much sooner.

Timing of Reaction Assessment   The timing and type of questions asked on a reaction questionnaire should be based on the information needed for evaluating and improving the training, the trainer(s), the processes, or the facility. Most reaction questionnaires are given to participants at the conclusion of training, while the training is still fresh and the audience is captive. However, a problem with giving them at this time is that the participant might be anxious to leave and might give incomplete or less-than-valid data. Also, trainees might not know whether the training is useful on the job until they go back to the job and try it.

An alternative is to send out a reaction questionnaire at some point after training. This delay gives the trainee time to see how training works in the actual job setting. However, the trainee might forget the specifics of the training. Also, there is no longer a captive audience, so response rate may be poor.

Another approach is to provide reaction questionnaires after segments of a training program or after each day in a multiday training session. In such situations, it might be possible to modify training that is in progress on the basis of trainees' responses. Of course, this system is more costly and requires a quicker turnaround time for analysis and feedback of the data.

Regardless of how often reaction evaluation takes place, the trainer should specify at the beginning that trainees will be asked to evaluate the training and state when this evaluation will occur. It not only helps clarify trainee expectations about what will happen during training but also acknowledges the organization's concern for how the trainees feel about the training. It is also important that the data gathered be used. Trainees and employees in the rest of the organization will quickly find out if the trainer is simply gathering data only to give the impression of concern about their reactions. Figure 9-2 provides a list of steps to consider when developing a reaction questionnaire.

Caution in Using Reaction Measures   A caution is in order regarding reaction questionnaires sent out to trainees some time after training asking them about the amount of transfer of training that has occurred on the job. Trainees tend to indicate that transfer has occurred when other measures suggest it did not.[22] Therefore, reaction measures should not be the only evaluation method used to determine transfer of training.

Reaction questionnaires are not meant to measure learning or transfer to the job. They do, however, provide the trainees with the opportunity to indicate how they felt about the learning. How interesting the training is found to be will affect their level of attention and motivation. What the trainees perceive the trainer to be doing well and not so well is also useful feedback for the trainer. This information can be used to make decisions about modifications to the training program.

Learning

Learning objectives are developed from the TNA. The difference between the individual's KSAs and the KSAs required for acceptable job performance defines the learning

Figure 9-2
Steps to Consider in Developing a Reaction Questionnaire

1. Determine what needs to be found out.
2. Develop a written set of questions to obtain the information.
3. Develop a scale to quantify respondents' data.
4. Make forms anonymous so that participants feel free to respond honestly.
5. Ask for information that might be useful in determining differences in reactions by subgroups taking the training (e.g., young vs. old; minority vs. nonminority). This could be valuable in determining effectiveness of training by different cultures, for example, which might be lost in an overall assessment. *Note:* Care must be taken when asking for this information. If you ask too many questions about race, gender, age, tenure, and so on, participants will begin to feel that they can be identified without their name on the questionnaire.
6. Allow space for additional comments to allow participants the opportunity to mention things you did not consider.
7. Decide the best time to give the questionnaire to get the information you want.
   a. If right after training, ask someone other than the instructor to administer and pick up the information.
   b. If some time later, develop a mechanism for obtaining a high response rate (e.g., encourage the supervisor to allow trainees to complete the questionnaire on company time).

that must occur. The person analysis serves as the pretraining measure of the person's KSAs. These results can be compared with a posttraining measure to determine whether learning has occurred and whether those changes can be attributed to training. The various ways of making such attributions will be discussed later in the chapter. As we noted, training can focus on three types of learning outcomes: knowledge, skills, and attitudes.

Knowledge Outcomes   Generally, the type of evaluation conducted in training is related to declarative knowledge. But remember that training can also focus on two higher-level knowledge outcomes: procedural and strategic.

Declarative Knowledge   If the goal of the training is to impart some sort of factual knowledge, such as "rules covering search and seizure" or "understanding the type of question that cannot be asked in an interview," a test can be developed to determine whether trainees acquired this declarative knowledge. Paper-and-pencil tests such as the multiple-choice test are often used. Multiple-choice tests offer many advantages. They are easy to administer and score and, when skillfully developed, can accurately measure knowledge.[23] Some trainees indicate that they are not good at taking multiple-choice tests. However, evidence suggests that such tests consistently correlate highly with other forms of testing. A big advantage of multiple-choice tests is their reliability. Also, because of the number of questions that can be asked, it is possible to cover a broader range of the content than with other methods.

The major difficulty with this type of test is in the construction of the items. A complete discussion on how to write good multiple-choice questions is beyond the scope of this text, but some general rules to consider in constructing questions are found in Figure 9-3. More comprehensive information can be found in *Evaluating Training Programs*, a book published by the American Society for Training and Development.[24] It might be wise to contact a local university and discuss the project with someone who has the appropriate background. Even small companies with limited budgets should be able to obtain such help from a supervised graduate student eager to get some real-world experience.

Procedural Knowledge   The second level of knowledge outcomes is procedural knowledge. Here, the learner begins to develop meaningful ways of organizing information into mental models. Mental models are also known as cognitive maps, knowledge structures, and task schemata. As noted in Chapter 4, experts develop more complex mental models for the way they organize their knowledge than do new learners. As a result, the expert can access the solution strategy more quickly.

There are several techniques for assessing how the trainee has organized procedural knowledge.[25] One method uses paired comparisons to determine how the trainee sees the relationship between topics. For example, trainees in a "train the trainer" course would be asked to indicate the relationships among several training concepts, such as instructional design, criterion development, needs assessment, organizational analysis,

Figure 9-3
Procedures for Developing a Multiple-Choice Test

1. Examine objectives to gain a clear understanding of the content area you wish to test.
2. Write the questions in a clear manner. Shorter is better.
3. Choose alternatives to the correct response from typical errors made during training. Make alternatives realistic.
4. Do not consistently make the correct response longer than the incorrect responses.
5. Provide four options. More than four takes longer to read, and it is difficult enough to write three reasonable alternatives along with the correct answer.
6. Pretest items by giving the test to those expected to know the material. Ask them for feedback on clarity. Note any questions that many of them get wrong.
7. Give revised items to a group of fully trained (experienced) employees and a group of untrained (inexperienced) employees. The former should score well, and the latter should do poorly.

and so on. Then, these relationships would be compared with the relationships identified by an expert. Another method (see Figure 9-4) uses a configuration of concepts that are linked. Some of the links are blank, and the trainee must place the appropriate concepts in the blanks next to the one that makes a best fit. Strategies for measuring these structures are too comprehensive to be discussed here, but several publications deal with this topic.[26]

Strategic Knowledge The category of strategic knowledge deals with the ability to develop and apply cognitive strategies used in problem solving. It assesses the trainee's level of understanding about the decisions or choices a trainee must make. Probed protocol analysis is one assessment method.[27] First, subject matter experts define a problem and the steps necessary to solve it. Trainees are then asked to explain step-by-step what they would do to solve the problem. Questions such as "Why would you do that?" "What would it mean if it did not help?" and "What other test could you do?" help determine the trainees' strategies. Once again, for more detailed information, several excellent publications are available.[28] One final

Figure 9-4 Test of Knowledge Organization for Civil Engineers

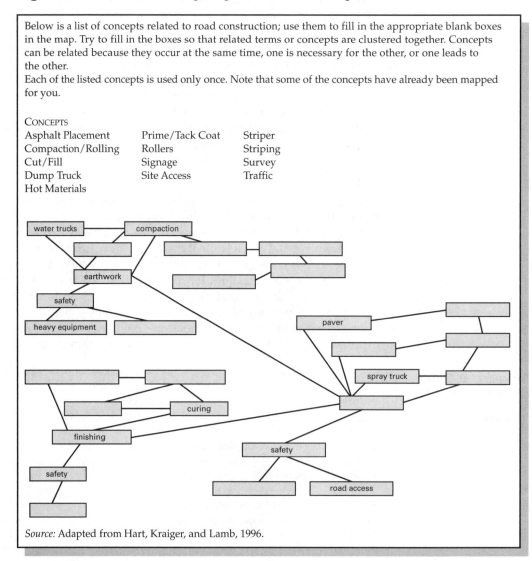

Below is a list of concepts related to road construction; use them to fill in the appropriate blank boxes in the map. Try to fill in the boxes so that related terms or concepts are clustered together. Concepts can be related because they occur at the same time, one is necessary for the other, or one leads to the other.
Each of the listed concepts is used only once. Note that some of the concepts have already been mapped for you.

CONCEPTS
Asphalt Placement   Prime/Tack Coat   Striper
Compaction/Rolling   Rollers   Striping
Cut/Fill   Signage   Survey
Dump Truck   Site Access   Traffic
Hot Materials

Source: Adapted from Hart, Kraiger, and Lamb, 1996.

note about cognitive (and other) tests: A common belief holds that a specific time limit needs to be given for a test. Understand that speed tests provide different information than power tests.[29] Speed tests should be given only if speed in retrieving and using information is an important job characteristic. If, however, the critical component is accuracy of retrieval and use, time limits should not be used. In general, power tests need some sort of time limit, as without one, some trainees will remain for twice the time of others to check and recheck their answers. A good approach is to indicate a general time limit (e.g., about one hour). When the time is up, ask, "How much time do you need to finish?" This question is usually enough incentive for those who are simply reluctant to hand the test in.

Skills   Determining whether a skill or a set of behaviors was learned is not the same as measuring whether it is used on the job. Obviously, if it is used on the job, it was learned. However, it might be learned but not be used on the job. Knowing that the skill was learned is important, particularly if it does not transfer to the job. In this situation, the focus is on lack of transfer to the job and not a learning problem.

Two levels of skill acquisition are compilation (lower level) and automaticity (higher level). Most training focuses on providing the skill training at the lower level, and hence evaluations tend to be at the compilation level.

Compilation   If the training being evaluated was in swimming, it is obvious that a paper-and-pencil test to determine the learning that has occurred does not apply. Similarly, if you wanted to evaluate the training of supervisors in interpersonal skills, a paper-and-pencil test could provide information regarding what the trainee understands about interpersonal skills, but it would not identify the trainee's actual interpersonal skills.

Developing behavioral tests and standards for scoring such tests can be difficult. A number of situations need to be created in which the trainee is required to demonstrate the target skill(s). The difficulty lies in developing scoring standards. Consider a study that examined the training of machinists.[30] It was noted that passing the training was more a function of the trainer who was running the course than of the trainees. Different trainers used different standards for passing.

To address this problem, a standardized method was needed to provide points based on criteria outlined in the training objectives. These criteria were based on tolerance requirements and finished specifications. These criteria, once developed, gave the trainers clear standards from which to evaluate, thereby eliminating trainer differences. For skills that have a specific output, such as a widget, assessment simply compares what was produced with what was required. For other skills, such as those required for conflict resolution, assessment could occur through the use of a structured scenario in which a person acts in an angry and aggressive manner and the trainee responds using the skills taught. These types of tests can be scored using multiple raters or standardized forms. Achieving inter-rater agreement is important in developing such tests. This consistency is accomplished through standardized methods of rating that are clear to the trainer or whoever is required to conduct the testing.

Automaticity   Skill-based training is generally evaluated at the compilation level. However, in some cases, the skill must be so well learned that it can be done quickly and without much thought. For this level of skill, the evaluation would need to be much more stringent about what constitutes successful performance. One method for determining whether the trainee reached automaticity would be a speed test that required performance to be completed within a certain time. Emergency procedures for pilots would be an example.

Attitudes   As noted earlier, attitudes are an important outcome of training. At the conclusion of training, it is useful to assess any changes in attitudes that were learning objectives. Numerous attitude scales are available through journals (*Personnel Psychology, Journal of Applied Psychology, Academy of Management Journal, Academy of Management Review, Academy of Management Executive*) and books (*Assessing Organizational Change, The Experience of Work, Buros Book of Mental Measurements*). Developing attitude scales requires care, and you should use existing scales whenever possible rather than attempting to develop one yourself. However, items in the survey might need to be reworded to reflect the specific training being done.

Assessing true attitude change is difficult. The primary assessment tool is a pre-/postmeasure of responses on an attitude scale. A scale measuring "attitude toward empowerment" is depicted in Figure 9-5. A comparison of responses before and after training that indicates an increase in positive attitude toward empowerment would suggest successful training. However, some doubts arise about such self-report measures, particularly if the trainees are identified. The new employee might see the wisdom in hiding a dislike of team-based work after a concentrated orientation espousing the value of teams. Going to great lengths to assure respondents of their anonymity encourages honesty in trainee self-reports.

Timing of Assessment of Learning   Depending on the duration of training, it might be desirable to assess learning periodically to determine how trainees are progressing. Periodic assessment would allow training to be modified if learning is not progressing as expected.

Assessment should also take place at the conclusion of training. If learning is not evaluated until sometime later, it is impossible to know how much was learned and then forgotten.

In the Palm Desert case, the measures that they took six months after training created a dilemma. Was the behavior ever learned, learned but forgotten, or learned but not transferred to the job?

Job Behavior Data

Once it is determined that learning took place, the next step is to determine whether the training transferred to the job. Assessment at this step is certainly more complex and is often ignored because of the difficulties of measurement.

Figure 9-5
Example of an
Attitudinal Measure

Attitudes Toward Empowerment					
Please indicate the degree to which you agree or disagree with the following statements.					
1 = Strongly disagree					
2 = Disagree					
3 = Neither agree nor disagree					
4 = Agree					
5 = Strongly agree					
1. Empowering employees is just another way to get more work done with fewer people. [Reverse scored]	1	2	3	4	5
2. Empowering employees allows everyone to contribute their ideas for the betterment of the company.	1	2	3	4	5
3. The empowerment program improved my relationship with my supervisor.	1	2	3	4	5
4. Empowerment brought more meaning to my life at this company.	1	2	3	4	5
5. Empowerment interventions should be introduced in other plants in this company.	1	2	3	4	5
6. The empowerment process provided a positive influence in labor–management relations.	1	2	3	4	5

Several methods can be used to assess job behavior. These methods were covered in depth in the discussion of TNA in Chapter 4, and, in fact the instrument used when conducting the needs assessment should serve well as the posttest evaluation tool. The primary sources of data are interviews, questionnaires, direct observation, and archival records of performance. Questionnaires are often preferred, for several reasons, including the following:

- Opinions can be obtained about specific behaviors from a large number of employees.
- Information can be tabulated to yield a numerical response.
- Respondents are anonymous, so it is more likely that they will be honest.
- Time to gather data is relatively short.

Because this method of evaluation is so common, it is important to understand how to develop effective questionnaires. Figure 9-6 provides some guidelines.

Performance appraisals can also be used to document job and performance changes. As was noted in Chapter 4, one useful technique is the 360-degree performance review. If a 360-degree appraisal is used annually, then trainees can examine

Figure 9-6
Guidelines for Writing an Effective Questionnaire

1. Write simply and clearly, and make the meaning obvious.

Bad: To what extent do supervisors provide information regarding the quality of performance of people at your level?

Good: How often does your boss give you feedback on your job?

2. Ask one question at a time.

Bad: Both the organization's goals and my role within the organization are clear.

Good: The organization's goals are clear.
My role within the organization is clear.

3. Provide discrete response options.

Bad: During the past three months, how often did you receive feedback on your work?

1	2	3	4	5
Rarely		Occasionally		Frequently

Good: During the past three months, how often did you receive feedback on your work?

1	2	3	4	5
Not once	1–3 times	About once a week	More than once a week	Once a day or more

4. Limit the number of response options.

Bad: What percentage of the time are you sure of what will be your compensation?

1	2	3	4	5	6	7	8	9	10
0%–10%	11%–20%	21%–30%	31%–40%	41%–50%	51%–60%	61%–70%	71%–80%	81%–90%	91%–100%

Good: What percentage of the time are you sure of what your compensation will be?

1	2	3	4	5
0%–20%	21%–40%	41%–60%	61%–80%	81%–100%

5. Match the response mode to the question.

Bad: To what extent are you satisfied with your job?

1	2	3	4	5
Strongly disagree	Disagree		Agree	Strongly agree

Good: To what extent are you satisfied with your job?

1	2	3	4	5
Not at all	A little bit		Quite a lot	Very much

their results after they receive training. Trainees can determine if they have improved by comparing their pre- and posttraining results.

Scripted Situations   Some recent research indicates that scripted situations might provide a better format for evaluating transfer of training than the more traditional behavioral questionnaires.[31] Scripted situations help the rater recall actual situations and the behaviors related to them rather than attempting to recall specific behaviors without the context provided. The rater is provided with several responses that might be elicited from the script and is asked to choose the one that describes the ratee's behavior. Research suggests that this method is useful in decreasing rating errors and improving validity.[32] An example of this method is depicted in Figure 9-7.

Finally, the trainer who includes sit ins as a later part of training can observe on-the-job performance of the trainee. As was discussed in Chapter 5, these sit-ins facilitate transfer[33] and also help the trainer determine the effectiveness of the training in facilitating the transfer of training to the job.

Attitudes   If attitudinal change is a goal of training, then it becomes necessary to assess the success of transfer and duration of the attitudinal change once the trainee is back on the job. As discussed earlier, such attitudinal change can be assessed through attitude surveys. The same instruments used in the needs analysis and learning assessment can be used. If respondents' anonymity is ensured in such surveys, responses are more likely to reflect true attitudes.

A study of steward training provides an example of the assessment of an attitude back on the job.[34] Training was designed to make union stewards more accessible to the rank and file by teaching them listening skills and how to interact more with the rank and file. Results indicated that when factors such as tenure as a union official and age were controlled, stewards who received the training behaved in a more participative manner and were more loyal to the union. For the union, loyalty is important because it translates into important behaviors that might not be measured directly, such as supporting the union's political candidates and attending union functions.[35]

Timing of Job Behavior Assessment   The wait time for assessing transfer of training depends on the training objectives. If the objective is to learn how to complete certain forms, simply auditing the work on the job before and after training would determine whether transfer took place. This could be done soon after training was complete. When learning objectives are more complex, such as learning how to solve problems or resolve conflict, wait time before assessment should be longer. The trainee will first need to become comfortable enough with the new behavior to exhibit it on a regular basis; then it will take more time for others to notice that the behavior has changed.

To understand this point, consider a more concrete change. Jack loses 10 pounds. First, the weight loss is gradual and often goes unnoticed. Even after Jack lost the weight, for some time people will say, "Gee, haven't you lost weight?" or "What is it

Figure 9-7
Scripted Situation Item for Evaluation of a School Superintendent

The following is a scenario regarding a school superintendent. To rate your superintendent, read the scenario and place an X next to the behavior you believe your superintendent would follow.

The administrator receives a letter from a parent objecting to the content of the science section on reproduction. The parent strongly objects to his daughter being exposed to such materials and demands that something be done. The administrator would most likely: (check one)

_____ Ask the teacher to provide handouts, materials, and curriculum content for review.

_____ Check the science curriculum for the board-approved approach to reproduction, and compare board guidelines with course content.

_____ Ask the head of the science department for an opinion about the teacher's lesson plan.

_____ Check to see whether the parent has made similar complaints in the past.

that's different about you?" If this uncertainty about specific changes happens with a concrete visual stimulus, imagine what happens when the stimuli are less concrete and not consistent. Some types of behavioral change might take a long time to be noticed.

To help get employees to notice the change in behavior, you can ask them to assess whether certain behaviors have changed. In our example, if asked, "Did Jack lose weight?" and he had lost 10 pounds, you would more than likely notice it then, even if you did not notice it before.

Organizational Results

Training objectives, whether proactive or reactive, are developed to solve an organizational problem—perhaps an expected increase in demand for new customer services in the proactive case, or too many grievances in the reactive case. The fact that a problem was identified (too many grievances) indicates a measurement of the "organizational result." This measurement would be used to determine any change after the training was completed. If it was initially determined that too many defective parts were being produced, the measurement of the "number of defective parts per 100 produced" would be used again after training to assess whether training was successful. This assessment is your organizational result.

It is important to assess this final level, because it is the reason for doing the training in the first place. In one sense, it is easier to measure than job behavior. Did the grievances decrease? Did quality improve? Did customer satisfaction increase? Did attitudes in the annual survey get more positive? Did subordinates' satisfaction with supervision improve? Such questions are relatively easily answered. The difficult question is, "Are the changes a result of training?" Perhaps the grievance rate dropped because of recent successful negotiations and the signing of a contract the union liked. Or if attitudes toward supervision improved but everyone recently received a large bonus, the improvement might be spill-off from the bonus and not the training. These examples explain why it is so important to gather information on all levels of the evaluation.

The links among organizational results, job behavior, and trainee KSAs should be clearly articulated in the TNA. This creates a model that specifies that if certain KSAs are developed and the employees use them on the job, then certain organizational results will occur. The occurrence of these things validates the model and provides some confidence that training caused these results. Thus, the difficult task of specifying how training should affect the results of the organization is already delineated before evaluation begins. TNAs are not always as thorough as they should be; therefore, it often falls to the evaluator to clarify the relationship among training, learning, job behavior, and organizational outcomes. For this reason, it is probably best to focus on organizational results as close to the trainee's work unit as possible. Results such as increased work unit productivity, quality, and decreased costs are more appropriate than increased organizational profitability, market share, and the like. Quantifying organizational results is not as onerous as it might seem at first glance.

Timing of Assessment of Organizational Results   Consistent tracking of the organizational performance gaps such as high scrap, number of grievances, or poor quality should take place at intervals throughout the training and beyond. At some point after the behavior is transferred to the job, it is reasonable to expect improvement. Tracking performance indices over time allows you to assess whether the training resulted in the desired changes to organizational results. You will need to also track any other organizational changes that might be affecting those results. For example, a downturn in the economy might result in the necessity for temporary layoffs. This could trigger an increase in grievances, even though the grievance training for supervisors was very effective. This is one of the difficulties of linking training to organizational results. There are a multitude of factors, other than employees' KSAs, that determine those results.

Relationship Among Levels of Outcomes

As suggested earlier, researchers have questioned the relationship among these four levels of evaluation. For example, some studies show reaction and learning outcomes to be strongly related to each other.[36] Others indicate little correlation between results of reaction questionnaires and measures of learning.[37] As noted earlier, a good response to the reaction questionnaire might mean only that the trainer had obtained the trainees' attention. This factor is only one of many in the learning process. The findings also indicate that the more the outcome is removed from the actual training, the smaller the relationship is between higher- and lower-level outcomes. Figure 9-8 illustrates the hierarchical nature of the outcomes and the factors that can influence these outcomes.

The research showing no relationship between the levels makes sense if we remember that organizational outcomes generally are the result of multiple causes.[38] For example, productivity is affected not only by the employees' KSAs, but also by the technology they work with, supplier reliability, interdependencies among work groups, and many other factors. Although improvements can occur in one area, declines can occur in another. When learning takes place but does not transfer to the job, the issues to be concerned with do not involve learning, but they do involve transfer. What structural constraints are being placed on trainees, so they do not behave properly? Beverly Geber, special projects editor for *Training* magazine, describes a situation in which training in communication skills at Hutchinson Technologies, a computer component manufacturer, was not transferring to the job for some of the employees.[39] An examination of the issue (through worker focus groups) disclosed that some employees were required to work in cramped space with poor lighting. These conditions made them irritable and unhappy. Did this situation affect their ability to communicate with their customers in a pleasant and upbeat manner? "You bet," said their human resource (HR) representative.

Despite all the above reasons that a researcher might not find a relationship among the four levels of evaluation, research has begun to show the existence of these linkages.[40] More research needs to be done, but evidence exists showing that reactions affect learning outcomes, and learning outcomes affect transfer to the job. Few studies have attempted to link transfer outcomes to organizational outcomes due to the significant problems of factoring out other variables related to those outcomes.

Figure 9-8
Types of Outcomes and Examples of Factors Affecting Those Outcomes

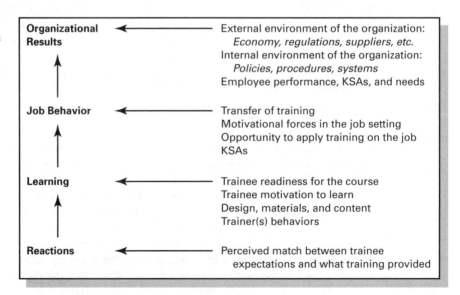

Evaluating the Costs of Training

Let's say you are able to show that your training caused a decrease in the number of grievances. You have data to show that participants are engaging in the new behaviors, and they have the desired knowledge and skills. Your examination of all four levels of evaluation provides evidence of cause and effect, and your use of appropriate designs (see Appendix 9-1) enhances the level of confidence in all of these outcomes. You might think that your job was done, but many executives still might ask, "So what?" Looking at the outcomes of training is only half the battle in evaluating its effectiveness. The other half is determining whether the results were worth the cost.

Cost/Benefit and Cost-Effectiveness Evaluations

Was the training cost worth the results? This question can be answered in either of the following two ways:[41]

- Cost/benefit evaluation
- Cost-effectiveness evaluation

Cost/Benefit Evaluation   A **cost/benefit evaluation** of training compares the monetary cost of training with the nonmonetary benefits. It is difficult to place a value on these benefits, which include attitudes and working relationships. The labor peace brought about by the reduction in grievances is difficult to assess, but it rates high in value compared with the cost of training. The conflict resolution skills learned by supervisors provide the nonmonetary benefit of better relationships between supervisors and union officials, and this is important. However, it is also possible to assess the reduction in grievances (for example) in a way that directly answers the cost-effectiveness question.

Cost-Effectiveness Evaluation   A **cost-effectiveness evaluation** compares the monetary costs of training with the financial benefits accrued from training. There are two approaches for assessing cost-effectiveness:

1. Cost savings, a calculation of the actual cost savings, based on the change in "results"
2. Utility analysis, an examination of value of overall improvement in the performance of the trained employees

The difference between the two is that the **cost savings analysis** only looks at the financial value of improvement in the problem that training was intended to correct (e.g., reduction in labor grievances). In contrast, utility analysis looks at all the ways in which the trainee's improved job performance will benefit the organization financially (e.g., reduced grievances, improved relations with labor force, less turnover).

Cost Savings Analysis (Results Focus)   The common types of costs associated with training programs were presented in Chapter 5, Table 5-4. These costs are compared with the savings that can be attributed to training. Let's look again at Table 5-4 on page 159.

Recall that the cost of training was $32,430. Now, determine how much is saved when training is completed. To perform this cost savings analysis, we must first determine the cost of the current situation (see Table 9-4). The company averaged 90 grievances per year. Seventy percent (63) of these go to the third step before settlement. The average time required by management (including HR managers, operational supervisors, etc.) to deal with a grievance that goes to the third step is 10 hours. The management wages ($50 per hour on average) add $500 to the cost of each grievance ($50 × 10). In addition, union representatives spend an average of 7.5 hours at $25 per hour, for a cost of $187.50 per grievance. The reason for this is that the union representative wages are considered paid time, as stipulated in the collective bargaining agreement. The total cost of wages to the company per grievance

Table 9-4 Cost Savings for Grievance Reduction Training

COSTS OF GRIEVANCES	PRETRAINING	POSTTRAINING
Management Time (for those going to third step) 10 h per grievance	10 h × 63 grievances = 630 h	10 h × 8 grievances = 80 h
Union Rep's Time (paid by management) 7.5 h per grievance	7.65 h × 63 grievances = 472 h	7.65 × 8 grievances = 60 h
Total Cost		
Management Time	630 h × $50 per h = $31,500	80 h × $50 per h = $4,000
Union Rep's Time	472 h × $25 per h = $11,812.50	60 h × $25 per h = $1,500
Total	**$43,312.50**	**$5,500.00**
Cost Savings		
Reduction in cost of grievances going to the third step		**$43,312.50 − $5,500.00 = $37 812.50**
Cost of training		−$32,430.00
Cost saving for the 1st year		$5,382.50
Return on Investment		
Calculating the ratio		$5,382.50/$32,430 = 0.166
Percent ROI		0.166 × 100 = **16.6%**

is $687.50. The total cost for those 63 grievances that go to the third step is $43,312.50. The cost of training is $32,430.00.

The data show a $37,812.50 return on a $32,430 investment. Therefore, in the first year, the cost saving is $5,382.50. Dividing the cost saving by the investment produces an ROI ratio of 0.166.[42] If the ratio is exactly 0, the training broke even. If it is below that, it costs more than it returns to the company. Multiplying the ratio by 100 provides the percent ROI. In this case, there is a 16.6 percent ROI for the first year. Most companies would be delighted if all their investments achieved this level of return. In addition, the nonmonetary benefits described earlier are also realized. Presenting this type of data to the corporate decision makers at budget preparation time is certainly more compelling than stating, "Thirty supervisors were given a five-day grievance reduction workshop."

Many training departments are beginning to see the importance of placing a monetary value on their training for several reasons:[43]

- HRD budgets are more easily justified and even expanded when HR can demonstrate that it is contributing to the profit.
- HRD specialists are more successful in containing costs.
- The image of the training department is improved by showing dollar value for training.

Recall Dave Palm from LensCrafters. Top management told him to demonstrate what they were getting in the way of "bang for the buck." Well, he did, and the result was that his training budget was doubled.[44] Training in Action 9-2 is a similar example. Here, Alberta Bell demonstrated the value of the training that prompted management not only to restore funding for the original training, but also to consider increasing it.

Because of the time and effort required to calculate the value of training, many small business managers simply do not do it. However, assessing the value of training is not an exact science, and it can be done more easily by means of estimates. Table 9-5 provides a simplified approach for small business.[45] When estimates are necessary in completing this form, it is useful to obtain them from those who will receive the report (usually top management). If you use their estimates, it is more likely that your final report will be credible. Of course, larger organizations can also use this method.

Alberta Bell of Edmonton, Alberta, was looking for ways to reduce the cost of its operations. Downsizing and cost cutting were necessary to meet the new competitive environment. One of the decisions made was to reduce the entry-level training program for its customer service representatives from two weeks to one week. This would save a great deal of money by reducing the cost of training and getting service representatives out "earning their keep" sooner.

The manager of training decided to assess the value of this decision. By gathering information from data already available, he calculated the average time necessary to complete a service call for those who attended the two-week and one-week training programs. Those from the two-week program completed a call on average in 11.4 minutes. Those in the one-week program took 14.5 minutes. This difference alone represented $50,000 in lost productivity for the first six weeks of work. He further analyzed the differences in increased errors, increased collectables, and service order errors. This difference was calculated at more than $50,000. The total loss exceeded $100,000.

He presented this information to upper management, who quickly restored the two-week training program and is considering making it longer.

Source: Adapted from Fitz-Enz, J. "Yes, you can weigh training's value." *Training* (July, 1994) pp. 54–58.

Utility Analysis In the previous example, training supervisors in grievance handling reduced the total number of grievances by 50 percent and the number going to the third step from 63 to 8. In this example, we calculated only the cost savings related to the change in third-step grievances. Utility analysis permits us to estimate the overall value to the organization of the supervisors' changes in behavior. In other words, if those trained are better performers, on average, and better performers are worth more in dollar terms, utility analysis allows us to estimate that increased worth. A general approach to utility is as follows:[46]

$$\Delta U = (N)(T)(D_T)(SD_Y) - C$$

where

ΔU = dollar value of improved performance
N = number of trainees
T = time the benefits will last
D_T = difference in performance between trained and untrained groups (in standard deviation units)
SD_Y = dollar value of untrained group's performance (in standard deviation units)
C = total cost of training the trained group

Some of the variables in the equation can be measured directly, whereas others must be estimated. For example, N, C, and D_T can be determined objectively. However, determining how long the benefits will last is really an estimate that will be more or less accurate, depending on the estimator's experience with training and the types of employees involved. Calculating the dollar value of the untrained group's performance falls somewhere in between. It is relatively easy to determine the compensation costs. However, it is often more difficult to translate their actual performance into dollar amounts. Recall our third-step grievance example. Even though we know what a third-step grievance costs in management labor compensation, we do not know the impact of those third-step grievances on the productivity of the work unit or the quality of the product/service. What to include in determining the dollar value of performance becomes a subjective decision. The final result will be an

Table 9-5
Training Investment Analysis Work Sheet

Objective: _____
_____

Audience: _____
_____

Returns measured over: _____ One year: _____
Other: _____

Part 1: Calculating the Revenue Produced by Training

Option A—Itemized Analysis

Increased sales:		_____	Additional sales per employee
	×	_____	Revenues (or margin) per sale
	×	_____	Number of employees
	=	_____	Revenue Produced by Training
Higher productivity:		_____	Percent increase in productivity
	×	_____	Cost per employee (salary plus benefits plus overhead)
	×	_____	Number of employees
	=	_____	Revenue Produced by Training
Reduced errors:		_____	Average cost per error
	×	_____	Number of errors avoided per employee
	×	_____	Number of employees
	=	_____	Revenue Produced by Training
Client retention:		_____	Average revenue per client
	×	_____	Number of clients retained
	=	_____	Revenue Produced by Training
Employee retention:		_____	Average cost of a new employee (training plus lost productivity
	×	_____	Number of employees retained
	=	_____	Revenue Produced by Training
Other:		_____	

Total Revenue Produced by Training:

$ _____

Option B—Summary Analysis

_____	−	_____	=	_____
Revenue		Revenue		Revenue
After		Without		Produced
Training		Training		byTraining

Part 2: Calculating the Return

_____	−	_____	=	_____
Revenue		Cost of		Total Return
Produced		Training		on Training
by Training				Investment

Source: Adapted from Hassett, J. "Simplifying ROI." *Training* (September 1992), pp. 53–57.

estimate of the value of the increased performance in dollars. Using the same example, an analysis of the possible utility is presented in Table 9-6.

Utility analysis is complex and beyond the scope of this text; what has been presented here is just a taste of that complexity. More complex models account for even more factors that might affect the true financial value of training outcomes.[47] The purpose here is to demonstrate the difficulties of getting a true picture of the total

Table 9-6
Calculation of the
Utility of the
Grievance Training

Formula: $\Delta U = (N)(T)(D_T)(SD_Y) - C$

$N = 30$

$T = 1$ year (an overly conservative estimate)

$$D_T = 0.2 = \frac{X_t - X_u}{SD(r_{yy})}$$

X_t = average job performance of the trained supervisors

X_u = average job performance of the untrained supervisors

SD = standard deviation of job performance for the untrained supervisors

r_{yy} = reliability of job performance measure

D_T is a measure of the improvement (in standard deviation units) in performance that trained supervisors will exhibit. Although obtaining the data is time-consuming (collecting the performance appraisal data for supervisors, trained and untrained), the calculations can be done easily on using a computer.

$$SD_Y = \$14,000 = 0.40 \times \$35,000$$

The equation assumes average salary of $35,000. The 0.40 comes from the 40% rule, which is a calculation based on 40% of the average salary of trainees. This rule comes from the Schmidt and Hunter research. This and other methods to calculate SD_Y can be found in Cascio (1991). According to the preceding information, the utility of the training based on this formula is

$$(30)(1)(0.2)(14,000) - 32,020 = \$51,980$$

Sources: Cascio, W. *Applied Psychology in Personnel Management* (1991), 4th ed. Upper Saddle River, NJ: Prentice Hall. Schmidt, F., and J. Hunter. "Individual differences in productivity: An empirical test of estimates derived from studies of selection procedure utility." *Journal of Applied Psychology* 68 (1983), pp. 407–14.

financial benefits associated with training outcomes. However, these complexities exist for any area of the business when you try to determine the effects of change. By becoming more quantitative in the assessment and description of training outcomes, training managers can put themselves on an equal footing with other managers in the organization.

One important note regarding the use of utility methods for gaining support for the training program being promoted: Some recent research has indicated that utility is not an effective method for garnering support for HR policies. In fact, the research concluded that using utility analysis to bolster the claim as to the value of a project actually decreased managerial support for the project.[48] Until it is clear why this tendency is the case, it might not be wise to use this particular type of analysis to sell a project. It still might be useful for showing the benefits after the fact.

When and What Type of Evaluation to Use

So, do we compute a comprehensive evaluation at all four levels in addition to a cost/benefit analysis for all training programs? No. To determine what evaluation should take place, ask the question, "Who is interested in these data?" The different levels of outcome evaluation are designed for different constituencies or customers. Note that in Table 9-7 the trainer is interested in the first three levels, because they reflect most directly on the training. Other trainers might also be interested in these data if the results show some relation to their training programs. Training managers are interested in all the information. Both reaction and learning data, when positive, can be used to evaluate the trainer and also promote the program to others. When the data are not positive, the training manager should be aware of this fact because it gives the trainer information to use to intervene and turn the program around. The

Table 9-7
Who Is Interested in
the Outcome Data

	OUTCOME DATA			
	REACTION	LEARNING	BEHAVIOR	RESULTS
Training Department				
Trainer	yes	yes	yes	no
Other trainers	perhaps	perhaps	perhaps	no
Training manager	yes	yes	yes	yes
Customers				
Trainees	yes	yes	yes	perhaps
Trainees' supervisor	not really	only if no transfer	yes	yes
Upper management	no	no	perhaps	yes

Source: Adapted from Camp, R. P., Blanchard, P. N., and Huszczo, G. E. *Toward a More Organizationally Effective Training Strategy and Practice* (1986). Upper Saddle River, NJ: Prentice Hall.

training manager's interest in the transfer of training is to evaluate the trainer's ability to promote the transfer. Care must be taken in using this information because many other factors may be present and operating to prevent transfer. Also, if transfer is favorable, the information is valuable in promoting the training program. These generalizations are also true for the organizational results. If the training manager is able to demonstrate positive results affecting the financial health of the company, the training department will be seen as a worthy part of the organization.

Trainees are interested in knowing whether others felt the same as they did during training. They are also interested in feedback on what they accomplished (learning) and may be interested in how useful it is to all trainees back on the job (behavior). A trainee's supervisor is interested in behavior and results. These are the supervisor's main reasons for sending subordinates to training in the first place. Upper management is interested in organizational results, although in cases where the results may not be measurable, behavior may be the focus.

Does the interest in different levels of evaluation among different customers mean that you need to gather information at all levels every time? Not at all. First, a considerable amount of work is required to evaluate every program offered. As with process data, it makes sense to gather the outcome data in some situations and not in others.

Again, the obvious question to ask in this regard is "What customer (if any) is interested in the information?" Although one of the major arguments for gathering the outcome data is to demonstrate the worth of the training department, some organizations go beyond that idea. In an examination of "companies with the best training evaluation practices," it was noted that none of them were evaluating training primarily to justify it or maintain a training budget.[49] They evaluated (particularly at the behavior and results levels) when requested to do so by the customer (top management or the particular department). Jack Phillips, founder of ROI Institute, a consulting firm that specializes in evaluation, suggests that organizations only evaluate 5 to 10 percent of their training at the ROI level.[50] Which ones? The ones that are high profile and/or are specifically requested by upper management. This selectivity is a function of the cost in developing such evaluations, because these type of evaluations[51]

- need to be customized for each situation,
- are costly and time consuming, and
- require cooperation from the customer.

Motorola, for example, evaluates only at the behavioral level and not at the results level. Executives at Motorola are willing to assume that if the employee is

TRAINING IN ACTION 9-3
What Companies Are Doing for Evaluation

After years of not evaluating their training, the U.S. Coast Guard decided to evaluate at the behavioral level, asking trainees and their supervisors three things: How well the trainees were able to perform the desired behaviors, how often they did those behaviors, and how important those behaviors were to being an effective employee. With the information provided in the evaluations, trainers were able to remove outdated training objectives and add job aids for some less frequent behaviors. Furthermore, the remaining training was refined, became more relevant, and provided more efficiency. This translated into a $3 million a year savings for the training department of the Coast Guard (Chevalier, 2004).

Texas Instruments noted that once trainees left training, it was difficult to obtain transfer of training information from them. It was generally ignored because of the time and expense of gathering this information. Then, an automated e-mail system was developed through which trainees, after being back on the job for 90 days, were contacted and asked to complete a survey related to transfer. This system increased the use of evaluations, reduced the time necessary to gather information, and provided a standardized process. Texas Instruments noted an improvement in the quantity and quality of participant

feedback. It would seem easy enough to include an e-mail to the trainees' supervisors for the same purpose (Overmyer-Day and Benson, 1996).

Century 21 decided to evaluate their sales training at the results level. After training, trainees were tracked through a sales performance system that identified the number of sales, listings, and commissions for each graduate. This was cross-referenced to the place they worked and their instructor. Findings were surprising. Trainees from certain offices outperformed trainees from other offices even though they had the same instructor. Examination of these results showed that the high-performing offices provided help when needed, had access to ongoing training, and had better support. To respond to this, Century 21 had its trainers still deliver the training but, in addition, was responsible for monitoring the environment in offices where trainees were sent. This monitoring was to see that every trainee was in an environment similar to that of the "high-performing trainees" identified earlier (Chevalier, 2004).

Booz Allen Hamilton, a consulting firm, recently decided to assess the ROI of its executive coaching program, which had been up and running for three years. The result? It was determined that the program's ROI was about $3 million per year (Ellis, 2005).

Sources: Chevalier, R. "Evaluation: The link between learning and performance." *Performance Improvement* 43 (2004), pp. 40–45. Overmyer-Day, D., and G. Benson. "Training success stories." *Training and Development* (June 1996), pp. 24–29. Ellis, K. "What is the ROI of ROI?" *Training*, 42, pp. 16–21.

exhibiting the appropriate behavior, the effect on the bottom line will be positive.[52] Training in Action 9-3 shows how various companies are dealing with evaluation, particularly behavior and results.

Certainly, all levels of data gathering are important at different times, and the training professional must be able to conduct an evaluation at every level. So, what and when should the trainer evaluate? The answer is that it depends on the organization and the attitudes and beliefs of upper management. If they perceive the training department as an effective tool of the organization and require only behavior-level evaluation, that is the evaluation to do.

However, this level still might require vigilance at the learning and reaction levels to ensure positive results. Darryl Jinkerson, director of evaluation services at Arthur Andersen, looks at the size and impact of the training before deciding how to evaluate it. Only those that are high profile, or for which the customer requests it, will be evaluated at the results level.[53] What if training is a one-time event and no desire is indicated to assess individual competence (e.g., a workshop on managing your career)? Such a situation provides simply no reason to evaluate.[54]

Can You Show That Training Is the Reason Change Has Occurred?

We have discussed in detail the types of measures you can use to help determine if training has been effective. However, it is not as simple as that, because change might have occurred for reasons not related to the training. This is where designing an appropriate evaluation becomes so important. Appendix 9-1 provides an examination of the various concerns in evaluation, such as those related to the validity (both internal and external) of the findings. It also provides several designs that can be useful to help assure you that your results are in fact valid.

FOCUS ON SMALL BUSINESS

For the small business owner, sending employees to training that is not effective could significantly affect the company's financial health. Consider the owner who is constantly terminating employees because they are unable (or unwilling) to do the job properly. They all receive training, and most, but not all, turn out to be ineffective. Why? If training is not evaluated, it is not possible to know whether employees are lost because the training is not effective or because some other factor is blocking effective performance.

The small-business owner might think it is not necessary to evaluate training, because whether or not it was effective will be obvious by changes observed on the job after training. Actually, this assessment is probably true; in a small business, it would soon be evident if recently trained employees were performing at the expected level. However, if training is a significant cost to the owner, evaluating learning before and after training can still be of value. After all, the trainees might be learning on the job and the training may not be adding anything to their KSAs.

Much of the training in a small business is done on the job. In such cases, evaluation is often simply an assessment of the trainee's ability to learn. Examining the training process is not considered. As we discussed in Chapter 6, on-the-job training requires trainer skills just like any other training. Simply placing a new employee with an experienced employee and expecting the experienced one to train is not wise. It can be worthwhile to evaluate the process of training that goes on, in addition to evaluating the outcomes, especially if the position is at a lower level where, because of turnover or promotion, a rather high number of employees receives training.

Beyond the above reasons for evaluation of training there are external pressures as well. The movement to quality standards, such as ISO creates a need for certification in several areas. As mentioned previously, one of the requirements is that the organization must maintain training records and periodically evaluate training. Training records can take the form of diplomas, certificates, licenses, experience records, resumes and so on. There is no specific method for evaluating training effectiveness. A popular method is an annual review of training's outcomes. Results of the review are recorded and are used as feedback for revising and updating the training program. Another method is a periodic assessment of individual employees.

David Alcock of Canadian Plastics Training Centre, in the Toronto area, says that even though few of the center's clients request an evaluation of training, such requests are on the increase. Most of the center's clients are small injection molding businesses. The need for certification seems to be the driving force behind the necessity to evaluate. Canadian Plastics Training conducts standardized injection molding training on its own site and provides a skill-based evaluation. A trainee who passes

"ISO makes training mandatory," says Don Villers, plant manager of the 160-employee Scepter Manufacturing plant in Scarborough, Ontario. "We train everyone from the shop floor to the front office." The plant has been ISO certified for over a decade and since then has moved well beyond the ISO training requirements.

In the company's rating system, supervisors are required to rate each of their employees on a scale from 1 to 10. An employee must reach 10 to be certified at that level and to be eligible for promotion. The rating system is not seen as punitive, but developmental. It is used as a needs analysis to identify skill deficiencies, then as a learning measure, and finally as a transfer of training measure.

What about results? According to Villers, "Defective parts dropped from 5 percent to 0.1 percent. Scrap also dropped 50 percent." He attributes this success primarily to training. As a result of the success, the training budget is 10 times the $6,000 per year that the company spent three years ago.

Source: Adapted from LeGault, M. "In-house training that gets results." *Canadian Plastics* (February 1997), pp. 14–18.

the skill-based test becomes certified as an injection molder. Generally, the company sends its employees for this training; however, some employees pay their own way to improve themselves.

One reason that these small companies do not evaluate is the cost. For in-house training done by Canadian Plastics Training, a late-1997 cost of evaluation for 20 employees to be trained to a higher-level classification was $25,000. This is similar to costs in the United States. The Center for Industrial Research and Service at Iowa State University suggests the cost to be $1,000 to $1,500 per employee.[55] Many small companies simply do not have those resources. Another issue noted by Alcock involves what the evaluation would be used for. For example, suppose a unionized shop wants to upgrade the skills of the workforce. Sending them to training would carry with it the union's blessing. Evaluating the learning, however, might be met with a great deal of resistance. The union leadership and rank and file might be concerned about the company knowing how well the employees did on a test. They might believe that the company's goal is to get rid of some employees based on test results. Otherwise, why evaluate? Convincing the union that evaluation is a way of assessing the effectiveness of training might be difficult to do, depending on the relationship between union and management. Training in Action 9-4 shows what one small company is doing.

Evaluation Beyond Learning

The discussion above focused primarily on learning. What about transfer of behavior and organizational results? In many ways, evaluation of transfer and organizational results is easier in a small company. After publishing the article on Scepter Manufacturing (see Training in Action 9-4),[56] Don Villers was asked how he knew that the drop in scrap and defective parts (results) was a function of training. His reply: "We are a small company, and it is the only thing that we changed." He makes an important point related to the examination of results in small businesses. When a small business does training, evidence of the impact can be much clearer and faster. Also, it should be easier to rule out alternative explanations for the change, without the need for the more complex designs discussed in Appendix 9-1.

SUMMARY

We began this chapter by discussing the importance of a comprehensive evaluation. We end it by suggesting that a comprehensive evaluation is not always necessary. Understanding what to consider before evaluating makes such decisions more logical and useful.

Evaluation can be complex and, in many cases, costly. For this reason, we suggested throughout this chapter that evaluation is useful and important, but not necessary at all levels all the time. Furthermore, good detective work can, in some cases, replace complex designs in assessing the validity of evaluation.

Deciding what training should be evaluated, and at what levels, will be easier if the organization is proactive. By examining the strategic plan, it is possible to identify those areas of training that require evaluation and the extent to which evaluating is necessary. Without such direction, the training department will need to identify its mission and goals as best it can and work from there to determine the training that needs to be evaluated. Even for a large organization, it is simply not practical to evaluate everything. All organizations need to determine what training they want to evaluate and how they will do so.

> ### THE TRAINING PROGRAM (FABRICS, INC.)
>
> We are now ready to examine the evaluation phase of the Fabrics, Inc., training. We presented the training, and it is time to do the evaluation. In the design phase of the training process, one of the outcomes was development of evaluation objectives. Although we developed and implemented the training, it is critical to remember that developing the tools for evaluation needs to be done concurrently with developing the training, not after it.
>
> Examination of the output of the evaluation phase of training indicated two types of evaluation: process and outcome. The process evaluation will consist of the trainer, during training, documenting the content phases and times taken in each of the training modules. These results will then be compared with the actual expectations regarding training content and times allotted.
>
> *(continued)*

For the outcome evaluation, four types are identified. The reaction questionnaire for trainers will model the one that was presented in Figure 9-1 of the text. For the training itself, the reaction questionnaire is shown in "Fabrics Reaction 1" below.

For learning, we need to revisit the learning objectives to determine what is required. We need a paper-and-pencil test for measuring knowledge (objectives 1 and 2 below) and two behavioral tests to measure active listening and conflict resolution skills (objectives 3 and 4). More specifically, the first two learning objectives (and the others related to the training but not developed here) are accommodated using the paper-and-pencil test. The content of this test is partially represented in "Fabrics Paper-and-Pencil Test" on page 356. But first let's look at the learning objectives.

Fabrics Reaction 1

Using the scale below, evaluate the training by circling the appropriate number to the right of the item.

1 = Strongly disagree
2 = Disagree
3 = Neither agree nor disagree
4 = Agree
5 = Strongly agree

Active Listening Skills

The training met the stated objectives.	1 2 3 4 5
The information provided was enough for me to understand the concepts being taught.	1 2 3 4 5
The practice sessions provided were sufficient to give me an idea of how to perform the skill.	1 2 3 4 5
The feedback provided was useful in helping me understand how to improve.	1 2 3 4 5
The training session kept my interest throughout.	1 2 3 4 5

Circle the response below that reflects your feelings about the pace of the session just completed.

1. Way too fast
2. A bit fast
3. Just right
4. A bit slow
5. Way too slow

What did you like best about this part of the training?

What would you change?

Comments:

Note: A similar scale would be used for each of the other components of training that were taught.

(continued)

The trainee will, <u>with no errors</u>, present in writing the four types of active listening, along with examples of each of the types, without using reference materials.

The trainee will, <u>with 100 percent accuracy</u>, provide in writing each step of the conflict resolution model, along with a relevant example, without help from any reference material.

After watching a role-play of an angry person and an employee using the conflict resolution model, the trainee will, without using reference materials, immediately provide feedback as to the effectiveness of the person using the conflict resolution model. <u>The trainee must identify four of the six errors.</u>

Fabrics Paper-and-Pencil Test

Evaluation of Learning

No specific time limit is set for this test, but you should be able to finish in about one hour.

Answers to the questions should be written in the booklet provided.

Please read each question carefully. Some of the questions contain more than one part.

1. List four types of active listening, and provide an example for each.
2. List the steps in the conflict resolution model. After each step, provide a relevant example of a phrase that could be used to represent that step.

And so forth for as many questions as needed

The next objective is partly related to skill development. Below are a number of standardized scenarios and guidelines to evaluate them. "Fabrics Scenario: Active Listening" is an example. But first, here is the objective.

When, in a role-play, the trainee is presented with an angry comment, the trainee will respond <u>immediately</u> using one of the appropriate active listening types. The trainee will then explain orally the technique used and why, with no help from reference material. <u>The trainee will be presented with five of these situations and be expected to correctly respond and explain a minimum of four techniques.</u>

Fabrics Scenario: Active Listening

This is read to the trainee: The following set of scenarios is designed to determine how well you, the trainee, have learned the active listening skills. There are three roles here: initiator, active listener (you, the trainee), and evaluator. The initiator is a nontrainee who speaks a conflict-provoking statement to you (the active listener). You, the trainee, listen to the statement, and then respond using active listening skills. The evaluator, who is trained in evaluating active listening, listens to your response and evaluates it based on the use of effective active listening skills.

Note: The following forms (initiator's role, active listener's role, evaluator's role) are given to the respective people, with the active listener's role being given to you, the trainee.

(continued)

The sheet below is for the person playing the initiator.

Initiator's Role

(The initiator is to be played by the same actor for all trainees.)

Instructions for the Initiator   Read the sentence describing the scenario carefully; wait until the trainee is ready, and then read the comment in bold under Scenario 1 angrily.

   Wait until you are told by the evaluator to move to the next scenario and repeat the above.

Test Scenario 1

You were just asked by your supervisor (the trainee) to serve on the same committee again. You are angry that they always ask you.

You start. Say angrily:

"OH, NO YOU DON'T. I'VE BEEN ON THAT COMMITTEE THREE YEARS IN A ROW AND IT TAKES UP TOO MUCH TIME!"

Test Scenario 2

Your supervisor just talked to you about following procedures. You think, Why me? After all, no one follows procedures.

You start. Say angrily:

"WHY ARE YOU PICKING ON ME ALL THE TIME? I'M NOT THE ONLY ONE WHO DOESN'T FOLLOW THESE STUPID PROCEDURES!"

Test Scenario 3

You were just asked by your supervisor for a second time today whether you will be attending the weekly meeting.

You say angrily:

"I ALREADY TOLD YOU, I CAN'T ATTEND THE WEEKLY MEETING BECAUSE I HAVE TO COMPLETE THE STAFF REPORTS FOR TOMORROW!"

And so forth (for a total of 5).

(*continued*)

The next sheet is for the trainee.

Trainee's (Active Listener) Role

Instructions for the trainee: This test will require you to respond to five different short scenarios in which you are a supervisor and you say something to a subordinate that elicits an angry response. You will be expected to respond using the skills of active listening. The description of each of the scenarios provides what you initially said to the subordinate. When you are ready for each of the scenarios to begin, nod your head to the initiator. At that time, the initiator will say something. You need to respond to the comment, and when complete, explain to the evaluator the rationale for your response.

Scenario 1

You asked a subordinate to continue working on a particular committee for another year. Listen; then respond using active listening. Nod your head when ready. . . .

Scenario 2

You just talked to a subordinate regarding the importance of following procedures. Listen; then respond using active listening. Nod your head when ready. . . .

Scenario 3

Today is the day of your weekly meeting. You asked if your subordinate would be attending the meeting; the answer was no. It is now time for the meeting and you call once more to check to see whether the subordinate can make the meeting. Listen; then respond using active listening. Nod your head when ready. . . .

And so forth (for a total of 5).

The next sheet is for the evaluator.

Evaluator's Role

Instructions to evaluator for scoring trainee responses: Trainee fails the scenario if the response is focused on the issue instead of reflecting what the initiator says. For example, a poor (fail) response to the first scenario would be something where the trainee responds to the concern by dealing with the issue **"But you are my best person for the job"** or **"You have to do it; I have no one else"** or **"Look, I am asking you as a favor to me."**

Appropriate responses reflect what the person is saying, as in the first scenario: **"So, you're saying that being on the committee interferes with your doing your job"** or **"You feel you have done your share regarding committee work."**

It is also important that the response does not sound like a mimic of what the person said. Although at this time we do not expect perfection regarding responses, the responses must, at a minimum, sound sincere. Refer to the tape recordings provided to understand the difference between what we consider mimicking and acceptable.

(continued)

For each of the five scenarios, there is an example of a poor (fail) response and an acceptable response. When the trainee explains his or her response, we expect the trainee to be able to identify the type of active listening response used (paraphrasing, decode and feedback, summarizing) and why it was chosen. Answers to why it was chosen are intended to show that they understand the different methods, and thus almost any answer is acceptable.

Scenario 1

The supervisor (trainee being tested) asked the subordinate to continue working on a particular committee for another year, and the subordinate responds. Listen to the supervisor's response and grade according to guidelines.

Unacceptable response: **"I am willing to talk about reducing the work you have to do if you will be on it."**

Acceptable response: **"YOU DON'T WANT TO BE ON THAT COMMITTEE AGAIN BECAUSE IT INTERFERES WITH YOUR WORK AND YOU FEEL YOU HAVE DONE YOUR SHARE."**

Scenario 2

The supervisor (trainee being tested) just talked to a subordinate regarding the importance of following procedures, and the subordinate responds. Listen to the supervisor's response and grade according to guidelines.

Unacceptable response: **"You are not the only one I have talked to about this."**

Acceptable response: **"YOU BELIEVE THAT YOU'RE THE ONLY ONE THAT I AM SINGLING OUT FOR NOT FOLLOWING PROCEDURES."**

Scenario 3

The supervisor (trainee being tested) called first thing in the morning and asked the subordinate if she would be attending the weekly meeting; the subordinate said, "No, I'm busy." The supervisor just called again at meeting time to check to see whether the subordinate could make the meeting, and the subordinate responds. Listen to the supervisor's response and grade.

Unacceptable response: **"The meeting will only be an hour."**

Acceptable response: **"YOU'RE NOT ABLE TO ATTEND THE MEETING BECAUSE YOU ARE COMPLETING STAFF REPORTS THAT ARE DUE TOMORROW."**

And so forth (for a total of 5).

Note that we do not provide the test for determining the knowledge part of this objective, where the trainee is asked to explain his or her response orally.

The next objective is skill related and has to do with conflict resolution. See "Fabrics Role-Play Conflict Resolution" for an example of this. The objective is:

"In a role-play of an angry employee, the trainee will calm the person using the steps in the conflict resolution model, <u>with help from a poster that lists the steps."</u>

(continued)

Fabrics Role-Play Conflict Resolution

Read the following to the trainee: The following role-play is designed to determine how well you, the trainee, have learned the conflict resolution skills. There are three roles here: initiator, active listener (you, the trainee), and evaluator. The initiator is a nontrainee who starts off very angry at something you did. You listen to what is said and respond using the conflict resolution model. The evaluator, who is trained in evaluating effective conflict resolution, listens to your response and evaluates it based on your effectiveness. The following forms (initiator's role, active listener's role, evaluator's role) are given to the respective people, with the active listener's role being given to you, the trainee.

The sheet below is for the person playing the initiator.

Initiator's Role

(The initiator is to be played by the same actor for all trainees.)

Instructions for the Initiator

- Read the role a couple of times and get in the mood suggested.
- Be sure you understand the issues, so you can present them without referring to the role.
- Once into the role, allow your own feelings to take over; if what the supervisor is saying makes you less angry, then act that way, and vice versa.
- Do not refer back to the role after the role-play begins; simply act the way you normally would do in such circumstances.
- Begin the role-play by presenting the points at the end of the role-play with anger.
- To elicit an assertive response, interrupt the trainee at least once after the trainee begins to present his or her point of view. If the trainee allows the interruption, interrupt again until the trainee becomes assertive and asks you not to interrupt (maximum of four interruptions).

The Role of the Initiator

Your name is Pat. You are the longest working machinist in the plant, with 25 years service. You taught many of those who are presently there, including most of those who were made supervisor recently. The company has been busy for the last number of years, and you have been called upon many times to provide the extra boost to get some projects out. You worked hard all your life and are starting to feel it in your bones. The work is getting harder and harder to complete, especially with the older lathes. With only three years to retirement, you are wishing you could afford to retire now. You are really worn out, that is, until you hear the news that the company just purchased one of those new computer-operated lathes. You feel confident that once you get to use the new machine you will be rejuvenated. In fact, the thought of getting to work on one of these new machines gives you goose bumps. You have not felt this excited in years. Actually, the thought of going back to school to learn about it is the most exciting thing, as it is making you feel young again. You are sorry that

(continued)

you missed today's meeting at which they were going to talk about the new equipment, but your car would not start.

"Hey, did you hear the news?" your friend Bill called out.

"I don't think so, what is it?" you replied.

"They just announced that Fred is going for training on the new computer-operated lathe. I guess he will be the one operating it."

"Are you sure?" you ask.

"Yep, it was announced at the circle meeting this morning. He was selected to operate it and will be going for a two-week training course next week."

You are furious. Fred was only just hired and is just a kid. You deserve first crack at the new machine, given your loyal service. Well, that is it. Your supervisor (the young guy you taught how to run a lathe before he got promoted) never did get along with you, and now this. Well, you are not going to take it. You walk into the supervisor's office and in a loud voice start off by saying:

"What do you think you are doing? How can you give the new lathe to Fred, after all the years I have been here? This is not fair and I am not going to sit still for it."

Be sure to continue the anger and bring up all the points mentioned in the role-play. Go over them again and again until the trainee calms you down.

The next sheet is for the trainee.

Trainee's Role

Instructions for the Trainee
- Read your role a few times and be sure you understand the issues, so you can present them without referring to the role.
- Do not refer back to the role after the role-play begins, but you can jot down a few points for reference.
- Use the conflict resolution model to deal with the issue.
- Nod at the initiator when you wish to begin.

The Role for the Trainee

You are the supervisor of a manufacturing firm and have about 10 subordinates. They are all lathe operators, and you were also one until you recently got promoted. Your subordinates are all good people, and with the exception of Pat, who has been here for 25 years and is a few years away from retirement, all are fairly young and have at most 10 years' service. Pat is a great machinist and knows more than everyone put together. He taught you the job when you had just started and, although you never really hit it off with him, you do respect his ability.

You are pretty excited these last few days, because the company just purchased a new computer-operated lathe. It is your understanding that you will be getting a new lathe each year until all are replaced. You are moving into the new age. Choosing only one of your

(continued)

machinists to go to training and be the first one on the new machine was a difficult decision. All were likely candidates, with the exception of Pat, who was too old to learn the new machine—computer stuff and all. Furthermore, why train Pat on a new machine when he will only be here a short time? It makes more sense to train those who will be able to use the new skills for the longest time. Anyway, Pat really knows how to operate the older machine better than anyone, so why move him? Finally, you came up with the perfect solution. The new guy, Fred, has not been trained on any machine yet, so training him on the new lathe would mean that no one else needed training for the time being. Putting anyone else on the new machine would mean training Fred on the old machine, then when they are phased out, retraining him on the computer-operated lathe. So you announced it today at your circle meeting. Everyone was pretty quiet, but they will get over it. Too bad Pat wasn't there. Wonder if he is sick?

The next sheet is for the evaluator.

Evaluator's Role

Instructions for the Evaluator

The trainee fails the scenario if the initial response is focused on the issue instead of reflecting what the initiator says. For example, a poor (fail) response would be if the first comment to Pat was **"I did not think you wanted it"** or **"It is probably too complicated for you"** or **"We value your contribution"** or **"You're the best we've got on the old machine, and we need you there."**

Keys to successfully passing this exercise are to

- actively listen to Pat (using the active listening skills) and
- question to obtain as much information as possible before dealing with the issue.

To be successful, it is expected that the trainee will use active listening and questions at least four to six times (preferably more) before moving to the trainee's point of view. The key is to note how much the initiator has calmed down.

- Be sure the trainee indicates respect (must have at least one phrase such as **"I can appreciate why you feel you should have the opportunity to receive the training. It makes sense that you believe after such long and loyal service you should receive some reward"**).
- Be assertive, not aggressive, if necessary to present points.

When interrupted, the trainee must use the proper assertive response to inhibit interruptions. The trainee is given four opportunities to be assertive, since the role requires interruptions until an assertive response is given (up to four). Note how that interruption is handled; the trainee needs to be assertive (for example, **"I have carefully listened to everything you have had to say; I think it only fair that now you give me a chance to respond, okay?"**).

- Provide the supervisor's points as "point of view," not correct point of view.

The role-play will begin with the initiator being angry. Response can be a summary of these points, paraphrase of one of them, or decode and feedback regarding emotion expressed,

(continued)

but not anything dealing with the specific issue. Below is a form to assist in the evaluation of the trainee.

Evaluator Report Form

Put a mark next to each of the responses in terms of their type. Try to jot down the words used in some of the cases to enable you to provide specific feedback.

Active Listening

Nonverbal behavior
Say more responses
Paraphrase
Decode and feedback
Summarize

Indicate Respect

Use of active listening
Questioning
Show acceptance of other's point of view

Be Assertive

Needs to be phrased in terms of YOUR POINT OF VIEW
My perception is . . .
It seems to me that . . .
It is my belief that . . . and so forth.

Provide Information

Use collaboration (problem solving) or compromise (negotiate). *Note:* Although this response is a part of the conflict resolution model, it is not part of the learning objectives for this training; therefore, it is not evaluated in this training program.

You will note that a standardized scoring key, examples of acceptable and unacceptable behavior of the trainee, and a checklist for different responses are provided for the evaluator.

The above are evaluations related to learning, but we still need to consider behavior (transfer of training) and organizational results. The owner in the Fabrics, Inc., case is not interested in doing any of this type of evaluation. Recall that we indicated that an evaluation using elaborate designs is nice but seldom happens in reality.

The owner in the Fabrics, Inc., case does not want us to assess any transfer of behaviors to the job. His argument is that his primary interest is in getting fewer complaints from employees and customers. He notes that in a small organization such as his, these changes (lowering of complaints) are proof enough that training was successful. We agree, so the evaluation will consist of gathering weekly archival information on complaints from customers and subordinates as a baseline (gathering it for two months prior to the training) and tracking it for six months after training is complete.

KEY TERMS

- Affective questionnaire
- Control group*
- Cost/benefit evaluation
- Cost-effectiveness evaluation
- Cost savings analysis
- External validity*
- History*
- Initial group differences
- Instrumentation*

- Internal referencing strategy (IRS)*
- Internal validity*
- Job behavior outcomes
- Learning outcomes
- Maturation*
- Organizational results
- Outcome evaluation
- Process evaluation

- Random assignment*
- Reaction outcomes
- Representative sampling*
- Single-case design*
- Statistical regression*
- Utility analysis
- Utility questionnaire

QUESTIONS FOR REVIEW

1. What is the relationship among the four levels of evaluation? Would you argue for examining all four levels if your boss suggested that you should look only at the last one (results) and that if it improved, you would know that training had some effect?

2. What is the difference between cost/benefit evaluation and cost-effectiveness evaluation? When would you use each, and why?

3. What is the difference between cost-effectiveness evaluation and utility analysis? When, if ever, would you use utility rather than cost-effectiveness? Why?

4. Assume that you were the training manager in the Westcan case (in Chapter 4). How would you suggest evaluating the training, assuming they were about to conduct it as suggested in the case? Be as specific as you can.

5. Of all the designs presented in Appendix 9-1, which one would you consider to be most effective while also being practical enough to convince an organization to adopt it? If your design involved representative sampling, how would you accomplish it?

EXERCISES

1. Examine the reaction questionnaire that your school uses. Is it designed to rate the course content or the instructors? Does it meet the requirements of a sound reaction questionnaire? Why or why not? Explain how you would improve it (if possible).

2. Break into small groups, with each group containing at least one member who previously received some type of training in an organization. Interview that person on what the training was designed to teach and how it was evaluated. Did the evaluation cover all the levels of outcomes? How did the trainee feel about the evaluation? Devise your own methods for evaluating each of the levels based on the person's description of the training.

3. Go to the role-play for active listening in the Fabrics, Inc., example. In groups of five or six, choose someone to be the initiator and someone to be the trainee. Have them go through the role-play while the rest evaluate the trainee's response on a scale of 1 to 7 (1 being poor and 7 being excellent). Now share your scores. Were they all exactly the same? If not, how could you make the instrument more reliable? If they were all the same, why was that? Is there anything you would suggest to make the evaluation process easier?

---

*These key terms appear in the Appendix.

CASE ANALYSIS

You run Tricky Nicky's Carpet Cleaning Co., which cleans carpets for businesses. On average, one carpet cleaner can clean six offices per eight-hour shift. Currently, 100 cleaners work for you, and they work 250 days per year. Supervisors inspect carpets when cleaners notify them that the carpet is done. Because of Nicky's "Satisfaction Guarantee," when a carpet does not meet the standard, it is redone immediately at no extra cost to the client. A recent analysis of the rework required found that, on average, one in every six carpets cleaned does not meet Nicky's standards.

The profit averages $20 a cleaning. You pay your cleaners $15 per hour. When you re-clean a carpet, it is done on overtime and you lose, on average, $20 in labor costs. On average, your profit is gone. In addition, there is an average cost of materials and equipment of $2.00 per office.

Your training manager conducted a needs assessment regarding this issue at your request. He reported that half the employees are not reaching the standard one in nine times, and the other half are not meeting the standard two in nine times, for an overall average of one in six $[(1/9 + 2/9)/2 = 1/6]$. The needs assessment also indicated that the cause was a lack of KSAs in both cases.

The training manager proposes a training program that he estimates will reduce everyone's errors to 1 carpet in 12 (half the current level). The training would take four hours and could handle 20 employees per session.

The costs below reflect implementing five training sessions of 20 employees each and assume 250 working days in a year.

Developmental Costs	
20 days of training manager's time for design and development at $40,000 per year	$ 3,200
Miscellaneous	$ 800
Direct Costs	
4 hours per session at $40,000 per year (trainer)	$ 400
Training facility and equipment	$ 500
Materials	$ 2,000
Refreshments	$ 600
Employee salaries at $20 per hour per employee (Nicky decides to do training on a Saturday and pay employees an extra $5 per hour as overtime)	$ 8,000
Lost profit (none because training is done on overtime)	0
Indirect Costs	
Evaluation of training; 10 days of training manager's time at $40,000 per year	$ 1,600
Material and equipment	$ 600
Clerical support—20 hours at $10 per hour	$ 200

CASE QUESTIONS

1. How much does the re-cleaning cost Nicky per year? Show all mathematical calculations.
2. If everyone is trained, how much will the training cost? How much will training cost if only the group with the most errors is trained? Show costs in a spreadsheet and all mathematical calculations.
3. If everyone is trained, what is the cost savings for the first year? If only the group with the highest re-cleaning requirements is trained, what is the cost savings for the first year? Show all mathematical calculations.

4. What is your recommendation for this training based on the expected return on investment? Should just the group with the most re-cleanings be trained or should both groups be trained? Provide a rationale for your recommendation that includes both the financial as well as other factors that may be important in making this decision. Show any mathematical calculations used.

5. Let's back up and assume that employees had the KSAs needed to clean the offices effectively. What other factors might you look at as potential causes of the re-cleaning problem?

WEB RESEARCH

Conduct a search of the Internet to identify eight distinct reasons for conducting an evaluation of training. Document the source of these reasons, and compare the list with reasons cited in the chapter.

Web Sites of Interest

Research Methods on the WWW—Questionnaires
http://www.slais.ubc.ca/resources/research_methods/questions.htm

Appendix 9-1

Evaluation: The Validity Issues

Once it is decided to evaluate training, it is important to be reasonably sure that the findings on the effectiveness of training will be valid. After all, evaluation is both time-consuming and costly.

Let's say that Sue is sent to a one-week training seminar on the operation of Windows. According to the needs analysis, she clearly did not know much about how to operate a computer in a Windows environment. After training, she is tested, and it is determined that she has learned a great deal. Training was effective. Perhaps—but several other factors could also result in her learning how to operate in a Windows environment. Her own interest in Windows might lead her to learn it on her own. The question is: "How certain is it that the improvement was a function of the training that you provided?" In other words, does the evaluation exhibit internal validity? Once internal validity is ensured, the next question is "Will the training be effective for other groups who go through the same training?" That is, does training show external validity? We will deal with internal and external validity separately. These "threats" are not specific to training evaluation but relate to evaluation in general. When we discuss each of the threats, we will indicate when it is not a serious threat in the training context.

Internal Validity

Internal validity is the confidence that the results of the evaluation are in fact correct. Even when an improvement is demonstrated after training, the concern is that perhaps the change occurred for reasons other than training. To address this problem, it is necessary to examine factors that might compromise the findings; these are called threats to internal validity.

History

History refers to events other than training that take place concurrently with the training program. The argument is that those other events caused learning to occur. Consider the example of Sue's computer training. Sue is eager to learn about computers, so she buys some books and works extra hard at home, and attends the training. At the end of training, she demonstrates that she has learned a great deal, but is this learning a function of training? It might just as well be that all her hard work at home caused her to learn so much.

In a half-day training seminar, is history likely to be a concern? Not really. What about a one-day seminar or a one-week seminar? The more that training is spread across time, the more likely history could be a factor in the learning that takes place.

Maturation Maturation refers to changes that occur because of the passage of time (e.g., growing older, hungrier, fatigued, bored). If Sue's one-week training program was so intense that she became tired, when it came time to take the posttraining test, her performance would not reflect how much she had learned. Making sure that the testing is done when trainees are fresh reduces this threat. Other maturation threats can usually be handled in a similar manner by being sure that training and testing are not so intense as to create physical or mental fatigue.

Testing Testing also has an influence on learning. Suppose the pretest and posttest of the knowledge, skills, and attitudes (KSAs) are the same test. The questions on the pretest could sensitize trainees to pay particular attention to certain issues. Furthermore, the questions might generate interest, and the trainees might later discuss many of them and work out the answers before or during training. Thus, learning demonstrated in the posttest may be a function not of the training, but of the pretest. In Sue's case, the needs analysis that served as the pretest for evaluation got her thinking about all the material contained in the test. Then, she focused on these issues in training. This situation presents less of a validity problem if pretests are given in every case and if they are comprehensive enough to cover all of the material taught. Comprehensive testing will also make it difficult for trainees to recall specific questions.

Instrumentation Instrumentation is also a concern. The problem arises if the same test is used in the pretest and posttest, as was already noted. If a different but equivalent test is used, however, the question becomes "Is it really equivalent?" Differences in instrumentation used could cause differences in the two scores. Also, if the rating requires judgments, the differences between pre- and posttest scores could be a function of different people doing the rating.

For Sue, the posttest was more difficult than the pretest, and even though she learned a great deal in the computer training, her posttest score was actually lower than the pretest, suggesting that she did not learn anything. If the test items for both tests were chosen randomly from a large population of items, it would not be much of a concern. For behavioral tests where raters make subjective decisions, this discrepancy may be more of a concern, but careful criteria development can help to deal with it.

Statistical Regression   **Statistical regression** is the tendency for those who score either very high or very low on a test to "regress to the middle" when taking the test again. This phenomenon, known as regression to the mean, occurs because no test is perfect and differences result as a function of measurement error. Those who are going to training will, by definition, score low for the KSAs to be covered in training and so will score low on their pretest. The tendency, therefore, will be for them to regress to the mean and improve their scores, irrespective of training. In the earlier example, Sue did not know much about computers. Imagine that she got all the questions on the pretest wrong. The likelihood of that happening twice is very low, so on another test she is bound to do better.

This threat to internal validity can be controlled through various evaluation designs that we will discuss later. In addition, the use of control groups and random assignment (when possible) goes a long way toward resolving statistical regression.

Initial Group Differences (Selection)   **Initial group differences** can also be a concern. For example, in some cases, to provide an effective evaluation, a comparison is made between the trainees and a similar group of employees who were not trained—known as the control group. It is important that the control group be similar in every way to the training group. Otherwise, the inherent differences between the groups might be the cause of differences after the training. Suppose that those selected for training are the up-and-coming stars of the department. After training, they may in fact perform much better than those not considered up and coming, but the problem is that they were better from the start and more motivated to improve. Therefore, if Sue is one of the highly motivated trainees, as are all her cohorts in training, they would potentially perform better even without training.

This problem does not arise if everyone is to be trained. The solution is simply to mix the two types, so both the group to be trained and the control group contain both types.

Loss of Group Members (Mortality)   In this situation, those who did poorly on the pretest are demoralized because of their low score and soon drop out of training. The control group remains intact. As a result, the trained group does better in the posttest than the control group, because the poorer-scoring members left the trained group, artificially raising the average score. The opposite could occur if, for some reason, members of the control group dropped out.

This situation becomes more of a problem when the groups are made up of volunteers. In an organizational setting, those who go to training are unlikely to drop out. Also, all department members who agree to be in the control group are a captive audience and are unlikely to refuse to take the posttest. Although some transfers and terminations do occur to affect the numbers of participants, they are usually not significant.

Diffusion of Training   When trainees interact with the control group in the workplace, they may share the knowledge or skill they are learning. For example, when Sue is back in the office, she shows a few of the other administrative assistants what she has learned. They are in the control group. When the posttest is given, they do as well as the trained group, because they were exposed to much of what went on in training. In this case, training would be seen as ineffective, when in fact it was effective. This would be especially true if certain quotas of trainees were selected from each department. When such sharing of information reduces differences between the groups in this way, determining the effectiveness of the training could be difficult.

Compensating Treatments   When the control group and training group come from different departments, administrators might be concerned that the control group is at an unfair disadvantage. Comments such as "Why do they receive the new training?" or "We are all expected to perform the same, but they get the help" would suggest that the control group feels slighted. To compensate for this inequity, the managers of the control group's department might offer special assistance or make special arrangements to help their group. For example, let's look at trainees who are learning how to install telephones more efficiently. Their productivity begins to rise, but because the supervisors of the control group feel sorry for the control group, they help the trainees to get the work done, thereby increasing the trainees' productivity. The evaluation would show no difference in productivity between the two groups after training is complete.

Compensatory Rivalry   If the training is being given to one particular intact work group, the other intact work group might see this situation as a challenge and compete for higher productivity. Although the trained group is working smarter and improving its productivity, the control group works harder still and perhaps equals the productivity of the trainees. The result is that, although the training is effective, it will not show up in the evaluation.

Demoralized Control Group   The control group could believe that it was made the control group because it was not as good as the training group. Rather than rivalry, the response could be to give up and actually reduce productivity. As a result, a difference between the two groups would be identified, but it would be a function of the drop in productivity and not the training. Even if training were effective, the test results would be exaggerated.

These threats to validity indicate the importance of tracking the process in the evaluation. Just as data are gathered about what is occurring in the training, it is also useful to gather data about what is going on with the control group.

External Validity

The evaluation must be internally valid before it can be externally valid. If evaluation indicated that training was successful and threats to internal validity were minimal, you would believe that the training was successful for that particular group. The next question is, "Will the training be effective for the rest of the employees slated to attend training?" **External validity** is the confidence that these findings will generalize to others who undergo the training. A number of factors threaten external validity.

Testing

If the training is evaluated initially by means of pre- and posttests, and if future training does not use the pretest, it can be difficult to conclude that future training would be as effective. Perhaps those in the initial training focused on particular material, because it was highlighted in the pretest. If the pretest is then not used, other trainees will not have the same cues. The solution is simple: Pretest everyone taking the training. Remember that pretest data can be gathered during the needs analysis.

Selection Suppose that a particular program designed to teach communication skills is highly effective with middle-level managers, but when a program with the same design is given to shop-floor workers, it does not work. Why? It might be differences in motivation or in entering KSAs, but remember that you cannot be sure that a training program that was successful with one group of trainees will be successful with all groups. Once it is successful with middle managers, it can be assumed that it will be successful with other, similar middle managers. However, if it is to be used to train entry-level accountants, you could not say with confidence that it would be successful (that it had external validity) until it was evaluated.

One of the authors was hired to assist in providing team skills to a large number of employees in a large manufacturing plant. The first few sessions with managers went reasonably well; the managers seemed to be involved and learned a great deal. After about a month, training began for the blue-collar workers, using the identical processes, which included a fair amount of theory. It soon became evident that trainees were bored, confused, and uninterested. In a discussion about the problem, the project leader commented, "I'm not surprised—this program was designed for executives." In retrospect, it is surprising that lower-level managers received the training so well, given that it was designed for executives.

Reaction to Evaluation In many situations, once the training is determined to be effective, the need for further evaluation is deemed unnecessary. Thus, some of the trainees who went through the program were evaluated and some were not. The very nature of evaluation causes more attention to be given to those who are evaluated. Recall the Hawthorne Studies that indicated the power of evaluation in an intervention. The Hawthorne Effect is explained by the following:[1]

- The trainees perceived the training as a novelty;
- The trainees felt themselves to be special because of being singled out for training;
- The trainees received specific feedback on how they were doing;
- The trainees knew they were being observed, so they wanted to perform to the best of their ability; and
- The enthusiasm of the instructor inspired the trainees to perform at a high level.

Whatever the mechanism, those who receive more attention might respond better as a function of that attention. As with the other threats to external validity, when the way groups are treated is changed, the training's external validity is jeopardized.

Multiple Techniques In clinical studies, a patient receives Dose A. It does not have an effect, so a month later she receives Dose B, which does not have an effect, so she receives Dose C and is cured. Did Dose C cure her? Perhaps, but it could also be that it was the combination of A, B, and C that resulted in the required effect. The use of multiple techniques could influence training when some component of the training is changed from one group to the next. For example, a group received one-on-one coaching and then video instruction. The members did poorly after receiving the coaching but excelled after receiving the video instruction, so video instruction became the method used to train future employees. It was not successful, however, because it was the combination of coaching and video instruction that resulted in the initial success.

What Does It All Mean?

It is useful to understand the preceding issues to recognize why it is difficult to suggest with certainty that training or any other intervention is the cause of any improvement. We cannot be absolutely certain about the internal or external validity when measuring things such as learning, behavior, and organizational results. Careful consideration of these issues, however, and the use of well-thought-out designs for the evaluation can improve the likelihood that training, when shown to be effective, is in fact effective (internal validity) and will be effective in the future (external validity). This information is useful for assessing training and, equally important, for assessing evaluations done by outside vendors.

Evaluation Design Issues

A number of texts provide excellent information on appropriate designs for conducting evaluations.[2] Unfortunately, many of their recommended designs are impractical in most organizational settings. Finding the time or resources to create a control group is difficult at best. Getting approval to do pretests on control groups takes away from productive time and is difficult to justify.

Scientifically valid research designs are difficult to implement, so organizations often use evaluation designs that are generally not acceptable to the scientific community.[3] However, it is still possible to have some confidence in the results with less rigorous designs. Some research designs are less than perfect, but it is possible to find ways of improving them. The two designs most often used, and most criticized by scientists, are the posttest-only and the pretest/posttest methods.[4]

Basic Designs

Posttest Only   The posttest-only method occurs when training is followed by a test of the KSAs. The posttest-only design is not appropriate in some instances. At other times, however, the method is completely acceptable.[5] The two possible goals of evaluation are

1. to determine whether change took place and
2. to determine whether a level of competence was reached.

If the goal of the training is the latter, a posttest-only design should suffice. If, for example, legal requirements state that everyone in the company who handles hazardous waste be trained to understand what to do in an emergency, then presumably this training needs only to provide a test at the end to confirm that all trainees reached the required level of knowledge. As more companies are required to be ISO 9000 (or equivalent) certified, it will be increasingly important to prove that employees possess the required skills. As a result, certification will become the goal of employee training, and in that case the posttest-only will suffice.

We frequently mention the value in doing a needs analysis. Conducting a needs analysis provides pretest data, making the posttest-only design moot. Giving the posttest automatically applies a pretest/posttest design. Furthermore, in the absence of a TNA, archival data may serve as the pretest. Performance appraisals, measures of quality, and the like might allow for some pre/post comparison. Although such historical data may not be ideal, it could provide some information as to the effectiveness of training. Alternatively, it is possible to identify an equivalent group and provide its members with the same posttest, thereby turning the design into a posttest only with control group. Suddenly, a much more meaningful design is created.

The posttest-only design as it stands is problematic for assessing change. A number of other competing causes could be responsible for the change, as noted in Table 9-8. Nevertheless, we would agree with other professionals that any evaluation is better than none.[6] Gathering any pretraining information that might suggest that the level of KSAs before training was lower than in the posttest would help to bolster the conclusion that training was effective.

Pretest/Posttest   The pretest/posttest design is the other method organizations frequently use. Here, a pretest is given (T_1), training is provided ($\times$), and then a posttest is given (T_2). This design is expressed as $T_1 \times T_2$.

This design can demonstrate that change has occurred. But even though it can be demonstrated that KSAs have changed, it is not possible to say that training is responsible for those changes. There are several threats to validity (see Table 9-8). For example, you might have been training a group of machine operators to operate new drill-press machines. Pretesting the trainees revealed that none knew how to operate the machine. After a three-day training session, a posttest showed that, on average, the trainees could operate the machine correctly 85 percent of the time. A big success? Not if the supervisor of the work group says that the ones without training can operate the machines correctly 95 percent of the time by just reading the manuals and practicing on their own. Several different reasons might explain why those who did not go to training are performing better on the job. Perhaps they already knew how to operate the machine. Perhaps a manufacturer's representative came and provided on-the-floor training to them. Or, it could be that your training somehow slowed down the learning process. Therefore, it would be useful to have a control group.

In many instances, using a control group is simply not an option. Does that mean that the trainer should not bother to do anything? Absolutely not! In fact, it is better to do something than nothing. We tend to focus on the negative aspects of the preexperimental designs rather than to examine ways of using them most effectively when other options do not exist.[7] The pre- post-no-control-group at least establishes that changes did take place. History can be examined through some detective work. Recall that Sue had learned a great deal about operating in a Windows environment according to the pretest/posttest. Did she do

Table 9-8 Sources of Invalidity

Techniques	Internal								External			
	History	Maturation	Testing	Instrumentation	Regression	Selection	Mortality	Interaction of Selection and Maturation	Testing	Selection	Relative Reaction to Evaluation	Multiple Techniques
Posttest Only (no control group)	–	–		–		–	–	–	–	–		
Pretest/Posttest (no control group)	–	–	–	–	?	+	+	–	–	–	?	
Posttest Only (with control group)	+	+	+	+	+	+	+	+	+	?	?	
Pretest/Posttest (with control group)	+	+	+	+	+	+	+	+	–	?	?	
Time Series Design	–	+	+	?	+	+	+	+	–	?	?	

Note: In the tables, a minus indicates a definite weakness, a plus indicates the factor is controlled, a question mark indicates a possible source of concern, and a blank indicates that the factor is not relevant.

It is with extreme reluctance that these summary tables are presented, because they are apt to be "too helpful" and to be depended upon in place of the more complex and qualified presentation in the text. No + or – indicator should be respected unless the reader comprehends why it is placed there. In particular, it is against the spirit of this presentation to create uncomprehended fears of, or confidence in, specific designs. These tables are based on random assignment, and we suggest that representative sampling is more appropriate when the small numbers are used as in organizational training. So for each of these designs, assume the representative sampling results in true equivalence of the group.

Source: Adapted from Campbell, D. T., and J. C. Stanley. *Experimental and Quasi-Experimental Designs for Research* (1963). Chicago: Rand McNally.

extra reading at home? Did she practice on her own irrespective of training expectations? Did she get some help from someone at the office or elsewhere? Simply asking her might indicate that none of those factors occurred, suggesting that it was in fact the training. This process may be particularly relevant for the small business, where size makes it easier to identify potential threats.

Internal Referencing Strategy Another way of dealing with the lack of a control group is to use the **internal referencing strategy (IRS)**.[8] With this method, include both relevant and nonrelevant test questions in the pre- and posttest. Here's how it works.

Both pretests and posttests contain questions that deal with the training content and questions that deal with related content not in the training. In the pretest, trainees will do poorly on both sets of questions. In the posttest, if training is effective, improvement should only be shown for the trained items. The nonrelevant items serve as a control. In their research on the IRS, Haccoun and Hamtiaux noted that the results obtained from the IRS design were identical to those obtained when a control group was used.[9] This method deals with many of the concerns that arise when a control group is used, and with several other concerns. Many of the threats to internal validity do not exist with the IRS because, with no control group to react in an inappropriate manner, issues such as diffusion of training, compensatory treatment, and compensatory rivalry are not a concern. The only threats are history, maturation, testing, statistical regression, and instrumentation.

As previously noted, history can be investigated through examination of the time frame in which training has occurred. Any events that potentially affected the trainees could be assessed as to their effect. Also, given that the relevant and nonrelevant items are similar in nature in the IRS, any historical event should affect both types of items in a similar manner. Maturation issues can be dealt with by ensuring that the training is designed to keep trainees interested and motivated, and to prevent them from becoming tired or fatigued. The reactive effect of testing can be dealt with if parallel tests are used. Parallel tests cover the same content but do not use identical questions. This technique does lead to another potential problem (instrumentation) that can be addressed. If all trainees receive a comprehensive pretest, then instrumentation is not an issue.

Instrumentation is a concern if two different tests are used. If a large pool of items is developed from which test items can be chosen at random, the result should be equivalent tests. Once again, it is important to note that in any evaluation, we can never be 100 percent sure that training has caused the improvement. We are not suggesting that this design take the place of more stringent designs when they are practical. It is appropriate, however, when the alternative is posttest-only or nothing. Again, some control is better than none at all.

One final note: The IRS design can be used to determine improvement in KSAs, but research indicates that it tends to show that training is not effective when, in fact, it is.[10] In other words, the training must provide a substantial improvement from pretest to posttest for it to be detected by this design.

More Complex Designs Two factors need to be considered when developing a sound evaluation design:

1. Control groups
2. Random assignment

The **control group** is a group of similar employees who do not receive the training. The control group is used to determine whether changes that take place in trainees also take place for those who do not receive training. If change occurs only in the trainees, it is probably a result of training. If it occurs in both trained and untrained groups, it is probably a result of some other factor.

Random assignment is the placement of employees in either the control group or the training group by chance, to ensure that the groups are equivalent. Random assignment is more applicable to experimental laboratories than to applied settings (such as in training) for two reasons. First, given the small number of employees placed in one group or the other, the theory of randomness is not likely to hold true. When we split a group of 60 employees into two groups of 30, it is quite likely that real differences will be present within the two groups. Random assignment works well when multiple groups of 30 are used, or when the total number of subjects is quite large (e.g., 500).

Second, it is unlikely that the organization can afford the luxury of randomly assigning employees to each group. The work still needs to be done, and managers would want some control over who will be in training at a specific time. For this reason, finding the best match of employees is important so that the control group contains a sample representative of employees who are in the training group. **Representative sampling** is matching employees in the control group and training group on factors such as age, tenure, and education to make the groups as equivalent as possible. The following discussion covers several designs that use control groups. We believe that assigning trainees through representative sampling is a more effective way of obtaining equivalent groups.

Posttest Only with Control Group The following represents posttesting only with a control group:

Trainee Group (representative sampling) $\times$ T_2

Control Group (representative sampling) T_2

This design and the following one are equivalent in terms of internal validity (see Table 9-8).

If for some reason a pretest was not conducted or if the trainer did not provide a pretest to a control group at the beginning of training, the trainees can be compared with a control group using a posttest-only design. Differences in test scores noted between the groups, if trainees do better, provide evidence of the success of the training. The tendency is to downplay the effectiveness of this design, because no pretest assessed the equivalence of the groups before training. But if representative sampling has resulted in the groups being equivalent, there is no need to have a pretest. Of course, there is greater confidence regarding the equivalence of the groups if there was a pretest.

Pretest/Posttest Only with Control Group   The expression for pretest/posttest with a control group is as follows:

Trainee Group (representative sampling) $T_1 \times T_2$

Control Group (representative sampling) $T_1 \quad T_2$

This design is one of the more favorable for eliminating threats to internal validity (see Table 9-8). Recall that we do not use random assignment in dividing the groups. So, how equivalent are they? A pretest can determine their level of equivalence. Equivalent pretests in both groups provide you with one more piece of evidence that the groups are equal, and posttest differences (if the trained group obtains higher scores) will suggest that training was successful.

Time Series Design   The time series design is represented by:

Trainee Group $T_1 \, T_2 \, T_3 \, T_4 \times T_5 \, T_6 \, T_7 \, T_8$

This design uses a series of measurements before and after training. In this way, the likelihood of internal validity threats such as testing or regression to the mean is minimized. Also, when everyone attends training at the same time (a one-shot training program), this design can be used whether the number is large or small. In such a case it could still be argued that with no control group, there are alternative reasons for any change. But in an applied setting, the goal is to be as sure as possible about the results, given organizational constraints. If enough measures are taken pre- and posttraining to deal with fluctuations in performance, changes after training are certainly suggestive of learning. Remember that in an applied setting, there will never be absolute certainty regarding the impact of training, but taking care to use the best possible design (considering constraints) is still better than doing nothing at all.

To make this design more powerful, consider adding a control group, expressed by:

Trainee Group $T_1 \, T_2 \, T_3 \, T_4 \times T_5 \, T_6 \, T_7 \, T_8$

Control Group $T_1 \, T_2 \, T_3 \, T_4 \quad T_5 \, T_6 \, T_7 \, T_8$

Multiple Baseline Design   Multiple baseline design is represented by:

Trainee Group A	$T_1 \, T_2 \, T_3 \times T_4 \, T_5 \, T_6 \, T_7 \, T_8 \, T_9 \, T_{10}$
Trainee Group B	$T_1 \, T_2 \, T_3 \, T_4 \, T_5 \times T_6 \, T_7 \, T_8 \, T_9 \, T_{10}$
Trainee Group C	$T_1 \, T_2 \, T_3 \, T_4 \, T_5 \, T_6 \, T_7 \times T_8 \, T_9 \, T_{10}$
Trainee Group D	$T_1 \, T_2 \, T_3 \, T_4 \, T_5 \, T_6 \, T_7 \, T_8 \, T_9 \times T_{10}$

In this design, multiple measures are taken much as in time series, but each group receives the training at a different time. Each untrained group serves as a control for the trained groups. This approach deals with many of the concerns when no control group is used. Here the ability to say that changes measured by the test are a result of the training is strong. If each group improves after training, it is difficult to argue that something else caused the change.

Choosing the Design to Use

Determining the true effect of training requires an investigation into the validity of evaluation results. Several methods are available, and the more complex the design, the more valid the results. There are other considerations when you are deciding on an evaluation design. Innovation can provide good substitutes when the best is not possible. Consider the multiple baseline design. It is a powerful design and certainly is a possibility if several employees need to receive the training over time.

However, what if multiple measures are not possible? The following design would address many of the same concerns, and although it is not as elaborate, it certainly deals with many of the concerns regarding outside influences causing the change. If pretest scores are all comparable and posttest scores indicate an improvement, these results are a strong argument for showing that training was responsible.

Trainee Group A	$T_1 \quad \times \quad T_2$		
Trainee Group B		$T_1 \quad \times \quad T_2$	
Trainee Group C			$T_1 \quad \times \quad T_2$
Trainee Group D			$\quad T_1 \quad \times \quad T_2$

We have already mentioned that most organizations do not evaluate all training at all levels. Furthermore, even when evaluating training, many organizations do not use pretest/posttest or control groups in a manner that would eliminate concerns about the validity of the results.

Dr. Dixon of George Washington University indicated that, of the companies she investigated in her article "New Routes to Evaluation," only one used designs that would deal with many of the validity issues. Other companies, including IBM and Johnson Controls, follow such procedures only when asked by particular departments or higher-level management, or when they can defray some of the high cost of developing reliable and valid tests by marketing the final product to other organizations.[11] The demand for certification in some skills (primarily because of ISO and others' requirements) created a need for these types of tests.

When you are evaluating training, if using control groups or pretesting is not possible, remember that other investigative methods can be used for assessing the likelihood that factors other than training account for any change in KSAs.

What About Small Business?

Single Case Designs We noted in Chapter 9 that, for small business, it is sometimes easier to infer cause and effect between training and outcomes. We also noted, however, that it is also useful at times to consider evaluation to ensure that training is having its effect on employee behavior. But traditional evaluation designs are very difficult to apply to a small business. So, is there an alternative? Consider the **single-case design.** It is often used to evaluate the training provided to professional counselors. But

managers can also use this method when the number of employees is small.[12]

The single-case design uses data from one individual and makes inferences based on that information. To increase confidence in the results, use the multiple baseline approach. Suppose that two supervisors need to be trained in active listening skills. Because the business is small, both cannot attend training at the same time. Using a predetermined checklist developed for evaluating the training, count the number of active listening phrases that each of them uses while talking to you. Take several measures over three or four weeks, then send one supervisor to training. Continue monitoring the active listening after the person returns. Did the number of active listening phrases increase for the trained supervisor and not the other supervisor? Now give the second supervisor training, and afterward, continue monitoring the conversations. If both employees improved after training, it can be inferred that the training was effective. Although this approach is suggested for the small business, it is also useful in any organization when only a few employees need to be trained.

Chapter 10

Key Areas of Organizational Training

Learning Objectives

After reading this chapter, you should be able to:

➤ Describe what organizations are doing in the following key areas of training and why this training is important:

- ◆ Orientation training
- ◆ Diversity training
- ◆ Sexual harassment training
- ◆ Team training
- ◆ Cross-cultural training

➤ Explain equity issues as they relate to training, specifically related to females in nontraditional jobs, the glass ceiling, and people with disabilities

➤ Describe issues that organizations need to consider related to basic skills training and safety training

---

CASE: The Competent Employee

Schrader-Bridgeport International (SBI) is a large manufacturing company with plants in North and South America, Europe, and Asia. It is a world leader in the design and manufacture of innovative engineered solutions to meet system, submodule, and component needs for industrial and automotive applications. Its sophistication in the engineering field, however, does not translate to sophistication in its management system. But perhaps you should judge for yourself.

A few years ago, nine males and one female—Ms. Conner—were hired at the same time for the position of "craftsmen." They were all graduates

(continued)

of a community college with a degree related to the job for which they had applied. Their job was to operate multispindle machines.

On joining SBI, the men were sent to Department 767, where special one-on-one, hands-on training took place for six months. This training taught them how to operate the machinery used at SBI, including how to load metal bars properly into the machines. Then they were transferred to Department 710, where they began operating the machines. Ms. Conner was placed directly into Department 710, and she did not receive the training.

On numerous occasions, George Schaefer, SBI's general supervisor in Department 710, stated explicitly that, in his view, women did not belong in the workplace at all. However, he admitted that Ms. Conner had "excellent mechanical ability," and he estimated that of the 10 persons hired from the community college training program, Ms. Conner was "probably number three from the top."

When one of the men's machines malfunctioned, supervisor Bruce Boyd would explain and demonstrate to the operator how to fix the machine and would permit the employee to assist and to learn how to get it going again. If Ms. Conner's machine malfunctioned, however, Boyd simply fixed it without showing or explaining what he did. When she asked to participate so she could learn, he "rolled his eyes" at her and refused. Ms. Conner then specifically asked General Supervisor Schaefer to see that she was provided with comparable training. He dismissed her request by responding that she had a high rate of absenteeism.

The machines that all 10 employees operated were idiosyncratic—each required its own particular techniques for it to perform well. New machine operators were typically assigned to a specific machine for a long period so they could learn how to keep that particular machine operating effectively. An inexperienced machine operator would advance to learning machine setup and unplanned tool setting only after gaining basic operating skills on a single machine. As a result, the machine operator's efficiency and productivity were greater.

Mr. Schaefer, however, repeatedly moved Ms. Conner from one machine to another. These machine changes caused her to spend a much greater proportion of her time on setup and unplanned tool setting than on production. She was always learning the idiosyncrasies of a new machine. From October through April, Ms. Conner spent 139.3 hours on machine setup and unplanned tool setting. The male operator who spent the most time on this task during that time period spent 82.5 hours. The male operator with the least amount of setup and unplanned-tool-setting time in the same period spent 12.1 hours.

Ms. Conner put up with a number of other things, such as being ridiculed, being forced to "mop up" the place, not receiving the same pay raise as the men, and so forth. She finally went to the personnel manager to complain. SBI had an antiharassment policy. The policy required investigation of employee complaints "thoroughly and promptly to the fullest extent practicable." However, the investigation conducted by the personnel manager consisted of asking supervisors Schaefer and Boyd about Ms. Conner. It is not surprising that the findings indicated no problem.[1]

OVERVIEW

In this chapter, we will explore four key areas of training, indicate why they are important, and discuss what organizations are doing. These areas are **orientation training, diversity training, sexual harassment** training, and team training. We will then describe some other types of training programs and issues that organizations need to be aware of.

Let's start by thinking back to the case above. It must be something from the 1950s or 1960s right? Well, no; it occurred in 1993. So was the company that "out of touch"? Perhaps, even though it did have an antiharassment policy. So what went wrong?

There might be several reasons why this company could not align the behavior of its employees with its policy. From an orientation perspective, none of the employees went through a formal orientation to the workplace when hired. Orientations provide new employees with information about rules, policies, procedures, and the workplace.[2] A well-designed orientation program for supervisors should help them understand the importance of treating everyone on the basis of ability and not gender. An orientation that included the procedures for airing a concern could have helped employees such as Ms. Conner deal with an issue before something serious occurred.

Let's examine this issue from a diversity training focus. Diversity training for managers would expose managers to the differences people from various cultures bring to the organization and why these differences should be valued. Gender differences would be a part of this discussion. Such a training topic would emphasize the value the organization puts on these differences. Messages of this kind from upper management, if sincere, do affect how gender and ethnic differences are treated in an organization.

This problem can also be viewed from a sexual harassment training perspective. Some of the things Ms. Conner endured were clearly sexual harassment. Given that an antiharassment policy was in place, harassment training might have been conducted. If so, the training was not taken seriously. Furthermore, the policy on investigating harassment was clearly flawed. The HR manager talked only to the two supervisors, which clearly was not of much value considering that they both seemed to be part of the problem.

From a team training perspective, you would probably uncover the negative attitude toward females during the needs analysis phase. The section on team training shows that attitudes among and toward team members are a vital factor in developing effective teams. Training can be designed to provide a forum for dealing with the issue.

In any event, no effective training took place at SBI in any of these areas (orientation, diversity, sexual harassment, or team training) so the harassment continued. We return to the case at the end of the chapter, but for now let's examine each of these key training areas in terms of why they are important, and what organizations are currently doing. Then we will provide some guidance in terms developing training in these four key training areas following our training model's five phases.

In addition to these four areas, another area that is of increasing importance is cross-cultural training. So, given its importance we will also discuss it in the same detail as the previously mentioned training areas.

In addition, for orientation training, we will take you through a hypothetical example to demonstrate how such a training program might be developed using our training model. It will, just like Fabrics, Inc., of earlier chapters, follow each of the phases, providing another example of how to develop training from start to finish.

ORIENTATION TRAINING (ONBOARDING)

An effective orientation is a way to assimilate new hires into the company environment. When done properly, it provides the new employee with information on what is required of them, as well as some history of the firm, the company's culture, and its strategic vision.[3] It begins the socialization process for new employees by helping them learn about the way the organization works and what it values. Orientations can be short (half or one day) or much longer (a week with periodic meetings for months thereafter). Some authors use the term *onboarding* to define the longer more in-depth orientations, others use the term specifically for managers, and still others simply use the terms *orientation* and *onboarding* interchangeably. Here, we will use the term *orientation* to represent both short and longer-term initial socialization processes of all employees.

Why spend time and money on an orientation? New employees will eventually learn about all the aspects of their job whether an orientation program exists or not.

Why It Is Important

From a learning theory perspective, we know that new learning is based on previous learning. New information is interpreted and understood in the context of what is already known. The best companies recognize that providing new employees with the information they need to understand the company and its expectations is a good investment. On the first day, the new employee is anxious to impress, nervous about what this new job is all about, and excited about what is in store. It is the new employee's first entry to the organization, so what happens on that first day and the next few days is critical. The first impression of the organization will be lasting, and it is important to orchestrate it in a manner that creates all the images and impressions that will enhance the effectiveness of the company and the employee.

Research shows that employees who attend orientation programs are more willing to adopt the organization's goals and values than those who do not.[4] Orientations also provide guidance to the new employee regarding management's expectations and inform the employee about job expectations. Effective orientations result in several positive outcomes for the organization, as depicted in Table 10-1. Higher commitment to the organization, increased job satisfaction, more job involvement, clear role understanding, and increased tenure are all outcomes of an effective orientation.[5]

What Organizations Are Doing

The orientation is one of the most common types of training programs.[6] It is also one of the most neglected.[7] It is often done haphazardly, with little thought to what should be included. This is true even at the executive level. Consider the survey that indicated that only 39 percent of senior executives were satisfied with their organization's efforts to orient them into the organization.[8] In some organizations, the orientation lasts a few

Table 10-1
Positive Outcomes Possible from an Effective Orientation

Reduced anxiety	A better understanding of expectations and formalized meeting of co-workers results in the new employee not feeling the higher level of anxiety associated with the first few days on the job.
Reduced role ambiguity	A structured opportunity to determine what is required on the job and a comfortable feeling about approaching the supervisor and co-workers to ask questions about the job provide an opportunity to clear up any misunderstandings about job requirements.
Reduced turnover	Substantial evidence indicates that effective orientations reduce turnover.
Improved job performance	A better understanding of job requirements and the willingness to ask for assistance result in fewer errors and the ability to get up to top production levels sooner; all of which translates to improved performance.
Higher level of commitment	Evidence suggests that those who receive effective orientations are more committed, more involved in their job, and more likely to take on the values of the organization.
More effective/efficient organization	The organization with more employees achieving optimal performance quicker, operating at a higher level of performance, showing a clearer understanding of their responsibilities, staying with the organization for a longer time, and being more committed to the values and objectives of the organization is definitely going to be more efficient, effective, and valuable to its shareholders.

hours; in others, it can be a few days. Large organizations often develop orientation packages but forget about revising them until they are far out of date. Small organizations frequently develop them with little thought, if they do them at all.[9] The positive outcomes identified by research suggest that the design and development of effective orientations is a good investment for most organizations.

Orientations do not require a long, drawn-out process to provide positive outcomes. Training in Action 10-1 describes an example of what Texas Instruments does in one day. A well-designed and implemented one-day orientation will be more effective than a poorly designed or outdated program that spans a year. Ohio Savings Bank is a second example of how an effective orientation can have positive effects on the bottom line. For the year before implementation of their new orientation program, turnover was 31 percent within the first 90 days of being hired. In the five months following the new orientation training, the turnover rate plummeted to only 4 percent within the first 90 days and remained well below the industry standard.[10]

TRAINING IN ACTION 10-1
Even a One-Day Orientation Can Have an Impact

Texas Instruments' HR department put on a two-hour orientation for its new assemblers. The new employees were told about the company, their job, and the performance requirements. They were then introduced to their supervisor, and after he gave the employees a short introduction to their job, they were on their own.

Management at Texas Instruments noted a high rate of tardiness and turnover in the assembly department. Management conducted a TNA and discovered that new hires experienced a high level of anxiety when they started the job, and this anxiety increased for the following reasons:

- New employees worried that they would not be able to meet production requirements.
- Old employees would tell new employees that they would never be able to reach performance requirements. This bit of hazing was considered a rite of passage.
- New employees were afraid to ask supervisors questions for fear of being seen as stupid.

Anxiety resulted in three important outcomes: low job satisfaction, tardiness, and high turnover.

Texas Instruments decided to see what could be done to affect these outcomes. They designed an additional six hours of orientation that consisted of four specific points. New hires were told the following:

1. They were highly likely to succeed, based on statistics that indicated that 99 percent of new employees met expectations. The new hires also viewed the learning curves for production, so they would understand that productivity would not be at the necessary level at first. Throughout the six hours, the new hires were constantly told that they all would succeed.
2. They needed to disregard the hazing (being told that they would never make it). They were told to take it in good humor but not to believe it.
3. They should take the initiative in talking with their supervisors, because the supervisors are busy and would probably not come to see how each of them is doing. Supervisors are open to questions, new workers are expected to ask questions, and no question is considered stupid.
4. They were told a bit about their supervisor (hobbies, personality, likes, and dislikes) to give the new employees a view of the supervisor as an approachable person.

The HR department wanted to be reasonably sure that any changes in turnover or tardiness could be attributed to the orientation. So, the next batch of new hires was separated into two groups: a control group (that received the typical two-hour orientation) and the experimental group (that received the two-hour along with the extra six hours of orientation).

The result was better than expected. The experimental group showed 50 percent less tardiness and absenteeism, 80 percent less waste, and a 50 percent reduction in overall training time during the first year.

Source: Ivancevich, J. *Human Resource Management* (1995). New York: Richard D. Irwin.

For larger, more complex companies or higher-level jobs, it is useful to spread the orientation over a longer time period. This approach minimizes the problem of information overload. It also ensures that opportunities for behaviors that management wants to encourage are practiced and feedback is given. At Bristol Myers Squibb, the orientation of their executives is intense but spreads over one to two months. Then, for the rest of the year, follow-up meetings are held to check progress and resolve any issues that have been identified.[11] At Pepsi Bottling Group, in addition to their comprehensive orientation, a peer coach is assigned to a new executive. A peer coach can provide long-term guidance, insights, and feedback without involving the new executive's boss—clearly a lower-risk environment.[12]

So, given the importance of the orientation, how long should it be? Having read to this point in the book, your anticipated answer is, "It all depends." The orientation is like any other training effort. In this next section, we will go back to our training model and demonstrate how to use it in the development of training. As you will see, we will use each of the phases (training needs analysis [TNA], design, development, implementation, and evaluation) to develop an orientation.

Using the Training Model to Develop Orientation Training

We will go through the phases of the training model, discuss the main points to consider in developing an orientation, and then provide a hypothetical example to help you see how it is done.

The Training Needs Analysis

You might think that a TNA is really not necessary for an orientation; after all, these are new employees, and there are obvious things you need to convey to them. This is exactly what Mecklenburg County thought.[13] They provided new employees with a half-day orientation related to showing new employees how to operate some of the organizational systems (phone, e-mail), how to complete important forms, what procedures to follow in an accident, and so forth. Reaction questionnaires at the end of the orientation indicated that the orientation was too long and boring. But the HRD department thought that such a response was to be expected. There were, after all, several mundane things that were necessary to learn even though they might be boring. So it was assumed that the orientation participants simply did not understand the importance of these things.

At one point, when the county was trying to change its image toward customers, someone in HR suggested they also treat new hires as customers. To do this, they would conduct a TNA and see what new hires wanted in the way of an orientation. The TNA included asking company executives, employees who had been through the present orientation, and new hires what they believed should be in an orientation. The resulting data indicated that the orientation would have to be even longer than a half-day to provide all the information identified as necessary. After much analysis, they put together a one-day orientation. Reaction questionnaires completed after the redesigned orientation indicated that 94 percent of the respondents thought the length was just right, and it was interesting. Why the change? One reason was that the TNA made it more relevant to their needs. So orientations, like any training, will be more relevant and therefore more interesting and motivating for participants when their needs are met.

Organizational, Operational, and Person Analysis   Recall from the training model that the TNA has three inputs: organizational analysis, operational analysis, and person analysis. Previously, we have discussed these analyses separately. Here they are combined, because that is how it happens in practice.

When a key performance indicator, such as productivity, tardiness, turnover, or employee satisfaction, is below expectations, a TNA is conducted to determine the causes.

The organizational analysis will determine any roadblocks in the system that prevents appropriate behaviors that affect these important outcomes. The operational and person analyses will determine any knowledge, skills, and attitude (KSA) deficiencies. As we have said before, issues such as productivity, turnover, and so forth, are likely to be caused by more than one thing. So it is unlikely that an orientation alone would solve the problem, especially since it deals only with new employees. You will need to determine the cause of the deficiency to know what, if any, training will be useful.

Imagine, for example, that you determined that production employees generally did not believe that quality was very important. This "attitude toward quality" would then become one area to include in an orientation program.* But remember, there may also be features in the system causing the discrepancy. Thus, adding a component to the orientation program that addresses the KSAs will not be enough. The organizational analysis will have identified the other barriers facilitating this negative attitude. You need to remove forces creating this attitude and add forces to change the attitude to a more positive one.

From your activities in the above paragraph, you know what barriers are being created by the system and the general KSA deficiencies. Now you need to identify the specific training needs (KSAs). You also need to determine what constraints will be placed on training. Gathering this information from company materials and upper management interviews is important to that end; therefore, you will need to return to the organizational analysis level for this information.

At the operational level, the supervisor can indicate the type of job-specific and nonspecific KSAs new employees should have. Keeping in mind that this is an orientation, and not technical job training, there are quite likely some basic points that the orientation should cover, such as early production expectations, policies and procedures that the department has in place, rules regarding absences, important dates and deadlines, how to use the phone and copy systems, and so forth. Supervisor interviews also allow you to determine what issues and requirements of the job might interfere with the goals identified by upper management. At the person analysis level, you will want to ask recent hires what company knowledge and operational procedures would have been most helpful when they started their jobs. Finally, asking those about to be hired what information they would like to know also provides important information. Do not assume that new hires know nothing about the firm. They might have conducted a search for information before being interviewed or even before applying for the job. Some new employees might be comfortable in a team environment; others arrive disillusioned by the experience. Remember, the key to a successful orientation is to make it interesting and relevant. Knowing where new hires stand on various issues (team approach) and what knowledge they have about the organization and their new jobs will help make the orientation relevant and interesting.

Some level of orientation training is generally indicated because you want the socialization process to begin as soon as possible. The length and intensity of the orientation will be, to a certain extent, based on the importance of the job, the size of the gap between the new hires' current KSAs and the organization's expected KSAs, competitive strategy, and many other factors. Within the same company, the amount and type of orientation training will differ across employee levels and groups. If your TNA shows that new hires have the general technical KSAs, but not the company-specific information they need to be effective and/or satisfied employees, this is clearly orientation material. If the new hires don't have the technical skills, then you are more likely looking at a selection or a technical training solution.

---

*Of course, you would also need to deal with the current employees through training and other interventions, depending on what the TNA revealed.

You are the training manager for a midsize company of 800 employees. The company projected a loss of market share for the second consecutive year. The VP of HR tells you that turnover among newly hired managers is much higher than the industry standard, and it has increased significantly over the last few years. He suggests that an orientation program may be needed and wants you to investigate. Obviously, your first task is to conduct a TNA. Assume the following results from your TNA:

- The competitive strategy of your company is to maintain dominant market share through producing high-quality products, in large volume, and within stringent cost parameters.
- The core values of the organization can be summed up in the phrase "quality products through teamwork."
- The entry- and midlevel managers are relied upon to develop effective production teams to continuously improve "end product quality" while meeting cost and volume goals.
- The low morale of new management hires in the manufacturing area leads to high rates of turnover and poor attendance, and this results in a demoralizing effect on the production teams.
- Warranty claims increased slightly each month over the last two years.
- Many of those who stay with the company and rise to midlevel manufacturing managers show little interest in working with new hires (indicating not enough time, little incentive, and a survival-of-the-fittest mentality).
- Poor performance in new hires stems primarily from a failure to align the activities of their work unit to the strategic direction of the company (they sacrifice quality for quantity).
- From the midlevel managers, you learn that managers are rewarded for quantity, not quality, and they feel a lot of pressure for productivity to remain high (this emphasis is confirmed by production team members).
- Exit interviews with managers who left the company after a relatively short tenure indicate that they knew little about the company

when they started, relied on advice from the production team, and experienced infrequent consultation with their boss (midlevel manager). A frequent response about company values was "everyone talks about quality, but the real pressure is on getting product out the door and keeping costs low." Policies and procedures were unclear, making it difficult to find out who is responsible for what.

Training Needs

In discussing the results with the VP of HR, other members of top management, and high-performing midlevel manufacturing managers, you determine that most new hires lack the following KSAs when they start the new job:

- *Attitude:* Strong belief in the mission and core values
- *Knowledge:* Clear understanding of the market strategy and goals of the company
- *Knowledge:* A picture of how the company operates and how their job contributes to achievement of the strategy and goals
- *Knowledge:* Clear understanding of performance expectations over the course of the first year
- *Knowledge:* Important company policies and procedures and who is responsible for key operations

Nontraining Needs

You also identified some nontraining needs that must be addressed before training can be truly effective. One of these issues was the reward system that did not support the commitment to quality. If quality is in fact important, you might suggest the following changes to the system so that it supports the quality core value:

- Provide managers with appraisals that give appropriate weighting to quality, quantity, and cost performance.
- Reward managers and workers only for reaching quality, quantity, and cost targets.
- Require operating units to produce and publicly display quality charts.

(continued)

Unless the discrepancy between what we want managers to do and what the reward system encourages them to do is resolved, the orientation, no matter how well designed and implemented, will make little difference. Once any nontraining needs are identified and addressed properly, you can start the design phase of your training.

Design

The training model identifies the design inputs as the training needs from the TNA, the organizational constraints, and the training methods based on learning theory. For the hypothetical example, we have identified the training needs, which include those mentioned above. But before we begin determining what the training methods to use and the order of training, we need to consider the constraints.

Organizational Constraints   Constraints are placed on training by the organization, the environment, and the trainee population. They include factors such as how much time will be available to deliver the training, what mode of delivery is best suited to the trainees, the level of technology in the organization, and the facilities available. The constraints will have been at least partially identified in the TNA. However, additional information will inevitably be required. Again, you will have to collect this information at the organizational, operational, and personal levels.

In our hypothetical situation, top management has deemed the orientation to be important. You are authorized to develop an effective management orientation that is cost-effective. There are specific dates that must be avoided for this training based on production schedules. However, you can work with the HR manager to ensure that no new management hires are brought in during these periods. This gives you more freedom in terms of the timing, length, and quality of the orientation (remembering that you still have a return on investment to think about). Based on your TNA and the above information, you determine that the orientation should take one full day and be periodically enhanced by meetings with the midlevel manager of the unit throughout the first six months.

Unfortunately for you, there is still the problem of when to offer the training. Your company has 800 employees, and 100 of them are management level. You are experiencing significant turnover of 15 percent (one of the reasons the orientation program is being developed). That means you have 15 new managers a year being hired. However, they don't all come in at the same time, and some replacements will be internal. So you're probably only getting about one a month. On the basis of this, you can't justify the cost of getting a trainer up to speed in all of the areas and 12 days a year of the trainer's salary. You solve this problem by incorporating in-house subject matter experts (SMEs) into the training design. Each SME spends an hour or two with the new hire covering the SME's area of expertise. These people may require some train-the-trainer activities before the start of orientation to ensure that they have the KSAs to be effective trainers. This is something you can look into as you are identifying the SMEs who will participate in the orientation. Your design strategy so far provides multiple benefits, as it

- addresses your cost-effectiveness issue because there is little added additional cost, as the SMEs are salaried and will "fit" the orientation module into their schedule,

(continued)

- provides experts in each of the areas covered by training rather than relying on the trainer to become an expert, and
- introduces the new hire to key people in the organization, helping to address one of the training needs.

Your organization has an adequate training facility, but you will only be training one or two people a month, and an office or small conference room will be better suited to your needs. You have only limited technology for developing the training. You do not have the capability of producing in-house video or computer-aided instruction of very high quality.

While you are reviewing your preliminary objectives, you note that initial learning of much of the material can be accomplished through reading or viewing a video. You know that some useful materials already exist. These would merely have to be duplicated for the training. Other materials might have to be produced by an outside vendor. You will keep this in mind as you develop your training objectives, knowing that you will have to do a cost-effectiveness analysis for outsourcing any of your training materials. All of the above will influence what the orientation will look like.

Training Objectives   The process part of the design model (page 153) calls for the development of training objectives. There are four categories of training objectives: reaction, learning, transfer, and organizational outcomes. We will focus primarily on the learning objectives. While there are many objectives to an orientation program, we will focus on just a few, as examples.

Continuing with your hypothetical trainer's job, you know that the new hires must develop a strong belief in the mission and values. Some prerequisite learning must occur. The new hire must first internalize the mission and values to articulate them when asked. Second, the new hire must develop a positive attitude toward them. A learning objective for the prerequisite learning is as follows:

- On completion of the orientation, all trainees, on request and with no assistance, will be able to state the mission statement and core values, with no errors.

Because the core values include teamwork, you need a learning objective related to the trainee's attitude toward teamwork. Recall that to affect attitudes, we do not train employees in attitudes per se, but rather provide information about teams that should result in a more positive attitude. You decide on the following:

- By the end of orientation, the trainee will be able to correctly list all the reasons why

using a team approach to achieve continuous improvement of the production system is more effective than using individuals to accomplish the same task.

The third learning objective states:

- On completion of the orientation, the trainee will be able to describe, to the satisfaction of a senior manager, how achievement of the mission and application of the core values will benefit society, the company, its employees, and customers.

New management employees also need to know the company's objectives and goals, and how their job relates to their achievement. You state this learning objective as follows:

- On completion of orientation, all trainees will be able to list the major goals and objectives of the company, without aids, and describe how their job relates to their

(continued)

achievement, in such a manner that anyone above them in the chain of command would approve of the statement.

The new employees probably would not be expected to learn the many policies and procedures of the organization by heart. Rather, they should have a general idea of what those policies and procedures are and know where their written descriptions could be located. A learning objective regarding a "procedure" in this case might read:

- When asked to describe one of the company's policies or procedures, the trainee, using the company reference manual for policies and procedures, will be able to indicate the correct answer 100 percent of the time.

Transfer of training objectives would include the following:

- Three months after the orientation, the manager will be evaluated as strongly supportive of the mission and core values by the immediate supervisor and production team members.

- Three months after completion of the orientation program, all trainees will be rated by their teammates as highly supportive of team activities.
- Within three months after orientation, all manager trainees will develop goals and objectives for their units that are aligned with those of the firm, as judged by their manager.
- On the first year performance evaluation, the trainee will be rated by the immediate supervisor as "always" or "nearly always" follows approved policy and procedure.

An organizational outcome objective is as follows:

- "The average level of turnover for the first year of employment will be 20 percent less than the current average."

On the basis of these and other objectives, you are now ready to consider the methods of instruction that will most likely ensure learning and transfer of the relevant knowledge and attitudes to the job. You note as you begin this process that the learning is focused on knowledge and attitudes. No skill development is included in your objectives.

Facilitate Learning   From learning theory, we know that the lecture and lecture/discussion would be useful for conveying some of the declarative knowledge. However, this type of knowledge can also be provided ahead of time in written form, with the class time used for practice, higher-level knowledge acquisition, attitude development, and explanation. So, based on the objectives you have developed, you need to make some design decisions.

On the basis of the deficiencies identified in the TNA and the constraints placed on you, you developed objectives. From these training objectives, you determine the methods of instruction:

- The face-to-face portion of the orientation will be the new hire's first day of work.
- Most of the declarative knowledge related to mission, values, market strategy, company goals, company operations, policies, and procedures will be learned from materials provided prior to arrival at orientation.

- Self-assessments for feedback purposes and formal preassessments of the informational learning can be done prior to and at the start of orientation.
- Orientation can be individually customized on the basis of the input and preassessment data.
- The face-to-face time will focus primarily on procedural and strategic knowledge and the learning designed to affect attitudes. Some time will be devoted to addressing

(continued)

any deficiencies noted from the preassessment. Some time will used to assess learning objectives at the end of each module.

Preorientation

You identified the following items that must occur prior to the new hire's arrival at orientation:

- Notify the new hire that the first day of work will consist of an orientation, and describe the program.
- Deliver the preorientation instructions, training, and assessment materials to the new hire.
- Instruct new hires to return the formal preassessment materials and any input into objectives and agenda.
- Modify objectives and agenda based on input from new hires and preassessment data.
- Identify and reserve the space that will be used.
- Reserve or acquire any equipment needed.

Orientation

Beginning   You developed the following goals and methods for the start of the orientation:

1. Create and maintain a positive attitude toward the orientation.
2. Demonstrate the need for, and the value of, the orientation
   - Introductions and welcome
   - Review the objectives (lecture/discussion)
   - Review the day's agenda: Show what learning occurs, and when. Discuss the usefulness of getting off to the right start. Ask for any additions or questions (lecture/discussion).

During   SMEs are identified and materials developed in the following areas:

- Company mission, goals, strategy, and core values: This presentation should be done by a high-level manager (perhaps the chief executive officer [CEO]). You decide to capture it on video and have a VP at the training session to answer questions.

- Company operations and how the new hire's job contributes to mission and strategy: The high-level manager covers company operations at the executive officer level. The director of manufacturing covers operations within the manufacturing area. The supervisor of the new hire covers operations within the department and in the new hire's unit.
- New hire's performance expectations for the first year: The supervisor presents this information.
- Company policy and procedures and people responsible for key operations: Trainer and the HR employment manager share responsibility for coverage of this material.

As you complete this list, you think of additional issues that need to be addressed in the development of the orientation, making these notes to yourself. Lunch and breaks need to be scheduled into the day. It would be nice if the entire training team could join the new hire for lunch. Each unit will be considered a module and will use a semiformal lecture/discussion format. Each module will contain some structured content, with the trainer determining on the basis of the trainee's responses how much additional coverage is needed. Sufficient time must be provided at the end to allow for coverage of additional areas of interest to the trainee. Learning aids in the form of handouts will be provided in each module.

End   After the last module and a break, the trainee tours the facility. During this time, you meet with the other members of the training team to review your assessments of the trainees' learning and plan the feedback session. You note the following issues that must be a part of the feedback session:

- Identify the learning that took place, and reinforce it. This assessment requires oral or written tests examining the learning expected (from learning objectives).
- Assess trainees' performance on the tests, and identify areas where additional learning is needed. Reassure trainees that with

(continued)

so much to retain in one sitting, you want to re-emphasize these areas.

- Initiate a group discussion on how the additional learning can be accomplished. Get the new hire to commit to a plan.
- Obtain public commitment from each member of the orientation team to be available to the new hire for assistance as needed.

- Have the supervisor inform new hire of weekly meetings for first month to review knowledge of the company and the job.
- Thank the new hire for the time and energy given during the orientation, and wish the new hire well on the new job.

Ensure Transfer   In the design phase, you also need to consider transfer of the knowledge and attitudes toward the job. The weekly meetings with the supervisor address this need in the short term. You will need to make sure that the new hire documents the plan for additional learning and gives it to the supervisor. This will form the agenda for the weekly meetings. At three months and six months, you will schedule half-day update sessions. You note that these will, by necessity, have to be custom-developed a few weeks before the sessions and based on the needs of the trainees. At these time intervals, you will have more trainees who have gone through the orientation, so you can use small group meetings. You decide that you will use your company intranet caucus to determine the types of information needed by the trainees and develop a system for prioritizing the lists.

The outputs from the design are the methods of instruction we determined are best for this situation (noted above) and the evaluation objectives (to be discussed shortly).

Development

At this point, you identified what needs to be done to facilitate learning and transfer and the instructional methods for your training (inputs to the Development Phase). Now you need to produce the instructional material, manuals, and so forth, and identify the specific equipment and facilities required. In developing the material, you will need to examine each objective carefully and compare it with the material as it is being developed to maximize the likelihood that the objective will be met.

Preorientation Training Plan

Develop a checklist for those in HR responsible for selection of new hires regarding preparing new hires for orientation. This checklist for the HR person should contain the following information:

- Reminder to inform each candidate, before making an employment offer, that if they are hired, they will attend an orientation program during the first day on the job.

- Once someone is selected for the job, notify the successful candidate that the first day of work will consist of an orientation, and describe the program.
- Prepare the notice of the orientation date, with purpose, objectives, and agenda. Indicate that the company's preorientation work is required, and that materials will be accessible on the company Web site once new hires receive a sign-on ID and password. Notice is

(continued)

included in the employment package given to the new hire on acceptance of the position.

- Call the new hire on the day after acceptance of the employment offer. Welcome the new hire to the company, and extend a reminder of the orientation and preorientation program. Ask if the new hire has any questions about the process. After answering any questions, provide a sign-on ID and password. Reiterate the date by which the formal preorientation assessment must be completed.
- Send preorientation instructions, training, and assessment materials (see below) to the new hire.

You now need to develop or acquire, and reproduce electronically, the following training materials:

- Orientation objectives and agenda, with an explanation of how objectives were developed.
- A mission statement, with an explanation of how achieving the mission will benefit society, the customers, and company stakeholders, including employees.
- A core values statement, with an explanation of why these values are held and how they benefit society, the customers, and company stakeholders, including employees.
- A general statement of the company's market strategy and goals. Because this information is proprietary, you will need to ensure that the new hire signs and turns in the company confidentiality agreement before receiving this material.
- An organizational chart with description of key operations, titles, names, and pictures of key personnel.
- A policies and procedures manual.
- Two self-assessment questionnaires for each topic area.
- An answer sheet to self-assessments.
- The formal preassessment questionnaire on the company Web site.

New hires are asked to complete the self-assessment questionnaires and provide ideas for the agenda and objectives of the orientation.

These are to be returned within three days. If they not received in two days, a reminder is sent out that the questionnaires must be returned the next day. From these questionnaires the following is done:

- Preassessment questionnaires are scored and feedback is provided to the new hire before the new hire attends the orientation.

Identify SMEs who will be the training team for this new hire.

- Modify objectives and agenda on the basis of input from the new hire and preassessment data. The team should consider new hire suggestions for additional objectives and agenda modification. If adopted, objectives are added and content and materials are developed. Content for modules is also modified by results of assessment, emphasizing areas where learning does not meet objectives.

Other preparations include the following:

- Identify and reserve the space that will be used.
- Reserve or acquire any equipment needed.
- New hire must have compatible computer hardware and software to access preorientation materials. If not, you must provide the loan of a company laptop.
- No additional equipment will be required; all handouts in modules will be hard copies.

In developing the content of the materials, you make a note that the following issues will have to be addressed:

- Provide information to create positive expectations for the orientation and the preorientation materials.
- Make the materials interesting and relevant to improve retention.
- Develop practice opportunities to allow for behavioral reproduction.
- Develop immediate feedback and reinforcement into materials to encourage learning.

(continued)

Orientation Training Plan

Beginning

- Introductions (yourself and the other SMEs) and welcome.
- Review objectives of the orientation (describe how they were developed). The involvement of top management, unit managers, and other new hires will enhance the credibility of the program.
- Review the agenda for the day, indicating the time frame and who will be the instructor for each portion of the orientation.

During From learning theory, we know that the lecture and lecture/discussion would be useful for conveying some of the declarative knowledge. However, some of this information will be provided ahead of time in written form with the class time used for practice and explanation. For example, you might ask the trainee to articulate the mission statement (delivered ahead of time to the trainee as part of the orientation manual). If the trainee encounters difficulty with the material, use successive approximations to both teach and build confidence. Perhaps ask the trainee to open the training manual to the page, and read the parts that are difficult to remember. During this process, you can ask the trainee to explain what the statement means. By discussing the meaning and underpinnings of the statement, the trainee will more easily retain it in memory. Explain that each trainee will be meeting with a corporate officer who will be discussing in greater detail the mission, values, goals, and objectives. Your goal at this time is to simply prepare the trainee in a general way for that session.

You also include a discussion of the positive aspects of teamwork in the orientation to support the idea that the organization operates this way. You point out that the orientation itself is a form of teamwork, because many people must coordinate their activities to achieve the common goal of successfully orienting new employees to the organization. In fact, the entire team will be coming together for dinner with the new hire(s) to welcome them to the company and answer their questions at the end of the day. Although exercises to highlight the points related to teamwork would be ideal, with so few trainees, your options will be limited and more abstract than concrete. However, the interactions of the training team at dinner will go a long way in demonstrating how teams work in your company.

When your part of the orientation is completed, you introduce the new hire to the next SME (a peer manager) who will discuss how teams operate, the general procedures for handling routine office matters, and general office protocol. This session is followed by a meeting with the HR representative, who will review policies and procedures related to compensation and benefits. This session is followed by a discussion with the high-level manager (preferably the CEO) about the mission, values, goals, and objectives. The trainee is then taken to lunch by the unit manager, who explains first-year job performance expectations. The manager also discusses how the new hire's job performance will affect the organization's goals and objectives. Providing an opportunity for the high-level and unit managers to answer questions considered important by the new employees ensures that these issues are addressed. These minisessions with individual SMEs continue until all your training components have been covered. The last SME returns the trainee to your office for evaluations and debriefing.

End Prior to this phase, you meet with the other SMEs to get their informal assessments of the degree to which the trainee met the training objectives. You begin the final phase of the program by asking the trainee to comment on the day's activities and which seemed the most valuable and why. You reassure the trainee that, because the one day of training covers a great deal, you will work together to develop some strategies for retaining the information. However, now you need to conduct a series of assessments to see whether the orientation training achieved its objectives.

Once the assessments are concluded, you make sure to provide the trainee with feedback. You identify the areas where the trainee did well and recognize any trainee accomplishments.

(continued)

Areas where the objectives are not fully met will be discussed further, and additional practice will be provided where needed and when time allows. Reassure the trainee that carrying the great deal of information conveyed during training back to the job without losing some of it will be difficult. Remind the trainee that orientation will conclude with dinner with the trainer and the supervisor to celebrate the beginning of the new job. At dinner, you work with the supervisor and new hire to develop strategies for transfer back to the job. At the end of dinner, congratulate the employee again and reaffirm that refresher sessions will be conducted during the first year.

At this point, we conclude our hypothetical example. Our intent with this example is to illustrate how the training process might play out. Obviously, it is difficult to illustrate the actual implementation of the training, so we will end the description of this hypothetical example here.

Ensure Transfer   Recall that in the design phase, you need to consider transfer of the knowledge and attitudes toward the job. Building in some refresher component is always a good idea. You cannot expect an employee on his first day or two to remember everything. Built-in refreshers keep the focus and provide structured times when the new employee can ask questions. Consider Corning, where the orientation lasts over a year, and the focus is on periodic structured interactions with the supervisor. So be sure to build in refresher sessions. At the refresher sessions, you will have more trainees who have gone through the orientation, so you can use small groups. In developing the content of these refresher sessions, use the new hires and their supervisors to determine training needs. For example, before the refresher session, you can ask the trainees to each submit a list of what is going well and what is not going so well. You can either do the same with the supervisors, or after combining all items onto a single list, ask the supervisor to review and identify any additional items and prioritize the list. The final, prioritized lists can then be used for the development of the refresher agenda.

Implementation

All the outputs from the development are the inputs for the implementation. As mentioned earlier, it is difficult to illustrate implementation in words. Thus, we just have a few reminders here from earlier portions of the book. Be sure to have a dry run to test out your plan. In addition to a few supervisors and a manager or two, select employees to attend the dry run from among those recently hired, who have shown a positive attitude toward the organization and their work. After revisions, on the basis of the dry run, you are ready to run your first orientation pilot. The pilot actually uses real new hires, but you gather data from them to make final refinements to the program. It would be helpful if all SMEs involved in the training could attend in entirety both the dry run and the pilot. This gives them input into the modifications and a complete understanding of the orientation program.

Evaluation

Although this stage is presented after implementation, development of the measures takes place at the same time as development of training. Recall that the output from the design phase is both "Identify alternative methods of instruction" and "Evaluation objectives." So evaluation measures are developed concurrently with the development of the training. The outputs here are both process and content measures. Again, we provide some reminders about what should be included in your evaluation plan.

Process Measures   Here you focus on measures to assess how closely the orientation training that was actually given matches the training that was developed. The types of measures you can use are

- interviews with new employees to ask what took place,
- sit-ins by orientation designers, and
- logs by the trainer.

Content Measures   Content measures deal with the four aspects of evaluation: reaction, learning, behavior, and results. They are based on the training objectives, so a review of those will clarify exactly what is necessary. As you can see, spending time developing good evaluation objectives makes development of the actual evaluation material much easier, as it clarifies exactly what must be assessed and how.

A reaction questionnaire should be developed to assess how trainees feel about the orientation in terms of its content and process. You might want to use a modified reaction questionnaire at the start of the refresher session and ask about the value of the orientation and what would make it better.

As indicated in the hypothetical example, learning should be measured through some assessment at the end of the orientation training. The assessment should measure the learning objectives presented at the start of training, which will require some oral tests and some written tests.

Examination of the transfer of training objectives indicates that measures of behavior will be assessed through various methods. One will be performance appraisals conducted by the employee's supervisor (measuring support of company's mission and core values, examining goals and objectives developed for their unit, and so forth). Another will be team members evaluating the manager's support of team activities. An organizational outcome will be to assess the level of manager turnover, as indicated by the objective developed at the beginning of the process.

DIVERSITY TRAINING

The makeup of the workplace continues to change. What was once predominantly white male is now a diverse group with many races and cultures and increasing numbers of women. As of 2000, 31 percent of the U.S. population was a member of a racial or ethnic minority group, and census projections indicate that by 2030, 40 percent of the U.S. population will be members of a racial or ethnic minority group.[14] There is a high percentage of older workers in the workforce now.[15] And, of course, women are continuing to increase as a percentage of the workforce.[16]

This diversity creates tension and conflicts in the workplace. One of the reasons is that supervisors (and people in general) tend to make decisions that favor those who are similar to themselves.[17] Thus, ratings of performance, promotion recommendations, and such are often biased in favor of those who are most similar to the person making the evaluation or recommendation. When employees perceive that decisions affecting their pay or status are biased by factors such as race or gender, they become upset. A recent study found that this similarity bias is directly related to a personal characteristic called "openness to dissimilarity."[18] People who are less open to differences between themselves and others are more likely to evaluate those who are different (in terms of ethnicity, gender, age, etc.) more harshly and those who are similar more favorably.

Why It Is Important

Consider the case at the beginning of the chapter. Ms. Conner, who was identified by her boss, George Schaefer, as "one of the best new hires," was continually thwarted when she tried to get help in order to be more effective. Even though Mr. Schaefer acknowledged that Ms. Conner was one of the best, he did nothing to help her be a productive employee. In fact, his attitude was that women did not belong in the workplace. Here is a motivated and talented worker who is being prevented from being as productive as she is capable of being. Is this practice good for the organization? Clearly not, and something needs to be done to ensure that all employees are nurtured to become highly effective employees.

Lack of acceptance by co-workers and management of those "different from themselves" leads to tension and biased treatment. Those "different" workers who are treated unfairly often quit, which can be costly to the organization if the numbers are high. The fact that the turnover of women in salaried jobs is double that of men, and the rate for black people is two-and-a-half times that of white males, supports the notion that being different is too often a disadvantage for those employees.[19] The costs to the organization for this type of turnover include the following:

- Loss of a productive employee who could end up with a competitor
- Expense to recruit a replacement
- Expense to retrain the replacement
- Loss of productivity during the preceding items

Furthermore, the resulting loss of reputation in the community entails its own costs (especially in metropolitan areas):

- Minorities and women will stop applying for jobs, reducing the pool from which to hire.
- Minorities and women will stop being customers or boycott the company.
- The stock price may drop.[20]

Finally, costs are associated with having legal action taken by such employees. These costs go beyond the cost of the settlement if you are found guilty and include the following:

- The hiring of legal staff to deal with the case
- Managers' time gathering the required information for a hearing
- Managers' time preparing to testify
- Managers' time testifying

When you consider all of these costs in addition to settlement costs, providing training to prevent such problems would seem the wise move. This is especially true considering that, if the company loses, it will not only incur all the costs indicated, but will also face the cost of training that is likely to be ordered by the human rights tribunal or the courts. Not all companies provide diversity training to their employees, however. A survey of more than 1,600 companies in North America that employ 100 or more people found that 25 percent did not provide diversity training. Another 24 percent provided this training on an as-needed basis, and the other 51 percent provided diversity training on a regular basis.[21]

Diversity training focuses on understanding the differences that are found among people of different backgrounds (race, age, ethnicity, gender). Diversity in organizations is a fact of life. Diversity training can help everyone in the company understand how differences can be useful to an organization. With the changing demographics in North America, organizations need to be effective in attracting, promoting, and retaining a diverse workforce in order to be competitive.[22] Advantages to an effective diverse workforce are noted in Table 10-2. Effective organizations that recognize the issues revolving around employing a diverse workforce do something to capitalize on the advantages and at the same time deal appropriately with any negative aspects of diversity.

Table 10-2
Advantages of an
Effective Diverse
Workforce

Larger applicant pool	An effective and diverse workforce that is well maintained will contribute to a good reputation, and more individuals will want to join the organization. It will mean that more people will apply for jobs, thus giving the organization a better likelihood of selecting employees. This will translate into a more effective workforce.
Reduced costs	An effective diverse workforce will result in fewer turnovers, which will translate into less rehiring because of quits.
	Also, the tension created in organizations that do not deal with diversity will not be present, and the outcomes of such tension (lower productivity, absenteeism, fighting, refusing to cooperate on projects, etc.) will not be present.
	Those organizations with effective diverse workforces will not incur the costs associated with paying for legal representation and settling lawsuits for discrimination.
Access to more markets	The North American population is more diverse. The more your organization reflects this diversity, the more likely a diverse customer base will be cultivated. Minorities and females will be attracted to an organization that employs a diverse workforce.
	As we become an international community with more international business, those organizations whose employees understand the culture of these international markets will do better.
Creative problem solving	The more diverse the group, the more diverse the ideas that are generated. Employees with different backgrounds are more likely to see issues from different perspectives, resulting in more creative ideas (other things being equal), which can result in better products and service.

Source: Adapted from Loudin, A. "Diversity pays." *Warehousing Management* (April 2000), pp. 30–33. "Diversity: A new tool for retention." *HR Focus* (June 2000), pp. 1–14. Hunsaker, P. *Training in Management Skills* (2001). Upper Saddle River, NJ: Prentice Hall.

What Organizations Are Doing

Think about the opening case. Would providing a formal training program in diversity help prevent the way Ms. Conner was treated? Would it put a company in a better position if it faces discrimination charges? An early and serious investment by companies in diversity training might help avoid time-consuming and costly fights with the human rights commission or the courts. However, just having a program is not enough.

Many North American companies implement policy and training programs to deal with diversity issues, but these efforts often do not change anything.[23] Why? Like any intervention, training is only a part of it. General Motors (GM) certainly provides training on this subject. Yet in July of 2000, an employee walked into a GM plant wearing a mock KKK robe and hood. The company immediately held meetings to tell employees that this behavior was not acceptable.[24] Was this action sufficient? GM articulates its employee guidelines in manuals and videos and has a hotline to deal with the diverse workplace and inappropriate behavior. Still, as one black man in the plant put it, "Sometimes it feels like this plant is run by white supremacists, but it is really worse for the women. They complain and are told to shut up, this is a man's job."[25]

So why are these programs not working? One factor is that many of these training programs have no mechanisms in place to support the training after it is over.[26] Recall the importance of identifying nontraining needs in the TNA and addressing these needs in order to ensure transfer of the training. Many diversity programs do not have any of these support mechanisms. Many of these programs also lack support from top management. Consider the study of 785 organizations in the United States. In that survey, only 11 percent of the organizations had diversity training initiated by the CEO. Another 50 percent indicated that their CEO was only minimally involved in the implementation of diversity training.[27] We indicated elsewhere the importance of upper management's support in any successful intervention. This involvement is probably more important for diversity training. Without strong support from upper management, many will see the training and policy as something the company requires from a legal standpoint, but not something that is really valued.

Which organizations have successful programs? The Bank of Montreal won the prestigious Catalyst Award for its effective diversity programs, promoted vigorously by its senior management.[28] Then there is IBM; it developed a diversity program that resulted in an increase in black executives (from 62 to 115) and female minority executives (from 17 to 54) in about two years.[29] Carrier Corp. formed diversity councils in all business units. It develops diversity business cases to assist in training and has successfully increased the percentage of black people in executive positions.[30] Companies such as Marriott International, American Express, and Coca-Cola have taken the next step and begun to focus on increasing supplier diversity by seeking out minority- and female-owned businesses.[31] The successful companies share an understanding that training alone is not enough. Two key additional elements are required:[32]

1. Top management commitment/involvement
2. Diversity success tied to performance appraisals

Both these ideas are utilized in the new Texaco training initiative on diversity. In response to a court order,[33] it trained 14,930 of its U.S. workforce (about 93%).[34] The training includes input from top management on the importance of diversity to its goal of excellence. They also tied managers' ability to promote diversity and equal opportunity within their departments to an incentive bonus plan.

So what does it take to see that diversity training is effective and results in a positive climate for everyone? Examining successful interventions that focused on diversity yielded the following factors as being important to include[35]

- top management support,
- training tailored to the needs of the organization,
- linking diversity to central operating goals,
- using trainers who were management or organizational development professionals,
- enrolling all levels of employees, including top managers,
- explicitly addressing individual behavior,
- training followed up and complemented by changes in human resource practices, and
- using other organizational development processes to ensure that training impacts corporate culture.

Table 10-3 provides information about what one successful company did.[36]

Using the Training Model to Develop Diversity Training

Once again we will go through the phases of the training model discussing some of the points to consider in developing diversity training. This is not meant to be complete, as that would simply require too much time and space. But it will provide some things to consider for each of the phases in the training model.

Training Needs Analysis

With diversity training, it is advisable to train everyone, so you can demonstrate that all employees are aware of the issues and know the company expectations. In

Table 10-3

Agenda for Ensuring Diversity Remains an Important Part of the Organization

Develop a broad diversity refresher training session, and implement throughout the plant.

Cover holidays that reflect diversity and publish throughout the plant.

Create a diversity council, and maintain its image by sharing what it does throughout the plant.

Write articles about diversity in the plant newsletter.

Set up a booth on diversity at the company picnic.

Invite nonmember managers to diversity council meetings.

Ask plant managers, on a monthly basis, to share information on what is going on in the way of diversity issues within their department.

Establish a mentoring program to provide employees with a source for help.

Continue to address the guidelines supervisors need to be aware of when appraising and making training and development decisions.

Address, in a timely manner, any concerns regarding diversity, and report back to the person affected.

Monitor the effect of diversity efforts, praise successes, and investigate the failures.

Chapter 4, we indicated that you might not have to do a TNA when you plan to train everyone. But for diversity training, there are good reasons for conducting at least a partial TNA. "Expected performance" is the way you expect your employees to respond to a diverse workforce. "Actual performance" is the current way they are behaving. You likely have examples of this from complaints and concerns expressed in interviews you had with employees to determine actual performance in regard to dealing with diverse employees.

One of the key reasons for conducting a TNA related to a diversity performance gap is the identification of nontraining needs. Remember that if there are things in the system that prevent appropriate behavior or encourage inappropriate behavior, no amount of training will be effective. In terms of nontraining needs, you must identify the roadblocks to successful implementation of diversity. A complaint expressed by many managers at diversity training is that the training does not take into consideration their concerns.[37] An output from the TNA in terms of training needs would be answer to these management concerns.

Nontraining needs would also help identify the requirements necessary to align the organizational systems and policies to support the diversity goals. Consider the following example. When a U.S. telephone company decided to provide females with the opportunity to become installation and repair workers, this was met with resistance from male workers. To be sure that the diversity training was effective required more than just training. Using Lewin's force-field analysis, all the forces pushing for the status quo (e.g., resisting the diversity program) were identified. To reduce these forces, training was provided. However, it is also important to increase or create strong forces to ensure transfer of the training, because the negative attitudes in males toward women in these jobs were deep-seated and very powerful. To effect change would require more than just providing KSAs. So, the phone company provided training but also instituted a zero tolerance* policy for harassment of women. There were a few who did not heed the policy, and their employment was terminated. The message spread throughout the workforce that the company was serious about the policy, and the incidence of harassment declined dramatically. Here a stronger force (job loss) was set up to counter the force of keeping the installation and repair job exclusively male. It was an important part of the intervention. Without a clear understanding of the nature and strength of the resistance, the intervention might have failed.

---

*We do not advocate a zero tolerance policy because you need to investigate all infractions and treat them on their merit; all behavior is not equal.

Below are some key aspects to consider in the TNA phase of diversity training.

1. Determine upper management's level of commitment to diversity. If top management is not committed, then the program is not likely to be successful. If the top management is committed, but significant segments of the rest of upper management are not, then training is indicated at this level. The American Institute for Managing Diversity suggests that such training include describing[38]

   - organizational culture and its impact on the change initiative;
   - steps involved in measuring how well people are managing diversity;
   - qualities of organizations that are beginning to managing diversity successfully;
   - the responses people have to managing diversity;
   - three approaches to managing diversity: affirmative action, understanding differences, and managing diversity; and
   - different motivations people have for implementing diversity.

2. Identify the organizational goals/objectives related to diversity.
3. Obtain a good cross section of attitudes and behaviors that reflect how the employees respond to diversity at their worksite. Determine the strength of these attitudes and behaviors.
4. Determine the forces supporting and resisting diversity.

As noted, it is critical to examine the policies and procedures (organizational analysis) of the organization and be sure they are aligned with the goals of training. One way to demonstrate the importance of diversity is to be sure that it is reflected in management performance appraisals. Having a number of performance goals for management that are tied to diversity demonstrate its importance. But even more important is that promotions and raises are also tied to some extent to these important goals.

Design

One of the inputs to the design phase is constraints. In diversity training, you will likely be training everyone, so the amount of time taken up by the training will be a constraint. You will need to balance the cost of the lost productivity against the value of the diversity training. This will involve making a careful match between the training objectives and the time needed to achieve those objectives. Related to this is the number of people you train at one time. The more people trained, the lower the per person cost of training. However, the larger the number, the more limits you place on the types of training methods you can use. Thus, you will have to examine the methods needed to achieve your objectives relative to the number of trainees that can be accommodated by the method. If training is to go beyond simply providing information, then the size of the training group will need to be controlled.

If because of the constraints related to cost and loss of productivity it is decided that large numbers of trainees need to be trained at the same time, then the focus would likely be limited to knowledge and attitudes. Thus, two learning objectives might be as follows:

- "After training, the trainee will be expected to pass a written test covering the benefits of diversity with a minimum of 80 percent.
- After training, the trainee will demonstrate an improved attitude toward people from diverse backgrounds by scoring at least 5 points higher on an attitude measure than they did prior to the training.

On the basis of these objectives, the method chosen would be the lecture method, perhaps augmented by video clips. Another design factor to demonstrate the training's importance would be to have a high-level company official kick off the training session. Also, use of additional audiovisual (AV) enhancements would be advisable to help keep employee interest.

Development/Implementation Issues

The primary method of instruction will be the lecture method with video clips and some AV for support. Things to be done are preparation of all the material required for the training and booking a lecture room large enough for the training. Development of the material and printing of any handouts will need to be completed. A set of video clips will need to be developed or purchased to augment the lecture. Additional AV tools will need to be created. A trainer or set of trainers with appropriate platform skills will need to be chosen.

We will conduct a dry run, given the importance of the training and the large audiences that will be present. You want to be sure that it is successful. We will forgo a pilot as the material is not that complex or in need of being integrated; it is primarily lecture and AV.

An introduction by a high-level company official (hopefully the president) is best done in person, but if this is not possible, have it on DVD. When Wisconsin Power and Light developed their diversity training, it included a VP or high-level manager opening each one-day session with an explanation of the importance of a workforce that values diversity.[40] It is also a good idea to have a senior manager available near the end to answer any questions and reinforce management's commitment to diversity.

Evaluation Issues

Not enough of the diversity training done in organizations is evaluated to know if it is effective.[41] Management might be concerned about evaluating training because they might discover that training is having no effect. The logic goes something like this: "It is better to provide the training, and if we get sued, we can point to the efforts of our training department as an indication of our commitment to diversity. But if it is evaluated and shown to have no effect, we are worse off in a court of law."[42] As we have noted earlier, however, that is looking at evaluation as a pass/fail system. The goal in evaluating diversity training is to provide input into the training process to create a continuous improvement system.

In our example, we would develop a "reaction" questionnaire to assess how the lectures were being received. Given the nature of lectures, it is important that employees find the lectures maintain their attention. We will also need to get trainee reactions to the video clips. For "learning," we need to develop a paper-and-pencil test (multiple choice) to assess employees' knowledge after the training. To assess behavioral change, we will monitor the complaints from minorities in the organization, expecting a drop. Finally, an improvement in "satisfaction with the diversity climate" will be the expected organizational results change.

SEXUAL HARASSMENT TRAINING

Sexual harassment is one specific type of behavior that diversity training attempts to eliminate. It deserves special attention because, although it has likely been going on for years, there were relatively few complaints in the past, even though it was against the law. In 1991, however, law clerk Anita Hill filed a sexual harassment complaint in the United States against Clarence Thomas, who at the time was a Supreme Court Justice nominee. Since then, it has become acceptable to file such complaints.

Sexual harassment is an unwelcome advance of a sexual nature and can take one of two forms: quid pro quo and hostile environment.

Quid pro quo harassment occurs if an employee higher in the organization makes an offer to a subordinate of some job perk (raise, promotion, or easier job) in return for sexual favors. If a supervisor sexually harasses a subordinate, the company can be considered liable, even if no one else was aware of the harassment.[43] If an employee is harassed by someone other than a supervisor (such as a co-worker or customer), the employer can still be liable if evidence shows that the employer was aware or should have been aware of the harassment.

When words, gestures, and/or behaviors make someone feel uncomfortable based on their gender, the result is a **hostile work environment.** The term comes from the U.S. Supreme Court ruling in *Meritor Savings Bank v. Vinson.*[44] In this case, Vinson was abused verbally and sexually over a number of years by her boss, but she was making good career progress. The court ruled that in this case, the verbal and sexual abuse was "unwelcome" and sufficiently severe and pervasive to be abusive. This notion of a "hostile work environment" is complex in terms of what is and is not considered sexual harassment. Sexual harassment training needs to define these concepts in ways that fit the specific workplace.

Why It Is Important

Although the number of complaints filed with the Equal Employment Opportunity Commission between 1997 and 2007 has declined about 20 percent (15,889 in 1997 and 12,510 in 2007), it is still quite high.[45] About 16 percent of these complaints were from men (up from 11.5% in 1997).[46] The cost to organizations for these complaints was $49 million in the year 2007, and this does not include the dollars that go to litigation.[47] As with diversity, not paying attention to sexual harassment can be expensive. Irrespective of the damages awarded, preparation and attendance at hearings, in addition to legal expenses, all take away from the bottom line for a company. Furthermore, it is estimated that the damage to a company's reputation from a sexual harassment charge can decrease the firm's market value on the stock exchange by 5 to 30 percent.[48]

Just how many employees are sexually harassed? Some data suggest that sexual harassment is fairly common in the workplace. One survey in the United States reported that 42 percent of the females and 15 percent of the males indicated being sexually harassed on the job.[49] In Canada, a survey showed that 48 percent indicated being sexually harassed in the previous year, with only 3 percent indicating that the harassment was of the quid pro quo type.[50]

To win a harassment suit in which the supervisor sexually harassed someone, the organization must prove that the supervisor's harassment was against the company's harassment policy. Therefore, maintaining such a policy is critical. The courts accept training supervisors in the use of these policies as compelling evidence of the company's concern regarding the issue.[51] In fact, the court previously held that if a company does not provide some kind of sexual harassment training to its employees, the company will be liable.[52]

But there are more than just the obvious costs associated with sexual harassment. Sexually harassed employees experience psychological distress and, in some cases, posttraumatic stress disorder, both of which interfere with productivity.[53] A more direct impact on productivity is that these employees experience higher levels of absenteeism and turnover.[54] Moreover, these outcomes manifest themselves in employees who, although experiencing sexual harassment, do not define it as such and therefore do not report it.[55] This troubling tendency suggests that vigilance on the part of management is critical to stamp out such behaviors.

None of the preceding points address the ethical issues. Allowing an employee to be sexually harassed by others in the company is morally and ethically reprehensible.

It is a part of a company's responsibility to the employees to protect their physical and psychological health while they are at the workplace.

What Organizations Are Doing

A survey of U.S. organizations indicated that more than 80 percent provided some type of sexual harassment training.[56] For many companies it is effective. A survey of 663 human resource practitioners indicated that in 500 of the responding organizations, sexual harassment complaints declined after initiating training. On the basis of the information from these organizations, an effective strategy for dealing with sexual harassment was developed, as depicted in Table 10-4.[57]

However, many organizations are not doing a good job in this area. For that reason, we continue to hear of flagrant violations. Consider two of these. The Sydney Frank Importing Company settled a complaint that awarded 100 women a total of $2.6 million for their sexual harassment complaints. The culprit? The owner/ president.[58] On January 9, 2006, the largest sexual harassment lawsuit ever, at $1 billion dollars, was filed in Manhattan against Dresdner Klienwort Wasserstein Services, the American branch of Dresdner Bank of Germany.[59]

Going back to the SBI case, we note that a procedure was in place for dealing with harassment. This procedure was correct in that it did not expect the harassed employee to report the allegation to the supervisor (who was the offender), but instead to the supervisor's boss. The problem was that the boss apparently lacked training and failed to take the complaint seriously. In fact, many companies conduct minimal training and even less evaluation of the outcomes of the training.[60] As a result, some states are now mandating training, even for businesses as small as 50 employees.[61]

As noted earlier, sexual harassment of the quid pro quo type is most obvious, and its definition is relatively clear. Defining sexual harassment when it relates to a hostile environment is difficult, and care in determining what is enforceable is important. Those who develop and conduct the training must not bring their own values into the training. Rather, they must present the company's guidelines and their application. It is important that the training does not create situations that are

Table 10-4
Effective Strategies for Dealing with Sexual Harassment

Develop a sexual harassment policy. In the policy, make it clear that sexual harassment will not be tolerated. Those guilty of it will suffer severe consequences. Post the policy throughout the company. Also make it a part of the employee handbook.

Obtain top management support. As with all change efforts, it is important that top management is seen as supporting the initiative.

Develop training. Most important here is that the training makes it clear what sexual harassment is and what it is not. Information sessions, videos, and group discussions are useful ways to provide this information.

Provide training to everyone. For large companies, online training would be useful. It is important that all levels of the organization receive the training, not just supervisors and/or their subordinates. Be sure to have the president or CEO kick off the training to show support. This can be via video if training is online or if the executive officer is unavailable at the time of the training sessions.

Evaluate the training. As with all training, evaluate it to be sure that employees do understand what acceptable and unacceptable behaviors are.

Develop a complaint process. Provide more than one contact person (HR person, peer, high-level manager). Recall the case at the start of the chapter. There was a complaint process in place, but it was ineffective. Providing a hotline for those who feel frustrated at trying to be heard is also a good idea.

Investigate all complaints quickly and confidentially. To prevent intimidation of witnesses or complainants, inform only those involved that there is an investigation.

Punish offenders severely. Those found guilty need to be punished, no matter who they are. This will reinforce the company's position on sexual harassment.

irrelevant and could quite likely lead to a backlash. For example, swearing on the shop floor might not be considered harassment.[62] However, the same behavior at the management level might be. The preceding should not be interpreted as implying fixed and absolute guidelines. For example, the company may set a policy that is more stringent than the law requires. If policy bans the use of foul language or the use of derogatory names, appropriate consequences for violating the policy can be enforced. However, what is being enforced is company policy, not sexual harassment, as defined by the courts.

Some organizations believe that sexual harassment training for nonsupervisors is unnecessary. All it will do is sensitize employees to the issue and perhaps create more complaints.[63] This line of thinking is an error. The truth is that this type of training might bring to the surface complaints that can be addressed in the early stages. Studies show that training can reduce both the number of complaints and the costs of settling complaints. Everyone needs to know the policy, how it is implemented, what types of behaviors are prohibited, and how to respond when an incident occurs.

Upper management might not believe that training is necessary for them. This position is irresponsible if they understand the law. As we pointed out, if they don't go through training, it leaves the company vulnerable to lawsuits. In addition, upper management often is unaware of what constitutes inappropriate behavior. Interviews with those who interact with upper management will help determine whether a problem exists at that level. Even if no specific problem is uncovered, training is a good idea for everyone.

For the small business, the costs associated with development of an effective sexual harassment policy need not be high, as Training in Action 10-2 indicates.

TRAINING IN ACTION 10-2
Sexual Harassment Training in the Small Business

Controlling sexual harassment does not have to be costly for the small business. There are also software applications retailing for about $100 that can help create a manual, such as Employee Manual Maker 3.0 by JIAN Tools for Sale, Inc., in Mountain View, California. The program, designed for companies with 100 or fewer employees, also has a sexual harassment questionnaire and discussion guide. Cheaper still, try networking with other companies and cutting and pasting from their policies.

After developing a policy, you should begin training. Brumberg Publications, Inc., of Brookline, Massachusetts, sells a $95 training video aimed at companies with 15 or fewer employees. Interactive Media of New York has a $425 interactive CD-ROM about harassment for supervisors at companies with fewer than 100 employees.

Judith Nitsch, a civil engineer at a small company, saw how to react effectively to offensive conduct. The same day her firm's chief engineer heard of a harassing remark, he sent a memo to all 35 employees that such conduct wouldn't be tolerated. It stopped.

When Nitsch opened her own firm in 1989, which now has 54 employees and $3.6 million in annual revenues, she also took a hard line. She not only created a sexual harassment policy but also named a male and a female employee to whom workers can report complaints directly. She says this has worked well.

Ultimately, however, the best defense isn't a board game, video, or strongly worded policy. To talk the talk, experts say, the boss must walk the walk. "If the senior people behave appropriately, that's the message that's communicated, irrespective of what's in the policy," says training consultant Lynn Revo-Cohen. Best of all, it doesn't cost a thing.

Source: Donovan, K. "Avoiding a time bomb: Sexual harassment: From videos to Web sites, new resources are available for small businesses." *Business Week Magazine* (October, 1997), p. 20.

Using the Training Model to Develop Sexual Harassment Training

As we indicated at the beginning of this section, sexual harassment is a component of an overall diversity program. Thus, the process followed using the training model in diversity training is much the same for sexual harassment training. Some additional points relating to sexual harassment training bear reinforcing here.

Training Needs Analysis

As part of the TNA, you need to examine the sexual harassment policy. If one does not exist, this is a nontraining need that must be addressed before training can be effective. The sexual harassment policy provides the information related to "expected behavior (performance)." An acceptable policy contains the points suggested in Table 10-5. Also, make sure that a process is in place and a committee set up to deal with complaints. The policy and guidelines provide the basis for much of the training. Part of the TNA would be an examination of the policy to identify the goals of training, the guidelines for the expected behaviors, and the nature of the content that the training will embrace. Actual performance would be reflected in behaviors that actually are occurring in the workplace. Complaints would provide this information.

To customize training to the environment of the company, you need to identify the types of problems that exist in the company. Use the committee set up to handle complaints to obtain initial information about problems and the effectiveness of the procedure for reporting problems. Remember, part of the TNA is used to identify not only training needs but also nontraining needs (roadblocks to transfer of training). Lack of an effective reporting procedure is one such roadblock (nontraining need). You can also meet with small, cross-sectional groups of employees. These groups should be homogeneous in terms of gender and level in the organization. Questions might include the following:

- What do you know about the issue of sexual harassment?
- Do you think anything you have ever done could be construed to be sexual harassment?
- Have you or anyone you know at this company ever been touched in a sexual manner?
- Have you heard about a supervisor indicating to a subordinate that sexual favors would help them get a raise, promotion, or any other perk?
- Do you know of anyone who might feel consistently uncomfortable in terms of the way co-workers or supervisors behave around her?

Table 10-5   What Experts Suggest Is Necessary to Include in a Sexual Harassment Policy

According to attorneys and experts, a sexual harassment policy protects your organization if it:
- states that the organization has a strong opposition to sexual harassment.
- explains what sexual harassment is with examples that employees will find relevant to their jobs.
- establishes a clear-cut procedure for reporting harassment, which does not limit the reporting to a supervisor in their department or in HR. There should be a committee of employees that has representatives from all levels of the organization, so an employee can talk to a peer if that is what makes them comfortable. Have a "hotline" dedicated to such reporting.
- warns potential perpetrators that violations could be punished by discipline that could include dismissal, no matter what level in the organization they are.
- pledges that investigations will be conducted promptly, and there will be no retaliation for reporting such issues.

Source: Ganzel, R. "What sexual harassment training really prevents." *Training* (October 1998), pp. 86–94.

With these groups, it is good to conclude with a statement similar to the following: "If anyone wishes to tell me anything else about this important issue, you can contact me personally, and we could meet to talk about it confidentially." It is a good idea to set up a schedule for times that employees could meet privately to discuss the issue.

Design

Constraints are much the same as for diversity training, primarily because you also want to train everyone. So, for our example, let's assume that the costs associated with being taken to court for sexual harassment, along with the personal costs to females, and the image the company wishes to portray cause upper management to insist that there be more than just lectures on the subject. They want some small group interactions. An example of an objective that might be developed beyond the type indicated in the diversity training is as follows:

> *The trainee will be able to identify the 5 violations of the company sexual harassment policy after viewing a video of employee interactions.*

The choice for training methods here could be a large group for providing information, coupled with smaller groups to discuss issues and examine videos of employee interactions to learn more about inappropriate behaviors.

Development/Implementation

Again, this is very similar to the diversity training except that there are plans for small-group interactions. Getting enough top-management support and involvement cannot be overstated. So, getting the president's commitment to show up for the kickoff of the training is important. Also developing some sexual harassment videos that demonstrate the various types of harassment will need to be completed. Get agendas set up for small-group discussions and obtain enough group facilitators to run these groups. Also, training of facilitators may be necessary.

For the same reasons given for diversity training, a dry run, but not a pilot, will be conducted.

Evaluation

Evaluations would be similar to the diversity training. However, for learning, videos similar to those used in the training program should be developed to test trainees on their ability to identify sexual harassment.

TEAM TRAINING

Teamwork is a pervasive part of organizational functioning in North America. A survey of *Fortune* 1000 organizations in the United States indicates that about 70 percent of them uses teams.[64] A survey of Canadian organizations indicates that a similar percentage (76%) uses teams.[65]

Why It Is Important

Use of teams seems to make a difference in the effectiveness of an organization. A common characteristic of North America's 100 best organizations is the effective use of teams.[66] A great deal of evidence indicates that effective teams can significantly improve the effectiveness of an organization. For example,

- Westinghouse Furniture Systems increased its productivity 74 percent in three years,[67]
- FedEx cut service errors by 13 percent,[68]

- Volvo's Kalamar plant reduced defects by 90 percent,[69] and
- Corning Cellular Ceramics decreased defect rates from 1,800 to 9 parts per million.[70]

In today's highly competitive environment, organizations are looking for ways to obtain an advantage. Effectively implementing the right kind of team concept can make the organization more responsive to customer needs, reduce the workforce by requiring fewer levels of management, reduce waste, improve quality and productivity, and make the company more competitive in other ways.

Work teams are also a benefit to employees, who are given the opportunity to be involved in more meaningful work.[71] More meaningful work leads to other positive organizational outcomes such as

- improved employee satisfaction and commitment,
- reduced absenteeism and turnover, and
- improved performance.

Organizations see a reason to be moving toward this style of management in ever-increasing numbers.

What Organizations Are Doing

The use of teams began in earnest a few decades ago under names such as quality of work life, quality circles, employee involvement, and so forth.[72] They all centered on getting workers more involved in their work and helping in a manner beyond what was traditionally expected. These efforts were met with skepticism, particularly by some unions that believed that it was simply a way for management to co-opt workers and reduce the workforce.[73] In some cases, this assessment was probably true. In those early years, many of these efforts failed.[74] The main reasons for failure were that, after initial team training, there was no[75]

- refresher training;
- evaluation and feedback of team efforts;
- alignment of systems, procedures, and organizational design to the team approach; and
- training of new members brought into the team.

From a transfer-of-training perspective, maintaining support from the top, removing roadblocks, and creating systems and practices that support the team process (performance appraisals, compensation systems, and so forth) are critical to the success of the program.[76]

Today, there are several successful team efforts; Training in Action 10-3 shows but one of these.[77] The transition from a hierarchical system to a flatter, more inclusive system is not easy, and training is one of the important ingredients for success. Coca-Cola's Baltimore syrup operation, for example, was a plant with high turnover, absenteeism, worn-out equipment, and an old-style management.[78] Mr. Bentley, the new plant manager, decided to change that. He promised to run the business competitively and provide the employees with the KSAs to do it now and in the future. Four years later, it emerged as a highly successful plant with cost savings of $1 million. This transformation was accomplished primarily through the use of teams. For a team to be effective, however, it must receive training. Training was the second part of Mr. Bentley's promise, and he came through on it.

The Coca-Cola training came in three categories: technical, interpersonal, and team. For the technical training, employees were encouraged to learn four different jobs to provide for flexibility in the organization. This increased knowledge also

Don Callahan, an hourly assembly worker, and Brian Large, a production engineer, were trying to determine why the warning light on the Dodge Intrepid was on when the system was working fine. Was this unique? If Dodge had built the Intrepid like most American cars are built, the problem would not have been fixed because the two workers would never have met. Brian would be too busy to contact anyone about the problem and Don would say it was not his problem. For this car, however, the manufacturing process depended on a team of workers, designers, and engineers collaborating on all stages of the car's development.

The collaboration resulted in the car reaching production a full year earlier than the average production cycle for Chrysler. It also required 40 percent fewer engineers. The total cost for the car from its inception was just over $1 billion, less than half of the cost of two other well-known team efforts—the Ford Taurus at $3 billion and the GM Saturn at $3.5 billion.

Source: Hunsaker, P. *Training in Management Skills* (2001). Upper Saddle River, NJ: Prentice Hall.

provided employees with a greater understanding of the operation of the plant, making them more valuable team members.

Interpersonal skills training was also provided because of the belief that, before anything can be done effectively, employees need to be able to interact effectively with others. All shop-floor employees, supervisors, and managers were trained together. This way, everyone was seen as a regular human being, not supervisor or worker. This approach helped employees work together as a team without necessarily seeing the other person as a boss or supervisor. The training included listening, handling conflict, and negotiation skills.

Team training included leadership, meeting management, group dynamics, and problem solving. As members are provided with these skills, they are also provided with additional skills to explore future career or retirement options. Self-assessment, résumé writing, and interview skills are all part of preparing employees for the future at Coke or anywhere else they decide to go. When people work for a company because they want to, rather than because they see no other options, it ensures that they stay because they enjoy their work and want to be part of the Coke team.

Using the Training Model to Develop Team Training

Because there are many types of teams, and many types of training involved in team training, rather than provide a specific example, we will speak in more general terms regarding each of the phases. The team concept usually surfaces when key organizational outcomes are not achieved, and one or more people in upper management suggest that implementing a team concept will "solve the problem." Of course, an experienced and knowledgeable training manager will suggest that a TNA would be required to fully understand the cause of the problem.

Training Needs Analysis

The first question to address in the TNA is "What organizational outcomes are not being achieved (expected behavior – actual performance), and to what degree are the work unit structure and job design responsible?" A team concept is just one possible approach to achieving the desired outcomes. Once the cause of the deficit in outcomes is understood, the next question becomes "Will some type of team concept sufficiently improve the outcomes, and if so, is it the best alternative?" Of the many types of team structure available, not all teams work equally well for achieving particular outcomes. Five of the major team types are listed here:[79]

1. Informal team (sense of togetherness and cooperation)
2. Traditional work units with a supervisor (more formal sense of togetherness and cooperation)
3. Problem-solving task forces, committees, or circles (teams outside of formal work unit)
4. Leadership teams, steering committees, and advisory boards (teams that integrate leadership from various areas of the company, such as management and union leadership)
5. Self-directed work teams (teams that are their own work unit, operating without a formal supervisor)

Space is not available here to describe each of these types in detail and to identify the tasks and situations for which they are best suited. We recommend the book *Tools for Team Excellence*, by Gregory Huszczo, as a good source for this information. Once you identify the type of team(s) required, you can then identify the KSAs needed by team members for the team to be effective.

Even though the different types of teams require some training that is unique, many of the KSAs are common to all types. Seven factors are generally found to be components of all effective teams:[80]

1. Clear sense of direction
2. Members with the talents necessary to achieve the team's purpose
3. Clear and enticing responsibilities
4. Reasonable and efficient operating procedures
5. Constructive interpersonal relationships
6. Active reinforcement systems
7. Constructive external relationships

As you can see, some of these components carry direct implications for the KSAs required of team members. They also identify the types of nontraining needs that must be addressed if the teams are to be successful. The TNA should describe what each of these components consists of for the team(s). This description will then determine the KSAs and nontraining needs.

Design/Development/Implementation Issues

Most training for teams requires KSA in addition to "team-building" modules. The KSA portion addresses deficiencies in item 2 in the preceding list (talents necessary to achieve the team's purpose). Knowledge acquired here is primarily declarative and procedural. Examples of the types of training/learning possibilities include the following:

- Listening skills
- Techniques for seeking input from others
- Communicating positively in conflict situations
- Problem-solving techniques
- Consensus decision making
- Conducting an effective meeting

Trainees are typically provided with lecturettes to convey the necessary knowledge, and then they participate in exercises that develop the skills. In addition to providing the lecturettes and facilitating the exercises, the trainer assesses the KSA development of the team as a whole. After the trainer is confident that the team shows sufficient development of KSAs, trainees are moved into a team-building module. During the team-building module, the trainer will be assessing the level of KSAs being applied, and at the conclusion, she will work with the team to assess its performance. If additional work on the KSAs is necessary, the trainer will provide that training; otherwise, the team will move on to the next set of KSAs or the next team-building module. This process allows the trainer to ensure that the appropriate level of learning occurs before moving to the next level. However, it also means that training must be done in small groups (teams), and this constraint will increase the cost of training.

If the company is changing from a traditional work flow to a team approach, the first types of training that are likely to be needed are informational (knowledge) and attitudinal. The first step is to reduce factors that may be creating resistance to the change. Here you would begin with a general orientation regarding the use of the teams. The orientation would provide everyone with the following:

- An understanding of why a team-based approach to work design is being implemented
- The advantages for the company and the employee of the type of teams being implemented
- The difficulties involved in moving to a team approach and the support the company will provide employees in meeting these challenges
- A basic understanding of how teams operate and any company guidelines for team operations (e.g., decision making, reporting relationships)

It would not be necessary to include intact teams at the same orientation session. However, it is important that everyone hears the same message. Thus, a thorough pilot of the orientation is important. Any team training conducted after the general orientation to team training should be done with intact teams.

Evaluation

Even though the organization holds a vested interest in the effectiveness of the team concept, the team itself is at least equally vested in its outcomes. Thus, particularly for team training, the team should be involved in the design and assessment of the evaluation phase. First, the team approach is most often designed to be an ongoing aspect of how the company does its business, so continuous improvement of team training is critical to the success of the company. Typically, the implementation of teams is beset with difficulties in the beginning because of the departure from the traditional, more comfortable work systems employees are used to. Therefore, it is important to examine each phase of the training process to identify what went well and what needs to be improved. Second, most team approaches are associated with a company's increased emphasis on quality and continuous improvement. Thus, from the TNA through implementation and evaluation, all phases must be carefully examined to provide a solid basis for understanding why desired outcomes were or were not achieved and to identify what corrective action is necessary.

Process and Content Evaluation   Our approach to evaluation of team training is to involve the team in the design of a reaction questionnaire that will be used at the end of each training module. This use of a reaction questionnaire to measure process differs from our previous discussions, in which the reaction questionnaire is used as an outcome measure. Even though it is also used here to assess outcomes (trainee reactions), the involvement of teams provides a unique opportunity to combine the two. Process evaluation is not only important for evaluating team training, but it is also a component of effective teams (it is part of the "reasonable and efficient operating procedures" component). Effective teams must periodically assess their process and their outcomes to make the necessary process improvements that will lead to performance improvement. So team training must include a component on evaluation of process and outcomes. By designing the reaction questionnaire to look at both processes and outcomes, you will be able to provide training while conducting a part of the evaluation.

As a trainer, you will need to spend some time discussing how to design a good reaction questionnaire. This process allows you to work with the team to design questions that measure the degree to which the team members feel that each learning objective was achieved. Each learning objective question is followed by questions about what seemed to be effective and what was less effective in that learning module. One advantage to this approach is that the team understands the meaning and intent of the questions (because they help design them); thus, the validity of the results is increased. The real advantage, however, is that the exercise is directly related to the team's need to develop evaluation procedures for their operation back on the job. Teams often encounter difficulty measuring the "soft" side of their operation (aspects such as interpersonal relationships, effective meetings, effective use of team's talent, etc.). The team's experience developing the reaction questionnaire is a good practice opportunity in preparation for developing an evaluation instrument for their "team process" back on the job.

After the trainees complete the reaction questionnaire, the trainer plays the role of a team leader and reviews the results with the team. The trainer may also identify outcomes that appear to be below standard, which the group did not identify. During this discussion, the trainer asks for clarification and seeks consensus about the results. The trainer then outlines the training process for the module and asks the trainees to help identify ways that improve the process. Once this task is completed, the trainer asks the team to review the evaluation process to identify practices that would be useful on the job.

More formal content evaluation is not necessary if the trainer did a thorough job. The trainer observes the team members using the knowledge and skill during their exercises. These observations combined with continuous coaching throughout the day, and the use of the feedback from the reaction questionnaire makes formal testing redundant. However, a trainer who is less confident in his abilities in this area may use more formal measures.

Transfer of training should be built into the team's own evaluation process. The trainer should schedule a meeting with the team about two weeks after training to review how things are going. Additionally, a meeting should be scheduled approximately six months after training is concluded. Organizational results should be reviewed at least every six months to identify teams that may be experiencing difficulties.

CROSS-CULTURAL TRAINING

Culture is the shared values, beliefs, attitudes, and behaviors that a society has in common. So, culture helps shape the behavior of its people and, of course, the way organizations operate. To understand some of the differences between cultures, it is useful to examine the work by Holfstede.[81] He identified five dimensions along which individuals from different cultures seem to differ: individualism/collectivism orientation, uncertainty orientation, goal orientation, power orientation, and time orientation.

Individualism focuses on individual goals and accomplishments. In these cultures, individuals have a high degree of self-respect and independence and focus on what is best for them. In an organizational setting, the employee expects to be rewarded for his own work. Collectivism is just the opposite. The group comes first; ahead of the individual's own interests. In a collectivist culture, organizations tend to have participative decision making, where the group has input into decisions. Uncertainty orientation focuses on how those in the culture feel about uncertainty. In an uncertainty acceptance culture, people are stimulated by change, and new opportunities excite them. Those in an uncertainty avoidance culture try their best to avoid uncertainty. So, organizations operating in an uncertainty accepting culture will be more flexible and encourage risk taking, whereas in uncertainty avoiding cultures, the organization would likely adopt a more hierarchical structure, with lots of rules and procedures. Goal orientation refers to what motivates the person in the culture. Aggressive goal behavior is focused on achievement, possessions, and assertiveness. Passive goal behavior is focused on social relationships, quality of life, and helping others. Organizations in the aggressive goal orientation culture are set up to value competitiveness and assertiveness and are primarily profit motivated. In a more passive goal orientation culture, employees prefer more fringe benefits that higher salaries. Power orientation is the degree with which people accept a power hierarchy in their society. Power respect cultures accept the power differences in the hierarchy. In these cultures, it is understood that those above in the hierarchy have the right to make decisions, and these decisions should not be questioned. Those in a power tolerance culture do not blindly accept decisions made by those in higher positions. In fact, they may choose not to follow a leader if these people believe that it is not in their best interest. Organizations in power respect cultures have employees who expect to be told what to do, whereas employees in power tolerance culture expect to be consulted. Finally, time orientation is the extent to which people have a long-term versus a short-term outlook on their life and work. In long-term orientation cultures, people focus on the future and value dedication, persistence, and hard work. The payoff is in the future. Short-term orientation cultures focus on the past and present, with emphasis on traditions and social obligations.[82] Table 10-6 provides examples of where various countries fall in terms of the above dimensions. There are, of course, other differences between cultures as well, and the above was simply to provide an example of the differences that exist. But just these basic differences highlight the importance of being aware of the culture you plan to be operating in.

Table 10-6
Cultural Values of Some Countries

Individualistic	Collectivistic
United States	Taiwan
Canada	Greece
Netherlands	Mexico
Great Britain	Singapore
Uncertainty Acceptance	**Uncertainty Avoidance**
Canada	Japan
United States	Israel
Denmark	Peru
India	Italy
Aggressive Goal Orientation	**Passive Goal Orientation**
Japan	Sweden
Germany	Norway
Italy	Denmark
United States	Chile
Power Tolerance	**Power Respect**
Israel	Mexico
United States	France
Norway	Japan
Austria	Brazil
Short-Term Orientation	**Long-Term Orientation**
Canada	China
United States	Japan
Pakistan	South Korea
Australia	India

Why It Is Important

North American businesses continue to expand, moving aggressively into markets around the world. These businesses require their employees to work in different countries and interact with varying cultures. Employees working in a foreign country are called expatriates. These expatriates range from sales staff to various professionals all the way to senior management.[83] To be effective, expatriates need to be aware of the differences between their home culture and the host country's culture, and act accordingly. If they do not, their behavior could lead to embarrassment, confusion, damage to the international relationship, and even loss of market share.[84] See Table 10-7 for some examples.

In the 1970s, many of the expatriates sent to other countries for an assignment either came back before the assignment was due to end, or, although they stayed the full duration, their effort was deemed a failure.[85] The problem often cited for the failure was the lack of cultural skills.[86] It has been estimated that these failures and unfinished assignments cost their organizations about 2 billion dollars per year.[87] So, for organizations to be effective in an international marketplace, their expatriates must operate successfully. An important part of the preparation for success working in a different country is training/orientation in the culture of that country.

What Organizations Are Doing

Today, most multinationals who use expatriates do offer some type of cross-cultural training.[88] However, in choosing an employee to represent the organization in a

Table 10-7   Examples of Lack of Cultural Awareness

The Japanese manager gave me his business card. I glanced at it and put it in my shirt pocket. Things deteriorated after that. Business card exchanges in Japan are very ceremonial. You have to acknowledge the card you have received, look at the logo, create conversation about it, and then do it in reverse. Everyone has to exchange cards before anyone can conduct any business. This can take a long time even if as few as four or five people are involved.

The recently transferred U.S. manager wanted to build his credibility with his native Japanese subordinates. He brought them together for a few hours to explain to them how much he had accomplished at his postings in the United States. Not a good idea. Behaving with humility is an important cultural norm in most Asian countries, including China, Japan, and Korea. These cultures also focus on the "we" not the "me." The manager should have been talking about the "team's" accomplishments not "his."

Bill went into the Latin American store confident that he had a product they would want to buy. He was surprised when he could not seem to close the deal. After over an hour, he left, confused about why he had not been able to convince the manager to buy his product. The simple concept of time is important. In Latin America, relationship is more important than how much time passes or how great the need for the product is. This differs from the mind-set in the United States that focuses on the task and instant gratification. The U.S. sales people go into the sales call wanting to know right away whether you want the product. But the Latin American person, no matter how wonderful that widget you're selling is, they're not going to buy from you today.

Even Walt Disney Co., a brand name recognized all over the world, was slow to recognize the importance of adapting to cultural differences when it opened its theme park in Paris. Initially, the park suffered financial losses. This may have been due to the fact that they didn't serve wine with their lunches. The cultural norms in the United States view wine as an alcoholic beverage with restrictions on when and to whom it can be served. The French culture views wine as a food and classifies it as such. Mealtime consumption of wine for the French is analogous to having coffee with breakfast for many Americans. But Disney executives either overlooked or neglected to provide the option of having wine served with lunch.

An American oil rig supervisor in Indonesia berated an employee who seemed to be taking much too long to take a boat to shore. This supervisor had no idea what was in store for him. In this culture, no one berates an Indonesian in public, so a mob of outraged workers chased the supervisor with axes.

U.S. and British negotiators found themselves in confusion when the head of the American company said that they were "tabling" the remaining key points and began to walk out of the meeting. In the United States, "tabling a motion" means to postpone discussing it, while the same phrase in Great Britain means to "bring it to the table for discussion."

And finally, imagine the trouble you could get into in Bulgaria, where nodding your head up and down means "no."

foreign subsidiary, many managers still consider the key component to be technical competence, with minimal attention being paid to the interpersonal skills and the domestic situations of potential expatriates.[89] This is in spite of research that suggests that failure in expatriate assignments is more likely due to family and personal issues and the lack of cross-cultural skills that enable people to adapt to their new environment.[90] Cross-cultural training does help in that regard, but this training needs to be for everyone in the family, not just the expatriate.

Given the costs associated with sending an expatriate to manage in another country, it is surprising that little in the way of evaluating success of these employees has been done. This is in spite of the fact that the failure rate (the percentage who return prematurely, without completing their assignment) in the United States is in the 20 to 40 percent range. In contrast, Japan has a failure rate that is less than 5 percent for their expatriates. One of the reasons for the difference is that Japanese expatriates receive far more orientation and language instruction than U.S. expatriates do.[91]

With the concern regarding failure rates, the high costs associated with expatriates, and the difficulty in obtaining qualified employees to accept these positions, organizations are looking to alternatives. Hiring of foreign nationals has been one alternative. In a survey of multinationals, more than half indicated that they were doing just that.[92] When someone is hired who already knows the culture, there is less chance for cultural problems, and the cost is considerably less than using an expatriate. Another alternative is the virtual expatriate. As an example, the head of an Asia-Pacific operation could be officially based in Singapore but actually live in Los Angeles. He could stay in an apartment when he visits Singapore and, at other times, communicate with his Singapore team via videoconferencing and other technologies.[93] McDonald's has also found it cost-effective to have the manager live in one country (Australia for example) and work in another (the entire Asian market). The virtual expatriate is able to keep his family (and himself) at home and communicate often via various technologies. The organization saves money, even with the costs associated with travel, and the manager is able to stay in his home country.

Notwithstanding these alternatives to expatriates, there will always be a need for them. These expatriates need to be prepared to deal with the culture of the host country. Despite all the warning signals about the frequent failure to adapt to a new culture, not all organizations send their business managers on any form of training to prepare them to operate effectively in the new environment. That said, those that do provide appropriate training do reap the benefits. See Training in Action 10-4 to see how McDonald's handles their foreign markets.

Using the Training Model to Develop Cross-Cultural Training

Training for an expatriate assignment is important for all the reasons mentioned earlier. This cross-cultural training/orientation needs to be developed in the same manner as any training.

Training Needs Analysis

In the development of cross-cultural training, the organizational outcomes not being achieved are future oriented (expected future performance in the foreign country – actual future performance in the foreign country). Expected performance is effective performance in the host country culture. This operational analysis information (describing how effective managers behave) would come from the host country. The person analysis is how the expatriate behaves presently. Some of the information in this analysis could come from experts in the specific culture, former expatriates, and the literature. However, it is also important to conduct interviews with host country employees. These

McDonald's goal is to have local nationals leading all of their markets. However, this is not always possible, especially in developing markets. Therefore, McDonald's will use seasoned leaders from developed markets as expatriates to initially lead the market to get it established and off to a strong start. Expatriates may also be used in support leadership roles as well in these markets (e.g., marketing, finance, supply chain, etc.). Expats understand that they have a dual role. One is to initially develop the market. The second major priority is to identify and develop local leaders who after some period of time will be able to replace the expatriate.

Expatriate assignments in a given market/location typically last from 3–5 years.

McDonald's typically takes the following steps to ensure the success of their expatriates. Step one is for the candidate to visit the market on their own to get exposed to the market, the culture and the team in place. During the visit they will get a very realistic view of the situation they are entering and business and personal challenges they will face. If they respond positively to the opportunity and express an interest in accepting the position, McDonald's will then arrange for their family to visit the market so they can assess the opportunity from their perspective.

During these visits, that may last 3 days to a week, they will have an opportunity to look at schools, real estate, shopping options, job prospects for spouse, etc. The visit usually includes tours, culture orientation sessions, visits with other expats, etc. The specific orientation provided depends on the needs of the employee and his/her family and, of course, on the actual location of the assignment.

With the high costs associated with expatriates, McDonald's, in some cases, uses virtual expatriates. Virtual expatriates are managers who are assigned to support a region or country, but remain in their own country. This works especially well when an individual's role involves a great deal of travel and, therefore, time away from home, so where they live is not as important. It is often less disruptive for their families and also less expensive to allow them to remain in their own country and travel to where they need to be vs. relocating them and paying them as expats. Technology enables them to communicate effectively and efficiently regardless of their distance from the market.

McDonald's is quite proud of their success rate with expatriates. Failure on assignments due to non-work issues, family issues, etc. does happen, but has been very infrequent. For the most part, McDonald's expatriates have performed and adjusted well to their assignments and find them to be incredible learning experiences both for them and their family.

Source: Personal communication with Neal Kulick, Vice President, Global Talent Management, McDonald's Corporation, 2915 Jorie Blvd./Oak Brook IL, September 2008.

employees can help identify problems that have occurred in the past with expatriates as well as identify methods for optimizing expatriate management performance. This step is often ignored.[94] The output here (training needs) would be the necessary items to be learned in order to be effective in the culture. The nontraining needs would be roadblocks that the organization in the host country had that would prevent the expatriate from being effective.

Design

One of the inputs to the design phase is constraints. In determining the type of training to provide and how long it should be, an important constraint is the cost versus benefit. Many organizations, although realizing that training is important, tend to be concerned about the cost of some training. One way to examine this is to look at the cost/benefit ratio of a short training program versus a more comprehensive training program. For example, say we are sending an executive to Asia for five years with his family. Being very conservative on the costs (1 million per year) means an investment of 5 million dollars. Even comprehensive training (costing 50,000 dollars) in terms of cost benefit ratio is only 1 percent of this 5 million dollar investment. When it is important that the expatriate be successful, this seems to be a small price to pay.

One of the objectives for the training will be to identify what behaviors are and are not appropriate in the culture. This can be measured by having the trainee watch a CD of various interactions between an expatriate and a host country employee. The trainee will stop the CD at each error committed by the expatriate (be 100% correct), explain the problem, and explain what should have been done.

To facilitate learning, the training will be in two parts: predeparture training (three days) and on-site training, which will take place after being on the job for four to six weeks and will be provided over a five-week period.

Development/Implementation

The training will utilize reading material, online discussion with current expatriates in the region, CDs, and role-plays. In the predeparture training, the focus is on providing

- cross-cultural awareness,
- cross-cultural communication skills, and
- business etiquette and procedures.

For the on-site training, there should be a review of the predeparture training, as often the hectic time prior to leaving for a foreign assignment causes one to lose her concentration. Then training will focus on questions that the expatriate and her family have now that they are living in the foreign country. This will take place a few times per week for a number of weeks.

Evaluation

Reaction questionnaires should be designed to rate the relevance and value of the training and should be completed just before beginning the on-site training. Learning will be measured by an online test of multiple-choice questions completed a week after training. Learning will also be evaluated at the end of training using multiple videos portraying various cultural gaffes. Behavior will be assessed from 360-degree performance appraisals completed on the expatriate after six months in the country. In the appraisals, there will be dimensions related to how the expatriate is fitting into the culture of the host country. Organizational results will be measured in terms of a drop in expatriates returning early from their assignments because of a frustration with their situation in the host country.

OTHER TRAINING PROGRAMS AND ISSUES

The types of training provided and the way they are managed affect almost every aspect of organizational life. Training can assist an employee in doing a job more effectively and can provide opportunities for promotion, transfers, increased pay, and employee well-being. It also prepares employees for dealing with emergencies and, in some cases, even saving lives. Let's examine a few of these types and the issues organizations need to consider.

Training and Equity

In the section on diversity training, we deal with ways the organization can improve the ability of a diverse group of employees to work together effectively. **Training equity** means providing equal access to training for all employees. Like hiring and promotion, training is a personnel decision that is subject to legal proscriptions and prescriptions. Even though we hope that the ethics of treating everyone equitably is the norm in the business world, unfortunately, many lawsuits are filed each year because an individual or group feels that it has been treated inequitably. Many of these suits are based on an employee not being selected for a particular position. It might seem like a selection issue, but many times, the organization's training practices played an important part in the outcome of the suit.

The majority of selection decisions within an organization involve current employees (transfers and promotions). Even if the promotion or transfer is based on who has the best set of KSAs for the new job, the company can be found guilty of unfair discrimination. This situation happens when one group of employees (e.g., minorities) is not provided with the same opportunities for training as another group (e.g., nonminorities).

Consider the female technician who worked for the Canadian Broadcasting Company (CBC).[95] She wanted to go on remote-location assignments, but was refused because many of these assignments took place at night and were not considered safe. When promotions came up at the CBC, she was not considered because one of the qualifications was a broad-based understanding of the types of assignments technicians go on. She never received the on-the-job training that going on remote assignments provided. The CBC's good intentions, which were meant to protect her, prevented her from developing important KSAs. This, in turn, inhibited her advancement. Training is an important part of the development of employees, whether they want transfers, promotions, or improved skills. It is the manager's responsibility to ensure that all employees are given opportunities to improve themselves and prepare for advancement.

In addition to the traditional performance review for the purpose of compensation and promotion decisions, many companies conduct a separate **developmental review.** This review provides the opportunity for the employee and supervisor to discuss career goals, areas of strength and weakness, and the opportunities for development that are open to the employee. This discussion benefits the organization because it helps develop employees for higher-level positions in the company. It benefits the employee because it provides opportunities to grow and develop. In addition to traditional types of training programs, development plans may include off-site seminars, on-the-job training, participation on a task force, a temporary assignment, or other ways the employee can develop the appropriate KSAs. The key is making sure that all supervisors understand the importance of providing all employees with opportunities on the basis of their current capabilities and developmental readiness, not on their gender, race, age, or other irrelevant criteria. Training in Action 10-5 provides an excellent example of an organization doing everything possible to provide opportunities for employees.

The Glass Ceiling

The **glass ceiling** is a metaphor for an invisible barrier that prevents minorities and women from moving up the corporate ladder. It is an example of how training and development opportunities can limit the ability of employees to advance in the company. Let's examine the glass ceiling for women. In the late 1980s, only about 2 percent of the corporate offices of the *Fortune* 500 companies were filled by women.[96] That has improved and was around 16 percent in 2005,[97] but considering the number of females in the workforce, it still seems rather low, especially in light of what Kraft Foods has accomplished. As one of the *Fortune* 500 companies, Kraft Foods takes equity seriously, with more than 26 percent of its corporate positions filled by women.[98] What is the difference between Kraft Foods and many others? One difference seems to be in the area of training. One of the main points, suggested by Kraft Foods executive vice president Mary Kay Haben, is the company's commitment to personal development and career advancement, both of which focus on training.

At Kraft Foods, employees meet with their supervisor once a year (formally) to discuss performance, developmental progress, and career aspirations. They meet again (informally) six months later to review how things are going. At Kraft Foods, executives seldom hire from the outside for management positions, so opportunities for moving up are available. When they do lose a senior manager to the competition,

Many women at Bell Telephone wanted to transfer from the operator's job to the more interesting and lucrative installation and repair jobs. When they applied, however, they failed to pass one of the required tests. Bell Telephone and the Communication Workers of Canada got together to work out a way the women could be more successful.

When women applied to the installation and repair department, they often were not accepted because they did not pass the electronics test. It was an important criterion for acceptance, because much of the work involved understanding and working on the components of a telephone and its accessories. Women did poorly on the test because they usually did not take such courses in high school or follow it as a hobby as

men seemed to do. Management and the union worked out an agreement in which operators could apply for a limited number of special training slots created in installation and repair. Successful candidates were required to be able to climb a ladder, have a valid driver's license, and pass a color vision test. Those who were successful were chosen on the basis of their seniority as operators.

Once accepted into a training slot, the operators received six months of on-the-job training in installation and repair. After training, they returned to their operator job until an opening became available. Then they applied like anyone else. The training the women received prepared them for the test and resulted in many operators being selected into the position.

Source: Martin, D. Personal communication. Communication Workers of Canada, Toronto, 1993.

they are able to fill the position within minutes.[99] To accomplish this level of preparedness, Kraft Foods developed an extensive human resource planning process with a heavy focus on preparing (training) employees for promotion. Part of this program takes place through an extensive mentoring program. Kraft Foods also formed a high-level committee that monitors how the company is doing regarding women and minorities at each level in the organization. When the committee identifies a problem in any area, it goes about solving it immediately. This example illustrates how a company can tie training to changes in the organizational environment to ensure equitable treatment for all employees.

People with Disabilities

Legislation in North America makes it unlawful, when hiring or training, to discriminate on the basis of a person's disability, whether physical or mental, if it does not prevent the person from doing the job. Basically, a job analysis describes the critical KSAs. On the basis of that information, it is possible to assess whether the disability will negatively affect job performance. If not, then the candidate must be provided with the same opportunity to be hired, promoted, or trained as anyone else.

Consider Mary, who is hearing impaired but able to speak and read lips. She applies for the job of accounting clerk. The job analysis identifies all the critical tasks and KSAs, and she meets all of them. However, although not a critical task, the job requires using the phone from time to time. Can the employer refuse to hire her on the basis of her inability to use a phone? Although each case needs to be examined on its merit, it would seem that such a refusal to hire her for the job would be illegal. According to the law, the company faces a **duty to accommodate.** It would require the company to purchase a special phone used by the hearing impaired.

Duty to accommodate requires the employer to help people with disabilities do their job. Remember, these employees possess the necessary KSAs to do the job but require some help in certain areas. Accommodation may come in the form of special desks for wheelchairs, large computer monitors for the visually impaired, removal of an unimportant task from a job (that the employee with a disability is not able to do), and so forth. Whether an employer needs to accommodate a person with a disability depends on whether it will result in **undue hardship** for the employer. Undue hardship is determined by factors such as cost of the accommodation, financial resources of the organization, number of employees, and effect of the accommodations on the operation of the company.

Irrespective of the legislation, there are nearly 85 million workers in the United States who are potential effective members of the workforce,[100] but only about 35 percent of them are working.[101] This leaves a huge untapped resource of potential talent. Just ask the owner of Habitat International, a supplier of artificial-grass-putting greens, indoor/outdoor carpet, and accent rugs to large retailers such as Home Depot and Meijers. Most of his workforce has some type of disability, yet he pays standard, or slightly above standard market rate for wages. This is not, as he says, because he is altruistic. He has practically no absenteeism or turnover. The defect rate is less than one-half of 1 percent. None of his disabled employees has been involved in an accident at work. The really good news is that his company routinely outperforms the competition two to one, and the profitability continues to grow.[102]

Many forget, before ruling out anyone, to conduct a job analysis to determine exactly what KSAs are needed. If the job analysis indicates that the job of operator requires answering phones and directing calls, someone who is legally blind can be considered. The main accommodation required in this situation is a phone in Braille. Training, however, may also require some changes to accommodate the special needs of someone who is blind. We return to that issue later.

So let us return to Mary, the hearing-impaired accounting clerk. She moved up to the highest level in nonmanagement accounting. Six years later, when she applies for the accounting manager position, she is turned down because she does not possess the requisite KSAs. Frank does demonstrate the required KSAs and gets the job, even though he has worked there three years less. However, Frank got those skills through training courses offered by the company. Mary was never told about those training opportunities. If the skills Mary is lacking were available through training and she was not told, the company failed to provide her with the same opportunities as other employees in the company were offered. This failure puts the company in a vulnerable legal position. Perhaps more important, the organization potentially missed out on a competent supervisor and instead faces an extremely angry accounting clerk.

The Training Dimension   For people with disabilities, accommodation on the job is necessary, and so is accommodation in training. Treating someone with special needs equitably in your training requires preparation. Consider, for example, proper furniture and accessibility to the training facility. The trainer might require additional training to talk to someone who is hearing impaired. Perhaps the organization could provide a certified sign-language interpreter. The best way to deal with this issue is to meet with those who have disabilities and ask them what they need.

Summing Up Training and Equity

Whether it involves not promoting a female to the job of technician, a minority or female to an executive position, or a hearing-impaired person to supervisor, the issue is the same: The organization is losing out on potential. The career and personal development of everyone in the organization needs to be a top priority. Although this point seems intuitive, a recent survey of organizations noted that about one-third provided no mentoring or coaching for employees, and 16 percent did not provide personal or developmental planning.[103] How many of the remaining companies are just "going through the motions" rather than doing it properly is also unknown. It is clear, however, that effort needs to go into helping all employees do their best if a company is going to compete. It makes good economic sense. To be sure that it happens, organizations need to consider the following:

- Obtain support from the top that identifies the importance of the issue of equity for all employees.
- Write clear descriptions of job requirements, and make them the focus of personnel decisions.
- Focus part of every manager's appraisal on the equitable treatment of employees.
- Assemble a steering committee that examines the issue and reports on progress each year.
- Establish a liaison and reporting procedure for dealing with issues of inequity.
- Provide extensive training to managers on issues related to equity at all levels.

Consider the implementation of an equity program as an intervention that will require training and changes in policies and procedures to ensure that the forces pushing in the direction of equity for all are stronger than those pushing against.

Basic Skills Training

Literacy training generally includes training in reading, writing, and basic arithmetic. The functionally illiterate cannot use those skills even at the most basic level (reading instructions, writing a report, balancing a checkbook, etc.). The problem may be getting worse as a result of the following factors:

- Lower standards in many high schools today
- More minorities and non-English-speaking immigrants entering the workforce
- The skill requirements for most jobs are increasing

In the United States, about 20 percent of the workforce is functionally illiterate.[104] This translates into a loss of about $60 billion a year in productivity, as measured by mistakes, accidents, and damage to equipment.[105]

As far back as 1983, a presidential report, *A Nation at Risk,* identified an inferior education system that would make it difficult for the United States to compete in an international marketplace.[106] Organizations find that, even when hiring high school graduates, they need to provide remedial skills training to get them ready for the job. One study indicated that of the new employees classified as requiring training in the basic skills, 67 percent did graduate from high school.[107] In addition to issues within the school system, immigration from non-English-speaking countries continues to increase. So new employees with English as a second language will be more prevalent, making reading and writing in English more problematic.

At the same time as skill levels were dropping, most jobs began to require more skills. A machinist now needs computer skills to operate the computerized machinery, and truck drivers need to understand logistics, inventory control, and flow analysis from the computer in their truck. Even parcel delivery requires data entry into a computer. Furthermore, many organizations are becoming ISO certified, thus requiring a new list of skills for the shop floor. Teamwork, which for years was the purview of management, is now also down on the shop floor, demanding that workers understand charts and know how to interact effectively with others.

It is necessary, then, for organizations to upgrade their employees' skills. Before they can, however, employees need to possess the basics. Just providing the basics can result in a positive financial impact. A survey of workplaces where literacy programs were installed revealed a drop in error rate in employees' work, an improvement in morale, and a general improvement in health and safety.[108] Another positive outcome of such training is the improvement of employees' self-efficacy. Recall the importance of self-efficacy for training. Those with poor literacy skills will likely show a low self-efficacy. Providing employees with these skills will definitely lead to positive effects.

Developing basic skills (or literacy) training is similar to developing any other training program. The first step is a TNA. Here, more than in other TNAs, the need to ensure confidentiality is critical.[109] Workers who are illiterate generally take great pains to hide it out of embarrassment and shame. It might be advisable to use an outside vendor in this case to ensure that few in the organization would know who requires literacy skills training. One company hired a consultant to provide outside assessment over a long period of time, to encourage everyone who thought that they might have a problem to go for assessment outside the workplace.

Outside vendors need not be the answer. Sea World succeeded via internal resources, through the use of company tutors. Trainees are given the option of a noncompany tutor, but most preferred someone from within the company. As with most things, no single way is always best.[110] The key is to keep the training relevant by using material that the employee uses every day. So for reading, use the memos received and typical instructions. This tie-in to actual work makes the success and value immediate. Some tips for improving employees' self-efficacy in literacy training are shown in Table 10-8.

Safety Training

In 2006, the Bureau of Labor Statistics reported 3.9 million job-related injuries.[111] Although this is down slightly from previous years, it is still very high. With all the technology and information available in North America, you might ask, "Why it is so high?" The answer is partly because safety training is often something the organization has to do (by law), rather than something they want to do. These organizations see safety efforts as a cost rather than as an investment. For example, an employee at Nu-Gro died because a forklift had its three safety devices bypassed, so they were not working. Why was this allowed to occur? Well, clearly, safety was not a priority, and likely it was seen as an obstacle to performance.

For many other organizations, a culture of safety is a requirement to be competitive in a global marketplace. In a survey of organizations considered to be on the cutting edge of safety training, it was noted that they developed this "culture of safety" rather than a number of different training courses on safety.[112] In such an organization, safety training is not considered a cost, but an investment. This distinction may seem minor, but it changes the focus by looking at the benefits of safety training—it is viewed as a cost savings—rather than seeing it as forced compliance with health and safety legislation. Evaluating training at the "results" level and identifying the cost savings in fewer accidents, less machine wear, lower compensation costs, and so forth, provide continued support for this proactive approach to safety. An example of this is Schneider Electric, a manufacturer of industrial controls in North America. It recently decided to focus on safety and make safe working habits a "condition of employment." An evaluation of the results

Table 10-8
Tips for Improving Self-Efficacy of Those Requiring Literacy Training

- Assure trainees that they are being asked to upgrade their KSAs because of their importance to the company.
- Do not call it "literacy training" or "basic skills training," as both can sound demeaning. Use a positive name that stresses job training.
- Make participation rewarding, not punishing. Pay them for the time, or conduct it on company time.
- Talk about "improving reading" rather than learning how to read.
- Indicate that the problem is widespread and that many similar employees have successfully completed the training.
- Provide early success stories so trainees can see that they are able to do it.
- Use company-related examples to ensure that the literacy training is not only meaningful, and therefore easier to learn, but also useful right away.

Source: Tyler, K. "Tips for structuring workplace literacy programs." *HR Magazine* 41 (1996), pp. 112–16.

proved enlightening. Medical incidents for its 15,000 employees dropped by 33 percent in one year, translating into a drop in workers' compensation premiums of $1 million.[113]

During years of consulting and training in organizations, we noted that most discussions with employees reveal how boring safety training can be. From what has been presented so far, it is safe to conclude that this impression does not bode well for learning. Valerie Overheul, president of Summit Training Source, suggests several ways to make training interesting.[114] She indicates that in many years of training employees in various safety skills, the one comment consistently made over the years is how interesting employees find the training, which is not like previous safety training. Valerie's recipe for increasing trainee motivation in safety training is to "jazz it up." Get trainees' attention through the use of humor, familiar music, action clips, and dynamic graphics. Be sure that the trainer is upbeat and interested in the topic. In a recent survey of the pulp and paper industry, where safety is a critical component of the job, one of the questions dealt with "obstacles to effective training." Fifty-two percent of the respondents indicated "boredom." The next closest response was scheduling, and only 22 percent indicated that it was an obstacle. These statistics reiterate a common theme in the text: Motivate trainees by making training interesting.

Training Workers from Different Cultures

Increased globalization and new technologies available for training have resulted in more training for more people in more countries. As noted in Chapter 7, there are many types of distance learning methods available to provide organizational training. Consequently, the question arises: Do you simply send North American–style training abroad, or do you need to be sensitive to cultural differences?

Training in North America often contains the following:

- Games, exercises, and role-plays to make it interesting
- A large interactive component that requires trainee participation through questioning and describing their experiences related to the training topic

These two design aspects of North American training can be problematic for some cultures. In Russia, for example, trainees see training as an opportunity to get ahead, and they are already motivated to learn.[115] Maintaining interest is not important, and games are unheard of. In Europe, trainees want the training, not things such as games and exercises that could be seen as a waste of time.[116]

A trainer in Norway noted that trainees were reluctant to become involved in discussions during the training. They preferred a highly structured training atmosphere.[117] In Russia, trainees respond better to self-study, especially if it is structured.[118] Chinese trainees expect a very formal lecture, with little interaction or questioning by trainees.[119]

Earlier in the chapter, we discussed the need for expatriates to understand the culture of the host country and operate effectively within it. To prepare the expatriate for her role in the host country, some type of training is advisable. But, if you've developed training in North America on company practices, interpersonal skills, and so on, do you need to adjust those programs when training employees from different cultures? The answer seems to be yes and no. First, according to Mike Davis, general manager of Oracle Corporation, North American training does have too much of an entertainment component, and toning it down may be beneficial. He says his European clients just want the nuts and bolts of training, not the flash.[120] They are already highly motivated to learn the material. This is particularly true of sales training, where cheerleading and giving prizes to trainees like a game show takes place.

What about involvement? In Asia, Alan Chute, the chief learning strategist for Lucent Technologies, says he asks the senior management for questions. If others have a question, they send it to the senior manager so he can ask it. This ensures that a junior person does not ask a better question than a senior manager.[121]

But, as we have emphasized in this text, involvement by trainees ensures understanding and improves retention. So what to do? It seems that those who do try to include a high level of interaction in their training abroad are successful. In Russia, for example, the discussions are received positively, but they need to be highly structured. Even icebreakers, role-plays, and exercises, which are viewed as taboo, seem to be enjoyed once they are tried, and trainees expect them in the future.[122] In China, questioning of instructors is simply not done. When Chuck Greenwood, from Drake University in Iowa, was teaching students in China, he suggested that they "act[123] like Americans" for the class and ask lots of questions. He found them eager to participate. A trainer from England asked a student in Korea if the training he was attending might not be Americanizing him. He answered: Of course, that is the whole point.[124] It seems that prolonged exposure to trainers who have an interactive style is infectious; given the advantages of the interactive style for adult learning, that is a positive thing.

So it would seem that more entertaining training methods might initially be more difficult to sell abroad. Note, however, that we do not adhere to the idea that entertainment alone is a good thing. We suggest that making training more interesting is a good idea, but it needs to be done in a way that is relevant to the topic. As for the interactive component, given its importance to learning, and given that it seems to be something other cultures can get used to and even enjoy, it should be considered as an important component of any learning. The implementation strategy, however, should be carefully developed to address the cultural issues of the group being trained.

What about training in North America, where organizations have multiple cultures to contend with in their training? Given the information above, it seems that games and interactive methods can be effective across many cultures. To increase acceptance, trainers should consider an orientation to training before those from different cultures attend their first regular training session. This would involve trainees learning the value of the novel training methods for retention and transfer back to the job. From the information above, this acceptance might not be all that difficult to generate.

So what is the conclusion? First, there are many factors to consider when training is developed by one culture and provided to another. Here we have addressed only two important components of North American training. There seems to be an acceptance of exercises that make the training interesting and get trainees involved in interactions with the trainer. But culture still needs to be considered in training those in other countries. In China, because it would be embarrassing to have a junior manager ask a better question than the senior manager, it might make sense to train one level in the organization at a time. Also, providing some type of orientation to training methods that are novel for the culture will increase the level of acceptance.

SUMMARY

This chapter examined in depth five of the more prevalent training practices taking place in organizations today: orientation, diversity, sexual harassment, team, and cross-cultural training. For the orientation, we discuss the importance of it and what organizations are doing. We also provide a hypothetical example, following the training model, to assist readers in understanding how to go about developing orientation training. For the other four training types, we again discuss the importance and what organizations are doing. Then, following the training model, we briefly outline the points to consider in developing such training.

Additional issues and training programs were discussed more generally and briefly. Equity was discussed in relationship to employment and training opportunities; employees are more often selected from within the organization than not. Even when promotions and transfers are based on the person's skills and potential, all employees, regardless of their race, gender, or disability, must be provided access to training and development opportunities. The importance of equitable access in preventing costly litigation is understood, but it is more important in terms of fair treatment and obtaining the best employees in all positions.

The need for highly skilled, continually learning employees requires a solid foundation of basic reading, writing, and arithmetic skills. More and more companies are taking it on themselves to provide these skills. However, employees experiencing functional illiteracy are unlikely to admit it unless organizations take the time to develop and market training that addresses these skills.

Many companies see safety training as a significant cost savings tool. In the past, it was generally presented in an uninteresting manner, leading to poor learning and transfer to the job. If safety training is to achieve its cost avoidance potential, it needs to be designed to arouse the interest of the trainees.

CASE: The Competent Employee (Conclusion)

Recall that Ms. Conner requested that the personnel manager investigate her complaints, and he found no merit to her complaint. As a result, she filed a civil action against SBI based on the treatment she endured. The judgment was in her favor, awarding her more than $500,000 in damages.[125] Clearly, much of this award was based on the hostile environment created by her managers and co-workers. However, consider the costs of simply going to court: time required for managers to get records together, preparations for trial, and legal representation. This potential expense alone is reason enough to motivate organizations to pay attention to such issues and provide appropriate training to see that it does not happen. But even more important are the ethics of fair treatment and the potential loss of a productive employee.

KEY TERMS

- Developmental review
- Diversity training
- Duty to accommodate
- Glass ceiling

- Hostile work environment
- Literacy training
- Orientation training
- Quid pro quo harassment

- Sexual harassment
- Training equity
- Undue hardship

QUESTIONS FOR REVIEW

1. What is an orientation designed to do? What are the characteristics of an effective orientation?
2. How are organizations dealing with diversity? Are the methods effective? Why or why not?
3. What are the important components of an effective sexual harassment strategy?
4. Why is team training necessary? What are the seven components of effective teams? What are some of the KSAs required of team members in effective teams?
5. How can training affect the selection of competent candidates for vacant positions? What would you recommend an organization do to ensure that everyone receives equitable opportunities for promotions?
6. In today's environment, why is it important for organizations to focus on training of basic literacy skills?
7. Why is safety training an important component of the training mix in so many companies? What is the biggest concern regarding safety training that was noted in the survey referenced in the chapter? Is it fixable, and if so how?

1. Over the next week, watch the instructors in the various classes you attend. Jot down notes about any differences you see in terms of how each instructor treats men, women, minorities, or people with disabilities. Share this information with a group, and generate a list of what differences exist and how you would deal with them. If you found no differences, indicate what specific things each instructor does to be sure that everyone in the class is treated equitably.

2. Break into small groups. Have each person think about a current job or one held in the past for which orientation training was provided.

   • If you never held a job that provided orientation training, just think of a job you held. Describe four things that good orientation training would include to make breaking into the job easier. Post these activities on an easel under the heading "Wish they had done."

   • If you went through an orientation training, think about the orientation and list two things that were good about the experience and two things you thought were a waste of time or boring.

   • Post these activities on an easel, with the positive under the heading "Glad they did" and the negative under the heading "Wish they hadn't done."

   • After everyone contributes, discuss how the "Glad they did" and the "Wish they had done" tie into the training model in terms of what you need to do right. Do the same for the "Wish they hadn't done" in terms of what to avoid.

3. Think about your role as a student in this class. Now think about students who are visually impaired, paraplegic, or hearing impaired. What kind(s) of accommodation(s) to the educational facilities (classroom) would need to be made for each to be successful? What changes (if any) should the teacher make to be sure that the person is getting full value of the training/education?

4. Break into small groups to discuss the following situation. The VP of human resources asked you, the director of training, to develop a sexual harassment training program for the company. During your needs analysis, you discover that most of the executives do not believe that they need this training and do not plan to attend. You identify a couple of instances in which an executive's behavior seems bordering on sexual harassment. You discuss your findings with the VP, who asks you to come back with a strategy for dealing with the resistance to training. Develop your response, and be prepared to present it to the rest of the class.

CASE ANALYSIS

ALL IT TAKES IS FOR GOOD MEN TO DO NOTHING

In 1987, Ms. Dillman was hired by IMP to work in Hangar 3 at North American International Airport as a seamstress in their fabric shop. After six months, the workload dropped, so Ms. Dillman approached her supervisor and asked for additional responsibilities. He sent her to the sheet metal shop. A number of months passed, and she approached the supervisor and asked if her classification could be changed from fabric worker to sheet metal technician; he complied.

At 20 years of age, she was the only woman out of about 100 employees working in Hangar 3. She often received special attention in terms of help and guidance, which she indicated she appreciated. But it was a male-dominated environment, and the language was crude and vulgar. Having pictures of naked women in the locker room was prohibited, but such pictures were posted and little was done about it. There was also evidence that in apprenticeship programs, men received extensive training, whereas women in the same programs received minimal training.

Mr. Pettipas was a long-time employee at IMP. In 1989, Ms. Dillman was assigned to work for him, and he was to provide her with on-the-job training. The first problem arose when Ms. Dillman made a mistake. Mr. Pettipas erupted in a torrent of verbal abuse directed at her. No one had ever heard him act so inappropriately. The incident caused Ms. Dillman to ask if she could be reassigned; the request was granted. When Mr. Pettipas was working in other hangars, things went fine. But when Mr. Pettipas was in her vicinity, he always made snide comments and insinuations. On one occasion, he screamed at her, calling her a tramp and troublemaker. He said she was not welcome in the workplace. Whenever he went by her, he would say something derogatory. By 1990, everyone in Hangar 3 knew of the situation between the two employees.

In late 1990, a series of meetings between Pettipas, Dillman, a company representative, and a union representative were held in an attempt to defuse the situation. But Mr. Pettipas refused to admit that he had done anything wrong. The union representative and manager involved agreed that a warning letter would be placed in Mr. Pettipas's file relating to his treatment of Ms. Dillman, and it would remain there for two years. In response, Mr. Pettipas went to see Mr. Rowe, the president and CEO of IMP, and convinced him to remove the letter. Mr. Pettipas then went around the hanger bragging to everyone that he had won.

All this had a devastating effect on Ms. Dillman, and in early May of 1991, she went on long-term disability for a few months. When she returned, she met with the HR manager to discuss the difficulty with Mr. Pettipas. He suggested that she take more time off, which she did.

In January of 1992, Ms. Dillman was transferred to another hangar, where she was involved with airframe construction. In the nine months she was there, the supervisor often complimented her on the quality of her work. None of her work was ever rejected. Then she received word that she was being transferred back to Hangar 3. Even though her own supervisor had nothing but praise for her work, the director of aircraft maintenance had given the order because "her work was not up to standard." When she questioned the director, he gave no specifics. When she indicated the problem regarding going back to Hangar 3, he promised to look into it. Nothing happened and she was sent back to Hangar 3.

She filed a complaint with the Nova Scotia Human Rights Commission. As a result of the commission's findings, IMP had to pay Ms. Dillman about $30,000. IMP was also ordered to provide training to all employees, on company time.

CASE QUESTIONS

Answer the following questions, assuming you have been contacted to provide this training.

1. Would a TNA be needed in this situation? Why or why not? If yes, who would you want to talk to?
2. Based on the case as presented above, what KSAs need to be trained?
3. Why has the commission insisted on training for the whole company when the problem is clearly only Mr. Pettipas? Elaborate.
4. For the training to be effective, what other things do you think need attention?
5. What would you suggest in the way of evaluation of the training? How would you convince top management that it would be worth it?

Source: I.M.P. Group Ltd. v. Dillman (1994), 24 C.H.R.R. D/322 (N.S. Bd.Inq.).

Chapter 11

Employee and Management Development

Learning Objectives

After reading this chapter, you should be able to:

➤ List the reasons why employee development is important in today's environment

➤ Describe the steps and process for setting up an employee development plan

➤ Describe who is responsible for an employee's development and what that individual should do

➤ Identify and describe the roles and responsibilities of managers at different levels in the organization

➤ Describe the general competencies and characteristics of effective managers

➤ List the important organizational factors that determine which managerial characteristics are desirable at a given time and situation

➤ Explain how management training needs are influenced by changes in organizational strategy

➤ Identify the various sources and types of training related to management development

➤ Identify the specific problems associated with training executives and some of the methods that can be used to deal with these problems

➤ Describe why development of executives is so critical to effective organizational functioning

CASE: *Linda Wachner Takes the Reins at Warnaco*

In 1986, Linda Wachner took over as CEO of Warnaco, a manufacturer of women's lingerie, which was experiencing financial difficulty. Wachner's goal was to take the company public and ensure its profitability in a hostile, competitive market and fairly stagnant economy. She knew that radical changes were needed to restore the company to competitiveness. Wachner took the company public, the stock rose 75 percent above its initial offering, the debt was cut by 40 percent, sales increased by 30 percent, earnings before taxes increased by 140 percent, and operating cash flow almost doubled. Wachner pursued an unrelenting focus on the company's performance, which was closely tied to her personal financial situation because she owned 10 percent of the stock.

As the only female CEO of a *Fortune* 500 company at the time, her leadership was subject to careful scrutiny. Wachner combined energy, drive, and enthusiasm with hard-core fiscal management. She maintained a focus on the customer and had high demands for her employees. Her employees viewed her as a tough boss, and they often felt that she expected too much. Although her "do it now" philosophy focused on responding to customer preferences in the short and long run, she also managed to reap considerable savings from cost cutting. For example, she reduced the corporate staff from 200 to 7. Some said that Wachner did not do a good job of managing people because of her single-minded focus on company profitability. She was unrelenting in getting to the point and requiring her colleagues to do the same.

"Have I yelled at meetings? No question. Do I think I've ever hurt anybody? I hope not. Look, I just want people to be good and I put enormous pressure on everyone to get this company moving in the right direction," she said. "I know I push very hard, but I do not push anybody harder than I push myself."

At the same time, she motivated her workers with praise for their work. She visited the stitch room almost daily, picking up and examining the fabric, lace, and trim the stitchers were working on, often commenting, "These are to die for." Maintaining the grueling schedule may have been difficult for employees, but Wachner emphasized creating an environment to which employees bring a high energy level and a focus on a common goal. Her determination created a hard-as-nails image, but it's a style that got the job done.

EMPLOYEE DEVELOPMENT

In the past, many employees stayed with the same organization for decades.[1] Development of employees in those days focused on a chosen few and was designed to help those chosen employees move up in the hierarchy. Of those chosen, many were promoted one or two levels and remained there until they retired. Management was not actively attempting to develop all its employees, but only those it took special interest in.

This has changed dramatically. In today's economy, employees have less loyalty to an organization and are quite willing to move to another organization to advance their careers. Some suggest that people expect to work for at least eightcompanies in their lifetime.[2] On top of that, there is a shortage of skilled workers in the labor pool. At the same time, skilled employees are becoming ever more important in the quest for high-quality goods and services in a competitive marketplace. Therefore, to attract and retain high-quality employees, successful organizations have taken the development of all employees more seriously.[3] Providing employees with opportunities to enhance their skills and develop their potential has replaced the traditional reward of promotion. Most employees respond positively to this opportunity.[4] But, that is not the only reason organizations are interested in employee development. To be effective, organizations need to become more flexible. Having employees who are able to do more than just one job on a moment's notice provides flexibility.[5] This involves a form of employee development called **cross training** (training on more than one job). Those who have developed their workforce through cross training have reaped the rewards. Consider Celestica, an IBM subsidiary, that achieved improvements in productivity, quality and lowered costs after introducing cross training.[6] RailCorp also boasts that cross training has led to a flexible workforce and improvements in output, defects, and downtime by as much as 40 percent.[7]

But, what is in it for the employee? Developing new skills is not likely to lead to a promotion, because current economic conditions, downsizing, mergers and acquisitions, and the resulting flatter organizations have made promotions less likely. As previously mentioned, most employees expect to move to a different organization a number of times in their career. By continuously upgrading their skills and by learning new ones, they will be much more marketable if they decide that they wish to move and more desirable to their present organization if they decide to stay.

When a company decides that it needs to reduce its workforce, those who are more flexible in what they can do are more valuable and hence likely to be retained. Some companies take this idea of flexibility very seriously. Harmon International Industries, for example, has an aggressive cross-training program. Employees have the opportunity to job rotate into as many jobs as possible. Therefore, if there is a downturn in one aspect of the company, they can move to another job. This program allows the company to provide its employees with job security, hence lower voluntary turnover and more committed, productive workers.[8]

Therefore, given the importance of employee development to the organization, the question is: How does an organization set up an effective development plan for its employees? The answer should not surprise you. It uses the training model that we have provided in the previous chapters. A few of the different types of development are discussed in the following section. However, no matter which type of development is being undertaken, the training process model is still a useful tool to use.

First, let's look at traditional employee development, which is focused on improving an employee's performance in the job they are currently in and helping them prepare for future jobs/goals they may have.

Development in the Current Job

It is in both the employees' and their supervisor's best interest if employees are performing at their best. Such development is critical to an effective organization. In this situation, an employee's development begins with a training needs analysis (TNA).

Training Needs Analysis

As noted in Chapter 4, the TNA can come from the traditional performance review. However, it is more meaningful if this performance review is focused only on development* and the organization has a culture of fostering the development of its employees.[9] While traditional performance measures are useful, perhaps more relevant to a developmental TNA are self-ratings and 360-degree feedback (360-DF, see Chapter 4). It is in the best interest of the employee to be as honest as possible when self-assessing, as the purpose of the process is to improve her performance and help her develop more skills. The 360-DF is also a useful tool for assessing needs in areas such as interpersonal communication, teamwork, and the like, where an employee is usually not aware of deficiencies.

---

*When the assessment focuses on pay raises or other administrative issues as well as development, it tends to distract from the developmental aspect.

An important part of this developmental process is the offer to help the employee develop skills for the future (personal development), not just for his present job. By dealing with these personal needs, the supervisor demonstrates concern for the employee, which should translate to an employee who is willing to meet the supervisor's needs to keep productivity at a high level. Not only that, but also those newly learned skills will quite likely be useful in the present job, or make the employee more valuable and flexible in the organization. Consider the production employee who is interested in taking courses to become a better listener. For a production line worker, being an effective listener is likely not in the job description. However, those skills, once learned, could make that employee more effective in many aspects of the job and able to perform additional duties related to the job (e.g., serve as an on-the-job training [OJT] trainer).

Design

Recall that one of the inputs to the design of training is constraints. A main constraint for employee development is that many aspects will be individually focused, especially when it comes to the employee's personal growth (not related to the specific job).

Training objectives are particularly valuable in employee development as they are not only useful for choosing the most relevant training, but also useful for providing goals for the employee. Recall the value of goal setting in the employee's success. One of the outputs is considering the alternative modes of instruction. Here, an issue is the individuality of the training. Some online training, coaching, and specific courses offered by institutions (universities or trade schools) may all be possibilities.

Development/Implementation

Since the type of training in the employee's development plan would be individualized based on the employee's needs and aspirations, the supervisor (with the help of HR*) needs to identify sources of training that might address the employee's needs. The main focus in this phase of the model would be on determining the value of various programs for meeting the employee's needs. In addition, the supervisor must make sure that the employee is given opportunities to obtain that training. Once again it is critical that the employee not only obtains the training to make him a more effective employee in his current job, but also provide the training to meet his personal growth needs.

Evaluation

It is important that the employee is satisfied with the training he receives from the development plan. Therefore, a process should be in place, so both the supervisor (and trainer) are aware of how the employee is reacting as he engages in and completes each aspect of the training. Equally important is the learning and transfer that occur as a result of the training. Any selected training programs should provide an assessment of the employee's knowledge, skills, and attitudes (KSAs) related to the program content. As for transfer to the job, the supervisor should track the employee's improvements and provide feedback. It may be necessary to provide "stretch" assignments for the employee, so he is able to demonstrate the ability to apply the KSAs in a meaningful situation.

Summing Up

This is the most typical type of development, albeit often not carried out very well. Care must be taken to not just focus on the specific job and ignore the employee's personal needs. Remember, the goal of development is to provide value to both the employees and the company. You want the employee's interest, motivation, and desire to perform at a high level. This is not likely if you ignore his needs. Furthermore,

---

*In fact, once the supervisor and employee have identified the training objectives/goals, HR may take over to help the employee determine the best course of action given what is available.

helping employees focus on their personal development can lead to employees thinking in different ways about what they have to offer.[10] Consider the line worker who is interested in improving her communication skills. After becoming proficient you suddenly have someone who can peer coach or train.

Job Rotation

Job rotation is a popular method of developing employee skills, and it can provide employees with a look at alternative career paths, as well as reduce boredom.[11] It requires the employee to be trained on one or more jobs other than his own. It has been suggested that job rotation keeps employees fresh, energized, and contributing.[12] Others have noted that when someone starts a new job in the rotation they bring fresh eyes on some of the problems that exist, and these fresh eyes come up with new ideas.[13]

But, let's look at job rotation as a means of development. Here, the goal is to make the employees more flexible in what they are capable of doing. This certainly benefits the company, in that the person is able to take more positions in case of an emergency, but it also benefits the employee because she is more valuable, meaning less likely to be laid off in a downturn.[14]

Training Needs Analysis

As job rotation puts someone in a job within the organization, there should be some documentation as to the job requirements (expected performance). If these are not comprehensive enough, then an operational analysis needs to be conducted to determine the KSAs required. The employee and supervisor can then work together to identify the employee's KSA deficiencies related to the job (potential actual performance).

An alternative way of assessing the competencies of the employee for the new job is to put the employee into the job and monitor her performance.[15] Having a supervisor or experienced peer watch the new employee and identify the areas where she is deficient is a form of TNA (expected performance—actual performance). The supervisor or experienced peer knows what is required for the job (expected performance) and through observation of the employee on the job can determine what the actual performance is. Interviewing the employee periodically as the process unfolds should provide you with additional insights as well as factors that inhibit performance (organizational analysis).

Design

A constraint for this training is that the number of employees requiring training is very low (often only one). The objectives in this case are based on what the employee needs to learn to be effective in this new job, based on the TNA. These objectives should be developed in conjunction with goals the supervisor and subordinate develop for the employee. The objectives for training and goals for the employee will be very similar, although the wording is likely to be different. From the objectives, and with consideration of the constraints noted earlier, the method of training will likely be OJT. However, this might be similar to apprenticeship training in which online learning, workshops, universities, and trade schools all offer possible supplemental knowledge and skill training, depending on the nature of the needs identified.

Development/Implementation

The issues related to the development of an OJT program were discussed in depth in Chapter 6. A few key things to keep in mind are discussed in the following paragraphs.

Development of OJT requires preparation just like any type of training. Those assigned to do the training need to have some trainer skills and understand the process of training. A method such as the Job Instructional Technique should be used, and the employee/supervisor doing the training needs to be familiar with that process.

In the implementation, it is very important that whoever is doing the OJT has been given the time to do it properly. If an employee has been assigned to do it, for example, he should not be expected to be as productive during the training process as he is at other times. The training he is doing must be considered an important part of his job.

Evaluation

Given that OJT training seldom has a real trainer, reactions to the trainer are particularly important. These reactions need to be assessed early in the program, perhaps after a few days, to address any trainer/trainee issues early on. The employee's overall reaction to the OJT experience can be assessed either in a discussion with the supervisor or by completing a reaction questionnaire at some point after the training is complete. Knowledge can be assessed through any of the methods identified in Chapter 9, but should be apparent in the employee's performance throughout the OJT program. The same is true for skills and attitudes. For OJT, transfer is built into the program as the person is actually doing the job. Periodic performance reviews should be conducted during the program. If done properly, the goals that were set during the objective setting would have a time frame for when the employee expects to be proficient (meeting her goals). Organizational results will depend on the reason for the job rotation training in the first place. If it is an organizational goal to become more flexible, then monitoring the ability to move employees to different jobs quickly would be an organizational result. If one of the goals was to reduce turnover by offering employees variety in jobs, then turnover would be the organizational result.

Summing It Up

As noted, job rotation has a number of advantages for both the employer and employee. There is evidence of reduced injuries related to repetitive strain and higher productivity.[16] There is also evidence that it can lead to an energized workforce; new tasks will encourage a new enthusiasm in employees. There may also be greater creativity. When employees assume new responsibilities, their minds are open to the opportunities within their tasks.[17] But to be successful, it must be approached as a developmental tool, keeping the employees' needs in mind. Furthermore, you need to follow the training process model if you want the job rotation process to be successful.

How useful is job rotation for production workers? Well, for a large North American auto manufacturer, it alleviates production workers' boredom, helps prevent repetitive strain injuries, and makes the organization more flexible. But, how important is it to the employee? See Training in Action 11-1 for the answer.

Special Assignments

Providing employees with the opportunity to take on **special assignments** can be an effective way to help them develop. It is also a way to keep them motivated and willing to remain in the organization.[18] Learning new things and being part of a hot issue (special assignment) will make the employee feel useful and part of something important. Once again, the process for development is provided in the training model.

TNA/Design

As stated earlier, the areas where an employee needs to develop should be identified in a developmental review session. These needs would be those that were agreed on by the supervisor and employee. Once these needs are identified, objectives (and corresponding goals for the employee) can be developed.

As with the other types of development, a constraint is that the required training may only be needed for one person. This will influence the type of training opportunities that are available. When this is the case, a useful approach is to put the person

TRAINING IN ACTION 11-1
Job Rotation Helps Everyone

A large North American manufacturer has a few thousand production line workers. Downtime on the line (for whatever reason) is expensive, so it is critical to keep the lines running. One of the ways to keep downtime to a minimum is to have employees cross-trained. That way, if, for any reason, employees cannot perform their duties, they can be quickly and easily replaced. This organization accomplishes this by having a comprehensive job rotation process in place. The production line workers rotate to four or more different jobs on a regular basis. That means there are always workers who are trained on more than one position on the line and able to take over if necessary.

But, what about the workers? Are they in favor of such a program? They should be, as job rotation helps deal with the boredom of a repetitive job. It also reduces the likelihood of physical trauma due to repetitive motion—an advantage to both the company and employees. Furthermore, it provides the workers with more skills, making them more valuable and marketable.

This might all be true, but what do these workers really think? When asked how important job rotation was to them, 43 percent said it was of the utmost importance and 38 percent said very important. Combined, that is 81 percent saying it was very important or better. Only six percent said of no importance. Clearly job rotation at this plant is a win-win situation.

on an already existing or newly created task force that requires the KSAs that the employee needs to develop. This has the advantage of giving her access to those who already have the desired KSAs. Alternatively, the supervisor could create a special assignment that will lead to her acquisition of the KSAs.

It is usually desirable to have the employee partake in some prerequisite learning that prepares her to engage in the assignment.

Ways of acquiring prerequisite KSAs might be to have the employee attend a training program currently offered by the company or to attend one offered through an outside vendor. A more likely choice would be to complete an e-learning course(s). There are likely to be many immediately available programs available through the Internet that can assist in meeting some of the knowledge objectives and perhaps even some of the skill objectives that are needed for the person to be ready for the special assignment. In some cases, the learning can take place concurrently with the assignment, depending on the type of needs and situation (task force is being set up immediately, special project needs to be started ASAP).

Development/Implementation

The task force or special assignment needs to be chosen carefully to ensure that the employee is able to achieve her development objectives. The supervisor also needs to monitor the employee's progress to ensure that the employee is getting the developmental aspect of the assignment. With a special assignment, the supervisor can serve as a mentor, providing some of the KSAs and directing the employee in how to develop others. If it is a task force that is being used for development, then the leader of that task force can assist in monitoring the progress of the employee. In consultation with the supervisor, the task force leader can also make sure that the employee is exposed to areas that she is expected to learn and provide her with help (coaching) where necessary.

Evaluation

Again, the reaction of the employee to the development experience is important. As with the other developmental approaches, the supervisor needs to assess reactions early and then periodically throughout the assignment. Evaluation of the KSAs and transfer of these to the job are important for determining the success of the developmental experience. Ways of assessing these are covered in depth in Chapter 9.

Summing It Up

Special assignments can last for months, or in the case of a task force, as long as the task force is in existence. It is important, once completed, that an evaluation takes place to determine how successful it was. Part of that evaluation would be determining how much the employee has learned and providing her with appropriate feedback.

The above-mentioned methods of development are not meant to be inclusive. There are many other methods available such as coaching (discussed below), shadowing, action learning, and so forth. The point is that whatever method is used the process is the same; use the training model.

Employee Development: Whose Responsibility Is It?

Responsibility for an employee's development goes beyond just the employee. The organization needs to reflect a culture of fostering employee development. Human resources (HR) is responsible for developing and maintaining the systems and practices that allow that culture to flourish. Supervisors are responsible for implementing the employee development systems and practices.

The Organization

For most companies, it is important that the organization reflect the importance of employees' development in everything they do. Top management must be supportive and help their subordinates develop. This type of support is reflected by the comments of Mr. Matsushita, founder of Matsushita Electronics. Matsushita Electronics produces products under the brand names of Panasonic, Technics, and Quasar. In 1978, Mr. Matsushita said

> When my company was still small I often told my employees that when customers asked, "What does your company make?" they should answer, "Matsushita Electronics is making men. We also make electrical appliances, but first and foremost our company makes men."[19]

Although Mr. Matsushita today employs many women, in his early days when his company was small, he only had male employees. The main point here is the importance he places on employee development. Support from the CEO leads to the waterfall effect. When the top boss supports the development of her direct reports and publicly describes its importance to the company, these people will in turn do the same with their subordinates, and so on. If developing employees to their fullest potential is not seen as a priority by upper management, then some managers might do it, but there will be many who will not. Therefore, make development a priority and have it as an important piece of the manager's own appraisal. Of course, this requires that the manager is not spread so thin with other work that she does not have time to conduct developmental assessments and help her employees progress.

Support systems can also be used to aid development. A Human Resource Information System (HRIS), for example, is useful for tracking employee development. Other organizational systems that are supportive of employee development include succession planning processes (where appropriate) and a reward system that recognizes increased employee competencies and value to the organization. All of these support a culture of employee development, reflecting the words of Mr. Matsushita.

Human Resources

The HR department is responsible for developing and maintaining the employee development systems and practices. These include the traditional things such as maintaining an up-to-date index of training programs available to employees (in-house, vendors, higher education, and trade schools), providing employees access to those programs, maintaining an up-to-date HRIS, and providing support to supervisors. Such support would include giving them training in areas related to employee development such as creating development plans, coaching employees, appraising performance, and so on.

In addition, the HR unit can assist in conducting TNAs, providing systems and methods for completing TNAs (assessment centers, testing, etc.) as well as training in how to conduct an effective TNA. An excellent model for the HR unit is British Petroleum Exploration. They provide employees with a personal development planning guidebook.[20] This guidebook provides a step-by-step process that helps the employee through the assessment of needs, goal setting, development planning, and action planning phases.

Immediate Supervisor

The importance of an immediate supervisor in the development of employees cannot be overstated. A survey of more than 500 engineers indicated that the key to improving the performance of technical employees is to improve the quality of the interaction between supervisors and subordinates. This can be accomplished through increased performance feedback and special job assignments, both developmental processes we have discussed.[21] Retaining other highly skilled workers can also be accomplished through the supervisors' behavior. According to Marcia Zidle, consultant with Change & Innovations, to retain highly skilled employees, supervisors should support training and development, provide special assignments, and rotate jobs and responsibilities.[22] Sound familiar?

The supervisor's position is the place where the organizational culture and HR systems and practices are put into action. Without proper implementation by the supervisor, employee development will not be successful. Beyond the role of assisting in the creation of the development plan and identifying programs where development objectives can be met, supervisors often have a direct role in the development of their employees. As discussed previously, supervisors can sometimes serve as the OJT trainer. Often, they are placed in the role of coach or mentor. We discuss these roles in more depth later. Supervisors are a cornerstone in the bridge to employee development. Keeping track of subordinates' interests and helping them fulfill their goals and aspirations will go far in retaining employees and keeping them productive.

Employee

Ultimately, of course, the responsibility for an employee's development rests with the employee. If the culture of the organization is supportive of developmental practices and the supervisor and HR are doing their jobs, development should progress reasonably well. In such cases, the employee is only required to be honest in the assessment process and motivated to develop and acquire new skills. However, that is the ideal and is often not the case. Sometimes, the employee needs to take the initiative for her own development. In such circumstances, she must

- be highly motivated and work at being an effective performer;
- ask for feedback on how she is doing in the job;
- ask for special assignments and/or training to develop specific competencies where she is weak;
- network with others from different departments, letting them know her interests;
- take on extra work, especially when it will provide a challenge and stretch her capabilities;
- let it be known that she is interested in developing herself to the fullest.

Doing these things should provide the employee with developmental opportunities, which she will need in order to become the best she can be.

Management Development?

The previous section refers to all employees. Development of both management and nonmanagement employees is necessary in today's environment if an organization is to be a success. The process for that development is the same for both.

But, we still feel it necessary to have a section on management development. Why is that? Do the processes and techniques already presented not apply to them? The answer is, of course, they do. However, several reasons prompt us to examine this part of the organizational community in more detail. Perhaps foremost is how important management development is in today's environment. Evidence indicates that companies that align their management development with their strategic planning are generally more competitive.[23] Therefore, we need to thoroughly understand such an important part of organizational competitiveness. Other related reasons include the following:

- Managers get a lot of training.
- Managers are accountable for success.
- Managers have complex jobs.

Managers Get a Lot of Training

One of the most frequent types of training provided by companies over the last several years is management development and executive leadership.[24] This is true across every industry from financial and banking institutions to manufacturing, communications, and utilities. For companies of all sizes, approximately 37 percent of all training budgets go toward management and executive training. Management training becomes slightly more important as the organization increases in size. Eighty-eight percent of firms report management development programs, compared with 90 percent that provide executive leadership training.[25] Thus, whether large or small, and regardless of the industry, management training is seen as a vital part of improving organizational performance. A training professional needs to understand a part of the business that is in such demand.

Managers Are Accountable for Success

Managers carry a different and more complex burden for ensuring the success of the enterprise than do nonmanagers. Think back to the opening case. How much responsibility does Ms. Wachner assume for the success of Warnaco relative to other employees? The business environment over the next decade is expected to place even more demands on management. Consider the following responsibilities of the manager of the new millennium:[26]

- Managers face a shrinking labor pool in terms of the skilled and educated. It is management's responsibility to grow and keep the talent necessary to be competitive.
- At the same time, more technologically sophisticated systems are being implemented, and management is responsible for ensuring that employees obtain the knowledge and skills required to perform their jobs.
- Managers must also deal with a more diverse workforce, see that diversity as strength, and not allow it to become a focus of divisiveness.
- Mergers, acquisitions, downsizing, and fast-paced changes must all be managed effectively.

In fact, it is management's responsibility to ensure that all systems and resources are integrated properly so the organization can achieve its objectives. No wonder companies place a high priority on developing the KSAs of their managers.

Managers Have Complex Jobs

Perhaps the most important reason to closely examine management development lies in the nature of managerial effectiveness. It is harder and more complex to ascertain what makes a manager effective than it is for most other targets of training and development. Thus, it is more difficult to assess needs, develop training content and methods, and, most certainly, to evaluate the effects of training. Was Ms. Wachner a good manager at Warnaco? What criteria would be used to decide this? Would everyone agree with those criteria?

Effective training requires an understanding of the employees' training needs before a training program can be designed. For management development, this is not easy. Typically, a manager's effectiveness is determined by how well her unit meets its objectives. However, determining her training needs from the performance of the unit is problematic. A complex alignment of many factors influences the unit's performance, and the manager can affect these factors in many ways. For example, Ms. Wachner's organization is successful. Would she be just as successful in a different company in a different industry? To understand a manager's development needs, first we must understand the context in which the manager and the unit operate. This context includes the strategic direction of the organization, the technology of the manager's unit, the human and financial resources available to the unit, and the unit's relationship to the rest of the organization.

Information about the context in which the manager must operate is collected from an organizational analysis, as discussed in Chapter 4. The operational analysis, also discussed in Chapter 4, identifies the managerial competencies required to create the appropriate match between the organization's strategy and the unit's structure, resources, and technology, so that the unit can achieve its objectives. To identify the manager's developmental needs, her KSAs and behavioral styles are compared with the competencies required for the job. The job in this case is the management position in a particular unit. Determining all these factors is difficult enough, but it becomes even more difficult when we realize how many different ways a manager might go about achieving the unit's objectives. Just identifying a manager's developmental needs is a complex task filled with ambiguities. Identifying or developing a training program to meet those needs is just as difficult and ambiguous.

OUR APPROACH TO MANAGEMENT DEVELOPMENT

An appropriate needs analysis can take place only when the managerial process is understood. This understanding is also required for the trainer to select the instructional strategy that will best meet the manager's developmental needs. Although we identify some sources from which training programs can be acquired or developed, they are not the focus of this chapter. Thousands of programs are available, and new management development programs are developed frequently as older ones fall out of favor—and then many years later suddenly reemerge as a "favored" approach. Instead, the focus of this chapter is on increasing your ability to determine management development needs. Our philosophy is that the educated consumer makes wiser choices. Understanding the match required between managers and their organizational context provides the following two long-lasting benefits to the training professional:

1. An increased ability to determine a manager's development needs
2. An increased ability to assess accurately whether a particular training program meets those needs

Thus, we provide an integrated framework (a model) for assessing managerial behavior within the organizational context. Again, doing so takes a systems perspective with which we look at the manager within both the unit and the organization.

GENERAL OVERVIEW OF THE MANAGERIAL JOB

A well-established principle of management holds that the effectiveness of a particular managerial style is contingent on other organizational variables.[27] That is, a successful managerial approach in one situation can be unsuccessful in another. How, then, can general statements be made about managerial duties and responsibilities across industries? Actually, no real contradiction arises here. The general activities carried out by managers seem to show more similarities than differences.[28] However, the frequency, relative importance, and manner in which these behaviors are performed differ greatly between organizations, even within the same industry. The first task is to understand the general makeup of the managerial job. With that understanding, we can turn our attention to some of the contextual factors that determine the frequency and style in which these activities are performed.

Managerial Roles

Research on managerial activity is integrated into general roles that are "customized" to fit into a particular management position in a particular organization.[29] Figure 11-1 illustrates the relationships among these roles, forming an integrated whole in which each role affects the others. One implication of this model is that managers must not only demonstrate the KSAs required to perform each role, but also the KSAs required for their integration. Although individual managers may give more or less importance to a particular role, eliminating or neglecting one role has consequences for performing other roles, and, therefore, on managerial effectiveness.

Mintzberg defines a manager as anyone who is in charge of an organization or one of its subunits. The manager's roles derive directly or indirectly from the formal authority and status granted to the position. The nature of the activities required of each role is described in Table 11-1.

Managers operate in a dynamic internal environment where they must act constantly to meet the challenges of new circumstances. Managers must not only adapt to new circumstances themselves, but also must coordinate their actions with other units that are also adapting. Typically, little time is available for careful planning and reflection.

Managers must have the knowledge and skills necessary to meet these challenges as soon as they arise. This is not to say that careful planning and reflective analysis are not important in organizations. Managers, however, often cannot take much time for

Figure 11-1
Mintzberg's
Managerial Roles

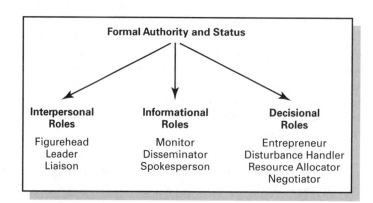

Table 11-1
Description of
Managerial Roles

ROLES	ACTIVITIES
Interpersonal	
Figurehead	Meets the routine, obligatory, social, and legal duties required of the head of a unit (e.g., attendance at social functions, meeting with politicians, buyers, or suppliers).
Leader	Maintains, develops, and motivates the human resources necessary to meet the needs of the unit.
Liaison	Develops and maintains a network of individuals outside the unit to acquire information and action of benefit to the unit.
Informational	
Monitor	Searches for and acquires information about the unit and its environment, so the manager becomes an information center for the unit and the organization; derives from liaison and leader roles.
Disseminator	Distributes selected information to others within the unit or organization; some of which is transformed through integration with other information.
Spokesperson	Distributes selected information to others outside the unit regarding plans, values, activities, and other elements of the unit and conveys the appropriate image of the unit.
Decisional	
Entrepreneur	Adjusts and proactively develops the unit to take advantage of the existing opportunities or meet anticipated threats in the environment; acts on the basis of inferences and conclusions drawn from the evaluation and integration of information gathered in the monitor role.
Disturbance handler	Reacts to meet the immediate demands of the unit (e.g., a wildcat strike, loss of a major customer).
Resource allocator	Evaluates and chooses among proposals; integrates and authorizes activities and resource utilization.
Negotiator	Bargains to acquire the resources to meet the needs of the unit and organization.

this important activity. For that reason, many organizations maintain staff units whose job is to provide the manager with recommendations based on careful planning and thoughtful reflection. A typical manager, however, must diagnose a situation quickly, develop an appropriate response, see that it is implemented, and move on to the next task. This process requires that the manager understand the organization, its strategies, and capabilities; how his unit fits into the puzzle; and how his behavior will influence events. The next section addresses many of these issues.

Organizational Factors

Managerial context refers to the alignment of an organization's environment, strategy, structure, and technology, as described in Chapter 2. These factors play a significant role in determining which managerial KSAs are necessary. Although many of the KSA requirements might be the same across organizations, different organizational contexts will require the KSAs to be used more or less frequently and in varying manners (or styles). The organizational analysis portion of a managerial needs analysis should carefully consider the factors discussed here and their relation to managerial requirements.

Integrating Strategy, Structure, and Technology

Organizations seek to maximize the integration of strategy, technology, structure, and HR through their design. Managers must monitor and manage these interactions within their unit to ensure that their unit's activities are integrated with the strategic direction and technological base of the organization. This integration is depicted in Table 11-2.

Table 11-2
Strategy,
Technology, and
Structure
Integration

	MARKET LEADER	COST LEADER
Technology	Nonroutine	Routine
Structure		
Design	Organic	Mechanistic
Decision making	Decentralized	Centralized

As discussed in Chapter 2, the market leader organization will be subject to a more uncertain environment and thus require more nonroutine technologies. Rapid changes in technology create high levels of complexity in market leader organizations. As a result, less job specialization, more coordination, and more decentralized decision making are the strategies. Conversely, recall from Chapter 2 that the cost leader strategy is more effective in environments with greater certainty. This type of strategy calls for more routinized technology, more centralized decision making, and reduced organizational complexity. These various strategies have direct implications for the skills, traits, and styles of managers within these different organizations.

Whereas a corporation or strategic business unit faces an array of environmental forces, the individual subunit will face only a portion of those forces directly and must respond appropriately to these direct forces. Even though the subunits must support the organization's strategy, effective management practice for a subunit varies according to its own environment and its role in the overall strategy. However, on a general level, the environment of the subunits tends to reflect the organization's strategic environment.

GENERAL CHARACTERISTICS OF MANAGERS

In the discussion of needs assessment in Chapter 4, we noted that an employee's duties and responsibilities must be understood to determine the KSAs required to perform those tasks. Unfortunately, much of the management development literature suggests that evidence of managerial effectiveness in one organization can be applied to other organizations. Whether this application is possible depends on the similarity of the organizational context. Remember our caution about copying other organizations without understanding the theory behind their practice. Nevertheless, the literature does identify many managerial characteristics that seem to be necessary for most managers.

The characteristics we discuss below are, like managerial roles, general in nature and thought to be applicable across most organizations. Later, we provide a model that can be used to integrate these general characteristics into various organizational contexts. As we review the empirical literature on managerial characteristics that are predictive of success, remember that the criteria used to determine "effectiveness" or "success" differ considerably across studies. However, some aspect of effectiveness or success is associated with these characteristics. Certainly, the frequency with which they are reported in the literature gives support to their organizational utility in certain contexts.

Management Styles

Several management theories attempt to demonstrate the relationship between managerial behavior and the situation in which that behavior occurs.[30] Although we will not explore each of these theories, there is a common thread running through most of them. **Managerial style** seems to be related to two dimensions of leader behavior: employee-oriented and task-oriented behaviors.[31] Research on path-goal theory further differentiates these two styles. The **employee-oriented style** has two types: participative and supportive. The **task-oriented style** also has two types: directive and achievement-oriented.[32]

Employee-oriented styles require higher levels of interpersonal skills (discussed in the next section). The **participative style** emphasizes involving subordinates in decision making, particularly in how they go about achieving their task. A **supportive style** is characterized by friendliness, empathy, and concern for meeting employees' needs.

Task-oriented styles require fewer human and more technical skills. In the **directive style,** subordinates are given instructions about what to do, how to do it, and when to do it. The **achievement style** emphasizes goal setting and high-performance expectations for subordinates.

Categories of Management Characteristics

In addition to a manager's style, which represents her actual behavior, factors related to the manager's cognitive makeup also affect her effectiveness. The research we examined[33] is organized into four major categories: conceptual knowledge/skill, technical knowledge/skill, interpersonal knowledge/skill, and personal traits. These categories are not independent of one another. Personal traits influence interpersonal skills, and both will affect how technical and conceptual activities are carried out. Most likely, the integration of all four categories into a whole determines the degree of a manager's success. Unfortunately, little research is available to tell us about how successful managers integrate these characteristics. For now, we will consider them separately.

Conceptual Knowledge and Skills

Conceptual knowledge and skills are the mental abilities required to analyze and diagnose complex situations and make correct decisions. They are essential and common to all (or nearly all) management positions. The following requirements are most frequently cited:

Planning and Decision Making

- Being aware of decision-making alternatives and being skilled in their use
- Setting priorities
- Forecasting events
- Integrating organizational policies, procedures, and objectives
- Adapting to legal, social, and political environments.

Organizing

- Developing appropriate organizational structures
- Coordinating separate but interrelated activities
- Scheduling activities to reach time, efficiency, and quality goals
- Allocating resources to maximize return on investment.

Controlling

- Knowing how to apply various control systems
- Developing control systems
- Developing and supporting initiatives
- Developing policy, procedures, and objectives.

Technical Knowledge and Skills

Technical knowledge and skills are necessary to carry out the operations of a particular functional area (e.g., marketing, engineering, HR). For example, a marketing manager will find that advertising, direct sales, and consumer psychology are areas in which technical knowledge and skills are expected. Also included in this category are general technical knowledge and skills required for managing any organizational unit. The most frequently mentioned are financial analysis, budgeting, managerial accounting, and marketing goods and services.

Interpersonal Knowledge and Skills

Interpersonal knowledge and skills, often called "human" skills, refer to the ability to work with, understand, and motivate others, both individually and in groups. As Mintzberg's research indicates, managers spend most of their time interacting with others. It is primarily the manager's interpersonal skills and knowledge of human behavior that determine her success in influencing others and developing information networks. Examples of knowledge and skill elements in this category include the following:

- Understanding individual differences
- Motivating subordinates
- Developing subordinates
- Building a work team and providing team leadership
- Managing conflict constructively
- Adjusting behavior to fit situational demands (behavioral flexibility)
- Presenting a position in a compelling fashion (persuasion)
- Listening effectively
- Showing awareness of social cues
- Maintaining objectivity in social situations

Personal Traits

Personal traits are not knowledge and skills, but rather qualities of the manager as a person. In some ways, personal traits could be thought of as attitudes, but they are more complex. A personal trait is a relatively permanent predisposition to behave in a particular way. Early leadership studies consistently failed to identify personality traits that predict successful leaders,[34] but research over the last 15 years found certain measurable characteristics that seem to be predictive of future success as a manager. It is important to remember that personal traits may change markedly over the course of a manager's career. The traits discussed here were characteristic of early career stages and were associated with managers' successes over the long term. However, the causal relationship is far from clear.

Early work by McClelland and his colleagues identified four need states that are predictive of effective managers. We focus on three: need for achievement (nAch), need for power (nPow), and need for autonomy (nAut). Those high in **nAch** possess a strong desire to assume personal responsibility, wish to receive concrete feedback on task performance, and demonstrate a single-minded preoccupation with task accomplishment.[35] Those high in **nAut** show a strong desire to work independently. For situations in which those with high nAut work alone, they prefer to control their own pace and procedure and not be hampered by excessive rules.[36] These individuals tend to resist working in groups and indicate their need to be personally responsible for outcomes. Those high in **nPow** desire to lead, influence, and control the people and things around them.[37]

Recent research describes these need states in terms of two general characteristics: drive and leadership motivation.[38] **Drive** includes nAch in addition to ambition, energy, and tenacity.[39] **Leadership motivation** relates primarily to nPow and distinguishes between a need for institutional power, which is directed toward organizational goals, and a need for personal power, which is focused on personal goals.[40] Institutional power needs are related to more successful managers, and personal power needs are related to less successful managers and nonmanagers. The research also shows that those with high nPow (institutional), moderately high nAch, and moderate to low nAut are generally the most effective managers.[41] In addition, likeableness, resistance to stress, and career orientation are generally found to be predictive of future success.

Recall that a common thread running through the management style literature is the existence of two general styles of management. A second common thread is that leaders/managers must adapt their style to fit the situations. A manager's ability to be flexible or adaptable with respect to style of management is also highly predictive of success.[42] This adaptability/flexibility characteristic is found in the literature as both a personal trait and a skill, and it is clearly a necessary component for long-term success as a manager. However, it might be required more in certain kinds of organizations than in others.

Integrating Managerial Roles and Characteristics

When examining the roles managers must perform and the characteristics needed for effective managers, it becomes possible to match characteristics with roles. Table 11-3 depicts such integration. For example, performing obligatory ceremonial duties (figurehead) will almost certainly require awareness of social cues, oral communication skills, and behavioral flexibility. The manager's personal traits, particularly likeableness and resistance to stress, are likely to influence how they respond to those situations; conversely, it is not likely that a manager's technical or conceptual knowledge/skill will be much of a factor in this role.

Table 11-3 serves as a heuristic device, relating a manager's knowledge, skills, and traits to various aspects of the manager's job. It is important to remember, however, that the precise nature of the roles and requisite managerial characteristics differ from organization to organization, and even within the same organization. In particular, the evidence is reasonably conclusive that the importance of the various roles, and consequently the associated knowledge and skills, differs from level to level within the organization's hierarchy.

Roles, KSAs, and Management Level

Lower-level managers primarily supervise and coordinate the work of nonmanagers. They are usually in daily contact with their subordinates and peers, and they are responsible for the day-to-day operations of their unit. They depend primarily on interpersonal and technical skills to get the job done.[43] Their roles are primarily leader, monitor, disseminator, disturbance handler, and negotiator. Usually other roles, requiring greater levels of conceptual skills, are unnecessary, with rules, policies, procedures, and upper management decisions taking their place.

Middle managers coordinate the activities of managers who report to them. The manager in the middle (or sometimes "in the muddle," as they like to say) performs

Table 11-3 Managerial Roles and Associated Management Characteristics

	KNOWLEDGE AND SKILLS			
MANAGERIAL ROLE	CONCEPTUAL	TECHNICAL	INTERPERSONAL	PERSONAL TRAITS
Interpersonal				
Figurehead			yes	yes
Leader	yes		yes	yes
Liaison	yes		yes	yes
Informational				
Monitor	yes	yes		yes
Disseminator	yes	yes	yes	
Spokesperson	yes	yes	yes	
Decisional				
Entrepreneur	yes	yes	yes	yes
Disturbance handler	yes	yes	yes	yes
Resource allocator	yes	yes	yes	yes
Negotiator	yes		yes	yes

the role of liaison, spokesperson, resource allocator, and entrepreneur, in addition to most of the roles performed by the lower-level manager. Interpersonal skills remain important, but technical skills decrease in importance. Conceptual skills are somewhat more important.

Top managers coordinate the activities of the organization through their middle managers. Conceptual skills are of primary importance at this level, particularly the entrepreneurial role. Leader behavior is also important here, as it instills a sense of direction and motivates those who report directly to the manager and to employees in general. Informational, liaison, and figurehead roles are predominant, and the focus of the other roles changes from inside to outside the organization.

Organizations emphasize different types of managerial KSAs at different levels and in different functional units. Each organization has its own context and specific expectations of managers within that context. Thus, even though it is generally helpful to know that supervisors typically are expected to rely on their technical knowledge and skills more than on their conceptual knowledge and skills, the relative importance will depend on the organizational context.

INTEGRATION: STRATEGIES AND MANAGEMENT CHARACTERISTICS

Combining research on organizational environment, strategy, structure, and technology with the research on leadership provides some general prescriptions for effective managerial characteristics at each extreme of the strategy continuum. In the most general sense, effective managers possess technical, interpersonal, and conceptual skills.[44] Leadership research adds the concepts of personal traits and style. We examine these factors and assess the degree to which each is more or less relevant in market and cost leader organizations. Table 11-4 provides a summary of this.

Technical Competence and Context

Research indicates that technical competence is an important foundation for effective management.[45] Both market leader and cost leader strategies require managers with high levels of technical competence, but the technical sophistication required of market leaders is much greater because they operate on the leading edge of technology. Many technologies capable of significant flexibility in application are also required, making the environment more complex and less predictable. Thus, market leader organizations are rated higher in the need for managers with technical skills, as noted in Table 11-4.

Table 11-4
Strategy and Managerial Characteristics Integration

CHARACTERISTICS	MARKET LEADER	COST LEADER
Skills		
Technical	More sophisticated and nonroutine	Less sophisticated and routine
Interpersonal	Higher	Lower
Conceptual	Higher	Lower
Traits		
Drive	High	High
Flexibility	Higher	Lower
Leader motive	High	High
Style		
Participative	Higher	Lower
Supportive	No difference	No difference
Achievement	Higher	Lower
Directive	Lower	Higher

Interpersonal Competence and Context

The market leader strategy uses a more organic, less formalized design that requires the manager to interact more with higher-level managers, subordinates, and peers. These interactions are critical to coordinating activities within and between units. In cost leader organizations, the centralization of decision making and the formalization of rules, procedures, and policies decrease the importance of many of the interpersonal skills. These characterizations reflect a relative difference in the two types of organizations and should not be construed in an all-or-none fashion. Effectiveness in these "human skills" generally differentiates between successful and unsuccessful managers,[46] but logic suggests this is more likely in market leader organizations, where considerably more interaction is required (see Table 11-4).

Conceptual Competence and Context

Again, the cost leader organization, by design, reduces the importance of managerial conceptual skills except at the higher levels of the organization, because of the routine technology, mechanistic design, centralized decision making, and formalized coordination systems. Market leader organizations, conversely, require managers with greater conceptual skills at all levels because of their more complex organization and the need to reduce barriers to creativity. In other words, conceptual skills are more important at all levels in the market leader compared with the cost leader organization. There is agreement that technical skills are more important at lower-level management positions, conceptual skills more important at higher levels, and human skills important at all levels.

Studies support the idea that interpersonal and conceptual skills are more predictive of managerial success than are technical skills.[47] This conclusion, of course, makes sense if technical activities decrease in frequency as a person moves from lower to higher management positions. The more effective managers are those who are able to handle the increasing demands of human and conceptual problems. In addition, individuals are typically hired or promoted to management positions on the basis of their technical competence at lower levels, so these skills are less likely to differentiate effective performers from ineffective performers. Particularly in technical units, new employees are rarely hired on the basis of interpersonal skills or ability to conceptualize complex organizational systems. When they are promoted to managerial positions, they are likely to need development in these areas.

Personal Traits and Context

For nearly all of the traits examined, no compelling evidence or logic suggests that managers high in these traits will be more or less effective in any particular organizational context. The only trait likely to be more useful in one organization than the other is flexibility. Because market leader organizations face more ambiguity and change than do cost leaders, the manager with higher levels of adaptability would likely be more effective than one who was less flexible. This point is reflected in Table 11-4.

Management Style and Context

Of the two employee-oriented styles, only the participative style is expected to show differences in effectiveness based on strategy. Logic suggests that participative styles are more effective in market leader organizations. Obviously, a decentralized structure promotes higher levels of participation in decision making. In the technical units of the market leader organization, this issue is especially important, because innovation and creativity are facilitated by multiple inputs and synergistic (working together) outcomes. In addition, because of the nonroutine nature of the technology, decisions relating to a particular area of that technology require the input of those who are most familiar with it.

We can expect the participative style to be less effective in the cost leader organization for several compelling reasons. For one, decisions are more centralized. The jobs are well defined by the routine technology, policies, procedures, and structure. Few reasons or opportunities arise that would promote the participation of employees in decisions that would meaningfully affect their job. Remember, we are talking about an organization at the extreme end of the continuum. Even here, we are not saying that no participation would take place, only that it would be of less value to the organization.

We find no logic to support the notion that a supportive style is more or less effective in either organizational context. Although employees are likely to be somewhat different in organizations at opposite ends of the strategy continuum, there is no justification for postulating differences in the need for friendliness, empathy, or concern from their managers. In other words, this style is effective in nearly all organizations.

For the task-oriented styles, clear structural reasons suggest differences in the effectiveness of the achievement versus directive styles. The achievement style is more effective for the market leader. Market leaders require managers to reduce some of the ambiguities of their unit's task, ambiguities created by the market leader's need to quickly identify and place new products or significant modifications of old products in the market. Therefore, the achievement-oriented manager clarifies goals, parameters, and performance expectations. For the cost leader, goals and expectations are well understood and standardized, leaving little need for the manager to exert effort in this area. In fact, subordinates are likely to see such behavior as redundant and negative.

Some amount of directive behavior will be useful in the market leader organization to the extent that it clarifies responsibilities and expectations. However, the detailed direction of who will do what, how, and when is contrary to the structural and technological systems of the market leader. For the cost leader, however, it is clearly important for the manager to monitor and ensure that the right people are doing the right things at the right time. In addition, the cost leader's design uses a centralized system in which operations are driven from the top. It is the manager's responsibility to ensure that changes in expectations are conveyed accurately to subordinates and that subordinates comply with the direction in a specific manner. We view the directive style as being more effective in the cost leader organization. Still, managers in such organizations must be discriminating in how it is applied. High- or adequately performing employees in this organization might find additional direction from the manager irritating. Conversely, in the market leader organization, employees might come to desire direction from their managers because of the absence of well-defined structure in their jobs. Nevertheless, the design of this organization favors the achievement style over the directive, providing employees with goals and objectives and giving them the autonomy to figure out the best way to achieve them (see Table 11-4).

The relationships described here between strategy and manager characteristics are generalizations, as are the relationships described among strategy, structure, and technology. Any given organization that adopts a market leader strategy will require some routine and some nonroutine technologies. The point is that they will experience a greater preponderance of nonroutine technologies than if they followed a cost leader strategy. Likewise, the managerial characteristics related here to organizational strategy point to those characteristics that will be most effective with the particular structural and technological characteristics of that strategy. Perhaps the best application of Table 11-4 is at the organizational subunit level. If the subunit is structured in ways consistent with the strategy, the managerial characteristics associated with the strategy are likely to be more effective. Consideration could be given to using this table in developing a managerial needs assessment where the organizational context of the manager's unit can be measured.

MANAGEMENT DEVELOPMENT IMPLICATIONS

The preceding model suggests that the first key to effective management is for managers to know and understand the context in which they operate. Then, on the basis of that knowledge, they have to know the effective skills, traits, and styles that will be effective in that context. Finally, they must assess to determine which of the KSAs are needed. All of these steps are important if a company is going to have managers who are effective in the environment in which they are placed. Management development needs to address the following:

- An understanding of context
- Self-awareness and diagnostic skills
- Managerial person analysis

An Understanding of Context

The most obvious implication of the context/management characteristics model is that effective managers must be able to adapt themselves and their unit to the needs of the organization. To do so, they need a clear understanding of the organization's strategy and their unit's part in that strategy. It is only with this understanding that managers can use their personal characteristics most effectively. Thus, the following are important parts of all developmental programs:

- Clarification of the organization's situation
- Strategy for coping with the situation
- How the various units fit into the strategy
- How the training program relates to these things

Organizations that develop their managers in this manner get a competitive advantage.[48] Too often, however, management development programs try to provide managers with skills, knowledge, styles, and traits without an understanding of the context in which they are to be applied. In the worst case, the development is inappropriate for some units; in the best case, in those units for which the development is appropriate, managers do not understand why it is appropriate.

Self-Awareness and Diagnostic Skills

Once managers understand what is needed from their unit and why, it is important that they understand how their own characteristics influence the activities within their unit and their unit's interaction with other units. This understanding requires self-awareness and diagnostic skills. By self-awareness, we mean the manager's ability to understand the cause-and-effect relationships between their behavior and others' actions.

Diagnostic skills are necessary to identify why gaps exist between what is expected of the unit and what actually occurs. Managers must be able to create the best match between their behavior and

- the structure/design of the unit and
- the characteristics of the subordinates.

Creating these matches requires the ability to diagnose the existence and cause of mismatches. Self-awareness and diagnostic skills are the basic requirements for managerial adaptability to changing conditions.

Once a manager understands the organizational context within which her unit operates and acquires the adaptability skills of self-awareness and diagnosis, she is ready to develop knowledge, skills, and styles. For this, a managerial person analysis is required.

Managerial Person Analysis

Identifying the required KSAs for a managerial job is difficult. It only gets more difficult, because once this identification is completed, you must now determine whether the managers possess the required KSAs. How do you go about determining a manager's style, traits, and ability to interact with peers, subordinates, and superiors? One method gaining considerable popularity is the 360-DF briefly described in Chapter 4. This approach requires a sample of those with whom the manager interacts to fill out an anonymous questionnaire about the manager. Responses are then analyzed and graphed to provide feedback to the manager. The results show where general agreement lies among subordinates, peers, and superiors concerning how the manager "comes across." These data, combined with the data from the unit's operations and other measurement tools, can be used to identify areas of development for each manager. It can also be used during training to help the manager identify the cause-and-effect relationships between her behavior and others' reactions. The manager, of course, should be involved in identifying her areas of strength and weakness.

This multiple-source feedback should be used only for development purposes, not for formal performance evaluations or for pay, promotion, or termination decisions.[49] If it is used for the latter purpose, the responses of those filling out the questionnaire are likely to change. Respondents who are friends will inflate the manager's score, rivals (peers and some of the superiors) will lower their ratings somewhat, and the staff support person the manager complained about would cut him to the bone. However, the research shows that when assessment occurs for developmental purposes, the validity of personal characteristics measurement is enhanced by the inclusion of supervisor, co-worker, subordinate, and customer ratings.[50]

Although 360-DF often results in positive comments about the manager, it can also provide powerful, uncomfortable, and surprising information. In addition to the characteristics discussed in this chapter, 360-DF provides feedback about several other personal characteristics that typically do not show up in the research on management effectiveness. For example, one manager learned that he stood too close to people when talking to them, and that little bits of saliva would fly out of his mouth when he spoke—not a good combination for a manager looking to advance his career. After feedback, he stood farther back and started speech therapy. Another manager, the head of Nestlé's Perrier operation, found out that when he moved from head of sales and marketing to the CEO position, people changed their interpretation of his behavior. His temper and occasional "public whippings" of senior managers that were previously tolerated and seen as demonstrating forceful management became frightening after he became CEO with the authority to fire anyone, and managers stopped coming to him with problems and ideas.[51]

Because of the sensitive nature of the data, feedback must be handled carefully by the training professional to ensure that the manager sees it as "legitimate" and "constructive." The most difficult comments to accept are those about interpersonal skills, such as "untrustworthy," "poor listener," and "uses poor judgment." These characteristics are seen as core competency skills, and nearly every manager assumes she is strong in these areas. The Center for Creative Leadership estimates that only about one-third of all managers accurately predict how others view them. Another third hold inflated views of their talents. The most surprises await these managers, because subordinates almost always rate them the least effective.[52] For some hard-core, control-oriented managers, it sometimes takes massive doses of feedback before the message finally sinks in. Many will attempt to dismiss the results as inaccurate, inappropriate, or irrelevant. The training professional's job is to help the manager come to terms with and accept the results. When results are consistent (e.g., most people rate the manager in the same way), it is more difficult for the manager to explain them away. The most important part of the feedback agent's job is helping the manager understand that her intentions are not the same as other people's interpretation of her behavior. Once the manager makes this association, she can then begin to explore what she might do differently to achieve the desired results.

SOURCES OF KNOWLEDGE/SKILL ACQUISITION

The most obvious source of management training is the organization itself. However, most companies use a combination of internal and external sources to provide their managers with the proper mix of developmental opportunities. A survey of training managers[53] showed 93 percent of the surveyed companies providing both internal and external training to supervisors and middle managers, and 63 percent providing such training for executives. Only about 15 percent of the firms said they developed internal courses for executives, while more than 60 percent did so for middle managers and supervisors. These numbers tell us that few firms rely only on internal training resources, especially for upper-level managers and executives. Those involved in management development must be familiar with training and development opportunities outside their organization and should be able to develop useful programs internally.

The following sections explore some of the more frequently discussed alternatives in the literature. This does not imply an endorsement of any particular source. Rather, we present them to demonstrate the variety of sources that are available.

Externally Based Training

Executive/management education programs at universities provide knowledge and skills of a general nature. These programs cover the range of management issues from traditional MBA functional areas to the development of strategic visioning skills. Other sources of management development activities include training vendors, consultants, and professional associations. They supply a wide variety of training activities ranging from broad-based, general-application programs to those that are narrowly focused on limited areas of skill and knowledge. When the education is narrowly focused, dealing with specific topics such as project management, team building, financial analysis, or effective communication, the managers typically stay in residence at the training site for a few days to several weeks. When the focus is broader, dealing with general management domains (e.g., executive MBA programs), the manager likely attends training for a few hours to a few days periodically over periods up to 24 months. Typically, the goal of broad-based programs is generic skill or content learning rather than job-specific skills. Personal insight is generally not a goal; classroom-based methods tend to be used rather than games and simulations.[54] Personal insight and job-specific KSAs are more typically addressed in the narrow-focus programs.

The principal advantages of externally based programs are as follows:

- They expose managers to the current thinking and theory in management.
- They remove organizational constraints in exploring new approaches.
- They allow interchange of ideas among managers from different organizational backgrounds.
- They cost less per person than internally developed programs.

Problems that may arise with externally based programs include the following:

- Inability to relate content to company-specific approaches
- Inconsistency of instructor effectiveness (some are excellent, others poor) and the inability of the contractor to choose the right instructor (more typical with executive MBA programs than with residential programs)
- Inability to specify expected company outcomes as a result of the training
- Extended time away from the job

- Failure of the manager's company to provide on-the-job reinforcement of concepts and skills
- Inability to control the content of the training (the company can choose the course or program, but not the content)

Despite these concerns, most companies see externally based management programs as valuable tools. Enrollment in traditional MBA education is up, and enrollment in the growing "for-profit" universities is up even more.[55] About 49 percent of companies utilize university-based residential or executive MBA programs, and most of these companies use some form of external short courses.[56] The primary reasons for utilizing these programs are the credibility of the organization offering the program, the nature of the program topic areas, and the managers' belief that it will meet their needs.

Corporate Universities

The growth of **corporate universities** is even greater than the growth of for-profit universities.[57] In an attempt to overcome some of the deficiencies of university-based education while maintaining many of its advantages, large corporations create their own internal "universities." Phillips Petroleum, General Electric, IBM, Motorola, McDonald's, and Xerox are just a few of the companies that have developed their own university-type education. According to Jeanne Meister, president of Corporate University Exchange, about 1,600 corporate universities exist in the United States.[58] The reason organizations are exploring this approach is that after examining the characteristics of university-based versus external, non-university-based formal educational programs for managers, they determined that they could do better internally.[59] The primary reasons are the following:

- The organization understands its own approach to management and can convey it better to its managers.
- Managers can obtain job-specific knowledge and skills.
- The company can ensure quality instruction.
- The courses are cost-effective because of the organization's size.

Dr. Bill Lee explains why American Airlines developed its own university in Training in Action 11-2.

Public and private universities draw a wide range of managers to their management development programs. The diversity of backgrounds and interests requires that the concepts and methods taught must be general in nature so as to be applicable across most situations. Although students are usually encouraged to apply these concepts and methods to their own organization, faculty members can do only a limited amount to facilitate the transfer of this knowledge back to students' jobs.

The corporate university, conversely, can integrate the technical, conceptual, and interpersonal skills within the context of the organization's strategy, structure, and technology. The company can control and shape the curriculum to meet its own needs and values, provide the same content to everyone, and schedule instruction to be convenient for the organization and the trainee.

Some problems, however, exist with the corporate university approach. Matching the curriculum to the needs of the organization remains a difficult task. Pressures within the organization might discourage training in some areas or the use of certain methods, while encouraging others. Although this situation reflects the political reality of the organization, it limits the organization's ability to develop new and more effective approaches. In addition, costs actually might be higher than for externally developed programs. Phillips, for example, found its costs to be about 50 percent more than for similar external training and education.[60]

This approach is possible only for large organizations. It is neither practical nor feasible for small- to moderate-sized businesses to create their own university that includes

American Airlines decided to develop a corporate university (CU), because training was fragmented and many departments operated as cottage industries. Departments were hiring their own outside consultants, vendors, and so forth. Dr. Bill Lee, during his tenure as Director of Measurement and Performance Analysis, stated, "We found that in many departments, the local management had contracts with the same off-the-shelf course providers and were all paying premium price." Other departments were hiring consultants to provide custom programs already developed by other departments. Before the CU was developed, this money came out of the operations budget, and no one was really tracking it.

"The CU is becoming a central clearinghouse for all material in the company, and is able to negotiate a better price with vendors and off-the-shelf providers as more and more departments come under the CU mantle," says Dr. Lee, "but there are still some groups that develop and provide their own training. We have reached out to them and offered to share what we have rather than trying to take them over. They have viewed that very positively and some groups have agreed to turn over their training to the CU because it is one less thing they have to manage. In many areas, such as publishing materials, we have saved thousands of dollars. In the area of government compliance we have saved literally millions by providing quality programs with consistent delivery."

Dr. Lee reported, "We are currently pursuing relationships with similar industries that are noncompetitive but have some of the same needs to reduce costs and maximize benefit."

Source: Personal communication with Dr. Bill Lee, former Director of Measurement and Performance Analysis, American Airlines Corporate FlagShip University, Fort Worth, Texas (September 2002).

faculty and attendance requirements. Smaller organizations must rely on public and private universities and on other external training and development suppliers.

Regardless of whether training is provided internally or through external sources, the training department needs to match the content of the training with the context within which the managers are to use it. Before adopting a management development program, the following questions are useful in assessing the match of a particular program to managers' needs.

1. Do the program outcomes meet an identified need?
2. Will the learning that results from the training be supported on the job?
3. Will behavior resulting from the training conform to the organization's policies, procedures, and norms?
4. Will the individuals receive any personal benefit from the training?
5. What is the cost/benefit ratio of the approach compared with that of alternative approaches?

Another important point is the evaluation of such training. It is one thing to train managers and discover that the training is of little or no value. It is quite another to continue to do so, wasting training dollars and credibility year after year.

Types of Management Development Programs

A description of the full diversity of management development approaches and techniques is beyond the scope of this chapter. However, the following descriptions cover various programs and techniques associated with the competencies of effective management described earlier. We are not necessarily advocating the use of any of them, but we are simply providing a glimpse of the diversity available. Those wishing to probe deeper into this area might begin with the references provided.

Knowledge/Skills Development: Conceptual

Ways to develop conceptual skills in managers include the following:

1. Management/business games, simulations, and case studies.
2. On-the-job training (OJT): Included in this are mentoring, coaching, action learning, job rotation, understudy training, and junior boards. Mentoring and understudy training are similar in that the manager works closely with a senior manager to develop or improve skills. Understudy training occurs when the manager is assigned as an assistant or adjunct to the senior manager; she learns by observing the senior manager and completing assignments of gradually increasing complexity and responsibility. Junior boards combine simulation and OJT techniques. A junior board of directors is created, composed of promising middle-level executives who are given critical issues related to the company's business and asked to provide senior management with recommendations.[61]
3. Decision making: Situations are diagnosed to determine the best approach to making a decision. For example, Vroom and Yetton provide a model in which the manager learns the relevant situational variables that determine whether the decision should be made by the manager alone, delegated to a group of subordinates, or handled somewhere in between.[62] Another approach to decision making is rational manager training, which uses simulations to develop managers' problem-solving and decision-making skills. A unique feature of this approach is the use of actual situations in the company for analysis, identification, and elimination of potential problems.
4. Managerial roles: This approach, based on Mintzberg's model, discussed earlier, is aimed at providing managers with an understanding of what they are doing and why. Through self-observation and understanding of our roles, effectiveness is increased.[63] A related approach, the incident technique, uses critical incidents from the organization, asking managers to identify the facts needed to address the incident.[64] Doing so develops the skills needed to perform the monitoring and disturbance-handler roles.

Knowledge/Skills Development: Technical

Technical training, especially professional skills training, is often purchased from outside sources.

1. Degree and certification programs: Degree programs in business and technical disciplines provide the technical foundation for most managers. In addition, technical knowledge and skills specific to a particular discipline are developed through external suppliers such as professional associations and through certificate training programs. For example, the Society for Human Resource Management provides training programs that prepare HR managers to take the certification examination. Other professional disciplines (e.g., accounting, finance, and engineering) provide similar types of programs. The American Society for Training and Development is in the initial phases of certification programs for trainers.
2. Workshops and seminars: These are offered on various topics by a wide range of providers (e.g., universities, professional associations, consultants, training companies). Larger companies that prefer internally developed workshops and seminars possess the resources to acquire high-level instructors and develop the appropriate training materials. These programs are also more easily tailored to fit the specific needs of the company.

Interpersonal Skills and Management Style

We combined these approaches, because it is difficult to separate management style from interpersonal skills. In fact, management styles are often addressed in training through emphasizing one or more interpersonal skills.

1. Interactive skills training: This approach uses simulations and feedback from observers to provide trainees with ways of interacting more effectively with others. The approach makes managers more aware of how their behavior influences the way others perceive and react to them.[65]

2. Grid management: The two most important managerial characteristics in this approach are the manager's concern for work outcomes and her concern for people (note the parallel here with "employee and task orientation"). The proposition here is that managers who have strong concerns in both of these areas are the best managers. Training focuses on developing the manager's ability to display these characteristics simultaneously. Even though the manager must respond to different situations with the appropriate behavior, it is the value orientation associated with a strong concern for both people and task that guides the manager's behavior.[66]

3. Workshops and seminars: Again, these are offered on various topics by a wide range of providers. These programs typically focus on a particular skill area, such as communication, managerial style, or team facilitation.

Developing Personal Traits   Development of personal traits can be a part of many management development programs. The following few programs focus specifically on trait development:

1. Role motivation: The object of this program is to develop six motivational states in managers: favorable attitude toward authority, desire to compete, assertiveness, desire to exercise power, desire for distinctiveness, and a sense of responsibility. These motives help managers deal with employee work deficiencies and meet organizational criteria for effectiveness (primarily in large organizations). It includes development of interpersonal skills but focuses primarily on self-examination and development of internal values.[67]

2. Need for achievement: This program of self-study, goal setting, and case analysis is designed to provide managers with an understanding of their nAch and development of that need so that it is focused on constructive behavior. This approach yielded the best results for small business owners, particularly at the early stages of their careers.[68]

TRAINING FOR EXECUTIVE-LEVEL MANAGEMENT

One of the reasons cited earlier for providing a chapter on management training is that "managers are accountable for success"; this is *especially* true at the senior level, as the success of the whole company is at stake here. Furthermore, at this level, it is absolutely critical to align training needs to the overall strategy, yet it is surprising how many companies still do not do it.[69] Consider the company that goes international. What do they do when they discover that their executives do not possess the KSAs necessary for such a venture? There are numerous examples of this.[70] Therefore, before any development takes place at this level, a thorough examination of the strategic direction needs to be undertaken. Once the direction is set, the KSAs required to meet the strategic direction (operational analysis) can be determined. These KSAs are then compared with each executive's performance capabilities (person analysis), and developmental plans for each executive can be determined.

Skills, Traits, and Leadership Style

An important duty for executives is to help formulate the strategic direction of the organization, plan for effective implementation of the plan, create mechanisms for ensuring that the strategic direction is followed, and track the progress of the change. These activities require strong conceptual skills in the entrepreneurial role and conceptual and interpersonal skills in the leader role.

President/CEO

The top executive must be effective in the role of entrepreneur (able to analyze the situation and choose the proper direction for the organization) and leader (able to implement the plan through others). Although both of these roles are important, the more important one is leadership. The literature is full of examples of top executives coming in and revamping the organization, making it into what they view it should be, and more importantly, getting the employees to buy into that vision. In fact, is that not what happened at Domtar (the opening case in Chapter 1)?

Even CEOs who are promoted from within need to examine the current environment and determine what changes in direction (if any) need to be taken. The important point is that the employees need to feel confident in the CEO's ability and buy into the executive's decisions regarding the direction the organization is taking. To inspire this kind of loyalty requires sound leadership skills. Of course, the importance of these skills will depend on the strategic direction being taken. The leadership skills for a CEO in a cost leader organization that is not making substantial changes in its strategic direction will not be as important as those for the CEO in a market leader that is beginning to move in a different direction.

Executives in General

One of the reasons for grooming internal higher-level managers to become executives is that they are already part of the organizational culture. These managers also possess many of the skills that are important to the type of organization they are in (e.g., market leader). This reasoning is especially applicable if management performance is based on a set of competencies. As long as promotion is based on sound appraisals and their development persists, these managers should continue to be effective when they are promoted to the executive level. However, there still must be a process to prepare them for the move.

Strategies for Development of Executives and Future Executives

Note that we are discussing two different levels of management here: development of executives and development of managers (preparing them for the executive level). Certain problems are specifically associated with training executives:

- These people are at the top of the organization, making it difficult for them to ask for help or even be aware they need it.
- Who is capable of helping them, or at least has the credibility to be listened to by these executives?
- These busy individuals work long hours and do not have much time for development.

Because of these issues, some strategies are better for executives and others are more likely to be used for developing managers to become executives in the future.[71] Finally, we would be remiss in not noting that both coaching and mentoring can be useful techniques for employees at all levels in the organization. After reading the material in these two areas in Chapter 6, you should be able to see the significant differences in how these techniques are applied at the managerial and executive levels compared to lower levels in the organization.

Coaching

Not long ago, coaching was only considered to be a method for correcting inadequate performance.[72] Not anymore. When Bob Peters was promoted to vice president of sales and marketing for American Science and Engineering, one of his perks was an executive coach.[73] An advantage of using a personal coach is that the coach can fit into the busy schedule of the executive. The credibility factor is also dealt with, as coaches are often experts from outside the organization. In a survey conducted by the International Coach Federation, more than 4,000 companies were using coaches for their executives.[74] For the CEO, a coach is the ideal training format. It can be done at the CEO's convenience, it is one-on-one, and it provides an opportunity for feedback from a professional. "It gets lonely at the top, and it's difficult to find someone to talk to about my concerns," says Ted Venners, chairman of KFx, a high-tech company in Denver.[75]

An advantage of this method is that it can be done in short meetings, phone conversations, and Internet communications when the executive has the time. It also focuses on specific areas identified as needing improvement. Again, the important first step is identifying the executive's specific developmental needs, which can be determined through 360-degree performance reviews.[76] The coach and executive mutually determine an action plan, followed by successive meetings and counseling by the coach.

For the manager, it is much more likely that any coaching would be done by the supervisor, although outside consultants are sometimes used for up-and-coming managers. Again, the personalized approach helps the manager focus on specific needs and improvements.

Mentoring

Coaching and mentoring are different in that mentoring is generally more of an ongoing relationship, and coaching is often for a shorter, more specific length of time. Also, meetings between a coach and the employee are generally more structured and regular than in mentoring.[77] Another difference for executives is that someone inside the company generally does the mentoring and an outside consultant often does the coaching.[78]

For the executive, "being a mentor" is an important developmental tool from which he can learn a great deal. By dealing with different mentees, the executive is given the opportunity to grow professionally by honing leadership skills and by learning how to work with various personality types and backgrounds.[79] Executives sometimes also have mentors. In cases where the executive is new to the organization, a senior executive could be assigned as a mentor to help get the new executive settled into his new role.

For managers who are potential executive material, being mentored is a valuable method for preparing them to be future executives. This one-on-one interaction allows the mentor to determine what is required to improve the mentee's effectiveness. Once the mentor identifies an area or competency that requires work, she can suggest relevant training. Also, the mentor can provide opportunities to work on special projects that require use of the competency. One real advantage of a mentoring program is that it keeps your talent at home.[80] In a study conducted by the Center for Creative Leadership, 77 percent of companies indicated development of a mentoring program improved their retention rate.

Executive Development Programs/Executive MBAs

This type of training can take place at the organization's leadership center or at a university (public or corporate). It mixes classroom learning with real-life problem solving. In such environments, the mix often includes both executives and middle managers. The training generally follows the boot camp philosophy championed by Noel Tichy or the less intense approach championed by Mintzberg.[81] The boot camp approach is designed to be stressful, which is generally what the executive's job is all about. Trainees are pushed to their limit, much like Navy SEAL or Special Forces

At the U.S. Postal Services' Advanced Leadership Program, one of the requirements is working on real Postal Service problems. At the end of week three of the training, a postal executive meets with each of the work teams that were formed at the beginning of training. The executive gives each of the teams a business problem. These problems are chosen from those submitted by executives from all across the country.

Over the course of the next three months, the teams work on the problems. When they return for the last week of the training, they present their solution to a panel of executives from the Postal Service. Generally, the solution is immaterial; it is the process that is important and where the learning takes place. So, where is the bonus?

It turns out that even though the important part of the exercise is the process of working out a solution, the solutions are often so innovative that they are implemented, and they save the company money.

A team from California was given the problem of workplace violence. The team determined that a common link to much of the violence was related to money problems. They recommended development of a four-hour workshop on how to manage money. This recommendation was implemented in California and the workplace environment improved.

Another group was challenged to increase retail income or reduce expenses in post offices. The group decided to put advertisements on the rolls of receipt paper they used. In that way, they could advertise their own products for free and hopefully increase revenue. Alternatively, they could sell the advertisement space to others, decreasing their cost for receipt paper. Although neither of these options has been adopted yet, it is estimated that the use of external advertising to defray the expenses of receipt rolls would save about $13 million per year.

Source: Delahoussaye, M. "Licking the leadership crisis." *Training* (January 2002), pp. 24–29.

training. Noel Tichy's point is that managers need to know how to operate in a stressful environment, so one is provided for them. Mintzberg does not agree. He says, "These managers live boot camp every day. The last thing in the world they need is more boot camp." Either way, both agree that the classroom is only a small part of learning. Most programs offer some sort of action learning to accompany the classroom work. Action learning provides trainees with real company problems to solve. For example, GE managers are in a classroom in the morning, then given a real problem from GE to work on in a team for the rest of the day (and often into the wee hours of the morning). Sometimes, these real-world projects provide a bonus for the company, as described in Training in Action 11-3.

Action Learning

Although often a part of executive training programs, action learning can also stand alone. It is effective because it focuses on exactly what managers and executives need to do—come up with effective solutions to complex problems, then implement and evaluate them. It requires working in teams (to problem solve) and on their own (researching the issue and gathering relevant data), both of which are important for effective managers and executives. The difference between traditional meetings to solve problems and action learning is the focus on the learning that takes place. To ensure that this learning happens, a facilitator is assigned to assist the team. The facilitator helps the team through debriefing after the meetings are over. Her focus would be on how members communicated with each other, how they provide feedback, and how well they are following their plan of action. She also gets them to reflect on how they are approaching the problem and how their basic assumptions might affect their view regarding the selection of a solution to the problem.[82] Once the group determines what specific training is required to help the team be more effective, "just-in-time" training is provided.[83]

The result: Not only do organizations get solutions to problems, but the team members develop skills necessary to be effective managers. And just as important, they learn how to continuously learn from the process.[84]

Job Rotation

For the executive, the job rotation takes on a different perspective than what we described earlier in the Employee Development section. The executive is usually not simply rotating to another executive's job, though this can happen. In many vertically integrated organizations (e.g., where the supplier is actually part of the same organization or a subsidiary), the job rotation might be to the supplier to see how the business operates from the supplier's point of view. Learning how the organization is perceived from the outside broadens the executive's perspective on its operation. A rotation to a foreign office would provide an international perspective.

Nonexecutive managers, being developed for executive roles, are often rotated through different departments in the organization. This approach allows the manager to operate in different roles and understand the different issues that arise. This is beneficial for the manager when she rotates back to her home department as she is better able to integrate her unit's activities with those of the rest of the company. In addition, having a good understanding of how each unit functions is a critical competency for someone who desires to be a corporate leader. After interviewing the company's top 120 leaders, Jerry Yelverton, executive vice president of Entergy, indicated that the single most important factor that led to these leaders' success was the variety of their experiences in different functions, business units, and even countries.[85] The other point these leaders made was that the earlier these opportunities started, the better it would be.

Special Job Assignments

Special job assignments, as discussed earlier, are a useful tool for both the executive and the manager, and they are more likely an outcome of coaching or mentoring. The coach helps the executive identify needs to improve his feedback skills. They decide that he will increase the number of feedback meetings with direct reports to improve these skills. These typically short-term assignments address specific skill deficiencies.

Team Building/Outward Bound

Whenever a team is formed, or several team members are replaced (especially if one is the CEO), some sort of team building is useful. Skills to operate effectively in a team are critical to effective executive functioning. For more in-depth team building, companies often send managers to Outward Bound programs like the "Wilderness Training Lab" presented in Chapter 3 as the opening case. Here, they can learn the importance of teams and how to operate effectively in one.

To Sum Up

Developing managers and executives to become more effective requires some combination of the above-mentioned methods to provide the experiences necessary. Methods not mentioned here also might be used from time to time in certain circumstances. To get an idea of what a developmental process in a large organization looks like, see Training in Action 11-4.

Succession Planning

Succession planning is a systematic and effective way to develop talent for the executive level of management. Recall that **succession planning** is the process of preparing employees at a lower level to replace someone at the next level. It is usually done for the positions critical to the effective functioning of the organization.

Steve Carlisle, a middle manager at GM, is being sent to Singapore as vice president of planning for its Asia Pacific region. This three- to five-year assignment is part of his ongoing development at GM. The developmental process for Steve started some time ago when he was a manager in Oshawa, Ontario, Canada.

As part of his development, he was given a temporary assignment in Warren, Michigan. This temporary job assignment later turned into a permanent one at the tech center in Warren.

Obtaining an advanced degree also played an important part in Steve's development. After a few years at the Warren plant, he was told that, to enhance his chances of continuing to move up at GM, he would need to go back to school. He was one of only a few who were sent by GM to MIT to receive an MBA. Steve received his full salary for the year it took to obtain the degree.

On return from MIT, Steve was promoted to group director of planning for the GM Truck Group in Warren. Then, in 2002, he got the news that he was going to the Asia Pacific region as part of his continued development.

Before leaving for Singapore, several alternative future assignments were discussed in preparing him for the current job rotation. Although no firm commitments could be made, general agreement pointed to future possibilities in his continued development upon his return.

For the President/CEO

It is surprising how many organizations do not develop succession plans for replacing their top person. Two reasons for this are that more immediate and important things need doing and the belief that it is always a good idea to go "outside" for a new CEO.[86] As for the first reason, it does take a great deal of time to implement and keep a succession plan up-to-date, but do the costs outweigh the benefits? The answer in most cases is no. As for the second reason, going outside for a new CEO should only be done when no talent can be found within the organization or when a major shift in thinking is required. As Philip Caldwell of Ford Motors said, "The best source of CEO candidates is the company itself. There are times when it makes sense to look outside, but in general you want successors to emerge from within the company."[87] After all, they know the organization and understand its culture and direction. Most important, if there is a good succession plan, knowing the potential candidate's skill set makes the likelihood of success much higher. Furthermore, without this option, many of the best employees will be looking outside for their promotion.

The process of succession planning for the top position should involve the following:

- Identification of the KSAs or competencies required for the CEO position
- Assessment of individuals with potential for filling the position
- Identification of areas where development is necessary
- A plan to provide the individual with opportunities to develop the areas identified as requiring improvement.

The job at the top is more difficult to assess in terms of KSAs and is, to a certain extent, based on the strategic direction of the organization. If a major change in direction is required, the CEO needs the KSAs to manage change more so than if the focus is to increase market sales. Think back to Domtar. Why was it in such poor shape financially when Royer took over? Why was Royer able to turn it around? Clearly, the KSAs Royer possessed had some relationship to the eventual success of Domtar.

Next, assessment of executives needs to be done and decisions regarding how to prepare and make the final choice for a replacement need to be made. Is it possible that Royer would have different expectations of those he considers potential replacements for himself?

Once developmental needs are determined, examine training delivery. An HR planning system makes succession planning much easier, and a good succession plan prepares organizations to deal with sudden and even planned personnel changes with minimal disruption. Therefore, with a succession plan, the assessment of the vice presidents (for the position of president) is an ongoing process of performance review. From the review, developmental activities to hone the executive's skills would be worked out with the CEO (the vice president's boss). In such scenarios, the change from one CEO to another is often smooth and immediate. The downside must also be considered. When more than one candidate is working toward the promotion, those who are not moved up may be not only disappointed but also angry, as Training in Action 11-5 indicates.

Therefore, as Training in Action 11-5 shows, in an effective succession planning process, where the best are constantly being groomed to become better, it is likely that when a promotion is made, some who do not get the promotion will leave. Good talent is lost. However, because the company is "growing the talent," two important things happen. First, the company gets first choice of the talent it has grown, which should translate into the best person. Second, the critical position is filled immediately, which is a real advantage.

For Executives in General

With all the money spent on management training, it is surprising that so little is spent on leadership development. A recent survey indicated that more than half the organizations either did not have executive development programs or only supplied them when needed.[88] Forty percent rate their approach to leadership development as low or very low.[89] This statistic is problematic for several reasons:[90]

- The pool of available managers to fill executive positions continues to shrink.
- The cost of recruiting outside talent is increasing at a high rate.
- The average company expects a 33 percent turnover of executives in the next five years.

This failure to prepare future executives is surprising, given the importance of having effective executives. One reason for this problem is the recent severe economic downturn and the continued downsizing in U.S. corporations.[91] Little attention is paid to succession planning when an organization is reducing employee numbers, and succession planning is the backbone of preparing future talent. Many of the middle managers

TRAINING IN ACTION 11-5
The Downside of an Effective Succession Planning Process

General Electric (GE) is widely known for its ability to develop executive talent. Recent CEO Jack Welch fortified this commitment to the development of high-level talent. His strong dedication to developing effective leaders is carried out through a comprehensive succession planning process. It is so effective that other companies, such as Polaris, emulate it. Each year, top executives at GE meet to review the talent requirements and discuss plans for developing its managers. In looking for his own replacement, Jack Welch, working with his board of directors, had some great talent to choose from.

When Jeff Immelt was chosen to succeed Jack Welch, Bob Nardelli was surprised and hurt. His record at GE was one of the best, and he simply did not understand why he did not get the job. As a result, Nardelli accepted a job as CEO of Home Depot, and one of the other candidates in the running, Jim McNerney, accepted the CEO position at 3M.

Sources: Gale, S. "Bringing good leaders to light." Training (June 2001), pp. 38–42. Tyler, J. "Succession planning: Charting a course for the future." Trustee 55 (2002), pp. 24–28.

who are let go in job cuts are potential future executives. This does not bode well for many organizations in North America when the economic conditions improve, but those that are paying attention to the issue will be the winners in the long run.

All of *Training* magazine's "top 50 training organizations" are constantly developing possible successors for their top positions through succession planning.[92] GE Lighting is one of those companies. In its succession planning process, executives meet twice a year to focus on the company's future needs, and then determine the developmental needs of managers targeted for advancement.[93]

Of course, these ideas are okay for the large organization that has the resources to fund them, but what about the small company?

FOCUS ON SMALL BUSINESS

For the small company, the senior manager/CEO or owner of the firm needs to take responsibility for the development of her managers. Some options include the following:[94]

- Clearly articulate a vision and goals for the organization and what these managers need to do to help you reach them.
- Help managers understand themselves and their shortcomings through feedback from the senior manager's own observations and the observations of others.
- Be sure that the assignments provided to these managers are in line with their developmental needs.
- Provide managers with opportunities to learn the total organization through job rotation or different projects.
- Be a positive role model and coach.
- Let them shadow an executive for a week or so to fully understand what the responsibilities are for senior management.

Some real advantages are available to the small business leader when it comes to training future executives. Because the company is small, doing all possible jobs and experiencing many of the issues that will arise are much more likely. Furthermore, under the guidance of the CEO, the manager surely will be learning what the CEO deems important because the CEO is the one who designs and implements the development program. Morgan McCall, professor of management at the University of Southern California, says that leaders grow better under good tutelage than in a classroom.[95] The key is for the CEO to take the development of managers seriously and to be that role model.

SUMMARY

Employee development is an important process for retaining employees and keeping them motivated. In addition, it creates more flexibility in terms of the company's ability to utilize employees in different ways. Benefits to the employee, beyond more interesting work and the sense of accomplishment in developing new competencies, include the increased value of the employee within the company and the employee's increased marketability outside the company.

Several approaches to employee development were discussed, including development in the current job, job rotation, and special assignments. Each of these uses the training process model, and examples were given of how this is applied to each alternative.

Responsibility for an employee's development is shared by the employee, the supervisor, the HR unit, and the organization. The organization needs to reflect a culture of fostering employee development. HR is responsible for developing and maintaining the systems and practices that allow that culture to flourish. Supervisors are responsible for implementing the employee development systems and practices. The employee is responsible for honestly evaluating her developmental needs and sharing those with the supervisor. The employee is also responsible for completing the developmental activities and accomplishing the goals that were mutually set with her supervisor.

All managers take on certain general roles, but the importance of these roles varies depending on the level of the manager and the type of strategy followed by the organization. Therefore, the development of managers needs to take these situations into account when determining what types of training to provide. The three main roles identified by Mintzberg are interpersonal, informational, and decisional. Within each of these roles are more specific roles: (1) figurehead, leader, and liaison are part of the interpersonal role; (2) monitor, disseminator, and spokesperson are part of the informational role; and (3) entrepreneurial, disturbance handler, resource allocator, and negotiator are part of the decisional role. For each of these specific roles, certain skills (conceptual, technical, and interpersonal) and traits are required. The key to effective management development is to determine the roles required for the position, and from these roles the relevant KSAs (operational analysis). Then, as in a traditional needs analysis, it is possible to assess the current KSAs of the managers (person analysis). The 360-DF, when used properly, is an effective tool for determining the managers' current KSA levels.

Several sources are used to obtain the relevant training for managers, from externally based programs to corporate universities. Conceptual, technical, interpersonal, and even personal traits can be developed through these programs.

Development of executives is critical to organizational functioning, but again it is often ignored. Special attention needs to be focused here, because executives are already at the top and likely feel competent or at least do not like to ask for help. It is difficult for someone who is a peer or lower to be credible enough to offer advice. Executives are also busy, often working long hours, making it difficult to find the time to receive any training. Executive coaching is one way to deal with these issues, and its use has grown at a tremendous rate over the last few years. Other methods are also available, and the key to smooth development is succession planning. An effective succession plan will allow all executives and high-level managers to be appraised constantly and provided with opportunities to develop using many of the methods mentioned, such as coaching, action learning, executive MBAs, and so forth.

KEY TERMS

- Achievement style
- Conceptual knowledge and skills
- Corporate universities
- Cross training
- Directive style
- Drive
- Employee-oriented style
- Executive/management education programs
- Interpersonal knowledge and skills
- Job rotation
- Leadership motivation
- Managerial context
- Managerial style
- Need for achievement (nAch)
- Need for autonomy (nAut)
- Need for power (nPow)
- Participative style
- Personal traits
- Special assignments
- Succession planning
- Supportive style
- Task-oriented style
- Technical knowledge and skills

QUESTIONS FOR REVIEW

1. Why is employee development so important in today's organization?
2. Why is it necessary to have so much of this chapter devoted to management training?
3. Compare and contrast the skills, traits, and management style for the manager in a cost leader versus market leader organization.

4. Why are corporations setting up their own universities? Explain in detail and indicate the advantages and disadvantages of this approach.
5. Why is it difficult to train executives? Explain five training methods and why they are useful for training executives.

EXERCISES

1. Put your role as a student into the context of a job. What type of development would you like to get to make you a more effective student in terms of (1) your grades, (2) a teammate in group projects, and (3) a student in the classroom? Are you aware of anyplace at the university where these skills are offered?
2. Bring a recent article (no more than a year old) that identifies KSAs that will be critical for managers in the immediate future. Be prepared to discuss the article and its management development implications in small groups or with the entire class.
3. Interview two managers with at least two years of management experience. One manager should come from a company whose strategy is toward the cost leader side and the other toward the market leader side. If possible, they should both be in the same functional area. Determine what management development they received from their company. Determine how satisfied they are with the development they have received so far. Provide an analysis of how consistent these two experiences are with what the text proposes. Bring the information back to class and be prepared to share it with others.
4. How does management education prepare a manager for her role? What are the ways in which management education occurs? Do some seem better to you than others? Why or why not? Can other forms of training substitute for management education? Why or why not?
5. Interview a manager with five or more years of experience. Record the manager's current position, previous positions, and education. Identify the manager's roles and responsibilities. Afterward, answer the following:

   - How do the roles and responsibilities compare with those described in the text?
   - Identify the KSAs required to meet this manager's roles and responsibilities.
   - How did the manager's previous experience and education prepare that manager for current roles and responsibilities?

6. Interview an HR person from a company to find out how the company's executives are developed. How are managers developed to fill executive positions? If the company uses a succession planning process, ask how it works and how often it is reviewed. If the company does not, ask how it determines whom to promote to executive positions when one becomes available. From the interview, answer the following questions:

   - How many different methods does the company use for developing executives? For developing managers?
   - If the company does use a succession plan, how does it work? Do you think it prepares the managers for the higher-level management positions? If the company does not use a succession plan, how does it fill higher-level positions?

WEB RESEARCH

Conduct an Internet search to find companies noted for best practices in management development. Describe what these best-practices companies do in management development. What are the similarities across companies? Describe any major differences. Be prepared to discuss this information in class.

WILL TEAMS WORK?

An automobile parts manufacturer was attempting to institute employee problem-solving teams to improve quality. This action was strongly encouraged by its biggest customer, a major automobile manufacturer. The competition in the original equipment manufacturing (OEM) business is especially fierce. The major automobile manufacturers (Ford, GM, DaimlerChrysler, Toyota, Honda, etc.) now demand high-quality parts at extremely low costs, and they often play one supplier against the other to force the OEM industry to meet their standards.

A TNA of middle- and first-level production managers was conducted. These managers were responsible for the operation of the parts production system, a system that is highly mechanized and somewhat automated. The labor force in this area is primarily high-school graduates, but many have less education. The managers' responsibility prior to the change was to ensure that the hourly workers did their jobs in the proper manner and that the right amount and type of parts were produced to meet the production schedule.

The TNA showed low technical knowledge among these managers, because they had been hired to monitor the hourly employees. They did not really understand the machinery and equipment and had never operated it. Most of them used a confrontational style in dealing with their subordinates, because they felt that if they took a gentler approach, the unionized workforce would take advantage of them. The managers were all selected on the basis of their high need to control their environment, strong desire to achieve, and willingness to work with others to get the job done. These traits still characterize this group of managers.

CASE QUESTIONS

1. What is the managerial context in which these managers will be operating? Do you think training designed to help managers understand the context they will be operating in will be helpful? Why or why not?
2. What types of competencies should be developed in the management training? Give your rationale.
3. What types of training should be used to provide the different competencies? How long will it take to provide this training? Give your rationale.
4. What are the alternatives to management development? Do you think one of these alternatives should be used? Why or why not?

REFERENCES

Chapter 1

1. "2008 Industry report." *Training* (November/December 2008), pp. 16–34.
2. Collins, C. J., and K. D. Clark. "Strategic human resource practices, top management social networks, and firm performance: The role of human resource practices in creating organizational competitive advantage." *The Academy of Management Journal* 46, no. 6 (December 2003), pp. 740–51. Bassi, L. J., and D. P. McMurrer. "Training investment can mean financial performance." *Training and Development* (May 1998), pp. 40–42. Lee, R. J. "Experience shows that training pays: Both agents and companies benefit, Mutual of Omaha study shows." *Training* (October 2006), p. 12.
3. Bersin, J. "Companies still struggle to tie training to business goals." *Training* (October, 2006), p. 22.
4. Katz, D., and R. L. Khan. *The Social Psychology of Organizations* (1978). New York: Wiley.
5. Weinstein, M. "What does the future hold?" *Training* (January 2007), pp. 18–22. "Talent management under the microscope." *Training* (May 2006), p. 15. Hall, B. "The top training priorities for 2005." *Training* (February 2005), pp. 24–29. Meisinger, S. "Challenges and opportunities for HR." *HR Magazine* 50, no. 5 (May 2004), p. 10. Hall, B., and S. Boehle. "The second annual Leaders of Learning Survey." *Training* (February 2004), pp. 27–33.
6. Hall and Boehle, op. cit. (2004).
7. Fullerton, H., Jr., and M. Tossi. "Labor force projections to 2010: Steady growth and changing composition." *Monthly Labor Review* 124, no. 11 (2001), pp. 21–38.
8. Cappelli, P. "Will there really be a labor shortage?" *Human Resource Management* 44, no. 2 (Summer 2005), pp. 143–149.
9. Carnevale, T. "The coming labor and skills shortage." *Training and Development* 59 no. 1 (January 2005), p. 36.
10. Anonymous. "Skilled labor shortage to be costly." *Manufacturing Engineering* 135, no. 1 (July 2005), p. 20.
11. Tyler, K. "Training revs up." *HR Magazine* (April 2005), pp. 58–63.
12. Quazi, H. A., and R. L. Jacobs. "Impact of ISO 9000 on training and development activities: An exploratory study." *The International Journal of Quality and Reliability Management* 21, no. 4, 5 (2004), p. 497.
13. Dolack, P. "ISO 9000 comes of age." *Chemical Marketing Reporter* 249 (1996), pp. 7–8. McAdam, R., and M. McKeown. "Life after ISO: An analysis of the impact of ISO 9000 and total quality management on small businesses in Northern Ireland." *Total Quality Management* 10, no. 2 (1999), pp. 229–41. Anderson, S. W., J. D. Daly, and M. F. Johnson. "Why firms seek ISO 9000 certification: Regulatory compliance or competitive advantage?" *Production and Operations Management* 8, no. 1 (1999), pp. 28–43.
14. Williamson, D. "ISO rating the sign of the times." *Windsor Star* (July 1997), p. F1.
15. Sample, J. *Avoiding Legal Liability: For Adult Educators, Human Resource Developers, and Instructional Designers* (2007). Melbourne, FL: Krieger Publishing.
16. Milciute, K., and B. Kleiner. "New legal developments concerning human resource management." *Management Research News* 26, no. 2–4 (2003), pp. 212–19.
17. Marbella, J. "Running the gauntlet: Diversity training is raising issues along with consciousness." *Baltimore Suit* (October 1994), pp. 1D, 6D.
18. Fleishman, E. "On the relation between abilities, learning, and human performance." *American Psychologist* 27 (1972), pp. 1017–32.
19. Dunnette, M. "Aptitudes, abilities, and skills." *The Handbook of Industrial and Organizational Psychology* (1976), edited by M. Dunnette. Chicago: Rand McNally.
20. Oskamp, S. *Attitudes and Opinions* (1991), 2d ed. Upper Saddle River, NJ: Prentice Hall.
21. *Webster's Universal Dictionary and Thesaurus* (1993). Toronto, Canada: Tormont Publications.
22. Kraiger, K., J. Ford, and E. Salas. "Application of cognitive, skill based and affective theories of learning outcomes to new methods of training evaluation." *Journal of Applied Psychology* 78, no. 2 (1993), pp. 311–28.
23. Dunnette, op. cit. (1976).
24. Oskamp, op. cit. (1991).
25. Chuvala, J., J. Gilmere, and T. Gillette. "The new kid on the training block." *Security Management* (August 1992), pp. 65–72.

Chapter 2

1. Mintzberg, H. "Crafting strategy." *Harvard Business Review* (July/August 1987) p. 66–76.
2. Ozone House, Inc. *Strategic Plan* (1999). Ann Arbor, MI: Ozone House, Inc.
3. http://www.hermanmiller.com/ (accessed June 21, 2008).
4. Miles, R., and C. Snow. *Organizational Strategy, Structure and Process* (1978). New York: McGraw-Hill.
5. Miller, D. "The structural and environmental correlates of business strategy." *Strategic Management Journal* (January/February 1987), pp. 55–76.
6. Porter, M. *Competitive Strategy: Techniques for Analyzing Industries and Competitors* (1980). New York: Free Press.
7. Miles and Snow, op. cit. (1978).

8. Duncan, B. "Characteristics of organizational environments and perceived uncertainty." *Administrative Science Quarterly* 17, no. 3 (1972), p.131–327.

9. Miles and Snow, op. cit. (1978).

10. Perrow, C. *Organizational Analysis: A Sociological View* (1970). Belmont, CA: Wadsworth. Thompson, J. D. *Organization in Action* (1967). New York: McGraw-Hill. Woodward, J. *Industrial Organization: Theory and Practice* (1965). London, U.K.: Oxford University.

11. Burns, T., and G. Stalker. *The Management of Innovation* (1961). London, U.K.: Tavistock.

12. David, F., J. Pearce, and W. Randolf. "Linking technology and structure to enhance group performance." *Journal of Applied Psychology* (April 1989), pp. 233–41.

13. Perrow, op. cit. (1970).

14. Mintzberg, H. *The Structuring of Organizations* (1979). Upper Saddle River, NJ: Prentice Hall, pp. 272–85. McDonough, E., and R. Leifer, "Using simultaneous structures to cope with uncertainty." *Academy of Management Journal* (December 1983), pp. 727–35.

15. Becker, B., and M. Huselid. "Overview: Strategic human resource management in five leading firms." *Human Resource Management* (Winter 1999), pp. 287–301.

16. Tichey, N. *Managing Strategic Change: Technical, Political, and Cultural Dynamics* (1983). New York: Wiley. Tichey, Fombrun, and Devanna, op. cit. (1992).

17. Rossett, A. "Training and organizational development: Separated at birth." *Training* (April 1996), pp. 53–59.

18. Lewin, K. "Quasi-stationary social equilibrium and the problem of permanent changes." *The Planning of Change*, edited by W. Bennis, D. Benne, and R. Chin. New York: Holt, Rinehart, and Winston.

19. Golembiewski, R., C. Proehl, and D. Sink. "Estimating the success of OD applications." *Training and Development Journal* (April 1982), pp. 86–95. Nicholas, J. "The comparative impact of organizational development interventions on hard criteria measures." *Academy of Management Review* (October 1982), pp. 531–42.

20. Goodman, P., and J. Dean. "Why productivity efforts fail." *Organizational Development: Theory, Practice, and Research* (1983), edited by W. French, C. Bell, and R. Zawacki. Plano, TX: Business Publications.

21. Schuler, R., and S. Jackson. "Linking competitive strategies with human resource management practices." *Academy of Management Executive* 1, no. 3 (1987), pp. 207–19.

22. Rossett, op. cit. (1996).

23. Ibid.

24. Hall, B. "Time to outsource?" *Training* (June 2004), p. 14.

25. Ackelsberg, R., and P. Arlow. "Small businesses do plan and it pays off." *Long Range Planning* 18 (1985), pp. 61–66. Bracker, J., B. Keats, and J. Pearson. "Planning and financial performance among small firms in a growth industry." *Strategic Management Journal* 9 (1988), pp. 591–603.

26. Sandberg, W., R. Robinson, and J. Pearce. "Why small businesses need a strategic plan." *Business and Economic Review* 48 (2001), pp. 12–15.

27. Wheelen, T., and J. Hunger. *Strategic Management and Business Policy* (1995). New York: Addison-Wesley.

28. Ackelsberg and Arlow, op. cit. (1985). Buchele. *Business Policy in Growing Firms* (1967). San Francisco, CA: Chandler. Gilmore, F. "Formulating strategy in smaller companies." *Harvard Business Review* 49 (1971), pp. 71–81.

29. Kargar, J., and R. Blumenthal. "Successful implementation of strategic decisions in small community banks." *Journal of Small Business Management* (April 1994), pp. 10–21.

30. Lang, J., R. Calantone, and D. Gudmundson. "Small firm information seeking as a response to environmental threats and opportunities." *Journal of Small Business Management* (January 1997), pp. 11–21.

31. Ibid.

32. O'Neal, H., and J. Duker. "Survival and failure in small businesses." *Journal of Small Business Management* (January 1986), pp. 30–37.

33. Kargar and Blumenthal, op. cit. (1994).

34. Anna Pentano, Human Resource Manager, personal communication (June 24, 2008).

Chapter 3

1. Deming, W. E. *Out of the Crisis* (1986). Cambridge, MA: Massachusetts Institute of Technology Press.

2. Dobyns, L., and C. Crawford-Mason. *Quality or Else* (1991). Boston, MA: Houghton Mifflin.

3. Lawler, E. E., S. A. Mohrman, and G. E. Ledford. *Creating High Performance Organizations: Practices and Results of Employee Involvement and Total Quality Management in Fortune 1000 Companies* (1995). San Francisco, CA: Jossey-Bass.

4. Maslow, A. H. *Motivation and Personality* (1954). New York: Harper & Row. Maslow, A. *Toward a Psychology of Being* (1968), 2nd ed. New York: Van Nostrand Reinhold.

5. Alderfer, C. "An empirical test of a new theory of human needs." *Organizational Behavior and Human Performance* 4, no. 2 (1969), pp. 142–75.

6. Ibid. Schneider, C. P., and C. Alderfer. "Three studies of measures of need satisfaction in organizations." *Administrative Science Quarterly* (December 1973), pp. 489–505.

7. Pavlov, I. P. *Lectures on the Principal Digestive Glands* (1897). St. Petersburg, Russia: Kushnereff. Pavlov, I. P. "Principal laws of the activity of the central nervous system as they find expression in conditioned reflexes." As reported by G. Murphy and J. Kovach in *Historical Introduction to Modern Psychology* (1912). New York: Harcourt Brace Jovanovich.

8. Thorndike, E. L. *The Elements of Psychology* (1905). New York: Seiler. Thorndike, E. L. "The psychology of learning." *Educational Psychology* (1913), vol. 2. New York: Teachers College, Columbia University Press. Thorndike, E. L. *Purposive Behavior in Animals and Men* (1932). New York: Appleton-Century-Crofts.

9. Skinner, B. F. *Science and Human Behavior* (1953). New York: Macmillan. Skinner, B. F. *The Technology of Teaching* (1968). New York: Appleton-Century-Crofts.

10. Ibid.

11. Grote, D. *Discipline Without Punishment* (1995). New York: AMACOM.

12. Vroom, V. *Work and Motivation* (1964). New York: Wiley.

13. Bandura, A. "Self-efficacy: Toward a unifying theory of behavioral change." *Psychological Review* 84 (1977a), pp. 191–215.

14. Gecas, V. "The social psychology of self-efficacy." *Annual Review of Sociology* 15 (1989), pp. 291–316. Gist, M. "Self-efficacy: Implications for organizational behavior and human resource management." *Academy of Management*

Review (July 1987), pp. 472–85. Manz, C. C., and H. P. Simms. "Vicarious learning: The influence of modeling on organizational behavior." *Academy of Management Review* 6 (1981), pp. 105–13.

15. Ford, J., E. Smith, D. Weissbein, S. Gully, and E. Salas. "Relationships of goal orientation, metacognitive activity, and practice strategies with learning outcomes and transfer." *Journal of Applied Psychology* 83 (1998), pp. 218–33. Locke, E. A., E. F. Lee, and P. Bobko. "Effect of self-efficacy, goals, and task strategies of task performance." *Journal of Applied Psychology* (May 1984), pp. 241–51.

16. Kozlowski, S., S. Gully, K. Brown, E. Salas, E. Smith, and E. Nason, "Effects of training goals and goal orientation traits on multidimensional training outcomes and performance adaptability." *Organizational Behavior and Human Decision Processes* 85 (2001), pp. 1–31. Colquitt, J., J. Lepine, and R. Noe. "Toward an integrative theory of training motivation: A meta-analytic path analysis of 20 years of research." *Journal of Applied Psychology* 85 (2000), pp. 678–707.

17. Ibid. Ford et al., op. cit. (1998).

18. Ibid. Kraiger, K., J. Ford, and E. Salas. "Application of cognitive, skill-based, and affective theories of learning outcomes to new methods of training evaluation." *Journal of Applied Psychology* 78, no. 2 (1993), pp. 311–28.

19. Schacter, D. *Searching for Memory: The Brain, the Mind and the Past* (1996). New York: Basic Books. Squire, L., A. Shimamura, and P. Graf. "Independence of recognition memory and priming effects: A neuropsychological analysis." *Journal of Experimental Psychology* 11 (1985), pp. 34–44. Squire, L., and S. Zola-Morgan. "The medial temporal lobe memory system." *Science* 253 (1991), pp. 1380–86.

20. Bruner, J. S. *Toward a Theory of Instruction* (1966). New York: Norton.

21. Gagné, R. M. *The Conditions of Learning* (1965). New York: Holt, Rinehart, and Winston.

22. Piaget, J. *The Construction of Reality in the Child* (1954). New York: Basic Books.

23. Skinner, B. F. *Beyond Freedom and Dignity* (1971). New York: Bantam/Vintage.

24. Knowles, M. F. "Adult learning: Theory and practice." *The Handbook of Human Resource Development* (1984), edited by D. A. Nadler. New York: Wiley. Knowles, M. F. *The Making of an Adult Educator* (1989). San Francisco, CA: Jossey-Bass.

25. Bandura, A. *Social Learning Theory* (1977b). Upper Saddle River, NJ: Prentice Hall. Bandura, op. cit. (1977a). Kraut, A. J. "Behavior modeling symposium: Developing managerial skills via modeling techniques." *Personnel Psychology* 29 (1976), pp. 325–28.

26. Gagné, R. M., L. Briggs, and W. Wager. *Principles of Instructional Design* (1992). Fort Worth, TX: Harcourt Brace Jovanovich.

27. Ibid.

28. Ibid.

29. Based on an example from Gagné et al. (1992).

30. Noe, R. A. "Trainee attributes and attitudes: Neglected influences on training effectiveness." *Academy of Management Review* 11 (1986), pp. 736–49. Kanfer, R. "Motivation theory and industrial and organizational psychology." *Handbook of Industrial and Organizational Psychology* (1991), vol. 1, edited by M. D. Dunnette and L. M. Hough. Palo Alto, CA: Consulting Psychologists Press.

31. Blum, M., and J. Naylor. *Industrial Psychology* (1956). New York: Harper Row.

32. Facteau, J., G. Dobbins, J. Russell, R. Ladd, and J. Kudisch. "The influence of general perceptions of the training environment on pretraining motivation and perceived training transfer." *Journal of Management* 21 (1995), pp. 1–5. Tracey, J., S. Tannenbaum, and M. Kavanaugh. "Applying trained skills on the job." *The Importance of the Work Environment* 80 (1995), pp. 239–52.

33. Coch, L., and J. French. "Overcoming resistance to change." *Human Relations* 1 (1948), pp. 512–32.

34. Facteau et al., op. cit. (1995).

35. Smith-Jentsch, K., E. Salas, and M. Brannick. "To transfer or not to transfer? Investigating the combined effects of trainee characteristics, team leader support, and team climate." *Journal of Applied Psychology* 86 (2001), pp. 279–92.

36. Jensen, A. R. *The g Factor: The Science of Mental Ability* (1998). Westport, CT: Praeger.

37. Kanfer, R., and P. Ackerman. "Motivation and cognitive abilities: An integrative aptitude/treatment interaction approach to skill acquisition." *Journal of Applied Psychology* 74 (1989), pp. 657–89.

38. Colquitt, J. and Simmings, M. Conscientiousness, goal orientation, and motivation to learn during the learning process: A longitudinal study. *Journal of Applied Psychology* 83 (1998), pp. 654–65.

39. Liebermann, S. and Hoffmann, S. The impact of practical relevance on training transfer: Evidence from a service quality training program for German bank clerks. *International Journal of Training and Development* 12 (2008), pp. 74–86.

40. Baltes, P. B., and S. L. Willis. "Toward psychological theories of aging." *Handbook on the Psychology of Aging* (1976), edited by J. E. Birren and K. W. Schaie. New York: Van Nostrand Reinhold. Griffin, G., A. Tough, W. Barnard, and D. Brundage. *The Design of Self-Directed Learning* (1980). Toronto: Ontario Institute for Studies in Education. Knowles, M. S. *The Adult Learner: A Neglected Species* (1978). Houston: Gulf Publishing. Pierce, J., D. Gardner, L. Cummings, and R. Dunham. "Organization-based self-esteem: Construct definition, measurement, and validation." *Academy of Management Journal* (September 1989), pp. 622–48.

41. Geddie, C., and B. Strickland. "From plateaus to progress: A model for career development." *Training* (June 1984), pp. 56–61. Leibowitz, Z. B., C. Farren, and B. L. Kaye. *Designing Career Development Systems* (1986). San Francisco, CA: Jossey-Bass.

42. Klein, H. J., R. A. Noe, and C. Wang. Motivation to learn and course outcomes: The impact of delivery mode, leaning goal orientaum, and perceived barriers and enablers. *Personnel Psychology* 59, no. 3 (2006), p. 665–94. Colquitt and Simmings, op. cit. (1998).

43. Dweck, C. S., and E. Leggett. "A social cognitive motivation and personality." *Psychological Review* 95 (1988), pp. 256–73.

44. Ibid. Hafsteinsson, L. G. "The interacting effect of self-efficacy and performance goal orientation on goal setting and performance." Masters Thesis (2002), submitted to the Virginia Polytechnic Institute and Virginia State University.

45. Seijts, G., G. Latham, K. Tasa, and B. Latham. Goal setting and goal orientation on two learning outcomes: An integration on two different yet related literatures. *Academy of Management Journal* 82 (1997), pp. 792–802.

46. Fisher, S. L., and J. K. Ford. "Differential effects of learner effort and goal orientation on two learning outcomes." *Personnel Psychology* 51 (1998), pp. 397–421. Phillips, J., and S. Gully. "The role of goal orientation, ability, need for achievement, and locus of control in the self-efficacy and goal setting process." *Journal of Applied Psychology* 82 (1997), pp. 792–802. Vande Walle, D., S. Ganesan, S. Challagalla, and S. Brown. "An integrated model of feedback seeking behavior: Disposition, context, and cognition." *Journal of Applied Psychology* 85 (2000), pp. 996–1003. Chiaburu, D., and S. Marinova. "What predicts skill transfer? An exploratory study of goal orientation, training self-efficacy, and organizational supports." *International Journal of Training and Development* 9 (2005), pp. 110–23.

47. Seijts, Latham, Tasa, and Latham, op. cit. (2004).

48. Ibid.

49. Knowles, op. cit. (1978). Knowles, op. cit. (1984). Tough, A. "New conclusions on why and how adults learn." *Training* (January 1979), pp. 8–10.

50. Knowles, op. cit. (1984).

51. Westmeyer, P. *Effective Teaching in Adult and Higher Education* (1988). Springfield, IL: Charles C. Thomas.

52. Klein, Noe, and Wang, op. cit. (2006).

53. Belmont, J., and E. Butterfield. "Learning strategies as determinants of memory deficiencies." *Cognitive Psychology* 2 (1971), pp. 411–20. Brown, A., and A. Palicsar. "Inducing strategic learning from texts by means of informed, self-control training." *Learning and Learning Disabilities* (April 1982), pp. 1–17.

54. Borkowski, J. "Sign of intelligence: Strategy generalization and metacognition." *The Growth of Reflection* (1985), edited by S. R. Yussen. New York: Academic Press. Kendall, C., J. Borkowski, and J. Cavanaugh. "Metamemory and the transfer of an interrogative strategy by EMR children." *Intelligence* 4 (1980), pp. 255–70. Walker, C. "Relative importance of domain knowledge and overall aptitude on acquisition of domain-related information." *Cognition and Instruction* 4 (1987), pp. 25–42.

55. Brookfield, S. *Developing Critical Thinkers* (1987). San Francisco, CA: Jossey-Bass. Knowles, op. cit. (1984). Marsick, V. *Learning in the Workplace: Theory and Practice* (1987). London, U.K.: Croom Helm.

Chapter 4

1. Rummler, G. "Determining needs." *Training and Development Handbook* (1987), edited by R. L. Craig. New York: McGraw-Hill.

2. Cascio, W. "Using utility analysis to assess training outcomes." *Training and Development in Organizations* (1989), edited by I. L. Goldstein, San Francisco, CA: Jossey-Bass. Cascio, W. *Costing Human Resources: The Financial Impact of Behavior in Organizations* (1991a). Boston, MA: PWS-Kent.

3. Galagan, P. A. "Training isn't the point." *Training and Development* (May 1999), pp. 28–29.

4. Korth, S. "Consolidating needs assessment and evaluation." *Performance Improvement* 40 (2001), pp. 38–43.

5. McGehee, W., and P. W. Thayer. *Training in Business and Industry* (1961). New York: Wiley.

6. McGehee and Thayer, op. cit. (1961).

7. Tannenbaum, S., and G. Yukl. "Training and development in work organizations." *American Review of Psychology* 43 (1992), pp. 399–441.

8. Brinkerhoff, R. "Increasing impact of training investments: An evaluation strategy for building organizational learning capability." *Industrial and Commercial Training* 38 (2006), pp. 302–07

9. Dayal, I., and J. Thomas. "Operation KPE: Developing a new organization." *Journal of Behavioral Science* 4 (1968), pp. 473–506.

10. McCormick, E. *Job Analysis* (1979). New York: AMACOM.

11. Kraiger, K., J. Ford, and E. Salas. "Application of cognitive based and affective theories of learning outcomes to new methods of training evaluation." *Journal of Applied Psychology* 78 (1993), pp. 311–28.

12. Shoben, E. J. "Applications of multidimensional scaling in cognitive psychology." *Applied Psychological Measurement* 7 (1983), pp. 473–90.

13. Davis, M., M. Curtis, and J. Tschetter. "Evaluating cognitive training outcomes: Validity and utility of structural assessment." *Journal of Business and Psychology* 18 (2003), pp. 191–206. Ford, J. K., and K. Kraiger. "The application of cognitive constructs and principles to the instructional systems model of training: Implications for needs assessment, design, and transfer." *International Review of Industrial and Organizational Psychology* 10, edited by C. L. Cooper and T. J. Robertson (1995), pp. 1–48. Goldsmith, P. E., and P. J. Johnson. "A structural assessment of classroom learning, in Pathfinder Associative Networks." *Studies in Knowledge Organization* (1990), edited by R. W. Schvaneveldt. Norwood, NJ: Ablex. Cook, N. M., and J. E. McDonald. "The application of psychological scaling techniques to knowledge elicitation for knowledge based systems." *International Journal of Man-Made Machine Studies* 28 (1987), pp. 533–50. Champagne, A. B., L. E. Klopfer, A. T. Desena, and D. A. Squires. "Structural representations of students' knowledge before and after science instruction." *Journal of Research in Science Technology* 18 (1981), pp. 97–111.

14. Shippmann, J., et al. "The practice of competency modeling." *Personnel Psychology* 53 (2000), pp. 703–40.

15. Cook, S. "Learning needs analysis: Part I: What is learning needs analysis?" *Training* (2005), pp. 64–70.

16. Montier, R., D. Alai, and D. Kramer. "Competency models develop top performance." *Training and Development* 60 (2006), pp. 47–50.

17. Parry, S. "Just what is a competency?" *Training* (1998), pp. 59–64.

18. Miller, L. "Editorial." *International Journal of Training and Development* 3 (1999), pp. 82–89.

19. Shippmann et al., op. cit. (2000).

20. Cardy, R., and Selvarajan, T. "Competencies: Alternative frameworks for competitive advantage." *Business Horizons*, 49 (2006). pp. 235–45.

21. Rothwell, W., and Lindholm, J. "Competency, identification, modeling, and assessment in the United States." *International Journal of Training and Development* 3 (1999), pp. 90–105.

22. Rothwell, W. "Competency based or a traditional approach to training." *Training and Development* 58 (2004), p. 46–57.

23. Shippmann et al., op. cit. (2000).

24. Rothwell, op. cit. (1999). Mirabile, R. "Everything you wanted to know about competency modeling." *Training and Development Journal* (August 1997), pp. 73–77.

25. Dalton, M. "Are competency models a waste?" *Training and Development* (October 1997), pp. 46–49.

26. Ibid.

27. Montier, Alai, and Kramer, op. cit. (2006).

28. Bernardin, H. J., and R. Beatty. *Performance Appraisal: Assessing Human Behavior at Work* (1984). Boston, MA: Kent.

29. Benedict, M. E., and E. L. Levine. "Delay and distortion: Tacit influences on performance appraisal." *Journal of Applied Psychology* 73 (1988), pp. 507–14. Longenecker, C. O., H. P. Sims, and D. A. Gioia. "Behind the mask: The politics of employee appraisal." *Academy of Management Executive* 1 (1987), pp. 183–93.

30. Payne, R., and D. Pugh. "Organizational structure and climate." *Handbook of Industrial and Organizational Psychology* (1976), edited by M. Dunnette. Chicago: Rand McNally.

31. Cascio, W. *Applied Psychology in Personnel Management* (1991b). Upper Saddle River, NJ: Prentice Hall.

32. Herbert, G., and D. Doverspike. "Performance appraisal in the training needs analysis process: A review and critique." *Public Personnel Management* 19 (1990), pp. 253–70.

33. Murphy, K. R., and J. N. Cleveland. *Performance Appraisal: An Organizational Perspective* (1991). Boston, MA: Allyn & Bacon.

34. Thorndike, E. L. "A constant error in psychological ratings." *Journal of Applied Psychology* 4 (1920), pp. 25–29.

35. Bass, B. "Reducing leniency in merit ratings." *Personnel Psychology* 9 (1956), pp. 359–69. Harris, M. M., and J. Schaubroek. "A meta-analysis of self-supervisor, self-peer, and peer-supervisor ratings." *Personnel Psychology* 41 (1988), pp. 43–62.

36. Farh, J., and G. Dobbins. "Effects of self-esteem on leniency bias in self-reports of performance: A structural equation analysis." *Personnel Psychology* 42 (1989), pp. 835–50.

37. Williams, J., and P. Levy. "The effects of perceived system knowledge on the agreement between self-ratings and supervisor ratings." *Personnel Psychology* 45 (1992), pp. 835–47.

38. McEnery, J., and J. McEnery. "Self-ratings in management training: A neglected opportunity?" *Journal of Occupational Psychology* 60 (1987), pp. 49–60.

39. Cheung, G. "Multifaceted conceptions of self-other ratings disagreement." *Personnel Psychology* 52 (1999), pp. 1–35.

40. London, M., and R. Beatty. "360-degree feedback as a competitive advantage." *Human Resource Management* 32 (1993), pp. 353–72.

41. Pollitt, D. "Alliance Unichem used 360-degree feedback to improve performance." *Human Resource Management International Digest* 12 (2004), pp. 27–30.

42. Brutus, S., M. London, and J. Martineau. "The impact of 360-degree feedback on planning for career development." *Journal of Management Development* 18 (1999), pp. 676–93.

43. Pfau, B., I. Kay, K. Nowack, and J. Ghorpade. "Does 360-degree feedback negatively affect company performance?" *HR Magazine* 47 (2000), pp. 54–60.

44. Maurer, T., D. Mitchell, and F. Barbeite. "Predictors of attitudes toward a 360-degree feedback system and involvement in post-feedback development activity." *Journal of Occupational and Organizational Psychology* 75 (2002), pp. 87–107.

45. Dalton, F. "Using 360-degree feedback mechanisms." *Occupational Health and Safety* 74 (2005), pp. 28–30.

46. Nunnaly, J. *Psychometric Theory* (1978). New York: McGraw-Hill.

47. Kropp, R., and E. Hankin. "Paper-and-pencil tests for evaluating instruction." *Evaluating Training Programs* (1975), edited by D. Kirkpatrick. Madison, WI: American Society of Training and Development.

48. Seashore, S., E. Lawler, P. Mirvis, and C. Cammann. *Assessing Organizational Change* (1983). New York: Wiley.

49. Cook, J., S. Hepworth, T. Wall, J. Toby, and P. Warr. *The Experience of Work: A Compendium and Review of 249 Measures and Their Use* (1981). New York: Academic Press.

50. Robinson, J., R. Athanasiou, and K. Head. *Measuring of Occupational Attitudes and Occupational Characteristics* (1976). Ann Arbor, MI: Institute for Social Research.

51. Ford, J. K., and R. A. Noe. "Self-assessed training needs: The effects of attitudes toward training, managerial level, and function." *Personnel Psychology* 40 (1987), pp. 39–53.

52. Fisher, C. "Transmission of negative and positive feedback to subordinates: A laboratory investigation." *Journal of Psychology* 64 (1979), pp. 533–40.

53. Carrol, S., and C. Schneier. *Performance Appraisal and Review Systems* (1982). Glenview, IL: Scott Foresman.

54. Michalak, D. F., and E. G. Yager. *Making the Training Process Work* (1979). New York: Harper & Row.

55. Brinkerhoff, op. cit. (2006).

56. Schneider, B., and A. Konz. "Strategic job analysis." *Human Resource Management* 28 (1989). pp. 51–63.

57. Ibid.

58. Casner, J. *Successful Training Strategies* (1989). San Francisco, CA: Jossey-Bass.

59. Burns, T., and G. M. Stalker. *The Management of Innovation* (1961). London, U.K.: Tavistock.

60. Mintzberg, H. "Crafting strategy." *Harvard Business Review* (July/August 1987), pp. 66–75.

61. Keats, B., and J. Bracker. "Toward a theory of small firm performance." *American Journal of Small Business* 4 (1988), pp. 35–43.

62. Kerr, G., S. A. Way, and J. W. Thacker. "Performance, HR practices and the HR manager in small entrepreneurial firms." *Journal of Small business Management and Entrepreneurship,* 20 (2007), pp. 55–68. Way, S. "High performance work systems and intermediate indicators of firm performance within the US small business sector." *Journal of Management,* 28 (2002), pp. 765–85.

63. Freel, M. S. "Patterns of innovation and skills in small firms." *Technovation* 25 (2005), p. 123.

64. Banks, M., A. Bures, and D. Champion. "Decision-making factors in small business: Training and development." *Journal of Small Business Management* (January 1987), pp. 19–26.

65. Fairfield-Sonn, J. "A strategic process model for small business training and development." *Journal of Small Business Management* (January 1987), pp. 11–18.

66. Lee, W., and D. Owens. "Rapid analysis model." *Performance Improvement Quarterly* 40 (2001), pp. 13–18. Rossett, A. *First Things Fast: A Handbook for Performance Analysis* (1998). New York: Pfeiffer.

67. The list is partially based on Rossett (1998).

Chapter 4 Appendix

1. Thorndike, R. L. *Personnel Selection: Test and Measurement Technique* (1949). New York: Wiley.

2. Blum, M. L., and J. C. Naylor. *Industrial Psychology: Its Theoretical and Social Foundation* (1968). New York: Harper & Row.

3. Ibid.

4. Ibid.

5. Nunnally, J. *Psychometric Theory* (1978). New York: McGraw-Hill.
6. Blum and Naylor, op. cit. (1968).

Chapter 5

1. Gavin, T. "Industry report." *Training* (October 2001), pp. 40–75.
2. Marquardt, M., N. Nissley, R. Ozag, and T. Taylor. "International briefing 6: Training and development in the United States." *International Journal of Training and Development* 4 (2000), pp. 138–49.
3. Mager, R. *Preparing Instructional Objectives* (1975). Belmont, CA: Pitman Learning.
4. Langdon, D. "Objectives? Get over them." *Training and Development* (February 1999), pp. 54–58. Stoneall, L. "The case for more flexible objectives." *Training and Development* (August 1992), pp. 67–69.
5. Stoneall, op. cit. (1992).
6. Langdon, op. cit. (1999).
7. Colquitt, J., J. LePine, and R. Noe. "Toward an integrative theory of training motivation: A meta-analytic path analysis of 20 years of research." *Journal of Applied Psychology* 85 (2000), pp. 678–707.
8. Lewis, J. "Answers to twenty questions on behavioral objectives." Educational Technology (March 1981), pp. 27–31.
9. Locke, E., K. Shaw, L. Saari, and G. Latham. "Goal setting and task performance." *Psychological Bulletin* 90 (1981), pp. 125–52.
10. Latham, G. P., and G. A. Yukl. "A review of research on the application of goal setting in organizations." *Academy of Management Journal* 18 (1981), pp. 824–45.
11. Lewis, op. cit. (1981).
12. Filipczak, B. "Old dogs, new tricks." *Training* 35 (1998), pp. 50–58.
13. Tossi, M. "Labor force projections to 2016: More workers in their golden years." *Monthly Labor Review* (November 2007), pp. 33–52.
14. Sleezer, C., and D. Denny. "Strategies for developing a high skilled workforce." *Performance Improvement Quarterly* 17 (2004), pp. 41–56.
15. Fullerton and Tossi, op. cit. (2001).
16. Felder, R. M., and L. K. Silverman, "Learning and teaching styles in engineering education." *Journal of Engineering Education* 78, no. 7 (1988), pp. 674–81. Litzinger, T. A., S. H. Lee, J. C. Wise, and R. M. Felder, "A Psychometric Study of the Index of Learning Styles." *Journal of Engineering Education* 96, no. 4 (2007), pp. 309–19.
17. Cronbach, L., and R. Snow. *Aptitude and Instructional Methods* (1977). New York: Irvington.
18. Goldstein, I. "Training in work organizations." *Annual Review of Psychology* 39 (1980), pp. 229–72.
19. Ryman, D., and R. Biersner. "Attitudes predictive of diving training success." *Personnel Psychology* 28 (1975), pp. 181–88.
20. Colquitt et al., op. cit. (2000).
21. Latham, G. P., and E. A. Locke. "Goal setting: A motivational technique that works." *Organizational Dynamics* 8 (1979), pp. 68–80. Locke et al., op. cit. (1981).
22. Dweck, C. S., and E. Leggett. "A social cognitive motivation and personality." *Psychological Review* 95 (1988), pp. 256–73.
23. Ibid. Hafsteinsson, L. G. "The interacting effect of self-efficacy and performance goal orientation on goal setting and performance." Masters Thesis (2002), submitted to the Virginia Polytechnic Institute and Virginia State University.
24. Seijts, G. H., G. Latham, K. Tasa, and B. Latham. "Goal setting and goal orientation: An integration of two different yet related literatures." *Academy of Management Journal* 47 (2004), pp. 227–39.
25. Fisher, S. L., and J. K. Ford. "Differential effects of learner effort and goal orientation on two learning outcomes." *Personnel Psychology* 51 (1998), pp. 397–421. Phillips, J., and S. Gully. "The role of goal orientation, ability, need for achievement, and locus of control in the self-efficacy and goal setting process." *Journal of Applied Psychology* 82 (1997), pp. 792–802. VandeWalle, D., S. Ganesan, S. Challagalla, and S. Brown. "An integrated model of feedback seeking behavior: Disposition, context, and cognition." *Journal of Applied Psychology* 85 (2000), pp. 996–1003. Chiaburu, D., and S. Marinova. "What predicts skill transfer? An exploratory study of goal orientation, training self-efficacy, and organizational supports." *International Journal of Training and Development* 9 (2005), pp. 110–23.
26. Seijts, Latham, Tasa, and Latham, op. cit. (2004).
27. Ibid.
28. Reigeluth, C. "What is instructional design theory and how is it changing?" *Instructional Design Theories and Models: An Overview of Their Current Status* (1999a), vol. 2, edited by C. Reigeluth. Mahwah, NJ: Lawrence Erlbaum Associates.
29. Klatzky, R. *Human Memory: Structures and Processes* (1975). San Francisco, CA: Freeman.
30. Lindsay, P., and D. Norman. *Human Information Processing: An Introduction to Psychology* (1972). New York: Academic Press.
31. Anderson, J. R., and G. H. Bower. "Recognition and retrieval processes in free recall." *Psychological Review* 79 (1972), pp. 97–123. Bandura, A. *Social Learning Theory* (1977), Upper Saddle River, NJ: Prentice Hall. Melton, A. W., and E. Martin. *Coding Processes in Human Memory* (1972). Washington, DC: Winston.
32. Anderson, J. R., and G. H. Bower. *Human Associative Memory* (1 1973). Washington, DC: Winston.
33. Cascio, W. *Managing Human Resources* (1995). New York: McGraw-Hill Ryerson.
34. Demster, F. "The spacing effect: A case study in the failure to apply the results of psychological research." *American Psychologist* 43 (1990), pp. 627–34.
35. Dipboye, R. "Organizational barriers to implementing a rational model of training." *Training for a Rapidly Changing Workplace* (1997), edited by M. Quinones and I. Ehrenstein. Washington, DC: American Psychological Association.
36. Donovan, J., and D. Radosevich. "A meta-analytic review of the distribution of practice effect: Now you see it, now you do not." *Journal of Applied Psychology* 84 (1999), pp. 795–804.
37. Ibid.
38. Baldwin, T., and K. Ford. "Transfer of training: A review and directions for future research." *Personnel Psychology* 41 (1988), pp. 63–105.
39. Winfred, A., J. Villado, P. Boatman, A. Bhupatkar, E. Day, and W. Bennett. "Complex skill acquisition decay, and transfer: The comparative effectiveness of massed and distributed practices." Paper presented at the 20th Annual SIOP Conference, SIOP Poster 28–22 (April 15–17, 2005), Los Angles, CA.
40. Adams, J. "Historical review and appraisal of research on the learning, retention, and transfer of human motor skills." *Psychological Bulletin* 101 (1987), pp. 41–74.

41. Naylor, J., and G. Briggs. "Effects of rehearsal of temporal and spatial aspects on the long-term retention of a procedural skill." *Journal of Applied Psychology* 47 (1963), pp. 120–26.

42. Blum, M., and J. Naylor. *Industrial Psychology, Its Theoretical and Social Foundations* (1968), New York: Harper & Row.

43. Atwater, S. "Proactive inhibition and associative facilitation as affected by the degree of prior learning." *Journal of Experimental Psychology* 46 (1953), pp. 400–4 Hagman, J. D., and A. M. Rose. "Retention of military tasks: A review." *Human Factors* 25 (1983), pp. 199–214. Mandler, G. "Transfer of training as a response to overlearning." *Journal of Experimental Psychology* 7 (1954), p. 7.

44. Schendel, J. D., and J. D. Hagman. "On sustaining procedural skills over a prolonged retention interval." *Journal of Applied Psychology* 67 (1982), pp. 605–10.

45. Clark, R., Colvin, F., and J. Sweller. *Efficiency in Learning: Evidence-based Guidelines to Manage Cognitive Load* (2006), San Francisco, CA: Jossey-Bass.

46. May, L., and W. Kahnweiler. "The effect of a mastery practice design on learning and transfer in behavior modeling training." *Personnel Psychology* 53 (2000), pp. 353–73.

47. Thorndike, E. L., and R. S. Woodworth. "The influence of improvement in one mental function upon the efficiency of other functions: Functions involving attention, observation, and discrimination." *Psychological Review* 8 (1901), pp. 553–64.

48. Locke, E., and G. Latham. *A Theory of Goal Setting and Task Performance* (1990). Upper Saddle River, NJ: Prentice Hall.

49. Martocchio, J. J., and J. Dulebohn. "Performance feedback effects in training: The role of perceived controllability." *Personnel Psychology* 47 (1994), pp. 357–73.

50. Bandura, A. "Social cognitive theory of self-regulation." *Organizational Behavior and Human Decision* 50 (1991), pp. 248–87.

51. Marx, R. D. "Relapse prevention for managerial training: A model for maintenance of behavior change." *Academy of Management Review* 7 (1982), pp. 433–41.

52. Brownell, K. D., G. Marlatt, E. Lichenstein, and G. Wilson. "Understanding and preventing relapse." *American Psychologist* 41 (1986), pp. 765–82.

53. Feldman, M. "Successful post-training skill application." *Training and Development Journal* 35 (1981), pp. 72–75. Wexley and Baldwin, op. cit. (1986).

54. Wexley, K., and T. Baldwin. "Post-training strategies for facilitating positive transfer: An empirical exploration." *Academy of Management Journal* 29 (1986), pp. 503–20.

55. Marx, R. "Improving management development through relapse prevention strategies." *Journal of Management Development* 5 (1986), pp. 27–40.

56. Wexley and Baldwin, op. cit. (1986).

57. Burke, L., and T. Baldwin. "Workforce training transfer: A study of the effect of relapse prevention training and transfer climate." *Human Resource Management* 38 (1999), pp. 227–42.

58. Cromwell, J., and J. Kolb. "An examination of work environment support factors affecting transfer of supervisory skills to the workplace." *Human Resource Development Quarterly* 15 (2004), pp. 449–71. Seyler, D., E. Holton, R. Bates, R. M. Burnett, and M. Carvalho. "Factors affecting motivation to transfer." *International Journal of Training and Development* 2 (1998), p. 16. Baldwin and Ford, op. cit. (1988).

59. Orpen, C. "The influence of the training environment on trainee motivation and perceived training quality." *International Journal of Training and Development* 3 (1999), pp. 34–43.

60. Noe, R. A., and S. L. Wilk. "Investigation of the factors that influence employees' participation in developmental activities." *Journal of Applied Psychology* 78 (1993), pp. 291–302.

61. Hicks, W. D., and R. J. Klimoski. "Entry into training programs and its effect on training outcomes: A field experiment." *Academy of Management Journal* 30 (1987), pp. 542–52.

62. Ibid.

63. Cromwell and Kolb, op. cit. (2004). Sayler et al., op. cit., (1998).

64. Bergman, T. "Job performance learning: A comprehensive approach to high-performance training design." *Employment Relations Today* (Winter 1993), pp. 399–409.

65. Wexley and Baldwin, op. cit. (1986).

66. Stark, C. "Ensuring skills transfer: A sensitive approach." *Training and Development Journal* (March 1986), pp. 50–51.

67. Ibid.

68. Orpen, op. cit. (1999).

69. Cromwell and Kolb, op. cit. (2004). Tracey, B., S. Tannenbaum, and M. Kavanaugh. "Applying trained skills on the job: The importance of the work environment." *Journal of Applied Psychology* 80 (1995), pp. 239–51.

70. Schneider, B. *Organizational Climate and Culture* (1990). San Francisco, CA: Jossey-Bass.

71. Orpen, op. cit. (1999).

72. Burke and Baldwin, op. cit. (1999).

73. Olsen, J. "The evaluation and enhancement of training transfer." *International Journal of Training and Development* 2 (1998), pp. 61–75.

74. Schein, E. H. *Organizational Culture and Leadership* (1985). San Francisco, CA: Jossey-Bass.

75. Tracey et al., op. cit. (1995).

76. Cascio, op. cit. (1995).

77. Thacker, J., and J. Cattaneo. *Survey of Personnel Practices in Canadian Organizations* (1992). Working Paper Series W92–04, ISSN 07146191. University of Windsor, Faculty of Business Administration.

78. Merrill, M. "Component display theory." *Instructional Design Theories and Models: An Overview of Their Current Status* (1983), edited by C. Reigeluth. Hillsdale NJ: Lawrence Erlbaum Associates.

79. Romiszowski, A. "The development of physical skills: Instruction in the psychomotor domain." *Instructional Design Theories and Models: An Overview of Their Current Status* (1999), vol. 2, edited by C. Reigeluth. Mahwah, NJ: Lawrence Erlbaum Associates.

80. Reigeluth, C. *Instructional Design Theories and Models: An Overview of Their Current Status* (1999b). Mahwah, NJ: Lawrence Erlbaum Associates.

81. Reigeluth, C. "Elaboration theory: Guidance for scope and sequence decisions." *Instructional Design Theories and Models: An Overview of Their Current Status.* (1999c), vol. 2, edited by C. Reigeluth. Mahwah, NJ: Lawrence Erlbaum Associates.

82. Gagné, R., L. Briggs, and W. Wager. *Principles of Instructional Design* (1988). New York: Holt, Rinehart, and Winston.

83. Reigeluth, C., op. cit. (1999a).

84. Reigeluth, C., op. cit. (1999c).

85. Ibid.

86. English, R., and C. Reigeluth. "Formative research on sequencing instruction with elaboration theory." *Education Technology, Research and Development* 44 (1996), pp. 23–44.

87. Carson H., and R. Curtis. "Applying instructional design theory to bibliographic instruction: Macro theory." *Research Strategies* 9 (1991), pp. 164–79. Reigeluth, C. "Lesson blueprints based on elaboration theory of instruction." *Instructional Theories* (1987), edited by C. Reigeluth. Hillsdale, NJ: Lawrence Erlbaum Associates. English and Reigeluth, op. cit. (1996).

88. Gagné, R., L. Briggs, and W. *Principles of Instructional Design* (1988). New York: Holt, Rinehart, and Winston.

89. Ibid.

90. Hornsby, J., and D. Kuratko. "Human resource management in small business: Critical issues for the 1990s." *Journal of Small Business Management* (July 1990), pp. 9–19.

91. Deshpande, S., and D. Golhar. "HRM practices in large and small manufacturing firms: A comparative study." *Journal of Small Business Management* (April 1994), pp. 49–56.

92. Ahire, S., and D. Golhar. "Quality management in large vs. small firms." *Journal of Small Business Management* (April 1996), pp. 1–13.

93. Kerr, G., S. A. Way, and J. W. Thacker. "Performance, HR practices, and the HR manager in small entrepreneurial firms." *Journal of Small Business Management and Entrepreneurship.* 20 (2007), pp. 55–68. Way, S. A. "High performance work systems and intermediate indicators of firm performance within the U.S. small business sector." *Journal of Management* 28 (2002), pp. 765–85.

94. McRae, C., A. Banks, A. Bures, and D. Champion. "Decision-making factors in small business: Training and development." *Journal of Small Business Management* (January 1987), pp. 19–25.

95. May and Kahnweiler, op. cit. (2000).

Chapter 6

1. Broadwell, M. *The Lecture Method of Instruction* (1980). Englewood Cliffs, NJ: Educational Technology Publications.

2. Brown, G. *Lecturing and Explaining* (1978). London, U.K.: Methuen & Co. Bligh, D. *What's the Use of Lectures?* (1974). Middlesex, England: Penguin Education.

3. Broadwell, op. cit. (1980).

4. Broadwell, M., and C. Dietrich. "How to get trainees into the action." *Training* (February 1996), pp. 52–56.

5. Ibid.

6. Johnstone, A., and F. Percival. "Attention breaks in lectures." *Education in Chemistry* 13 (1976), pp. 273–304. Lloyd, D. "A concept of improvement of learning response in the taught lesson." *Visual Education* (Winter 1968), pp. 23–25. Maddox, H., and E. Hook. "Performance decrement in the lecture." *Educational Research* 28 (1975), pp. 17–30.

7. Killian, D. *The Impact of Flight Simulators on U.S. Airlines* (1976). Fort Worth, TX: American Airlines Flight Academy. Mecham, M. "Cathay refines approach to simulator training." *Aviation Week and Space Technology* (January 1994), pp. 35–37.

8. Killian, op. cit. (1976). Parsons, H. M. *Man–Machine System Experiment* (1972), Baltimore, MD: Johns Hopkins University Press.

9. Erwin, D. E. "Psychological fidelity in simulated work environments." *Proceedings of the American Psychological Association* (1978). Toronto, Canada.

10. Edwards, D., C. Hahn, and E. Fleishman. "Evaluation of laboratory methods for the study of driver behavior: Relations between simulator and street performance." *Journal of Applied Psychology* 62 (1980), pp. 559–66.

11. Fink, C. D., and E. L. Shriver. "Simulators for maintenance training: Some issues, problems, and areas for future research." *AFHRL Technical Report*, Brooks Air Force Base, Texas (1978), pp. 78–127.

12. Barrett, G., T. Benko, and G. Riddle. "Programmable simulator speeds operator training." *Bell Laboratories Record* 59, no. 7 (1981), pp. 213–16.

13. Paffet, J. A. "Ships' officers use simulators to learn vessel operation." *Minicomputer News* 4, no. 8 (1978), pp. 11–13.

14. Slack, K. "Training for the real thing." *Training and Development* (May 1993), pp. 79–89.

15. Davis, L. "Evolving alternative organizational designs: Their sociotechnical bases." *Human Relations* 30 (1973), pp. 261–71. Walton, R. "From Hawthorne to Topeka and Kalmar." *Man and Work in Society* (1975), edited by E. Cass and F. Zimmer. New York: Van Nostrand Reinhold Co.

16. Barbian, J. "Get simulated." *Training* (February 2001), pp. 67–70.

17. Dakin, S., and G. Wood. "Learn TQM principles using jumbled proverbs." *Quality Progress* (October 1995), pp. 92–95. Kaplan, R., M. Lombardo, and M. Mazique. "A mirror for managers: Using simulation to develop management teams." *Journal of Applied Behavioral Science* 21 (1985), pp. 241–53. Goudy, R. "Two years of management experience in two challenging weeks." *ABA Banking Journal* 73, no. 6 (1981), pp. 74–77. Groth, J., and C. Phillips. "What would you do if a crisis hit your firm?" *Management World* 7, no. 3 (1978), pp. 12–16. Zemke, R. "Can games and simulations improve your training power?" *Training* 19, no. 2 (1982), pp. 24–31.

18. Faria, T., Personal communication (2002).

19. Argyris, C. "Some limitations of the case method: Experiences in a management development program." *Academy of Management Review* 5 (1980), pp. 291–98.

20. Pigors, P., and F. Pigors. "The case method." *Training and Development Handbook: A Guide to Human Resource Development* (1987), edited by R. Craig. New York: McGraw-Hill, pp. 414–29.

21. Argyris, C. "Some limitations to the case method: Experience in a management development program." *Academy of Management Review* 5 (1980), pp. 291–98.

22. Engel, H. *Handbook of Creative Learning Exercises* (1973). Houston, TX: Gulf.

23. Wohlking, W. "Role playing." *Training and Development Handbook* (1976), edited by R. L. Craig. New York: McGraw-Hill.

24. Huegli, J., and H. Tschirgi. "Preparing the student for the initial job interview: Skills and methods." *American Business Communication Association Bulletin* 42, no. 4 (1980), pp. 10–13. Goldstein, op. cit. (1993). Wexley, K., and G. Latham. *Developing and Training Human Resources in Organizations* (1991), 2nd ed. New York: HarperCollins. Sims, H., and C. Manz. "Modeling influences on employee behavior." *Personnel Journal* 61, no. 1 (1982), pp. 58–65.

25. Burke, M., and R. Day. "A cumulative study of the effectiveness of managerial training." *Journal of Applied*

Psychology 71 (1986), pp. 232–45. Decker, P., and B. Nathen. *Behavior Modeling Training: Principles and Applications* (1985), New York: Praeger. Huegli and Tschirgi, op. cit. (1980). Latham, G., and C. Frayne. "Self-management training for increased job attendance: A follow-up and replication." *Journal of Applied Psychology* 74 (1989), pp. 411–16. Smith, P. "Management modeling training to improve morale and customer satisfaction." *Personnel Psychology* 29 (1976), pp. 251–59.

26. Taylor, P. J., D. F. Russ-Eft, and D. W. Chan. "A meta-analytic review of behavior modeling training." *Journal of Applied Psychology* 90, no. 4 (2005), pp. 692–709.

27. Hequet, M. "Video shakeout." *Training* (September 1996), pp. 46–50.

28. Taylor et al., op. cit. (2005).

29. Solem, A. R. "Human relations training: A comparison of case studies." *Personnel Administration* 23 (1960), pp. 29–37. Fazio, R., and M. Zanna. "Direct experience and attitude–behavior consistency." *Advances in Experimental Social Psychology* (1981), edited by L. Berkowitz. New York: Academic Press.

30. Van Gundy, A., ed. *101 Great Games and Activities* (1988). San Francisco, CA: Jossey-Bass/Pfeiffer.

31. Swamidass, P. "New directions for on-the-job training." *Training Strategies for Tomorrow* 17, no. 1 (2003), pp. 10–12.

32. Suzik, H. "On-the-job training: Do it right." *Quality* 38 (1999), pp. 84–85.

33. Gold, L. "Job instruction: Four steps to success." *Training and Development Journal* (September 1981), pp. 28–32.

34. Ibid.

35. *National Apprenticeship Training Program* (1987). Washington, DC: Employment and Training Administration, Department of Labor.

36. Ontario Training and Adjustment Board. *Apprentice Information* (1995). Toronto, Canada: Queens' Printer.

37. Finnerty, M. "Coaching for growth and development." *The Training and Development Handbook* (1996), edited by R. Craig. New York: McGraw-Hill.

38. Orth, C. D., H. E. Wilkinson, and R. C. Benfari. "The manager's role as coach and mentor." *Organizational Dynamics* 15, no. 4 (1987), pp. 66–74.

39. Evered, R., and J. Selman. "Coaching and the art of management." *Organizational Dynamics* 18, no. 2 (1989), pp. 16–32.

40. Feldman, D. "Career coaching: What HR professionals and managers need to know." *Human Resource Planning* 24 (2001), pp. 26–35.

41. Schneider, S. "Coach or mentor? It depends . . ." *Human Resources* (November 2004), p. 42.

42. Phillips-Jones, L. "Establishing a formalized mentoring program." *Training and Development Journal* (February 2004), pp. 38–42.

43. ———. "Lack of mentoring increases mid-level defections." *Corporate Financing Week* (March 2005), p. 1.

44. Gordon, E. E., R. Morgan, and J. Ponticell. "The individualized training alternative." *Training and Development* (September 1995), pp. 52–60.

45. Filipczak, B. "Training on the cheap." *Training* (May 1996), pp. 28–34.

46. Van Buren, M. *The 2001 ASTD State of the Industry Report Training and Development* (February 2001), pp. 19–20.

47. Ibid.

48. Honeycutt, E., Jr., T. McCarty, and V. Howe. "Sales technology applications: Self-paced video enhanced training: A case study." *Journal of Personal Selling and Sales Management* 13, no. 1 (1993), pp. 73–79.

49. Ibid.

50. Gagné, R. *The Conditions of Learning* (1977). New York: Holt, Rinehart, and Winston.

Chapter 7

1. "Interaction has its attraction." *Personnel Journal* (July 1995), pp. 27–28.

2. Gordon, S. E. *Systematic Training Program Design* (1994). Upper Saddle River, NJ: Prentice Hall.

3. Van Buren, M. "The 2001 ASTD state of the industry report." *Training and Development* (February 2001), pp. 19–20.

4. "2007 Industry report." *Training* (November/December 2007), pp. 9–24.

5. Ibid.

6. Ibid.

7. Ibid.

8. Agnvall, E. "Just-in-time training: With MP3 players, iPods and other mobile devices, employee training is truly on the go." *HR Magazine* (May 2006), pp. 66–72.

9. Op. cit. Industry report, 2007.

10. Rosenberg, M. J. "Learning meets Web 2.0: Collaborative learning." *Handbook For Learning Professionals* (2008), edited by E. Biech.

11. Forlenza, D. "Computer-based training." *Professional Safety* (May 1995), pp. 27–29.

12. Steel-Johnson, D., and B. Hyde. "Advanced technologies in training: Intelligent tutoring systems and virtual reality." *Training for a Rapidly Changing Workplace* (1997), edited by M. Quinones and A. Ehrenstein. Washington, DC: American Psychological Association.

13. Ibid.

14. Seidel, R., O. Park, and R. Perez. "Expertise of ICAI: Development requirements." *Computers in Human Behavior* 4 (1988), pp. 235–56.

15. Ong, J., and S. Ramachandran. "Intelligent tutoring systems." *The What and the How. ASTD Learning Circuits* (2000). Available at http://www.learningcircuits.orgfeb2000/org.html

16. D'Mello, S. K., S. D. Craig, A. Witherspoon, A. McDaniel, and A. Graesser. "Automatic detection of learners affect from conversational cues." *User Modeling and User-Adapted Interaction* 18 (2008), pp. 45–80.

17. McQuiggan, S. W., B. W. Mott, and J. C. Lester. Modeling self-efficacy in intelligent tutoring systems: An inductive approach. *User Modeling and User-Adapted Interaction.* 18 (2008), pp. 81–126.

18. Ibid.

19. Anonymous "Industry report." *Training* (November-December 2008), pp. 16–34.

20. "Nugget introduces food safety training and certification through CD-ROM." *Restaurant Hospitality* 83 (1999), pp. S6–S7.

21. Grunberg, D. "Multimedia training." *Franchising World* 31 (1999), p. 50.

22. 2004. http://www.medtrng.com

23. "Put SPIMM in your CBT." *Training* (February 1993), pp. 12, 14.

24. Johnson, G. "Brewing the perfect blend." *Training* (2003), pp. 31–34.

25. Marquardt, M. *Technology-Based Learning* (1999). Boca Raton FL: CRC Press.

26. Steel-Johnson, D., and B. Hyde. "Advanced technologies in training: Intelligent tutoring systems and virtual reality." *Training for a Rapidly Changing Workplace* (1997), edited by M. Quinones and A. Ehrenstein. Washington, DC: American Psychological Association.

27. Fister, S. "Tech trends." *Training* (August 1999), pp. 24–26.

28. Field, S., RTI International. Personal communication (2002).

29. Lee, W. *Multimedia-Based Instructional Design: Computer-Based Training, Web-Based Training, and Distance Broadcast Training* (2000), San Francisco, CA: Jossey-Bass.

30. CNN News. October 20, 2006. http://www.cnn.com/video/#/video/tech/2006/10/20/explorers.virtusphere.cnn

31. University of Pennsylvania. "New Virtual Reality Array Allows Immersive Experience Without the Disorienting 3-D Goggles." *Science Daily*. 2003, May 14. Retrieved July 16, 2008, from http://www.sciencedaily.com

32. Chapman, B. "Learning technology primer." *Handbook for Workplace Learning Professionals* (2008), edited by E. Biech. Alexandria, VA: ASTD Press.

33. Ibid.

34. Ibid.

35. Blumenthal, R., L. Meiskey, S. Dooley, and R. Sparks. "Reducing developmental costs with intelligent tutoring system shells," paper presented at the Workshop on Architectures and Methods for Designing Cost-Effective and Reusable ITSs, Montreal (June 1996).

36. Ibid.

37. Baynton, D. "Cyber learning fortunes." *Training* 38 (2001), pp. 22–23.

38. "Release of the virtual reality training decision tool." 1997. News release, http://www.rti.org/news/news

39. Ibid.

40. Nash, N. J., and M. Vettori. "The relative practical effectiveness of programmed instruction." *Personnel Psychology* 24 (1971), pp. 397–418. Burns, T. "Multimedia and quality." *Quality Progress* (February 1997), pp. 77–84. Stauffer, D. "High-tech training a huge win in Marriott's high-touch culture." 7 (1999). http://www.traininguniversity.com. Fletcher, D. *Intelligent Tutoring Systems: Then and Now*, workshop on Advanced Training Technologies and Learning Environments held at NASA, Langley Research Center (March 1999), NASA/CP-1999-209339.

41. Fletcher, op. cit. (1999).

42. Kearsley, G. *Training and Technology* (1984), Reading, MA: Addison-Wesley.

43. Jensen, E. Personal communication (January 31, 2002).

44. Johnson, op. cit. (2003).

45. Bonk C. J., K. J. Kim, and T. Zeng. "Future directions of blended learning in higher education and workplace learning settings." *Handbook of Blended Learning: Global Perspectives, Local Designs* (2005), edited by C. J. Bonk and C. R. Graham. San Francisco, CA: Pfeiffer.

46. Sitzmann, T., K. Kraiger, D. Stewart, and R. Wissher. "The comparative effectiveness of Web-based and classroom instruction: A meta-analysis." *Personnel Psychology* 59 (2006), pp. 623–65.

Chapter 8

1. Davis, I. K., and J. Hagman. "What is right and wrong with your training room environment." *Training* (July 1976), p. 28.

2. Chaddock, P. "How do your trainers grow?" *Training and Development Journal* (March 1971), pp. 2–7.

3. Curry, T. "Why not use your line managers as management trainers?" *Training and Development Journal* (November 1977), pp. 43–47.

4. Rothwell, W., and H. Kazanas. *Improving on-the-Job Training* (1994). San Francisco, CA: Jossey-Bass.

5. Ibid.

6. Anonymous. "Training flexes small firm's competitive muscle." *Management Services* 45 (2001), pp. 6–7.

7. Freel, M. "Patterns of innovation and skills in small firms." *Technovation* 25 (2005), pp. 123–25.

8. Kerr, G., S. Way, and J. W. Thacker. "Performance, HR practices and the HR manager in small, entrepreneurial firms." *Proceedings of the Administrative Science Association of Canada* (June 5–8, 2004), Quebec City, Quebec.

9. Blumfield, M. "Learning to share." *Training* (April 1997), pp. 38–42.

10. Anfuso, D. "Trainers prove many heads are greater than one." *Workforce* 78 (1999), pp. 60–65.

11. Tyler, K. "E-learning: Not just for e-normous companies anymore." *HR Magazine* 46 (2001), pp. 82–88.

12. Harris, P. "Small businesses bask in training's spotlight." *Training and Development* 59 (2005), pp. 46–52.

13. Leeds, L. Personal communication. *Western Learning Systems* (2002).

14. Filipczak, B. "Training on the cheap." *Training* (May 1996), pp. 28–34.

15. Abella, K. *Building Successful Training Programs* (1986). Reading, MA: Addison-Wesley.

16. Jolles, R. *How to Run Seminars and Workshops* (1993). New York: Wiley.

17. Ibid.

18. Johnstone, A. H., and F. Percival. "Attention breaks in lectures." *Education in Chemistry* 13 (1976), pp. 273–304. Lloyd, D. H. "A concept of improvement of learning in the taught lesson." *Visual Education* (1968), pp. 23–25. Maddox, H., and E. Hook. "Performance decrement in the lecture." *Educational Research* 28 (1975), pp. 17–30.

19. Palmer, A. "Models of behavioral change." *The 1981 Annual Handbook for Group Facilitators* (1981), edited by J. E. Jones and J. W. Pfeiffer. San Diego, CA: University Associates Press.

20. Pfeiffer, J. W., and J. E. Jones. *The 1980 Annual Handbook for Group Facilitators* (1980), San Diego, CA: University Associates Press.

21. Ibid.

22. Abella, op. cit. (1986).

Chapter 9

1. Brandenburg, D., and E. Shultz. The status of evaluation of training: An update. Presentation at the National Society of Performance and Instruction Conference, April 1988, Washington DC.

2. McLaughlin, D. J. "The turning point in human resource management." *Strategic Human Resource Management* (1986), edited by F. W. Folkes. Upper Saddle River, NJ: Prentice Hall.

3. Olsen, J. "The evaluation and enhancement of training transfer." *International Journal of Training and Development*, 2 (1998), pp. 61–75.

4. Bersin, J. "Companies still struggle to tie training to business goals." *Training* (October 2006), p. 22.

5. Goldwasser, D. "Beyond ROI." *Training* (January 2001), pp. 82–90. Geber, op. cit. (1995).

6. Purcell, A. "20/20 ROI." *Training and Development* (July 2000), pp. 28–33.

7. Meals, D., and J. W. Rogers. "Matching human resource management to strategy." *Strategic Human Resource Management* (1986), edited by F. K. Folkes. Upper Saddle River, NJ: Prentice Hall.

8. "2008 Industry report." *Training* (November/December 2008), pp. 16-34.

9. Spitzer, D. "Embracing evaluation." *Training* (June 1999), pp. 42–47.

10. Geber, B. "Does your training make a difference? Prove it!" *Training* (March 1995), pp. 27–34.

11. Ibid.

12. Ellis, K. "What is the ROI of ROI?" *Training* 42 (2005), pp. 16–21.

13. Geis, G. "Formative evaluation: Developmental testing and expert review." *Performance and Instruction* (May 1987), pp. 1–7.

14. Ibid.

15. Kirkpatrick, D. L. "Techniques for evaluating training programs." *Training and Development Journal* 33, no. 6 (1979), pp. 78–92. Kirkpatrick, D. L. "Evaluating in-house training programs." *More Evaluating Training Programs—A Collection of Articles from Training and Development Journal* (1987), edited by D. L. Kirkpatrick. Alexandria, VA: American Society for Training and Development. Kirkpatrick, D. L. *Evaluation of Training Programs: The Four Levels* (1998), 2nd ed. San Francisco, CA: Berret-Koehler Publishers.

16. Alliger, G., S. Tannenbaum, W. Bennett, H. Traver, and A. Shortland. "A meta-analysis of the relationship among training outcomes." *Personnel Psychology* 50 (1997), pp. 341–58. Alliger, G., and E. Janak. "Kirkpatrick's levels of training criteria: Thirty years later." *Personnel Psychology* 42 (1989), pp. 331–42.

17. Blanchard, P. N., and J. W. Thacker. Organizational Strategy and Management Development. Paper presented at the Global Business Trends Conference of the Academy of Business Administration, 1998, Acapulco, Mexico.

18. Korth, S. "Consolidating needs assessment and evaluation." *Performance Improvement* 40 (2001), pp. 38–43.

19. Hamblin, A. C. *Evaluation and Control of Training* (1974). New York: McGraw-Hill.

20. Saari, L., T. Johnson, S. McLaughlin, and D. Zimmerlie. "A survey of management training and education practices in U.S. companies." *Personnel Psychology* 41 (1988), pp. 731–43. Sloman, M. "Learning evaluation or not?" *Training and Development* 58 (2004), p. 45. Yancey, G. B., and L. Kelly. "The inappropriateness of using participants' reactions to evaluate effectiveness of training." *Psychological Reports* 66 (1990), pp. 937–38. Wexley, K., and G. Yukl. *Organizational Behavior and Industrial Psychology: Readings with Commentary* (1975). New York: Oxford University Press.

21. Alliger et al., op. cit. (1997).

22. Conroy, M., and M. Ross. "Getting what you want by revising what you had." *Journal of Personality and Social Psychology* 47 (1984), pp. 738–48. Dixon, N. "The relationship between training responses on participant reaction forms and post test scores." *Human Resource Development Quarterly* 1, no. 2 (1990), pp. 129–37.

23. Nunnally, J. C. *Psychometric Theory* (1978). New York: McGraw-Hill.

24. Kropp, R., and E. Hankin. "Paper-and-pencil tests for evaluating instruction." *Evaluating Training Programs* (1975), edited by D. Kirkpatrick. Madison, WI: American Society of Training and Development.

25. Flanagan, D. L. *Techniques for Eliciting and Representing Knowledge Structures and Mental Models* (1990). Unpublished manuscript. Orlando, FL: Naval Training Systems Training Center.

26. Davis, M. A., M. B. Curtis, and J. D. Tschetter. "Evaluating cognitive training outcomes: Validity and utility of structural knowledge assessment." *Journal of Business and Psychology*, 18 (2003), pp. 191–206. Kraiger, K., E. Salas, and J. Cannon-Bowers. "Measuring knowledge organization as a method for assessing learning during training." *Human Factors* 37 (1995), pp. 804–16. Kraiger, K., J. K. Ford, and E. Salas. "Application of cognitive, skill based, and affective theories of learning outcomes to new methods of training evaluation." *Journal of Applied Psychology* 28 (2003), pp. 311–28. Goldsmith, T. E., P. J. Johnson, and W. H. Acton "Assessing structural knowledge." *Journal of Educational Psychology* 83 (1991), pp. 88–96. Flannagan, op. cit. (1990).

27. Means, B., and S. Gott. "Cognitive task analysis as a basis for tutor development: Articulating abstract knowledge representations." *Intelligence Tutoring Systems: Lessons Learned* (1998), edited by J. Psotka, L. Massey, and S. Mutter. Hillsdale, NJ: Erlbaum.

28. Kraiger et al., op. cit. (1995). Gill, R. S., S. Gordon, J. B. Moore, and C. Arbera. "The role of conceptual structure in problem solving." *Proceedings of the Annual Meeting of the American Society of Engineering Education* (1988). Washington, DC: American Society of Engineering Education Means and Gott, op. cit. (1988).

29. Ackerman, P. L., and L. G. Humphreys. "Individual differences theory in industrial and organizational psychology." *Handbook of Industrial and Organizational Psychology* (1990), 2nd ed., edited by M. D. Dunnette and L. M. Hough. Palo Alto, CA: Consulting Psychology Press. Lord, F. "A study of speed factors in tests and academic grades." *Psychometrika*, 21 (1956), pp. 31–50.

30. Gordon, M. E., and J. F. Isenberg. "Validation of an experimental training criterion for machinists." *Journal of Industrial Teacher Education* 12 (1956), pp. 72–78.

31. Ostroff, C. "Training effectiveness measures and scoring schemes: A comparison." *Personnel Psychology* 44 (1991), pp. 353–74.

32. King, L., J. Hunter, and F. Schmidt. "Halo in a multidimensional forced choice performance evaluation scale." *Journal of Applied Psychology* 65 (1980), pp. 507–16.

33. Stark, C. "Ensuring skills transfer: A sensitive approach." *Training and Development Journal* (March 1986), pp. 50–51.

34. Thacker, J. W., and M. Fields. Evaluation of steward training: Did it do what you wanted it to? *Proceedings of the 44th Annual Meeting of the Industrial Relations Research Association* (January 1992). New Orleans, LA.

35. Thacker, J. W., M. Fields, and L. Barclay. "Union commitment: An examination of antecedent and outcome factors." *Journal of Occupational Psychology* 63 (1990), pp. 17–20.

36. Clement, R. W. "Testing the hierarchy theory of training evaluation: An expanded role for trainee reactions." *Public Personnel Management Journal* 11 (1982), pp. 176–84.

37. Dixon, op. cit. (1990).

38. Holton, E. "The flawed four-level evaluation model." *Human Resource Development Quarterly* 7 (1996), p. 21. Blanchard and Thacker, op. cit. (1998).

39. Geber, op. cit. (1995).

40. Alliger et al., op. cit. (1997). Colquitt, J. A., J. A. LePine, and R. A. Noe. "Towards an integrative theory of training motivation: A meta-analytical path analysis of 20 years of research." *Journal of Applied Psychology* 85 (2000), pp. 678–707. Liebermann, S., and S. Hoffmann. "The impact of practical relevance on training transfer: Evidence from a service quality training program for German bank clerks." *International Journal of Training and Development.* 12, no. 2 (2008), pp. 74–86.

41. Cascio, W. *Applied Psychology in Personnel Management* (2005), 6th ed. Upper Saddle River, NJ: Prentice Hall.

42. Phillips, J. "ROI: The search for best practices." *Training and Development* 51, no. 2 (1996), pp. 42–47.

43. Geber, op. cit. (1995).

44. Purcell, op. cit. (2000).

45. Hassett, J. "Simplifying ROI." *Training* (September 1992), pp. 53–57.

46. Cascio, op. cit. (2005).

47. Cascio, W. "Using utility analysis to assess training outcomes." *Training and Development in Organizations* (1989), edited by I. Goldstein. San Francisco, CA: Jossey-Bass.

48. Whyte, G., and G. Latham. "The futility of utility analysis revisited: When even an expert fails." *Personnel Psychology* 50 (1997), pp. 601–10. Latham, G., and G. Whyte. "The futility of utility analysis." *Personnel Psychology* 47 (1994), pp. 31–46.

49. Dixon, N. "New routes to evaluation." *Training and Development* (May 1996), pp. 82–85.

50. Ellis, K. "What's the ROI of ROI?" *Training* 42 (2005), p. 16–21.

51. Dixon, op. cit. (1996).

52. Blanchard et al., op. cit. (2000).

53. Geber, op. cit. (1995).

54. Sackett, P. R., and E. J. Mullen. "Beyond formal experimental design: Toward an expanded view of the training evaluation process." *Personnel Psychology* 46 (1993), pp. 613–27.

55. Tvrik, B. "Cost and benefits of ISO 9000 Registration." *CIRS News* 32, no. 1 (Fall 1997). Center for Industrial Research and Service, Iowa State University.

56. LeGault, M. "In-house training that gets results." *Canadian Plastics* (February 1997), pp. 14–18.

Chapter 9 Appendix

1. Goldstein, I. L. "Training in work organizations." *Handbook of Industrial and Organizational Psychology* (1991), 2nd ed., edited by M. D. Dunnette and L. M. Hough. Palo Alto, CA: Consulting Psychologists Press.

2. Cook, T. D., D. T. Campbell, and L. Peracchio. "Quasi-experimentation." *Handbook of Industrial and Organizational Psychology* (1990), 2nd ed., edited by M. D. Dunnette and L. M. Hough. Palo Alto, CA: Consulting Psychologists Press. Cook, T. D., and D. T. Campbell. *Quasi-Experimentation: Design and Analysis Issues for Field Settings* (1979). Chicago: Rand McNally. Campbell, D. T., and J. C. Stanley. *Experimental and Quasi-experimental Designs for Research* (1963). Chicago: Rand McNally.

3. Camp, R. P., P. N. Blanchard, and G. E. Huszczo. *Toward a More Organizationally Effective Training Strategy and Practice* (1986). Upper Saddle River, NJ: Prentice Hall.

4. Wexley, K. N., and G. P. Latham. *Developing and Training Human Resources in Organizations* (1981). Glenview, IL: Scott, Foresman.

5. Sackett and Mullen, op. cit. (1993).

6. Ibid.

7. Ibid.

8. Haccoun, R., and T. Hamtiaux. "Optimizing knowledge tests for inferring learning acquisition levels in single group training evaluation designs: The internal referencing strategy." *Personnel Psychology* 47 (1994), pp. 593–604.

9. Ibid.

10. Ibid.

11. Dixon, N. Personal communication (July 1997). Associate Professor, George Washington University, Department of Administrative Sciences.

12. White, L., D. Rosenthal, and C. Fleuridas. "Accountable supervision through systematic data collection: Using single case designs." *Counselor Education and Supervision* 33 (1993), pp. 32–37.

Chapter 10

1. Adapted from: *Conner v. Schrader-Bridgeport International, Inc.*, 4th cir. (September 2000). No. 98-2055.

2. Fisher, C. "Organizational socialization: An integrative review." *Research in Personnel and Human Resource Management* 4 (1986), pp. 104–45.

3. Katz, D. "Bringing Hires Aboard: 'Onboarding' new hires helps assimilate and empower them before they even begin work." *Financial Planner* (August 1, 2008).

4. Klein, H., and N. Weaver. "The effectiveness of an organizational-level orientation training program in the socialization of new hires." *Personnel Psychology* 53 (2000), pp. 47–66.

5. Allen, N., and J. Meyer. "Organizational socialization tactics: A longitudinal analysis of links to newcomers' commitment and role orientation." *Academy of Management Journal* 33 (1990), pp. 847–58. Bauer, T., E. Morrison, and R. Callister. "Organizational socialization: A review and directions for future research." *Research in Personnel and Human Resource Management* 16 (1998), pp. 149–214. Saks, A. "The relationship between the amount of helpfulness of entry training and work outcomes." *Human Relations* 49 (1996), pp. 429–51.

6. Bassi, L., and M. Van Buren. "The 1998 ASTD state of the industry report." *Training and Development* 52 (1998), pp. 21–43.

7. Tyler, K. "Take new employee training off the back burner." *HR Magazine* (May 1998), pp. 49–57.

8. Wells, S. "Diving in." *HR Magazine* 50 (2005), pp. 54–60.

9. Tyler, op. cit. (1988).

10. Galvin, T. "Training top 100: Best practices." *Training* 40 (2003), pp. 60–61.

11. Wells, op. cit. (2005).

12. Derven, M. "Management onboarding." *Training and Development* 62 (2008), pp. 49–53.

13. McGillicuddy, J. "Making a first good impression." *Public Management* 81 (1999), pp. 15–18.

14. Curtis, E. F., J. L. Dreachslin, and M. Sinioris. "Diversity and cultural competence training in health care organizations: Hallmarks of success." *The Health Care Manager* 26, no. 3 (2007), p. 255.

15. Sleezer, C., and D. Denny. "Strategies for developing a high skilled workforce." *Performance Improvement Quarterly* 17 (2004), pp. 41–56.

16. Fullerton, B., and M. Tossi. "Labor force projections to 2010: Steady growth and changing composition." *Monthly Labor Review* 124 (2001), pp. 21–38.

17. Tsui, A. S., and C. A. O'Reilly. "Beyond simple demographic effects: The importance of relational demography in superior-subordinate dyads." *Academy of Management Journal* 29 (1989), pp. 586–99. Wayne, S. J., and R. C. Linden. "Effects of impression management on performance ratings: A longitudinal study." *Academy of Management Journal* 38 (1995), pp. 232–60.

18. Hartel, C. E., S. S. Douthitt, G. Hartel, and S. Y. Douthitt. "Equally qualified but unequally perceived: Openness to perceived dissimilarity as a predictor of race and sex discrimination in performance judgments." *Human Resource Development Quarterly* 10, no. 1 (1999), pp. 79–89.

19. Gilbert, J. "An empirical examination of resources in a diverse environment." *Public Personnel Management* (2000), pp. 175–84.

20. Wright, P., S. Ferris, J. S. Hiller, and M. Kroll. "Competitiveness through management of diversity: Effects on stock price valuation." *Academy of Management Journal* 38 (1995), pp. 272–87.

21. Galvin, T. "Industry report." *Training* (October 2001), pp. 40–75.

22. Naisbitt, J., and P. Aburdene. *Megatrends* (2000). New York: Avon.

23. Kalev, E., F. Dobbin, E. Kelly. "Best practices or best guesses? Assessing the efficacy of corporate affirmative action and diversity policies." *American Sociological Review* 7 (2006), pp. 589–618. Gilbert, J., and J. Ivancevich. "Valuing diversity: A tale of two organizations." *Academy of Management Executive* 14 (2000), pp. 93–105.

24. Lords, E. "Sex, race charges hit GM in Pontiac." *Detroit Free Press* (August 2001), pp. 1A, 11A.

25. Ibid.

26. Nancherla, A. "Nobody's perfect: Diversity training study finds common flaws." *Training and Development* 62 (2008). pp. 20–21.

27. Rynes, S., and B. Rosen. "A field survey of factors affecting the adoption and perceived success of diversity training." *Personnel Psychology* 48 (1995), pp. 247–70.

28. Lilley, W. "Banking on equity." *Report on Business Magazine* 65 (April 1995), p. 69.

29. Grossman, R. "Is diversity working?" *HR Magazine* (March 2001), pp. 46–50.

30. Ibid.

31. Prince, C. J. "Doing diversity." *Chief Executive* no. 207 (2005), pp. 46–50.

32. Ibid.

33. *Roberts et al. v. Texaco, Inc.* (1994). Civ. 2015.

34. Texaco. Second Annual Report of the Equity and Fairness Task Force (June 1999).

35. Curtis, E., J. Dreachslin, and M. Sinioris. "Diversity and cultural competence training in health care organizations: Hallmarks of success." *The Health Care Manager* 26, no. 3 (2007), p. 255.

36. Gilbert, J., and J. Ivancevich. "Valuing diversity: A tale of two organizations." *Academy of Management Executive* 14 (2004), pp. 93–105.

37. Nancherla, op. cit. (2008).

38. Loudin, A. "Diversity pays." *Warehousing Management* 7 (2000), pp. 30–33.

39. Harris, T. M. "Impacting student perceptions of and attitudes toward race in the interracial communication course." *Communication Education* 52, no. 3/4 (2003), p. 311. Hood J. N., H. J. Muller, and P. Seitz. "Attitudes of Hispanics and Anglos surrounding a workforce diversity intervention." *Hispanic Journal of Behavioral Science* 23, no. 4 (2001), p. 444.

40. Mueller, N. L. "Wisconsin Power and Light's model diversity program." *Training and Development* (March 1996), pp. 57–60.

41. De Meuse, K., T. Hostager, and K. O'Neill. "A longitudinal evaluation of senior managers' perceptions and attitudes of a workplace diversity training program from HR." *Human Resource Planning* 30 (2007), pp. 38–46.

42. Mueller, op. cit. (1996).

43. "Court holds employer liable for harassment by supervisor." *Daily Labor Report* (June 1987), pp. A1, D1–5.

44. *Meritor Savings Bank v. Vinson.* (1986). 477 U.S. 57.

45. http://www.eeoc.gov/stats/harass.html

46. Ibid.

47. Ibid.

48. Foy, N. "Sexual harassment can threaten your bottom line." *Financial Times* (September 2000), p. 27.

49. Flynn, K. "Preventative medicine for sexual harassment." *Personnel* 68 (1991), p. 17.

50. "Study: Many employers unaware of subtle sexual harassment." *Halifax Daily News* (March 2001), p. 12.

51. Johnson, M. "Anti-harassment training to shelter yourself from suits." *HR Magazine* 44 (1999), pp. 76–81.

52. Ganzel, R. "What sexual harassment training really prevents." *Training* (October 1998), pp. 86–94.

53. Magley, V., C. Hulin, L. Fitzgerald, and M. DeNardo. "Outcomes of self-labeling sexual harassment." *Journal of Applied Psychology* 84 (1999), pp. 390–402.

54. Ibid.

55. Ibid.

56. "Industry report." *Training* (October 1999), p. 57.

57. Moore, H., R. Gatlin-Watts, and J. Cangelosi. "Eight steps to a sexual-harassment-free workplace." *Training and Development* (April 1998), pp. 12–13.

58. Cicmanec, A., and B. Kleiner. "A statistical look at judicial decisions regarding employment law." *Managerial Law* 44 (2002), pp. 3–9.

59. Lindenberger, L. "Ignoring sexual harassment just got more expensive: Five tips to prevent lawsuits." *Office Solutions* 24 (2007), p. 42.

60. Bingham, S., and L. Scherer. "The unexpected effects of a sexual harassment educational program." *Journal of Applied Behavioral Science* 37 (2001), pp. 125–53.

61. Sramcik, T. "Heading off harassment." *Motor Age* 124 (2005), pp. 126–32.

62. Ganzel, op. cit. (1998).

63. Johnson, M. "Use antiharassment training to shelter yourself from suits." *HR Magazine* 44 (1999), pp. 76–81.

64. Tata, J. "Autonomous work teams: An examination of cultural and structural constraints." *Work Study* 49 (2000), pp. 187–93.

65. Way, S., and J. Thacker. "Trends in human resource management." *HR Professional: Research Forum* (August/September 2000).

66. Hunsaker, P. *Training in Management Skill* (2001). Upper Saddle River, NJ: Prentice Hall.

67. Whetten, D., and K. Cameron. *Developing Management Skills* (2002). Upper Saddle River, NJ: Prentice Hall.

68. Ibid.

69. Ibid.

70. Ibid.

71. Neuman, G., and J. Wright. "Team effectiveness: Beyond skills and ability." *Journal of Applied Psychology* 84 (1999), pp. 376–89.

72. Cutcher-Gershenfeld, J., T. Kochan, and A. Verma. "Recent developments in U.S. employee involvement initiatives: Erosion or diffusion." Paper presented at the Pacific Rim Labor Policy Conference, Vancouver, Canada (June 1987), pp. 25–26.

73. Wells, D. *Soft Sell* (1986). Ottawa, Canada: Canadian Centre for Policy Alternatives.

74. Cutcher-Gershenfeld et al., op. cit. (1987). Greenberg, P., and E. Glaser. "Viewpoints of labor leaders regarding quality of work life improvement programs." *International Review of Applied Psychology* 30 (1981), pp. 157–74.

75. Goodman, P., and J. Dean. *Organizational Development: Theory Practice and Research* (1983), edited by W. French, C. Bell, and R. Zawacki. Plano, TX: Business Publications, Inc.

76. Anonymous. "Why teams don't work." *Sales and Marketing Management* (April 1993), p. 12.

77. Hunsaker, P. *Training in Management Skills* (2001). Upper Saddle River, NJ: Prentice Hall.

78. Phillips, S. "Team training puts fizz in Coke plant's future." *Personnel Journal* 75 (1996), pp. 87–94.

79. Huszczo, G. *Tools for Team Excellence* (1996). Palo Alto, CA: Davis Black.

80. Ibid.

81. Hofstede, G. "The business of international business culture." *International Business Review* 3 (1994), pp. 1–14.

82. Griffen, R., and M. Pustay. *International Business* (2007). Upper Saddle River, NJ: Prentice Hall.

83. Hallcrow, A. "Expats: The squandered resource." *Workforce* 78 (1999), pp. 42–46.

84. Minter, R. "Preparation of expatriates for global assignments." *Journal of Diversity Management* 3 (2008), pp. 37–42.

85. Minter, R. "Preparation of expatriates for global assignments: Revisited." *Journal of Diversity Management* 3 (2008), pp. 37–44.

86. Brian, J. H. "Pre-departure training for international business managers." *Industrial and Commercial Training* 39. (2007), pp. 9–17.

87. Tung, R. "Selection and training of personnel for overseas assignments." *Columbia Journal of World Business.* 16 (1981), pp. 18–78.

88. Luthans, K., and Farner, S. "Expatriate development: The use of 360-degree feedback." *The Journal of Management Development* 21 (2002), pp. 780–93.

89. Anderson, B. "Expatriate selection: Good management or good luck?" *The International Journal of Human Resource Management* 16 (2005), pp. 567–83.

90. Hurn, op. cit. (2007).

91. Treven, S. "Human resources management in the global environment." *Journal of American Academy of Business* 8 (2006), pp. 120–26.

92. Ettorre, B. "Let's hear it for local talent." *Management Review* 83 (1994), p. 9.

93. Flynn, J. "E-mail, cellphones and frequent-flier miles let 'virtual' expats work abroad but live at home." *Wall Street Journal* (October 25, 1999), p. A.26.

94. Vance, C., Yongsun, P. "One size fits all in expatriate pre-departure training?: Comparing the host country voices of Mexican, Indonesian and US workers." *Journal of Management Development* 21 (2002), pp. 557–71.

95. *Pay for lost opportunities* (1988). Canadian Human Rights Advocate 4.

96. Haben, M. K. "Shattering the glass ceiling." *Executive Speeches* 15 (2001), pp. 4–10.

97. Laff, M. "The invisible wall." *Training and Development* 61 (2007), pp. 32–38.

98. Haben, op. cit. (2001).

99. Ibid.

100. Nelton, S. "Can-do attitudes and the disabled." *Nations Business* (May 1998), pp. 35–37.

101. Morris, G. "The next great hiring frontier." *Wall Street Journal* (September 2005), p. B2.

102. Ibid.

103. Salopek, J. "Arrested development." *Training and Development* 52 (1998), pp. 65–66.

104. Hays, S. "The ABCs of workplace literacy." *Workforce* 78 (1999), pp. 70–74.

105. Ibid.

106. Barron, K., and A. Marsh. "The skills gap." *Forbes* (February 1998), pp. 44–45.

107. Ibid.

108. "Workplace literacy training pays off." *OH&S Canada* 14 (1998), p. 8.

109. Tyler, op. cit. (1996).

110. Ibid.

111. Bureau of Labor Statistics. Workplace injury and illness summary. 2007 U.S. Department of Labor. http://www.bls.gov/news.release/osh.nr0.htm

112. Overheul, V. "A cure for boredom." *Occupational Health and Safety* 70 (2001), pp. 192–95.

113. Anonymous. "Increasing employee safety awareness on and off the job." *Electrical Apparatus* 58 (2001), p. 34.

114. Ibid.

115. Thach, L. "Training in Russia." *Training and Development* 50 (1996), pp. 34–38.

116. Filpczak, B. "Think locally, train globally." *Training* 34 (1997), pp. 40–46.

117. Ibid.

118. Thach, op. cit. (1996).

119. Filpczak, op. cit. (1997).

120. Ibid.

121. Ibid.

122. Thach, op. cit. (1996).

123. Filpczak, op. cit. (1997).

124. Ibid.

125. "Workplace literacy training pays off." *OH&S Canada* 14 (1998), p. 8.

Chapter 11

1. Ready, D., and J. Conger. "How to fill the talent gap: Global companies face a perfect storm when it comes to finding the employees they need." *Wall Street Journal* (September 15, 2007), p. R.4.

2. Ibid.

3. Moses, B. "Employee career planning programs: What's in it for organizations." *HR Professional* (September 1985), p. 1.

4. Dessler, G., and N. Cole. *Human Resource Management in Canada* (2005). Toronto, Canada: Pearson Education.

5. Nembhard, D., and H. Nembhard. "A real options model for workforce cross training." *The Engineering Economist* 50 (2005), pp. 95–117.

6. Dyck, R., and N. Halpem. "Team based organizations at Celestica." *Journal for Quality and Participation* 22 (1999), pp. 36–40.

7. Dalton, G. "The collective stretch." *Management Review* 87 (1998), pp. 54–59.

8. Martinez, M. "To have and to hold." *HR Magazine* 43 (1998), pp. 130–7.

9. Benedict, M., and E. Levine. "Delay and distortion: Tacit influences on performance appraisal." *Journal of Applied Psychology* 73 (1988), pp. 507–14.

10. Taylor, D., and D. Edge. "Personal development plans: Unlocking the future." *Career Development International* 2 (1997), pp. 21–23.

11. Fiester, M., A. Collis, and N. Cossack. "Job rotation, total rewards, measuring value." *HR Magazine* 53 (2008), pp. 33–34.

12. Anonymous. "Energize and enhance employee value with job rotation." *HR Focus* 85 (2008), p. 6.

13. Ibid.

14. *Martinez*, op. cit. (1998).

15. Eriksson, T., and J. Ortega. "The adoption of job rotation: Testing the theories." *Industrial & Labor Relations Review* 59 (2006), pp. 653–66.

16. Walker, S., J. Davis, and D. Desai. "Postural assessments and job rotation: A survey of one company's assembly line supervisors." *Professional Safety* 53 (2008), pp. 32–37.

17. Perry, W. "The value of on-the-job rotation." *Supervisory Management* 38 (1993), p. 6.

18. Zidle, M. "Retention hooks for keeping your knowledge workers." *Management* 50 (1998), pp. 21–23.

19. Matsushita, K. *My Management Philosophy* (1978). Tokyo: PHP Institute, Inc.

20. Tucker, R., and M. Moravec. "Do it yourself career development." *Training* (February 1992), pp. 48–52.

21. Gautschi, T., and R. Anderson. "Keys to the productivity of technical employees." *Industrial Management* 35 (1993), p. 21.

22. Zidle, op. cit. (1998).

23. Burack, E., W. Hochwarter, and N. Mathys. "The new management development paradigm." *Human Resource Planning* 20 (1997), pp. 14–21.

24. "Industry report." *Training* (October 2002). "Industry report." *Training* (October 2001). "Industry report." *Training* (1996). "Industry report." *Training* (1995).

25. *Training*, op. cit. (2002).

26. Cascio, W., and R. Zammuto. *Societal Trends and Staffing Policies* (1987). Denver, CO: University of Colorado Press. Offerman, L., and M. Gowing. "Organizations of the future: Changes and challenges." *American Psychologist* 45 (1990), pp. 95–108. Patel, D. "Managing talent." *HR Magazine* (March 2002), pp. 112–13. Pater, R. "Leadership skills for the 21st century." *Occupational Health and Safety* (March 2002), pp. 6–15.

27. Howell, J., P. Dorfman, and S. Kerr. "Moderating variables in leadership research." *Academy of Management Review* 11 (1986), pp. 88–102. Morden, T. "Leadership as competence." *Management Decision* 35 (1997), pp. 519–26.

28. Campbell, J., M. Dunnette, E. Lawler III, and K. Weick, Jr. *Managerial Behavior, Performance, and Effectiveness* (1970). New York: McGraw-Hill.

29. Mintzberg, H. "The manager's job: Folklore and fact." *Harvard Business Review* 53, no. 4 (1975), pp. 49–61.

30. Wexley, K., and G. Latham. *Developing and Training Human Resources in Organizations* (1991), 2nd ed. New York: HarperCollins.

31. Karmel, B. "Leadership: A challenge to traditional research methods and assumptions." *Academy of Management Review* (July 1978), pp. 477–79. Schein, E. *Organizational Psychology* (1980), 3rd ed. Upper Saddle River, NJ: Prentice Hall.

32. House, R. "A path-goal theory of leadership." *Administrative Science Quarterly* (September 1971), pp. 321–38. House, R., and T. Mitchell. "Path-goal theory of leadership." *Journal of Contemporary Business* (Autumn 1974), p. 83. Keller, R. "A test of the path-goal theory of leadership with need for clarity as a moderator in research and development organizations." *Journal of Applied Psychology* (April 1989), pp. 208–12. Mathieu, J. "A test of subordinates' achievement and affiliation needs as moderators of a leader's path-goal relationships." *Basic and Applied Social Psychology* (June 1990), pp. 179–89.

33. The primary and secondary researches we examined that led us to the conclusions in this section are: Andrews, J. "The achievement motive and advancement in two types of organizations." *Journal of Personality and Social Psychology* 6 (1967), pp. 163–68. Bass, B. *Handbook of Leadership* (1990). New York: Free Press. Bennis, W., and B. Nanus. *Leaders: The Strategies for Taking Charge* (1985). New York: Harper & Row. Birch, D., and J. Veroff. *Motivation: A Study of Action* (1966). Monterey, CA: Brooks/Cole. Bray, D. "New data from the management progress study." *Assessment and Development* 1 (1973), p. 3. Bray, D., R. Campbell, and D. Grant. *Formative Years in Business: A Long-Term AT&T Study of Managerial Lives* (1974). New York: Wiley. Bray, D., and D. Grant. "The assessment center in the measurement of potential for business management." *Psychological Monographs* 80 (1966), pp. 1–27. Brown, W., and N. Karagozoglu. "Leading the way to faster new product development." *The Executive* 7 (1993), p. 1. Byham, W. "Starting an assessment center." *Personnel Administrator* 25, no. 2 (1980), pp. 27–32. Gupta, A. "Contingency linkages between strategy and general manager characteristics: A conceptual examination." *Academy of Management Review* 9 (1984), pp. 399–412. Gupta, A., and V. Govindarajan. "Business unit strategy, managerial characteristics, and business unit effectiveness at strategy implementation." *Academy of Management Journal* 27 (1984), pp. 25–41. Howard, A., and D. Bray. *Managerial Lives in Transition: Advancing Age and Changing Times* (1988). New York: Guilford Press. Katz, R. "Skills of an effective administrator." *Harvard Business Review* (September/October 1974), p. 90. Kirkpatrick, S., and E. Locke. "Leadership: Do traits matter?" *The Executive* 5 (1991), p. 2. Kouzes, J., and B. Posner. *The Leadership Challenge: How to Get Things Done in Organizations* (1988). San Francisco, CA: Jossey-Bass. Luthans, F., R. Hodgetts, and S. Rosenkrantz. *Real Managers* (1988). Cambridge, MA: Ballinger Press. McCauley, C., M. Lombardo, and C. Usher. "Diagnosing management development needs: An instrument based on how managers develop." *Journal of Management* 15 (1989), p. 3. McClelland, D. *The Achieving Society* (1961). New York: Van Nostrand. McClelland, D., and D. Burnham. "Power is the great motivator." *Harvard Business Review* 54, no. 2 (1976), pp. 100–10. McClelland, D., and R. Boyatzis. "Leadership motive pattern and long-term success in management." *Journal of Applied Psychology* 67 (1982), pp. 737–43. Miner, J. "Twenty years of research on role-motivation theory of managerial effectiveness." *Personnel Psychology* 31 (1978), pp. 739–60. Niehoff, M., and M. Romans. "Needs assessment as step one toward

enhancing productivity." *Personnel Administrator* (May 1982), pp. 35–39. Porter, L., and L. McKibbin. *Future of Management Education and Development: Drift or Thrust into the 21st Century?* (1988). New York: McGraw-Hill. Smith, K., and J. Harrison. "In search of excellent leaders." *The Handbook of Strategy* (1986), edited by W. Guth. New York: Warren, Gorham & Lamont. Starcevich, M., and J. Sykes. "Internal advanced management programs for executive development: The experience of Phillips Petroleum." *Personnel Administrator* (June 1982), pp. 27–33. Tornton, G., and W. Byham. *Assessment Centers and Managerial Performance* (1982). New York: Academic Press. Zaleznik, A. "Power and politics in organizational life." *Harvard Business Review* 48 (1970), pp. 47–60.

34. Bass, B. *Stogdill's Handbook of Leadership: A Survey of Theory and Research* (1981), revised and expanded. New York: Free Press.

35. McClelland, D. *The Achieving Society* (1961). New York: Van Nostrand.

36. Birch, D., and J. Veroff. *Motivation: A Study of Action* (1966). Monterey, CA: Brooks/Cole.

37. McClelland, D., and D. Burnham. "Power is the great motivator." *Harvard Business Review* 54, no. 2 (1976), pp. 100–10.

38. Kirkpatrick, S., and E. Locke. "Leadership: Do traits matter?" *The Executive* 5 (1991), p. 2.

39. For ambition, see Howard, A., and D. Bray. *Managerial Lives in Transition: Advancing Age and Changing Times* (1988). New York: Guilford Press. For energy, see Kouzes, J., and B. Posner. *The Leadership Challenge: How to Get Things Done in Organizations* (1988). San Francisco, CA: Jossey-Bass. For tenacity, see Bass, B. *Handbook of Leadership* (1990). New York: Free Press.

40. McClelland, D., and R. Boyatzis. "Leadership motive pattern and long-term success in management." *Journal of Applied Psychology* 67 (1982), pp. 737–43. Miner, J. "Twenty years of research on role-motivation theory of managerial effectiveness." *Personnel Psychology* 31 (1978), pp. 739–60.

41. Andrews, J. "The achievement motive and advancement in two types of organizations." *Journal of Personality and Social Psychology* 6 (1967), pp. 163–68. Zaleznik, A. "Power and politics in organizational life." *Harvard Business Review* 48 (1970), pp. 47–60.

42. McCauley, C., M. Lombardo, and C. Usher. "Diagnosing management development needs: An instrument based on how managers develop." *Journal of Management* 15 (1989), p. 3. Smith, K., and J. Harrison. "In search of excellent leaders." *The Handbook of Strategy* (1986), edited by W. Guth. New York: Warren, Gorham & Lamont. Weiss, W. "Leadership." *Supervision* 60 (1999), pp. 6–9.

43. Coleman, E., and M. Campbell. *Supervisors: A Corporate Resource* (1975). New York: AMACOM.

44. Katz, R. "Skills of an effective administrator." *Harvard Business Review* (September/October 1974).

45. Bennis, W., and B. Nanus. *Leaders: The Strategies for Taking Charge* (1985). New York: Harper and Row. Smith, K., and J. Harrison. "In search of excellent leaders." *The Handbook of Strategy* (1986), edited by W. Guth. New York: Warren, Gorham & Lamont.

46. Brown, W., and N. Karagozoglu. "Leading the way to faster new product development." *The Executive* 7 (1993), p. 1. McCauley, C., M. Lombardo, and C. Usher. "Diagnosing management development needs: An instrument based on

how managers develop." *Journal of Management* 15 (1989), p. 3. Kirkpatrick, S., and E. Locke. "Leadership: Do traits matter?" *The Executive* 5 (1991), p. 2.

47. Luthans, F., R. Hodgetts, and S. Rosenkrantz. *Real Managers* (1988). Cambridge, MA: Ballinger Press. McCauley et al., op. cit. (1989). McClelland, D., and D. Burnham. "Power is the great motivator." *Harvard Business Review* 54, no. 2 (1976), pp. 100–10. Porter, L., and L. McKibbin. *Future of Management Education and Development: Drift or Thrust into the 21st Century?* (1988). New York: McGraw-Hill.

48. Bruack et al., op. cit. (1997).

49. Frisch, M. "Going around in circles with 360 tools: Have they grown too popular for their own good?" *Human Resource Planning* 24 (2001), pp. 7–8.

50. Waldman, D., F. Yammarino, and B. Avolio. "A multiple level investigation of personnel ratings." *Personnel Psychology* 43 (1990), pp. 811–35.

51. O'Reilly, B. "360-feedback can change your life." *Fortune* (October 1994), p. 17.

52. Ibid.

53. "State of the industry report." *Training and Development* (January 1998), pp. 22–43.

54. Hall, op. cit. (1986).

55. Schleede, J. "The future of management education." *Mid-American Journal of Business* 17 (2002), pp. 5–8.

56. *Training and Development*, op. cit. (1998).

57. Ibid.

58. Schleede, op. cit. (2002).

59. Eurich, N. *Corporate Classroom: The Learning Process* (1985). Princeton, NJ: Carnegie Foundation for the Advancement of Teaching. Starcevich, M., and J. Sykes. "Internal advanced management programs for executive development: The experience of Phillips Petroleum." *Personnel Administrator* (June 1982), pp. 27–33.

60. Camp, R., P. Blanchard., and G. Huszczo. *Toward a More Organizationally Effective Training Strategy and Practice* (1986). Upper Saddle River, NJ: Prentice Hall, pp. 285–86.

61. Mintzberg, op. cit. (1975). Roberts, T. *Developing Effective Managers* (1974). Stratford-upon-Avon: Edward Fox and Son.

62. Vroom, V., and A. Jago. *The New Leadership: Managing Participation in Organizations* (1988). Upper Saddle River, NJ: Prentice Hall. Vroom, V., and P. Yetton. *Leadership and Decision Making* (1973). Pittsburgh, PA: University of Pittsburgh Press.

63. Mintzberg, op. cit. (1975).

64. Pigors, P., and F. Pigors. "Case method." *Training and Development Handbook: A Guide to Human Resource Development* (1987), edited by R. Craig. New York: McGraw-Hill.

65. Rackham, N., and T. Morgan. *Behavior Analysis in Training* (1977). Maidenhead, England: McGraw-Hill.

66. Blake, R., and J. Mouton. *The Managerial Grid III: The Key to Leadership Excellence* (1985). Houston, TX: Gulf Publishing. Yukl, G. *Leadership in Organizations* (1989). Upper Saddle River, NJ: Prentice Hall.

67. Minor, J. "Twenty years of research on role motivation theory of managerial effectiveness." *Personnel Psychology* 31 (1978), pp. 739–60.

68. McClelland, op. cit. (1961). McClelland and Burnham, op. cit. (1976). Miron and McClelland, op. cit. (1979).

69. Wellins, R., and W. Byham. "The leadership gap." *Training* (March 2001), pp. 98–106.

70. Ibid.

71. Thach, E. "14 ways to groom executives." *Training* (August 1998), pp. 52–55. Zemke, R., and S. Zemke. "Where do leaders come from?" *Training* (August 2001), pp. 44–48.

72. Tomlinson, A. "The coaching explosion." *Canadian HR Reporter* 15 (2002), p. 7.

73. Bolch, M. "Proactive coaching." *Training* (May 2001), pp. 58–66.

74. Ibid.

75. Ibid.

76. Caironi, P. "Coaches coach, players play, and companies win." *TIP* 40 (2002), pp. 37–44.

77. Feldman, D. "Career coaching: What HR professionals and managers need to know." *Human Resource Planning* 24 (June 2001), pp. 26–35.

78. Thach, op. cit. (1998).

79. Thach, op. cit. (1998).

80. Murphy, S., and E. Ensher. "Establish a great mentoring relationship." *Training and Development* 60 (2006), pp. 27–28. Barbian, J. "The road best traveled." *Training* (May 2002), pp. 38–42.

81. Zemke and Zemke, op. cit. (2001).

82. Zemke and Zemke, op. cit. (2001).

83. Peters, J., and P. Smith. "Action learning and the leadership development challenge." *Journal of Workplace Learning* 10 (1998), pp. 284–91.

84. Ibid.

85. Yelverton, J. "Adaptive skills: Seven keys to developing top managers." *Vital Speeches of the Day* 63 (1997), pp. 725–27.

86. Tyler, L. "Succession planning: Charting a course for the future." *Trustee* 55 (2002), pp. 24–28.

87. Ibid.

88. Galvin, T. "Industry report." *Training* (October 2001), pp. 40–75.

89. Wellins and Byham, op. cit. (2001).

90. Grossman, R. "Heirs unapparent." *HR Magazine* (February 1999), pp. 36–44.

91. Ibid.

92. Galvin, T. "Birds of a feather." *Training* (March 2001), pp. 58–68.

93. Ibid.

94. Tarley, M. "Leadership development for small organizations." *Training and Development* 56 (2002), pp. 52–55. Zemke and Zemke, op. cit. (2001).

95. Zemke and Zemke, op. cit. (2001).

GLOSSARY

360-Degree Performance Review A performance appraisal that uses supervisor, peer, subordinate, and sometimes customer ratings.

Accommodation The process of changing our cognitive map of the world to correspond with our experience in it.

Achievement Style A personal trait that emphasizes goal setting and high-performance expectations for subordinates.

Actual Criterion In relation to the needs analysis process it is what is used to measure an employee's KSAs.

Actual Organizational Performance (AOP) The performance level of the organization, department, or unit.

Actual Performance (AP) The actual level of performance by an individual in the job.

Affective Questionnaire A type of reaction questionnaire that measures general feelings about training.

Analysis Phase A process of data gathering and causal analysis to identify both training, and nontraining needs and their priorities.

Anticipatory Learning Learning that occurs when a person finds out what consequences are associated with a behavior (or set of behaviors) without actually engaging in the behavior or receiving the consequences.

Apprenticeship Training A formal type of on-the-job-training in which trainees receive training from journeymen and knowledge through classroom instruction.

Assessment Center A method of testing that utilizes many types of tests (personality, simulations, cognitive) and multiple raters.

Assimilation The incorporation of new experience into our existing cognitive map.

Attention Getting a person to focus where you want her to.

Attitudes Employee beliefs and opinions that support or inhibit behavior.

Audiovisual Aids Any physical, mechanical, or electronic media used to provide or assist instruction.

Automaticity A higher level of skill acquisition in which a high level of performance is achieved without conscious thought about each action.

Behavior Modeling The process of learning through watching, and then imitating a model that provides an example of the behavior to be learned.

Behavioral Methods Activities that allow the trainee to practice behavior in a real or simulated fashion.

Behavioral Reproduction A part of social learning theory in which learning is translated into behavior through practice.

Behavioral Test A quantitative measure of behavior.

Bias A predisposition to evaluate a person or object in a particular manner (e.g., more or less favorably than the objective evidence supports).

Bias in Performance Ratings The portion of the actual criterion that is not correlated with the ultimate criterion but is correlated with other variables used by raters in their subjective judgments.

Business Games Simulations that attempt to represent the way an industry, company, or unit of a company functions.

Capital Resources The holdings an organization has, such as property, equipment, finances, and so on.

Case Study A description of events, typically from actual situations, that simulates decision-making situations that trainees might encounter in their jobs.

Classical Conditioning The association of a generalized response to some signal in the environment.

Climate The perception of salient characteristics of the organization such as company policies, reward systems, behaviors of management, and so forth.

Closed-Ended Question A question that asks for a specific answer.

Coaching The process of providing one-on-one guidance and instruction to improve knowledge, skills, and work performance.

Cognition The mental processing of information.

Cognitive Load The amount of information a person must process during a given time period.

Cognitive Methods Approaches to training that provide verbal or written information, demonstrate relationships among concepts, or provide rules on how to do something.

Cognitive Organization A process in Social Learning Theory in which new learning is organized into the existing cognitive structure through associations with previously stored information.

Cognitive Process A mental activity such as information storage, retrieval, or use. Thinking and decision making are cognitive processes.

Cognitive Structure The way that our brains organize and classify what we learn.

Cognitive Test A measure of knowledge.

Competency A cluster of related knowledge, skills, and attitudes required for a person to be successful in performing a group of related tasks. Valid measures of a competency will differentiate among high, medium, and low performers.

Competitive Strategy The set of plans created to position an organization in the marketplace (e.g., cost leader, market leader).

Compilation A lower level of skill development associated with newly learned behaviors that the person must consciously think about to perform well.

Computer-Based Training (CBT) Training that uses a computer or other electronic memory devices to provide instruction.

Conceptual Knowledge and Skills The mental abilities required to analyze and diagnose complex situations and make the right decisions.

Conditions (as related to training objectives)   The situational factors that should be present when the training objectives are measured. These would include anything that will clarify what is required for the objective to be achieved (such as the time period when measurement will occur, the aids that can be used, and any hindrances that must be overcome).

Content Validity   The use of an expert to determine that the outcome (e.g., test) is representative of the domain of information/situations it purports to represent.

Control Group   A group of similar employees who do not receive the training.

Core Technology   The main activities associated with producing the organization's principal products and services.

Corporate Universities   The term used for learning centers created by corporations in an attempt to overcome some of the deficiencies of university-based education while maintaining many of its advantages.

Cost Leader   A competitive strategy with the goal of being the low-cost provider in the industry.

Cost Savings Analysis   A method of evaluation that compares the monetary cost of training with the financial benefits accrued from training, using only factors that training focused on correcting.

Cost/Benefit Evaluation   A method of evaluation that compares the actual costs of training with nonmonetary benefits, such as a better relationship between management and nonmanagement.

Cost-Effectiveness Evaluation   A method of evaluation that compares the monetary cost of training with the financial benefits accrued from training.

Criteria   The standards from which decisions can be evaluated.

Criterion Contamination   The portion of the actual criterion that is not related to the ultimate criterion (true performance).

Criterion Deficiency   The portion of the ultimate criterion that is not measured by the actual criterion.

Criterion Relevancy   The portion of the ultimate criterion that we are able to measure with our actual criterion.

Cross Training   A process in which several employees in a work unit are trained to do each other's jobs.

Culture   A pattern of basic assumptions invented, discovered, or developed by a group within the organization.

Decision Autonomy   The level of freedom to make decisions, as determined by the structure of the organization.

Declarative Knowledge   A person's store of factual information.

Delivery System   The method chosen to deliver computer-based training.

Demonstration   A visual display of how to do something or how something works.

Design Phase   A systematic process for the objectives of training and the most effective means of (given organizational constraints) achieving the objectives.

Design Theory   General models for how to design training, such as how material should be organized and presented.

Development   The learning of KSAs (an outcome of training and other experiences).

Development Phase   A process of formulating an instructional strategy, within the constraints of the organization, to meet a set of training objectives.

Developmental Review   The opportunity for the employee and supervisor to discuss career goals, areas of strength and weakness, and the opportunities for development that are open to the employee.

Direct Question   A question asked by the trainer and directed to a particular trainee.

Directive Style   A managerial style that tells subordinates what to do, how to do it, and when it should be done.

Diversity Training   Training that focuses on understanding the differences that are found among people of different backgrounds (race, age, ethnicity, gender).

Division of Labor   The way in which work is organized and divided (e.g., process, function, geography, customer).

Drive   A personality characteristic that is a combination of nAch, ambition, energy, and tenacity.

Dry Run   A step prior to piloting the training, where developers of the training determine the value and clarity of the various pieces of the training program in a controlled setting.

Duty to Accommodate   Governmental requirements for the employer to adjust working conditions and/or requirements of the job to allow a person with a disability, who that is otherwise capable, to do the job.

Dynamic Media   Sequentially moving stimuli, where the information is presented in a continuously moving progression from beginning to end.

Dysfluencies   Filler sounds used when talking, such as um, uh, etc.

Education   Experience that is designed to provide more general learning that is not specific to a job.

E-Learning   The delivery of training through electronic media.

Employee-Oriented Style   A style of management in which the manager focuses on the subordinate's personal needs; and is made up of two types: participative and supportive.

Environment   The physical surroundings in which performance (individual or organizational) must occur, including barriers and aids to performance, and objects and events (cues) that might be seen as indicating that performance will be rewarded or punished.

Environmental Complexity   The number of factors in the environment and how interrelated they are.

Environmental Stability   The rate at which key factors in the environment change; the more rapid the change, the more unstable the environment.

Environmental Uncertainty   The combination of complexity and stability factors in the business environment. When the environment is more complex and unstable, it is more uncertain. When it is simpler and more stable, it is more certain.

Equipment Simulators   Mechanical devices that require trainees to use the same procedures, movements, or decision processes they would use with equipment back on the job.

ERG Theory   A theory of motivational needs, derived by Alderfer from the work of Maslow, and describing three types of need: existence, relatedness, and growth.

Error (Measurement)   The portion of the actual criterion measure that, although not correlated with the ultimate criterion, is also not correlated with other variables (bias).

Evaluation Phase   Determining training's success in meeting the training design and outcome objectives.

Executive/Management Education Programs   University programs that cover the range of management issues, from traditional MBA programs to building strategically effective organizations.

Existence Needs Lower-level needs in the ERG model representing physiological and security needs.

Expectancy Theory A motivation theory using cognitive processes as a means of determining the best course of action for achieving one's goals.

Expected Organizational Performance (EOP) The level or goal that has been set and is expected of the organization, department, or unit in key performance areas (e.g., profits, market share, absenteeism).

Expected Performance (EP) The level of performance expected of an employee holding a particular job.

Expert Knowledge Base A component of an intelligent tutoring system that stores the correct answers to the knowledge being taught.

External Validity The confidence that the results of an evaluation can be generalized to other groups of trainees.

Extinction A form of punishment in which something desirable is removed.

Force-Field Analysis An analysis of the counterbalancing forces that hold a situation in place, with the purpose of identifying the forces that must be weakened if change is to occur.

Glass Ceiling An invisible barrier that prevents minorities and women from moving up the corporate ladder.

Group Characteristic Bias The portion of the actual criterion not correlated with the ultimate criterion but correlated with factors related to group membership.

Group Dynamics The process whereby the group determines and enforces its norms.

Growth Needs Higher-level needs in the ERG model that include feelings of self-worth and competency, and achieving one's potential.

Guided Discovery The process of leading trainees to discover for themselves answers to questions that, at first, they are unable to answer. This is accomplished by having the trainers ask successively more basic questions. Each question is designed to bring the trainees closer to "discovering" the answer to the original question.

Halo Effect An error in rating performance in which evaluation in one dimension influences all other dimensions.

History Changes that are noted in the evaluation of training could be caused by other factors that took place concurrently with the training.

Hostile Work Environment A type of sexual harassment in which words, gestures, and/or behaviors make someone feel uncomfortable based on their gender.

HR Strategy The set of tactics that HR will use to support the competitive strategy.

HRD Strategy The set of tactics that HRD will use to support the HR strategy.

Icebreaker A game or exercise that prompts trainees to get involved in meeting and talking with others.

Identical Elements A training experience that is designed to match the actual job experience as closely as possible.

Implementation Phase Putting a training program into action through pilot testing and the actual training.

In-Basket Technique A simulation that provides trainees with a packet of written information and requests, such as memos, messages, and reports that typically would be handled in a given position.

Incident Process A simulation in which trainees are given only a brief description of the problem and must gather additional information from the trainer (and perhaps others) by asking specific questions.

Instructional Strategy The order, timing, and combination of methods and elements used in the training program.

Instrumentation Changes noted in the evaluation of training could occur because the posttest is not really the same as the pretest; they are not equivalent.

Intelligent Tutoring System (ITS) A sophisticated form of programmed instruction.

Interactive Multimedia Training The integration of video, graphics, photos, animation, and sound to produce a complex training environment with which trainees can interact.

Internal Referencing Strategy (IRS) A way of dealing with the lack of a control group, in which both relevant and nonrelevant test questions in the pre- and posttests are included.

Internal Strategy A plan for changing the organization to align it with its competitive strategy.

Internal Validity The degree of confidence one can have that the results of an evaluation are, in fact, correct.

Interpersonal Knowledge and Skills The competencies required to interact with others in an effective manner.

Intranet A communication tool similar to the Internet, but accessible only to a specific company's employees.

ISO The International Organization for Standardization (ISO), is located in Geneva, Switzerland, and has developed a set of worldwide standards to ensure consistency in product quality by all companies that become certified.

Job Aid A set of instructions, diagrams, or other form of providing information that is available at the job site to provide guidance to the worker.

Job Behavior Outcomes The degree to which behaviors learned in training are transferred back to the employee's job.

Job Expectation Technique A method of clarifying job expectations for a particular position by having the supervisor meet with the incumbent for the sole purpose of clarifying for both exactly what is required on the job.

Job Instruction Technique (JIT) A structured approach to on-the-job training that uses a behavioral strategy with a focus on skill development. It consists of four steps—prepare, present, try out, and follow up.

Job Rotation The periodic shifting of an employee from one job to another; requiring the employee to do a different set of tasks.

Job-Duty-Task Method A structured, task-oriented job analysis method.

Knowledge An organized body of facts, principles, procedures, and information that has been acquired over the years.

Knowledge Base The things that the trainee will need to know for a particular training program.

Knowledge of Predictor Bias The bias that occurs from knowing how successful a person was in an earlier situation (test/training) that influences how you rate the success of the person at a later time.

Knowledge of Results The trainee's understanding of how he or she has performed during training. This is typically achieved through feedback from the trainer and is a key component in the design of training that will facilitate transfer back to the job.

KSAs This is an acronym that stands for knowledge, skills, and attitudes.

Law of Effect Behavior followed by satisfying experiences tends to be repeated, and behavior followed by annoyance or dissatisfaction tends to be avoided.

Leadership Motivation A form of nPow that is directed toward organizational goals and is distinguished from a need for personal power, which is focused on personal goals.

Learning A relatively permanent change in cognition resulting from experience and directly influencing behavior.

Learning Goal Orientation The degree to which an individual is predisposed toward a learning goal rather than a performance goal. In other words, the focus of the individual is on learning rather than achieving some performance standard.

Learning Management System (LMS) Software of varying degrees of sophistication that manages the delivery of training content and monitors and records trainee activity.

Learning Objectives A description of the KSA outcomes that trainees are expected to acquire throughout the training program, and the ways that learning will be demonstrated.

Learning Outcomes A determination of the degree to which the learning objectives were met.

Learning Point An important piece of information that a trainee must acquire to accomplish the learning objective.

Lecture/Discussion Method A method of conveying knowledge that is supported, reinforced, and expanded on through interactions both among the trainees and between the trainees and the trainer.

Lecturette A form of conveying knowledge that has the same characteristics as the lecture but usually lasts less than 20 minutes.

Literacy Training Educational experiences that provide the basic skills of reading, writing, and arithmetic.

Local Area Network (LAN) An electronic connection among various computers and a central server.

Managerial Context The alignment of an organization's environment, strategy, structure, and technology.

Managerial Style A manager's preference for behavior that falls along a continuum running from employee-oriented to task-oriented behaviors.

Market Leader A competitive business strategy with the goal of finding and exploiting new product and market opportunities.

Massed Practice Training that is done all at once with no substantial rest periods.

Maturation Changes noted in the evaluation of training could be because of other factors related to the passage of time, such as growing older, hungrier, fatigued, and bored.

Mechanistic Design An organizational structure characterized by highly defined tasks, rigid and detailed procedures, high reliance on authority, and vertical communication channels.

Mentoring A form of coaching in which an ongoing relationship is developed between a senior and a junior employee.

Micro Theory of Instructional Design A guide for designing training.

Motivation The direction, persistence, and amount of effort expended by an individual to achieve a specified outcome.

Multiple Role-play Similar to a single role-play except that all trainees are in groups, with each group acting out the role-play simultaneously.

nAch A personal trait characterized by a strong desire to assume personal responsibility, to receive concrete feedback on task performance, and to single-mindedly pursue task accomplishment.

nAut A personal trait characterized by a strong desire to work independently.

Needs Theory Theories of motivation describing the various types of human needs that motivate behavior.

Negative Reinforcement Behavior that results in removing something you find annoying, frustrating, or unpleasant.

Negative Transfer A situation in which a person performs less well on the job after he or she has received training than he or she did before receiving training.

Nonroutine Technology Tasks with outcomes that are difficult to predict, where problems occur often and unexpectedly, and solutions are not readily available but need to be developed on a case-by-case basis.

Nonverbal Cues Body language and facial expressions used when interacting with others.

nPow A personal trait characterized by a desire to lead, influence, and control people and things.

On-the-Job Training (OJT) The use of more experienced and skilled employees, whether co-workers or supervisors, to train less skilled or less experienced employees.

Open Systems Model A model that depicts the dynamic relationship an organization has with its environment.

Open-Ended Question A question that seeks an opinion and has no right or wrong answers.

Operant Conditioning A type of learning where specific types of behavior are reinforced.

Operational Analysis An examination of specific jobs to determine the requirements, in terms of the tasks required to be done, and the KSAs needed to do them, to get the job done. It is analogous to a job analysis.

Opportunity Bias The portion of the actual criterion not correlated with the ultimate criterion but correlated with variables beyond the control of the performer.

Organic Design An organization characterized by flexibility in its rules and procedures, loosely defined tasks, high reliance on expertise, and horizontal communication channels.

Organizational Analysis An examination of an organization's strategy, its goals/objectives, and the systems and practices in place to determine how they affect employee performance.

Organizational Design The number and formality of rules, policies, and procedures created to direct employee behavior.

Organizational Development A field of study that deals with creating and implementing planned change.

Organizational Environment The internal characteristics of an organization, including structures (e.g., organic or mechanistic) and designs (e.g., workflow, division of labor, pay systems, and reward policies).

Organizational Mission A general statement that articulates why the organization exists and its commitments.

Organizational Performance Gap The difference between the organization's expected performance and its actual performance on key performance indicators (e.g., profit, market share, absenteeism).

Organizational Results The degree to which training outcomes can be linked to key outcomes for the organization.

Organizational Strategy   An organization's attempt to optimize the match between its mission, what is occurring (or is projected to occur) in the external environment, and the organization's internal operations.

Organizational Structure   The manner in which an organization organizes itself to get its work accomplished. This includes how labor is divided; the rules, policies, and procedures used for making decisions; and how activities of the various units are coordinated.

Orientation Training   Training designed for new employees to allow them to understand how the company operates, its policies and procedures and to familiarize the employee with their new work environment.

Outcome Evaluation   A measure of the outcomes attributable to training and their value.

Overhead Question   A question directed by the trainer toward the whole group rather than at one person in particular.

Overlearning   Providing trainees with continued practice far beyond the point at which they perform the task successfully.

Part Learning   A way of organizing training in which the whole task to be learned is broken down into parts that are taught separately before being put together and taught as a whole.

Participative Style   The involvement of subordinates in decision making, particularly in how they go about achieving their task.

Performance Gap (PG)   The difference between a person's expected level of performance and the actual level of performance. Also called **Performance Deficiency.**

Performance Goal Orientation   The degree to which an individual is predisposed toward a performance goal rather than a learning goal. In other words, the focus of the individual is on achieving some performance standard rather than learning.

Performance Management Systems (PMS)   Software that links an employee's competencies from a learning management system to other HR systems such as annual performance reviews and compensation.

Performance Model   This model (see Figure 3.1) shows that a person's performance depends on the interaction of motivation, KSAs, and environment.

Person Analysis   An examination of the employees in the jobs to determine whether they have the required KSAs to perform at the expected level.

Personal Traits   A relatively permanent predisposition to behave in a particular way.

Physical Fidelity   The degree to which the simulation replicates, as closely as possible, the physical aspects of the equipment and operating environment trainees will find at their job site.

Pilot Program   The implementation of a training program in a controlled setting, provided to specially selected trainees, to get feedback for any possible program modifications.

Positive Reinforcement   Behavior that results in something desirable happening to you—it can be tangible, psychological, or some combination of the two.

Positive Transfer   This occurs when a person performs better after he or she received training than he or she did before training.

Proactive Strategy   The long-term plans for achieving the organization's goals and objectives given the future expectations in the environment.

Proactive TNA   A TNA focusing on a performance problem anticipated in the future.

Procedural Knowledge   A person's understanding about how and when to apply the facts that have been learned.

Process Evaluation   An examination of the way training was conducted to determine if it met the expectations based on the design.

Process Theories   Motivational theories that describe how a person translates his needs into behavior designed to satisfy those needs.

Program Development Plan   A detailed plan that outlines the methods, material, equipment, facilities, and trainers for a training program.

Programmed Instruction (PI)   A method of self-paced learning managed by both the trainee and the learning system (e.g., computer program or text).

Progressive Part Training   A number of tasks are taught by teaching the first task, then the first and second tasks, then the first, second, and third tasks, and so forth, until the total activity has been taught.

Psychological Fidelity   The degree to which the simulation replicates, as closely as possible, the psychological conditions under which the equipment is operated (such as time pressures and conflicting demands).

Punishment   Behavior that results in something undesirable happening to you—it can be tangible or psychological or both and can come from the environment or be self-administered.

Quid Pro Quo Harassment   A form of sexual harassment in which an employee higher in the organization makes an offer of some job perquisite or raise to a subordinate in return for sexual favors.

Random Assignment   The placement of employees in either a control group or a training group by chance to ensure that the groups are equivalent.

Reaction Outcomes   A determination of the trainee's perceptions, emotions, and subjective evaluations of the training experience.

Reactive Strategy   Plans for achieving the organization's immediate goals and objectives in response to current environmental conditions.

Reactive TNA   A type of TNA that focuses on a performance problem that currently exists.

Reinforcement Theory   A theory of motivation that uses the Law of Effect to predict behavior.

Relapse Prevention   The process of helping transfer training to the job by preparing trainees for the problems associated with the transfer.

Relatedness Needs   A person's need to be valued and accepted by others.

Relay Question   A question from a trainee that the trainer redirects back to the trainee group.

Reliability   The consistency of a measurement.

Representative Sampling   The matching of employees in the control group and training group on a number of factors such as age, tenure, and education to make the groups as equivalent as possible.

Resistance to Learning   A natural tendency in adults to resist learning new processes, systems, or information, stemming from a fear of the unknown, and the possible losses to the individual that the new learning signifies.

Retention   The process of storing information in the brain and being able to access what has been stored. This is a key measure of learning.

Reverse Question   A question that the trainer redirects to the trainee who asked it.

Role Rotation   A type of role-play in which, after the characters interact for a period of time, the trainer will stop the role-play and discuss what happened so far and what can be learned from it, then continue with other trainees.

Role-play   An enactment (or simulation) of a scenario in which each participant is given a part to act out.

Routine Technology   Tasks with outcomes that are highly predictable, demonstrate few problems, and use well-structured, well-defined solutions when problems do occur.

Self-Efficacy   A belief about our ability to perform successfully.

Self-Paced Learning   A type of training in which trainees move through the training as quickly as they are able to learn the material.

Self-Ratings   A type of performance appraisal that ratees complete on themselves.

Sexual Harassment   An unwelcome advance of a sexual nature.

Single Role-play   A type of role-play in which one group of trainees role-plays for the rest, providing a visual demonstration of some learning point.

Single-Case Design   A method of evaluation in which a single person is measured pre- and posttraining, and inferences are made as to the learning that took place.

Sit In   A process to assist in transfer of training that involves the trainer observing job behaviors and providing feedback.

Skills   The capacities that are developed as a result of training and experience that are needed to perform a set of interrelated tasks.

Small Business   An organization that has fewer than 100 employees.

Social Learning Theory   A cognitive theory of learning that incorporates anticipatory learning.

Spaced Practice   A way of organizing training so that trainees practice what they have learned with rest periods specifically designed into the program.

Split Half Reliability   A measure of reliability that splits the test/scale in half and correlates the results of one half with those of the other.

Spontaneous Role-play   A type of role-play in which the role-play is loosely constructed and one of the participants plays himself while the other(s) play people with whom the first trainee interacted in the past, or will in the future.

Standards   In relation to training objectives, this refers to the level of performance that must be shown by the trainee to signify that the training objective has been achieved.

Static Media   Presentations of fixed text or images, such as printed matter, overhead transparencies, pictures/slides, and computer-generated projections.

Statistical Regression   Changes noted in the evaluation of training could occur because trainees had such low scores in the pretest that they improved simply because getting worse was almost impossible; they regressed to the mean.

Straight Lecture   A method of presenting information in which the trainer speaks to the trainees and might include the use of audiovisual aids.

Strategic Job Analysis   A type of job analysis that examines the KSAs required for effective performance in a job as it is expected to exist in the future.

Strategic Knowledge   A person's awareness of what she knows and the internal rules that have been learned for accessing the relevant facts and procedures to be applied toward achieving some goal.

Strategic Planning   A proactive process used to decide how best to meet the demands of the environment.

Structured Role-play   A type of role-play that provides trainees with more detail about the situation and more detailed descriptions of each character's attitudes, needs, opinions, and so on.

Succession Planning   A process for identifying and developing high-potential employees (often executives or high-level managers) for promotion to key positions. In a more general sense, it is the planning process to identify and prepare employees at a lower level to replace someone at the next level.

Supportive Style   A personal trait characterized by friendliness, empathy, and concern for meeting employees' needs.

Symbolic Coding   A process in Social Learning Theory in which the brain translates external information into meaningful internal symbols (such as language).

Symbolic Rehearsal   A process in Social Learning Theory in which the person is able to increase the retention of newly learned material through visualization or imagining of how some set of knowledge or skill will be used.

Task Complexity   The level of difficulty in performing a task.

Task Organization   The degree to which tasks are interrelated.

Task-Oriented Job Analysis   A type of job analysis that determines the tasks necessary to do the job, then from these, determines the KSAs necessary to perform the tasks.

Task-Oriented Style   A manager's preference for behavior that focuses on the work the subordinate does; made up of two types: directive or achievement-oriented.

Technical Knowledge and Skills   The knowledge and skills needed to perform the functional and general management aspects of the organizational unit.

Test Retest Reliability   A measure of reliability that administers the same test/scale at two different times and correlates the results of the two times.

Theory   A theory is an abstraction that allows one to make sense of a large number of facts related to an issue.

Trainee Model   A component of an intelligent tutoring system that stores the information about how the trainee is responding and what the trainee seems to know.

Training   The organized and systematic process of providing an opportunity to learn KSAs for current or future jobs.

Training Equity   The degree to which all employees are provided equal access to training.

Training Needs Analysis (TNA)   A process of data gathering and causal analysis related to a performance gap and occurring in the analysis phase of the Training Process Model. The results of an effective TNA identify training needs and nontraining needs related to eliminating the performance gap.

Training Objectives   The specific outcomes that are expected to be realized from training.

Training Plan   This is a term used interchangeably with instructional strategy. A training plan describes the order, timing, and combination of methods and elements used in the training program.

Training Scenario Generator   A component of an intelligent tutoring system that determines the order and level of difficulty of the problems that are presented to the trainee.

Training Session Manager   A component of an intelligent tutoring system that interprets trainees' responses and responds with more information, coaching, or tutoring.

Transfer of Training The degree to which the KSAs the trainee acquires in training are used when the trainee returns to her workstation.

Triggering Event The identification of an actual or potential organizational performance gap by a key member of the organization.

Ultimate Criterion A theoretical construct denoting a true and exact measure of an object (this is an impossible task).

Undue Hardship An argument that allows an exception to the duty to accommodate. The employer provides evidence that accommodating the particular employee will place undue hardship on the organization.

User Interface The equipment that allows the trainee to interact with the intelligent tutoring system.

Utility Analysis A method of evaluation that compares the monetary cost of training with all the financial benefits accrued from the resulting change in behavior.

Utility Questionnaire A type of reaction questionnaire that reflects beliefs about the value of training.

Valence The attractiveness of outcomes to an individual.

Validity The degree to which a measurement actually measures what it is intended to measure.

Virtual Reality (VR) Training A type of training in which an artificial, three-dimensional environment is used to simulate real situations.

Whole Learning A way of organizing the training activities so that the task to be trained is kept intact and taught as a complete unit.

Work Sample An actual part of a job is constructed as a test, and measures of effectiveness are developed.

Worker-Oriented Job Analysis A method of job analysis that focuses only on the KSAs required to get the job done.

Zero Transfer This occurs when a person performs no differently after he or she received training than he or she did before training.